PERSPECTIVES ON SUPPLIER INNOVATION

Theories, Concepts and Empirical Insights on Open Innovation and the Integration of Suppliers

Series on Technology Management*

Series Editor: J. Tidd (University of Sussex, UK)   ISSN 0219-9823

*The complete list of the published volumes in the series can be found at
http://www.worldscibooks.com/series/stm_series.shtml

SERIES ON TECHNOLOGY MANAGEMENT – VOL. 18

PERSPECTIVES ON SUPPLIER INNOVATION

Theories, Concepts and Empirical Insights on Open Innovation and the Integration of Suppliers

editors

Alexander Brem
University of Erlangen-Nuremberg, Germany

Joe Tidd
University of Sussex, UK

Imperial College Press

ICP

Published by

Imperial College Press
57 Shelton Street
Covent Garden
London WC2H 9HE

Distributed by

World Scientific Publishing Co. Pte. Ltd.
5 Toh Tuck Link, Singapore 596224
USA office: 27 Warren Street, Suite 401-402, Hackensack, NJ 07601
UK office: 57 Shelton Street, Covent Garden, London WC2H 9HE

Library of Congress Cataloging-in-Publication Data
Perspectives on supplier innovation : theories, concepts and empirical insights on open innovation
    and the integration of suppliers / edited by Alexander Brem & Joe Tidd.
      p. cm. -- (Series on technology management, ISSN 0219-9823 ; v. 18)
    Includes bibliographical references and index.
    ISBN-13 978-1-84816-899-2 -- ISBN-10 1-84816-899-3
    1. Diffusion of innovations. 2. Technological innovations. 3. Strategic alliances (Business)
4. Interorganizational relations. 5. Industrial procurement.
    I. Brem, Alexander. II. Tidd, Joseph, 1960–
    HD45.P435 2012
    658.701--dc23

                                           2012005377

British Library Cataloguing-in-Publication Data
A catalogue record for this book is available from the British Library.

In-house Editor: Alisha Nguyen

Printed in Singapore by B & Jo Enterprise Pte Ltd

Preface

Open innovation is not a new topic anymore but there are still some areas that have not attracted enough research. In particular, Gassmann (2006) mentioned the importance of supplier integration in 2006; however, to date there are few publications on this subject.

Against this background and based on our experience in research and consulting, we invited theoretical and conceptual papers on supplier integration and challenges at the firm level for a Special Issue of the *International Journal of Innovation Management*. The results were two issues of the *International Journal of Innovation Management* published in August 2010 (Volume 14, Number 4) and February 2011 (Volume 15, Number 1).

The response was surprising as well as encouraging: 51 abstracts from all over the world were submitted. Our assumption was confirmed: There is still less research dealing with suppliers because the linkage to customers has been the dominant theme in research over the last few years. Unsurprisingly, it was hard to choose the 'best' papers suitable for the scope of the Special Issue with a sufficiently high scientific level and relevance to practice: Finally, 16 papers were published in the two special issues.

For this book, we chose the best papers from all of the initial submissions. The book is divided into three parts:

- Theories and concepts
- Empirical findings based on quantitative research
- Insights from case study research

The structure of this book shows that research on supplier innovation is still in its early stages as most of the research is still qualitative. We hope to encourage discussions about theory and practice — any feedback on these chapters is very welcome!

Finally, we would like to thank all 30 reviewers for their constructive comments, which helped to improve the quality of the contributions. Moreover, we would like to thank the editorial team at Imperial College Press (Alisha Nguyen and Venkatesh Sandhya) for their support and encouragement.

Contents

Introduction

Alexander Brem
University of Erlangen Nuremberg, Germany

Joe Tidd
University of Sussex, UK

Open innovation describes an innovation paradigm shift from a closed-to an open-innovation model (Chesbrough, 2003). With this idea, the term "open innovation" has become one of the most commonly used buzzwords of recent years, with a plethora of research. These days, many companies are already using open-innovation principles in practice as well, especially when it comes to the integration of customers. However, the concept has been criticized for being too prescriptive and for offering little new to innovation research or practice (Trott and Hartmann, 2009). For instance, the lead-user concept (von Hippel 1988, 2005) has become one of the most important trends in innovation management in the last ten years, but questions have arisen over whether open innovation is anything more than the lead-user concept [see the *International Journal of Innovation Management,* Special Issue on User Innovation, 2008, **12**(3)].

Hardly anybody outside any company knows its products and processes better than its suppliers (Bessant, 2003; Petersen *et al.*, 2003; von Hippel, 1988). Research confirms that the intensive integration of suppliers in the value-creation process positively influences the success of a company, particularly in highly competitive industries (Wingert, 1997). This is a result of the progressing reduction in the depth of value creation for manufacturers and the increasing transfer of know-how to suppliers. In multilevel business-to-business relationships, suppliers often have the best, or the only, access and comprehensive knowledge about the end users (Groher, 2003). A practical example for supplier integration is the use of guest engineers (Maylor, 2001). Therefore, suppliers determine the scope of possible innovation, which most companies do not actively use, yet. The main risk for suppliers is the danger of releasing or using confidential expertise gleaned from other sources, therefore reciprocal trust is critical for this to work (Groher, 2003). Tools such as the continuous improvement model or collaborative engineering already involve suppliers, but mostly at an operative level only. Hence, suppliers are an important source for open innovation.

The **first part** of this book is on the theories and concepts for supplier innovation and consists of four chapters:

Gianiodis, Ellis, and Secchi introduce an advanced typology of open innovation. As a first step toward such a framework, they provide a critical review of previous research on conceptualization, antecedents, and consequences of open innovation. They then offer a typology describing four open-innovation strategies: (1) innovation seeker, (2) innovation provider, (3) intermediary, and (4) open innovator, which emerge through unique combinations of sources of innovation, firm attributes, mechanisms of inter-organizational exchange, and which produce varying outcomes. Finally, they discuss their typology's implications for theory and practice, and advance some potential research avenues.

Brem and Schuster conducted a bibliographic analysis of papers on supplier innovation. Based on their findings, they made a systematic content analysis of journal articles, contributions, books, and conference proceedings. To do so, they searched Thomson Reuter's *Web of Science* database for articles whose titles, keywords, or abstracts contain 'innovation' and 'supplier.' Their analysis shows that four areas interact in supplier innovation, namely importance, requirements, management, and the outcomes of supplier innovation.

Bahemia and Squire developed a conceptual framework of inbound open innovation at the new product development (NPD) project level to assess factors that help determine the degree of openness along three dimensions. They argue that the margin of managerial action is not only constrained to the decision to open up an NPD project to a wide range of different types of external partners (the breadth dimension), but it is equally important to consider the depth of the relationships with different types of external partners (the depth dimension), and the balance between the development of new and long-standing relationships with these external partners (the ambidexterity dimension). These three dimensions are the levers for managing an inbound-open-innovation strategy during an NPD project. Finally, they identified a range of contingencies that potentially have a bearing on the appropriate calibration of the breadth, depth, and ambidexterity dimensions of an open-innovation strategy. They argue that appropriate calibration of the three dimensions of inbound open innovation is determined by the type of innovation (radical versus incremental), product complexity (discrete versus complex), and the appropriability regime (tight versus weak).

The chapter by Erzurumlu is concerned with how open innovation through inter-firm collaboration and strategic alliances may generate value for competing suppliers by stimulating the adoption of new component innovation by the downstream supply chain. The analysis specifically examines three types of firm interaction representing different levels of open innovation. First, in a joint venture, fully integrated suppliers would develop and market the component. Second, in a development alliance, partially integrated suppliers share the development outcomes, but compete in marketing. Finally, independent suppliers do not form any kind of collaborative formation. The findings reveal that the value of open innovation is derived not only from technology development, but also how well it stimulates a downstream original equipment manufacturer to invest.

The **second part** of the book deals with empirical findings based on quantitative research.

Schiele, Feldmann, and Hüttinger studied the antecedents of supplier innovativeness and supplier pricing. Based on a literature review, they identified two different types of antecedents: (1) 'technical' antecedents, which include the capabilities of suppliers to innovate (such as their level of R&D investment), and (2) 'behavioral' antecedents, which focus on the position of the buyer as a supplier's preferred customer. They hypothesize that the two antecedents influence supplier innovativeness in a positive way. Furthermore, they analyze supplier pricing behavior. They assume that suppliers' awareness of their capabilities to innovate might provoke them to charge unfair prices, while preferred customer status may reverse this tendency and lead to more benevolent supplier pricing behavior. They test the conceptual framework using a sample of 166 buyer–supplier relations. They found that technical and behavioral antecedents can explain supplier innovativeness to a large extent, with the role of preferred customer status being less relevant. Remarkably, whereas they expected that suppliers who are involved in innovation would be found to charge higher prices for their contributions to newly developed products, their results show that this effect is not statistically significant. The missing link between supplier pricing and supplier innovativeness can encourage firms to engage in collaborative innovation, because buyers do not need to fear being overcharged. Implementing a preferred customer policy can improve conditions for innovating with suppliers.

Peerally and Cantwell examined data on the textile-based Mauritius export processing zone (MEPZ) collected just prior to the demise of the preferential trade agreement (PTA) with Europe and they compared the acquisition and absorption of innovative technological capabilities (ITCs) of domestic firms and Asian-owned subsidiaries through domestic, Asian, and European-based supplier linkages. Their results show that there are significant differences in learning for innovation from suppliers by MEPZ domestic firms and Asian-owned subsidiaries. The study firstly reveals that domestic supplier firms in a developing sub-Saharan country, such as Mauritius, can be an important source of ITCs to both domestic firms and foreign subsidiaries. Secondly, despite the presence of appropriate policies and institutions, Asian-owned subsidiaries did not fully harness learning opportunities and absorb acquired ITCs through supplier linkages in order to create new technology locally. They conjecture that their learning strategy was dictated by their foreseen exit from the MEPZ due to the anticipated end of the PTA. Thirdly, domestic firms exhibited a higher commitment to the acquisition and absorption of ITCs through supplier linkages and to the development of local ITCs. They infer that their learning strategy is a consequence of their need to continue to thrive and expand post-PTA.

Yun and Avvari investigated the relationship between external open-innovation factors and internal open-innovation factors, termed the 'open-innovation attitude', in two different clusters in South Korea. They propose that certain 'internal open-innovation factors' such as 'attitude', known as the open-innovation attitude, along with other open-innovation factors, can affect overall innovation performance. The study has several interesting results-among them the result that external open-innovation factors and firm size have positive and significant effects on a firm's innovative performance. As they looked into results based on the two clusters, the results were different from each other. In Banwol-Sihwa Cluster, external open innovation, firm size, and R&D intensity did not have any significant effect on firms' innovation performance. However, in Goomi cluster external open innovation, and firm size had a positive and significant effect on firms' innovative performance. While there was a correlation between external open innovation and the internal open-innovation attitude in both clusters other results had significant differences for the role of clusters or Innovation systems in open innovation. The paper discusses the implications for open-innovation and also for policy and for firms' innovation strategies.

The chapter by Podmetina, Smirnova, Väätänen, and Torkkeli analyzes cooperation with external partners (using the example of suppliers) and their role for open-innovation implementation. Open innovation includes inbound innovation (the search for and acquisition of external knowledge, R&D, and technology), outbound innovation (the promotion of internal innovation through external commercialization channels), and coupled processes (the combination of inbound and outbound innovation). Results based on a survey of 206 Russian companies show that companies with more open and sophisticated innovation strategies tend to place a higher importance on cooperation with suppliers. In addition, the effects of partner location were evident in the data analysis. Companies value cooperation with domestic suppliers more than with foreign suppliers. The results are crucially important to managers because they show how cooperation matters for companies

with different innovation strategies. These insights are essential especially now, when the internationalization of Russian companies is
increasing on the international markets and their business strategies
are interesting for other participants of the European markets.

Teichert and Bouncken researched innovation in the context of
internal and external alignment. This is particularly the case for supplier innovation, as new product concepts and strategies must cope
with supply-chain interfaces. Suppliers' strategies are often confronted
by innovation rigidities resulting from a manufacturer's need to manage the integration of several components from various suppliers into
a coherent innovation. Suppliers can follow different innovation strategies derived from deliberate planning or emerging as suppliers incrementally learn and experiment. A survey of 241 suppliers illustrates
that the effects of these strategieson market success depends on the
level of the rigidities. The survey results also illustrated that two
dynamic capabilities, planning capability and innovation orientation,
act as intermediary variables for increasing success under specific
rigidity conditions. The findings further illustrate that dynamic capabilities can be enhanced by an adequate strategy.

Tiemann, Sick, and Leker present the results from an empirical survey of chemical suppliers, which examines the influence of customer
relationship functions on supplier involvement in customer new product development from the supplier's perspective. Using multiple regression analysis, they demonstrated a positive influence between direct
functions (e.g., profit and volume) of the customer relationship and
supplier involvement in customer NPD. Differentiating between innovative and non-innovative suppliers leads to distinctive differences.
While the direct functions are a strong predictor for supplier involvement in the non-innovative supplier group, in the innovative group
only indirect functions (innovation, market, scout, and access functions)
influence supplier involvement. These results show that mutual support
in the NPD and open network are the imperative triggers for the
involvement of innovative suppliers. The results show theoretical as well
as practical implications for supplier involvement in customer NPD.

The **third part** of the book discusses insights from case study
research.

Paasi, Luoma, Valkokari and Lee empirically studied firms' practices of knowledge and intellectual property (IP) management in customer–supplier relationships. The work applies the qualitative methodology of multiple case studies, and the material was collected in semi-structured interviews with management personnel at 36 organizations in Finland and in the Netherlands. Almost every firm had innovation relationships with their customers and suppliers, but the forms these relationships took, and the kinds of practices they involved, varied greatly. As a result, the firms considered the management of knowledge and IP in these relationships to be very challenging. They argue that by distinguishing knowledge management in the exploration phase of new business from knowledge management in the exploitation phase of innovation, firms could manage the knowledge and IP better. Accordingly, the paper introduced three propositions to support knowledge and IP management in customer–supplier relationships.

Sjödin and Eriksson explored how process firms can organize and manage supplier integration and open-innovation practices when developing and installing new process technology. By means of a literature review and a case study of two process firms, a collaborative lifecycle perspective on procurement was adopted. Their results show that process firms utilize different interconnected cooperative procurement procedures in different stages of the equipment lifecycle, in order to enhance integration both in buyer–supplier dyads and among suppliers in the project network. The lifecycle-based procurement model that they developed can serve as an illustrative framework, guiding practitioners in organizing and managing supplier integration and open-innovation practices.

Aune and Gressetvold researched a taxonomy for organizing innovation processes with suppliers. The empirical data consists of a case study of Norske Skog Skogn, the paper mill owned by the world's second largest producer of newsprint, and one of its suppliers, ABB, the global engineering company. The chapter considers a variety of approaches to organizing innovation processes with suppliers. The taxonomy may be useful in initiatives to increase awareness of the organization of innovation processes and to improve the performance of innovation processes.

Jörgensen, Bergenholtz, Goduscheit, and Rasmussen stated that the literature on innovation emphasizes the potential for organizations to collaborate and network instead of carrying out innovation individually. Integrating suppliers, customers, and other organizations into the innovation process is hence perceived as a key to success in innovation management (Chesbrough, 2003). Although the merits of network-based innovation are widely acknowledged, the managerial challenges of the initial integration of external organizations in an innovation network are somewhat neglected in the literature. The aim of this chapter is to address the challenges that an organization faces when integrating a plurality of suppliers, customers, and other organizations into the fuzzy front end of the innovation process.

Colombo, Dell' Era and Frattini adopt the point of view of an NPD service provider to investigate the approaches that can be employed in order to favor knowledge exchange with clients, throughout the service delivery process. The research relies on a multiple case study, which focuses on three collaborative projects undertaken by a world-leading provider of NPD services with some of its most important clients. The analysis reveals important findings. First, the NPD service provider uses standard approaches, both for process and organizational variables, to address two critical barriers for the successful completion of the inter-organizational relationship: the tacit nature of the knowledge to be exchanged and the difficulties in predicting the content of collaboration activities. Second, in implementing these approaches, the NPD service provider takes into account the distinctive characteristics of each client and the peculiarities of the specific collaborative project. Besides providing several practical insights that will be useful for managers working for NPD service providers, the paper contributes to the academic debate, e.g., by investigating the importance of trust in successful inter-organizational knowledge-exchange processes.

Edoff, Norström, and Wretås discuss offshore outsourcing in the context of cost reduction, by utilizing the suppliers´ economies of scale and lower wages. However, as outsourced tasks become more complex and require innovative practices, cultural differences become exposed. Cultural aspects are important to consider in securing efficiency and innovation in offshore outsourcing. Nevertheless, the cultural influence has only been studied to a limited extent. With this in mind, a case study was designed to explore the cultural interface between a Swedish high-tech company and its Indian service provider. The study was based on 40 in-depth interviews, observations, and business review documentation. The phenomenon of culture was examined through a literature review of organizational culture, national culture, and contextual factors. Their results show that by understanding, relating to, and managing cultural differences in a systematic manner, companies can gain competitive advantages.

Using process research of how multiple firms participated in the development of a groundbreaking anti-influenza drug, Newey found that firms needed to develop both supplier- and customer-types of absorptive capacity. Inbound open innovation involved customer absorptive capacity and outbound innovation required supplier absorptive capacity. In each case absorptive capacity needed to be leveraged differently.

Remneland-Wikhamn, Ljungberg, Bergquist, and Kuschel carried out a comparative case study of iPhones and Android phones. The notion of generative capacity washighlighted inresearch on open innovation, suggesting that it is generativity rather than openness that drives the platforms' aggregated wealth. These two cases from the mobile phone industry illustrate that innovation initiatives can successfully approach generativity in different ways and that both openness and control are important elements to facilitate stakeholder contributions.

Brunswicker and Hutschek linked relevant concepts of cognitive psychology and management theory — such as analogical problem-solving and the principle of isomorphism — with open innovation as the front end. They discuss the relevant dimensions for the systematic search for innovation in different industries. A piloted framework was presented, which assists firms in systematically and interactively searching for external innovation inputs in distant industries. This framework supports an external innovation search in unrelated industries for a fuzzy customer problem. The results of this participatory action research indicate that a systematic and interactive search process is of practical value to innovation managers. It also points out the contingencies of a cross-industry innovation search.

In a concluding chapter, we show the future paths for supplier innovation.

References

Bessant, J. (2003). *High Involvement Innovation: Building and Sustaining Competitive Advantage Through Continuous Change*, John Wiley, Chichester.

Bilgram, V., Brem, A. and Voigt, K.-I. (2008). User-centric innovations in new product development — Systematic identification of lead users harnessing interactive and collaborative online-tools, *International Journal of Innovation Management*, **12**(3), 419–458.

Chesbrough, H. (2003). *Open Innovation: The New Imperative for Creating and Profiting From Technology*, Harvard Business School Press, Boston, MA.

Groher, E. (2003). *Lieferantenintegration. Gestaltung der Integration von Lieferanten in den Produktentstehungsprozess*, TCW, München.

Maylor, H. (2001). Assessing relationship between practice changes and process: improvement in new product development, *Omega — International Journal of Management Science*, **29**(1), 85–96.

Petersen, K.J., Handfield, R.B. and Ragatz, G.L. (2003). A model of supplier integration into new product development, *Journal of Product Innovation Management*, **20**, 284–299.

Trott, P. and Hartmann, D. (2009). Why 'open innovation' is old wine in new bottles, *International Journal of Innovation Management*, **13**(4), 715–736.

vonHippel, E. (1988). *The Sources of Innovation*, Oxford University Press, New York.

vonHippel, E. (2005). *Democratizing Innovation*, MIT Press, Cambridge, MA.

Wingert, G.M. (1997). *Wettbewerbsvorteile durch Lieferantenintegration*, Gabler Verlag, Wiesbaden.

Part I

Theories and Concepts

Chapter 1

Advancing a Typology of Open Innovation

Peter Gianiodis*
College of Business & Behavioral Science, Department
of Management, Clemson University, USA

Scott C. Ellis
Department of Marketing and Supply Chain Management,
Gatton College of Business and Economics
University of Kentucky, USA

Enrico Secchi
College of Business & Behavioral Science, Department
of Management, Clemson University, USA

Introduction

Firms have adopted different systems of innovation in the face of increased global competition. Traditionally, firms have used a 'closed' approach, leveraging internal research and design capabilities to innovate. Recently, firms have adopted a more 'open' approach to innovation through the exchange of knowledge, resources, or capabilities with external partners. Firms who embrace open innovation are able to scale down internal research and development resources, while expanding the scope of their innovation activities. Examples abound of firms shifting towards open innovation (OI); for example,

---

*Corresponding author

Merck (Chesbrough, 2003c) has leveraged OI to achieve product innovation while reducing the numbers of research and design staff. In addition, Procter & Gamble (Dodgson *et al.*, 2006) and Xerox (Chesbrough, 2003b) have successfully adopted various forms of OI to increase revenues by incorporating innovation from external networks and selling existing intellectual property, respectively.

The promise of open-innovation systems has motivated scholars from a diverse set of disciplines — finance (Higgins and Rodriguez, 2006), economics (Cassiman and Veugelers, 2006), marketing (Di Maria and Finotto, 2008), and strategic management (Almirall and Casadesus-Masanell, 2010), just to name a few — to investigate this burgeoning phenomenon. As a consequence, researchers have applied diverse social and organizational theories to investigate the antecedents and consequences of OI; for example, researchers have used network theory to examine the effects of network centrality (Dahlander and Wallin, 2006) and uncertainty (Terwiesch and Xu, 2008), transaction cost economics to examine governance structure (van de Vrande *et al.*, 2006), and learning theory to examine absorptive capacity (Gassmann and Enkel, 2004; Laursen and Salter, 2006), and search capability (Kirschbaum 2005). These diverse views have fostered conceptualizations that emphasize different aspects of this phenomenon. In general, conceptualizations of OI tend to incorporate notions of: (1) inflows and outflows of knowledge, (2) the permeability of firm boundaries, (3) a firm's deliberate adoption practices, and (4) factors that influence the success of OI adoption. However, research models vary in how they apply OI concepts, including the parties involved, the type of transaction, and commercial outcomes. Our review suggests that, despite the early momentum, greater progress in OI is hampered by disparate definitions of constructs, conceptualizations, and findings across previous studies and the lack of a unifying framework that integrates this body of research.

Towards a theory of open innovation, we develop a typology of OI strategies that integrates existing research. In doing so, we contribute to the body of OI literature in several important ways (see Fig. 1). First, we provide a thorough review of the literature that examines OI at the strategic level. Through our review, we develop a theoretically grounded definition of open innovation, summarize the salient aspects already investigated, and provide a holistic view of the extant, multi-disciplinary

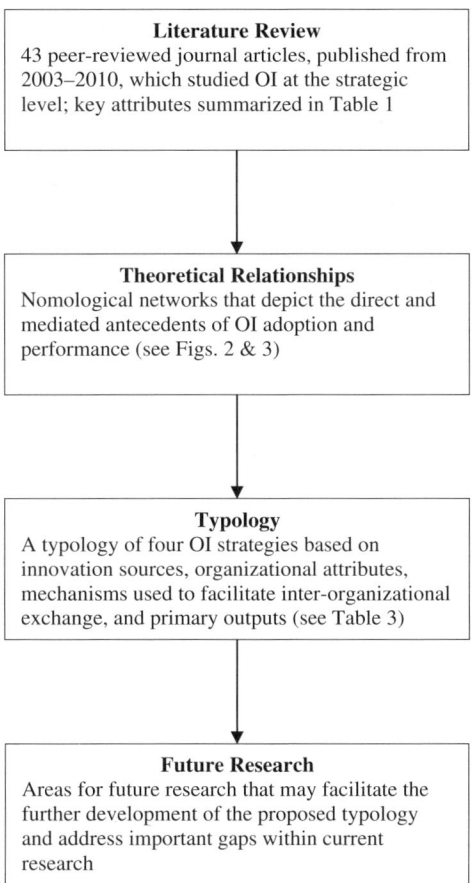

Fig. 1. Overview of Research Contributions.

research as it relates to two OI dependent variables: adoption and performance. In addition, we develop a typology detailing four OI strategies — the *innovation seeker*, the *innovation provider*, the *open innovator*, and *intermediary* strategies — that emerge through unique combinations of innovation sources, firm attributes, mechanisms of inter-organizational exchange, and which produce varying outcomes. These strategies represent four distinct pathways for firms to ensure the appropriability of their innovation capabilities. Lastly, our typology acts as a catalyst for researchers to investigate several avenues for future OI research. In particular, we identify several areas of conceptual development through the integration of complementary research; this richer theory, in turn, motivates large-scale empirical investigation.

The remainder of this chapter is organized as follows. In the next section, we review the OI literature, including theories that have influenced OI research and the development of existing OI definitions. Further, we develop a nomological network that synthesizes extant OI adoption and OI performance research. Then, we develop a typology of open-innovation strategies. We conclude our study with a brief discussion of the limitations of our study and present a comprehensive agenda for future OI research.

Literature Review

Scope and structure of the review

Given its importance in understanding organizational evolution and adaptation, innovation is one of the most researched areas in organizational studies attracting a diverse set of disciplines — economics, organization theory, strategic management, sociology, just to name a few. During the past century, researchers have made significant progress developing and testing a rich body of theory. Conducting a comprehensive review of the organizational innovation literature would be a major undertaking, beyond the scope of this paper. Thus, although drawing extensively from established theories of innovation, we confine our review to the developing body of literature investigating one form of innovation: open innovation.

We employed a two-stage approach to identify a comprehensive set of scholarly publications that form the basis of our review. Initially, we performed a search of key terms in the EBSCO, JSTOR, and Science Direct databases, and in the Google Scholar search engine. The search was performed using the keys 'open innovation', 'innovation outsourcing', 'innovation providers', and 'innovation networks'. Drawing from the sample of studies from the first stage, we subsequently expanded our search using forward and backward citation indices. We continued our search process until we identified an exhaustive set of studies. We adopted three boundary criteria for this review. First, we excluded studies that do not explicitly reference *open innovation*; thus, our review includes only articles published after 2003, when the term was coined (Chesbrough, 2003a, 2003b, 2003c). Second, because our study's primary focus is to better understand the implications of OI adoption for a firm's business model or within its value chain (Chesbrough, 2006a; Chesbrough, 2007; Christensen *et al.*, 2005), we required that the included articles consider *open innovation* at a strategic level. Finally, although OI has gained significant traction in the popular press and with consulting firms, we only included papers published in peer-reviewed scholarly journals.

Table 1 lists the resulting set of 43 studies that comprise our literature review and, for each study, presents the following key attributes: (1) unit of analysis, (2) exchange partners, (3) sample frame, (4) theoretical lens, (5) method, (6) constructs, (7) discipline, (8) locus of innovation, (9) research focus, and (10) research findings. Within this table, the *unit of analysis* is the level at which the analysis is conducted (firm, dyad, network, project). The field for *exchange partners* refers to the type of organizations engaged in the technology transaction and the nature of the inter-organizational tie. Whereas exchange partners include firms (F), communities (C), user communities (UC), and universities (U), the inter-organizational relationship may be vertical (V) or horizontal (H). *Sample frame* indicates whether the study investigated OI within a specific industry or across industries, and the *theoretical lens* refers to the specific theories used to examine the OI phenomenon. The *method* field indicates whether the study is theoretical, analytical, or empirical; for the last case, we describe the employed methodology (i.e., qualitative or quantitative). *Constructs* refer to the building blocks of the relations under study; these may be actual constructs, as operationalized within empirical studies, or implicit concepts derived from the relations and conclusions of the study. *Discipline* indicates the main reference field and stream of literature to which the research belongs. The *locus of innovation* field describes the innovation source and specifies whether the knowledge originates inside a firm (internal) or is acquired from external sources (external). Finally, the *research focus* and *findings* fields synthesize the central idea and primary conclusions of the study, respectively.

Table 1. Literature Review.

No.	Author (year)	UoA[3]	Exchange partners[4]	Sample frame	Theoretical lens	Method[5]	Constructs	Discipline	Locus of innovation	Research focus	Findings
1	Almirall and Casadesus-Masanell (2009)	N/C	F-F (H)	—	Evolutionary	A	Innovation strategy Partnership type (fixed/flexible) Complexity	Strategy	Both	Investigate the benefits and costs of OI in different situations	When changing partner is not an option, open innovation leads to better performance if complexity is low. When it is possible to change partners, as the partner opportunity set expands so does the minimum level of complexity, and open innovation leads to better performance.
2	Chesbrough (2003a)	P	—	Across	Innovation	E(C)	—	Strategy	Both	Show examples of companies that launched OI experiments	Many different approaches to OI are possible. The experiments examined were highly successful.

(*Continued*)

Table 1. (*Continued*)

No.	Author (year)	UoA[3]	Exchange partners[4]	Sample frame	Theoretical lens	Method[5]	Constructs	Discipline	Locus of innovation	Research focus	Findings
3	Chesbrough (2003b)	F	F-F (V)		Innovation	E(C)	Partnership	Strategy	Both	Illustrate how companies like Adobe are successful by establishing a standard	Adobe was successful because it leveraged partnerships to create a platform. Traditional measures of innovation performance (such as number of patents) do not capture the dynamics of these innovation processes.
4	Chesbrough (2003c)	F	F-F (H)	Within	Innovation	E(Qt)	Spin-off performance Complementarities (market and technical) Governance	Strategy	Internal	Identify the drivers of spin-off success in relation to governance choice	The presence of people from Xerox in the board of the spin-off is more important for the performance than the equity structure.

(*Continued*)

Table 1. (*Continued*)

No.	Author (year)	UoA[3]	Exchange partners[4]	Sample frame	Theoretical lens	Method[5]	Constructs	Discipline	Locus of innovation	Research focus	Findings
5	Chesbrough (2003d)	F	—	—	Innovation	T	—	Strategy	Both	Provide a general introduction to the concept of OI	The role of R&D extends beyond the boundaries of a single firm.
6	Chesbrough (2003e)	F	—	—	Innovation	T	—	Strategy	Both	Describe OI	Relying solely on internal R&D is no longer viable in the current environment.
7	Chesbrough (2006)	F	—	—	Innovation	T	Technical and market uncertainty Innovation performance	Strategy	Both	Development of metrics to manage open innovation	New metrics are needed to manage false positives and to react to the environment.

(*Continued*)

Table 1. (*Continued*)

No.	Author (year)	UoA[3]	Exchange partners[4]	Sample frame	Theoretical lens	Method[5]	Constructs	Discipline	Locus of innovation	Research focus	Findings
8	Chesbrough and Crowther (2006)	F	—	Across	Innovation	E(C)	Openness Practices adopted	Strategy	Both	Identify and interview early adopters of OI outside high-tech industries	Approaches to OI in non high-tech markets: — Using external technology to reduce time-to-market. — Identifying potential areas in which the next breakthrough will come.
9	Chesbrough and Schwartz (2007)	N	F-F (H&V)	—	Innovation	E(C)	Partnership objective Business requirements Implications for design Capabilities	Strategy	Both	Evaluate the potential of co-development practices	Few companies articulate what they expect to gain from their network and how they will secure gains. Leveraging network through co-development partnerships can be an important source of innovation.

(*Continued*)

Table 1. (*Continued*)

No.	Author (year)	UoA³	Exchange partners⁴	Sample frame	Theoretical lens	Method⁵	Constructs	Discipline	Locus of innovation	Research focus	Findings
10	Christensen *et al.* (2005)	D	F-F (V)	Within	Other (industrial dynamics)	E(C)	Access to technology; Complementary assets	Entrepreneurship	Internal	Study the role of complementarities in the implementation of OI strategy	The small technology firms had access to university research, but lacked the complementary assets to bring technology to maturity; they had to integrate into the existing value chains and choose niche markets.
11	Cooke (2005)	N/C	—	Across	Social networks; Dynamic capabilities	E(C)	Characteristics of network — Specialization — Diversification	Strategy	—	Highlight the importance of local networks to be able to succeed in global competition	Microcosms enable the macrocosm to function: globalization can work only with strong localization.

(*Continued*)

Table 1. (*Continued*)

No.	Author (year)	UoA[3]	Exchange partners[4]	Sample frame	Theoretical lens	Method[5]	Constructs	Discipline	Locus of innovation	Research focus	Findings
12	Dahlander *et al.* (2008)	—	F-C	—	Social networks	T	—	Entrepreneurship	External	Examine the issues of firm exploitation of online communities	Online communities are a valuable source of innovation. Governance and symbolic value creation are the main themes in the literature on managing open communities from a firm's perspective.
13	Dahlander and Wallin (2006)	D	F-C (H)	Within	Social networks	E(Qt)	Centrality Prestige Eigenvector (connection to central individuals) Firm connection Type of affiliation	Policy	External	Understand the dynamics of OS networks, and the differences between industry-sponsored participants and regular ones	User communities can be seen as complementary assets, which enable firms to take advantage of knowledge outside the firm. Firm-sponsored individuals have a resource advantage compared to

(*Continued*)

P. Gianiodis, S.C. Ellis and E. Secchi

Table 1. (*Continued*)

No.	Author (year)	UoA[3]	Exchange partners[4]	Sample frame	Theoretical lens	Method[5]	Constructs	Discipline	Locus of innovation	Research focus	Findings
											hobbyists, which allows them to reach a centrality position in the network. Individuals from companies that have incorporated OS in their business model have a significant influence in the community. In a situation like FOSS neither integration nor contractual strategies are feasible, and the boundaries between core and complementary assets are blurred.

(*Continued*)

Table 1. (*Continued*)

No.	Author (year)	UoA³	Exchange partners⁴	Sample frame	Theoretical lens	Method⁵	Constructs	Discipline	Locus of innovation	Research focus	Findings
14	Di Maria and Finotto (2008)	F	F-UC (V)	Across	User innovation	E(C)	—	Marketing	External	Study the effect of user communities by unifying marketing and innovation literature	The development of brand communities or other types of user communities can be a valuable source of innovation.
15	Dittrich and Duysters (2007)	N/C	F-F (V)	Within	Learning social networks	E(Qt)	Exploration/ exploitation- Partner's capabilities- Type of partner- Alliance type	Management	—	Investigate how rapid technological change can be faced through the establishment of innovation networks	Nokia tends to internally produce technologies that are considered to be part of their core (mobile handsets, network technology, and middleware). With the advent of UMTS, Nokia established many agreements characterized by weak ties, indicating a growth in the importance of exploration activities.

(*Continued*)

Table 1. (*Continued*)

No.	Author (year)	UoA[3]	Exchange partners[4]	Sample frame	Theoretical lens	Method[5]	Constructs	Discipline	Locus of innovation	Research focus	Findings
											Nokia has moved from formal buyer–supplier relations to a networking activity characteristic of open innovation.
16	Dodgson *et al.* (2006)	P	—	Within	Learning	E(C)	Organizational changes Technical changes	Strategy	Both	Explore the challenges that P&G had to face to move towards an OI model	Innovation Technologies (IvT) impact the creation of knowledge. Moving towards OI required organizational and technological changes.
17	Fetterhoff and Voelkel (2006)	P	—	Within	Innovation	E(C)	Five stages of OI 1. Seeking opportunities 2. Evaluating market potential 3. Recruiting partners	Strategy	External	Explore an effective method of employing OI	Pressures to incorporate external knowledge are increasing.

(*Continued*)

Table 1. (*Continued*)

No.	Author (year)	UoA[3]	Exchange partners[4]	Sample frame	Theoretical lens	Method[5]	Constructs	Discipline	Locus of innovation	Research focus	Findings
							4. Capturing value 5. Extending the innovation offering				Many companies will have to face the challenges of OI.
18	Gassmann, Sandmeier and Wecht (2006)	P	F-UC (V)	Within	User innovation	E(C)	Creativity Resource efficiency Effectiveness of front-end	Strategy	Both	Integrate customer inputs in NPD front-end	An effective NPD front-end enables both creativity and resource efficiency. XP (Extreme Programming)-type methodologies can be used to resolve the tension between creativity and resource efficiency (systematic probe and learn approach involving customers).

(*Continued*)

Table 1. (*Continued*)

No.	Author (year)	UoA[3]	Exchange partners[4]	Sample frame	Theoretical lens	Method[5]	Constructs	Discipline	Locus of innovation	Research focus	Findings
19	Gruber and Henkel (2006)	F	F-C (H)	Within	Evolutionary (organizational ecology)	E(Qt)	Liabilities of newness; Liabilities of smallness; Market-entry barriers; Participation in OSS	Entrepreneurship	Both	Explore how OSS-based new companies are affected by three challenges of venture management	Participation in OSS forums (the choice to open proprietary software) helps in offsetting liabilities and market barriers.
20	Henkel (2006)	F	F-C (H)	Within	Other (information trading)	E(Qt)	Share of code revealed to the public; Firm size; Firm policies; Proprietary complementary assets; Experience in embedded Linux; Support factors; Reputation; GPL	Strategy	Internal	Understand the dynamics of "free revealing" in embedded Linux firms	Firm size negatively affects share of code revealed. Firm policies only partially affect sharing. Complementary assets do not affect sharing. Experience significantly affects sharing. Reputation and development factors affect sharing. GPL and marketing factors do not affect sharing.

(Continued)

Table 1. (*Continued*)

No.	Author (year)	UoA[3]	Exchange partners[4]	Sample frame	Theoretical lens	Method[5]	Constructs	Discipline	Locus of innovation	Research focus	Findings
21	Hienerth (2006)	N/C	F-UC (V)	Within	NPD	E(C)	Stages of user innovations commercialization: Stage I) Start Stage II) Community building Stage III) Commercialization Stage IV) Market expansion	Entrepreneurship	External	Understand the dynamics of user innovation, development, and evolution	User-innovators commercialize their own innovations under certain conditions: — Individual needs, competitive ambitions. — Lead-users are the ones that may end up commercializing their innovations. — Ability to offset economies of scale by creating a niche.

(*Continued*)

Table 1. (*Continued*)

No.	Author (year)	UoA[3]	Exchange partners[4]	Sample frame	Theoretical lens	Method[5]	Constructs	Discipline	Locus of innovation	Research focus	Findings
22	Higgins and Rodriguez (2006)	D	F-F (H)	Within	Other (mergers)	E(Qt)	Desperation index Complementarities: — Prior set of experiences in therapeutic area — Alliance experience with target firm Cumulative abnormal returns Change in research pipeline	Finance	External	Understand how information on the target company before the acquisition contributes to the positive outcome of the acquisition (+ returns)	The amount of information gathering activities performed prior to merger positively affects performance after the merger. Level of desperation of the buying company has a negative effect on performance after the merger. Acquisition is a viable strategy to acquire external innovation.

(*Continued*)

Table 1. (*Continued*)

No.	Author (year)	UoA[3]	Exchange partners[4]	Sample frame	Theoretical lens	Method[5]	Constructs	Discipline	Locus of innovation	Research focus	Findings
23	Hurmelinna et al. (2007)	F	—	Across	Appropriability regimes	E(Qt)	Strength of appropriability regime (IPR and tacitness of knowledge) Knowledge flows within a company Positive network externalities available Level of standardization	Strategy		Understand the effect of managerial decisions on appropriability regimes and subsequently on knowledge flows	A strong Intellectual Property Regime (IPR) increases internal knowledge sharing. The stronger the appropriability regime, the more the company has positive network externalities.
24	Kaiser and Müller-Seitz (2008)	N/C	F-UC (H)	Within	Social networks Motivation (psych)	E(GT)	Extrinsic motivation Intrinsic motivation Degree of participation	Strategy	Internal	Understand the motivational drivers and performance outcome of the IT-mediated participation of lead-users in software development	Flow states provide intrinsic motivation: — Freedom to engage. — Freedom of speech. — Having impact. — Reciprocal social exchange.

(*Continued*)

P. Gianiodis, S.C. Ellis and E. Secchi

Table 1. (*Continued*)

No.	Author (year)	UoA[3]	Exchange partners[4]	Sample frame	Theoretical lens	Method[5]	Constructs	Discipline	Locus of innovation	Research focus	Findings
											External motivation: — Ability to signal competence. — Obtaining support.
25	Kirschbaum (2005)	P	—	Within	Innovation	E(C)	Search strategy	Strategy	Both	Understand the drivers of OI success at DSM	DSM innovation strategy is based on: — Systematically scanning the environment for new opportunities. — The management of projects with an "intrapreneurial" mindset. — Leveraging the skills of experienced management when projects reach maturity.

(*Continued*)

Table 1. (*Continued*)

No.	Author (year)	UoA[3]	Exchange partners[4]	Sample frame	Theoretical lens	Method[5]	Constructs	Discipline	Locus of innovation	Research focus	Findings
26	Laursen and Salter (2006)	F	—	Across (manufacturing)	Social networks Institutional theory Evolutionary economics	E(Qt)	External search Novelty of innovation Openness Absorptive capacity Innovative performance	Strategy	External	Empirically examine the effect of open innovation	External search breadth is curvilin early related to innovative performance (inverted U-shape). External search depth is curvilin early related to innovative performance (inverted U-shape). No support for relation between internal R&D and external search breadth and depth. External search provides advantages, but over-searching can negatively affect innovative performance; external search depth is associated with radical innovation.

(*Continued*)

Table 1. (*Continued*)

No.	Author (year)	UoA[3]	Exchange partners[4]	Sample frame	Theoretical lens	Method[5]	Constructs	Discipline	Locus of innovation	Research focus	Findings
27	Lettl *et al.* (2006)	P	F-UC (V)	Within	User innovation	E(C)	— User characteristics — User roles — Interaction type between firm and user — Typology of knowledge gained from users — Outcomes	Strategy	External	Show how users can be an important source of innovation	Users had a need and in all four cases looked for technologies outside their immediate field. Users had a highly entrepreneurial attitude and behavior, and exhibited ability in managing the extended networks of people involved. Users also took over a developer or co-developer role in the innovation process. The firms that were able to incorporate users' efforts in their

(*Continued*)

Table 1. (*Continued*)

No.	Author (year)	UoA[3]	Exchange partners[4]	Sample frame	Theoretical lens	Method[5]	Constructs	Discipline	Locus of innovation	Research focus	Findings
											development benefited in terms of product innovation, process, and technology.
28	Lichtenthaler (2006)	F	—	—	Exploration/ exploitation	T	Internal technology exploitation External technology exploitation	Strategy	External	Develop an integrated approach to technology exploitation	Four technology exploitation strategies can be adopted in the context of OI: — Internal technology exploitation. — Integrated technology exploitation. — No technology exploitation. — External technology exploitation.

(*Continued*)

P. Gianiodis, S.C. Ellis and E. Secchi

Table 1. (*Continued*)

No.	Author (year)	UoA[3]	Exchange partners[4]	Sample frame	Theoretical lens	Method[5]	Constructs	Discipline	Locus of innovation	Research focus	Findings
29	Lichtenthaler (2008)	F	—	Within	Learning	E(Qt)	Extent of external technology acquisition Extent of external technology commercialization Industry Country Financial performance R&D intensity Emphasis on radical innovation Diversification	Strategy	Both	Classify firms according to their innovation strategy	Clusters: 1) Closed innovators, 2) Closed innovators that acquire a considerable part of their technology from external sources, 3) Absorbing innovators, 4) Desorbing innovators, 5) Balanced innovators, 6) Open innovators. The largest cluster is still that of the closed innovators.

(*Continued*)

Table 1. (*Continued*)

No.	Author (year)	UoA[3]	Exchange partners[4]	Sample frame	Theoretical lens	Method[5]	Constructs	Discipline	Locus of innovation	Research focus	Findings
											Firms with higher revenues, more product variety, and a CV unit are more likely to be open innovators.
30	Lichtenthaler and Ernst (2006)	F	—	—	Other (knowledge management)	T	Attitudes to externally carrying out knowledge management tasks: 1) Not-invented-here (NIH) 2) Buy-in (BI) 3) All-stored-here (ASH) 4) Relate-out (RO) 5) Only-used-here (OUH) 6) Sell-out (SO)	Strategy	Both	Expand the previous literature on NIH syndrome by including other attitudes that play a role in technology adoption	The six syndromes identify overly positive or negative attitudes towards the external performance of knowledge management tasks. It is difficult to gain competitive advantage with a biased decision-making process

(*Continued*)

Table 1. (*Continued*)

No.	Author (year)	UoA[3]	Exchange partners[4]	Sample frame	Theoretical lens	Method[5]	Constructs	Discipline	Locus of innovation	Research focus	Findings
31	Lichtenthaler and Ernst (2007)	F	F-F (H&V)	Across	Innovation	E(Qt)	Revenues from licensing and selling tech. Knowledge Strategic functions of outbound OI	Strategy	Internal	Provide a quantitative evaluation of the magnitude and characteristics of the External Technology Commercialization (ETC) phenomenon	Outbound OI is limited in comparison to traditional R&D. Strategic role of OI is considered more important than monetary returns.
32	Lokshin et al. (2008)	F	—	Across	Learning	E(Qt)	Ratio of internal to external R&D (R&D intensity, external and internal) Labor productivity	Economics	Both	Analyze the role of complementarities between internal and external R&D	Increasing external R&D can be beneficial. External and internal R&D are complementary — external R&D expenditure leads to diminished expenditure on labor productivity only in the presence of adequate internal R&D expenditure.

(*Continued*)

Table 1. (*Continued*)

No.	Author (year)	UoA[3]	Exchange partners[4]	Sample frame	Theoretical lens	Method[5]	Constructs	Discipline	Locus of innovation	Research focus	Findings
33	Perkmann and Walsh (2007)	D	F-U (H)	—	Social networks	T	University-industry relationship types: — Research partnerships — Research services	Management	External	Creating a roadmap for research in F-U relationships in an open-innovation context	The more a sector is science based, the more it will use partnerships. Consulting (service) activities of universities play an important role for SMEs.
34	Piller and Walcher (2006)	P	F-UC (V)	Within	User innovation	E(C)	Initiative characteristics (task specificity and degree of elaboration). Performance of user contribution	Strategy	External	Evaluate the effectiveness of TIC competitions in NPD	Users are willing to participate in development.
35	Prugl and Schreier (2006)	Pj	F-UC (V)	Within	User innovation	E(C)	Development toolkits available to users (openness)	Strategy	External	Understand how the development of tools that allow the users to modify the product affects the innovation process	Users spent an equivalent of 36.6 full time programmers' time in development activities. The most innovative designs came from users.

(*Continued*)

Table 1. (*Continued*)

No.	Author (year)	UoA[3]	Exchange partners[4]	Sample frame	Theoretical lens	Method[5]	Constructs	Discipline	Locus of innovation	Research focus	Findings
36	Terwiesch and Xu (2008)	Pj	F-F (V)	—	NPD	A	Type of project-expertise-based-ideation projects- trial and error projects expertise, effort, uncertainty Number of trials	Strategy	External	Understand what type of innovation problems are most suited for innovation contests Determine the optimal design of the innovation contest, given the type of innovation problem	High uncertainty can lead to solver underinvestment. Using filtering mechanisms (like first-round screening) the seeker can reduce the underinvestment problem. In this case a large pool of initial contestants can be beneficial.
37	van de Vrande *et al.* (2006)	F	F-F (H&V)	—	Other (TCE, RO)	T	Governance mode Information asymmetry Technological distance	Strategy	External	Understand when firms prefer alliances and partnerships over acquisitions	Under high uncertainty, companies will try to use reversible technology sourcing strategies.

(*Continued*)

Table 1. (*Continued*)

No.	Author (year)	UoA[3]	Exchange partners[4]	Sample frame	Theoretical lens	Method[5]	Constructs	Discipline	Locus of innovation	Research focus	Findings
											The more the technological distance between firms, the more VC will be preferred to strategic alliances, and strategic alliances to acquisitions. The more the information asymmetry, the less close the relationship.
38	van der Meer (2007)	F	—	Across	Innovation	E(Qt)	Factors that hamper innovation Innovation strategy	Strategy	Both	Analyze diffusion and perception of OI models in the Netherlands	Very small diffusion of OI models apart from a group of pioneers. Innovative SMEs are more naturally suited to engage in OI.

(*Continued*)

P. Gianiodis, S.C. Ellis and E. Secchi

Table 1. (*Continued*)

No.	Author (year)	UoA[3]	Exchange partners[4]	Sample frame	Theoretical lens	Method[5]	Constructs	Discipline	Locus of innovation	Research focus	Findings
39	von Hippel and von Krogh (2006)	F	—	Within	Other (collective action)	T	Model of innovation incentives — Private investment model — Collective action model — Private-collective model	Strategy	Internal	Understand when companies freely reveal their technological knowledge	There are several incentives that promote free revealing behavior. As an alternative to completely closed and completely open, a private-collective model is optimal.
40	West and Lakhani (2008)	N/C	—	—	Social networks	T	Community	Strategy	—	Generate a better definition for the community construct in OI literature	The term "community" is used many different ways in OI literature. The relative position of firms with respect to innovation communities is an area of increasing importance.

(*Continued*)

Table 1. (*Continued*)

No.	Author (year)	UoA[3]	Exchange partners[4]	Sample frame	Theoretical lens	Method[5]	Constructs	Discipline	Locus of innovation	Research focus	Findings
41	West and O'Mahony (2008)	N/C	F-C (V)	Within	Social networks	E(GT)	Form of openness — transparency — accessibility — proprietary model; Dimensions of participation architecture — production — governance — intellectual property	Strategy	External	Understand how firm-sponsored innovation communities differ from autonomous ones	Sponsors of communities face tension between control and openness. The choices on the three dimensions qualify the way in which firms deal with the tension. Three groups of communities are classifiable according to their degree of openness.
42	West *et al.* (2006)	F	F-C (V)	Within	Appropriability regimes	E(GT)	Motivation to contribute; Incorporation of external knowledge; OI approach	Strategy	Internal	Understand how and why firms commit their IP and HR investment in efforts that will benefit others (i.e. developing open technology)	Classification of OI through the structural relationship of R&D contributors: — Pooled R&D (Mozilla, OSDL): firms donate IP to the project

(*Continued*)

P. Gianiodis, S.C. Ellis and E. Secchi

Table 1. (*Continued*)

No.	Author (year)	UoA[3]	Exchange partners[4]	Sample frame	Theoretical lens	Method[5]	Constructs	Discipline	Locus of innovation	Research focus	Findings
											while reaping the common benefits (sale of a related product). Spillovers re not controllable. Contributions arrive from external participants who are not part of any of the consortium companies. — Spinouts: transforming internal development processes into open external, more visible, ones.

(*Continued*)

Table 1. (*Continued*)

No.	Author (year)	UoA³	Exchange partners⁴	Sample frame	Theoretical lens	Method⁵	Constructs	Discipline	Locus of innovation	Research focus	Findings
43	Witzeman et al. (2006)	F	—	Across	Other (strategic planning)	E(Ql)	Approaches to levels of external technology sourcing — Cost and SCM — Strategic Partnering — Extended networks — Integrated external innovation	Strategy	External	Develop a framework for making OI decisions	Harnessing external innovation requires a change in the overall strategic planning process.

³Unit of Analysis. C: Community; D: Dyad; F: Firm; N: Network; P: OI Program; Pj: Project.

⁴F-F: Firm-to-Firm relation; F-C: Firm–Community relation; F-UC: Firm–User Community relation; F-U: Firm–University relation. V: Vertical relationship (e.g. buyer-supplier); H: Horizontal relation.

⁵A: Analytical; E: Empirical (Qt: Quantitative; Ql: Qualitative; C: Case study; GT: Grounded Theory); T: Theoretical.

P. Gianiodis, S.C. Ellis and E. Secchi

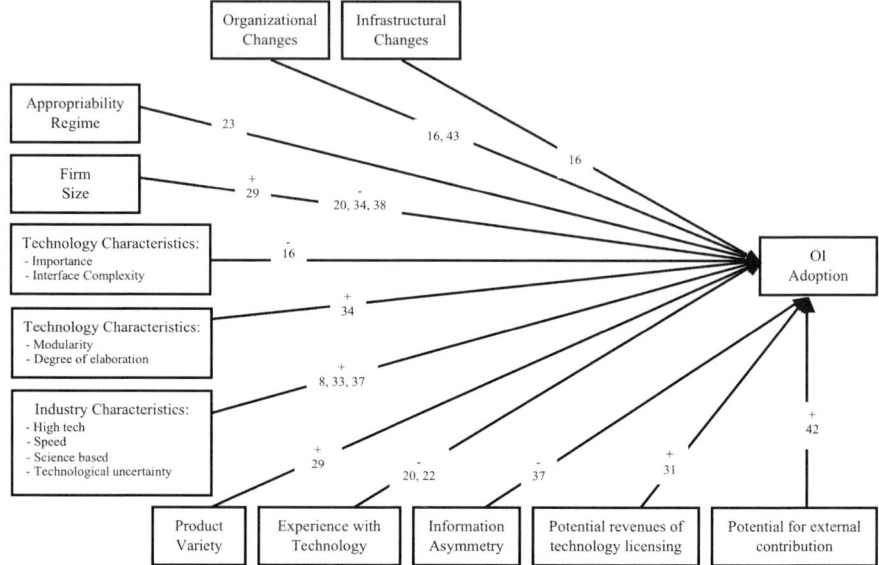

Fig. 2. Antecedents of OI Adoption.

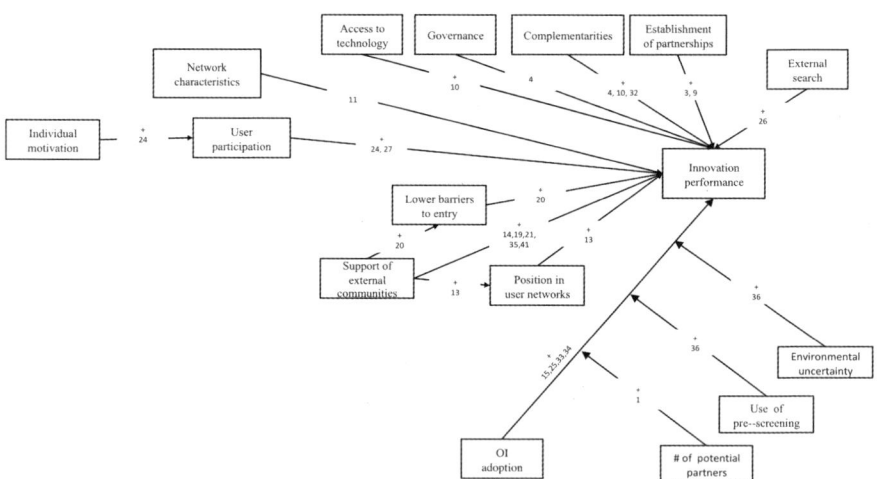

Fig. 3. Antecedents of Innovation Performance.

To complement Table 1, Figs 2 and 3 summarize the theoretical relationships between the constructs identified in our review. Figure 2 summarizes conceptual developments and empirical findings related to OI adoption, and Fig. 3 synthesizes prior OI research related to innovation performance. We link the table and figures using a consistent numbering scheme such that the numbers in Figs 2 and 3 correspond with studies listed in Table 1; we associate specific studies with each relationship presented in the figures. This approach allows readers to gain insight into the studies that address specific aspects of OI and also facilitates an assessment of the breadth and depth of extant OI research. Whenever possible, we denote the nature of the relation using a plus or minus sign. We omit the direction for studies in which the relation between constructs was not articulated.

Defining open innovation

Extant research on OI employs a variety of theoretical approaches, which have fostered (1) the consideration of a wide array of disparate principles and constructs (see Figs 2 and 3), and (2) the development of a variety of definitions of open innovation (see Table 2). Despite this diversity in conceptualization across disparate studies, we identify several themes that emerge from extant definitions of open innovation and prior research and suggest that these themes may serve as the basis for a unifying definition of OI.

A significant body of OI research draws explicitly or tacitly from organizational learning theory (March, 1991) and the notion of absorptive capacity (Cohen and Levinthal, 1990; Zahra and George, 2002). For example, Gassmann and Enkel (2004) identify three archetypes of knowledge flows in open-innovation environments: (1) outside-in flows, (2) inside-out flows, and (3) bi-directional flows, and they suggest that these knowledge flows are critical to firms' innovation processes. Similarly, Lichtenthaler (2008) empirically derives strategic approaches to OI using two criteria: the extent of external technology acquisition and exploitation. Related studies consider how absorptive capacity influences firms' existing innovation processes (Cohen and Levinthal, 1990). In particular, researchers have considered the linkage between absorptive capacity and innovation acquisition (Christensen *et al.*, 2005; Dittrich

Table 2.   Open-innovation Definitions.

Definition	Source
Open innovation is the use of purposive inflows and outflows of knowledge to accelerate internal innovation, and expand the markets for external use of innovation, respectively. [This paradigm] assumes that firms can and should use external ideas as well as internal ideas, and internal and external paths to market, as they look to advance their technology.	Chesbrough *et al.*, 2006, p. 1
Open innovation means that the company needs to open up its solid boundaries to let valuable knowledge flow in from the outside in order to create opportunities for cooperative innovation processes with partners, customers and/or suppliers. It also includes the exploitation of ideas and IP in order to bring them to market faster than competitors can.	Gassmann and Enkel, 2004, p. 2
An open-innovation approach refers to systematically relying on a firm's dynamic capabilities of internally and externally carrying out the major technology management tasks, i.e. technology acquisition and technology exploitation, along the innovation process.	Lichtenthaler, 2008, p. 148
The system is referred to as open because the boundaries of the product development funnel are permeable. Some ideas from innovation projects are initiated by other parties before entering the internal funnel; other projects leave the funnel and are further developed by other parties.	Dittrich and Duysters, 2007, p. 512

(Continued)

Table 2. (*Continued*)

This means that innovation can be regarded as resulting from distributed inter-organizational networks, rather than from single firms.	Perkmann and Walsh, 2007, p. 259
We define open innovation as systematically encouraging and exploring a wide range of internal and external sources for innovation opportunities, consciously integrating that exploration with firm capabilities and resources, and broadly exploiting those opportunities through multiple channels.	West *et al.*, 2006, p. 320
[T]here exist a rapidly growing number of innovation processes that rely on the outside world to create opportunities and then select the best from among these alternatives for further development. This approach is often referred to as *open innovation.*	Terwiesch and Xu, 2008, p. 1529

and Duysters, 2007; Dodgson *et al.*, 2006; Lokshin *et al.*, 2008). These studies, in conjunction with the definitions of OI, which explicitly cite 'inflows and outflows of knowledge' (Chesbrough *et al.*, 2006) and 'knowledge flow' (Gassmann and Enkel, 2004), suggest that inflows and outflows of knowledge are particularly germane to a definition of open innovation.

Consistent with organizational learning theory, several studies cite the permeability of organizational and innovation process boundaries as a salient aspect of OI. Traditional views of R&D, for example the *development tunnel* (Hayes *et al.*, 1988), hold that successful innovation requires control; this assumption is the cornerstone of what Chesbrough (2003b) refers to as the old paradigm of closed innovation. Within this paradigm, competitive advantage stems from the possession of unique knowledge, which firms safeguard as exclusive intellectual property. Firms purposely limit and tightly control flows of information across organizational boundaries; boundary-spanning activity is accompanied with exhaustive contracting or buffeted by long-standing partner relations (Teece, 2000). In contrast, Chesbrough's (2003d) conceptualization of the innovation funnel decouples the loci of innovation, new product development (NPD), and commercialization, holding that firms enhance innovation performance through acquisition and commercialization of innovation within a broader, external innovation network. Dittrich and Duysters (2007) extend this notion of permeability by suggesting that the boundaries of the innovation creation process, rather than the organization, are critical to OI success. Thus, organizational permeability is a precondition for enacting and exploiting an OI business model (Chesbrough, 2006). Organizational permeability creates issues of appropriation; drawing upon the concept of an appropriability regime (Teece, 1986), researchers have demonstrated how firms benefit from OI by deploying complementary assets, and through the effective use of contracting and intellectual property management (Dahlander and Wallin, 2006).

Although researchers posit that OI has implications at all levels of the firm, the main thrust of the research considers its strategic impact. For example, extant OI research has studied how (1) top-down managerial initiatives and business growth goals (Chesbrough and Crowther, 2006), (2) research awards and business performance metrics (Chesbrough, 2003e), (3) corporate culture (West *et al.*, 2006), and (4) boundary-spanning leadership (Fleming and Waguespack, 2007) affect the transfer of innovation across organizational boundaries. Empirically, research findings indicate that innovation search capabilities significantly influence innovation performance (Laursen and Salter, 2006). Similarly, case-based research suggests that a firm's ability to manage strategic alliances, spin-offs, and license agreements is critical to the commercialization of innovation outside the firm's traditional channels (Chesbrough, 2003b).

Consistent with our review, we suggest that three themes emerge from extant OI research: (2) open innovation requires inflows or outflows of knowledge and innovation, (2) an organization must have permeable boundaries that allow knowledge and innovation flows into and out of it, and (3) open innovation is a 'firm-level' strategy that enables organizations to capture value. Consistent with these emergent themes, we define an open-innovation strategy as a *business model that is designed to purposefully allow and facilitate knowledge and technology transfers across organizational boundaries.*

Nomological network of open innovation

We organize our discussion of the literature into sections in accordance with the two primary dependent variables: OI adoption and innovation performance. As suggested in Fig. 2 several factors affect a firm's decision to adopt OI practices and subsequently the magnitude of it usage. Contextual factors such as the characteristics of the environment (Perkmann and Walsh, 2007; Van de Vrande *et al.*, 2006), the firm (Henkel, 2006; Higgins and Rodriguez, 2006), or the technology (Dodgson *et al.*, 2006; Piller and Walcher, 2006), are important preconditions to OI adoption. Figure 3 indicates that several factors in addition to OI adoption affect innovation performance, including industry structure (Henkel, 2006), inter-firm relational attributes (Dahlander *et al.*, 2008), organizational activities (Laursen and Salter, 2006), and user and user community involvement (Kaiser and Muller-Seitz 2008). Next, we elaborate on the elements and relationship in Figs. 2 and 3.

Open-innovation adoption

Firms face the choice of whether to and the degree to which they adopt OI strategies. Research has identified three broad categories of determinants of OI adoption: firm characteristics, technology considerations, and external environmental conditions (Gassmann and Enkel, 2004; Perkmann and Walsh, 2007). Each affects 'organizational fit' — the extent to which critical firm-level characteristics (i.e., systems, processes, structures, and incentives) are aligned with external environmental conditions.

Firm characteristics. Firm characteristics play a prominent role in determining OI adoption. For many firms, changes to organizational structure and existing processes must take place in order to facilitate OI adoption (Dodgson *et al.*, 2006; Witzeman *et al.*, 2006). Antiquated organizational structures and systems supporting closed-innovation strategies are oriented towards knowledge management and storage; whereas, OI strategies require networking and knowledge exchange capabilities (Dodgson *et al.*, 2006). Indeed, the reshaping of practices and technology goes beyond the adoption of specific practices and instead requires that the firm reshape its entire business model. Previous research suggests that firm size affects the innovation approach; however, to date, findings are equivocal. Lichtenthaler (2008) found that larger firms are more likely to leverage OI strategies as a means to ward off competitive pressure from smaller and more entrepreneurial firms. In contrast, other studies found that smaller firms are more likely to engage in OI practices (Henkel, 2006; Van der Meer, 2007). Because OI is an emerging phenomenon, the choice of research settings and methods may explain these conflicting findings. Additionally, the degree of a firm's product variety may help explain OI adoption; the more varied a firm's product offerings, the less likely the firm is to rely completely on internal innovation (Lichtenthaler, 2008). Another important firm-level factor relates to experience with the focal technology. As with size, the findings are not clear, especially when industry considerations are taken into effect. Henkel (2006) found that experience with embedding Linux into a product lowers the need to exchange knowledge with the community; however, Higgins and Rodriguez (2006) found that the familiarity with another firm's technology increases the likelihood that mergers may be used to acquire such technology.

Technology considerations. In addition to firm characteristics, OI research suggests that the type of technology employed by a firm is also likely to impact the adoption of an OI strategy. Modular technologies are better suited for OI methods; whereas, technologies with complex interfaces make OI adoption more difficult (Gassmann and Enkel, 2004). Also firms will try to protect core technologies by making them inaccessible to external partners, limiting open-innovation exchanges (Dodgson *et al.*, 2006). Lastly, research has yet to explore the relation between technology portfolio management and OI adoption. In a broader perspective, prior to adopting an OI strategy, firms must understand the *appropriability regime* in which they will transact such that they can effectively minimize the risks of replication or emulation from potential imitators and capture value through innovation (Hurmelinna *et al.*, 2007).

External environmental conditions: The third broad consideration regarding OI adoption relates to external environmental conditions. Consistent with Chesbrough's (2003b) concept of 'erosion factors', research has examined how environmental changes have undermined the functionality of the closed model. Industry characteristics such as industry speed (i.e. the length of product life cycles, the frequency of changes in industry structure, and the development of new markets) and the high- or low-tech nature are likely antecedents of the decision to adopt OI strategies (Chesbrough and Crowther, 2006). Although OI is generally associated most closely with high-tech industries research has begun to examine OI in more traditional sectors. The prominence of OI in high-tech industries is explained by their higher *clockspeed* (Eisenhardt and Brown, 1998; Fine, 1998); high-tech industries are more research intensive, which makes firms more active searchers for innovation. Research posits that technological uncertainty, often associated with industries with fast cycles and a high *clockspeed*, increases the likelihood that firms will employ a more open approach to innovation (Van de Vrande *et al.*, 2006).

Open-innovation performance

A complementary body of research has investigated the performance effects of OI adoption. In line with mainstream innovation research, scholars have conceptualized OI performance in a variety of ways depending upon the unit of analysis and specific OI processes under investigation. In general, researchers have broadly considered innovation performance in terms of: (1) incremental and radical innovation (Chesbrough and Crowther, 2006; Laursen and Salter, 2006; Lettl *et al.*, 2006), (2) commercialization and value appropriation (Chesbrough, 2003b; Cooke, 2005; Henkel, 2006; Hurmelinna *et al.*, 2007; Lichtenthaler and Ernst, 2007; West *et al.*, 2006), and (3) labor productivity (Lokshin *et al.*, 2008) and efficiency gains through innovation contests (Terwiesch and Xu, 2008) and open-source communities (Dahlander and Wallin, 2006; Di Maria and Finotto, 2008; Gruber and Henkel, 2006; West and O'Mahony, 2008). Consistent with extant research, we adopt a broad view of OI performance and as suggested in Fig. 3 consider many environmental, firm-specific, and technological factors that affect innovation performance.

Firms simultaneously seek incremental innovation to enhance existing product offerings, while searching for radical solutions to open new, fertile markets. Researchers have examined the extent to which OI practices affect a firm's innovation portfolio (i.e. incremental vs. radical innovation). Instituting OI practices denotes a firm's commitment to external search and reliance upon its absorptive capacity efficacy. External search, in terms of breadth and depth, drives the number and type of strategic partners available for collaboration. Laursen and Salter (2005) found that the breadth and depth of search have a curvilinear (inverted U-shaped) effect on both incremental and radical innovation; whereas the consideration of external sources (i.e. breadth) and intensive interaction within search channels (i.e. depth) initially contribute to innovation, the bounded rationality and managerial attention limits suggest that over-search, i.e., an excessive breadth and depth of search, is detrimental to innovation performance. Similarly, drawing on the notion of diminishing returns from extensive search, Cooke (2005) suggested that a robust regional network is critical to successful innovation. In a similar vein Almirall and Casadesus (2010) employed an analytical approach to show how the number of available partners (i.e. a 'flexible partnership' regime) leads to more innovative end-products, which embody greater customer value. Broadening innovation networks increases the likelihood of finding innovative solutions (Almirall and Casadesus-Masanell, 2010).

Complementary to external search, research suggests that a firm's absorptive capacity influences its ability to develop innovation.

Absorptive capacity is predicated on shared understanding whereby common language, norms, and culture facilitate the efficient transfer of knowledge across functional and firm boundaries (Cohen and Levinthal, 1990). A certain amount of internal knowledge is a prerequisite for effectively leveraging external sources (Lokshin *et al.*, 2008). Laursen and Salter (2006) identify R&D intensity as a proxy for absorptive capacity and argue that investments in R&D enable firms to identify promising new innovations and subsequently improve the effectiveness of search activities. However, empirical findings regarding absorptive capacity are mixed; Laursen and Salter (2006) show that the interaction of R&D intensity and search negatively affects innovation suggesting that firms view R&D intensity and search capabilities as substitutes rather than complements. Conversely, Lokshin and his colleagues (2008) find that greater R&D intensity allow firms to benefit most from increases in external R&D.

Users may also contribute to both radical and incremental innovation (Kaiser and Muller-Seitz, 2008). Lettl and colleagues (2006) found that user-innovators: (1) were motivated by severe problems that existing technology did not address, (2) were open to adopt new technology that facilitated problem resolution, (3) maintained access to inter-disciplinary tacit knowledge, and (4) were intrinsically motivated to invent new solutions. Importantly, the same study found that establishing linkages with innovative users enabled manufacturers to develop more innovative products while decreasing development times and costs. Related research suggests that company-provided toolkits, which facilitate access to customers' novel ideas, may effectively enhance innovation performance (Piller and Walcher, 2006).

In addition to facilitating incremental and radical solutions, OI performance may denote commercialization and value appropriation by the inventing firm. One factor influencing successful commercialization is the presence of complementarities — firm-specific resources valued by a partnering firm (Teece, 1986). The presence of complementary assets underlies the notion of technological or commercial 'fit' or 'match' between firms. In general, extant research suggests that the presence of complementarities allows firms to simultaneously exploit their own and their partners' core competencies. In

Chesbrough's (2003b) investigation of Xerox spin-offs, he found, contrary to expectations, that complementarities (i.e. market and technical relatedness) have no effect on spin-off revenue growth. In related research Christensen *et al.* (2005) and Cooke (2005) examined the inter-relationships amongst complementarities, product life cycle (PLC), and commercialization. Their qualitative analysis of the consumer electronics and biotechnology industries suggests that the effectiveness of specific approaches to commercialization is conditioned by the PLC stage. In particular Christensen *et al.* (2005) emphasize how, with embryonic product technologies, entrepreneurial firms sought strategic partnerships within high-end markets to carve out niche positions. However, as the product technology matured, the same firms sought ties with large, mass marketers of mainstream consumer electronics (Christensen *et al.*, 2005).

In addition to complementarities and stage of the PLC, specific firm strategies and the governance of the partnerships affect commercialization and value appropriation. In contrast to closed-innovation systems, where proprietary innovation is prominent, open innovation espouses the exploitation of both internal and external intellectual property (Hurmelinna *et al.*, 2007). Accordingly, research suggests that a key aspect of an OI strategy is the protection of intellectual property. Strong intellectual property rights may protect first-mover advantage, facilitate product marketing, legitimize product technology, enhance a firm's image, and increase licensing opportunities (Hurmelinna *et al.*, 2007, p. 136). However, tight protection may also be harmful: patents may reveal important innovation information to competitors and strong protection may impede knowledge transfer to partners even when transfer is desirable. Related studies consider the effects of free revealing on appropriability. For example, Henkel (2006) suggests that under certain conditions firms may reveal their innovations without protection in order to attain collaborative benefits from a wider community. Similarly, von Hippel and von Krogh (2006) propose that free revealing may generate excess profits when: (1) the innovation is similar to others, (2) patents yield little revenue, and (3) there are other non-monetary benefits to revealing the innovation (i.e. providing a public good).

A final OI performance outcome relates to gaining greater efficiencies within a firm's existing innovation system. Research has found that strategic partnerships have a positive effect on internal labor efficiencies; in OI settings, internal human capital can leverage external knowledge sources to create a stronger pipeline and bring innovation to market more efficiently (Lokshin *et al.*, 2008). Similarly, the development of close partnerships facilitates efficiencies within the new product development and commercialization processes (Chesbrough and Schwartz, 2007). For example, Adobe's ability to establish partnerships with companies willing to support their platform ultimately determined its success (Chesbrough, 2003c). Firms may foster further efficiencies within their innovation processes through the use of innovation contests. Using analytical methods Terwiesch and Xu (2008) found that firms may customize contest design and reward structures to optimize firms' expected profits across different types of innovation projects.

Research into open-source software (OSS) (i.e. software without proprietary standards) indicates that firms may leverage software development communities to realize efficiencies within the software development process. Many global firms leverage OSS in their operations or are otherwise affected by the spread of OSS (Henkel, 2006). Of importance is a firm's commitment to OSS online communities. Some firms actually employ programmers to participate in such communities, contribute to them and at the same time leverage their collective power (Dahlander and Wallin, 2006). Others directly sponsor the development and functioning of online communities to create a highly productive external locus of innovation, constantly improving their software at a rate that would not be achievable otherwise (West and O'Mahony, 2008). Further reliance on open-source communities can significantly lower barriers to entry for start-up firms (Henkel, 2006) or lower development costs for the software components of high-tech products (Gruber and Henkel, 2006).

Concluding remarks

Our synthesis of the OI literature includes a diverse set of issues investigated, constructs considered, and relations. However, because most studies are exploratory in nature, relying upon small samples and primarily qualitative data, there remains significant opportunity for theory development and empirical investigation. Specifically many of the constructs remain loosely defined or are undefined, creating underspecified research models. In fact, the few comprehensive empirical studies have generally addressed a narrower set of questions concerning a limited set of practices or firm characteristics. In the next section, we present a comprehensive typology of OI strategies, which will address these shortcomings in the OI literature.

A Typology of Open-Innovation Strategies

Firms enact strategies, such as adopting new business models, to best position themselves with changes in their external environment. Consistent with research on strategic positioning and fit (Ansari *et al.*, 2010; Siggelkow, 2002), it has been found that firm adoption of and efficacy with OI is a function of (1) the flow of knowledge within an industry, (2) an industry's product life cycle, (3) and the specific activities that a firm currently performs within the industry's value chain. Firms' pursuit of OI is highly contextual; they employ various OI strategies, which evolve over time to meet changes in the external environmental. Given OI's contextual nature, firms will implement different strategies within an industry value chain, and will adopt these strategies at varying rates and magnitudes (Almirall and Casadesus-Masanell, 2010). In building a framework to explain OI adoption and performance, we identify four distinctive strategies rooted in inter-firm exchange incorporated in the various transactions within an industry's value chain: *innovation seeker*, *innovation provider*, *intermediary*, and *open innovator*.

---

[1]We designate *innovation providers* as organizations rather than firms to reflect the broad nature of research-focused entities and the term includes universities, government labs, non-profit think tanks, as well as private firms.

Within an industry's value chain, an *innovation seeker* is a firm searching for innovation solutions beyond its boundaries. Firms purchase technological solutions in markets for innovation to supplement or complement existing technology portfolios (Teece, 2000). Examples of *innovation seekers* abound; software companies participate in open-source communities to gain access to critical innovative solutions. Similarly, pharmaceutical companies procure solutions by jointly developing technology with strategic partners or by acquiring the smaller companies, which developed it (Dahlander and Wallin, 2006; Higgins and Rodriguez, 2006).

The counterpart to an innovation seeker is an *innovation provider*: an organization[1] that distributes innovation solutions. These organizations exploit their technological discoveries not to build commercial solutions, but rather to sell them as 'products' to partners, who then reconfigure the technologies to package them as final products (Markman *et al.*, 2009b). Such organizations leverage their technology to gain access to complementary assets and better market access (Christensen *et al.*, 2005). Further, partnering with larger firms provides access to innovation networks, which can play a fundamental role in the success of small-to-medium enterprises (SMEs).

At the center of many innovation seeker and innovation provider exchanges is an *intermediary*: a firm which acts as an innovation broker (Terwiesch and Xu, 2008). The presence of intermediaries helps explain the explosive growth of OI by firms across various industries and economic regions; they act as catalysts for market exchange and have influenced shifts in many firms away from the traditional closed model of innovation. Although some intermediary firms have gained strong market positions — Innocentive, Yet2.com, Nine Sigma, just to name a few — researchers have yet to fully incorporate the role of intermediaries in models of OI, or empirically examine their effect on OI adoption or performance (Almirall and Casadesus-Masanell, 2010).

The last distinct OI strategy, which we term *open innovator*, is actually an aggregation of two other innovation strategies. Firms, especially multi-unit conglomerates, can create synergies between

Table 3. Open-innovation Strategic Positioning.

OI Strategy	Exemplar Firm	Sources	Attributes	Mechanisms	Outputs
Innovation seeker	P&G Eli Lilly	External	Absorptive capacity Exploration abilities (search)	Leveraging user innovation Outsourcing and alliances Mergers and acquisitions	Product Process Service
Innovation provider	ICEPower	Internal	Valuable portfolio of innovation Internal innovation capabilities	Venture capital Licensing and alliances	Raw innovation and technology Intellectual property
Intermediary	Innocentive Nine Sigma	External	Connectedness Network embeddedness	Auctions Partnerships Membership	Match of seeker and provider
Open innovator	Xerox IBM	External Internal	Internal innovation capabilities or portfolio Absorptive capacity Searching abilities Boundary-spanning abilities	Outsourcing and alliances Mergers and acquisitions Venture capital Licensing	Knowledge flows

internal and external knowledge creation activities, which facilitate occasions where they act as innovation seekers (i.e. to 'fill' technology gaps) and innovation providers (i.e. to appropriate a non-core technology or divest a particular technological trajectory). These firms leverage their extensive partnerships to continuously exchange knowledge through boundary expanding activities (Teece, 2000). Table 3 summarizes the important features of the four distinct OI strategies including: sources, attributes, mechanisms, and the outputs generated by each strategy. In the following sections we elaborate further on these important characteristics for the four strategies and their position within an OI network.

Innovation seeker

The innovation-seeker strategy is a product of increased worker mobility and the diffusion of knowledge, which makes firm reliance solely upon internal R&D more difficult. In addition, research suggests that external environmental pressures, stemming from technological discontinuity or the entry of potential rivals, often trigger an external search (Markman *et al.*, 2009a). Firm boundary spanning provides opportunities to expand the scope and range of ideas and potential innovative solutions, and also opens pathways to help stimulate internal R&D efforts. Many firms do not have the capacity needed to sustain a competitive advantage and must rely upon external sources to fill critical capability and product gaps (Almirall and Casadesus-Masanell, 2010). OI seeking behavior has only intensified due to drastic changes in how firms manage their internal R&D, which has evolved into a center of coordination and assimilation of external knowledge (Chesbrough, 2003a). Research has identified three principal mechanisms of exchange employed by OI seekers: leveraging user-based innovation, innovation outsourcing and strategic alliances, and integrating acquired firms (Cassiman and Veugelers, 2006; Higgins and Rodriguez, 2006). In general an OI seekers' external search starts with their existing network; they engage suppliers, strategic partners, and other affiliated network members, who are familiar with the focal firm's technology portfolio and innovation systems. Not surprisingly OI adoption is generally enhanced when a firm has an expansive network of partner relationships.

Firms leverage users to help them enhance existing offerings or develop new product or service extensions. Although not entirely new, the employment of user-based innovation has experienced significant growth during the last decade (Von Hippel, 2005). User forums such as online communities, clubs, or blogs constitute new repositories of potential ideas that complement the traditional ways of interacting with customers (Dahlander *et al.*, 2008). Examples abound in which user communities or individual 'lead' users have provided innovative solutions to improve current product offerings or new products under development (Lettl *et al.*, 2006). For example, BMW provided customers with user 'toolkits' as a means to improve in-car online services, and Staples held a customer-focused competition that generated 8,300 submissions by actual customers (Von Hippel, 2005). Thus, firms ignore user-based innovation at their peril; in the kayak industry, when incumbent firms passed on important user-based innovations, a select group of user-innovators started new ventures and successfully competed based on these innovations (Hienerth, 2006).

OI seekers also tend to outsource to a varying degree their R&D processes. Substantial costs to maintain large R&D units compel firms to seek more efficient means of product and service innovation. Outsourcing can take the form of an initial bid on the open market, considering all possible sources, or firms can restrict their search to existing partners and suppliers. While open bids may yield greater savings, appropriation considerations render this approach far from risk free. In fact, research suggests that OI seekers are more likely to work with trusted partners, who are already knowledgeable about the firms' innovation systems (Cassiman and Veugelers, 2006). Despite the risks, outsourcing innovation outside the circle of existing relationships can yield novel solutions, which may not be readily available to competitors (Terwiesch and Xu, 2008). Three broad methods for outsourcing innovation exist: (1) direct contact with a specified innovation provider; (2) organize a contest or an auction in the open market; or (3) use an intermediary to act as a filter between the innovation seeker and the provider (Saur-Amaral and Amaral, 2008). OI seekers most often use an intermediary because it is more efficient; outsourcing the search process enables them to focus their R&D efforts, enhancing their existing core competencies (Christensen, 2006; Teece, 2000).

In addition to outsourcing innovation seeking activities, firms engage in OI via strategic alliances and mergers and acquisitions. Strategic alliances give firms the ability to tap into complementary technologies, capabilities, and assets, which can enhance both early value chain activities (i.e. R&D), as well as product and service offerings (Markman *et al.*, 2009b). Many OI seekers employ strategic partnerships to gain access to intellectual property, which may enhance R&D efforts or product offerings of the seeker firm. In addition, alliance partners provide asset complementarity, which gives greater R&D efficiencies. Mergers and acquisitions broaden product and market scope, and enable firms to gain efficiencies from combined synergies. For example, in industries as varied as pharmaceuticals, consumer products, and information technology, firms have procured external innovation through mergers and acquisitions (Higgins and Rodriguez, 2006; Oliveira *et al.*, 2003). In the context of OI, the preferred method has been the acquisition of SMEs who have pioneered a promising technology but do not have sufficient resources to fully exploit their discoveries. In general, SMEs lack the financial capital or adequate infrastructure to independently commercialize many of their discoveries, which makes selling to innovation seekers an efficient way to benefit from their inventions (Oliveira *et al.*, 2003).

What distinguishes innovation seeking behavior is the efficacy of a firm's absorptive capacity; firms must be able to assimilate, deploy, and exploit externally acquired innovation to be innovation seekers (Zahra and George, 2002). Firms that have drastically stripped down their internal R&D activities (except for rare cases, like Cisco Systems, Inc.) have greater difficulties in incorporating third-party solutions into their technology portfolios and product offerings. Also, the often cited 'not invented here' syndrome plays a substantial role in the internal resistance to external innovation solutions (Lichtenthaler and Ernst, 2006). The transition to an OI strategy as any paradigm change requires a substantial change in a firm's culture (Dodgson *et al.*, 2006). In order to play the OI game in a substantive way, a company — even a company only interested in acquiring external technology — has to develop a set of skills and practices for the absorption and integration of external knowledge.

Innovation provider

Innovation providers, the second OI strategy, evolved from heavy investment in R&D during much of the twentieth century; these firms have a wellspring of innovation solutions waiting for a champion or partner to commercialize them. OI providers aim to tap into heretofore underused pathways to exploit their R&D (Markman *et al.*, 2009b). OI providers are broadly one of two types of organizations: large, global firms and SMEs, including non-profit organizations. The first group consists of large (i.e. Fortune 500-level), global firms such as Xerox and IBM, who have extensive intellectual property (IP) portfolios, which contain underutilized technologies. These IP portfolios are the outcome of extensive R&D investment; yet, for a variety of reasons, these investments yielded technology that the firms were unable to commercialize independently. These firms now view their large IP portfolios as potential cash cows, and they seek partners to either sell the IP directly or to develop jointly commercially viable products.

Large firms are susceptible to significant changes in strategic focus, where R&D projects are either temporarily shut down or completely abandoned. Yet, these projects often yield viable technologies, which may only need complementary assets from strategic partners to produce marketable products. The deployment of venture financing shapes innovation providers, especially global firms. Venturing consists of financing new enterprises based on technology generated by joint R&D efforts. The firm has a financial stake in the new venture; the founders of the new company usually come from the parent company; and often, the technical staff and the board of directors are composed of former or current members of the parent (Bray and Lee, 2000; Chesbrough, 2003b; Van de Vrande *et al.*, 2006). Hence, global firms have extensively employed licensing strategies, launched 'spin-off' companies, and financed SMEs to tap into underutilized revenue sources derived from their large IP portfolios.

The second group includes SMEs with strong technological positions in niche markets; such providers seek to fully exploit their IP across multiple domains. As noted, SMEs lack adequate financial capital and infrastructure assets to launch extensive product lines, and must rely on external financing to broaden their business scope. They employ innovation provider behavior by transacting with intra-industry or inter-industry partners willing to exploit their IP. Unlike global firms, SMEs leverage venture capital to conduct boundary spanning via strategic alliances; it is a systematic way of bringing technology to market (Chesbrough, 2003b). The second group also consists of nonprofit organizations with broad research missions. For example, research universities are a major source of technological discoveries because of their extensive research infrastructure — faculty scientists, labs, graduate students, etc. — enabling them to perform research exploration activities. However, like SMEs, they lack the requisite organizational structure, mission, and culture to successfully commercialize their discoveries (Markman, 2009b; Perkmann and Walsh, 2007). As global firms, which possess large IP portfolios, universities have accumulated an extensive cache of technologies and need external partners to commercialize them.[2]

Regardless of the type of provider, one thing is certain: an extensive IP portfolio is a necessary condition for implementing an innovation provider strategy. The search for an external path to the market is due to the realization that most IP held is underdeployed. Organizations realize that without external partners there is little chance of these technologies reaching the market because their current business model or strategic focus does not support commercialization (Christensen *et al.*, 2005). For example, research found that in global firms such as Procter & Gamble and the Dow Chemical

---

[2]Since the passage of the Bayh-Dole Act of 1980 granting American universities the right to exploit inventions derived from federally funded research, there has been explosive growth in technology transfer activity. Other countries (most notably within the EU), have also followed this public policy program.

Company more than 80% of their patents went unused (Chesbrough *et al.*, 2006). Executing an innovation provider strategy in response to this type of business opportunity requires formal organizational processes characterized by an adaptive organizational structure, the active management (i.e. systematic review) of IP portfolios, and a dedicated OI function (Chesbrough, 2006a). Out-licensing is the most common outcome of OI provider activity because it provides two primary benefits: a residual income from an underutilized asset and a low risk that the strategic partner will encroach on the licensing firm's core technology domains. In addition, the OI provider generally has limited involvement with the strategic partners and, thus, limited control of the technological trajectory of the licensed technology.

Intermediary

The third OI strategy, *intermediary*, is a product of the first two OI strategies; innovation seekers and providers often need a third party to help broker the exchange. Intermediaries, or innovation brokers, facilitate a search and make markets for innovation much like investment banks make markets for trading other commodities. Intermediaries are firms that create a point of contact between OI seekers and providers (Teece, 2000). In a recent review of innovation brokerage, Winch and Courtney (2007) defined an innovation broker as 'an organization acting as a member of a network of actors in an industrial sector that is focused neither on the generation nor the implementation of innovations, but on enabling other organizations to innovate' (p. 751). Innovation brokers have a unique set of capabilities consisting of human capital with (1) an understanding of basic and applied science; (2) marketing expertise to gauge commercial potential, able to discriminate which innovations are potentially useful to solve specific problems, coupled with the ability to link problems and solutions in different industries, and (3) network contacts who occupy an adequate position in the network and enable the matching of complementarities across multiple partners.

There is an extensive literature that has explored the role of brokers in formal innovation systems and networks, especially the diffusion of cutting-edge technology (Burt, 2004; Gould and Fernandez, 1989). By filling structural holes in the network, brokers are able to connect nodes that were heretofore not engaged (Burt, 2004). Innovation brokers, much like most human capital-intensive services (e.g. consulting), have two organizational forms: generalists and specialists. Generalists build expertise in multiple industries, offering cradle-to-grave services that facilitate technology exchange. For example, Nine Sigma advises SMEs on how best to protect their IP and identify potential partners most likely to purchase their innovation. In contrast specialist firms focus on one particular industry or a few exclusive technology domains. For example, Pharmalicensing works exclusively in the life sciences industries. The literature has recognized the difference in organizational forms and formal strategies arising from the span of the brokerage activity. Organizations that connect entities in the same industries are said to perform within-group brokerage (Winch and Courtney, 2007) while organizations that link entities in different industries, markets, or sectors are said to engage in between-groups brokerage (Gould and Fernandez, 1989). In the latter case, the ability to identify breakthrough solutions across varying contexts is most important.

Although research on innovation brokers is rapidly growing, most research has been conducted at the network level, and their effect on the strategies of innovation seekers and providers has not yet been systematically examined. Intuitively it is likely that intermediaries influence the efficacy of OI performance; both innovation seekers and providers can enhance their positions by employing intermediaries. Organizational theory supports this notion; intermediaries are likened to boundary-spanning knowledge brokers in organizational research (Pewlowski and Ourso, 2004). The social network literature demonstrates how brokers create connections between different communities without being a full member of them (Brown and Duguid, 1991). The same theoretical basis can be applied to innovation brokers, who boundary span established communities of practice, create weak ties in multiple communities, and translate knowledge coming from different environment (Pawlowski and Ourso, 2004).

Open innovator

An *open innovator* is a product of increased scaling of OI practices; these firms behave both as OI seekers and providers. They possess both access to technology (i.e. IP portfolios), and the requisite capabilities (i.e. absorptive capacity), and gaps in their innovation systems, which make them buyers and sellers of innovation. Open innovators are usually large, global firms, which have dedicated R&D divisions, while at the same time looking for external technologies to incorporate. Xerox, the focus of much of Chesbrough's first book, is a good example of a firm employing this strategy (Chesbrough, 2003a). Given that such companies are often big corporations, they tend to finance spin-offs in order to bring some of their innovations to market, while relying on mergers and acquisitions to procure interesting innovations (Chesbrough, 2003b).

Conclusions and Future Perspectives

Our review of the extant literature posits that firms may enhance their innovation capabilities and outcomes through the effective management of inflows and outflows of knowledge and innovation. Critical to this view is (1) the logical separation of the locus of idea generation, new product development, and commercialization within an industry's value chain, and (2) the recognition that each of these stages of innovation may occur within or outside a firm's boundaries. In conclusion, we find that previous research considers many determinants of OI adoption and innovation performance; however, our review suggests that construct definitions, the operationalization of constructs, and the large-scale empirical study of relations amongst constructs are in the formative stages of development. Further, because OI research is at the formative stage of development, studies tend to be theory building, employing interviews and case-based methodologies, rather than theory testing in nature. As such, the OI stream of research represents a rich area for future scholarly investigation.

The empirical investigation of OI strategies represents a promising avenue for future research. Building on a tradition of OI studies that espouse the importance of inflows and outflows of knowledge and innovation acquisition and exploitation, we have developed a typology with four OI strategies. In contrast to previous research, however, we explicitly recognize the intermediary strategy in addition to innovation seekers and providers. While our typology draws from previous research, we suggest that new insights may be gained by operationalizing these strategies and studying the linkages amongst these strategies, the requisite capabilities that support these strategies, and the context (i.e. rate, magnitude, etc.) in which firms adopt each strategy. Additionally, including the intermediary function in OI models may explain how: (1) the linkage between search and innovation affects performance (Laursen and Salter, 2006), (2) the complementary relationship between internal R&D and absorptive capacity affects OI adoption and performance (Cassiman and Veugelers, 2006), and (3) the various costs associated with each OI strategy — innovation seeker, innovation provider, and open innovators — affect firm performance (Almirall and Casadesus-Masanell, 2010). Similarly, the rise of intermediaries may significantly affect the horizontal and vertical structure of existing supply chains.

Firms adopt OI practices in order to develop new or enhance existing streams of revenues. However, the extant literature suggests that firms may also leverage OI mechanisms to influence the development of standards (Fleming and Waguespack, 2007), spin off new ventures that support the former parent's primary business (Chesbrough, 2003b), and distribute the risks associated with costly investment in new product development (Christensen *et al.*, 2005). Further, the extant literature provides little guidance into the substitutability of various mechanisms to achieve given strategic goals. For example, our review indicates many innovation sources (e.g. universities, research institutions, customers, suppliers, and lead-users) use various mechanisms to transfer technology (e.g. outsourcing, acquisition, strategic alliance, licensing, acquisitions, and auctions); yet, it remains unclear if or when specific source-mechanism combinations will yield superior innovation performance because of the level of product-market competition, the complexity of the technology, and the level of market or technical uncertainty.

Finally we acknowledge that we have bounded our review to include only those studies of OI that adopt a strategic view of this phenomenon. While the OI literature is in its formative stages of development we note that several mature streams of research lie adjacent to this field. For example, studies of OI have drawn from the social network (Fleming and Waguespack, 2007), entrepreneurship (Chesbrough, 2003b), exploration and exploitation (Dittrich and Duysters, 2007), and absorptive capacity (Christensen *et al.*, 2005) streams of literature. However, other overlapping mature streams of research, such as studies of supplier involvement in new product development, have not made substantive inroads into OI discourse. Consistent with the principles of OI, future researchers should continue to integrate insights from related streams of literature into their empirical studies. Only when OI research fully incorporates these research streams will it achieve a theory that fully explains how firms develop, acquire, assimilate, and exploit existing and potential innovation portfolios.

References

Almirall, E. and Casadesus-Masanell, R. (2010). Open vs. closed innovation: A model of discovery and divergence, *Academy of Management Review*, **35**(2), 27–47.

Ansari, S.M., Fiss, P.C. and Zajac, E.J. (2010). Made to fit: How practices vary as they diffuse, *Academy of Management Review*, **35**(1), 67–92.

Bray, M.J. and Lee, J.N. (2000). University revenues from technology transfer licensing fees vs. equity positions, *Journal of Business Venturing*, **15**(5–6), 385–392.

Brown, J.S. and Duguid, P. (1991). Organizational learning and communities-of-practice: Toward a unified view of working, learning and innovation, *Organization Science*, **2**(1), 40–57.

Burt, R.S. (2004). Structural holes and good ideas, *American Journal of Sociology*, **110**(2), 349–399.

Cassiman, B. and Veugelers, R. (2006). In search of complementarity in innovation strategy: Internal R&D and external knowledge acquisition, *Management Science*, **52**(1), 68.

Chesbrough, H.W. (2003a). *Open Innovation: The New Imperative for Creating and Profiting from Technology*, Harvard Business School Press, Cambridge, MA.

Chesbrough, H.W. (2003b). The governance and performance of Xerox's technology spin-off companies, *Research Policy*, **32**(3), 403–421.

Chesbrough, H.W. (2003c). The era of open innovation, *Sloan Management Review*, **44**(3), 35–41.

Chesbrough, H.W. (2003d). A better way to innovate, *Harvard Business Review*, **81**(7), 12–13.

Chesbrough, H.W. (2003e). Open platform innovation: Creating value from internal and external innovation, *Intel Technology Journal*, 7(3), 5–9.

Chesbrough, H.W. (2006a). *Open Business Models: How to Thrive in the New Innovation Landscape*, Harvard Business School Press, Cambridge, MA.

Chesbrough, H.W. (2006b). "New puzzles and new findings," in Chesbrough, H.W., Vanhaverbeke, W. and West, J. (eds), *Open Innovation: Researching a New Paradigm*, Oxford University Press, New York.

Chesbrough, H.W. (2007). Business model innovation: It's not just about technology anymore, *Strategy and Leadership*, **35**(6), 12–17.

Chesbrough, H.W. and Crowther, A.K. (2006). Beyond high tech: Early adopters of open innovation in other industries, *R&D Management*, **36**(3), 229–236.

Chesbrough, H.W. and Schwartz, K. (2007). Innovating business models with co-development partnerships, *Research–Technology Management*, **50**(1), 55–59.

Chesbrough, H.W., Vanhaverbeke, W. and West, J. (2006). *Open Innovation: Researching a New Paradigm*, Oxford University Press, New York.

Christensen, J.F. (2006). "Whither core competency for the large corporation in an open innovation world?" in Chesbrough, H.W., Vanhaverbeke, W., and West, J. (eds), *Open Innovation: Researching a New Paradigm*, Oxford University Press, New York.

Christensen, J.F., Olesen, M.H. and Kjær, J.S. (2005). The industrial dynamics of open innovation — Evidence from the transformation of consumer electronics, *Research Policy*, **34**(10), 1533–1549.

Cohen, W.M. and Levinthal, D.A. (1990). Absorptive capacity: A new perspective on learning and innovation, *Administrative Science Quarterly*, **35**(1), 128–152.

Cooke, P. (2005). "Regional knowledge capabilities and open innovation: Regional innovation systems and clusters in the asymmetric knowledge economy," in anonymous, *Clusters, Networks and Innovation*, Oxford University Press, New York.

Dahlander, L., Frederiksen, L. and Rullani, F. (2008). Online communities and open innovation: Governance and symbolic value creation, *Industry and Innovation*, **15**(2), 115–123.

Dahlander, L. and Wallin, M.W. (2006). A man on the inside: Unlocking communities as complementary assets, *Research Policy*, **35**(8), 1243–1259.

Di Maria, E. and Finotto, V. (2008). Communities of consumption and made in Italy, *Industry and Innovation*, **15**(2), 179–197.

Dittrich, K. and Duysters, G. (2007). Networking as a means to strategy change: The case of open innovation in mobile telephony, *Journal of Product Innovation Management*, **24**(6), 510–521.

Dodgson, M., Gann, D., Salter, A. and Campus, S.K. (2006). The role of technology in the shift towards open innovation: The case of Procter & Gamble, *R&D Management*, **36**(3), 333–346.

Eisenhardt, K.M. and Brown, S.L. (1998). Time pacing: Competing in markets that won't stand still, *Harvard Business Review*, **76**(2), 59–69.

Fine, C.H. (1998). *Clockspeed: Winning Industry Control in the Age of Temporary Advantage*, Basic Books, New York.

Fleming, L. and Waguespack, D.M. (2007). Brokerage, boundary spanning, and leadership in open innovation communities, *Organization Science*, **18**(2), 165.

Gassmann, O. and Enkel, E. (2004). Towards a theory of open innovation: Three core process archetypes, in *Proceedings of the R&D Management Conference in Sesimbra, Portugal*.

Gould, R.V. and Fernandez, R.M. (1989). Structures of mediation: A formal approach to brokerage in transaction networks, *Sociological Methodology*, **19**, 89–126.

Gruber, M. and Henkel, J. (2006). New ventures based on open innovation — An empirical analysis of start-up firms in embedded Linux, *International Journal of Technology Management*, **33**(4), 356–372.

Hayes, R.H., Wheelwright, S.C. and Clark, K.B. (1988). *Dynamic Manufacturing: Creating the Learning Organization,* Free Press, New York.

Henkel, J. (2006). Selective revealing in open innovation processes: The case of embedded Linux, *Research Policy,* **35**(7), 953–969.

Hienerth, C. (2006). The commercialization of user innovations: The development of the rodeo kayak industry, *R&D Management,* **36**(3), 273–294.

Higgins, M.J. and Rodriguez, D. (2006). The outsourcing of R&D through acquisitions in the pharmaceutical industry, *Journal of Financial Economics,* **80**(2), 351–383.

Hurmelinna, P., Kyläheiko, K. and Jauhiainen, T. (2007). The Janus face of the appropriability regime in the protection of innovations: Theoretical re-appraisal and empirical analysis, *Technovation,* **27**(3):133–144.

Kaiser, S. and Muller-Seitz, G. (2008). Leveraging lead user knowledge in software development — The case of weblog technology, *Industry and Innovation,* **15**(2), 199–221.

Kirschbaum, R. (2005). Open innovation in practice, *Research Technology Management,* **48**(4), 24–28.

Laursen, K. and Salter, A. (2006). Open for innovation: The role of openness in explaining innovation performance among UK manufacturing firms, *Strategic Management Journal,* **27**(2), 131–150.

Lettl, C., Herstatt, C. and Gemuenden, H.G. (2006). Users' contributions to radical innovation: Evidence from four cases in the field of medical equipment technology, *R&D Management,* **36**(3), 251–272.

Lichtenthaler, U. (2006). Technology exploitation strategies in the context of open innovation, *International Journal of Technology Intelligence and Planning,* **2**(1), 1–21.

Lichtenthaler, U. (2008). Open innovation in practice: An analysis of strategic approaches to technology transactions, *IEEE Transactions on Engineering Management,* **55**(1): 148–157.

Lichtenthaler, U. and Ernst, H. (2006). Attitudes to externally organizing knowledge management tasks: A review, reconsideration and extension of the NIH syndrome, *R&D Management,* **36**(4), 367–386.

Lichtenthaler, U. and Ernst, H. (2007). External technology commercialization in large firms: Results of a quantitative benchmarking study, *R&D Management,* **37**(5), 383–397.

Lokshin, B., Belderbos, R. and Carree, M. (2008). The productivity effects of internal and external R&D: Evidence from a dynamic panel data model, *Oxford Bulletin of Economics and Statistics,* **70**(3), 399–413.

March, J.G. (1991). Exploration and exploitation in organizational learning, *Organization Science,* 71–87.

Markman, G.D., Gianiodis, P.T. and Buchholtz, A.K. (2009a). Factor-market rivalry, *Academy of Management Review,* **34**(3), 423–441.

Markman, G.D., Gianiodis, P.T. and Phan, P.H. (2009b). Supply-side innovation and technology commercialization, *Journal of Management Studies,* **46**(4), 625–649.

Oliveira, P., Roth, A.V. and Ponte, K.M. (2003). Cross-border mergers and acquisitions as a tool to transfer knowledge and foster competitive capabilities, *International Journal of Technology, Policy and Management,* **3**(2), 204–223.

Perkmann, M. and Walsh, K. (2007). University–industry relationships and open innovation: Towards a research agenda, *International Journal of Management Reviews,* **9**(4), 259–280.

Piller, F.T. and Walcher, D. (2006). Toolkits for idea competitions: a novel method to integrate users in new product development, *R&D Management,* **36**(3), 307–318.

Saur-Amaral, I. and Amaral, P. (2008). Contract innovation organizations: An idiosyncratic approach to open innovation, *Universidade de Aveiro, Documentos de Trabalho em Gestão,* working papers in management.

Siggelkow, N. (2002). Evolution toward fit, *Administrative Science Quarterly,* **47**(1), 125–159.

Teece, D.J. (1986). Profiting from technological innovation: Implications for integration, collaboration, licensing and public policy, *Research Policy,* **15**(6), 285–305.

Teece, D.J. (2000). *Managing Intellectual Capital: Organizational, Strategic, and Policy Dimensions,* Oxford University Press, New York.

Terwiesch, C. and Xu, Y. (2008). Innovation contests, open innovation, and multiagent problem solving, *Management Science,* **54**(9), 1529–1553.

Van de Vrande, V., Lemmens, C. and Vanhaverbeke, W. (2006). Choosing governance modes for external technology sourcing, *R&D Management,* **36**(3), 347–363.

Van der Meer, H. (2007). Open innovation the Dutch treat: Challenges in thinking in business models, *Creativity and Innovation Management,* **16**(2), 192–202.

Von Hippel, E.A. (2005). *Democratizing Innovation,* MIT Press, Cambridge, MA.

West, J., Gallagher, S. and Square, O.W. (2006). Challenges of open innovation: The paradox of firm investment in open-source software, *R&D Management,* **36**(3), 319–331.

Winch, G.M. and Courtney, R. (2007). The organization of innovation brokers: An international review, *Technology Analysis and Strategic Management,* **19**(6), 747–763.

Zahra, S.A. and George, G. (2002). Absorptive capacity: A review, reconceptualization, and extension, *Academy of Management Review,* **27**(2), 185–203.

Chapter 2

Open Innovation and the Integration of Suppliers — Literature Review and Discussion on Supplier Innovation

Alexander Brem and Gerd Schuster
University of Erlangen-Nuremberg, Germany

Introduction

There is no commonly accepted definition of open innovation to date — at least no other than general typologies (e.g. Gianiodis *et al.*, 2010). This is certainly one of the main reasons for the fact that there is a plethora of research on open innovation but no common direction — this is stated in other recently published papers, which call for a stimulation of research in and examination of open innovation (e.g. lli *et al.*, 2010; Dahlander and Gann, 2010) and especially in the area of organizational capabilities for the management of open innovation processes (Lichtenthaler, 2011). In this context, we believe that there is a clear linkage of open innovation and supply chain management, different to some other comments on this subject, especially from Badawy (2011): The supply chain is the lifeline of a company offering all different interfaces that are necessary to integrate relevant players and their ideas from outside the company. Suppliers especially form an essential part of the supply chain and they are a valuable source of innovation and, hence, show a "real-case" application of open innovation.

This results from the unique position of the supplier as an expert in the least parts of the joint value proposal (Bessant *et al.*, 2003). And this is not just true in industries where companies work closely together, such as the automotive industry, in which value-creation activities are shifted to suppliers. Hence, from our point of view, supply chain management can be viewed as a source or tool for open innovation to get in touch with potential idea providers, e.g. suppliers as initiators of innovation, and not just as a means of getting new materials (Klioutch and Leker, 2011). This is in line with several studies on the integration of suppliers in product development and open innovation, which show that early and extensive supplier involvement leads to superior performance (e.g. Petersen *et al.*, 2003; John, 2009; Bonaccorsi & Lipparini, 1994; Rosenzweig *et al.*, 2003). The same results can be found in supply chain publications as well, e.g. a supply chain study by IBM discovered that 41% of the participants found collaborations with customers and suppliers to have the most significant effect on reducing product development time-to-market (Butner and Bourdé, 2004). However, one of the main challenges remains — how to find efficient mechanisms to identify adequate suppliers. New forms of value creation within the supply chain, where boundaries between production and consumption of value are highly overlapping, may help to check if such close collaborations are working (Remneland-Wikham *et al.*, 2011). In analogy to the search for lead users, this can be pursued with collaborative online tools (Bilgram *et al.*, 2009). In comparison to the integration of customers and users through the lead-user concept, there is less research regarding the role of suppliers in the context of open innovation (Brem, 2008). With this book, several insights are given into this under-researched topic of supplier innovation. Most of them either focus on empirical findings based on quantitative research or insights from case study research. Just four chapters focus on theory and concepts, of which this chapter will introduce a conceptual framework based on a bibliographic analysis including a review of current debates.

Methodology

To establish a framework for supplier innovation, we conducted a bibliographic analysis of papers with this aim. Based on our findings, we made a systematic content analysis of journal articles, contributions, books, and conference proceedings. Therefore, we searched Thomson Reuters's *Web of Science* database[1] for articles whose titles, keywords, or abstracts contain 'innovation' and 'supplier'.

The application of this method, formerly also introduced by Dahlander and Gann (2010) to review open-innovation literature, found 429 publications of which some have no direct linkage with supplier innovation. A follow-up screening of abstracts and full texts resulted in 95 papers, which are in scope for our research focus. For a first (less academic) bibliographic summary we always focused on the primary topic of the studies and finally picked the most specific in terms of topic (scope) and extent of the research (scale).

We will highlight some findings and discuss those papers in detail that we think are of especial interest in the context of this book. These results are part of a meta-analysis, which will be introduced in 2012. The full references of the articles are given in the bibliography at the end of this chapter.

Results

Before we go into the detail of the results of our bibliographic analysis, we want to introduce some notable general findings and statistics.

Firstly, authors of research about supplier innovation tend to publish in selected outlet journals. We found that there is a clear focus on two periodicals: the *Journal of Product Innovation Management* and the *International Journal of Technology Management*. In Table 1, we rank the top ten periodicals in which most of the papers were published.

Secondly, there are a considerable number of (quantitative) empirical studies. In total, we found 16 empirical studies that directly refer to the topic of supplier innovation and supplier involvement in the context of open innovation. A list of empirical studies is shown in Table 2.

---

[1]Thomson Reuters's *Web of Science* is considered to be one of the most comprehensive databases for scholarly work and includes many journal publications. Although not all journals are included, the *Web of Science* typically includes the most prominent journals in a field.

Table 1.   Most Common Outlet Journals.

No.	Journal	Number of published papers
1	*Journal of Product Innovation Management*	19
2	*International Journal of Technology Management*	15
3	*Journal of Operations Management*	7
4	*IEEE Transactions on Engineering Management*	7
5	*Industrial Management and Data Systems*	6
6	*Technovation*	6
7	*Research-Technology Management*	5
8	*International Journal of Production Research*	4
9	*Journal of Engineering and Technology Management*	4
10	*International Journal of Production Economics*	2

It is interesting that the majority of the empirical studies mainly focus on two topics: the importance of supplier innovation and the outcome of supplier innovation. This makes sense as these topics are of a measurable nature and can thus be tested empirically. Moreover, we found that the empirical samples are absolutely diverse in both geographical extent and organizational type. For example, the empirical studies include research about 251 established manufacturers in Hong Kong (Lau *et al.*, 2007), 781 international manufacturing firms operating in Spain (Un, Cuervo-Cazurra, and Asakawa, 2010) and 161 production suppliers to car and truck manufacturers in the Swedish automotive industry (Wynstra, Corswant, and Wetzels, 2010). Additionally, researchers also studied supplier innovation in smaller and less established firms, e.g. 137 Chinese manufacturing SMEs (Zeng, Xie, and Tam, 2010), 25 small and medium-sized car suppliers from Italy (Calabrese, 2002), and recently even in start-up firms (Song *et al.*, 2011; Neyens, Faems, and Sels, 2010).

Table 2. Some Examples of (Quantitative) Empirical Studies on Supplier Innovation.

Authors(s)	Year	Title
Vanrossum and Cabo	1995	The contribution of research institutes in EUREKA projects
Bidault and Despres	1998	New product development and early supplier involvement (ESI): The drivers of ESI adoption
Chiesa and Manzini	1998	Profiting from the virtual organization of technological innovation: Suggestions from an empirical study
Ulrich and Ellison	1999	Holistic customer requirements and the design-select decision
Zairi	1999	Effective TQM implementation through supplier partnerships: A benchmarking study of advanced manufacturing technology systems
Calabrese	2002	Small-medium car suppliers and behavioural models in innovation
Ulrich and Ellison	2005	Beyond make-buy: Internalization and integration of design and production
Lau *et al.*	2007	Supply chain product co-development, product modularity and product performance — Empirical evidence from Hong Kong manufacturers
Song and Thieme	2009	The role of suppliers in market intelligence gathering for radical and incremental innovation
Azadegan and Dooley	2010	Supplier innovativeness, organizational learning styles and manufacturer performance: An empirical assessment
Neyens, Faems, and Sels	2010	The impact of continuous and discontinuous alliance strategies on startup innovation performance
Un, Cuervo-Cazurra, and Asakawa	2010	R&D collaborations and product innovation

(*Continued*)

Table 2. (*Continued*)

Authors(s)	Year	Title
Wynstra, Corswant, and Wetzels	2010	In chains? An empirical study of antecedents of supplier product development activity in the automotive industry
Zeng, Xie, and Tam	2010	Relationship between cooperation networks and innovation performance of SMEs
Lau	2011	Supplier and customer involvement on new product performance — Contextual factors and an empirical test from manufacturer perspective
Song, Song, and Di Benedetto	2011	Resources, supplier investment, product launch advantages, and first product performance

Thirdly, there are also a considerable number of (qualitative) case studies. In total, we identified 12 case studies that directly refer to the topic of supplier innovation and supplier involvement in the context of open innovation. A list of the case studies is shown in Table 3.

In contrast, the topics of the (qualitative) case studies are not (as in the quantitative empirical studies) about the importance and outcome of supplier innovation but mainly the requirements and the management of supplier innovation. The case studies include research about different industries of both renowned companies and less prominent ones. For example, van Echtelt (2008) studied the integration of suppliers at a manufacturer in the copier and printer industry and in eight projects, in which four manufacturers from different industries involve multiple suppliers (van Echtelt, 2007). Unsurprisingly, the case studies also include examples from the automotive industry where many of the value-creation activities are shifted to suppliers. Five in-depth case studies of a European automotive manufacturer and three first-tier suppliers are described in the work of Nellore and Balachandra (2001) and another European car-maker and two of its suppliers were studied by Caputo and Zirpoli (2002). A very interesting piece of research was conducted by Petersen,

Handfield, and Ragatz (2003). They carried out 17 case studies in Japanese and American manufacturing firms, each of which had at least one successful and one unsuccessful supplier integration experience. The results have been further validated using data from 84 American, European, and Australian firms, which were selected because this set of companies was considered best in class in the areas of supplier integration in new product development.

Other case studies in Table 3 were conducted in the food-processing industry (Tsekouras, 2006), the UK aerospace and defense sector (Reed and Walsh, 2002), and the wind-turbine industry (Andersen and Drejer, 2009).

Table 3. Some Examples of Case Study Research on Supplier Innovation.

Author(s)	Year	Title
Harryson *et al.*	1997	From experience — How Canon and Sony drive product innovation through networking and application-focused R&D
Nellore and Balachandra	2001	Factors influencing success in integrated product development (IPD) projects
Caputo and Zirpoli	2002	Supplier involvement in automotive component design: Outsourcing strategies and supply chain management
Reed and Walsh	2002	Enhancing technological capability through supplier development: A study of the UK aerospace industry
Petersen, Handfield, and Ragatz	2003	A model of supplier integration into new product development
McIvor, Humphreys, and Cadden	2006	Supplier involvement in product development in the electronics industry: A case study
Tsekouras	2006	Gaining competitive advantage through knowledge integration in a European industrialising economy
van Echtelt *et al.*	2007	Strategic and operational management of supplier involvement in new product development: A contingency perspective

(Continued)

Table 3. (*Continued*)

Author(s)	Year	Title
van Echtelt *et al.*	2008	Managing supplier involvement in new product development: A multiple case study
Andersen and Drejer	2009	Together we share? Competitive and collaborative supplier interests in product development
Egbetokun *et al.*	2009	What drives innovation? Inferences from an industrywide survey in Nigeria
Keizer and Halman	2009	Risks in major innovation projects, a multiple case study within a world's leading company in the fast moving consumer goods

Having examined the identified articles in detail we found that the 95 papers in scope can be distinguished into four topics with certain contextual interdependencies. Hence, we split our results into the following categories:

(a) the importance of supplier innovation,
(b) the requirements for supplier innovation,
(c) managing supplier innovation,
(d) supplier innovation outcome.

In the following, we will explain each of these categories in detail.

(a) *Importance of supplier innovation*

These papers discuss the importance of supplier innovation in different ways (see Table 4); however, they have in common their support of the general importance of supplier innovation. For instance, Spaeth *et al.* (2010) extend the current open-innovation literature with a push model of open innovation and a focus on supplier innovation. Therefore, voluntarily created knowledge from outside the company pushes the knowledge into a firm's innovation process. This push model is enabled through four contexts, which are preemptive generosity, continuous commitment, adaptive governance structure, and low entry barriers. Hence, suppliers

Table 4. Selected Journal Articles Regarding the Importance of Supplier Innovation.

Author(s)	Year	Title
Bonaccorsi and Lipparini	1994	Strategic partnerships in new product development — An Italian case study
Tidd	1995	Development of novel products through intraorganizational and interorganizational networks — The case of home automation
McCutcheon, Grant, and Hartley	1997	Determinants of new product designers' satisfaction with suppliers' contributions
Harryson	1997	From experience — How Canon and Sony drive product innovation through networking and application-focused R&D
Schoening *et al.*	1998	The influence of government science and technology policies on new product development in the US, UK, South Korea and Taiwan
Zairi	1999	Effective TQM implementation through supplier partnerships: A benchmarking study of advanced manufacturing technology systems
Reed and Walsh	2002	Enhancing technological capability through supplier development: A study of the UK aerospace industry
Calabrese	2002	Small-medium car suppliers and behavioural models in innovation
Alam	2003	Commercial innovations from consulting engineering firms: An empirical exploration of a novel source of new product ideas
Ulrich and Ellison	2005	Beyond make-buy: Internalization and integration of design and production
Sharma	2005	Collaborative product innovation: Integrating elements of CPI via PLM framework

(Continued)

Table 4. (*Continued*)

Author(s)	Year	Title
Nieto and Santamaria	2007	The importance of diverse collaborative networks for the novelty of product innovation
Knudsen	2007	The relative importance of interfirm relationships and knowledge transfer for new product development success
Song and Di Benedetto	2008	Supplier's involvement and success of radical new product development in new ventures
Lee, Chen, and Tong	2008	Developing new products in a network with efficiency and innovation
Wagner	2009	Getting Innovation from suppliers
Egbetokun *et al.*	2009	What drives innovation? Inferences from an industrywide survey in Nigeria
Zeng, Xie, and Tam	2010	Relationship between cooperation networks and innovation performance of SMEs
Wynstra, Corswant, and Wetzels	2010	In chains? An empirical study of antecedents of supplier product development activity in the automotive industry
Wink	2010	Restructuring European aeronautics SMEs: The role of formal examination knowledge
Talke and Hultink	2010	Managing diffusion barriers when launching new products
Spaeth, Stuermer, and Krogh	2010	Enabling knowledge creation through outsiders: Towards a push model of open innovation
Traitler, Watzke, and Saguy	2011	Reinventing R&D in an open innovation ecosystem
Song, Song, and Di Benedetto	2011	Resources, supplier investment, product launch advantages, and first product performance

who want to be part of future development projects should market their cooperativeness strategically as this factor is more influential for companies than their technical competence (McCutcheon *et al.*, 1997). The sharing of supplementary knowledge with external partners has a positive effect on innovation performance as Knudsen (2007) discovered. In this context Schoening *et al.* (1998) state that networks of colleague firms, suppliers, and customers were the most important sources for new product development projects. This is supported by the results of Alam (2003) and of Talke and Hultink (2010), who did an interesting review of diffusion research and stakeholder theory. As a result, they found that customers, dealers, suppliers, and competitors have a strong influence on innovation diffusion. This is supported by other studies as well, e.g. by Egbetokun (2009) in an African context or by Bonaccorsi and Lipparini (1994). Tidd (1995) argues that companies from the United States, Europe, and Japan are different in their organizational approaches to networks of alliances. Thus, European firms tend to overlook the potential for new products as they tend to be more narrowly focused than companies from the United States or Japan. Another notable result is Zheng *et al.* (2010) who showed that the vertical and horizontal cooperation with customers, suppliers, and other firms plays a more distinct role in the innovation process of SMEs than horizontal cooperation with research institutions, universities or colleges, and government agencies. This is indeed surprising as the paper is based on an analysis of Chinese companies. Against this background, Traitler *et al.* (2011) mention universities, research institutes and centers, start-ups, and individual inventers as potential partners for such "sharing-is-winning" models. Facing the international context of supplier innovation, Wynstra *et al.* (2010) state that supply chains can be useful metaphors to understand the distribution of regular production activities between firms; however, they arguably apply less to the distribution of product development activities. Such new ventures include their suppliers in the production of their first product as this is beneficial to the later success of the product (Song *et al.*, 2011). Moreover, in the same context, it was found that contingency conditions moderate the achieved levels of supplier involvement and that a direct relationship between the achieved level of involvement and performance exists (Song and Di Benedetto, 2008). Finally, large companies utilize supplier development to promote their technology management processes (Reed and Walsh, 2002).

(b) *Requirements for supplier innovation*

These papers discuss the requirements for supplier innovation (see Table 5). This is especially shown in the context of lean production (So and Sun, 2011) and in combination with IT systems such as customer relationship management systems (Lin *et al.*, 2010) and information-communication technologies (Awazu *et al.*, 2009). The use of innovation software is in general often recommended but the usage rate especially in SMEs is very low (Kohn and Hüsig, 2006).

Table 5. Selected Journal Articles Regarding the Requirements of Supplier Innovation.

Author(s)	Year	Title
Straker	2000	The customer and supplier innovation team guidebook
Pilkington and Dyerson	2002	Extending simultaneous engineering: Electric vehicle supply chains and new product development
Tatikonda and Stock	2003	Product technology transfer in the upstream supply chain
McIvor and Humphreys	2004	Early supplier involvement in the design process: Lessons from the electronics industry
Horn	2005	The changing nature of innovation
McIvor, Humphreys, and Cadden	2006	Supplier involvement in product development in the electronics industry: A case study
Kohn and Hüsig	2006	Potential benefits, current supply, utilization and barriers to adoption: An exploratory study on German SMEs and innovation software
Awazu *et al.*	2009	Information-communication technologies open up innovation

(*Continued*)

Table 5. (*Continued*)

Author(s)	Year	Title
Andersen and Drejer	2009	Together we share? Competitive and collaborative supplier interests in product development
Lin, Chen, and Chiu	2010	Customer relationship management and innovation capability: An empirical study
So and Sun	2011	An extension of IDT in examining the relationship between electronic-enabled supply chain integration and the adoption of lean production

McIvor *et al.* (2006) indicate that the degree of early supplier involvement must be taken into consideration: namely the depth of integration, the information exchange as well as the (existing) buyer–supplier relationships. Pilkington and Dyerson (2002) spotted the need for an extension of existing simultaneous engineering and supply chain management approaches in the context of the development of electric vehicles: The demands of these products force the car manufacturers to extend their supplier network beyond their existing boundaries into new networks. They consider that this phenomenon will become more common as environmental pressures will increase in the near future. In such cases, competitors often have to work together. A recent study by Anderson and Drejer (2009) regarding competitive supplier interests leads to three propositions: How such supplier rivalry and specialization influences roles, coordination patterns, and communication in different product development projects.

(c) *Managing supplier innovation*

We have given an overview of the importance and requirements for successful supplier innovation, but how do companies manage the innovation activities of their suppliers successfully? Let us have a look at the current debates in the literature.

Keizer and Halman (2009) argue that the reliability of suppliers is important and that this must be managed. Hence, project teams and innovation managers must seek to tick off early and any issues that continuously require team and management attention have to be managed under collaborative principles. Another interesting finding was researched by Duysters and Lokshin (2011), who suggest having a 'radar function' of links to various different partners in accessing novel information. Caputo and Zirpoli (2002) and Beecham and Hayes (1998) highlight that the role of managing innovative suppliers is specific to the automotive industry. In this context, Feng *et al.* (2011) offer a decision method for selecting suppliers from a short list.

When customer needs are translated into corporate technology development plans, which should stimulate and plan innovation activities along the supply chain, the speed and accuracy of the information to be gathered is extremely critical for successful new product development. The study by Vojak and Suarez-Nunez (2004) reveals that multidimensional problems occur when information (from customers) flows upstream on the supply chain and products flow downstream. Material, component, and system suppliers, who sell to industrial markets, struggle with getting the right market information for the development of successful user-driven innovation. As a result, companies who have to manage supplier innovation have two options: (a) collaboratively coordinate technology planning with suppliers to avoid failures in information sharing in the supply chain process, or (b) when information from original equipment manufacturers is restricted for competitive reasons, the number of failures can be reduced by the enrichment of information flows. To study these failures Vojak and Suarez-Nunez apply a methodology known from supply chain management: Analogous to the order decision problem of the 'order quantity bullwhip', they define the technology planning problem as 'product attribute bullwhip', which is crucial for every company managing supplier innovation in a user-driven environment (e.g. the telecommunications industry).

In contrast to the 'product attribute bullwhip' problem of companies' innovations, which are driven by user-centered design and product attributes, Verganti (2008) showed that the innovation process in this field hardly starts from a close observation of user needs for design-intensive manufacturers. These firms instead aim to change the emotional and symbolic content of a product. Therefore, he studied the ability of a manufacturer to understand and influence the emergence of new product meanings and manage the collaboration with suppliers for design-driven (radical) innovation.

Furthermore, van Echtelt *et al.* (2007) found that successful supplier involvement strongly depends on the coordinated design, execution, and evaluation of strategic long-term processes and operational short-term processes. Hence, they suggest a different approach to supplier involvement depending on firm size and environmental uncertainty. Many other articles study the decisions of companies regarding make-or-buy innovation (e.g. Ulrich and Ellison, 1999 and Petersen *et al.*, 2005). Concerning this phenomenon, Petersen *et al.* (2005) found some important relations: e.g. the increased knowledge of a supplier results in better information sharing and involvement of suppliers; moreover, the sharing of technological information leads to higher supplier involvement.

(d) *Supplier innovation outcome*

The supplier innovation outcome is related to success measures. Hence, it is a part of analysis that is very popular among practitioners. As already stated above, Knudsen (2007) discovered that the sharing of knowledge with external partners has a positive effect on a firm's innovation performance. In addition to this result other authors also researched the outcome of supplier innovation, see Table 7.

For example, Primo and Amundson (2002) measured the level of supplier involvement on a new product development project as contingent on the level of technical difficulty of the project. Lau (2011) extends prior studies of the contextual dimensions of product modularity, product innovativeness, and internal coordination for such involvement. A very interesting study for supplier innovation outcome research was completed by Frishammar and Horte (2005). They carried out a comprehensive empirical examination as to whether the management of external information is associated with innovation performance. On the one hand, they discovered that scanning customers,

Table 6.   Selected Journal Articles Regarding the Management of Supplier Innovation.

Author(s)	Year	Title
Wasservogel	1994	Materials in automobiles — A new distribution of roles between clients and suppliers
Chiesa and Manzini	1998	Profiting from the virtual organization of technological innovation: Suggestions from an empirical study
Beecham and Cordey-Hayes	1998	Partnering and knowledge transfer in the UK motor industry
Ulrich and Ellison	1999	Holistic customer requirements and the design-select decision
Nellore and Balachandra	2001	Factors influencing success in integrated product development (IPD) projects
Caputo and Zirpoli	2002	Supplier involvement in automotive component design: Outsourcing strategies and supply chain management
Petersen, Handfield, and Ragatz	2003	A model of supplier integration into new product development
Lin	2004	Original equipment manufacturers (OEM) manufacturing strategy for network innovation agility: The case of Taiwanese manufacturing networks
Vojak and Suarez-Nunez	2004	Product attribute bullwhip in the technology planning process and a methodology to reduce it
Petersen, Handfield, and Ragatz	2005	Supplier integration into new product development: Coordinating product, process and supply chain design

(*Continued*)

Table 6. (*Continued*)

Author(s)	Year	Title
Damanpour and Wischnevsky	2006	Research on innovation in organizations: Distinguishing innovation-generating from innovation-adopting organizations
van Echtelt, Wynstra, and van Weele	2007	Strategic and operational manageme of supplier involvement in new product development: A contingency perspective
Verganti	2008	Design, meanings, and radical innovation: A metamodel and a research agenda
van Echtelt *et al.*	2008	Managing supplier involvement in new product development: A multiple-case study
Slowinski *et al.*	2009	Effective practices for sourcing innovation
Keizer and Halman	2009	Risks in major innovation projects, a multiple case study within a world's leading company in the fast moving consumer goods
Feng, Fan, and Li	2011	A decision method for supplier selection in multi-service outsourcing
Duysters and Lokshin	2011	Determinants of alliance portfolio complexity and its effect on innovative performance of companies

suppliers, and competitors proved to be negatively correlated with innovation performance while, on the other hand, cross-functional integration in the form of collaboration (e.g. with suppliers) proved to be significantly correlated with innovation performance. Frishammar and Horte profoundly discovered the concept of knowledge integration. They unexpectedly found that it is collaboration, in the form of an unstructured, 'affective, volitional, mutual/shared process where

Table 7.   Selected Journal Articles Regarding the Outcome of Supplier Innovation.

Author(s)	Year	Title
Vanrossum and Cabo	1995	The contribution of research institutes in EUREKA projects
Bidault and Despres	1998	New product development and early supplier involvement (ESI): The drivers of ESI adoption
Primo and Amundson	2002	An exploratory study of the effects of supplier relationships on new product development outcomes
Miozzo and Dewick	2004	Networks and innovation in European construction: Benefits from inter-organisational cooperation in a fragmented industry
Bommer and Jalajas	2004	Innovation sources of large and small technology-based firms
Frishammar and Horte	2005	Managing external information in manufacturing firms: The impact on innovation performance
Tsekouras	2006	Gaining competitive advantage through knowledge integration in a European industrialising economy
Lau, Yam, and Tang	2007	Supply chain product co-development, product modularity and product performance — Empirical evidence from Hong Kong manufacturers
Song and Thieme	2009	The role of suppliers in market intelligence gathering for radical and incremental innovation
Neyens, Faems, and Sels	2010	The impact of continuous and discontinuous alliance strategies on startup innovation performance
Azadegan and Dooley	2010	Supplier innovativeness, organizational learning styles and manufacturer performance: An empirical assessment

(Continued)

Table 7. (*Continued*)

Author(s)	Year	Title
Un, Cuervo-Cazurra, and Asakawa	2010	R&D collaborations and product innovation
Lau	2011	Supplier and customer involvement on new product performance Contextual factors and an empirical test from manufacturer perspective

two or more departments work together, have mutual understanding, have a common vision, share resources, and achieve collective goals' (Kahn, 1996, p. 139), which is positively related to innovation performance. However, interaction as a structured and formally coordinated activity between departments including routine meetings, planned teleconferencing, memoranda, and the flow of standard documentation (Kahn, 1996) was proven to be insignificantly correlated.

Moreover, decision-making based on information from the industry environment is significantly correlated with innovation performance. Finally, Bommer and Jalajas (2004) compare small and medium-sized enterprises with large companies, where they found that professionals in large firms valued suppliers much more highly than in smaller firms.

Discussion

Supplier involvement is often examined with regards to strategic sourcing and the relationship between buyer and supplier. Our analysis shows that four areas may interact with regard to supplier innovation. We propose a conceptual framework for further studies on supplier innovation on the basis of these results (see Fig. 1).

Hence, we suggest that there are four stages, namely, importance, requirements, management, and the outcome of supplier innovation. We found — based on our literature review — that from stage 1 (understanding the importance of supplier innovation) to stage 4

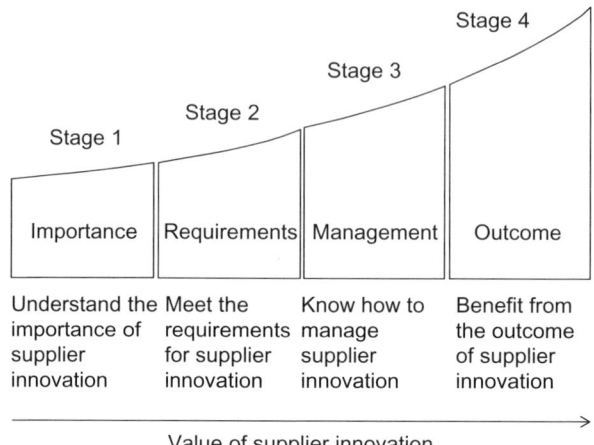

Fig. 1.   The Value Stages of Supplier Innovation.

(the benefit from the outcome of supplier innovation) there is an increased value of supplier innovation and the involvement of suppliers concerning open innovation. Thus, from step to step, we assume an increasing learning curve, which results in a higher value of supplier innovation.

The importance of supplier innovation refers to the mental process that suppliers are perceived as sources of innovation, not just as goods or services providers. Obviously not all suppliers will fit into this category; however, if at least some of them do this process is worth further effort. As there is professional supplier management in most companies, a mechanism to identify compatible suppliers must be individually determined. Without the acknowledgment of this assumption, there will be no success in supplier innovation.

Based on this understanding, there is a need for defining and understanding the requirements for supplier innovation. Both sides must ensure that they have senior management support. Moreover, there has to be a fit in the companies' strategies, the culture of innovative collaboration, and, of course, in the technical fundamental standards. The last point especially refers to information technology systems like customer relationship management or enterprise resource planning.

This area may be seen as the groundwork on which all further joint collaborative projects will be based.

Even if corporations understand the importance and requirements of supplier innovation they still have to manage the involvement of suppliers in an appropriate way. There are two main decisions that have to be made by management: Firstly, to understand the right time for supplier involvement and to decide in which phase of the supply chain a supplier should be involved (e.g. late involvement in a design-driven industry but very early involvement in a product-attribute-driven industry) and secondly, to decide the extent of supplier involvement (e.g. comprehensive involvement as system supplier or limited involvement as a parts supplier).

Based on this, supplier involvement in most studies we reviewed is considered as a boosting factor for internal capabilities and firm performance. The importance of supplier innovation is highly appreciated in start-ups and large companies, but not in small and medium-sized companies. Still, several important questions regarding supplier involvement in new product development remain unanswered.

All elements of our framework show interesting opportunities for future research. On the one hand, it might show interesting insights for further single-element research. On the other hand, process-oriented research may result in a better understanding of the correlations between these elements. In general, additional distinctions in branches, industries, and company sizes are suggested. Finally, we see many research opportunities based on supplier innovation, which will hopefully attract scholars from all over the world.

References

Alam, I. (2003). Commercial innovations from consulting engineering firms: An empirical exploration of a novel source of new product ideas, *Journal of Product Innovation Management*, **20**(4), 300–313.

Andersen, P.H. and Drejer, I. (2009). Together we share? Competitive and collaborative supplier interests in product development, *Technovation*, **29**(10), 690–703.

Awazu, Y., Baloh, P., Desouza, K.C., Wecht, C.H., Kim, J. and Jha, S. (2009). Information-communication technologies open up innovation, *Research-Technology Management*, **52**(1), 51–58.

Azadegan, A. and Dooley, K.J. (2010). Supplier innovativeness, organizational learning styles and manufacturer performance: An empirical assessment, *Journal of Operations Management*, **28**(6), 488–505.

Badawy, M.K. (2011). Is open innovation a field of study or a communication barrier to theory development? A perspective, *Technovation*, **31**(1), 65–67.

Beecham, M.A. and Cordey-Hayes, M. (1998). Partnering and knowledge transfer in the UK motor industry, *Technovation*, **18**(3), 191–205.

Bessant, J., Kaplinsky, R. and Lamming, R. (2003). Putting supply chain learning into practice, *International Journal of Operations and Production Management*, **23**(2), 167–184.

Bidault, F. and Despres, C. (1998). New product development and early supplier involvement (ESI): The drivers of ESI adoption, *International Journal of Technology Management*, **15**(1–2), 49–69.

Bilgram, V., Brem, A., and Voigt, K.-I. (2008). User-centric innovations in new product development — Systematic identification of lead-users harnessing interactive and collaborative online tools, *International Journal of Innovation Management*, **12**(3), 419–458.

Bommer, M. and Jalajas, D.S. (2004). Innovation sources of large and small technology-based firms, *IEEE Transactions on Engineering Management*, **51**(1), 13–18.

Bonaccorsi, A. and Lipparini, A. (1994). Strategic partnerships in new product development: An Italian case study, *Journal of Product Innovation Management*, **11**(2), 134–145.

Brem, A. (2008). *The Boundaries of Innovation and Entrepreneurship — Conceptual Background and Selected Theoretical and Empirical Aspects*, Gabler, Wiesbaden.

Butner, K. and Bourdé, M. (2004). Energize your supply chain network — New competitive advantage from existing investments, IBM. Available at http://www-935.ibm.com/services/au/igs/pdf/g510-3563-energize-your-supply-chain-network.pdf

Calabrese, G. (2002). Small–medium car suppliers and behavioural models in innovation, *Technology Analysis & Strategic Management*, **14**(2), 217–225.

Caputo, M. and Zirpoli, F. (2002). Supplier involvement in automotive component design: Outsourcing strategies and supply chain management, *International Journal of Technology Management*, **23**(1–3), 129–154.

Chiesa, V. and Manzini, R. (1998). Profiting from the virtual organization of technological innovation: Suggestions from an empirical study, *International Journal of Technology Management*, **15**(1–2), 109–123.

Dahlander, L. and Gann, D.M. (2010). How open is innovation? *Research Policy*, **39**(6), 699–709.

Damanpour, F. and Wischnevsky, J.D. (2006). Research on innovation in organizations: Distinguishing innovation-generating from innovation-adopting organizations, *Journal of Engineering and Technology Management*, **23**(4), 269–291.

Duysters, G. and Lokshin, B. (2011). Determinants of alliance portfolio complexity and its effect on innovative performance of companies, *Journal of Product Innovation Management*, **28**(4), 570–585.

Egbetokun, A.A., Siyanbola, W.O., Sanni, M., Olamade, O.O., Adeniyi, A.A. and Irefin, I.A. (2009). What drives innovation? Inferences from an industrywide survey in Nigeria, *International Journal of Technology Management*, **45**(1–2), 123–140.

Feng, B., Fan, Z.-P. and Li, Y. (2011). A decision method for supplier selection in multi-service outsourcing, *International Journal of Production Economics*, **132**(2), 240–250.

Frishammar, J. and Horte, S.A. (2005). Managing external information in manufacturing firms: The impact on innovation performance, *Journal of Product Innovation Management*, **22**(3), 251–266.

Gianiodis, P., Ellis, S.C. and Secchi, E. (2010). Advancing a typology of open innovation, *International Journal of Innovation Management*, **14**(4), 531–572.

Harryson, S.J. (1997). From experience — How Canon and Sony drive product innovation through networking and application-focused R&D, *Journal of Product Innovation Management*, **14**(4), 288–295.

Horn, P.M. (2005). The changing nature of innovation, *Research-Technology Management*, **48**(6), 28.

Ili, S., Albers, A. and Miller, S. (2010). Open innovation in the automotive industry, *R&D Management*, **40**(3), 246–255.

John, S. (2010). *Integration von Lieferanten in die Produktentwicklung: Risiken und Risikomanagement in vertikalen Entwicklungskooperationen — Eine konzeptionelle und empirische Untersuchung,* Dr. Hut, München.

Kahn, K.B. (1996). Interdepartmental integration: A definition with implications for product development performance, *Journal of Product Innovation Management,* **13**(2), 137–151.

Keizer, J.A. and Halman, J.I.M. (2009). Risks in major innovation projects, a multiple case study within a world's leading company in the fast moving consumer goods, *International Journal of Technology Management,* **48**(4), 499–517.

Klioutch, I. and Leker, J. (2011). Supplier involvement in customer new product development: New insights from the supplier's perspective, *International Journal of Innovation Management,* **15**(1), 231–248.

Knudsen, M.P. (2007). The relative importance of interfirm relationships and knowledge transfer for new product development success, *Journal of Product Innovation Management,* **24**(2), 117–138.

Kohn, S. and Hüsig, S. (2006). Potential benefits, current supply, utilization and barriers to adoption: An exploratory study on German SMEs and innovation software, *Technovation,* **26**(8), 988–998.

Lau, A.K.W. (2011). Supplier and customer involvement on new product performance: Contextual factors and an empirical test from manufacturer perspective, *Industrial Management and Data Systems,* **111**(5–6), 910–942.

Lau, A.K.W., Yam, R.C.M. and Tang, E.P.Y. (2007). Supply chain product co-development, product modularity and product performance — Empirical evidence from Hong Kong manufacturers, *Industrial Management and Data Systems,* **107**(7), 1036–1065.

Lee, A.H.I., Chen, H.H. and Tong, Y. (2008). Developing new products in a network with efficiency and innovation, *International Journal of Production Research,* **46**(17), 4687–4707.

Lichtenthaler, U. (2011). Open Innovation: Past research, current debates, and future directions, *Academy of Management Perspectives,* **25**(1), 75–93.

Lin, B.W. (2004). Original equipment manufacturers (OEM) manufacturing strategy for network innovation agility: The case of Taiwanese manufacturing networks, *International Journal of Production Research,* **42**(5), 943–957.

Lin, R.-J., Chen, R.-H. and Chiu, K.-S. (2010). Customer relationship management and innovation capability: An empirical study, *Industrial Management and Data Systems*, **110**(1–2), 111–133.

McCutcheon, D.M., Grant, R.A. and Hartley, J. (1997). Determinants of new product designers' satisfaction with suppliers' contributions, *Journal of Engineering and Technology Management*, **14**(3–4), 273–290.

McIvor, R. and Humphreys, P. (2004). Early supplier involvement in the design process: Lessons from the electronics industry, *Omega-International Journal of Management Science*, **32**(3), 179–199.

McIvor, R., Humphreys, P. and Cadden, T. (2006). Supplier involvement in product development in the electronics industry: A case study, *Journal of Engineering and Technology Management*, **23**(4), 374–397.

Miozzo, M. and Dewick, P. (2004). Networks and innovation in European construction: Benefits from inter-organisational cooperation in a fragmented industry, *International Journal of Technology Management*, **27**(1), 68–92.

Nellore, R. and Balachandra, R. (2001). Factors influencing success in integrated product development (IPD) projects, *IEEE Transactions on Engineering Management*, **48**(2), 164–174.

Neyens, I., Faems, D. and Sels, L. (2010). The impact of continuous and discontinuous alliance strategies on startup innovation performance, *International Journal of Technology Management*, **52**(3–4), 392–410.

Nieto, M.J. and Santamaria, L. (2007). The importance of diverse collaborative networks for the novelty of product innovation, *Technovation*, **27**(6–7), 367–377.

Petersen, K.J., Handfield, R.B. and Ragatz, G.L. (2003). A model of supplier integration into new product development, *Journal of Product Innovation Management*, **20**(4), 284–299.

Petersen, K.J., Handfield, R.B., and Ragatz, G.L. (2005). Supplier integration into new product development: Coordinating product, process and supply chain design, *Journal of Operations Management*, **23**(3–4), 371–388.

Pilkington, A. and Dyerson, R. (2002). Extending simultaneous engineering: Electric vehicle supply chains and new product development, *International Journal of Technology Management*, **23**(1–3), 74–88.

Primo, M.A.M. and Amundson, S.D. (2002). An exploratory study of the effects of supplier relationships on new product development outcomes, *Journal of Operations Management*, **20**(1), 33–52.

Reed, F.M. and Walsh, K. (2002). Enhancing technological capability through supplier development: A study of the UK aerospace industry, *IEEE Transactions on Engineering Management*, **49**(3), 231–242.

Remneland-Wikhamn, B., Ljungberg, J., Bergquist, M. and Kuschel, J. (2011). Open innovation, generativity and the supplier as peer: The case of iPhone and Android, *International Journal of Innovation Management*, **15**(1), 205–230.

Rosenzweig, E.D., Roth, A.V. and Dean, J.W. Jr. (2003). The influence of an integration strategy on competitive capabilities and business performance: An exploratory study of consumer products manufacturer, *Journal of Operations Management*, **21**(4), 437–456.

Schoening, N.C., Souder, W.E., Lee, J. and Cooper, R. (1998). The influence of government science and technology policies on new product development in the US, UK, South Korea and Taiwan, *International Journal of Technology Management*, **15**(8), 821–835.

Sharma, A. (2005). Collaborative product innovation: Integrating elements of CPI via PLM framework, *Computer-Aided Design*, **37**(13), 1425–1434.

Slowinski, G., Hummel, E., Gupta, A. and Gilmont, E.R. (2009). Effective practices for sourcing innovation, *Research-Technology Management*, **52**(1), 27–34.

So, S. and Sun, H. (2011). An extension of IDT in examining the relationship between electronic-enabled supply chain integration and the adoption of lean production, *International Journal of Production Research*, **49**(2), 447–466.

Song, L.Z., Song, M., and Di Benedetto, C.A. (2011). Resources, supplier investment, product launch advantages, and first product performance, *Journal of Operations Management*, **29**(1–2), 86–104.

Song, M. and Di Benedetto, C.A. (2008). Supplier's involvement and success of radical new product development in new ventures, *Journal of Operations Management*, **26**(1), 1–22.

Song, M. and Thieme, J. (2009). The role of suppliers in market intelligence gathering for radical and incremental innovation, *Journal of Product Innovation Management*, **26**(1), 43–57.

Spaeth, S., Stuermer, M. and Krogh, G. (2010). Enabling knowledge creation through outsiders: Towards a push model of open innovation, *International Journal of Technology Management*, **52**(3–4), 411–431.

Straker, D.M. (2000). The customer and supplier innovation team guide-book, *Quality Progress*, **33**(12), 124.

Talke, K. and Hultink, E.J. (2010). Managing diffusion barriers when launching new products, *Journal of Product Innovation Management*, **27**(4), 537–553.

Tatikonda, M.V. and Stock, G.N. (2003). Product technology transfer in the upstream supply chain, *Journal of Product Innovation Management*, **20**(6), 444–467.

Tidd, J. (1995). Development of novel products through intraorganizational and interorganizational networks — The case of home automation, *Journal of Product Innovation Management*, **12**(4), 307–322.

Traitler, H., Watzke, H.J. and Saguy, I.S. (2011). Reinventing R&D in an open innovation ecosystem, *Journal of Food Science*, **76**(2), 62–68.

Tsekouras, G. (2006). Gaining competitive advantage through knowledge integration in a European industrialising economy, *International Journal of Technology Management*, **36**(1–3), 126–147.

Ulrich, K.T. and Ellison, D.J. (1999). Holistic customer requirements and the design-select decision, *Management Science*, **45**(5), 641–658.

Ulrich, K.T. and Ellison, D.J. (2005). Beyond make-buy: Internalization and integration of design and production, *Production and Operations Management*, **14**(3), 315–330.

Un, C.A., Cuervo-Cazurra, A. and Asakawa, K. (2010). R&D collaborations and product innovation, *Journal of Product Innovation Management*, **27**(5), 673–689.

Van Echtelt, F.E.A., Wynstra, F. and van Weele, A.J. (2007). Strategic and operational management of supplier involvement in new product development: A contingency perspective, *IEEE Transactions on Engineering Management*, **54**(4), 644–661.

Van Echtelt, F.E.A., Wynstra, F., van Weele, A.J. and Duysters, G. (2008). Managing supplier involvement in new product development: A multiple-case study, *Journal of Product Innovation Management*, **25**(2), 180–201.

Vanrossum, W. and Cabo, P.G. (1995). The contribution of research institutes in EUREKA projects, *International Journal of Technology Management*, **10**(7–8), 853–866.

Verganti, R. (2008). Design, meanings, and radical innovation: A metamodel and a research agenda, *Journal of Product Innovation Management*, **25**(5), 436–456.

Vojak, B.A. and Suarez-Nunez, C.A. (2004). Product attribute bullwhip in the technology planning process and a methodology to reduce it, *IEEE Transactions on Engineering Management*, **51**(3), 288–299.

Wagner, S. M. (2009). Getting innovation from suppliers, *Research-Technology Management*, **52**(1), 8–9.

Wasservogel, F. (1994). Materials in automobiles — A new distribution of roles between clients and suppliers, *Revue de Métallurgie-Cahiers d'Informations Techniques*, **91**(10), 1415–1422.

Wink, R. (2010). Restructuring European aeronautics SMEs: The role of formal examination knowledge, *International Journal of Technology Management*, **50**(3–4), 380–392.

Wynstra, F., Corswant, F. and Wetzels, M. (2010). In chains? An empirical study of antecedents of supplier product development activity in the automotive industry, *Journal of Product Innovation Management*, **27**(5), 625–639.

Zairi, M. (1999). Effective TQM implementation through supplier partnerships: A benchmarking study of advanced manufacturing technology systems, *International Journal of Industrial Engineering: Theory, Applications and Practice*, **6**(3), 254–264.

Zeng, S.X., Xie, X.M. and Tam, C.M. (2010). Relationship between cooperation networks and innovation performance of SMEs, *Technovation*, **30**(3), 181–194.

Chapter 3

Managing Open Innovation
in New Product Development Projects:
A Contingent Perspective

Hanna Bahemia
Manchester Business School,
The University of Manchester, UK

Brian Squire
School of Management,
The University of Bath, UK

Introduction

Adoption of open innovation is recognition that new product development (NPD) performance can no longer be solely determined by internal R&D functions but also depends on the contributions of a broad
range of external players from individual customers to large research
institutes. Firms opening their innovation process in both inbound (i.e.
the acquisition of knowledge from external parties) and outbound (i.e.
the commercialisation of technology to other companies) directions
have been shown to achieve higher profitability than internally focussed
organisations (Chesbrough, 2006; Lichtenthaler and Ernst, 2009).

   Perhaps unsurprisingly, there is growing interest in examining the
effectiveness of open innovation. The popular press has held up examples of successful product introductions, such as Olay Regenerative
cream care and Pringles Print Crisps, which were developed within an
open innovation framework (Huston and Sakkab, 2006). Although
open innovation was initially studied in large high-tech multinational
enterprises, there is evidence that this strategy has also been embraced

by small and medium enterprises (SMEs) in both the manufacturing and service sectors (Van de Vrande *et al.*, 2009). The majority of studies on open innovation in the academic literature have shown the value-generating effects of integrating a broad range of external parties, including suppliers, customers, competitors, consultants, research institutes and universities, in the innovation process (Faems *et al.*, 2005; Love and Roper, 1999; Tether, 2002; Tether and Tajar, 2008). More recently, however, studies have also warned that diminishing returns to performance set in when firms open their innovation processes to external sources of knowledge too far (Laursen and Salter, 2006; Rothaermel and Deeds, 2006; Leiponen and Helfat, 2010).

While there is little doubt as to the value of these studies, their focus has been on the role of open innovation at the level of the firm. Thus they make the implicit assumption that the choice of an open innovation strategy is determined at the level of the organisation and do not provide advice on the degree to which managers should engage external parties during the course of any single (NPD) project. Arguably, such a micro-level of analysis may be beneficial where the objectives and conditions of individual NPD projects vary substantially within the same organisation and where each requires a differing degree of openness.

The objective of this chapter is to develop a conceptual framework to aid understanding of the extent to which different contingencies affect inbound open innovation during an NPD project. We argue that the decision for managers is not solely a binary choice of whether to adopt open innovation at a *firm* level (e.g. Chesbrough, 2006; Lichtenthaler and Ernst, 2009) but also the extent to which each individual NPD project should engage with external parties. More specifically we adopt contingency theory to examine how three dimensions of inbound open innovation — breadth, depth and ambidexterity — might vary across different contexts. It is shown that these three dimensions of inbound open innovation can vary significantly at the level of the NPD project and that they are affected by the type of innovation, the product complexity and appropriability regime.

The remainder of this chapter is organised as follows. First, we present contingency theory as an appropriate theoretical lens to develop the conceptual model (Lawrence and Lorsch, 1967;

Donaldson, 2001). We review the literature on inbound open innovation and summarise the limitations of the conceptualisation of inbound open innovation, which is measured along a single dimension in the majority of studies. We then proceed to justify the relevance of a multidimensional approach for measuring the inbound open innovation construct. A conceptual model and propositions, supporting a contingent perspective of open innovation for NPD projects, are developed for future empirical work. Finally, we discuss the theoretical contributions of the conceptual model as well as its implications for future research and for managers.

Theoretical Lens: Contingency Theory

Contingency theory states that there is no one best way to organise and that any one way of organising is not effective under all conditions (Galbraith, 1973). The theory holds that organisations will alter their structure in response to changing contextual factors to maintain high performance, which is the so-called contextual — response — performance model (Lawrence and Lorsch, 1967; Donaldson, 2001). Contextual variables represent situational factors that are either exogenous or endogenous to the organisation or managers. In this model contextual variables represent endogenous factors of any new product development (NPD) project such as the types of innovation (i.e. incremental or radical), product complexity (i.e. discrete or complex) and the appropriability regime (i.e. strong or weak). Response variables are the actions taken by managers in reaction to such contingency factors and here they represent the calibration of the three dimensions (breadth, depth and ambidexterity) of inbound open innovation at an NPD project level. Finally, performance variables measure the effectiveness of the fit between the context and the response and are measured by the performance of the new product.

Literature Review

Critics have argued that the so-called emergence of a new paradigm of open innovation, as described by Chesbrough in 2003, appears to be a case of old wine in new bottles (Trott and Hartmann, 2009). The notion that firms need to integrate different types of external parties such as suppliers, customers, universities and research institutes is not a new idea in the innovation literature. However, the differentiating factor between previous studies on inter-firm collaborative innovation models and those of open innovation, as posited by Chesbrough (2003), is an emphasis on the importance of striking a balance between the inbound and outbound dimensions of an open innovation strategy.

The origins of inter-firm R&D collaboration can be found in studies examining the integration of various external parties, including suppliers (Hakansson and Eriksson, 1993; Petersen *et al.*, 2003; Ragatz *et al.*, 2002; Handfield and Lawson, 2007), customers (Hippel, 1978; Cooper and Kleinschmidt, 1987; Atuahene-Gima, 1995), competitors (Hamel, 1991) and universities (Gerwin *et al.*, 1992; Santoro, 2000), into the innovation process. The focus was constrained to the role of a single type of external party as befitting specific streams of research, for example supply chain management (suppliers), marketing (customers, competitors) and research policy (universities, private and public research institutes). Consequently, the synergistic effect of opening the innovation process to a diverse set of external actors was not as well understood.

The open innovation literature differs in that studies have purposefully sought to examine the concurrent effect of inputs from a range of external parties. Firms that possess a heterogeneous network of different types of external parties, such as suppliers, customers, consultants, competitors, universities, public and private research institutes, have been found to have better innovation performance as synergies emerge from a networked approach to innovation (Becker and Dietz, 2004; Miotti and Sachwald, 2003; Nieto and Santamaria, 2007; Belderbos *et al.*, 2004; Tether, 2002). As the number of different types of external partner increases, so does the innovation performance of new products (Faems *et al.*, 2005; Roper *et al.*, 2008; Tether and Tajar, 2008). Amara and Landry (2005) have also suggested that when firms rely on a large variety of external sources of information, they are more likely to develop more innovative products.

More recently, scholars have started to explore some of the limits to open innovation. The risk associated with inbound open innovation is primarily related to the potential costs to the organisation. For example, the direct cost of technology acquisitions from third parties has been found to be larger than their indirect value-generating effect; consequently, the net effect on firm performance is negative (Faems *et al.*, 2009). More broadly, the relation between the number of alliances across different types of collaboration (e.g. suppliers, universities, research institutes) and the rate of new product development can have an inverted U shape, where there are diminishing returns as the number of parties involved in the open innovation process becomes too large (Rothaermel and Deeds, 2006).

Furthermore, Laursen and Salter (2006) have examined the extent to which the use of external sources of knowledge affects innovation performance; those firms searching widely and deeply across several external sources of knowledge, at a firm level, tend to be more innovative. However, beyond some point, diminishing returns set in and there is a negative relation for innovation performance due to the high costs of searching. Similarly, Leiponen and Helfat (2010) support the presence of diminishing returns when firms access a very large number of different types of knowledge sources during the innovation process. Therefore, the cost implication of an inbound open innovation strategy is an inherent threat to its success. In this respect, a judicious calibration of the degree of openness to external parties, *at an NPD project level*, is necessary. It appears that the diminishing return of an inbound open strategy, *at a firm level*, may potentially be a consequence of the long-run cumulative effects of opening up unnecessarily the innovation process too far *at a NPD project level*.

Measuring Inbound Open Innovation

The measurement of inbound open innovation broadly fits into one of two types. First, openness can be measured in terms of R&D partnership and cooperation (Becker and Dietz, 2004; Miotti and Sachwald, 2003; Belderbos *et al.*, 2004). Second, openness can be equated to the number of external sources of information used during the innovation process (Amara and Landry, 2005; Laursen and Salter, 2006; Roper *et al.*, 2008). Table 1 indicates the heterogeneous measurement approaches and shows that the majority of studies focus exclusively on the breadth dimension of inbound open innovation. Breadth measures the degree of openness in terms of the number of different external parties involved in the innovation process. Studies have found a number of different parties, such as suppliers, clients, universities etc., and have evolved from studying a relatively small variety of external parties to many different sources. The research clearly indicates the degree of possible variance along this dimension, both for scholars and for industry.

Table 1 also indicates that two prior studies have identified depth as a second dimension of inbound open innovation (Laursen and Salter, 2006; Oerlemans and Knoben, 2010). This dimension refers to the importance of the external parties and is measured according to the extent to which a specific source was used during the innovation process. Importance is, however, only one dimension of the depth of any relationship and we suggest this construct could be refined by examining the level of cooperation and integration between the firm and those external parties involved in the innovation process. This has the advantage of drawing on the substantial body of literature pertaining to supplier involvement in new product development, where it is common practice to assess relationships in terms of cooperation and integration (Droge *et al.*, 2004; Petersen *et al.*, 2005; Jayaram, 2008).

In addition to refining the measures of breadth and depth, we suggest a final dimension of inbound open innovation. Drawing on March's (1991) seminal work on exploration and exploitation, scholars have recently demonstrated the practical advantages of developing ambidextrous inter-firm relations by including both new and existing parties within an alliance structure (Lin, *et al.*, 2007; Tiwana, 2008). Ambidextrous alliances will generate better and more radical innovation outcomes for alliances where at least 20% of the partners are new (Lin *et al.*, 2007). Similarly, we suggest that the number of new versus existing partners is an important dimension of inbound open innovation and refer to this as 'ambidexterity'. Ambidextrous open innovation

Table 1. Measurement Approaches for Inbound Open Innovation.

Paper	Definition of openness	Supplier	Client	Rival	University	Public Research Institute	Private Research Institute	Consultant	Generally available sources	Others	Unit of analysis	Dimension
Becker and Dietz, (2004)	R&D cooperation	✓	✓	✓	✓						Firm	Breadth
Miotti and Sachwald, (2003)	R&D partnerships	✓	✓	✓	✓						Firm	Breadth
Nieto and Santamaria (2007)	Collaboration	✓	✓	✓	✓	✓					Firm	Breadth
Belderbos, Carree, Lokshin (2004)	R&D cooperation	✓	✓	✓	✓						Firm	Breadth
Faems, Looy and Debackere (2005)	Collaboration	✓	✓	✓	✓	✓		✓			Firm	Breadth
Roper Du, Love (2008)	Knowledge sourcing	✓	✓	✓	✓			✓			Firm	Breadth

(*Continued*)

H. Bahemia and B. Squire

Table 1. (*Continued*)

Paper	Definition of openness	Supplier	Client	Rival	University	Public Research Institute	Private Research Institute	Consultant	Generally available sources	Others	Unit of analysis	Dimension
Tether and Tajar (2008)	Sources of information	✓	✓	✓	✓	✓	✓	✓			Firm	Breadth
Tether 2002	Joint R&D	✓	✓	✓	✓	✓	✓	✓			Firm	Breadth
Rothaermel and Deeds (2006)	Alliances	✓	✓	✓	✓	✓	✓				Firm	Breadth
Amara and Landry (2005)	Sources of information	✓	✓	✓	✓	✓	✓	✓	✓		Firm	Breadth
Laursen and Salter (2006)	Sources of knowledge	✓	✓	✓	✓	✓	✓	✓	✓	✓	Firm	Breadth Depth
Leiponen and Helfat (2010)	Sources of knowledge	✓	✓	✓	✓	✓	✓	✓	✓	✓	Firm	Breadth
Oerlemans and Knoben (2010)	Inter organisational relationship (IORs)	✓	✓	✓	✓	✓	✓	✓	✓		Firm	Breadth Depth

projects include both new and existing external partners and we will argue that there are clear outcomes for the performance of new products. Each of these three dimensions will be explored in greater depth in the following sections.

Dimension one of inbound open innovation: breadth

Based on Table 1, we define the breadth dimension of inbound open innovation as the number of different types of external parties involved in the innovation process. Previous studies, showing the value-generating effect of opening up the innovation process to different types of external parties, have focused primarily on the role of traditional players (suppliers, customers, competitors, consultants, commercial laboratories, research institutes and universities). In this conceptual chapter, we further refine the breadth dimension of inbound open innovation by incorporating these traditional players alongside three new types of external parties.

First, we identify small players such as start-ups, entrepreneurs and individual innovators as being a distinct category of external players with whom innovating firms may potentially cooperate. Previous studies have highlighted that smaller players achieve a higher level of creativity, speed and flexibility during the innovation process (Bower and Christensen, 1995). For example in the pharmaceutical industry, large companies collaborate extensively with specialist biotech start-ups during the innovation process (Galambos and Sturchio, 1998). In the ITC sector, collaboration with smaller players is becoming a viable alternative path for bringing new technologies to market. For example, the collaboration between Nokia and a high-tech entrepreneur, to produce nano-enabled solutions to increase energy density and to shorten the charge/discharge cycles of the energy storage systems for mobile phones, illustrates the potential of individual entrepreneurs to contribute to product outcomes in the context of a networked approach to innovation (Nokia, 2009).

Second, we add open innovation intermediaries to the list of possible external parties. Intermediaries have recently emerged as a central actor in the open innovation network and exist to help innovating companies search for information about potential collaborators in the network (Verona *et al.*, 2006; Sieg *et al.*, 2010). Companies such as IDEO, InnoCentive, Invention Machine, Spigit, CrowdSpirit, BrainReactions, YourEncore and CommuniSpace act as knowledge brokers between a pool of specialised experts and innovating firms (Diener and Piller, 2009). For example, Mattel Toys relies on idea brokers like the Big Idea Group to invite inventors to submit ideas (Chesbrough, 2003). In the UK, 100% Open is an open innovation agency in the market, which provides open innovation service to companies such as Oracle, Virgin Atlantic, Tesco, Orange, the Discovery Channel, Cancer Research UK, McLaren, Pfizer and BT. Similarly, Procter & Gamble connects with a global community of experts through the platform of InnoCentive. The platform acts as an effective link to bridge the gap between innovating firms and a wide range of potential solution providers widely dispersed in a global network (Huston and Sakkab, 2006).

The final type of external party included in the breadth dimension is members of the public. Many firms have developed crowd-sourcing initiatives by launching idea generation contests for members of the public (Surowiecki, 2004; Pisano and Verganti, 2008). Firms are using dedicated websites and networking sites, such as Facebook and Twitter, to encourage the public to participate in the innovation process and generate new ideas. For example, recent reports from the US automotive industry have indicated that Local Motors, a company bases in the US, has built a new racing car called the rally fighter, targeted at the American community of off-road racers, by using open source techniques and by harnessing on the wisdom of the crowd (*The Sunday Times*, 2009). Car enthuasts and members of the crowd have submitted their ideas for the development of every aspect of the car by email or Twitter. Many firms such as Adidas, BMW and Boeing are also leveraging the potential of crowd-sourcing initiatives in their innovation processes to stimulate the generation of new ideas (Berthon *et al.*, 2007; Sawhney and Prandelli, 2000; Piller and Walcher, 2006).

To the best knowledge of the authors, previous studies on inbound open innovation have not incorporated these three aforementioned players alongside traditional ones when measuring the breadth of openness. The emergence of these actors in the network is a relatively

recent phenomenon but all have been shown to have at least an anec-
dotal impact on innovation performance. In summary, the breadth of
open innovation represents the relation between the innovating firm
and traditional external parties (suppliers, customers, competitors,
universities, consultants, commercial laboratories, private and public
research institutes), as well as with emerging parties (smaller players,
open innovation intermediaries and members of the crowd).

Dimension two of inbound open innovation: Depth

Table 1 highlights that studies on open innovation focus primarily on
the breadth dimension rather than the depth of the relation a between
firm and the external parties involved in the innovation process. It is
to be underlined that although Laursen and Salter (2006) and
Oerlemans and Knoben (2010) dichotomise openness into two
components, breadth and depth, their definition of depth is limited
to the importance of the sources of knowledge and inter-organisational
relations, respectively. The innovation literature acknowledges this
deficit, suggesting future research to investigate the depth of the relation with external factors from a relational perspective as for example
the level of cooperation (Becker and Dietz, 2004; Nieto and Santamaria,
2007; Oerlemans and Knoben, 2010).

While the depth of inter-firm relations, from a relational perspective, is largely absent from the open innovation literature, it has been
discussed extensively in the alliance and supply chain management
literatures. The latter fields are highly relevant in helping to explore
and define the depth dimension of inbound open innovation. There
is a strong parallel between these strands of the literature and that of
open innovation where the common denominator is a focus on inter-
firm relations. In the supply chain literature, the depth of inter-firm
collaboration is measured by the extent and timing of involvement
(Brown and Eisenhardt, 1995; Ittner and Larcker, 1997; Swink,
1999; Gerwin and Barrowman, 2002; Mishra *et al.*, 2009). An early
and high level of integration of suppliers is a critical success factor for
the performance of the NPD project leading to reduction of costs,
shorter development cycles and improved product manufacturability

(Bonaccorsi and Lipparini, 1994; Ragatz *et al.*, 1997; Droge *et al.*, 2004; Petersen *et al.*, 2005; Jayaram, 2008). Past research has also associated early and close integration of suppliers in the NPD process with superior product performance (Gupta and Wilemon, 1990; Clark and Fujimoto, 1989). Similarly, the alliance literature suggests that a high level of coordination, communication and bonding skills between the firm and alliance partners forms part of an alliance management capability, which exerts a positive influence on performance outcomes at both the alliance and firm levels (Schreiner *et al.*, 2009). Therefore, based on the above, aside from the breadth dimension of inbound open innovation (i.e. the degree of openness to different types of external parties), the level of cooperation and integration between the focal firm and the different types of external parties represents the depth dimension, which managers use for effective implementation of an inbound open innovation strategy.

Dimension three of inbound open innovation: Ambidexterity

In addition to the previous two dimensions, we argue that inbound open innovation is also determined by the degree of ambidexterity. In the field of technological innovation, exploration and exploitation theory (March, 1991) has been widely used as a framework to represent different organisational learning strategies for acquiring various competences. The balance between the exploration of new competences and the exploitation of existing competences represents an ambidextrous approach. This approach yields better performance as each of these strategic orientations has inherent weaknesses that may be overcome in combination (He and Wong, 2004; Levinthal and March, 1993; Tushman and O'Reilly, 1996).

On the one hand, an exploitation strategy refers to the exploitation of existing knowledge, skills and processes, while on the other hand, an exploration strategy refers to the investment of resources to acquire new knowledge, skills and processes that will enhance variation and experimentation (March, 1991). Previous studies have applied the exploitation–exploration framework to differentiate between cooperation with long-standing partners as opposed to cooperation with new external partners. Although an alliance represents only one of the many forms of inter-firm relation, it is fertile ground for exploring the third dimension of open innovation because both streams of research — on open innovation and alliances — consider the inter-organisational relation perspective. There is a broad consensus in the alliance literature about the importance of achieving ambidexterity in inter-firm relations by developing relations with a mix of long-standing and new partners.

Collaboration with new partners is classified as an exploration strategy whereas collaboration with existing partners is associated with an exploitation strategy (Lin *et al.*, 2007; Beckman *et al.*, 2004; Lavie and Rosenkopf, 2006; Dittrich and Duysters, 2007; Tiwana, 2008). Ambidexterity has been measured empirically when a firm achieves a balance in exploring at least 20% of new alliances while simultaneously exploiting 80% of existing alliances (Lin *et al.*, 2007). Large firms exhibiting this ambidextrous capability achieve higher performance when operating in turbulent environments (Lin *et al.*, 2007). Similarly, Kogut and Zander (1993) provided evidence that firms benefit from combining current knowledge already present in the firm's existing network partners, with new knowledge reached by extending the boundary of the firm's network to new partners.

Social capital theory, and more specifically the theory of the strength of weak ties, sheds light on the benefits of teaming up with new partners where new possibilities and ideas are more likely to be generated from weak ties than from strong ties (Granovetter, 1973). Firms are in a better position to generate novelties when they renew their inter-firm relations in an agile way, initiating collaboration with new players while at the same time relying on long-standing partners (Capaldo, 2007). From this perspective, we argue that the capability of managers to develop a balance between the exploitation of long-standing relations and the exploration of new ones during an NPD project forms the ambidexterity dimension of inbound open innovation.

In summary, the breadth, depth and ambidexterity dimensions represent the multiple facets of inbound open innovation. We argue that these three dimensions are managerially relevant and determinable during the course of an NPD project and therefore represent our 'response' variables. We have refined the breadth dimension by including both traditional and new players creating a list of eleven potential types of external actors. The depth dimension captures the timing and level of cooperation and integration with the different types of external actors involved in an NPD project. Finally, the ambidexterity dimension represents the capability of managers to strike a balance between the exploitation of long-standing inter-firm relations and the exploration of new ones during an NPD project. Therefore, we argue that the effectiveness of inbound open innovation during an NPD project is not solely restricted to a decision regarding the degree of openness to different types of external actors (as described in earlier studies) but equally to the capability of managers to regulate the depth and ambidexterity of these inter-firm relations.

Development of a Contingency Framework for Inbound Open Innovation

Following the refinement of the inbound open innovation construct, we develop a conceptual model to address the main objective of this chapter, which is to develop a contingency view of inbound open innovation at the NPD project level. We argue that the relation between the three dimensions of inbound open innovation and new product performance, which is defined as the financial success of new products, is moderated by three contingencies: the type of innovation (incremental or radical), product complexity (complex or discrete) and the appropriability regime (strong or weak) (see Figure 2). In the next section, we explain how the breadth, depth and ambidexterity dimensions of inbound open innovation influence the performance of new products, followed by the moderating effect of these contingencies.

The effect of the breadth dimension on NPD performance

Firms enter into inter-firm collaborative arrangements for innovation to access strategic resources, as well as to reduce the cost and risk of internal R&D. The complexities of technology, the rising cost of

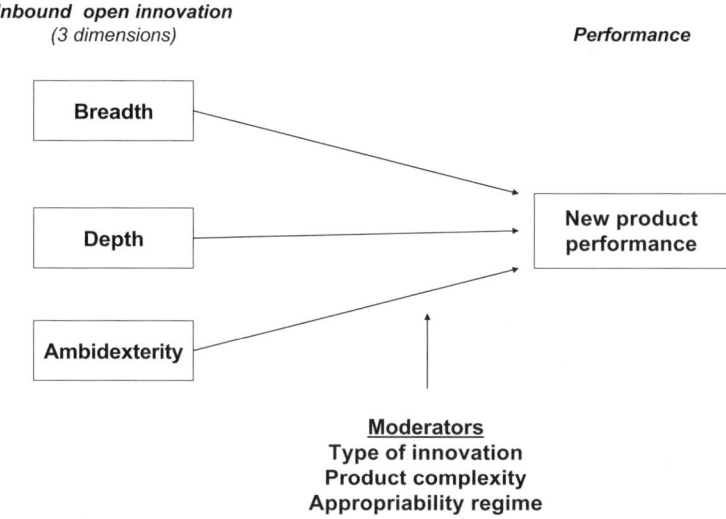

Fig. 2. Dimensions and Moderators of Inbound Open Innovation.

R&D and the pressure for speed to market are the drivers leading firms to embrace an inter-firm cooperative R&D strategy to capture key knowledge resources distributed in a global network (Tether, 2002). There is a broad consensus in the literature that simultaneous collaboration with suppliers, customers, competitors and universities leads to a positive effect on innovation performance (Becker and Dietz, 2004; Miotti and Sachwald, 2003; Nieto and Santamaria, 2007; Belderbos *et al.*, 2004; Faems *et al.*, 2005). Some scholars have integrated consultants as a new type of external partner alongside suppliers, customers, competitors and universities (Faems *et al.*, 2005). Other scholars have brought further accuracy by integrating public and private research institutes with the traditional types of inter-firm relation such as suppliers, customers, competitors, consultants and universities (Tether and Tajar, 2008; Tether, 2002). All these studies have shown similar results regarding the positive exponential effect on innovation performance when the number of different types of external parties increases. Roper *et al.* (2008) have shown evidence of a direct link between the sourcing of knowledge from external parties (suppliers, customers, consultants, competitors, universities and research institutes) for innovation and business growth and productivity. The foregoing studies suggest that a diverse range of external partners will have a positive effect on innovation performance.

Despite evidence that openness to different types of external knowledge sources is likely to result in better performance, the emergence of diminishing returns offers a more nuanced view (Laursen and Salter, 2006; Leiponen and Helfat, 2009). Diminishing returns may be explained by the fact that for the transaction costs associated with multiple channels of information there exists a break-even point beyond which costs offset any marginal gains to innovation outcomes (Laursen and Salter, 2006). Based on these arguments, it is expected that the breadth dimension of open innovation is curvilinearly related to the performance of new products. This leads to our first proposition:

Proposition 1: There is an inverted U relation between the breadth dimension of inbound open innovation and the performance of new products.

The effect of the depth dimension on NPD performance

As discussed earlier, there is dearth of studies in the open innovation literature that look at the level of cooperation or integration with different types of external parties involved in the NPD process (the depth dimension). Nevertheless, we apply research from the supply chain and strategic alliances literature to provide support for the correlation between the depth of inter-firm relations and NPD performance. There is support that an early and high level of integration with both customers and suppliers yields superior performance in the lead time of NPD projects, the design performance of new products and overall firm performance (Droge *et al.*, 2004; Petersen *et al.*, 2005; Jayaram, 2008). Prior studies have emphasised that deep cooperation, coordination and communication between firms and their alliance partners positively affect performance outcomes (Mohr and Spekman, 1994; Das and Teng, 1998; Dyer and Singh, 1998; Schreiner *et al.*, 2009). Littler *et al.* (1995) examined the key success factors for collaborative NPD projects with any external partner such as a supplier, customer or competitor and found that frequent communication together with trust between the firm and the third parties involved in the innovation process is linked with the likelihood of success. Similarly, Bstieler (2006) reported that the formation of trust (based on shared problem-solving and high communication) is the differentiating variable between high- and low-performing collaborative relations in new product development. Based on this line of reasoning, we argue that increasing the level of cooperation and integration with a broad range of external parties will positively affect the performance of new products.

Proposition 2: There is a positive relation between the depth dimension of inbound open innovation and the performance of new products.

The effect of the ambidexterity dimension on NPD performance

It has been suggested that firms that succeed in simultaneously managing exploration and exploitation strategies can develop an ambidextrous capability, which in turn can pave the way to better firm performance (Tushman and O'Reilly, 1996; Eisenhardth and Martin, 2000). Katila and Ahuja (2002) found a positive effect on new product development when firms combine both exploitation and exploration learning strategies, while He and Wong (2004) found a similar effect of ambidexterity on firm performance. In an uncertain environment where there is a greater need for flexibility, an ambidextrous approach to organisational learning is achieved through the development of relations with new external alliance partners as well as the exploitation of long-standing ones (Lin *et al.*, 2007). Goerzen (2007) argued that repeated partnerships are associated with lower firm performance, particularly in technologically uncertain environments and it is necessary to balance this negative effect with the exploration of relations with new partners. Moreover, firms exhibiting an ambidextrous approach, in exploiting current alliances while simultaneously exploring new ones, achieve higher performance at the level of the alliances (Lin *et al.*, 2007).

A dual network architecture, where a small core of strong ties is integrated with a large periphery of weak ties, does have a positive effect on the innovation capability of a firm (Capaldo, 2007). Firms are in a better position to innovate because the integration of weak ties represented by cooperation with new partners is an effective mechanism to reduce the risk of redundancy, which stifles innovation and creativity. This leads us to suggest that the balance between the exploitation of long-standing relations and the exploration of new relations during NPD (the ambidexterity dimension) will exert a positive effect on the performance of new products.

Proposition 3: There is a positive relation between the ambidexterity dimension of inbound open innovation and the performance of new products.

The moderating role of the type of innovation

The choice of the three moderators is primarily motivated by a specific concern to align the levels of theory, measurement and analysis (Rousseau, 1985). The level of the contingency theory, which this chapter aims to develop, is at the NPD project level. As suggested in the literature, the levels of theory, measurement and analysis must be aligned to minimise 'fallacies of the wrong level' (Hitt *et al.*, 2007). In this respect, the boundary of the moderators is restricted to the level of a new product development project and variables located at the firm level are excluded as potential candidates in order to capture the moderating effect. The three moderators, namely, the type of innovation, product complexity and the appropriability regime, which are described in the next section, do not traverse higher level of analysis than the NPD project itself. For this reason we exclude firm-*level* strategic and cultural factors such as absorptive capacity and organisational leadership.

We propose that the type of innovation moderates two of the dimensions of the open innovation–performance relation: breadth and ambidexterity. Scholars have investigated the link between the type of innovation (incremental or radical) and the choice of the type of partner (Miotti *et al.*, 2003; Amara and Landry, 2005; Belderbos *et al.*, 2004). Results indicate that vertical cooperation (for example with suppliers or customers) is efficient for innovation new to the firm, while cooperation with external partners providing science research capabilities (for example with universities and public and private research institutions) is efficient for innovation new to the industry (Belderbos *et al.*, 2004; Miotti and Sachwald, 2003). Indeed, the use of market sources (such as suppliers, clients or competitors) decreases the likelihood of world premiere innovation. Products or processes embodying radical innovation require more research-based sources of information such as universities, federal government agencies and research laboratories (Amara and Landry, 2005).

Based on our earlier definition of the breadth dimension of inbound open innovation, it appears the broader the degree of openness to external parties who are market based (suppliers, small players, customers, members of the crowd, competitors, consultants, commercial laboratories or open innovation intermediaries), the higher will be the generation of innovation that is new to the firm (incremental innovation). In contrast, a narrow degree of openness to external parties who are research based (universities and private and public research institutes) is more likely to lead to industry innovation (radical innovation). Thus, we propose that the type of innovation will moderate the relation between the breadth of open innovation and the performance of new products. Projects developing incremental innovation will seek to collaborate with a broader and more diverse number of external partners compared to projects aiming at radical products.

Proposition 4a: The inverted U relation between the breadth dimension of inbound open innovation and NPD performance is moderated by the type of innovation.

Furthermore, the type of innovation also influences the ambidexterity dimension of an open innovation strategy. On a broad level, the exploitation of competences (i.e. existing technologies, skills and processes) leads to the development of incremental innovation and hinders radical innovation (Christensen and Bower, 1996; Danneels, 2002). Atuahene-Gima (2005) found that competence exploitation is positively related to incremental innovation performance and negatively related to radical innovation performance, while competence exploration is negatively related to incremental innovation performance and positively related to radical performance innovation. We posit that the ambidexterity–performance relation is moderated by the type of innovation. For radical innovation, the balance between exploration and exploitation will be shifted towards exploration while for incremental innovation the focus will remain squarely on exploiting existing relations.

Proposition 4b: The relation between the ambidexterity dimension of inbound open innovation and NPD performance is moderated by the type of innovation.

The moderating role of product complexity

Complex products are characterised by a high number of components and a high level of interaction among the components (Mondragon *et al.*, 2009). Transaction cost logic suggests that the internal management of complex products will reduce coordination costs, uncertainty and opportunism (Klein *et al.*, 1978). Novak and Eppinger (2001) find evidence of the benefits gained by firms when they concentrate the production of complex products in-house. On the other hand, there are several examples illustrating the extent to which coordination with multiple parties when managing complex products can lead to product failure and delay in time to market. The development of the 787 Dreamliner typifies a complex NPD project where multiple suppliers located in Japan, Italy and the USA collaborated on different components. This extensive collaboration with external parties divested Boeing of a degree of control in the development of the Dreamliner, leading to delay in the development cycle and increased development cost (Lunsford, 2007, 2008). Based on this evidence, it is proposed that projects involving complex products are less likely to involve a broad range of external parties in order to maintain control and therefore that the breadth–performance relation is moderated by the degree of complexity of a new product.

Proposition 5a: The inverted U relation between the breadth dimension of open innovation and NPD performance is moderated by product complexity.

There is a dearth of empirical research on the interaction effect between the exploitation of long-standing relations and the simultaneous exploration of new relations when firms develop complex products. However, following the argument that weak ties facilitate the generation of new knowledge (Capaldo, 2007), it appears that when firms develop complex products with a high number of components, the innovation often rests in the interplay between several of these components. Complexity exerts further pressure on internal R&D to be at the forefront of innovation for many components. However, in a highly turbulent technological environment, it becomes difficult for a single firm to keep abreast of the innovation development of multiple components (Chesbrough, 2006). In this respect, firms may have to leverage the knowledge of outsiders out of necessity, as they are not in a position to generate innovation for a wide range of components in-house.

Moreover, there is evidence from case studies of successful complex products that were jointly developed with new external parties instead of long-standing ones. An example of a complex product is the cellular mobile communication system (Davies and Brady, 1998). Nokia's strategy illustrates clearly the importance of the ambidexterity dimension for open innovation. From 2001–2002, 88.4% of the partners who collaborated with Nokia were completely new partners (Dittrich, 2008). This implies that Nokia has relied on an agile innovation strategy, which focuses on the strength of weak ties, for the development of a complex product despite the associated risks. This leads us to predict that for complex products, firms are more likely to collaborate with new external parties rather than long-standing ones.

Proposition 5b: The relation between the ambidexterity dimension of open innovation and NPD performance is moderated by the level of complexity of a new product.

The moderating role of the appropriability regime

In an open innovation business model, there is a higher risk of inadvertently losing intellectual capital during the interaction process with external parties. This risk is driven by the high mobility of knowledge in the network and is amplified when firms open up to external parties without any prior protection of the ideas. In NPD projects, a strong appropriability regime (i.e. patent protection) is an important mechanism for protecting firms against such loss (Levin *et al.*, 1987). In the event that the appropriability regime is weak, firms benefit from developing the innovation in-house (Teece, 1986). Recent results from a survey of manufacturing firms in the UK reveal that the hazards of the loss of intellectual property (IP) due to a weak appropriability regime, act as a disincentive for firms to open up the innovation process to external sources of knowledge (Laursen and Salter, 2005). The study suggests that a strong appropriability regime is an enabler to an open innovation strategy because the risk of losing IP is mitigated (Laursen and Salter, 2005). Therefore, following this line of reasoning, at the project level, it appears that firms will tend to open further to different types of external partners on condition that the appropriability regime is strong, thus reducing the risk of loss of IP. Other scholars suggested that for technology-based firms, the risks of opening up to external firms are high; new ideas are protected by secrecy, leading these firms to limit interaction with external firms (Gans and Stern, 2003). This leads us to formulate the proposition that the absence of formal institutional mechanisms (i.e. patents) and the use of informal mechanisms during an NPD project (i.e. secrecy and first-move advantage) will inhibit firms from opening up to external parties in order to protect ideas from competitors and potential imitators.

In a similar vein, we can also deduce that, in the context of a weak appropriability regime, firms will tend to be less agile and will privilege interactions with long-standing parties rather than new ones due to the behavioural uncertainty of new external parties. Scholars have argued that trust is a key factor in the performance of alliances when the level of behavioural uncertainty is high (Krishnan and Martin, 2005). Furthermore, a high level of trust differentiates high-performing collaborative relations from low-performing collaborative relations during the process of new product development (Bstieler, 2006). In new exchange relations, the level of trust is inherently fragile due to the lack of a basis for assessing the partners' motives (Gulati, 1995; Larson, 1992; Uzzi, 1997). This implies that, in the event that the appropriability regime is weak and informal, firms will tend to restrict collaboration with new external partners as a preventive measure to mitigate the risk of knowledge leakage and spill-over.

Proposition 6a: The inverted U relation between the breadth dimension of open innovation and NPD performance is moderated by the strength of the appropriability regime.

Proposition 6b: The relation between the ambidexterity dimension of open innovation and NPD performance is moderated by the strength of the appropriability regime.

Discussion and Conclusion

In this section, we will discuss the potential contributions of our conceptual model. We developed a framework to test a contingency theory of inbound open innovation at the NPD project level. As described in the first part of this chapter, the cost implication of inbound open innovation is an inherent threat to its success (Faems *et al.*, 2009; Rothaermel and Deeds, 2006). Although successful organisations have adopted open innovation *at a firm level* (Chesbrough, 2003; Lichtenthaler and Ernst, 2009), it appears that a more nuanced and judicious approach may be necessary *at an NPD project level* where more openness is not necessarily better. This conceptual chapter has made three contributions to the literature on inbound open innovation.

Firstly, there has been an attempt to refine the conceptualisation of the breadth dimension of the inbound open innovation construct. We have proposed including those emerging actors who have recently started to play a more prominent role in innovation networks. These emerging actors were not integrated in the breadth dimension in extant studies on open innovation (Becker and Dietz, 2004; Miotti and Sachwald, 2003; Nieto and Santamaria, 2007; Belderbos *et al.*, 2004; Faems *et al.*, 2005; Love and Roper, 1999; Tether and Tajar, 2008; Tether, 2002; Leiponen and Helfat, 2010). More specifically, we included actors such as smaller players (i.e. high-tech entrepreneurs and start-ups), open innovation intermediaries and members of the public (crowd sourcing) in the conceptualisation of the breadth dimension of open innovation alongside the traditional players such as suppliers, customers, competitors, consultants, commercial laboratories, universities and public and private research institutes.

Secondly, the majority of studies on inbound open innovation are confined only to the correlation between the breadth of opening up to a broad range of external parties and overall innovation performance. For the strategic recommendation of opening up innovation to all these different types of external parties (the breadth dimension), there is little understanding of the management of other facets linked to inbound open innovation. In this chapter, there has been an attempt to conceptualise the inbound open innovation construct as multidimensional, linking disparate stands of research (such as supply chain management and social networks) as a means of uncovering the underlying dimensions that have not been previously formalised.

By identifying two further dimensions of the inbound open innovation construct (depth and ambidexterity), we argue that the margin of managerial action is not constrained to the decision to open up an innovation project to a wide range of different types of external parties (the breadth dimension). Instead, it is also important to consider the level of cooperation and integration with different types of external parties (the depth dimension) and the development of new and long-standing relations (the ambidexterity dimension), which are the additional dimensions of inbound open innovation that managers can proactively regulate in their inbound open innovation strategies.

Thirdly, we address the lack of a contingent approach to inbound open innovation. We identify a range of contingencies, which potentially have a bearing on the appropriate calibration of the breadth, depth and ambidexterity dimensions of an open innovation strategy. The literature has remained silent on those multiple contingencies inherently present in any NPD project (i.e. the type of innovation, product complexity and the appropriability regime), which potentially influence the implementation of an inbound open innovation strategy of an NPD project. This is because most of the studies on inter-firm collaboration predominantly focus their analysis *at the firm level* rather than at the *NPD project level*. Following the rationale of traditional contingency theory, the appropriate answer to the question of this chapter: 'To what extent should a firm adjust the three dimensions of inbound open innovation at a NPD project level?' is 'It all depends.' We argue that the appropriate calibration of the three dimensions of inbound open innovation will be shaped by the type of innovation (radical versus incremental), product complexity (discrete versus complex) and the appropriability regime (tight versus weak).

In summary, this chapter is a point of departure for future empirical studies to test the propositions that we have put forward. It is suggested that future empirical work controls for technological and market turbulence, as these variables are likely to affect the way that an open innovation strategy at a project level is implemented. Our model is a preliminary building block to explore further dimensions of the inbound open innovation strategy construct as well as other contingencies at an NPD project level. For example, the extent to which the breadth, depth and ambidexterity dimensions vary across different stages of an innovation process are not well understood. The type of knowledge (i.e. codified or tacit) may have a bearing on these dimensions of an open innovation strategy.

As this chapter is aimed at building theory, it is suggested that empirical research starts with in-depth case studies within firms that have embraced an open innovation strategy for radical or incremental innovation. The objective of these case studies would be to uncover the interaction of other contingencies, which might potentially be present at a project level. Furthermore, this approach will provide the opportunity to test the propositions presented in this conceptual model as well as to identify the presence of any other significant variables. For the refinement of the conceptual model from case studies, further empirical testing (surveys) will progress the generalisability of a contingent theory of inbound open innovation. The testing of this conceptual framework will address previous calls from scholars to focus further on the development of a contingency theory for open innovation (Fredberg *et al.*, 2008). Future empirical work on a contingent perspective to inbound open innovation within an NPD project will help further refine managers' understanding of the importance of adjusting the extent of openness according to characteristics of the project. It will raise awareness that the success of this strategy is dependent on their adaptive capability to calibrate the breadth, depth and ambidexterity dimensions in response to the contingencies of their NPD projects.

Managerial implications

Generally, open innovation is considered to be a firm-level strategy. On the other hand, our conceptual chapter offers an alternative managerial view by exploring the dynamics of open innovation at the project level. Managers have a broad choice of different partners with whom they can potentially collaborate during their NPD projects. Choices include the number of partners, the types of partner and whether to exploit existing partners or search for new ones. Moreover, managers must make critical decisions over the extent and timing of the involvement of each partner. To capture these decisions we introduce three dimensions of open innovation: breadth, depth and ambidexterity. We suggest that the orchestration of these dimensions determines the success of an NPD project. To aid such orchestration we identify critical contingencies that influence the extent to which the three dimensions will influence success. By acknowledging these three dimensions and the contingencies, this chapter suggests that the success of an open innovation strategy for NPD projects rests on the capability of managers to build, orchestrate and integrate the breadth, ambidexterity and depth dimensions of an open innovation strategy in reaction to contingent factors such as the type of innovation, product complexity and the strength of the appropriability regime. The difference in managerial decisions in orchestrating these three dimensions of open innovation in relation to these contingencies is likely to lead to heterogeneity in performance at the project level.

References

Amara, N. and Landry, R.J. (2005). Sources of information as determinants of novelty of innovation in manufacturing firms: Evidence from the 1999 statistics Canada innovation survey, *Technovation*, **25**(3), 245–259.

Atuahene-Gima, K. (1995). An exploratory analysis of the impact of market orientation on new product performance: A contingency approach, *The Journal of Product Innovation Management*, **12**(4), 275.

Atuahene-Gima, K. (2005). Resolving the capability rigidity paradox in new product innovation, *Journal of Marketing*, **69**(4), 61–83.

Becker, W. and Dietz, J.R. (2004). R&D cooperation and innovation activities of firms: Evidence for the German manufacturing industry, *Research Policy*, **33**(2), 209.

Beckman, C.M., Haunschild, P.R. *et al.* (2004). Friends or strangers? Firm-specific uncertainty, market uncertainty, and network partner selection, *Organization Science*, **15**(3), 259–275.

Belderbos, R., Carree, M. *et al.* (2004a). Cooperative R&D and firm performance, *Research Policy*, **33**(10), 1477–1492.

Belderbos, R., Carree, M. *et al.* (2004b). Heterogeneity in R&D cooperation strategies, *International Journal of Industrial Organization*, **22**(8/9), 1237–1263.

Berthon, P.R., Pitt, L.F. *et al.* (2007). When customers get clever: Managerial approaches to dealing with creative consumers, *Business Horizons*, **50**(1), 39–47.

Bonaccorsi, A. and Lipparini, A. (1994). Strategic partnerships in new product development: An Italian case study, *The Journal of Product Innovation Management*, **11**(2), 134–145.

Bower, J.L. and Christensen, C.M. (1995). Disruptive technologies: Catching the wave, *Harvard Business Review*, **73**(1), 43–53.

Brown, S.L. and Eisenhardt, K.M. (1995). Product development: Past research, present findings and future directions, *Academy of Management Review*, **20**(2), 343–378.

Bstieler, L. (2006). Trust formation in collaborative new product development, *Journal of Product Innovation Management*, **23**(1), 56–72.

Capaldo, A. (2007). Network structure and innovation: The leveraging of a dual network as a distinctive relational capability, *Strategic Management Journal*, **28**(6), 585–608.

Chesbrough, H. (2003a). *Open Innovation: The New Imperative for Creating and Profiting From Technology*, Harvard Business Press, Boston, MA.

Chesbrough, H.W. (2003b). A better way to innovate, *Harvard Business Review*, **81**(7), 12–13.

Chesbrough, H. (2006). *Open Innovation: Researching a New Paradigm*, Oxford University Press, Oxford, UK.

Chesbrough, H. and Crowther, A.K. (2006). Beyond high tech: Early adopters of open innovation in other industries, *R&D Management*, **36**(3), 229–236.

Christensen, C.M. and Bower, J.L. (1996). Customer power, strategic investment and the failure of leading firms, *Strategic Management Journal*, **17**(March), 197–218.

Clark, K.B. and Fujimoto, T. (1989). Lead time in automobile product development explaining the Japanese advantage, *Journal of Engineering and Technology Management*, **6**(1), 25–58.

Cooper, R.G., Kleinschmidt, E.J. (1987). What makes a new product a winner: Success factors at the project level, *R&D Management*, (**17**)3, 175–189.

Dahlander, L. and Gann, D.M. (2010). How open is innovation? *Research Policy*, **39**(6), 699–709.

Danneels, E. (2002). The Dynamics of product innovation and firm competencies, *Strategic Management Journal*, **23**(12), 1095–1121.

Das, T.K. and Bing-Sheng, T. (1998). Between trust and control: Developing confidence in partner cooperation in alliances, *Academy of Management Review*, **23**(3), 491–512.

Davies, A. and Brady, T. (1998). Policies for a complex product system, *Futures*, **30**(4), 293.

Diener, K. and Piller, F. (2009). Facets of open innovation: Development of a conceptual framework conference proceedings. *16th International Product Development Management Conference.*

Dittrich, K. (2008). "Nokia's strategic change by means of alliance networks. A case of adopting the open innovation paradigm?" in Sivarajadhanavel, P. and Vellingiri, D. (eds), *Open Innovation: The Networked R and D*, Icfai's Professional Reference Book Series, Icfai University Press, Chennai, India.

Dittrich, K. and Duysters, G. (2007). Networking as a means to strategy change: The case of open innovation in mobile telephony, *Journal of Product Innovation Management*, **24**(6), 510–521.

Donaldson, L. (2001). *The Contingency Theory of Organizations*, Sage Publications, London.

Droge, C., Jayaram, J. *et al.* (2004). The effects of internal versus external integration practices on time-based performance and overall firm performance, *Journal of Operations Management*, **22**(6), 557–573.

Dyer, J.H. and Chu, W. (2003). The role of trustworthiness in reducing transaction costs and improving performance: Empirical evidence from the United States, Japan, and Korea, *Organization Science*, **14**(1), 57–68.

Dyer, J.H. and Singh, H. (1998). The relational view: Cooperative strategy and sources of interorganizational competitive advantage, *Academy of Management Review*, **23**(4), 660–679.

Faems, D., Van Looy, B. *et al.* (2005). Interorganizational collaboration and innovation: Toward a portfolio approach, *Journal of Product Innovation Management*, **22**(3), 238–250.

Faems, D., De Visser, M. and Van Looy, B. (2009). Technology alliance portfolios and financial performance: Disentangling value enhancing and cost increasing effects of open innovation, *16ᵗʰ International Product Development Management Conference*.

Fetterhoff, T.J., Voelkel, D. (2006). Managing open innovation in biotechnology, *Research Technology Management*, **49**(3), 14.

Fredberg, T., Elmquist, M. and Ollila, S. (2008). *Managing Open Innovation: Present Findings and Future Directions*, VINNOVA, The Swedish Governmental Agency for Innovation Systems.

Galambos, L. and Sturchio, J. (1998). Pharmaceutical firms and the transition to biotechnology: A study in strategic innovation, *Business History Review*, **72**(2), 250.

Galbraith, J. (1973). *Designing Complex Organizations*, Addison-Wesley Publishing Co Reading, MA.

Gans, J.S. and Stern, S. (2003). The product market and the market for "ideas": Commercialization strategies for technology entrepreneurs, *Research Policy*, **32**(2), 333–350.

Gerwin, D., Kumar, V. and Pal, S. (1992). Transfer of advanced manufacturing technology from Canadian universities to industry, *Technology Transfer*, **12**, 57–67.

Goerzen, A. (2007). Alliance networks and firm performance: The impact of repeated partnerships, *Strategic Management Journal*, **28**(5), 487–509.

Granovetter, M.S. (1973). The strength of weak ties, *American Journal of Sociology*, **78**(6), 1360–1380.

Gulati, R. (1995). Does familiarity breed trust? The implications of repeated ties for contractual choice in alliances, *Academy of Management Journal*, **38**(1), 85–112.

Gupta, A.K. and Wilemon, D.L. (1990). Accelerating the development of Technology-based new product, *California Management Review*, **32**(2), 24–44.

Hakansson, H.K. and Eriksson, A.-K. (1993). Getting innovations out of supplier networks, *Journal of Business-to-Business Marketing*, **1**(3), 3.

Hakansson, H.K., Havila, V. *et al.* (1999). Learning in networks, *Industrial Marketing Management*, **28**(5), 443–452.

Hamel, G. (1991). Competition for competence and inter-partner learning within international strategic alliances, *Strategic Management Journal*, **12**(4), 83–103.

Handfield, R. and Lawson, B. (2007). Integrating suppliers into new product development, *Research Technology Management*, **50** (5), 44.

He, Z.L. and Wong, P. K. (2004). Exploration vs. exploitation: An empirical test of the ambidexterity hypothesis, *Organization Science*, **15**(4), 481–494.

Hippel, E.v. (1978). Successful industrial products from customer ideas, *Journal of Marketing*, **42**(1), 39.

Hitt, M., Beamish, P., Jackson, S., Mathieu, J. (2007). Building theoretical and empirical bridges across levels: Multilevel research in management, *Academy of Management Journal*, (6), 1385.

Huston, L. and Sakkab, N. (2006). Connect and develop, *Harvard Business Review*, **84**(3), 58–66.

Ittner, C.D. and Larcker, D.F. (1997). Product development cycle time and organizational performance, *Journal of Marketing Research*, **34**(1), 13–23.

Jayaram, J. (2008). Supplier involvement in new product development projects: Dimensionality and contingency effects, *International Journal of Production Research*, **46**(13), 3717.

Katila, R. and Ahuja, G. (2002). Something old, something new: A longitudinal study of behaviour and new product, *Academy of Management Journal*, **45**(6), 1183–1194.

Klein, B., Crawford, R.G. *et al.* (1978). Vertical integration, appropriable rents and the competitive contracting process, *Journal of Law and Economics*, **21**(2), 297–326.

Kogut, B. and Zander, U. (1993). Knowledge of the firm and the evolutionary theory of the multinational corporation, *Journal of International Business Studies*, **24**(4), 625–645.

Krishnan, R., Martin, X. *et al.* (2006). When does trust matter to alliance performance? *Academy of Management Journal*, **49**(5), 894–917.

Larson, A. (1992). Network dyads in entrepreneurial settings: A study of the governance of exchange relationships, *Administrative Science Quarterly*, **37**(1), 76–104.

Lavie, D. and Rosenkopf, L. (2006). Balancing exploration and exploitation in alliance formation, *Academy of Management Journal*, **49**(4), 797–818.

Laursen, K. and Salter, A. (2005). The paradox of openness: Appropriability and the use of external sources of knowledge for innovation, *Academy of Management Conference*, August 5–10, Honolulu, HI.

Laursen, K. and Salter, A. (2006). Open for innovation: The role of openness in explaining innovation performance among UK manufacturing firms, *Strategic Management Journal*, **27**(2), 131–150.

Lawrence, P.R. and Lorsch, J.W. (1967). *Organisation and Environment: Managing Differentiation and Integration*, Graduate School of Business Administration, Harvard University, Boston, MA.

Leiponen, A. and Helfat, C.E. (2010). Innovation objectives, knowledge sources, and the benefits of breadth, *Strategic Management Journal*, **31**(2), 224–236.

Levin, R.C., Klevorick, A.K. *et al.* (1987). Appropriating the returns from industrial research and development; comments and discussion, *Brookings Papers on Economic Activity*, 783.

Levinthal, D.A. and March, J.G. (1993). The myopia of learning, *Strategic Management Journal*, **14**, 95–112.

Lichtenthaler, U. and Ernst, H. (2009). Opening up the innovation process: The role of technology aggressiveness, *R&D Management*, **39**(1), 38–54.

Lin, Z., Haibin, Y. *et al.* (2007). The performance consequences of ambidexterity in strategic alliance formations: Empirical investigation and computational theorizing, *Management Science*, **53**(10), 1645–1658.

Littler, D., Leverick, F. *et al.* (1995). Factors affecting the process of collaborative product development: A study of UK manufacturers of information and communications technology products, *Journal of Product Innovation Management*, **12**(1), 16–32.

Love, J.H. and Roper, S. (1999). The determinants of innovation: R&D, technology transfer and networking effects, *Review of Industrial Organization*, **15**(1).

Lunsford, J.L. (2007). Boeing in embarrassing setback, says 787 dreamliner will be delayed, *Wall Street Journal*, October 11.

Lunsford, J.L. (2008). Boeing moves to solve 787 delays, *Wall Street Journal*, March 29–30.

March, J.G. (1991). Exploration and exploitation in organizational learning, *Organization Science*, **2**(1), 71–87.

Miotti, L. and Sachwald, F.d.r. (2003). Cooperative R&D: Why and with whom? An integrated framework of analysis, *Research Policy*, **32**(8), 1481.

Mishra, A.A. and Shah, R. (2009). In union lies strength: Collaborative competence in new product development and its performance effects, *Journal of Operations Management*, **27**(4), 324–338.

Mohr, J. and Spekman, R. (1994). Characteristics of partnership success: Partnership attributes, communication behaviour and conflict resolution techniques, *Strategic Management Journal*, **15**(2), 135–152.

Mondragon, C. *et al.* (2009). Managing technology for highly complex critical modular systems: The case of automotive by-wire systems, *International Journal of Production Economics*, **118**(2), 473–485.

Nieto, M.a.J.s. and Santamaria, L. (2007). The importance of diverse collaborative networks for the novelty of product innovation, *Technovation*, **27**(6/7), 367–377.

Nokia (2009). Open innovation Newsletter, *Open Threads*, Nokia Research Centre (NRC). Available at http://research.nokia.com/files/OT_1_09.pdf.

Novak, S. and Eppinger, S.D. (2001). Sourcing By design: Product complexity and the supply chain, *Management Science*, **47**(1), 189.

Oerlemans, L.A.G. and Knoben, J. (2010). Configurations of knowledge transfer relations: An empirically based taxonomy and its determinants, *Journal of Engineering & Technology Management*, **27**(1/2), 33–51.

Petersen, K.J., Handfield, R.B. *et al.* (2003). A model of supplier integration into new product development, *Journal of Product Innovation Management*, **20**(4), 284–299.

Petersen, K.J., Handfield, R.B. *et al.* (2005). Supplier integration into new product development: Coordinating product, process and supply chain design, *Journal of Operations Management*, **23**(3–4), 371–388.

Piller, F.T. and Walcher, D. (2006). Toolkits for idea competitions: A novel method to integrate users in new product development, *R&D Management*, **36**(3), 307–318.

Pisano, G.P. and Verganti, R. (2008). Which kind of collaboration is right for you? *Harvard Business Review*, **86**(12), 78–86.

Ragatz, G.L., Handfield, R.B. *et al.* (1997). Success factors for integrating suppliers into new product development, *The Journal of Product Innovation Management*, **14**(3), 190–202.

Ragatz, G.L., Handfield, R.B. *et al.* (2002). Benefits associated with supplier integration into new product development under conditions of technology uncertainty, *Journal of Business Research*, **55**(5), 389–400.

Roper, S., Du, J. *et al.* (2008). Modelling the innovation value chain, *Research Policy*, **37**(6/7), 961.

Rothaermel, F.T. and Deeds, D.L. (2006). Alliance type, alliance experience and alliance management capability in high-technology ventures, *Journal of Business Venturing*, **21**(4), 429–460.

Rousseau, D.M. (1985). "Issues of level in organizational research: Multi-level and cross-level perspectives," in Cummings, L.L. and Staw, B.M. (eds), *Research in Organizational Behavior*, JAI Press, Greenwich, CT, Vol. 7, pp. 1–37.

Santoro, M.D. (2000). Success breeds success: The linkage between relationship intensity and tangible outcomes in industry–university collaborative ventures, *Journal of High Technology Management Research*, **11**(2), 255–273.

Sawhney, M. and Prandelli, E. (2000). Communities of creation: Managing distributed innovation in turbulent markets, *California Management Review*, **42**(4), 24–54.

Schreiner, M., Kale, P. *et al.* (2009). What really is alliance management capability and how does it impact alliance outcomes and success? *Strategic Management Journal*, **30**(13), 1395–1419.

Sieg, J.H., Wallin, M.W. and von Krogh, G. (2010). Managerial challenges in open innovation: A study of innovation intermediation in the chemical industry, *R&D Management*, **40**(3), 281–291.

Surowiecki, J. (2004). *The Wisdom of Crowds*, Random House Large Print and Doubleday, New York.

Swink, M. (1999). Threats to new product manufacturability and the effects of development team integration processes, *Journal of Operations Management*, **17**(6), 691–709.

Teece, D.J. (1986). Profiting from technological innovation: Implications for integration, collaboration, licensing and public policy, *Research Policy*, **15**(6), 285.

Tether, B.S. and Tajar, A. (2008). Beyond industry university links: Sourcing knowledge for innovation from consultants, private research organisations and the public science-base, *Research Policy*, **37**(6/7).

The Suday Times (2009). The bruiser built tweet by Tweet, November 29. Available at www.timesonline.co.uk/lingears

Tiwana, A. (2008). Do bridging ties complement strong ties? An empirical examination of alliance ambidexterity, *Strategic Management Journal*, **29**(3), 251.

Trott, P. and Hartmann, D. (2009). Why open innovation is old wine in new bottles, *International Journal of Innovation Management*, **13**(4), 715–736.

Tushman, M.L. and O'Reilly, C.A. (1996). Ambidextrous organizations: managing evolutionary and revolutionary change, *California Management Review*, **38**(4), 8–30.

Van De Vrande, V., De Jong, P.J. and Vanhaverbeke, W. (2009). Open innovation in SMEs: Trends, motives and management challenges, *Technovation*, **29**(6/7), 423–437.

Verona, G., Prandelli, E. and Sawhney, M. (2006). Innovation and virtual environments: Towards virtual knowledge brokers, *Organization Studies*, **27**(6), 755–788.

Chapter 4

Collaborative Product Development for Competing Suppliers

S. Sinan Erzurumlu

Technology, Operations and Information Management Division
Babson College, USA

Introduction

Collaboration has proliferated in various industries such as electronics, manufacturing, IT, and pharmaceutical since the early 1980s. However, at the same time competition in these industries has become stiffer than ever before. The increase in collaboration is because, first, innovation requires a more in-depth understanding of current technology and firms are becoming increasingly specialized (Baldwin and Clark, 2000). Second, firms are inextricably linked by the dynamics of the supply chain. Therefore, they seek ways of utilizing internal and external sources of ideas and skills through open innovation (Chesbrough, 2003) though partnering firms may be competitors in the market (Hamel *et al.*, 1989). This study is concerned with how open innovation through inter-firm collaboration and strategic alliances may generate value for firms by stimulating the adoption of new product innovation by the downstream supply chain. Of particular interest to this research is the effect of supplier collaboration and strategic alliance formation between competing suppliers on a downstream original equipment manufacturer (OEM) (Brandenburger and Nalebuff, 1995).

While existing research has long been interested in understanding value creation due to open innovation, the purpose of this research is to develop a better understanding of the effect of open innovation on the dynamics of the supply chain. To achieve this, this study is specifically interested in the strategic consequences of collaboration and strategic alliances on the investment and production decisions of two competing upstream suppliers and a complementary downstream OEM. The theoretical model presented in this study considers several important parameters, including the OEM's investment in cost-reducing or demand-enhancing innovation, the investments of the suppliers in new product development (NPD), and the extent to which the suppliers can stimulate the OEM's investment through collaboration. The analysis explores how the development and investment decisions by the suppliers alter a downstream OEM's adoption decisions and investments to provide a complementary product or service, and discusses how the OEM could affect the suppliers' collaboration and new product development processes. It further characterizes the critical conditions for collaboration and alliances under which it may be beneficial for the competing suppliers to collaborate rather than compete.

The chapter is organized as follows. First, the motivation behind open innovation, inter-firm collaboration and alliances, and their purpose as a strategic asset in a co-creation context are discussed as the conceptual basis of this study. The chapter then details the theoretical modeling framework and explains different collaborative structures and alliances. It first considers a situation in which fully integrated suppliers would form a joint venture to develop and market a component. Then it considers how the outcome for the OEM and partially integrated suppliers would change if they co-develop the component but compete in marketing and sales to the OEM. Finally, it considers the situation where independent suppliers may choose not to form an alliance but compete to develop and market a component individually. The chapter analyzes the effect of each these types of collaboration on the investment decisions of the supply chain and it presents the research results. Specifically, the analysis articulates the tradeoff between reduced profits due to the collaboration and the increase in demand as a result of stimulating the OEM's investment. It finds the optimal supplier cooperation that would induce supply chain coordination between the profit maximizing suppliers and OEM. The final section summarizes the major results, highlights some limitations of the study, and provides directions for future research.

Open Innovation and the Supply Chain

The concept of openness requires a paradigm shift from ownership to value creation and value capture (de Wit *et al.*, 2007). Open innovation enables more effective use of resources and capacities, better matching of capabilities with market needs, and benchmarking to improve efficiency. Various aspects of open innovation include: globalization of innovation, early supplier integration, user innovation, and external commercialization and application of technology (Gassmann, 2006; Bilgram *et al.*, 2008; Erzurumlu *et al.*, 2010). In this context, most prior research on open innovation is limited to theoretical considerations and case studies (Dodgson *et al.*, 2006; Drummond and Perkins, 2009; Aylen, 2010), whereas other lines of research have focused on technology acquisition and exploitation (Lichtenthaler and Ernst, 2009).

According to a supply chain survey conducted by IBM and *Industry Week*, 40% of respondents found collaborations with customers and suppliers to have the most significant effect on product development (*Industry Week*, 2007). The degree of cooperation and the scope of supplier involvement may increase awareness of the organization of the innovation process and improve the performance of the innovation process (Aune and Gressetvold, 2011). However, a few complexities and challenges are apparent. Innovators frequently and freely reveal proprietary information about both information-based products and physical products they have developed (von Hippel and von Krogh, 2006). So long as it is in a firm's best interest to be innovative in terms of technology and business model, in order to maximize performance it needs to find a balance between development of organizational capabilities and the openness of innovation strategies (Kolk and Püüman, 2008; Paasi *et al.*, 2010). While open innovation is rewarding, firms must analyze its consequences (Olleros, 2007) and they must be able to impose barriers upon innovative users or collaboration partners to protect their core competences (Braun and Herstatt, 2008). Different degrees of open innovation as well as closed innovation must be implemented depending on the portfolio of internal and external assets (Lazzarotti and Manzini, 2009) and the depth of the relations with different types of external parties (Bahemia and Squire, 2010).

The utilization of external resources can play a critical role in value creation and traditional business strategy (Chesbrough and Appleyard, 2007) as long as the organization can successfully identify the external sourcing method so as to manage the effect of external sources on technology innovation (Kang and Kang, 2009). For example, partial integration, accompanied by appropriate transfer prices and incentive design, promotes an open-innovation platform and improves strategic capabilities by linking key parts of the supply chain (Jacobides and Billinger, 2006). A firm may post an innovation-related problem to a population of independent agents but it also needs to determine the strategy so as to benefit from open innovation (Terwiesch and Xu, 2008; Erat and Krishnan, 2011). Therefore, innovation management needs appropriate methods and practices, and the metrics to monitor investment and the effect of open versus the closed innovation approaches (Enkel and Lenz, 2009; Bergman *et al.*, 2009). This study aims to further examine the strategic use of open innovation to provide the right incentives to the right participants without any competitive surrender. The analysis in this study investigates different perspectives of open innovation and presents a decision framework to help companies find the right formation and business strategy.

Inter-firm Collaboration and Strategic Alliances

The critical elements of an open-innovation strategy include inter-firm collaboration, partial or full integration, and the creation of alliances for capturing ideas generated externally and facilitating open-innovation commercialization (Vapola *et al.*, 2008). As long as the benefits of a strategic alliance between firms outweigh its risks such as the revelation of technical information and competitive compromise, collaboration between competing firms could be beneficial for various reasons. A collaborating firm's knowledge and expertise can reduce development risks and help a participating firm to allocate its resources more efficiently (Kogut, 1991; Mazzarol and Reboud, 2008). Firms can exploit each other's resources (Pfeffer and Novak, 1976; Das and Teng, 2000; Perks, 2004), increase purchasing power (Granot and Sosic, 2005), or acquire inter-firm knowledge (Rosenkopf and Almeida, 2003). A compilation of different perspectives of strategic alliances such as economic, real options, learning, and relational can be found in Reuer (2004).

The purpose and benefits of a strategic alliance may not be limited to these reasons. The manner in which a customer firm adopts a component technology depends not only on the value of the innovation but also on the dynamic capabilities of the source and the vertical interactions in the supply chain (Teece *et al.*, 1997; Perks, 2004). Therefore, the alliance members have to evaluate their decisions in joining an alliance (Granot and Sosic, 2005) and find coordination mechanisms to align their individual–alliance member incentives (Nault and Tyagi, 2001). There are considerable asymmetries in new product development alliances with regard to the effects of alliance, partner, and firm characteristics on the gains of the partner firms (Kalaignanam *et al.*, 2007). Similarly, a merger could affect the profits of other participating and non-participating firms (Deneckere and Davidson, 1985; Braid, 1999; Brito, 2003). The competitive intensity affects open innovation and the resources committed by the participants to product and market development in both inbound and outbound open-innovation processes (Lichtenthaler, 2009). This research is based on the premise that the fundamental nature of open innovation through inter-firm collaboration or alliance changes the dynamics of the supply chain.

Therefore, the scope of this study is to further explore the strategic effect of collaboration and supplier integration on the profits and decisions of the supply chain participants. Although firms use open innovation as a result of their internal weaknesses in innovation (Keupp and Gassmann, 2009), what may be important in determining how they co-create could be the activities and the consequences of the decisions. Individual development increases the investment in the market while decreasing investment in product development (Amaldoss and Rapoport, 2005). A merger between two naturally differentiated downstream dealers affects their interaction with a common supplier and the attractiveness of merging depends upon the extent to which the end demand can be stimulated by either an upstream supplier or the dealers (Gilbert *et al.*, 2006, 2007). Open-innovation initiatives can give a supplier a more active role as a peer producer and facilitate supplier contributions (Björn *et al.*, 2011). The types of R&D collaboration, which differ in terms of the breadth of the new knowledge provided to the firm and in the ease of access to this new knowledge, result in different effects on product innovation (Un *et al.*, 2010). This study specifically considers a situation in which collaboration between two upstream competing suppliers can play a significant role in stimulating a downstream OEM to invest in demand-stimulating activities. Further, it particularly examines supplier investment in development effort and extends the discussion on the attractiveness of collaboration to other types of supplier cooperation.

In this research framework the inter-firm collaboration and independent development may also suggest a second source for the downstream OEM. There are various uses of second sourcing. Firms can use second sourcing as a commitment not to act opportunistically when a monopolist firm is unable to commit to long-term contracts (Farrell and Gallini, 1988; Klotz and Chatterjee, 1995). In a networked environment the entry of a second source can enlarge the user base and increase network benefits (Conner, 1995). A buyer can use a second entrant supplier to provide information about the incumbent's costs (Demski *et al.*, 1987). Nonetheless, second sourcing may result in less expected profits (Riordan and Sappington, 1989). To manage the potential gains from a second production source, firms have to evaluate the supply chain dynamics in the presence of a second source. This study examines the effect of a second source on the tradeoff between increased competition and higher downstream investment and analyzes the suppliers' decisions regarding alliance formation.

This study is, in summary, concerned with game-theoretic interactions within competitor-based strategic NPD alliances whose purpose is to substantially create value through collaboration and open innovation. It enhances our understanding of the factors influencing the way competing firms interact throughout NPD collaboration. In particular, it explains how such interactions in closed versus open innovation develop, even when the resources and capabilities are not a concern for the firms, and it provides a detailed metrics framework that unravels the optimal NPD collaboration for the participants in the supply chain.

The Model

A good example of the interaction between collaboration and competition comes from the tire industry. In recent years there has been an alliance between the world's two big tire developers and manufacturers, Michelin and Goodyear, to develop a run-flat tire technology, which has attracted the close attention of big tire manufacturers for the past few decades (Goodyear, 2010). Michelin created a run-flat tire technology named the PAX System, which allows driving at a speed of up to 50 miles per hour for 100–150 miles after a tire is punctured. Although Michelin's achievements in the technological developments for the PAX System has increased anticipation that the PAX System will be the next biggest technological achievement in the tire industry, Michelin has agreed to collaborate with a major competitor, Goodyear, on the development of run-flat tire technology, but commercialize it competitively (*Business Week*, 2004).

Further, Michelin needed to involve the major car manufacturers in the development process to accommodate a complementary new platform for the run-flat tires. Therefore, inter-firm collaboration in the development and competition in the marketing of the run-flat tire with Goodyear have enhanced the credibility and adoption rate of the technology by car manufacturers. The manufacturers increased their investment to accommodate the new tire technology and enhance consumer demand for cars with the PAX System because the collaboration of the Michelin–Goodyear alliance would not only generate a better technology but sales competition would also dampen tire prices.

Similar collaborations and open innovation are also common in other industries. For example, two major competitors, Intel and AMD, have collaborated on the development of graphics technology for microprocessors to expedite the development and motivate the adoption of the technology by manufacturers (Softpedia, 2008). Nokia effectively uses an open-innovation strategy in the development of new products and services and in setting technology standards for mobile communication applications (Dittrich and Duysters, 2007).

This study provides a technical model to augment understanding of the factors underlying and influencing the way new product development collaboration occurs. Several papers in economics, marketing and supply chain operations that study the interaction between vertical firms have used a similar analytical research methodology to examine coordination problems (Jeuland and Shugan, 1983; McGuire and Staelin, 1983; Aghion and Tirole, 1994) and the effect of innovation of one of the firms on its channel partners (Gupta and Loulou, 1998; Gilbert and Cvsa, 2003; Bhaskaran and Krishnan, 2009). Comprehensive reviews can be found in Tsay *et al.* (1998) and Kouvelis *et al.* (2006). This methodology is reasonable for explaining the consequences of collaboration and competition because the modeling framework in this paper studies the interaction as a duopoly in the upstream supply chain and a bilateral monopoly in the downstream supply chain. Therefore, regarding the scope of the research this study uses some of the modeling elements from this research stream, which are common to much of the literature on incentive issues and collaboration in the supply chain.

The modeling framework in this study differs from this stream and extends beyond inter-firm collaboration based on tactical decisions (prices and quantities) by examining different types of supplier cooperation and degrees of open innovation. The model considers a supply chain in which two suppliers, say supplier 1 and supplier 2, interact with a downstream OEM in two consecutive stages: development and marketing. They first develop and then market a breakthrough component, which will be used in the complementary product of the OEM. This is a reasonable representation since the primary focus of this research is to understand how an upstream firm's commitment to collaboration affects its downstream channel partner's investment in innovation.

In the development stage, the suppliers either decide on collaboration or stay independent; then, they simultaneously choose their investment level in the technology development. Since the formation decision is made infrequently relative to investment and pricing and it is fully observed, it is reasonable to assume that this decision precedes all decisions about development and marketing. The study is concerned with three types of collaborative formations regarding different levels of open innovation. First, in a joint venture the suppliers are fully integrated and form a monopoly in order to collaborate in the development and marketing of the component. Second, in a development alliance they agree on partial integration, where they individually develop the component and share the technological outcome but after successful development they compete in marketing. Finally, independent suppliers do not form any kind of collaborative formation in development and marketing; hence, they compete with each other.

Under any type of cooperation, a supplier $i (i \varepsilon \{1, 2\})$ could successfully develop the component technology with probability P_i, which is determined by its investment level in technology development. Unless a supplier has the breakthrough technology, it will not sell any components and earn zero profits. The novelty of this approach lies in representing the strategic interactions in a stylized two-stage model. Using a model with a substitute component would not add many insights but would tremendously complicate the analysis. Therefore, it is reasonable to assume that the suppliers do not offer a substitute component that could match the conformance quality of the breakthrough.

Subsequently, depending on the type of cooperation the OEM will decide whether or not to accommodate the breakthrough technology. This is critical since the OEM's participation is complementary to the component technology. That is, if the OEM refuses to participate the component technology would not be utilized. After the OEM agrees to adopt the component, it chooses its investment level r in innovation relating to a cost reduction or a demand enhancement to improve the perceived value of the product before observing the outcome of the development stage (Gupta and Loulou, 1998).

The consecutive marketing stage is concerned with the quantity decisions of the suppliers and the OEM. The OEM procures the component only from these suppliers to use in its final product. The supplier i delivers a component production capacity of q_i at a wholesale price of w_i. The OEM then sells the final products on the consumer market. The OEM's marginal cost of production c is assumed to be constant and for ease of exposition, each supplier's marginal production cost is normalized to zero. Although the assumption of constant production cost is simple, this is a reasonable assumption since, in practice, there could be production costs that are constant for the volume of production for a range of outputs and any new component technology may be integrated into the OEM's current production process without any additional costs.

The method of analysis uses backward induction and will assume that the suppliers have chosen a type of cooperation. It will examine the production decisions with a single and dual supplier source for the component. The analysis will then examine the development stage for the investment decisions of the suppliers and the OEM. In both stages, the suppliers play a simultaneous non-cooperative game with complete information.

In the single-supplier case the OEM will choose the product quantity q to maximize its profit function $\pi_{oem}(q) = q(p(q) - w - (c - r))$ where w is the single-supplier wholesale price and the price function is determined by $p(q) = 1 - q$. Note that for ease of exposition the potential market-size constant in the price function is normalized to 1. Solving the manufacturer's profit function, the optimal quantity that maximizes the manufacturer's profits is

$$q^* = \frac{1 - c - w + r}{2} \tag{1}$$

The wholesale price is determined by the total capacity. Since the suppliers are capacity constrained, the wholesale price they could charge is the maximum price at which the OEM will accept the entire supplier capacity, denoted by $w(q, r) = 1 - 2q - c + r$. In a monopoly supplier market, the supplier maximizes its profits $\pi(q, r) = qw(q, r)$ by determining the wholesale price for the optimal quantity of the OEM in (1),

$$w^* = \frac{1 - c + r}{2} \tag{2}$$

Hence, the profits for a single supplier and the OEM are found as

$$\pi^{1S}(r) = \frac{(1 - c + r)^2}{8} \tag{3}$$

$$\pi_{oem}^{1S}(r) = \frac{(1 - c + r)}{16} \tag{4}$$

where the superscript $1S$ in the model denotes the single-supplier case and the subscript oem represents the profit functions of the OEM. Later the superscript $2S$ is used for the two-supplier case.

With two suppliers, although the absolute performance of each component could be identical, consumers may perceive one component better in conformance quality due to brand recognition. For the model to reflect this, it encompasses the asymmetric nature of consumer preferences. That is, though the component from supplier 1 is a perfect substitute for the component from supplier 2, supplier 2's component is only an imperfect substitute for supplier 1's component, without loss of generality. The degree of substitutability between two products with a component from separate suppliers is represented with the parameter $v \in [0,1]$.

Let p_i and q_i be the market clearing prices and the quantities for the products with a component from supplier i. The suppliers' inverse demand functions are given by $p_1(q_1, q_2) = 1 - q_1 - v(1 - q_1 - q_2)$. and $p_2(q_1, q_2) = v(1 - q_1 - q_2)$. The OEM chooses the product quantities q_1 and q_2 to maximize its profit function $\pi_{oem}(q_1, q_2) = q_1(p_1 - w_1 - (c - r)) + q_2(p_2 - w_2 - (c - r))$. Solving the manufacturer's profit function the optimal quantities are

$$q_1^* = \frac{1 - v - w_1 + w_2}{2(1 - v)}; \quad q_2^* = \frac{v w_1 - w_2 - (c - r)(1 - v)}{2v(1 - v)} \tag{5}$$

In the duopoly supplier market, the suppliers maximize their profits, $\pi_1(w_1, w_2) = w_1 q_1(w_1, w_2)$ and $\pi_2(w_1, w_2) = w_2 q_2(w_1, w_2)$, simultaneously, where w_1 and w_2 are the supplier's wholesale prices. The suppliers would offer the following optimal wholesale prices

$$w_1^* = \frac{(1 - v)(2 - c + r)}{4 - v}; \quad w_2^* = \frac{(1 - v)(v - 2c + 2r)}{4 - v} \tag{6}$$

Note that $q_1, w_1 > 0$ for all parameter values, but $q_2 > 0$ and $w_2 > 0$ for $v \geq 2(c - r)$. When $v < 2(c - r)$, supplier 2 earns zero profits, but stays in the market and exerts pressure on supplier 1. The model considers a situation in which both suppliers compete with non-negative production quantities and assumes that $v \geq 2(c - r)$. Consequently, the profits for each supplier and the OEM in a duopoly are

$$\pi_1^{2S}(r) = \frac{(1 - v)(2 - c + r)^2}{2(4 - v)^2}; \quad \pi_2^{2S}(r) = \frac{(1 - v)(v - 2c + 2r)^2}{2v(4 - v)^2} \tag{7}$$

$$\pi_{\text{oem}}^{2S}(r) = \frac{((c - r)^2 + v) - 2v(c - r)(8 + v)}{4v(4 - v)^2} \tag{8}$$

Next the model considers the development stage by incorporating the supplier's investment in technology development and the OEM's investment in demand cost reduction (demand enhancement). With the new component technology, the OEM would have to incur fixed costs to develop a new production process with reduced marginal costs or increase the perceived value of the final product. For example, the car manufacturers had to change the design of their cars and build a new manufacturing platform for cars with the PAX tire. The total fixed costs of development for the OEM to achieve a production cost reduction (demand enhancement) of r would be

$$I_r(r) = Kr^2 \qquad (9)$$

where K is a parameter that determines how costly it is to stimulate cost reduction (demand enhancement) with higher investment. In other words, the parameter K demonstrates the relative ease with which demand can be stimulated by investment. Note that the investment function is increasing and convex because the investment level requires higher fixed costs when the OEM aims to influence a greater cost reduction (demand enhancement). Similarly, although the probability of development failure decreases with the supplier's investment, supplier i must invest the following amount to achieve a probability of development success P_i

$$Ip(P_i) = MP_i^2 \qquad (10)$$

The investment function in the probability of successful development, P, is increasing and convex. Since M reflects the relative ease of improving the probability of development, for ease of exposition, such a parameter can be incorporated in the total probability by setting M to 1 in the model.

The remainder of this section unravels the optimal investment by the OEM under each type of supplier formation: joint venture (JV), development alliance (DA), and independent development (ID). The study discusses the merits and mechanics of each type of formation for the suppliers and the OEM.

Joint venture

Mergers and joint ventures are common business ventures and represent open innovation in which suppliers are fully integrated. Hence, in a joint venture two collaborating suppliers integrate their tangible and intangible assets to establish one venture to develop a component and later market it.

To maintain focus on how collaboration influences the technology development stage, the model utilizes a revenue- and cost-sharing agreement between the two suppliers in the joint venture.

Thus, $\pi_1^{1S}(r) = \phi \pi^{1S}(r)$ and $\pi_2^{1S}(r) = (1-\phi)\pi^{1S}(r)$, where π^{1S} is computed in (3) ϕ denotes the equilibrium revenue-sharing parameter and is determined as a function of the bargaining between participating suppliers. Subsequently, with the Nash bargaining structure (Nash, 1950), the analysis obtains the equilibrium $\phi^* = 1/2$ in this modeling framework. Although end consumers perceive one component better in quality, this simple result supports the fact that in the upstream supply chain participating suppliers and the OEM are fully informed about the quality of the rival's component. Therefore, the components produced by each supplier are deemed perfectly substitutable. This implies the equitable allocation of the costs and earnings among the participants, $\pi_1^{1S}(r) = \pi^{1S}(r) = \frac{1}{2}\pi^{1S}(r)$.

Since the OEM deals with a single firm in the joint venture, the profit function for each supplier i that jointly invests P for technology development would be

$$\pi_i^{JV}(P,r) = P\pi_i^{1S}(r) - \frac{1}{2}I_p(P) \tag{11}$$

Further, the OEM maximizes the following expected profit function by investing r

$$\pi_{oem}^{JV}(P,r) = P\pi_{oem}^{1S}(r) - I_r(r) \tag{12}$$

where π_{oem}^{1S} is computed in (4). Maximizing the profit function in (12), the optimal investment that the OEM would choose for cost reduction (demand enhancement) is

$$r^{JV} = \frac{P(1-C)}{16K - p} \tag{13}$$

To ensure that the OEM can only make feasible investments, $0 < r^{JV} < c$, the restriction $K > K^{JV} = \frac{P}{16c}$ is imposed. This condition also establishes that the respective profit functions of the suppliers and the

OEM are concave in the decisions over which they have control and rules out any case in which it is extremely cheap to reduce costs. Gupta and Loulou (1998) in their analysis of how channel structure influences an innovation decision show that this relationship is satisfied by practical investment opportunities.

Development alliance

Under the collaborative formation of a development alliance the suppliers are partially integrated. That is, each supplier develops the component technology separately by investing P_1 and P_2. If the development stage results in success for any of the suppliers, both suppliers gain access to the new technology. Therefore, the component market is guaranteed to be a duopoly after successful development. However, in the marketing stage each supplier chooses its capacity individually and uses its own marketing assets. In this formation, the expected profit function of supplier i is

$$\pi_i^{DA}(P_1, P_2, r) = (P_1 P_2 + P_1(1 - P_2) + P_2(1 - P_1))\pi_i^{2S}(r) - I_p(P_i) \quad (14)$$

and the OEM's expected profit function becomes

$$\pi_{oem}^{DA}(P_1, P_2, r) = (P_1 P_2 + P_1(1 - P_2) + P_2(1 - P_1))\pi_{oem}^{2S}(r) - I_r(r) \quad (15)$$

Similar to the joint venture, the OEM's profits in (15) are maximized and the optimal investment by the OEM is

$$r^{DA} = \frac{(P_1(1 - P_2) + P_2)(v(8 - v) - c(4 = 5v))}{4Kv(4 - v)^2 - (P_1(1 - P_2) + P_2)(4 + 5v)} \quad (16)$$

To insure that the OEM only invests a feasible amount, $0 < r^{DA} < c$, and all profits are concave, $K > K^{DA} = \frac{(P_1(1-P_2)+P_2)(8+v)}{4c(4-v)^2}$.

Independent development

Finally, the model considers the case where the suppliers choose not to collaborate in the development and marketing stages. They make individual investments at each stage. If both suppliers successfully develop, they compete for the OEM's demand. Nevertheless, if there is only one successful supplier, the supplier with the new component would obtain a monopoly position and ask for the monopoly price to maximize its profits. The expected profit functions of independent supplier 1 and supplier 2 are, respectively,

$$\pi_1^{ID}(P_1,P_2,r) = P_1 P_2 \pi_1^{2S}(r) + P_1(1-P_2)\pi^{1S}(r) - I_p(P_1)$$
$$\pi_2^{ID}(P_1,P_2,r) = P_1 P_2 \pi_2^{2S}(r) + P_2(1-P_1)\pi^{1S}(r) - I_p(P_2)$$
(17)

and the OEM's expected profit function is

$$\pi_{oem}^{ID}(P_1,P_2,r) = P_1 P_2 \pi_{oem}^{2S}(r) + (P_1(1-P_2)+P_2(1-P_1))\pi_{oem}^{1S}(r) - I_r(r)$$
(18)

Maximizing (18) with respect to r, the optimal amount of cost reduction is

$$r^{ID} = \frac{v(4-v)^2(P_2 - c(P_1+P_2)) + vP_1(16+2vP_2(10-v)-v(8-v)) - 2P_1 P_2 c(8-v((8-v)v-6))}{4Kv(4-v)^2 - (P_1(1-P_2)+P_2)(4+5v)}$$
(19)

A feasible amount of investment, $0 < r^{ID} < c$, imposes that $K > K^{ID} = \frac{P_2(4-v)^2+P_1(16-4v(2-5P_2)+v^2(1-2P_2))}{16c(4-v)^2}$.

Before the analysis for each type of cooperation, Lemma 1 characterizes the optimal formation for the suppliers and the OEM when the component technology already exists and no investment by the OEM is needed, i.e. $r = 0$, to demonstrate the conflict of interest between the suppliers and the OEM.

Lemma 1. *When there is a breakthrough component that can be commercialized immediately, the suppliers earn the highest profits if they form a monopoly, but the OEM would earn higher profits sourcing from a duopoly supplier market.*

The results can be easily shown by comparing the profit functions of the suppliers, (3) with (7), and the OEM, (4) with (8), for the single-supplier and two-supplier markets. When the component technology is ready for commercialization and the OEM can accommodate the component at no cost, it would favor a duopoly supplier market because competition in procurement would always reduce the component prices for the OEM. Conversely, the suppliers would choose a monopoly so as to maximize their profits. Further, when the OEM makes a positive investment to accommodate the component technology, its investment decision could change the suppliers' collaboration strategy. In the next section the study examines the optimal decisions of the suppliers and the OEM under each type of formation and the positive investment by each participant.

Analysis

The analysis to follow investigates the supply chain under each type of formation and examines the interrelated interaction of supplier cooperation and the investment levels of the OEM in cost reduction (demand enhancement) and the suppliers in technology development. In order to develop some intuition, the analysis studies the case under which the suppliers have already made significant progress in the technology development. That is, the development stage would not change much with further investment by the suppliers. For example, Michelin and Goodyear have been working to commercialize the run-flat tire technology since the early 1980s and have displayed their competencies and potential to succeed through patents they have acquired on related technologies. This is represented in this modeling framework with the assumption that the probability of successful development is a fixed exogenous parameter, i.e. $P_1 = P_2 = P$. The analysis in the next section allows for the possibility of supplier investment in technology development through the decision variable P.

Equilibria analysis for the OEM and the suppliers

This section examines the adoption of the technology by the downstream OEM and the pivotal role of the supplier formation on the decision of each participant when investments by the suppliers are known. Proposition 1 describes the conditions for the supplier formation that will generate the optimal profits for the OEM.

Proposition 1. The supplier formation, optimal profits and investment level of the OEM

For the three types of supplier formation (joint venture, development alliance, and independent development), for all values of c, v, and P such that $v \geq 2(c - r)$:

i)   *When $K \geq K^{DA}$, the OEM's equilibrium investment and profits are the highest with a development alliance.*
ii) *When $K^{ID} \leq K < K^{DA}$, the OEM's equilibrium investment and profits are the highest with independent suppliers.*
iii) *When $K^{JV} \leq K < K^{ID}$, the OEM could only invest in the joint venture.*
iv) *The cost coefficients for the OEM's investment K^{JV}, K^{ID}, and K^{DA} increase with the probability of successful technology development P.*

Here,

$$K^{JV} = \frac{P}{16c}, \qquad K^{DA} = \frac{(P(2-P))(8+v)}{4c(4-v)^2},$$

and

$$K^{ID} = \frac{P(4-v)^2 + P(16 - 4v(2 - 5P)) + v^2(1 - 2P))}{16c(4-v)^2}$$

The proof of Proposition 1 is achieved by comparing the OEM's profits and investments under each type of formation. Proposition 1 shows that the OEM chooses the supplier formation depending on the type of component sourcing and its investment cost. Dual sourcing is the supplier's commitment to low wholesale prices because it exacerbates price competition in the marketing stage and results in a surge in total capacity. In other words, suppliers may be better off with partial supplier integration than full integration when integration provides the incentive for the OEM to accommodate the technology ($r^{DA} > r^{ID} > r^{JV}$). This incentive becomes more important when the investment cost for the OEM is high. However, the positive effect of the supplier formation is not as attractive when the investment cost for the OEM is low ($K \downarrow$) or the suppliers are more likely to develop the technology ($P \uparrow$). The benefits of a development alliance might be obtained with formations less competitive or uncompetitive in the marketing stage, such as a joint venture.

Further, the following proposition summarizes the effects of the focal parameters (the investment cost incurred by the OEM and the likelihood of successful development) on the supply chain.

Proposition 2. Sensitivity of the profits of the suppliers and the OEM

For any type of supplier formation (joint venture, development alliance, and independent development) the profits and investment levels of the OEM and the profits of the suppliers decrease with the OEM's investment cost, K, and increase with the probability of successful technology development, P.

The proof is straightforward from the first-order conditions. Proposition 2 shows how the profits of the supply chain are affected by the characteristics of the investments. Regardless of the formation, the investment cost incurred by the OEM and the likelihood of successful development have a similar effect on the participants of the supply chain. A high likelihood of successful technology development positively induces the OEM to invest and this increases the profits of all participants. A high cost for the OEM's investment adversely affects the investment level and reduces earnings.

Recall that the OEM's participation is complementary in this context, but it is intriguing to examine the conditions in which the suppliers would agree with the OEM's formation decision. Unfortunately, the profit functions for differentiated suppliers are more sophisticated and do not allow interpretable results. However, the model can identify equilibrium conditions for specific values of v and characterize the response functions of the OEM and the suppliers with first-order conditions. To better understand the suppliers' decisions, the analysis considers the situation for two identical suppliers ($v = 1$). This can be true when two firms with similar complementary assets that have already invested in the development of a technology may offer relatively similar products, which is common in the telecommunications industry.

The next corollary follows from Proposition 1 by setting $v = 1$ and comparing the total profits and investment levels of the OEM for each type of formation. It further characterizes the optimal profits and investment level for the OEM with identical suppliers. For the OEM's investment to be non-negative and feasible in each formation, assume that $K > \underline{K} = \frac{P(2-P)}{9}$, which is increasing in the probability of success. This condition also implies that it should not be too cheap to develop the new technology.

Corollary 1. Optimal profits and investment level of the OEM with identical suppliers

For the three types of supplier formation, for all values of c, P, and K ($> \underline{K}$), the OEM's profits and the equilibrium investment level are the highest in a development alliance with identical suppliers, i.e. $v = 1$.

Proof: Assume $v = 1$ for identical suppliers. The analysis for the joint venture and the OEM's investment in (13) do not change since the suppliers already evenly share the costs and revenues in a joint venture. Nevertheless, in a development alliance or with two independent suppliers, the OEM would procure the same amount from each supplier. Technically, $q_1^* = q_2^*$ when $w_1^* = w_2^*$. Maximizing the suppliers' profits, the optimal wholesale price is $w^{2S} = \frac{1-c+r}{3}$ and the profits of each supplier in a duopoly and the OEM are $\pi^{2S}(r) = \frac{(1-c+r)^2}{18}$ and $\pi^{2S}_{oem}(r) = \frac{1}{4} + \frac{(1-c+r)^2}{9}$, respectively.

Consequently, using the profit functions in (15) for the development alliance and in (18) for independent development, the optimal investment levels of the OEM for a development alliance and for independent suppliers, respectively, are

$$ r_{is}^{DA} = \frac{P(2-P)(1-c)}{9K - P(2-P)}; \quad r_{is}^{ID} = \frac{P(9-P)(1-c)}{72K - P(9-P)} \tag{20} $$

where the subscript is denotes identical suppliers. Comparing the profit and investment levels, $\pi^{DA}_{oem}(P, P, r_{is}^{DA}) > \pi^{ID}_{oem}(P, P, r_{is}^{ID}) > \pi^{JV}_{oem}(P, P, r^{JV})$ and $r_{is}^{DA} > r_{is}^{ID} > r^{JV}$. ∎

Since the likelihood of successful development is exogenous, Corollary 1 shows that the OEM maximizes its profits in a development alliance from marketing competition since the identical suppliers not only guarantee a duopoly market as for independent suppliers, but they also share the outcome of the technology development. However, this outcome may not be true for the suppliers. It is possible to compare the profits of the identical suppliers under each type of formation and find the necessary conditions for the optimal formation. Proposition 3 characterizes the optimal supplier formations.

Proposition 3. The supplier formation and optimal profits for identical suppliers

When the suppliers are identical ($v = 1$), for the three types of supplier formation, for all values of c and P:

i) *If $K \geq K_{UB}$, the suppliers would earn the highest profits in a development alliance.*

ii) *If $K_{LB} \leq K < K_{UB}$, the suppliers would not participate in any form of collaborative formation and they would develop the technology and market the component independently.*

iii) *If $K < K_{LB}$, the suppliers would earn the highest profits in a joint venture.*

Here, the lower bound $K_{\mathrm{LB}} = \frac{P(36-18P+7\sqrt{(P-2)(9-5P)})}{36}$ *and the upper bound*

$K_{\mathrm{UB}} = \frac{P(48-24P+7\sqrt{2(P-2)(9-5P)})}{48}$.

Proof: It is straightforward by comparing the profit functions of a development alliance and a joint venture to show that there exists a threshold $\overline{K} = \frac{(12+7\sqrt{2})P(2-P)}{24}$ such that for supplier i when $K < \overline{K}, \pi_i^{\mathrm{JV}}\left(r^{\mathrm{JV}}\right) > \pi_i^{\mathrm{DA}}\left(r_{\mathrm{is}}^{\mathrm{DA}}\right)$; and when $K \geq \overline{K}, \pi_i^{\mathrm{JV}}\left(r^{\mathrm{JV}}\right) \leq \pi_i^{\mathrm{DA}}\left(r_{\mathrm{is}}^{\mathrm{DA}}\right)$. Comparing the profits of a supplier in collaboration with the profits from independent development and for all values of the parameters, $0 < P < 1$ and $0 < c < 1$, $\pi_i^{\mathrm{DA}}\left(r_{\mathrm{is}}^{\mathrm{DA}}\right) > 0, \pi_i^{\mathrm{ID}}\left(r_{\mathrm{is}}^{\mathrm{DA}}\right) > 0$, and $\pi_i^{\mathrm{JV}}\left(r^{\mathrm{JV}}\right) > 0$. When $K < \overline{K}, \pi_i^{\mathrm{JV}}\left(r^{\mathrm{JV}}\right) < \pi_i^{\mathrm{ID}}\left(r_{\mathrm{is}}^{\mathrm{DA}}\right)$ for $K_{\mathrm{LB}} < K < \overline{K}$. And similarly, when $K \geq \overline{K}, \pi_i^{\mathrm{JV}}\left(r^{\mathrm{JV}}\right) > \pi_i^{\mathrm{ID}}\left(r_{\mathrm{is}}^{\mathrm{DA}}\right)$ for $K_{\mathrm{LB}} > K > \overline{K}$.   ∎

Similar to Proposition 1, Proposition 3 presents the main tradeoff between profits and the OEM's investment for identical suppliers. When the OEM incurs high investment costs, the suppliers are concerned about motivating the OEM to invest. Although increased duopoly competition hurts the profits of the suppliers in a development alliance, the reduced wholesale prices enhance the OEM's incentive to invest. Therefore, the suppliers could find partial integration profitable as long as the OEM's cost-reducing or demand-enhancing investment justifies any loss due to marketing competition.

In addition to supplier integration, part *ii)* of Proposition 3 identifies the conditions under which the identical suppliers may choose not to participate in any formation and operate independently. From a supplier's perspective, when it develops and markets independently, there is not only the possibility of becoming a monopoly (if its rival fails) but it will also attract more downstream investment than if it were a single supplier. Although the OEM does not invest as much as it would in a development alliance, it does not reduce its investment level as low as in a joint venture. Hence, independent development could be the optimal decision for the suppliers when the level of probability of successful development does not justify a joint venture for the OEM and the investment cost makes the development alliance suboptimal.

Hence, these findings characterize the coordination of the supply chain through high collaborative formations in the development and marketing of a new technology. This can be interpreted in the context of the alliance between the close competitors, Michelin and Goodyear. Michelin's attempts to work with major car manufacturers were not successful until it signed up with Goodyear to collaborate on the run-flat tire technology. Collaboration and past individual investment in R&D by both firms improved the likelihood of success and motivated the downstream car manufacturers, Ford and Honda, which also agreed to work only with the duopoly market for the run-flat tire.

Numerical example for differentiated suppliers

The analysis has so far examined the situation for identical suppliers. To better illustrate the effect of collaboration on the profitability of differentiated suppliers, a numerical analysis considers the interpretation of the optimal decisions for other values of v. In Fig. 1 a selective example is displayed for $c = 0.2$ and $v = 0.6$. In the result below, the effect of the collaboration on the supplier profits is summarized.

Result 1. *i) When the OEM's investment costs ($K > K^{DA}$) are high and the probability of successful development, P, is low, the development alliance dominates independent development and a joint venture for the suppliers. ii) When the technology development stage is more efficient (lower K and higher P), the suppliers choose formations that are less competitive in the development and marketing stages.*

Within the range for higher values of K (implying that the OEM has to incur high investment costs) and lower values of the probability of successful technology development, P, the suppliers choose partial integration through a development alliance. But, a development alliance is not justified when the development stage is more efficient, i.e. the likelihood of successful technology development is high or it is relatively affordable for the OEM to consider the new technology. Since an efficient development stage motivates the OEM to invest, it may need no additional incentives. Then the suppliers could find it

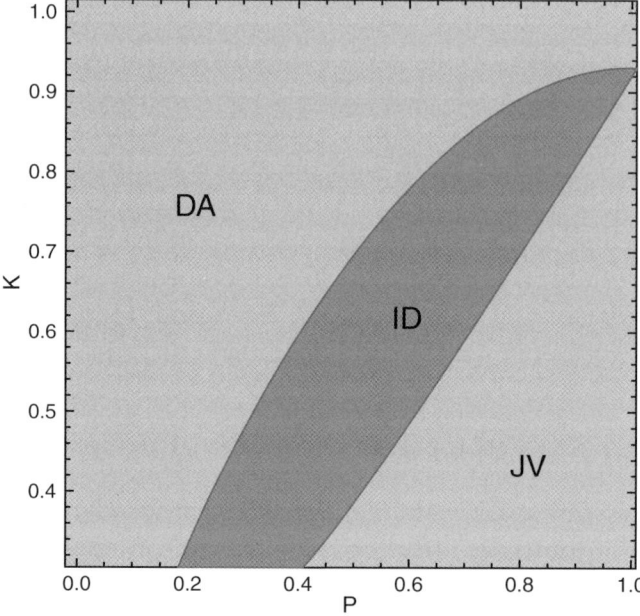

Fig. 1. Optimal Supplier Formation ($c = 0.2$, $v = 0.6$).

more profitable to develop independently in anticipation of monopoly profits ($K^{ID} \leq K < K^{DA}$). Further, when the OEM incurs minimal investment costs, the suppliers could form a joint venture ($K^{JV} \leq K < K^{ID}$. Note that Proposition 1 shows that the OEM would react to this situation by reducing its investment amount. This result can be observed for the regions ID and JV for higher values of P and lower values of K in Fig. 1.

In general, these results suggest that if the operational factors affecting the level of technology development and investment costs are not sufficient to induce participation of the downstream supply chain, the supplier formation can indeed coordinate the supply chain and improve total profits. The OEM's investment could justify the adverse consequences of a collaborative formation. Further, it is noteworthy that the suppliers in the model do not obtain any synergy through collaborative development. Yet, they could benefit from partial integration with competition in the marketing stage in the absence of such synergies in production and development.

Supplier investment in technology development

Thus far, the research has focused on the efforts to identify the conditions when collaboration between suppliers would stimulate the downstream OEM's investment without any explicit consideration of the supplier investment in technology development. It is worth noting that a supplier could make such an investment to improve its probability of success with respect to the competitor, especially if it is developing individually. To capture this effect, in this section the suppliers simultaneously select their investment levels in technology development after they agree on the type of collaborative formation.

To model this decision, the probability of successful technology development is endogenously decided by the suppliers. The optimal investment level of supplier $i \in \{1,2\}$ under formation type $j \in \{JV,DA,ID\}$, denoted by $P_{ij}(c,r,v)$, are computed using (11), (14), and (17). For example, P_{1DA} denotes the investment level for the success of the technology development by supplier 1 in a development alliance. In the remainder of this section the analysis is based on closed-form solutions (the closed-form expressions are sophisticated and available from the author). When they are too complicated, the results are demonstrated with numerical examples. The numerical analysis presents a selection of the results but similar results with the entire sets of values that the model parameters can take have been tested and confirmed.

First, the analysis examines in more detail how firms at different levels of the supply chain affect the operational dynamics of the others. The following proposition characterizes the effect of a supplier's investment on the OEM's investment in cost reduction and profits and extends Proposition 2 for endogenous values of P_1 and P_2.

Proposition 4. Impact of supplier investment on the OEM

The investment level by the suppliers in technology development positively induces the OEM to invest in cost reduction (demand enhancement)

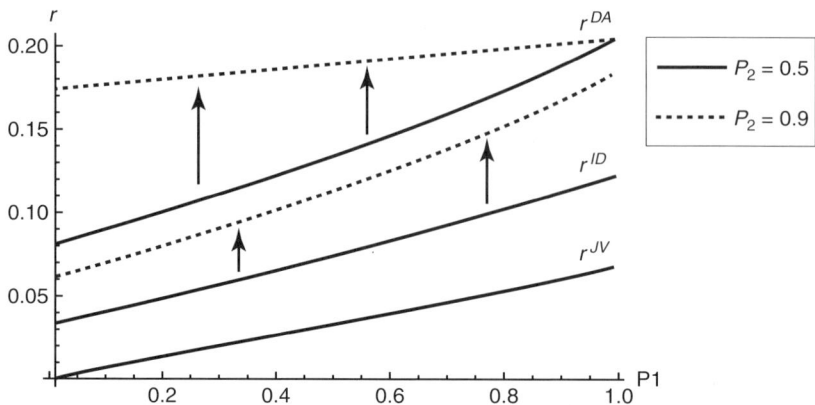

Fig. 2. The Effect of Supplier Investment in Technology Development on the OEM's Investment ($c = 0.2$, $v = 0.4$, $K = 0.8$).

under each type of supplier formation (joint venture, development alliance, and independent development).

   This result can be easily proved by considering the sensitivity analysis of the optimal cost reduction (demand enhancement) in (13), (16), and (19) with respect to P_{1j} and P_{2j}. Proposition 4 shows how the upstream investment in the supply chain positively affects downstream investment decisions. In particular, the OEM is always positively induced to invest when there is a higher likelihood for technology development success, which is due to a higher level of supplier investment in the development stage.

   Figure 2 illustrates this result and further shows that with increasing r^j the OEM is more sensitive and responsive to supplier investment for cases in which both suppliers could meet the OEM's demand. Further, if the suppliers develop with closer individual probabilities, the OEM is less indifferent to the formation of the dual source. This finding is shown in Fig. 2 where r^{DA} and r^{ID} approach each other for higher values for the second supplier's probability of successful development ($P_2 = 0.9$). Hence, the OEM is less likely to make a high investment when there is a development alliance because there is a greater probability of obtaining a dual source through independent suppliers.

Analogously, the OEM's investment has a drastic influence on the suppliers' investment decisions. This effect is examined in a numerical example and summarized in the following result.

Result 2. *An increase in the investment level by the OEM, r, positively stimulates supplier investment thus increasing the probability of successful development, P1 and P2, for each type of supplier formation.*

According to Result 2, downstream investment in the supply chain positively affects investment by the upstream suppliers. This is illustrated by the positive slopes of the P curves with r under different formations, as shown in Fig. 3. The OEM's cost reduction (demand enhancement) has a greater positive effect on supplier investment in formations with a single supplier such as independent development and joint ventures than a dual source like development alliances because the profitability of a monopoly induces more investment by the suppliers. Further, to make up for the lack of price competition, the suppliers have to invest the most in a joint venture.

Although collaboration stimulates the OEM to invest (Proposition 4), which in return improves the supplier's investment, collaborating suppliers may not be equally motivated due to the imbalance between reduced benefits and investment costs. In particular, in a development alliance supplier 2, whose component is an imperfect substitute, may be significantly less interested in investment due to the future position of its own component in the market. This is seen as the difference between P_{1DA} and P_{2DA} for different values of r in Fig. 3. This issue is eliminated in a joint venture with a revenue-sharing mechanism.

Note that Fig. 2 demonstrates that the OEM invests the highest amount for a development alliance whilst Fig. 3 shows that the suppliers invest the least in a development alliance. Because the partial integration of a development alliance improves the OEM's investment the suppliers are less concerned about making high levels of investment to motivate the OEM. In other words, Proposition 4 and Result 2 support the finding that the collaborative formation of the suppliers could justify the OEM's investment and coordinate the

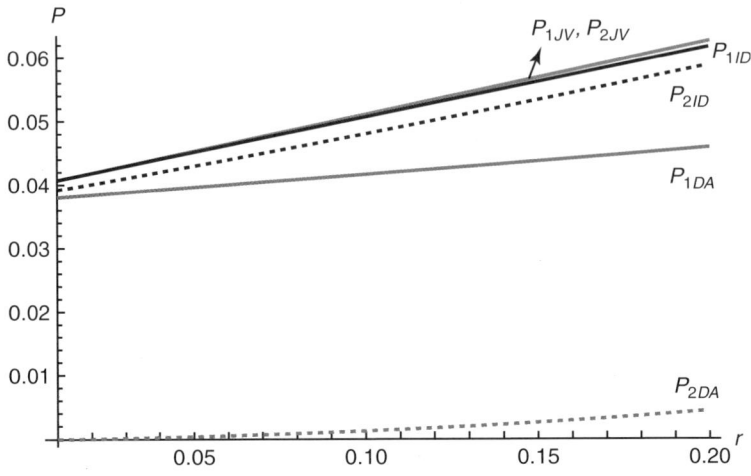

Fig. 3. The Effect of the OEM's Investment in Cost Reduction on Supplier Investment in Technology Development ($c = 0.2$, $v = 0.4$, $K = 0.8$).

supply chain so long as the formation could provide sufficient operational benefits.

Finally, in addition to the interrelated relationship between the investments of the supplier and the OEM, the analysis examines the effect of factors such as the unit production cost of the final product and the degree of component substitutability on the supplier investment. It is intuitive that the lower the unit production cost, the higher the supplier investment level, as shown by the decreasing P_{ij} with c in Fig. 4, since an OEM with low production costs is more willing to participate. The effect of the unit production cost on supplier investment under each formation leads to the next result.

Result 3. *For the three types of supplier formation, the suppliers of a joint venture (full integration) are the most sensitive to the OEM's unit production cost and the least sensitive are the suppliers in a development alliance (partial integration).*

As shown in Fig. 4, a high unit production cost affects an independent supplier or a joint venture more adversely than a development alliance, because, first, the investment-stimulating effect of

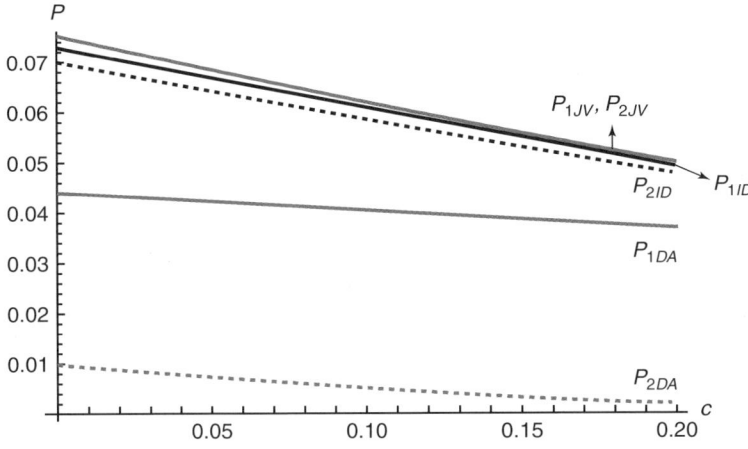

Fig. 4. The Effect of the OEM's Unit Production Cost on Supplier Investment in Technology Development ($v = 0.4$, $r = 0.1$, $K = 0.8$).

competition in a development alliance is missing and second, the OEM is more concerned about paying the monopoly wholesale price. Figure 4 suggests that partially integrated suppliers are less susceptible to changes in production costs because the OEM is more inclined to make a relatively high investment despite the increasing unit cost. Therefore, the fully integrated suppliers of a joint venture have to make up by investing the most. When there are extremely high costs all suppliers would quit development.

Another factor is the degree of component substitutability. Figure 5 illustrates the effect of substitutability on supplier investment. The analysis does not consider a joint venture since the suppliers in a joint venture always offer a single product in this model. The following result summarizes the situation for suppliers in the other two formations.

Result 4. *The degree of component substitutability, v, reduces the investment level in technology development for a supplier with a relatively higher-valued component but may or may not reduce the investment level for a supplier with a relatively lower-valued component.*

According to Result 4 the investment level of supplier 1, whose component is perceived to be of higher value by consumers, decreases

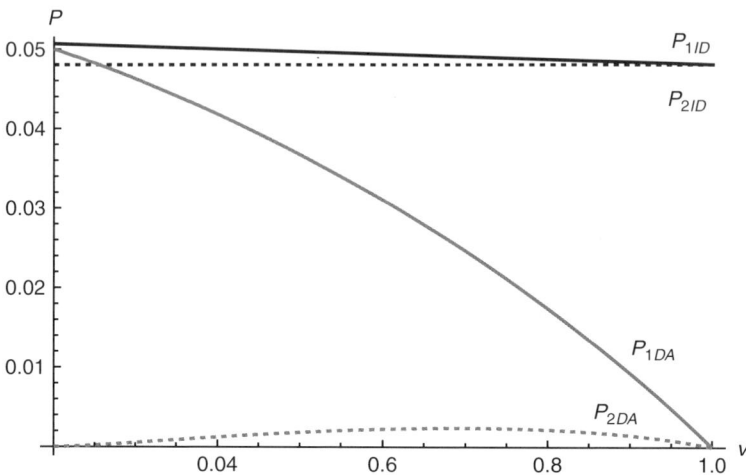

Fig. 5. The Effect of the OEM's Unit Production Cost on Supplier Investment in Technology Development ($c = 0.2$, $r = 0.1$, $K = 0.8$).

with v because highly substitutable components would imply close competition in the following marketing stage and hurt the future profits for supplier 1 more than for supplier 2. Accordingly, the suppliers in a development alliance invest significantly less than independent suppliers because an independent supplier may earn a monopoly position whereas in a development alliance stiffer competition would certainly follow the development stage.

Figure 5 further illustrates that supplier 2 with a component of lower perceived quality would increase investment if it had a closer substitute but any further increase in the degree of substitutability would have the opposite effect. This may seem like a counterintuitive result, but when two products are closer in perceived value for the consumer, price competition dramatically reduces the profits for both suppliers. Consequently, a development alliance would cause more harm than it provides benefits to the suppliers. Suppliers do not invest in development if they have perfect substitutes. In contrast, independent suppliers with perfect substitutes invest the same amount due to marketing competition. Hence, no integration may result in a higher investment level.

Conclusion and Outlook

Open innovation and collaboration in a supply chain could be very beneficial to the participants for various operational and financial reasons. Open innovation through inter-firm collaboration is a strategic asset for the firms besides the exploitation of tangible and intangible assets. Participating firms have to consider the effect of their cooperation on the supply chain dynamics. Since participants alter their decisions relative to the characteristics of the cooperation, the type of inter-firm collaboration has a significant effect on the profitability of all supply chain members. This is especially significant in a competitive market where firms depend on each other's resources or a complementary technology is required for continuous development.

This research examines the strategic incentives for open innovation in a supply chain and specifically studies three types of firm interaction with different levels of open innovation. The study in particular considers the collaboration decisions faced by two competing suppliers in the development and marketing stages and their effect on the OEM's adoption of the component technology and investment in a complementary technology. It examines three types of firm interaction representing different levels of supplier integration and open innovation: joint venture (full integration), development alliance (partial integration), and independent development (no integration). Whereas the study examines several situational factors that determine the specific way in which the suppliers might decide on the degree of collaboration, it particularly focuses on the OEM's investment in cost reduction, the probability of development success for the suppliers, and the extent to which the suppliers can stimulate the OEM's investment through the type of collaboration. These factors that affect the post-alliance market structure are intimately linked and exhibit strong interactions that are readily seen in practice.

The study presents several results. First, the research shows that a central consideration in selecting the type of supplier formation (joint venture, development alliance, or independent development) is the positive value generated by the OEM's investment, but inter-firm collaboration should not lead to competitive surrender in order to attract the manufacturer's innovation efforts for the component. The analysis finds the critical conditions by paying attention to suppliers who exploit the OEM's investment decision in cost reduction (demand enhancement) by choosing whether to collaborate or compete in the technology development and marketing stages. Based on these conditions, the results suggest that while the decision to compete in marketing reduces supplier profits, it stimulates the OEM's investment, which in return increases consumer demand for the final product and thereby the earnings for the suppliers. Further, the likelihood of a collaboration is greater if the OEM has a more efficient production process, i.e. the OEM incurs lower investment costs or if the suppliers are very likely to develop the technology.

A second point that the analysis shows is that investments at different levels of the supply chain affect each other depending on the type of collaboration. In particular, suppliers earn the highest profits with a monopoly such as a joint venture. However, the results show that they may improve their profits with a development alliance by providing the downstream firm with the right incentive to invest. This result highlights the strategic use of open innovation to coordinate the supply chain by managing the effect of collaboration on the adoption and investment decisions of the entire supply chain. In other words, open innovation can be profitable if the OEM's effect on enhancing demand and increased competition are matched correctly.

Finally, the study examines the suppliers' investments in technology development, which depend on factors such as the OEM's unit production cost and the degree of component substitutability. The numerical results show that independent development, i.e. closed innovation, is most affected by the cost structure of the downstream supply chain and an efficient OEM due to potential high future earnings. However, firms are less affected by the cost structure of the OEM when they provide an incentive to the OEM by increasing the level of "openness" in innovation activities. Further, when innovation results in components that are relatively close substitutes, open innovation is not the best option since stiff competition in marketing would hurt the profits of the suppliers. Hence, open innovation should be avoided unless the OEM's investment is relatively large and the two products are sufficiently differentiated.

The study develops an analytical framework for understanding cooperation decisions. This methodology is reasonable in providing a better understanding of the consequences of collaboration and competition. To focus attention on how an upstream firm's commitment to collaboration affects its downstream channel partner's investment in innovation, the modeling framework studies the interaction as a duopoly in the upstream supply chain and a bilateral monopoly in the downstream supply chain, leaving the effects of competition in downstream markets to future research. The modeling framework in this study contributes to the literature on inter-firm collaboration based on tactical decisions (prices and quantities) by studying a game-theoretic model of different supplier formations and degrees of open innovation.

Although the model has made some stylized assumptions in order to study the central question, the limitations of this framework and their influence on the results need to be acknowledged, and the results of this paper identify potential directions for future research. First and foremost, competition in downstream markets might change the incentives for upstream innovators to collaborate and the levels of investment in innovation. However, downstream manufacturers might react collaboratively to facilitate upstream innovation so as to obtain an innovative component for their products. Thus, it would be interesting to study whether the presence of a downstream competitor improves the extent of open innovation in the supply chain. Further, the model only considers two suppliers. This limits the applicability of the model to other alliance formations with n suppliers. Also, suppliers in the model do not create synergy through collaboration. Even though the results already highlight a counterintuitive interaction between firms without synergy, the operational synergy and compatibility between suppliers could extend managers' understanding of supplier interactions at the operational level.

Another limitation of the model is that firms have complete information about the new technology and demand. However, most OEMs are not well informed about technological progress and may not correctly assess the likelihood of a successful development. In addition, suppliers may not appraise the rival's likelihood of success. A different model that allows information asymmetry between suppliers or between the OEM and the suppliers could alter the suppliers' formation and the OEM's investment decisions, and hence, yield different results. Further, demand uncertainty may change the interaction between the two levels of the supply chain since the downstream manufacturer's incentive to invest in innovation will be driven by its anticipated demand.

Finally, the outcome of the component quality at the technology development stage is the same for both suppliers, but one supplier may obtain a component of relatively higher quality and this would change the dynamics of the development stage and the collaboration decision. Although the intrinsic nature of the degree of substitutability in the model partially explains the difference in a component's perceived quality between suppliers, further analysis with a specific focus on component quality may provide additional insights. Investigating these issues will enhance the understanding of collaboration decisions in supply chains.

References

Aghion, P. and Tirole, J. (1994). The management of innovation, *Quarterly Journal of Economics*, **109**(4), 1185–1209.

Amaldoss, W. and Rapoport, A. (2005). Collaborative product and market development: Theoretical implications and experimental evidence, *Marketing Science*, **24**(3), 396–414.

Aune, T.B. and Gressetvold, E. (2011). Supplier involvement in innovation processes: A taxonomy, *International Journal of Innovation Management*, **15**(1), 121–143.

Aylen, J. (2010). Open versus closed innovation: Development of the wide strip mill for steel in the United States during the 1920s, *R&D Management*, **40**(1), 67–80.

Baldwin, C.Y. and Clark, K.B. (2000). *Design Rules, Volume 1: The Power of Modularity*, MIT Press, Cambridge, MA.

Bahemia, H. and Squire, B. (2010). A contingent perspective of open innovation in new product development projects, *International Journal of Innovation Management*, **15**(1), 121–143.

Bergman, J., Jantunen, A. and Saksa, J. (2009). Enabling open innovation process through interactive methods: Scenarios and group decision support systems, *International Journal of Innovation Management*, **13**(1), 139–156.

Bhaskaran, S.R. and Krishnan, V. (2009). Effort, revenue and cost sharing mechanisms for collaborative product development, *Management Science*, **55**(7), 1–18.

Bilgram, V., Brem, A. and Voigt, K. (2008). User-centric innovations in new product development systematic identification of lead users harnessing interactive and collaborative online-tools, *International Journal of Innovation Management*, **12**(3), 419–458.

Björn, R., Ljunberg, J., Bergquist, M. and Kuschel, J. (2011). Open innovation, generativity and the supplier as peer: The case of iPhone and Android, *International Journal of Innovation Management*, **15**(1), 205–230.

Braid, R.M. (1999). The price and profit effects of horizontal mergers in two-dimensional spatial competition, *Economics Letters*, **62**(1), 113–119.

Brandenburger, A. and Nalebuff, B. (1995). The right game: Use game theory to shape strategy, *Harvard Business Review*, **73**(4), 57–71.

Braun, V. and Herstatt, C. (2008). The freedom fighters: How incumbent corporations are attempting to control user-innovation, *International Journal of Innovation Management*, **12**(3), 543–572.

Brito, D. (2003). Preemptive mergers under spatial competition, *International Journal of Industrial Organization*, **21**(10), 1601–1622.

Business Week (2004). Michelin: New rubber hits the road, August 16.

Chesbrough, H.W. (2003). *Open Innovation: The New Imperative for Creating and Profiting from Technology*, Harvard Business School Press, Cambridge, MA.

Chesbrough, H.W. and Appleyard, M.M. (2007). Open innovation and strategy, *California Management Review*, **50**(1), 57–76.

Conner, K. (1995). Obtaining strategic advantage from being imitated: When can encouraging clones pay? *Management Science*, **41**(2), 209–225.

Das, T.K. and Teng, B.S. (2000). A resource-based theory of strategic alliances, *Journal of Management*, **26**(1), 31–61.

de Wit, J., Dankbaar, B. and Vissers, G. (2007). Open innovation: The new way of knowledge transfer? *Journal of Business Chemistry*, **4**, 1–17.

Demski, J.S., Sappington, D.E.M. and Spiller, P.T. (1987). Managing supplier switching, *The RAND Journal of Economics*, **18**(1), 77–97.

Deneckere, R. and Davidson, C. (1985). Incentives to form coalitions with Bertrand competition, *The RAND Journal of Economics*, **16**(4), 473–486.

Dittrich, K. and Duysters, G. (2007). Networking as a means to strategy change: The case of open innovation in mobile telephony, *Journal of Product Innovation Management*, **24**(6), 510–521.

Dodgson, M., Gann, D. and Salter, A. (2006). The role of technology in the shift towards open innovation: The case of Procter & Gamble, *R&D Management*, **36**(3), 333–346.

Drummond, M. and Perkins, C. (2009). In search of, *Inventors' Digest*, **25**(1), 30–32.

Enkel, E. and Lenz, A. (2009). Open innovation metrics system, *Proceedings of the R&D Management Conference*, Vienna, Austria, June 21–24.

Erat, S. and Krishnan, V. (2011). Managing delegated search over design spaces, *Management Science*, **57**(10).

Erzurumlu, S., Gilbert, S.M., and Ramachandran, K. (2010). To share or to compete: Managing revenue streams for innovations in markets with network effects, *Technology Operation Management*, **1**(2), 37–55.

Farrell, J. and Gallini, N.T. (1988). Second-sourcing as a commitment: Monopoly incentives to attract competition, *The Quarterly Journal of Economics*, **103**(4), 673–694.

Gassmann, O. (2006). Opening up the innovation process: Towards an agenda, *R&D Management*, **36**(3), 223–228.

Gilbert, S.M. and Cvsa, V. (2003). Strategic commitment to price to stimulate downstream innovation in a supply chain, *European Journal of Operational Research*, **150**, 617–639.

Gilbert, S.M., Xia, Y. and Yu, G. (2006). Strategic outsourcing for competing OEMs that face cost reduction opportunities, *IIE Transactions*, **38**(11), 903–915.

Gilbert, S.M., Xia, Y. and Yu, G. (2007). The strategic effects of a merger upon supplier interactions, *Naval Research Logistics*, **54**(2), 162–175.

Goodyear. (2010). History by year. Available at Goodyear Corporate website, http://www.goodyear.com/corporate/history/history_byyear.html

Granot, D. and Sosic, G. (2005). Formation of alliances in internet-based supply exchanges, *Management Science*, **51**(1), 92–105.

Gupta, S. and Loulou, R. (1998). Process innovation, product differentiation, and channel structure: Strategic incentives in a duopoly, *Marketing Science*, **17**(4), 301–316.

Hamel, G., Doz, Y.L. and Prahalad, C.K. (1989). Collaborate with your competitors and win, *Harvard Business Review*, **67**(1), 133–139.

Industry Week. (2007). A team effort, January.

Jacobides, M.G. and Billinger, S. (2006). Designing the boundaries of the firm: From "make, buy, or ally" to the dynamic benefits of vertical architecture, *Organization Science*, **17**(2), 249–261.

Jeuland, A.P. and Shugan, S.M. (1983). Managing channel profits, *Marketing Science*, **2**(3), 239–272.

Kalaignanam, K., Shankar, V. and Varadarajan, R. (2007). Asymmetric new product development alliances: Win-win or win-lose partnerships? *Management Science*, **53**(3), 357–374.

Kang, K.H. and Kang, J. (2009). How do firms source external knowledge for innovation? Analysing effects of different knowledge sourcing methods, *International Journal of Innovation Management*, **13**(1), 1–17.

Keupp, M.M. and Gassmann, O. (2009). Determinants and archetype users of open innovation, *R&D Management*, **39**(4), 331–341.

Klotz, D.E. and Chatterjee, K. (1995). Dual sourcing in repeated procurement competitions, *Management Science*, **41**(8), 1317–1327.

Kogut, B. (1991). Joint ventures and the option to expand and acquire, *Management Science*, **37**(1), 19–33.

Kolk, A. and Püüman, K. (2008). Co-development of open innovation strategy and dynamic capabilities as a source of corporate growth, *Working Papers in Economics*, **25**(168–180), 73–83.

Kouvelis, P., Chambers, C. and Wang, H. (2006). Supply chain management research and production and operations management: Review, trends, and opportunities, *Production and Operations Management*, **15**(3), 449–469.

Lazzarotti, V. and Manzini, R. (2009). Different modes of open innovation: A theoretical framework and an empirical study, *International Journal of Innovation Management*, **13**(4), 615–636.

Lichtenthaler, U. (2009). Outbound open innovation and its effect on firm performance: Examining environmental influences, *R&D Management*, **39**(4), 317–330.

Lichtenthaler, U. and Ernst, H. (2009). Opening up the innovation process: The role of technology aggressiveness, *R&D Management*, **39**(1), 38–54.

Mazzarol, T. and Reboud, S. (2008). The role of complementary actors in the development of innovation in small firms, *International Journal of Innovation Management*, **12**(2), 223–253.

McGuire, T.W. and Staelin, R. (1983). An industry equilibrium analysis of downstream vertical integration, *Marketing Science*, **2**(2), 161–191.

Nash, J.J. (1950). The bargaining problem, *Econometrica*, **18**(2), 155–162.

Nault, B.R. and Tyagi, R.K. (2001). Implementable mechanisms to coordinate horizontal alliances, *Management Science*, **47**(6), 787–799.

Olleros, F.X. (2007). The power of non-contractual innovation, *International Journal of Innovation Management*, **11**(1), 93–113.

Paasi, J., Luoma, T., Valkokari, K. and Lee, N. (2010). Knowledge and intellectual property management in customer–supplier relationships, *International Journal of Innovation Management*, **14**(4), 629–654.

Perks, H. (2004). Exploring processes of resource exchange and co-creation in strategic partnering for new product development, *International Journal of Innovation Management*, **8**(1), 37–61.

Pfeffer, J. and Novak, P. (1976). Joint venture and internationalisation interdependence, *Administrative Science Quarterly*, **4**(2), 398–418.

Reuer, J.J. (2004). *Strategic Alliances: Theory and Evidence*, Oxford University Press, Oxford, UK.

Riordan, M.H. and Sappington, D.E.M. (1989). Second sourcing, *The RAND Journal of Economics*, **20**(1), 41–58.

Rosenkopf, L. and Almeida, P. (2003). Overcoming local search through alliances and mobility, *Management Science*, **49**(6), 751–766.

Softpedia (2008). AMD and Intel working on further development of havok physics technology. Available at http://news.softpedia.com/news/AMD-and-Intel-working-on-further-development-of-havok-physics-technology-88068.shtml.

Teece, D., Pisano, G. and Shuen, A. (1997). *Dynamic Capabilities and Strategic Management*, Oxford University Press, Oxford, UK.

Terwiesch, C. and Xu, Y. (2008). Innovation contests, open innovation, and multiagent problem solving, *Management Science*, **54**(9), 1529–1543.

Tsay, A., Nahmias, S. and Agrawal, N. (1998). "Modeling supply chain contracts: A review," in Tayur, S. Ganeshan, R. and M. Magazine (eds), *Quantitative Models for Supply Chain Management*, Kluwer, Boston, MA.

Un, C.A. Cuervo-Cazurra, A. and Asakawa, K. (2010). R&D collaborations and product innovation, *Journal of Product Innovation Management*, **27**(5), 673–689.

Vapola, T., Tossavainen, P. and Gabrielsson, M. (2008). The battleship strategy: The complementing role of born globals in MNC's new opportunity creation, *Journal of International Entrepreneurship*, **6**(1), 1–21.

von Hippel, E. and von Krogh, G. (2006). Free revealing and the private-collective model for innovation incentives, *R&D Management*, **36**(3), 295–306.

Part II

Empirical Findings Based on Quantitative Research

Chapter 5

Supplier Innovativeness and Supplier Pricing: The Role of Preferred-Customer Status

Holger Schiele*, Jasper Veldman, and Lisa Hüttinger
Operations, Organisation and Human Resources,
University of Twente, The Netherlands

Introduction

In recent years, innovation has increasingly been analysed from an 'open innovation' perspective, with the argument that innovation develops through the interplay of different parties from different organisations (von Hippel, 1988; Edquist, 1997; Freeman and Soete, 1997; Steinle and Schiele, 2002; Chesbrough, 2003; Trott and Hartmann, 2009). A panel study involving the largest R&D investors worldwide revealed that the proportion of firms that rely heavily on external support for innovation increased from 20% a decade ago to 85% at the beginning of the new millennium (Roberts, 2001). Another longitudinal study involving a large sample of firms further supported the presence of a paradigm shift from a closed to an open innovation model (Poot *et al.*, 2009). This change reflects not only the establishment of horizontal alliances, whose number has stagnated since the mid-1980s (Hagedoorn, 2002), but also the increasing role that suppliers play in the innovation process. However, whereas the role and integration of downstream

* Corresponding author

parties (i.e. customers) and midstream partners (i.e. alliances) have been widely researched, and despite the substantial effects that can be expected from supplier involvement (e.g., see Ragatz *et al.*, 2002), the upstream part of open innovation (i.e. the innovativeness of a supplier during a successful early supplier integration in innovation processes with the buyer) has received much less attention (Johnsen, 2009).

Upstream open innovation poses several new managerial challenges. Thus, one branch of the literature has focussed on the effects that the selection of (un)suitable suppliers can have (Hartley *et al.*, 1997a; Flynn *et al.*, 2000; Primo and Amundson, 2002; Wognum *et al.*, 2002; Petroni and Panciroli, 2002; Rutten, 2003; Zsidisin and Smith, 2005). Most of these studies, nonetheless, focus on project management issues and on the technological capabilities of suppliers. The role of behavioural factors is less well understood. One important behavioural factor is preferred-customer status, which refers to buyer attractiveness from a supplier's point of view. Some authors show that a high level of customer attractiveness helps to ensure the prime commitment of capable suppliers, which is one of the preconditions for their engagement in innovation projects (Christiansen and Maltz, 2002; Koppelmann, 2000; Leenders and Blenkhorn, 1988; Ellegaard *et al.*, 2003; Wynstra *et al.*, 2003; Mortensen *et al.*, 2008). Although there have already been preliminary attempts to study the role of preferred-customer status, this literature is based on case studies rather than on a quantitative analysis of the relation between supplier innovativeness and preferred-customer status. Thus, a primary objective of this paper is to quantitatively assess the effect of supplier capabilities and preferred-customer status on the generation of innovation in buyer–supplier relations.

To gain competitive advantage, more and more buyers are entering into close relations with strategically relevant sellers striving for a network of 'innovation-suppliers' (Schiele, 2006; Wagner, 2009). From a buyer's perspective, such close ties can lead to dependency — which, in turn, can lead to opportunistic behaviour (Pfeffer and Salancik, 1978; Provan and Skinner, 1989; Cool and Henderson, 1998). Having dependent buyers might inspire suppliers to exhibit less benevolent pricing behaviour. Particularly in practice, the belief exists among purchasers that sellers will ask for overly high prices once established as strategic or development partners (Corsten and Felde, 2005).

This fear of being exploited is one reason why buyers might refrain from integrating a supplier into their internal processes and eventually failing to fully access the supplier's power of innovation. In order to pave the way for further upstream open innovation, it is crucial to address the fear that supplier integration may actually end up being too expensive for the buying firm. Therefore, we test the assumption that preferred-customer status with an innovative supplier can eliminate the pricing-induced barrier to collaboration. With this in mind, the second objective of this chapter is to test how suppliers' innovative capabilities and preferred-customer status affect supplier pricing behaviour.

We construct and test the conceptual framework using a sample of 166 buyer–supplier relations in a business-to-business context. We find that technical antecedents (i.e. supplier innovation capability) and behavioural antecedents (i.e. when the buyer is a preferred customer) can largely explain supplier innovativeness, understood as a supplier's contribution in a joint innovation process with a buyer. Behavioural antecedents operationalised through the preferred-customer variable have a stronger effect than technical antecedents. Remarkably, whereas we expected that suppliers might charge higher prices for their contribution to a newly developed product once they were involved in innovation, our results show that this relation is not statistically significant. Further, pricing even becomes more benevolent as the attractiveness of the buying firm for its suppliers increases.

On a theoretical level, these results underline the importance of one specific behavioural antecedent (i.e. preferred-customer status) and its effect on supplier innovation and pricing. Much of the research on collaborative innovation has focussed on technical antecedents as well as on project organisation and project manager capabilities (e.g. Gerwin and Ferris, 2004). Our results alert researchers to the need to dedicate more effort to analysing the status of the parties involved (i.e. preferred- versus not-preferred-customer status).

Further, by not finding evidence of an innovativeness–pricing trade-off, our results will encourage firms to engage in collaborative innovation with suppliers. Supporting the feasibility of collaboration may crucially contribute to the further development of the theory and practice of upstream open innovation. The implications of these results for both the innovation and the pricing literature will be discussed in the final part of the article.

This paper is structured as follows. First, we will derive our hypotheses regarding the relation between supplier capability and buyers' preferred-customer status on the one hand and supplier innovativeness and supplier pricing behaviour on the other hand. We will then explain our method of empirical analysis and discuss the results of our survey.

Hypothesis Development

Innovation by suppliers

Firms in many industries face increasing global competition and markets that demand more frequent innovation. As a result, during the 1990s, a fundamental change seems to have occurred in the way innovation is generated. According to the concept of innovation discussed by Håkansson and Eriksson (1993), ideas are developed in close exchanges with a series of network partners. In contrast to 'inventor-' or 'laboratory-innovation', this 'network-innovation' occurs when different actors from different organisations with distinct knowledge bases combine knowledge, information, skills and other resources to improve an existing product or to create a new one (Freeman and Soete, 1997; Steinle and Schiele, 2002; Servatius, 2004; Lazzarotti and Manzini, 2009). In pursuit of innovation, buyers often purchase key products from a single supplier or a handful of suppliers and enter into a partnering-style collaborative relation with them. This implies that innovation as a product of a joint buyer–seller process is often gained either through the integration of a supplier into a new product development process or in the context of a continuous improvement process. Research shows that suppliers increase buyers' product and project success by mobilising their capabilities to innovate and develop products when involved in the innovation process early on (Primo and Amundson, 2002). In a major benchmarking study, a particular commitment to innovation through purchasing was identified as a key feature that distinguishes successful firms from underperforming ones compared to their industry rivals (Goffre *et al.*, 2005). It follows that a firm's competitive position is significantly influenced by its ability to engage in a network approach to innovation.

According to Ragatz *et al.* (2002), suppliers complement internal capabilities in the achievement of high performance according to different indicators, such as reductions in concept-to-customer cycle time, costs and quality problems — and the improvement of overall design efforts. Hence, to select the right suppliers is essential. The expectations for an innovative supplier have been operationalised by highlighting the ability of the supplier to design new products or make changes to existing products and the level of technological capabilities that the supplier possesses and is willing to use. Without the required competencies for supporting processes of innovation, a supplier may not be able to play an actively contributing role. Along the same lines, Cabral and Traill (1999) identified suppliers' R&D activities and other technological activities as determinants of a supplier's innovativeness. Furthermore, a supplier's design capabilities and process and product expertise are important factors in the identification of innovative contributors (Croom, 1999; Ellram, 1990; Koppelmann, 2000). Another feature that determines the innovativeness of a supplier from the buyer's perspective is the willingness of the supplier to support collaborative processes in product development and process improvement — not in general but with a particular buyer (Krause *et al.*, 2001; Schiele, 2006). The effective integration of such suppliers into new product development teams provides an external source of ideas and solutions for the buying firm, which should facilitate problem-solving and enhance the innovation process, leading to the development of successful new processes and products (Chakrabarti and Hauschild, 1989; Smith and Reinertsen, 1991). If these suppliers are not sufficiently competent, integration efforts are doomed to fail. This line of reasoning leads to the following hypothesis:

Hypothesis 1. *Supplier technical capability positively influences supplier innovativeness.*

Pricing behaviour in industrial markets

The issue of pricing in industrial marketing has received little academic investigation (Hinterhuber, 2004). A description of the pricing behaviour of suppliers in industrial markets must take into account that pricing in business-to-business markets is a result of interaction. In industrial markets, price-setting is an enduring matching process that occurs between buyer and seller (Jain and Laric, 1979). Note that we specifically address the concept of 'pricing' as opposed to 'price' to emphasise the dynamic nature of prices as well as, for example, the additional charges often requested during transactions (Elmaghraby and Keskinocak, 2003). Because prices in these markets are set during the transaction, business relations are an important issue in price determination and consequently affect supplier pricing behaviour (Gadde *et al.*, 2002). In the existing literature on buyer–seller relation models, relations have been characterised as ranging from markets to hierarchies (Thorelli, 1986) or from price-centred, short-term arm's-length relations with limited interaction between buyer and supplier to partnering-style collaborative relations (Dwyer *et al.*, 1987). The latter type of relation is characterised as a long-term, interaction-intensive relation and has also been termed a quasi-hierarchy due to the high levels of interdependence between buyers and sellers (Dyer, 2000; Sako, 1992). From a buyer's perspective, those business relations are used to influence supplier pricing behaviour (Gadde and Håkansson, 2001; Gadde *et al.*, 2002). For instance, buyers deploy multiple arm's-length supplier relations as a mechanism for reducing costs. Because competition is created in this way, the extent to which sellers can reach an optimal price is constrained (Skouras *et al.*, 2005). If a supplier, however, exhibits exceptional capabilities and expertise, that supplier might act in a manner similar to that of an oligopolistic or even a monopolistic firm. A supplier's level of competitiveness may create a form of dependence for the buyer as the number of high-capability suppliers is limited. Hence, the pricing behaviour of suppliers with high levels of capability can be more assertive and dictating (Corsten and Felde, 2005). Therefore, we hypothesise the following:

Hypothesis 2. *Supplier capability negatively influences supplier benevolent pricing.*

When a high-skilled supplier is an important strategic resource, the buying firm will often enter into a partnership based on coordination rather than competition to access external sources of technology and innovation and thereby create a competitive edge (Clark, 1989; Hartley *et al.*, 1997b; Ragatz *et al.*, 1997; Handfield *et al.*, 1999; Wasti and Liker, 1997; Primo and Amundson, 2002; Tracey, 2004). Because strategic collaboration increases supplier specificity, potential competitors and alternative sources of supply are gradually eliminated (Laaksonen *et al.*, 2008). For instance, a supplier who has been entrusted with development tasks during innovation processes deepens its knowledge of the product or technology. The buyer and other competitors, on the other hand, run the risk of gradually losing their full understanding of the progress that the supplier has made in solving the problem at hand (Cohen and Levinthal, 1990). Thus, partial or quasi-vertical integration as a fertile ground for innovation fosters the buyer's dependence on the specific supplier, whereas the bargaining power in price negotiations is likely to decrease. Due to this unbalanced power situation, suppliers 'may easily shift cost towards the buyer and extract additional profits from the relationship' (Corsten and Felde, 2005, p. 450). In this context, Forker and Stannack (2000) found that 'competition' might be more effective than 'cooperation' in many buyer–supplier exchange relations. Observing strategic partnerships, researchers conclude that except in ideal cases, ' "win-win" outcomes in transactions are an illusion and ideal normative mutuality in business relationships can rarely be achieved' (Cox, 2004, p. 417). Following this view, buyers often believe that there is a trade-off between innovation-enhancing relations with suppliers on the one hand and their pricing behaviour on the other. Buying firms seem to be convinced that a supplier will abuse the relation and show an attitude of moral hazard, asking for exaggerated prices once innovation is jointly developed (Cousins and Crone, 2003). The assumption exists that innovation enables the supplier to charge premium prices (Koufteros *et al.*, 2002). Various authors support this view by stating that increasing power on the part of the supplier could lead to opportunistic behaviour and relation conflicts (Lonsdale, 2001; Heide and John, 1988; Kumar *et al.*, 1995). The following hypothesis can thus be posited:

Hypothesis 3. *Supplier innovativeness negatively influences supplier benevolent pricing.*

Preferred customer

Whereas supplier capability may be considered as an important technical antecedent to both supplier innovativeness and supplier benevolent pricing, it can be argued that behavioural antecedents play an important role as well. From the buyer's point of view, there is a trade-off between supplier innovativeness and supplier pricing due to power imbalances between sellers and buyers. Firms that search for external sources of technology to generate competitive advantage willingly establish close ties with strategic suppliers but simultaneously may have to pay for it (e.g. due to increasing prices). For buyers, one way of dealing with a high level of dependence in (and because of) innovation processes is to become attractive to such a supplier (Lusch and Brown, 1996). This would enable the buying firm to exploit supplier innovativeness and enjoy acceptable pricing behaviour at the same time. The idea is fairly straightforward: if the buyer is sufficiently interesting to the supplier, the latter will not abuse its position of power.

Some preliminary attempts to study customer attractiveness have already appeared in the literature. Christiansen and Maltz (2002), for example, conducted case studies of several small Danish firms that were trying to become 'interesting customers' to their large international suppliers. In a case study of new product development, Wynstra *et al.* (2003) concluded that the buyer should actively try to become interesting to the supplier. From a conceptual point of view, Koppelmann (2000) encourages 'procurement marketing', while Leenders and Blenkhorn (1988) mention the need to motivate a supplier to satisfy novel demands and label it 'reverse marketing'. Ellegaard *et al.* (2003), again drawing on a case study, highlight the particular importance of customer attractiveness in complex industrial buyer–supplier relations. Customer attractiveness for suppliers, however, may not be seen as a static condition but instead may change according to the maturity of the relation (Mortensen *et al.*, 2008), which is why 'industrial customers must be aware of the status of their supplier's satisfaction' (Essig and Amann, 2009, p. 104). The satisfaction of the supplier determines the quality of the buyer–seller relation and is directly linked to value creation. The assumption that supplier satisfaction benefits buyers and the entire supply chain through enhanced supplier performance was empirically tested by Benton and Maloni (2005), who stress the importance of a relationship-driven supply chain strategy. From a different perspective but concerning the same phenomenon, Helm *et al.* (2006) analysed suppliers' willingness to discontinue serving unattractive customers, which could be seen as the ultimate act of non-preferential customer treatment.

Adjusting the relational approach and becoming a 'preferred customer' for its key suppliers might create various advantages for the buying firm. 'A firm has preferred-customer status with a supplier, if the supplier offers the buyer preferential resource allocation' (Steinle and Schiele, 2008, p. 11). Once a particular customer offers more to a supplier than it does to the other customers, the perceived relation quality may increase. As a result, the supplier will be prepared and motivated to offer even more functions to the customer and commit itself fully to the relationship (Ellegaard *et al.*, 2003; Walter *et al.*, 2003). This is a major reason why reverse-marketing buyers need to enhance their level of customer attractiveness and obtain better services and support from their suppliers. According to Christiansen and Maltz (2002), being an interesting customer for suppliers guarantees the attention and loyalty of the latter. Additionally, it ensures the open exchange of knowledge and information, which in turn provides the basis for inter-organisational innovative capabilities. In other words, the supplier is more motivated to participate in and devote resources to product development and the improvement of manufacturing processes. The supplier might, for example, put its best employees at the preferred customer's disposal, adapt its capacity to its partner's wishes and give priority to its most attractive buyer when offering promising and innovative ideas. Thus, close collaboration and long-term partnerships with leading suppliers in an industry, with whom the buyer enjoys preferred-customer status, may represent a viable means of gaining access to their innovation resources in the context of new product development.

Hypothesis 4. *Preferred-customer status positively influences supplier innovativeness.*

Empirical results also indicate that strong buyer–seller ties not only influence innovation outcomes but also affect inventory reduction, quality improvement and cost efficiency (Milas, 2006). In fact, firms tend to place equal importance on quality, reliability, performance and supplier prices (Tracey and Tan, 2001). With regard to the latter, surveys may even underestimate the importance placed on supplier price: 'Although managers say that quality is the most important attribute for a supplier, they actually choose suppliers based largely on cost' (Verma and Pullman, 1998, p. 739). Therefore, buying firms tend to avoid poor relations with highly competitive suppliers, acting negatively *vis-à-vis* customers with regard to pricing behaviour. Preferred-customer status, however, might mitigate the negative impact that dependence imbalances have on suppliers' pricing behaviour. If one partner sees the other as an important strategic resource, it may adjust its interpretation of costs and revenues. By reconsidering the value of the relation, it may increase the significance of price decreases for both parties and other factors like trust and complementary resources (Laaksonen *et al.*, 2008). Research has already shown that there is a chance of offsetting the disadvantage of dependence on a supplier and the resulting less benevolent pricing behaviour if a relation based on trust and commitment is developed (Geyskens *et al.*, 1996). The reason is that trust and commitment, as the premises of a good relation between a customer and supplier and the drivers of supplier satisfaction, reduce the uncertainty of the latter's actions or other relational risks and serve as an additional safeguard against opportunism in power-driven relations (Corsten and Felde, 2005; Essig and Amann, 2009). In addition, the results of some authors, who claim that prices in long-lasting relations tend to remain constant over time (Blinder *et al.*, 1998; Chappell *et al.*, 1993; Hall *et al.*, 2000), support Hypothesis 5. The complete research model containing all hypothesised relations is provided in Fig. 1.

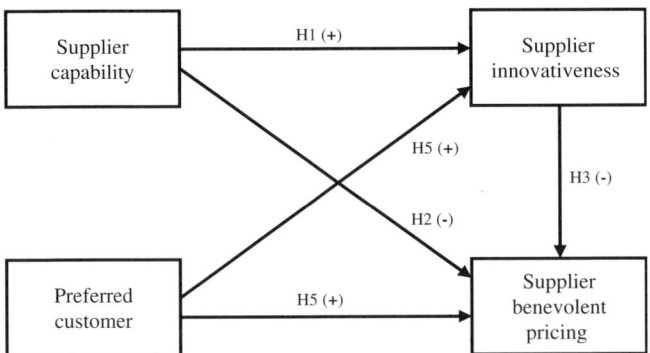

Fig. 1. Research Model.

Hypothesis 5. Preferred-customer status will lead to more supplier benevolent pricing.

Methodology

Data collection

We designed a quantitative study using a survey of purchasing managers in Germany and Austria.

Questionnaire development

The survey we administered consisted of two main parts. We first asked the respondents to assess and characterise selected suppliers. The respondents were then asked to indicate basic data on their firm and their position in the firm.

One common problem with surveys assessing relation issues in a buyer–supplier environment is the frequent incidence of non-normally distributed data. This causes problems in statistical analysis and makes it difficult to reveal any significant effect. For instance, asking firms to assess their most important customer or their largest supplier usually leads to biased scores. Firms that do not have (very) good relations with such important partners may find it difficult to persist in the market at all (so that they will not be included in any sample). To obtain the desired distribution when comparing two suppliers, we adopted the suggestion by Ulaga and Eggert (2006). The respondents were asked to assess a supplier with excellent performance in product and process innovation and a supplier who has exhibited disappointing innovativeness (i.e. a supplier who has failed to contribute according to expectations). The respondents were asked to write down the names of these two firms on a separate sheet of paper and then to answer the questionnaire for both suppliers. As a check of content validity, the instrument was pre-tested intensively with a sample of five academics knowledgeable in the field of buyer–supplier relations and with seven practitioners. The pre-test resulted in a few minor changes.

Sampling procedure

We collected data using a survey administered by the German and Austrian associations of materials management, purchasing and logistics — the BME and BMÖ, respectively. Members received an invitation to participate via email and via a newsletter that contained the link to a web page with the questionnaire. Because we did not have direct access to the two associations' databases, it was not possible to assess non-response bias. In addition to the associations' members, the contacts of a consulting firm were included in the survey. No significant differences between these groups of respondents could be identified, nor were there differences between early and late respondents. The web page containing the questionnaire was opened 440 times. We received 121 questionnaires (constituting a response rate of 27%) with data about 242 suppliers. However, we used casewise replacement so that only fully completed questionnaires were used for analysis. This resulted in a final sample of 166 cases for analysis (it can be demonstrated that the use of mean substitution does not qualitatively affect our results). The questionnaire was distributed in German.

Sample and respondent characteristics

Most respondents represent industries that are typically strongly developed in German-speaking countries: 26.8% were mechanical engineering and machine-building; 22.2% electrical and electronic engineering; 9.2% chemical, rubber and plastics; 10.5% vehicles and 31.3% other industries (including 7.8% services). No differences were observed between industries or between industry and services. Respondent firms were of notable size, averaging 4,697 employees (with a median of 930 employees) and a yearly turnover of 1.475 billion euros (with a median of 260 million). The sample can be considered high-tech; the average R&D expenditure was 8.1% of turnover. Concerning the respondent profile, we note that 47.8% of the respondents were purchasing managers, 35.5% were purchasers and 16.7% served other functions, including senior management.

Measurement development

For our survey, we employed proven measures from the literature as much as possible. To measure the preferred-customer concept, we adopted an instrument developed by Ganesan (1994), who measured a 'vendor's benevolence' in a retail channel study. As in Ganesan (1994) we used five items that, for example, refer to whether the supplier has made sacrifices in the past, cares for the buyer and dedicates its 'best resources' to the buyer. The items thus not only cover a certain emotion attached to the relation (e.g. 'caring' and 'being on the buyer's side') but also whether the supplier is willing to make an effort towards this relation (e.g. 'sacrificing' and 'letting the best resources work for the buyer'). The four supplier innovativeness measures were based on a study by Krause *et al.* (2001). The measures are formulated in such a way that they focus on collaborative innovation rather than innovation that is fully detached from the buyer–supplier relation. They emphasise, for example, willingness to use technological capability on behalf of the buyer, willingness to share important technological information and proactiveness with respect to approaching the buyer with innovations. As we explained above, we focussed our research on the (non-traditional) dynamic concept of pricing behaviour instead of the static concept of price. Solid scales for this concept could not be identified in the literature as there has not been much research into pricing in industrial markets (Hinterhuber, 2004). In fact, a review of almost one thousand papers from the business-to-business domain found less than 3% of them elaborating on pricing (LaPlaca, 1997). Therefore, we designed a supplier benevolent pricing construct, pre-tested it with academics and practitioners and finally employed it after minor corrections. The three items include a direct comparison with competitors, acceptability of prices and conditions, and fairness of pricing behaviour with respect to additional services such as spares or addenda.

The constructs preferred customer, supplier innovativeness and benevolent pricing were reflective in nature. Supplier capability, how-ever, was modelled as a formative construct composed of three items, which were inspired by Schiele (2006). R&D expenses were used as a way to capture suppliers' absorptive capacity. Previous studies revealed a significant influence of R&D intensity on supplier innovativeness (Cabral and Traill, 1999). Similarly, the availability of required quality certificates was included because the positive results of quality audits have been unveiled as antecedents of supplier innovativeness (Croom, 1999). As the third item of the construct 'supplier capability', the project management capabilities of the supplier were included (Petroni and Panciroli, 2002). All items on the questionnaire were based on a five-point Likert scale except for one of the supplier capa-bility items (size of R&D expenses). The complete list of items can be found in the appendix.

Results

Measurement model

We first assessed the reliability of the individual items by inspecting the standardised path loadings with their intended constructs (see Table 1). To assess the convergent validity of the reflective constructs (preferred customer, supplier innovativeness and benevolent pricing), we examined the Average Variance Extracted (AVE) and Composite Reliability (CR) indicators. As we show in Table 2, all values exceeded the recommended thresholds of 0.5 for AVE and 0.7 for CR

Table 1.   Descriptive Statistics and Reliability at the Item Level.

		Mean	S.D.	Standardised path loadings	S.D. of the path loading	t-statistic
Preferred customer	PC1	3.60	1.24	0.771	0.034	22.90
	PC2	3.90	1.13	0.915	0.011	83.13
	PC3	3.75	1.19	0.899	0.015	60.18
	PC4	3.60	1.11	0.907	0.011	85.64
	PC5	3.44	1.13	0.878	0.015	56.88
Supplier capability	SC1	3.75	1.41	—	—	—
	SC2	3.35	1.25	—	—	—
	SC3	6.99	8.16	—	—	—
Supplier innovativeness	IS1	3.59	1.21	0.888	0.017	53.45
	IS2	3.41	1.23	0.833	0.021	40.55
	IS3	3.66	1.30	0.914	0.011	84.25
	IS4	2.85	1.42	0.885	0.011	77.99
Supplier benevolent pricing	PR1	3.18	1.20	0.571	0.105	5.42
	PR2	3.45	1.00	0.869	0.028	31.41
	PR3	3.72	1.25	0.766	0.051	15.14

Note: Path-loading information cannot be given for the supplier capability construct due to its formative nature. All other constructs are reflective.

(Nunnally, 1978; Fornell and Larcker, 1981; Bagozzi and Yi, 1988; Henseler *et al.*, 2009). In addition we report Cronbach's alpha values in Table 2.

We assessed discriminant validity by testing the Fornell and Larcker criterion (Fornell and Larcker, 1981). For this purpose, we conducted a principal component analysis (with varimax rotation), which we omit for brevity. The items all score higher on their intended constructs than on the other constructs. Furthermore, the smallest AVE exceeds the squared correlation between each pair of factors. This indicates a satisfactory level of discriminant validity.

Table 2. Convergent Validity, Reliability Assessment and Correlations.[a]

	AVE[b]	CR[b]	1. Preferred customer	2. Supplier innovativeness	3. Supplier benevolent pricing	4. Supplier capability
1. Preferred customer	0.767	0.942	*0.923*			
2. Supplier innovativeness	0.775	0.932	0.727	*0.903*		
3. Supplier benevolent pricing	0.556	0.785	0.484	0.344	*0.636*	
4. Supplier capability	—	—	0.503	0.640	0.178	—

[a] On the diagonal, Cronbach's α values are provided (in italics) except for the formative construct (supplier capability). Off-diagonal values are the Pearson correlations. All correlations are significant ($p \leq 0.01$).
[b] AVE = average variance extracted; CR = composite reliability.

Structural model

To test the hypotheses, partial least squares (PLS) structural equation modelling was used (Fornell and Cha, 1994). Specifically, we used SmartPLS software (Ringle *et al.*, 2005), which is a well-known software package for the simultaneous testing of both reflective and formative scales. PLS also allows the researchers to relax the stringent distributional assumptions generally imposed on other (co-variance-based) structural equation modelling approaches. The preferred-customer variable was right-skewed and slightly kurtotic despite the respondents' assessment of both 'good' and 'bad' suppliers. As a result, a co-variance-based approach could only be applied using the ADF algorithm. However, this algorithm produces very misleading results except for very large sample sizes. With our model, about 950 datasets would have been recommended (Hoogland and Boomsma, 1998; Boomsma and Hoogland, 2001).

We employed a bootstrapping procedure with replacement using 1,000 rounds. The standardised path coefficients associated with the structural model are given in Fig. 2. Predictive validity within the model is fairly high; 62.9% of the variance in supplier innovativeness is explained by supplier capability and preferred-customer status,

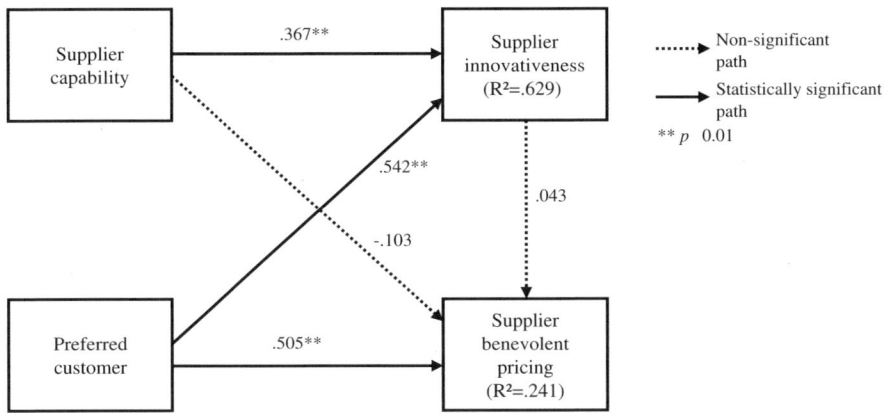

Fig. 2. PLS Results of the Structural Model.

and 24.1% of the variance in supplier benevolent pricing is explained by supplier capability, supplier innovativeness and preferred-customer status. All estimates have high statistical power exceeding 0.9.

Hypothesis 1 states that supplier capability positively influences supplier innovativeness. This hypothesis is strongly supported: the path is positive and significant ($\beta = .367$, $p \leq 0.01$). In Hypothesis 2, we stated that supplier capability negatively influences supplier benevolent pricing. Although the effect was negative, it was not statistically significant ($\beta = -.103$, $p > 0.1$). In addition, no empirical support could be found for Hypothesis 3: supplier innovativeness did not negatively influence supplier benevolent pricing ($\beta = .043$, $p > 0.1$). In Hypotheses 4 and 5, we propose that preferred-customer status has a positive influence on both supplier innovativeness and supplier benevolent pricing. Both paths were found to be positive and significant ($\beta = .542$ and $.505$, respectively, $p \leq 0.01$). Hence, Hypotheses 4 and 5 are supported. See Table 3 and Fig. 2 for a summary of our results.

Recently, a call has been made for a more 'customer-centric science', which in particular would include reports not only of significance, but also on effect size (Aguinis *et al.*, 2010). Following this request, we assessed effect size using Cohen's effect-size test

Table 3. Impact of the Antecedents of Supplier Innovativeness and Supplier Benevolent Pricing.

Hypothesised path	Path coefficient (*t*-value)	Total effect (*t*-value)
Supplier innovativeness → Supplier benevolent pricing	.043 (.69)	.043 (.44)
Preferred customer → Supplier benevolent pricing	.505 (6.47)**	.528 (8.82)**
Preferred customer → Supplier innovativeness	.542 (10.68)**	.542 (10.68)**
Supplier capability → Supplier benevolent pricing	−.103 (1.39)	−.087 (1.07)
Supplier capability → Supplier innovativeness	.367 (6.82)**	.367 (6.82)**

**p < 0.01 (one-sided).

(Cohen, 1992). We eliminated one hypothesised path at a time and calculated f^2 using

$$f^2 = \frac{R^2_{incl} - R^2_{excl}}{1 - R^2_{incl}}$$

where the subscript 'incl' ('excl') on R^2 indicates if the hypothesised path was included (excluded). The (statistically significant) path of supplier capability → supplier innovativeness has an f^2 of 0.27, which indicates a medium effect size (Cohen, 1992). The (statistically significant) path of preferred-customer status → supplier innovativeness has an f^2 of 0.58, which indicates a very high effect size. The path of preferred-customer status → supplier benevolent pricing behaviour has a medium effect size (f^2 of 0.15).

Discussion and Conclusion

In the current study, we hypothesised that the innovation capability of a supplier and the degree to which a buyer is seen as a preferred customer influence supplier innovativeness and benevolent pricing behaviour. We furthermore expected that supplier capability and innovativeness would have a negative influence on supplier benevolent pricing. Our study provides mixed results with respect to these hypotheses. We find that the positive effect of supplier capability on supplier innovativeness is statistically significant (Hypothesis 1), indicating a medium effect size in terms of Cohen's f^2. This finding supports the large body of literature that assumes that suppliers' innovative capabilities positively contribute to their innovativeness — more generally for the supplier itself as well as in particular buyer–supplier relations (e.g. Cabral and Traill, 1999; Krause *et al.*, 2001; Ragatz *et al.*, 2002).

However, we could not find any evidence of the assumed negative relationship between supplier capability and supplier benevolent pricing (Hypothesis 2). A possible explanation would involve a situation of lock-in, i.e. when the buyer has only one single source for a component and is fully dependent on this supplier. Drawing from social exchange theory, Narasimhan *et al.* (2009) conjecture that in a lock-in situation the optimal pricing strategy for the supplier is one in which it does not take opportunistic advantage of its buyer. The supportive argument is that the return for the supplier is higher in the long term, as a non-opportunistic pricing strategy means that the buyer will not develop an alternative component in-house or support a rival supplier in acquiring the required capabilities.

Also, we could not find any evidence of the hypothesised negative relationship between supplier innovativeness and benevolent pricing behaviour (Hypothesis 3). We based our hypothesis on the proposition that an innovative supplier might expose itself to moral hazard and opportunistic behaviour with less benevolent pricing as a potential outcome. However, considering our finding with respect to Hypothesis 2 (i.e. supplier capability does not appear to negatively influence benevolent pricing), the absence of any significant relation between supplier innovativeness and benevolent pricing is less surprising: in our sample, capable suppliers did not necessarily exhibit less benevolent pricing behaviour, even if they are shown to be more innovative than their competitors. One explanation for the absence of (post-innovation) price adjustments and overcharging by suppliers could be that the cost of price adjustments in industrial markets is generally high, also for the seller who needs to engage in intensive negotiations and preparation (Zbaracki et al., 2004). Another aspect is the observation that in business-to-business markets that involve innovative products, suppliers develop a multi-period perspective. In a study conducted at a Siemens company, Schumacher et al. (2008) found that suppliers were even willing to reduce prices on existing materials in order to become involved in new product development activities for future generation products.

In addition to the examination of the effects of the technical antecedent supplier capability we also examined the behavioural antecedent preferred-customer status. The role of preferred-customer status often appears to be neglected or at least underestimated in current innovation, operations management and marketing literature. In contrast, our study found preferential customer treatment to be important: preferred-customer status has a positive influence on supplier innovativeness, with a very high effect size (Hypothesis 4). Furthermore, being a customer of choice positively influences benevolent pricing behaviour (Hypothesis 5), exhibiting a medium effect size. Suppliers have to make choices with whom to partner and they apparently tend to choose their preferred customers. The failure to consider preferred-customer status with suppliers may provide a new explanation for the often observed phenomenon of supplier obstructionism in collaborative development (Hartley et al., 1997a; Flynn et al., 2000; Primo et al., 2002; Wognum et al., 2002; Petroni and Panciroli, 2002; Rutten, 2003; Zsidisin and Smith, 2005). This finding is in line with Christiansen and Maltz (2002) and Walter et al. (2001), who also consider what the buyer can offer to the supplier. They conclude that since close buyer–supplier relations can benefit knowledge transfer and product innovation the buyer should therefore become interesting for the supplier.

There are several important conclusions to be drawn from our results, which show that the antecedents of supplier innovativeness are not purely technical in nature (i.e. supplier capability) but also depend on behavioural factors (i.e. preferred-customer status).

Moreover, when we compare effect sizes, with our sample the behavioural antecedents were more contributory than the technical antecedents in explaining the variance in supplier contribution to innovation. The prevalence of behavioural over technical factors also supports the increasing academic interest in 'behavioural operations management' (e.g. Bendoly *et al.*, 2006; Gino and Pisano, 2008; Loch and Wu, 2007). Behavioural operations management's main claim is that buyers and suppliers tend to make decisions that go beyond the classical viewpoint of economics, namely that actors are fully rational or can be induced to behave rationally. Instead, human behaviour and cognition and their influence on decision-making have to be taken into account. In our study, rather than emphasising the importance of innovation capabilities *per se*, for instance, as expressed by research budgets, we also see that the behavioural factor 'preferred-customer status' is a highly important determinant, alerting us to the need to extend our research beyond technical matters. While research on customer attractiveness is in its early stages and it would be merely speculative to make any judgement on the importance of rational as opposed to non-rational explanations for the phenomenon, behavioural management aspects clearly deserve a more thorough analysis in future research. Also the relevance of corporate culture in collaborative new product development has recently been stressed (Zunk and Marchner, 2009; Schiele, 2010).

This paper's contribution to the existing literature can thus be summarised as follows:

1. Whereas most studies in innovation management and beyond focus on the more technical antecedents of supplier innovativeness, we are, to the best of our knowledge, the first to identify the positive effect of the behavioural antecedent 'preferred-customer status'.
2. This study is also unique in the way it tests the innovativeness–pricing relation. Because we did not identify any significant link between the two variables, this should encourage firms to engage in upstream open innovation. This finding may remove a large practical obstacle to buyer–supplier collaboration in innovation.

We can also identify several managerial implications. Having established that there appear to be few reasons to prevent buyer–supplier collaboration for innovation due to pricing problems, it is worth exploring the importance of being a preferred customer when innovating with suppliers. First, firms would profit from assessing their portfolio of suppliers and identifying their status with the key suppliers. Since our data stresses that the behavioural component has a larger effect than the technical competence of a supplier, it could be concluded that the 'best' supplier is not always the best partner for every firm. Rather than trying to collaborate with world-leading suppliers, if there is no chance of ever becoming a preferred customer of such a firm, it may be more advisable to team up with a slightly less competent supplier, provided it honours the buyer with the privileges of preferential customer treatment. Carrying this line of thought forward, the ultimate managerial consequence would be to phase out those suppliers where the buying firm sees no chance of achieving preferential treatment and closely integrating the remaining strategic suppliers.

The preferred-customer phenomenon also has a strategic implication: in oligopolistic supply markets where a limited number of key suppliers is responsible for most innovation, being the first buyer to actively pursue a preferred-customer policy may contribute to achieving a sustainable competitive advantage. A pioneering firm would reorganise its portfolio of partners and establish a strong network with partners that award it with preferred-customer status. A competing firm recognising the importance of customer attractiveness too late may discover that in the meantime all key suppliers in the industry have already selected their preferred customers and established close ties to the firm's competitors. In an open innovation environment a strategy of innovation leadership may by then be no longer possible.

Future Research and Limitations

Our results shed new light on the open-innovation debate and particularly on the role and behaviour of suppliers. Our conclusions hint at several avenues for future research. We have yet to fully grasp the factors that influence preferred-customer status. Up to now, we have treated preferred-customer status as a stand-alone factor without discussing its determinants, i.e. the cardinal question of how to become a preferred customer. An interesting research direction would be to address these determinants and the various circumstances under which the determinant preferred-customer status can vary. To extend our understanding of how to become a preferred customer, knowledge not only from management theory, but also from diverse fields such as marketing and psychology could be integrated. Particular challenges arise for firms that are *a priori* unattractive due to their small size or which are located in peripheral areas outside the main industry clusters (Steinle and Schiele, 2008). Other fruitful research paths elaborating on the preferred-customer phenomenon relate to its implications for operations, supplier development and innovation. For instance, it could be rewarding to distinguish between buying innovation and co-developing innovative solutions and to distinguish between product and process innovation. Assuming that process innovation is more socially embedded and that industries characterised by process innovation are more supplier-driven (Pavitt, 1984), the importance of being a preferred customer in such a setting could be strong.

Investigating the buyer–supplier dyad (and the potential differences between them) would be necessary to further advance our understanding of supply chain innovation. Hald *et al.* (2009), for example, argue that mutual attraction is important in developing relations. It would be interesting to see whether mutual attraction is also a necessary condition for collaborative product and process innovation, and under which circumstances (if any) asymmetries remain beneficial.

Finally, another interesting research direction would be a more in-depth study of the role of pricing in innovation contexts. Traditionally, operations management researchers place pricing in supply chain management higher on the research agenda (e.g., see Dong *et al.*, 2009). The role of pricing in innovation management research, however, appears to be somewhat marginal. For example, researchers could examine the role of time in the pricing-innovation relation, using questions such as: 'Does innovation follow pricing or does pricing follow innovation?'

Our results are subject to several limitations. First of all, our respondents are all purchasing managers from buying firms. Whereas this approach might provide more objective responses to questions that assess suppliers (i.e. supplier capability and supplier innovativeness), the degree to which these buyers are actual preferred customers might be somewhat debatable because the buyers' and suppliers' perceptions of this status are not necessarily aligned. Second (and along these lines), it is unclear whether or not a supplier actually changes its behaviour towards its customer because of the customer's status in this regard. The barriers with which a supplier is confronted before and during a transaction, for example, might limit its degree of freedom to establish strong ties during the innovation process. Third, our research involves an indirect measurement of R&D performance (i.e. we focussed on the buyer's assessment of supplier innovativeness). It is important to extend this research by measuring actual (compared to perceptual) performance indicators.

References

Aguinis, H., Werner, S., Abbott, J., Angert, C., Park, J. and Kohlhausen, D. (2010). Customer-centric science: Reporting significant research results with rigor, relevance, and practical impact in mind, *Organizational Research Methods*, forthcoming.

Bagozzi, R. and Yi, Y. (1988). On the evaluation of structural equation models, *Journal of the Academy of Marketing Sciences*, **16**(1), 74–94.

Bendoly, E., Donohue, K. and Schultz, K.L. (2006). Behavior in operations management: Assessing recent findings and revisiting old assumptions, *Journal of Operations Management*, **24**(6), 737–752.

Benton, W.C. and Maloni, M. (2005). The influence of power driven buyer/ seller relationships on supply chain satisfaction, *Journal of Operations Management*, **23**, 1–22.

Blinder, A.S., Canetti, E.R.D., Lebow, D.E. and Rudd, J.B. (1998). *Asking about Prices: A New Approach to Understanding Price Stickiness*, Russell Sage Foundation, New York.

Boomsma, A. and Hoogland, J.J. (2001). "The robustness of Lisrel modeling revisited," in Cudeck, R., du_Toit, S., Sörbom, D. (eds), *Structural Equation Modeling: Present and Future. A Festschrift in Honour of Karl Jöreskog*, Scientific Software International, Chicago, pp. 139–168.

Cabral, J.E.O. and Traill, W.B. (1999). Determinants of a firm's likelihood to innovate and intensity of innovation in the Brazilian food industry, *Journal on Chain and Network Science*, 1(1), 33–48.

Chakrabarti, A.K. and Hauschild, J. (1989). The division of labour in innovation management, *R&D Management*, 19, 161–171.

Chappell, W.F., Mayer, W.J. and Shughart, W.F. (1993). Firm heterogeneity and production flexibility: Evidence from price-cost margins of large and small firms, *Bulletin of Economic Research*, 45(3), 229–244.

Chesbrough, H.W. (2003). The era of open innovation, *Sloan Management Review*, 44(3), 35–41.

Chin, W. (1998). "The partial least squares modeling approach to structural equation modeling," in Marcoulides, G. (ed.), *Modern Methods for Business Research*, Lawrence Erlbaum Associates, Mahwah, NJ, pp. 295–336.

Christiansen, P.E. and Maltz, A. (2002). Becoming an "interesting" customer: Procurement strategies for buyers without leverage, *International Journal of Logistics: Research and Applications*, 5(2), 177–195.

Clark, K.B. (1989). Project scope and project performance: The effects of parts strategy and supplier involvement on product development, *Management Science*, 35(10), 1247–1263.

Cohen, J.W. (1992). A power primer, *Psychological Bulletin*, 112(1), 155–159.

Cohen, W.M. and Levinthal, D.A. (1990). Absorptive capacity: A new perspective on learning and innovation, *Administrative Science Quarterly*, 35(1), 128–152.

Cool, K. and Henderson, J. (1998). Power and firm profitability in supply chains: French manufacturing industry in 1993, *Strategic Management Journal*, 19, 909–926.

Corsten, D. and Felde, J. (2005). Exploring the performance effects of key-supplier collaboration. An empirical investigation in Swiss buyer–supplier relationships, *International Journal of Physical Distribution and Logistics Management*, 35(6), 217–234.

Cousins, P.D. and Crone, M.J. (2003). Strategic models for the development of obligation based inter-firm relationships, *International Journal of Operations and Production Management*, **23**(12), 1447–1474.

Cox, A. (2004). Business relationship alignment: On the commensurability of value capture and mutuality in buyer and supplier exchange, *Supply Chain Management: An International Journal*, **9**(5), 410–420.

Croom, S. (1999). The dyadic capabilities concept: Examining the processes of key supplier involvement in collaborative product development, *European Journal of Purchasing and Supply Management*, **7**(1), 29–37.

Dong, L., Narasimhan, C. and Zhu, K. (2009). Product line pricing in a supply chain, *Management Science*, **55**(10), 1704–1717.

Dwyer, F.R., Schurr, P.H. and Oh, S. (1987). Developing buyer–supplier relationships, *Journal of Marketing*, **51**(2), 11–27.

Dyer, J.H. (2000). *Collaborative Advantage: Winning Through Extended Enterprise Supplier Networks*, Oxford University Press, Oxford, UK.

Edquist, C. (1997). "Systems of innovation approaches — Their emergence and characteristics," in Edquist, C. (ed.), *Systems of Innovation. Technologies, institutions and Organizations*, Pinter, London, Washington, pp. 1–35.

Ellegaard, C., Johansen, J. and Drejer, A. (2003). Managing industrial buyer–supplier relations — The case for attractiveness, *Integrated Manufacturing Systems*, **14**(4), 346–356.

Ellram, L.M. (1990). The supplier selection decision in strategic partnerships, *Journal of Purchasing and Materials Management*, **20**(4), 8–14.

Elmaghraby, W. and Keskinocak, P. (2003). Dynamic pricing in the presence of inventory considerations: Research overview, current practices, and future directions, *Management Science*, **49**(10), 1287–1309.

Essig, M. and Amann, M. (2009). Supplier satisfaction: Conceptual basics and explorative findings, *Journal of Purchasing and Supply Management*, **15**, 103–113.

Flynn, B.B., Flynn, E.J., Amundson, S.D. and Schroeder, R.G. (2000). Team characteristics as enablers of fast product development speed, *Advances in Interdisciplinary Studies of Work Teams*, **5**, 133–169.

Forker, L.B. and Stannack, P. (2000). Cooperation versus competition: Do buyers and suppliers really see eye-to-eye? *European Journal of Purchasing and Supply Management*, **6**, 31–40

Fornell, C. and Cha, J. (1994). "Partial least squares," in Bagozzi, R.P. (ed.), *Advanced Methods of Marketing Research*, Blackwell, Cambridge, MA, pp. 52–78.

Fornell, C. and Larcker, D.F. (1981). Structural equation models with unobservable variables and measurement error: Algebra and statistics, *Journal of Marketing Research*, **18**(3), 382–388.

Freeman, C. and Soete, L. (1997). *The Economics of Industrial Innovation*, 3rd edn., Continuum, London, Washington.

Gadde, L.E. and Håkansson, H. (2001). *Supply Network Strategies*, Wiley, Chichester.

Gadde, L.E., Harrison, D. and Håkansson, H. (2002). Price in a relational context, *Journal of Customer Behaviour*, **1**(3), 317–334.

Ganesan, S. (1994). Determinants of long-term orientation in buyer–seller relationships, *Journal of Marketing*, **58**(2), 1–19.

Gerwin, D. and Ferris, J.S. (2004). Organizing new product development projects in strategic alliances, *Organization Science*, **15**(1), 22–37.

Geyskens, I., Steenkamp, J.B.E.M., Scheer, L.K. and Kumar, N. (1996). The effects of trust and interdependence on relationship commitment: A trans-Atlantic study, *International Journal of Research in Marketing*, **13**(4), S. 303–317.

Gino, F. and Pisano, G. (2008). Toward a theory of behavioral operations, *Manufacturing & Service Operations Management*, **10**(4), 676–691.

Goffre, J., Plaizier, W. and Schade, J. (2005). Scaling new heights. What separates the leaders from the followers in procurement today? A major benchmarking study offers some answers, *CPO Agenda*, **1**(1), 54–58.

Hagedoorn, J. (2002). Inter-firm R&D partnerships: An overview of major trends and patterns since 1960, *Research Policy*, **31**, 477–492.

Håkansson, H. and Eriksson, A. (1993). Getting innovations out of supplier networks, *Journal of Business-to-Business Marketing*, **1**(3), 3–34.

Hald, K.S., Cordón, C., Vollmann, T.E. (2009). Towards an understanding of attraction in buyer–supplier relationships, *Industrial Marketing Management*, **38**, 960–970.

Hall, S., Walsh, M. and Yates, A. (2000). Are UK companies' prices sticky? *Oxford Economic Papers*, **52**, 425–446.

Handfield, R.B., Ragatz, G.L., Petersen, K.J. and Monczka, R.M. (1999). Involving suppliers in new product development, *California Management Review*, **42**(1), 59–82.

Hartley, J.L., Zirger, B.J. and Kamath, R.R. (1997a) Managing the buyer–supplier interface for on-time performance in product development, *Journal of Operations Management*, **15**, 57–70.

Hartley, J.L., Meredith, J.R., McCutcheon, D. and Kamath, R.R. (1997b). Suppliers' contributions to product development: An exploratory study, *IEEE Transactions on Engineering Management*, **44**(3), 258–267.

Heide, J.B. and John, G. (1988). The role of dependence balancing in safeguarding transaction-specific assets in conventional channels, *Journal of Marketing*, **52**(1), 20–35.

Helm, S., Rolfes, L. and Günter, B. (2006). Suppliers' willingness to end unprofitable customer relationships: An exploratory investigation in the German mechanical engineering sector, *European Journal of Marketing*, **40**(3/4), 366–383.

Henseler, J., Ringle, C.M. and Sikovics, R. (2009). The use of partial least square path modeling in international marketing, *Advances in International Marketing*, **20**, 277–319.

Hinterhuber, A. (2004). Towards value-based pricing — An integrative framework for decision making, *Industrial Marketing Management*, **33**, 765–778.

Hoogland, J.J. and Boomsma, A. (1998). Robustness studies in covariance structure modeling: An overview and a meta-analysis, *Sociological Methods & Research*, **26**(3), 329–367.

Jain, S.C. and Laric, M.V. (1979). A framework for strategic industrial pricing, *Industrial Marketing Management*, **8**(1), 75–80.

Johnsen, T.E. (2009). Supplier involvement in new product development and innovation: Taking stock and looking to the future, *Journal of Purchasing and Supply Management*, **15**, 187–197.

Koppelmann, U. (2000). *Beschaffungsmarketing* [Supply Marketing], 3rd edn., Springer, Berlin.

Koufteros, X.A., Vonderembse, M.A. and Doll, W.J. (2002). Integrated product development practices and competitive capabilities: The effects of uncertainty, equivocality, and platform strategy, *Journal of Operations Management*, **20**(4), 331–355.

Krause, D.R., Pagell, M. and Curkovic, S. (2001). Toward a measure of competitive priorities for purchasing, *Journal of Operations Management*, **19**, 497–512.

Kumar, N., Scheer, L.K. and Steenkamp, J.E.M. (1995). The effect of perceived interdependence on dealer attitudes, *Journal of Marketing Research*, **32**(3), 348–356.

Laaksonen, T., Pajunen, K. and Kulmala, H.I. (2008). Co-evolution of trust and dependence in customer–supplier relationships, *Industrial Marketing Management*, **37**, 910–920.

LaPlaca, P.J. (1997). Contributions to marketing theory and practice from Industrial Marketing Management, *Journal of Business Research*, **38**(3), 179–198.

Lazzarotti, V., and Manzini, R. (2009). Different modes of open innovation: A theoretical framework and empirical study, *International Journal of Innovation Management*, **13**(4), 615–636

Leenders, M.R. and Blenkhorn, D.L. (1988). *Reverse Marketing: The New Buyer–Supplier Relationship*, Free Press, New York.

Loch, C.H. and Wu, Y. (2007). Behavioral operations management, *Foundations and Trends in Technology, Information and Operations Management*, **1**(3), 121–232.

Lonsdale, C. (2001). Locked-in to supplier dominance: On the dangers of asset specificity for the outsourcing decision, *The Journal of Supply Chain Management*, **37**(2), 22–27.

Lusch, R.F. and Brown, J.R. (1996). Interdependency, contracting, and relational behavior in marketing channels, *Journal of Marketing*, **60**(4), 19–38.

Milas, M.J. (2006). *The Economic Value of Supplier Working Relations with Automotive Original Equipment Manufacturers*, Eastern Michigan University, Department of Economics, Ypsilanti.

Mortensen, M.H., Freytag, P.V. and Arlbjørn, J.S. (2008). Attractiveness in supply chains: A process and matureness perspective, *International Journal of Physical Distribution and Logistics Management*, **38**(10), 799–815.

Narasimhan, R., Nair, A., Griffith, D.A., Arlbjørn, J.S. and Bendoly, E. (2009). Lock-in situations in supply chains: A social exchange theoretic study of sourcing arrangements in buyer–supplier relationships, *Journal of Operations Management*, **27**, 374–389.

Nunnally, J.C. (1978). *Psychometric Theory*, 2nd edn., McGraw-Hill, New York.

Pavitt, K. (1984). Sectoral patterns of technical change: Towards a taxonomy and a theory, *Research Policy*, **13**, 343–373.

Petroni, A. and Panciroli, B. (2002). Innovation as a determinant of suppliers' roles and performances: An empirical study in the food machinery industry, *European Journal of Purchasing and Supply Management*, **8**, 135–149.

Pfeffer, J. and Salancik, G.R. (1978). *The External Control of Organizations*, Harper & Row, New York.

Poot, T., Faems, D. and Vanhaverbeke, W. (2009). Toward a dynamic perspective on open innovation: A longitudinal assessment of the adoption of internal and external innovation strategies in The Netherlands, *International Journal of Innovation Management*, **13**(2), 177–200.

Primo, M.A.M. and Amundson, S.D. (2002). An exploratory study of the effects of supplier relationships on new product development outcomes, *Journal of Operations Management*, **20**(1), 33–52.

Provan, K.G. and Skinner, S.J. (1989). Interorganizational dependence and control as predictors of opportunism in dealer–supplier relations, *Academy of Management Journal*, **32**(1), 202–212.

Ragatz, G.L., Handfield, R.B. and Scannell, T.V. (1997). Success factors for integrating suppliers into new product development, *Journal of Product Innovation Management*, **14**(3), 190–202.

Ragatz, G.L., Handfield, R.B. and Petersen, K.J. (2002). Benefits associated with supplier integration into new product development under conditions of technology uncertainty, *Journal of Business Research*, **55**, 389–400.

Ringle, C.M., Wende, S. and Will, A. (2005). SmartPLS 2.0 M3. Available at http://www.smartpls.de.

Ringle, C.M., Sarstedt, M. and Mooi, E.A. (2009). Response-based segmentation using finite mixture partial least squares, *Annals of Information Systems*, **8**, 19–49.

Roberts, E.B. (2001). Benchmarking global strategic management of technology. Survey of the world's largest R&D performers reveals, among other trends, a greater reliance upon external sources of technology, *Research-Technology Management*, **44**(2), 25–36.

Rutten, R. (2003). *Knowledge and Innovation in Regional Industry: An Entrepreneurial Coalition*, Taylor & Francis Ltd, London.

Sako, M. (1992). *Prices, Quality and Trust. Inter-firm Relations in Britain and Japan*, Cambridge University Press, Cambridge, UK.

Schiele, H. (2006). How to distinguish innovative suppliers? Identifying innovative suppliers as new task for purchasing, *Industrial Marketing Management*, **35**, 925–935.

Schiele, H. (2010). Early supplier integration: The dual role of purchasing in new product development. *R&D Management*, **40**(2), 138–153.

Servatius, H. (2004). Next practice des innovationsmanagements [Next practice in the management of innovation], *Information Management & Consulting*, **19** (October), 53–60.

Skouras, T., Avlonitis, G.J. and Indounas, K.A. (2005). Economics and marketing on pricing: How and why do they differ? *Journal of Product & Brand Management*, **14**(6), 362–374.

Smith, P.G. and Reinertsen, D.G. (1991). *Developing Products in Half the Time*, Van Nostrand, New York.

Steinle, C. and Schiele, H (2002). When do industries cluster? *Research Policy*, **31**, 849–858.

Steinle, C. and Schiele, H. (2008). Limits to global sourcing? Strategic consequences of dependency on international suppliers. Cluster theory, resource-based view and case studies, *Journal of Purchasing and Supply Management*, **14**(1), 3–14.

Thorelli, H.B. (1986). Networks: Between markets and hierarchies, *Strategic Management Journal*, 7(1), 37–51.

Tracey, M. (2004). A holistic approach to new product development: New insights, *The Journal of Supply Chain Management*, **40**(4), 37–55.

Tracey, M. and Tan, C.L. (2001). Empirical analysis of supplier selection and involvement, customer satisfaction, and firm performance, *Supply Chain Management: An International Journal*, **6**(4), 174–188.

Trott, P. and Hartmann, D. (2009). Why 'open innovation' is old wine in new bottles, *International Journal of Innovation Management*, **13**(4), 715–736.

Ulaga, W. and Eggert, A. (2006). Value-based differentiation in business relationships: Gaining and sustaining key supplier status, *Journal of Marketing*, **70**(1), 119–136.

Verma, R. and Pullman, M.E. (1998). An analysis of supplier selection process, *Omega*, **26**(6), 739–750.

Von Hippel, E. (1988). *The Sources of Innovation*, Oxford University Press, New York.

Wagner, S.M. (2009). Getting innovation from suppliers, *Research-Technology Management*, **52**(1), 8–9.

Walter A., Ritter, T. and Gemünden, H.G. (2001). Value creation in buyer–seller relationships, *Industrial Marketing Management*, **30**, 365–377.

Walter, A., Müller, T.A., Helfert, G. and Ritter, T. (2003). Functions of industrial relationships and their impact on relationship quality, *Industrial Marketing Management*, **32**, 159–169.

Wasti, S.N. and Liker, J.K. (1997). Risky business or competitive power? Supplier involvement in Japanese product design, *Journal of Product Innovation Management*, **14**, 337–355.

Wognum, P., Fisscher, O.A., and Weenink, S.A. (2002). Balanced relationships: Management of client–supplier relationships in product development, *Technovation*, **22**, 341–351.

Wynstra, F., Weggeman, M. and van Weele, A. (2003). Exploring purchasing integration in product development, *Industrial Marketing Management*, **32**(1), 69–83.

Zbaracki, M.J., Ritson, M., Levy, D., Dutta, S. and Bergen, M. (2004). Managerial and customer costs of price adjustment: Direct evidence from industrial markets, *Review of Economics and Statistics*, **86**(2), 514–533.

Zsidisin, G.A. and Smith, M.E. (2005). Managing supply risk with early supplier involvement: A case study and research propositions, *The Journal of Supply Chain Management*, **41**, 44–57.

Zunk, B.M. and Marchner, A. (2009). Verbesserung der Kooperation zwischen Beschaffung und Produktentwicklung: Beziehungsmanagementmaßnahmen in Technologieunternehmen [Measures of relationship management for improving the cooperation between procurement and product development in technology companies], *Zeitschrift für wirtschaftlichen Fabrikbetrieb*, **104**(12), 1087–1092.

Appendix: Measures

Table 4. Survey Questions

Supplier innovativeness (IS)	The level of technological capability the supplier possesses and is willing to use for our products is high	IS1
	The supplier is willing to share key technological information	IS2
	This supplier is capable of supporting collaborative processes in product development and process improvement	IS3
	This supplier is frequently proactive in approaching us with innovations	IS4
Supplier capability (SC)	The supplier obtained relevant quality certificates (e.g. ISO TS 16949 in the automotive industry)	SC1
	This supplier has well-developed project management capabilities	SC2
	Please indicate the magnitude of this supplier's R&D expenditure in relation to annual sales	SC3
Preferred customer (PC)	This supplier has made sacrifices for us in the past	PC1
	This supplier cares for us	PC2
	When there are shortages, this supplier has gone out on a limb for us	PC3
	We feel this supplier is on our side	PC4
	The best resources of this supplier work for us	PC5
Supplier benevolent pricing (PR)	This supplier is very expensive compared to direct competitors *(reverse coded)*	PR1
	With this supplier we always get acceptable prices and conditions	PR2
	This supplier has exhibited unfair pricing behaviour (e.g. with spares or addenda) *(reverse coded)*	PR3

Chapter 6

The Effect of Trade Policy Regimes on Firms' Learning From Suppliers How to Innovate

*Jahan Ara Peerally**
Department of International Business
HEC Montréal, Canada

John Cantwell
Rutgers Business School
Rutgers University, USA

Introduction

Different perspectives of technology have been explored and emphasised over the past century mainly for their pivotal roles in economic development. These perspectives have since evolved and branched out into several distinct, yet interrelated, theories. Such evolutionary theory gave rise to the innovative technological capability (ITC) development approach advocating that firms' ability to successfully generate and manage technical change (Bell and Pavitt, 1995) plays a key role in the industrial success of developing countries (Lall, 1993a).

Past evidence has established that domestic firms of developing countries need to move beyond 'elementary learning' (Lall, 1980) and 'passive learning-by-doing' (Bell and Pavitt, 1995) in order to

---
*Corresponding author

create higher levels of capabilities and innovate. The same fact applies to foreign subsidiaries located in developing countries. Comparative studies between the ITCs of domestic firms and foreign subsidiaries in developing countries are abundant and have mixed results (for example Chen, 1983; Katz, 1984; Wignaraja, 1998; Rasiah, 2004a, 2004b, 2004c, 2006; Rasiah and Rasagam, 2004; Rasiah and Tamale, 2004; Figueiredo, 2005; Liu *et al.*, 2009). Non-comparative case study analysis has sometimes shown that domestic firms fail to upgrade capabilities and innovate (Bell *et al.*, 1982) while in other cases foreign subsidiaries also fail to do so (Hobday and Rush, 2007).

Developing country firms learn to innovate in various ways and through linkages with different local or international actors such as parent firms, customers, suppliers, joint-venture partners, subcontractors and research institutes (Lundvall, 1988; von Hippel, 1988). Through these external sources of knowledge, firms accumulate and create new ITCs in their organisation. Learning processes are therefore linked to the trajectories of incremental technical change through the accumulated stock of knowledge in firms (Malerba, 1992). Despite the abundance of studies on the various dynamisms and factors involved in the acquisition of ITCs through external sources — both at the developed and developing country levels — little is known about the learning processes in firms that have subsisted under the protection of a temporary preferential trade agreement (PTA). Consequently, the existing empirical evidence does not provide evidence on learning to innovate by developing country firms and foreign subsidiaries under such temporary PTAs, nor on the role of domestic suppliers as a source of knowledge and innovation.

The structure of the chapter is as follows: the next section describes the research questions and objectives of the study; it is followed by a section that surveys the literature related to the acquisition of ITCs from suppliers and presents the hypotheses. There is a section, which explains the analytical framework of the study followed by a section that describes the data, the methodology and variables used to test the hypotheses. A section presents and discusses the statistical results of the study and the final section concludes with the contributions and policy lessons of the study.

Research Questions and Objectives

The contemporary approach to the ITCs' empirical field can be summarised by the synthesis put forward by Lall (1993b). He states that the traditional link between foreign direct investment (FDI) and innovation in developing countries has been loosened. He acknowledges that multinational enterprises (MNEs) from the developed world have been the main sources of innovation for firms in developing countries. However, he highlights that other sources of innovation have emerged in the form of new intermediaries and suppliers, specialised sellers of engineering, consultancy and equipment that have little interest in opening foreign subsidiaries in developing countries. In this connection, he firstly affirms that the local development of ITC in developing countries often requires more than just access to international technology flows. The assimilation, adaptation and further development of the imported knowledge usually involve a process of building new ITCs that do not exist in developing countries. Secondly, ITC development is determined at the national level by the trade policy and industry policy regimes and by investments in skills, information flows, infrastructure and supporting institutions. Finally, he states that at the micro-level, ITC development is also the outcome of firm-level efforts to build new organisational and technical skills.

Lall's (1993b) synthesis provides the basis for our three research questions:

(1) Which suppliers — domestic or foreign-based — are the most significant sources of ITCs for domestic firms and Asian-owned subsidiaries in the Mauritius export processing zone (MEPZ)?
(2) Did domestic firms and Asian-owned subsidiaries in the MEPZ, which operated under a temporary PTA, equally acquire and absorb ITCs through these supplier linkages during their operating lifetime, in order to create new technology locally?
(3) If yes, what are the determinants for the absorptive capacity of acquired ITCs from suppliers?

Thus, our first research objective is to determine which supplier linkages are the most significant sources of ITCs for MEPZ domestic firms and Asian-owned subsidiaries. Our focus is primarily on backward linkages with domestic suppliers and foreign suppliers based in Asia and Europe of both inputs and equipment. However, we also include in our analysis ITC acquisition from parent company linkages, i.e. horizontal linkages, as a moderating measure, since studies (such as Ernst and Kim, 2002; Hobday and Rush, 2007) have demonstrated that parent companies of foreign subsidiaries in some cases allow, and in other cases do not allow, the latter to independently acquire and absorb ITCs.

Our second objective is to determine whether the acquired ITCs from supplier linkages have contributed to local ITC development in the MEPZ domestic firms and Asian-owned subsidiaries. This objective is key in answering our second research question. The MEPZ has been subject to major capital flight from Asian-owned subsidiaries since 2005 due to the redundancy of the PTA, namely the Cotonou Agreement,[1] with Europe and the end of the Multi Fibre Agreement (MFA) (WIR, 2006).[2] However, domestic firms have continued their integration and expansion in the MEPZ and regionally post 2005.

---

[1] Of the preferential agreements, the most significant to Mauritius' industrial development was the privileged, duty-free access granted to textiles and clothing products to the European market following the signing, in 1975, of the Lomé Convention, also known as the Cotonou Agreement. This duty-free preferential access was in part an important factor in attracting significant foreign investors, largely from the Hong Kong Special Administrative Region (SAR) to the MEPZ during its initial setting up stage. Furthermore, at the time these firms profited from an abundant cheap labour supply and also from lax labour legislation. In fact, it was not until 1993 that legislation was passed to promote better working conditions in the MEPZ (Torres, 2001).

[2] 'The Multi Fibre Agreement (MFA), established in 1973, set up an elaborate system of quotas organised by product and country. In practice, the agreement limited exports of textiles and apparel from developing countries. In 1995, the Agreement on Textiles and Clothing (AITC), a multilateral trade regime established under WTO auspices replaced the MFA. By phasing out quotas and discriminatory import practices, the AITC aimed to fully integrate the textile and apparel trades into WTO rules by 2005. The dismantling of the MFA particularly threatens manufacturers who previously enjoyed privileged access to the European and North American markets by putting them in direct competition with highly competitive exporters from Asia', (Cammett, 2007).

Based on these two aforementioned facts, we conjecture that Asian-owned subsidiaries had foreseen their exit from the MEPZ and therefore, unlike domestic firms, did not fully harness learning through supplier linkages. In this light, our second objective is to determine whether our conjecture has any validity by testing if the ITCs acquired through suppliers have been equally absorbed by domestic firms and Asian-owned subsidiaries. It should be noted that our purpose is to understand the effects, if any, of temporary PTAs on ITC acquisition and absorption from suppliers by domestic firms and foreign subsidiaries in the MEPZ and to use the data collected to provide policy insights for other similar country contexts and produce some of the initial building blocks for future research.

Third, in the case where learning from suppliers has led to local ITC development, the objective is to assess the firm-level determinants for this absorptive capacity. This assessment conveys the efforts, if any, made by MEPZ firms and subsidiaries in order to build new organisational and technical skills by learning from suppliers.

We use data on both domestic firms and Asian-owned subsidiaries collected in 2002–2003, that is just prior to these changes in trade policies, to address these objectives and answer our research questions.

Literature Review and Hypotheses

Firms learn in various ways including through linkages with different local or international actors such as parent firms, customers, suppliers, joint-venture partners, subcontractors and research institutes (Lundvall, 1988; von Hippel, 1988). The literature on learning is vast and comprises various approaches and terminologies put forward by similarly numerous scholars and authors: *learning-by-doing* (Arrow, 1962; David, 1975; Rosenberg, 1976; Silverberg *et al.*, 1988; Malerba, 1992; von Hippel and Tyre, 1995); *learning-before-doing* (Pisano, 1996); *learning-by-using* (Rosenberg, 1982; Malerba, 1992; Tyre and Orlikowski, 1996); *learning through linkages* (Lundvall, 1988; von Hippel, 1988) and *learning-by-searching* or *learning in R&D* (Sahal, 1981; Nelson and Winter, 1982; Dosi, 1988; Dosi *et al.*, 1988; Cohen and Levinthal, 1989).

This paper firstly focuses on ITC acquisition by MEPZ domestic firms and Asian-owned subsidiaries through *learning-by-interacting* with domestic, Asia- and Europe-based suppliers. The relation between manufacturers and their suppliers is recognised as a key element in their internal improvement process. Several studies have confirmed that user–supplier collaboration in new product development, for example, helps to improve quality and reduces costs and lead times (Clark, 1998; Clark and Fujimoto, 1991). Similarly, the evidence on user–supplier (customer–supplier or user–producer) relations establishes that innovation and capabilities are created through such linkages (Lundvall, 1992; Busby and Fan, 1993; Larsson, 1993). In fact, agile manufacturing (Goldman and Nagel, 1992) and extended manufacturing (Busby and Fan, 1993) are examples of outcomes from inter-firm linkages involving collaborative design and production activities by innovative customers and suppliers.

For the MEPZ textile firms, all inputs — goods in semi-finished or finished forms and technology used in manufacturing — are imported from foreign suppliers for users to utilise, process and transform into textile products. Some of these textile products (such as dyes and fabrics) are supplied to downstream MEPZ firms for further processing into finished garments. Subsequently, firms within the MEPZ interact both with local and foreign suppliers, but to varying degrees depending on their position in the value chain.

Secondly, the paper focuses on ITC creation, that is through *learning-by-doing, using* and *searching* as well as through conscious investment in human resources, physical resources and time with the aim of improving technological mastery and learning (Dahlman and Westphal, 1981, p. 13). As Romijn (1997: 1) explains, the latter involves:

> *practical, shop floor-based problem-solving involved in setting, running, maintaining, repairing, and making minor changes to technology in response to local conditions that are different from the circumstances under which the technology was developed.*

Being for the most part a development economics issue, local ITC development has very often only involved the analysis of domestic firms (for example Fransman and King, 1984; Romijn, 1997, 1999; Jonker *et al.*, 2006). Lately, several studies have compared the ITCs of foreign subsidiaries and domestic firms in developing countries. However, they do not specifically compare the ITCs acquired through supplier linkages.

Empirical studies (such as Reuber *et al.*, 1973 and Lall, 1980), which investigate specifically the role of domestic suppliers, suggest that MNEs can be quite active in establishing local supplier firms when host governments promote the indigenisation of inputs. In some cases, the roles are inversed whereby the MNEs encourage domestic firms to upgrade their production methods, quality levels and distribution channels in order to meet their requirements. Thus, some positive linkages and spill-overs result from suppliers being compelled to meet the higher standards of quality, reliability and speed of delivery of the MNEs (for example Brash, 1966; Katz, 1969; Ivarsson and Alvstam, 2009). Furthermore, it must be noted that the existing studies on user–supplier linkages are either on advanced users of technology such as von Hippel's (1976) scientific and medical instrument sectors or on developed countries' users and suppliers (for example Hines, 1994, studied supplier networks located in Japan, UK and the US). As Chen (2009) argues these models are insufficient to account for the catching-up of low- and medium technology industries in some newly industrialised countries that do not share the characteristics of high-tech industries.

Hence, the contemporary literature on the creation of ITCs has shown that MNE subsidiaries have the capacity to generate positive spill-over effects to domestic supplier firms. Studies regarding the capacity for domestic supplier firms to generate positive spill-over effects to MNE subsidiaries are lacking apart from Hobday (1996). He found, in the case of the Malaysian electronic industry, that the number of backward linkages between MNEs and new domestic suppliers were too low for the technological innovative needs of the MNEs.

Additionally, the existing theoretical and empirical literature does not provide answers or evidence about the impact of temporary PTAs on the development of ITCs in domestic firms and foreign subsidiaries. The only existing study on ITC and PTAs compares the ITC of firms in a liberalised trade regime with those that operate under one that has protected trading policies (Rasiah, 2009).

In view of the abovementioned lack of existing empirical evidence regarding the effect of temporary PTAs and the role of domestic suppliers as sources of ITCs, we base our hypotheses on the MEPZ events pre- and post-PTA with Europe.

Domestic firms

At the micro-level, firms can acquire ITCs from other firms in the industry, industrial and technology institutions, research organisations and universities. This paper specifically investigates linkages with suppliers firms in the local and global textile industry. In the case of MEPZ domestic firms, it is expected that higher levels of ITCs were acquired through suppliers located in more technologically advanced locations, namely Asia and Europe. We contend that by virtue of the fact that parent companies of domestic MEPZ firms and domestic suppliers are found in a less advanced national technological system i.e. Mauritius, that their levels of transferred ITCs will be lower. Nevertheless, it is expected that there was ITC acquisition by domestic MEPZ firms through these two linkages due to geographical and cultural proximity, but to a lower extent. Therefore, although the parent company of domestic firms is where production activities and other firm-level ITCs usually originate in the internal network of multi-unit or vertically integrated textile groups, unlike the parent company of Asian-owned subsidiaries, the former are assumed to be less technologically advanced. The same argument is applied to domestic suppliers. Furthermore, if the MEPZ textile industry is to thrive post-PTA with Europe, it implies that domestic suppliers would have also had to actively upgrade their capability and knowledge base in order to provide advanced services and support to their MEPZ customers since a synergistic relation would ensure the survival of all concerned. Hence, Asia- and Europe-based suppliers are deemed as being the most important sources of technological knowledge for domestic firms in the MEPZ since they have access to major resources and global networks, which domestic suppliers may not have access to. Thus, our hypothesis is as follows.

Hypothesis 1a: For domestic MEPZ textile firms, Asia- and Europe-based suppliers provide more technological leadership in the acquisition of ITCs than domestic suppliers.

However, in view of their need to remain globally competitive post-PTA with Europe, domestic firms should be able to rely on their pool of acquired and created ITCs. These ITCs are also crucial to the current process of regionalisation and globalisation undertaken by MEPZ domestic firms.

Under the national innovation system school of thought, it is argued that ITC development and creation in domestic firms of developing countries is most dependent on two levels of effort (Lall, 1993b). Firstly, there are efforts at the micro-level: firms creating new organisational and technical skills, generating new information, developing unique specialisations and linkages with suppliers, buyers and institutions, which we discussed earlier in the paper. Secondly, there are efforts at the national level: devising optimal policies on trade and industry, and investing in skills, information flows, infrastructure and supporting institutions. It must therefore be noted that past and current Mauritian governments have actively supported the development and upgrading of the MEPZ textile industry since its inception. This fact coupled with the need for domestic MEPZ firms to survive in the face of international competition leads to the postulation that domestic firms were well poised to actively develop the absorptive capacity to assimilate, adapt and improve the acquired ITCs through supplier linkages. Consequently, we hypothesise that:

Hypothesis 1b: For domestic MEPZ textile firms, the disaggregated acquired ITCs through domestic, Europe- and Asia-based supplier linkages are significantly and positively correlated to their overall levels of created ITCs.

Asian-owned subsidiaries

The motive for Asian-owned subsidiaries in locating production in Mauritius in the 1960s, 1970s and 1980s was to take advantage of the PTA with Europe and circumvent quotas imposed by the MFA. Unlike domestic firms, they serve both the Asian and the European markets. Therefore, production activities were maintained in their home country to serve the Asian market. Domestic firms serve primarily the European market, followed by the American market. They, however, do not export to Asia. During their operating lifetime in the MEPZ, Asian-owned subsidiaries needed ITCs that would allow them to export efficiently to the EU. However, actively engaging in the acquisition and creation of advanced ITCs and creating a core ITC hub in the MEPZ for future purposes is argued as being redundant since they likely foresaw their exit from the MEPZ in view of the phasing out of the MFA and the PTA. We therefore postulate that the Asian parent companies controlled the ITC development trajectory of their MEPZ subsidiaries by being their main source of ITCs. Yet, we also posit that cultural and business links with Asia enabled them to efficiently harness ITCs through Asia-based supplier linkages. Therefore our hypothesis is:

Hypothesis 2a: For Asian-owned subsidiaries, parent companies and Asia-based suppliers provide more technological leadership in the acquisition of ITCs than Europe-based suppliers and domestic suppliers.

As it is an established fact that Asian-owned subsidiaries exited the MEPZ post-PTA with Europe and post-MFA, we also argue that they did not actively engage in local ITC creation. Our conjecture is that they did not invest in years of learning and 'hard-slogging' (Hobday, 1995) which would allow them to incrementally move to more advanced levels of ITCs like domestic firms. Hence our next hypothesis is:

Hypothesis 2b: In the case of Asian-owned subsidiaries, the disaggregated acquired ITCs through supplier linkages are not significantly correlated to their levels of created ITCs.

Based on the findings related to the above hypotheses, we then proceed to meet the third objective of the study, which is to ascertain

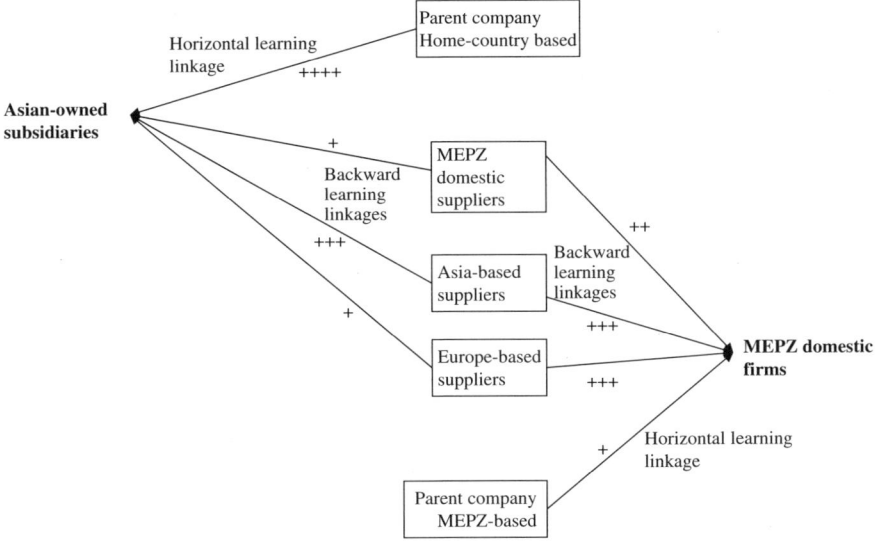

++++, +++, ++, +: denotes degree of innovative technological capabilities acquired through linkages.

Fig. 1. The ITC Learning Linkages for MEPZ Domestic Textile Firms and Asian-Owned Subsidiaries.

the determinants of the absorptive capacity for acquired ITCs from supplier linkages.

By investigating the role of both domestic and foreign supplier linkages in ITC acquisition and creation, a clearer and holistic understanding of inter-firm technological learning linkages was developed for the MEPZ textile industry, which has so far evolved under a temporary PTA. We examine, as shown in Fig. 1, the learning and acquisition of ITCs by MEPZ domestic firms and Asian-owned subsidiaries from (1) the parent company, (2) domestic suppliers, (3) Asia-based suppliers and (4) Europe-based suppliers.

Analytical Framework

We analyse the acquisition and creation of ITCs in the MEPZ by using Bell and Pavitt's (1995) framework for the creation and accumulation of firm-level capabilities, which also integrates Lall's (1992) taxonomy of ITCs. Bell and Pavitt's framework enables the identification and differentiation of the types and levels of ITC for each firm. They use a fine disaggregation of the different levels and types of ITCs, which has been adapted, as shown in Table 1, to this study. The framework is therefore based on actual activities performed by MEPZ domestic textile and Asian-owned subsidiaries.

The framework comprises investment, capital goods supply and production capabilities. *Investment capabilities* include skills, knowledge and resources required for commissioning or expanding a new facility, securing and disbursing loans and finances, active monitoring and control of feasibility studies, project preparation and implementation, training and recruitment and engaging in detailed engineering. *Capital goods supply capabilities* consist of the skills and resources needed to modify, adapt or produce new capital goods that embody locally created new technology. *Production capabilities* include skills, knowledge and resources related to: (1) process technology with activities ranging from internal quality control measures, the optimum use of equipment, sound maintenance awareness to improvements in equipment and processes; and (2) product technology involving mastering product design, improving product quality and developing new products.

The framework also disaggregates the functional area of capabilities into different levels of ITCs. The levels of capabilities range from the basic operation capability at Level 1 to advanced innovative capability at Level 4.

Basic operation capability refers to the capability to produce goods at a given measure of efficiency and input requirements. At this level, the firm's capability is mainly in technology-using skills and knowledge with simple organisation arrangements for routine production. Basic operation capability therefore does not entail any form of innovative capability.

The subsequent levels of capabilities (Levels 2–4) are derived from innovative capabilities whereby the firm's capability is mainly in technology-changing skills, knowledge, and experiences with increasingly complex organisational arrangements. Thus, firms which have acquired and created innovative ITCs are able to generate and manage technical change geared at modifying, improving and creating

Table 1. A framework for Measuring Acquired and Created ITCs by Domestic Firms and Asian-Owned Subsidiaries in the MEPZ Textile Industry.

Functions	Investment function		Capital goods supply	Production function	
Main activities	Decision-making and control	Project management	Equipment and machinery in yarn, fabric and garment (CMT*) manufacturing	Process and production organisation in yarn, fabric and garment (CMT*) manufacturing	Product centred: yarn, fabric, garment and accessories
Capability level					
Routine production capabilities					
Level 1: Basic operation capability	Basic activities such as engaging prime contractor and disbursing finances from bank in setting up a new production plant or customising existing production facilities	Project preparation and implementation when undertaking orders from clients and buyers	Maintenance awareness and systematic preventative measures. Servicing of unchanging items of plant and machinery. Replication of simple equipment spare parts	Routine operation and testing. Basic maintenance of given facilities. Continuous efficiency improvement from accumulated experience in existing task	Replication of product samples from clients and of fixed specificities and design. Product quality enforced through client QC‡ systems
Innovative technological capabilities					
Level 2: Basic innovative capability	Active monitoring and control of feasibility studies, technology choice, technology sourcing and project scheduling	Running feasibility studies before choosing and buying technology. Providing project management services to primary and support departments and to clients	Modification of equipment and machinery such as in-house adaptation to pressure foot and guides in garment manufacturing. In-house repair and troubleshooting of equipment	Integrated automatic/semi-automatic processes in production. Minor adaptation to processes and production to suit different production lines. Internal defect rates measurement	Minor adaptation to suit differences in market needs. Incremental improvement in product quality based on informal feedback from buyer and supplier. In-house QC‡ to maintain existing quality standards

(*Continued*)

Table 1. (*Continued*)

Functions	Investment function		Capital goods supply	Production function	
Level 3: Intermediate innovative capability	Search, evaluation and selection of technology and raw material sources. Undertaking tenders and negotiations. Conducting overall project management	Project management of joint-venture and cooperative-agreement projects. Detailed engineering in major textile projects. Project scheduling and management. Commissioning. Formalised training programs and recruitment processes	Original use of equipment and machinery. Innovative reverse engineering. Innovative reconfiguration of computer-aided/controlled equipment and machinery to modify capabilities and broaden utilisation	ISO certification. Flexible and multi-skilled production line. Full-scale automation with computer-aided/controlled systems. Develop new process specifications through full optimisation of knowledge from technology transfers, linkages and public sources	Sampling unit for designing garment samples and facilitating their production. Feasibility studies. Laboratory for testing durability and quality of new dyes, yarns and fabrics in isolation and when applied to each other
Level 4: Advanced innovative capability	Involves full capabilities in coordinating, supporting and managing the development of new production systems and components	Overall project management in large-scale investments such as creating and commissioning new production facilities. Involves full capabilities in providing project management services, turnkey solutions and advanced training to sister companies or subsidiaries	Set up of R&D centre for the design of original equipment and development of new textile technologies	R&D related to process and production organisation for designing, selecting and extensively justifying yarn, fabric and garment manufacturing techniques for specific end uses. Develop full-scale new production processes and standards	Set up R&D centre for generating innovative textile designs and textile technological skills (product attributes). Related product R&D in creating cost-effective, high-performing, functionally appropriate and aesthetically pleasing yarns, fabrics and garments

Notes: Adapted from Bell and Pavitt (1995) and based on authors' own research and elaboration.

* Cut, make and trim

‡ Quality control

products, processes, production organisation or equipment. The extent of their innovative capabilities, however, depends upon the level the firms have reached. Therefore at Level 2 the innovative capabilities of a firm are basic and its ability to modify, improve and create products, processes, production organisation or equipment is incremental and simple in nature. A firm will have intermediate innovative capability at Level 3 and therefore a higher ability to generate and manage technical change, for example by engaging in various types of product and process design and engineering or through original use of equipment and machinery. Finally at Level 4, the firm has an advanced innovative capability, which is likely to involve R&D-related efforts to generate innovation in products, equipment, machinery and process and production organisation.

The framework provides a basis for describing and measuring the acquired and created levels of ITCs by MEPZ domestic textile firms and foreign subsidiaries.

Data, Methodology and Variables

A list of all MEPZ domestic firms and Asian-owned subsidiaries was derived from the Ministry of Industry and Commerce database and their population was 45 and 26, respectively. They were all targeted for data collection through face-to-face interviews with directors or production managers. The response rate was positive at 86.6% for domestic firms and 77% for Asian-owned subsidiaries. The domestic firms and Asian-owned subsidiaries belonged to two industry sectors: fabric (including spinning and dyeing) and garment (including knitwear) manufacturing; therefore the firms represent a complete cross section of the industry.

The ownership of the domestic firms and Asian-owned subsidiaries was determined by the equity structure. Domestic firms are 100% Mauritian in financial equity structure. All Asian-owned subsidiaries had a majority of foreign equity — that is more than 50.1%[3] — as part

---

[3] We adopt the same definition as Dunning (1995) to describe a foreign subsidiary as foreign investment involving at least a 50.1% holding.

of their financial structure. Our stratified samples consist of 39 domestic firms and 20 Asian-owned subsidiaries. A description of the sampled domestic firms and Asian-owned subsidiaries is provided in Table 2. The regional grouping of countries as Asian was derived from the classification proposed by the United Nations Statistics Division.[4]

Dependent variables: A measure of created and acquired ITCs

A measure of the acquired and created ITCs for each firm was derived from the framework described in the previous section (Table 1) and operationalised into ITC indices. These indices are for each area of ITC namely investment capabilities, production capabilities, capital good supply capabilities and finally there is a composite technological capabilities index, which combines the former three sets of capabilities. ITC indices have been used in several studies (for example Westphal *et al.*, 1990; Lall 1992; Bell and Pavitt, 1995; Dutrénit and Vera-Cruz, 2006; Wignaraja, 1998, 2002, 2008) and are a well-accepted 'tried-and-tested' measure for analysing firm-level innovative capabilities. Bell and Pavitt's (1995) framework integrates Lall's (1992) taxonomy of innovative capabilities, which has also been successfully used in empirical work on developing countries. Studies include for example, Lall *et al.* (1994) in Ghana, Biggs *et al.* (1995) in Kenya, Zimbabwe and Ghana, Pietrobelli (1997) in Chile and more recently Wignaraja (2002) in Mauritius and Sri Lanka (2008).

Created ITC indices

In our study, the respondents rated the ITCs that their firm has created since the time when it started operations in the MEPZ. The rating was on a scale of 1 to 5 where 1 equals to no capability at all and 5 equals to a very high capability when compared to international

---

[4]Available from http://unstats.un.org/unsd/methods/m49/m49regin.htm

Table 2. MEPZ Sampled Domestic Firms and Asian-Owned Subsidiaries and Their Linkages.

Firms surveyed	MEPZ textile industry: fabric and garment domestic firms and Asian-owned subsidiaries		Fabric domestic firms and Asian-owned subsidiaries* (Upstream firms)		Garment firms and Asian-owned subsidiaries (Downstream firms)	
	#	%	#	%	#	%
Domestic firms	39	66.1	7	53.8	24	63.2
Asian-owned subsidiaries	20	33.9	6	46.2	14	36.8
Sample size (N)	59	100	13	100	38	100

Linkages	Parent companies		Domestic suppliers		Europe-based suppliers		Asia-based suppliers	
	#	%	#	%	#	%	#	%
Domestic firms	13	41.9	30	73.2	22	71.0	31	62
Asian-owned subsidiaries	18	58.1	11	26.8	9	29.0	19	38
Total	31	100	41	100	31	100	50	100

Regional grouping of Asian-owned subsidiaries	# and Country	%
	2 Chinese	10
	14 Hong Kong	70
	1 India	5
	2 Singapore	10
	1 Taiwan	5
Total	20	100

Notes: *It can be observed from the data that two Asian-owned subsidiaries do not have parent companies. In effect they are considered as foreign firms (see for example Rasiah, 2004a) as opposed to foreign subsidiaries that are integrated within a multinational enterprise's network. These foreign firms are nevertheless included in the analysis, where applicable, since they are considered as having access to resources and networks, which domestic firms may not benefit from.

standards.[5] Values were assigned for (A) each function: (1) the investment function comprising decision-making and control and project management, (2) the capital goods supply function comprising equipment and machinery in yarn, fabric and garment manufacturing and (3) the production function comprising process and production organisation and product centred; and for (B) each capability level: basic operation capability, basic innovative capability, intermediate innovative capability and advanced innovative capability.

An index for each function was then computed by averaging the ratings assigned. Thus, for investment capabilities (IVT_IND), an average value was computed based on the rates assigned for each cell under the columns decision-making and control and project management of Table 1. The same principle was applied for computing the capital goods supply indices (CG_IND) and the production and process capabilities indices (PP_IND). The overall created technological capabilities indices (ITC_IND) were computed in the same manner; however, they include all of the three functions for MEPZ domestic firms and Asian-owned subsidiaries.

Acquired ITCs indices

The same method for computing created ITC indices was used to measure (1) the overall innovative capabilities that were acquired by domestic and Asian-owned subsidiaries through parent and supplier linkages and (2) the disaggregated ITCs that were acquired through parent and supplier linkages. The latter involves separating the overall capability indices into each functional area of the ITCs, namely, investment, capital goods supply and production capabilities. The

---

[5]Since the data was collected through face-to-face interviews, every attempt was made to reduce respondents' errors in self-reporting the rates for each function under each capability level. The operationalisation of the indices adopted in this study is based on perceptual data as is the case in most ITC studies. Therefore, our findings could be to some extent the outcome of subjective bias from respondents. While we explicitly recognise this risk, we believe that perceptual data still offers relevant insights for both scholars and policy-makers.

respondents were asked to rate the ITCs that their firm or foreign subsidiary had acquired through each type of linkage since the time they started operations in the MEPZ. As with the measurement of created ITCs, the rating was on a scale of 1 to 5 where 1 equals no capability acquired at all and 5 equals to a very high capability acquired when compared to international standards. The scores were self-assigned by the firms.

The dependent variables — created, acquired and disaggregated acquired ITCs — and their indices are listed and described in Table 3.

It must also be noted that linkages with suppliers who are foreign-owned but operate locally within the MEPZ were also investigated but removed due to their very low occurrence.

Independent and control variables

The size of the firm, age of firm, level of foreign equity, number of engineers and technicians in the firm, training budget and external technological assistance are important independent variables for determining the local ITC development of firms and foreign subsidiaries. They represent the factors that Dahlman and Westphal (1981) described as leading to technological mastery, learning and innovative capabilities.

The study includes five variables (see Annex 1 for an overview and the frequency distributions of the independent and control variables):

(1) *Age*, measured as the number of years the firm or subsidiary has been in operation in the MEPZ
(2) *Training budget*, measured as the expenditure on employee training as a percentage of sales
(3) *External technical assistance*, which is the number of times the firm or subsidiary has used an external technical consultant or local technology institution during a three-year period prior to data collection
(4) The number of *engineers and technicians* in the domestic firm or Asian-owned subsidiary. This variable serves a dual purpose since

Table 3. Description of Dependent Variables.

Dependent Variable 1: Indices for the overall levels of created technological capabilities by MEPZ domestic firms and Asian-owned subsidiaries over their operating lifetime

Investment capability index IVT_IND	Average value of scores[+] for investment function comprising decision-making and control and project management
Capital goods supply capability index CG_IND	Average value of scores[+] for capital goods supply function comprising equipment and machinery in yarn, fabric and garment manufacturing
Production capability index PP_IND	Average value of scores[+] for production function comprising (1) process and production organisation in yarn, fabric and garment manufacturing and (2) product centred: yarn, fabric, garment and accessories
Technological capability index ITC_IND	Composite index based on average value of all functions in the firm or subsidiary and for all capability levels

Dependent Variable 2: Indices for the overall levels of acquired technological capabilities through linkages by MEPZ domestic firms and Asian-owned subsidiaries over their operating lifetime*

AQ_ITC_PC[‡]	Composite index based on average value of all functions in the firm or subsidiary and for all capability levels denoting overall acquired capabilities from parent company linkages
AQ_ITC_DS	Composite index based on average value of all functions in the firm or subsidiary and for all capability levels denoting overall acquired capabilities from domestic supplier linkages
AQ_ITC_AS	Composite index based on average value of all functions in the firm or subsidiary and for all capability levels denoting overall acquired capabilities from Asia-based supplier linkages
AQ_ITC_EU	Composite index based on average value of all functions in the firm or subsidiary and for all capability levels denoting overall acquired capabilities from Europe-based supplier linkages

(Continued)

Table 3.   (*Continued*)

Dependent Variable 3: Indices for the disaggregated acquired technological capabilities through linkages by MEPZ domestic firms and Asian-owned subsidiaries over their operating lifetime*

AQ_PC_IVT_ IND‡	Acquired investment capabilities from parent company linkages
AQ_DS_IVT_IND	Acquired investment capabilities from domestic supplier linkages
AQ_AS_IVT_IND	Acquired investment capabilities from Asia-based supplier linkages
AQ_EU_IVT_IND	Acquired investment capabilities from Europe-based supplier linkages
AQ_PC_CG_IND‡	Acquired capital goods supply capabilities from parent company linkages
AQ_DS_CG_IND	Acquired capital goods supply capabilities from domestic supplier linkages
AQ_AS_CG_IND	Acquired capital goods supply capabilities from Asia-based supplier linkages
AQ_EU_CG_IND	Acquired capital goods supply capabilities from Europe-based supplier linkages
AQ_PC_PP_IND†	Acquired production capabilities from parent company linkages
AQ_DS_PP_IND	Acquired production capabilities from domestic supplier linkages
AQ_AS_PP_IND	Acquired production capabilities from Asia-based supplier linkages
AQ_EU_PP_IND	Acquired production capabilities from Europe-based supplier linkages

Notes:
† Average value range from 1–5
* Based on average value of scores ranging from 1–5
‡ Used as a moderating measure

it denotes the intensity of internal skills of the firm or subsidiary, as well as acting as a proxy for firm or subsidiary size.[6]

(5) A dummy control variable — *textile industry sector* — where fabric firms or subsidiaries were assigned a value of 1 and garment firms or subsidiaries were assigned a value of 0. This control variable was required since the domestic fabric firms and subsidiaries in our samples are also suppliers to the garment firms and subsidiaries analysed. The inclusion of fabric firms and subsidiaries in our sample was necessary as they are important players in the industry and they also interact with foreign-based suppliers.

Statistical Results and Discussion

Acquired ITCs through supplier linkages

To compare supplier linkages, we used the non-parametric statistical Wilcoxon signed ranks test, since our samples for linkages are of differing small sizes (see Table 2). For the same reason, the statistical significance was determined by using the exact variant as opposed to the asymptotic variant. We also used the one-tailed test since we use directional hypotheses. The results for domestic firms and Asian-owned subsidiaries are reported in Tables 4 and 5, respectively. The tables show the test statistic (denoted by T — the smaller of the two sums of ranks), Z scores and the exact significance for the paired samples. We also calculated the effect size (denoted by r) for the statistically significant results. When using the Wilcoxon signed ranks test, an r-value of 0.3 and 0.5 based on Cohen's criteria suggest a medium and large effect, respectively (Field, 2009).

The results in Table 4 firstly reveal that domestic firms have acquired a statistically and significantly higher level of investment capabilities from Asia-based suppliers than from domestic suppliers (p value = 0.018; $r = -0.27$) and Europe-based suppliers (p value = 0.031; $r = -0.27$). Secondly, it can also be observed that a statistically

---

[6]The variables size and number of engineers and technicians in the firm were highly correlated.

Table 4. Wilcoxon Signed Ranks Test Results for Domestic MEPZ Firms.

		T	Z	Exact Sig. (1-tailed)	$r^{\dagger}$
Investment capabilities indices	AQ_AS_IVT_IND > AQ_DS_IVT_IND	49.5	-2.077	0.018*	-0.27
	AQ_EU_IVT_IND < AQ_DS_IVT_IND	7	-1.841	0.035*	-0.26
	AQ_EU_IVT_IND < AQ_AS_IVT_IND	4	-1.973	0.031*	-0.27
	AQ_AS_IVT_IND > AQ_PC_IVT_IND	18.5	-1.292	0.107	
	AQ_EU_IVT_IND < AQ_PC_IVT_IND	10.5	-1.053	0.172	
	AQ_DS_IVT_IND < AQ_PC_IVT_IND	16	-0.771	0.238	
Capital goods supply capabilities indices	AQ_DS_CG_IND = AQ_PC_CG_IND	3	0.000	0.625	
	AQ_AS_CG_IND = AQ_PC_CG_IND	3	0.000	0.625	
	AQ_EU_CG_IND < AQ_PC_CG_IND	0	-1.604	0.125	
	AQ_AS_CG_IND < AQ_DS_CG_IND	3	-1.225	0.125	
	AQ_EU_CG_IND < AQ_DS_CG_IND	4	-0.368	0.438	
	AQ_EU_CG_IND < AQ_AS_CG_IND	2	-0.577	0.5	

(Continued)

Table 4. (*Continued*)

		T	Z	Exact Sig. (1-tailed)	$r^\dagger$
Production capabilities indices	AQ_DS_PP_IND > AQ_PC_PP_IND	10	-0.676	0.289	
	AQ_AS_PP_IND > AQ_PC_PP_IND	16	-0.280	0.406	
	AQ_EU_PP_IND < AQ_PC_PP_IND	7	-1.542	0.074	
	AQ_AS_PP_IND < AQ_DS_PP_IND	78.5	-0.994	0.167	
	AQ_EU_PP_IND < AQ_DS_PP_IND	7	*-2.515*	*0.004**	**-0.35**
	AQ_EU_PP_IND < AQ_AS_PP_IND	19.5	-1.202	0.128	
Technological capabilities indices	AQ_ITC_DS > AQ_ITC_PC	14	-0.560	0.32	
	AQ_ITC_AS > AQ_ITC_PC	22.5	-0.934	0.187	
	AQ_ITC_EU < AQ_ITC_PC	6	-1.680	0.055	
	AQ_ITC_AS > AQ_ITC_DS	30	-1.186	0.122	
	AQ_ITC_EU < AQ_ITC_DS	3	*-2.826*	*0.001**	**-0.39**
	AQ_ITC_EU < AQ_ITC_AS	40	-0.785	0.232	

Notes:
† Authors' calculations

Table 5. Wilcoxon Signed Ranks Test Results for MEPZ Asian-Owned Subsidiaries.

		T	Z	Exact Sig. (1-tailed)	$r^\dagger$
Investment capabilities indices	AQ_DS_IVT_IND < AQ_PC_IVT_IND	12	−1.588	0.065	
	AQ_AS_IVT_IND < AQ_PC_IVT_IND	*16.5*	*−2.266*	*0.011**	−0.36
	AQ_EU_IVT_IND < AQ_PC_IVT_IND	13	−0.169	0.445	
	AQ_AS_IVT_IND < AQ_DS_IVT_IND	7	−1.183	0.148	
	AQ_EU_IVT_IND < AQ_DS_IVT_IND	3	−0.730	0.312	
	AQ_EU_IVT_IND < AQ_AS_IVT_IND	4.5	−0.813	0.25	
Capital goods supply capabilities indices	AQ_DS_CG_IND = AQ_PC_CG_IND	0	0.000	1	
	AQ_AS_CG_IND = AQ_PC_CG_IND	0	0.000	1	
	AQ_EU_CG_IND = AQ_PC_CG_IND	0	0.000	1	
	AQ_AS_CG_IND = AQ_DS_CG_IND	0	0.000	1	
	AQ_EU_CG_IND = AQ_DS_CG_IND	0	0.000	1	
	AQ_EU_CG_IND = AQ_AS_CG_IND	0	0.000	1	

(*Continued*)

Table 5. (Continued)

		T	Z	Exact Sig. (1-tailed)	r†
Production capabilities indices	AQ_DS_PP_IND > AQ_PC_PP_IND	10.5	−1.738	0.044*	−0.31
	AQ_AS_PP_IND > AQ_PC_PP_IND	16	−2.295	0.01*	−0.37
	AQ_EU_PP_IND < AQ_PC_PP_IND	8.5	−0.933	0.188	
	AQ_AS_PP_IND < AQ_DS_PP_IND	6.5	−1.270	0.117	
	AQ_EU_PP_IND < AQ_DS_PP_IND	3	−0.730	0.312	
	AQ_EU_PP_IND < AQ_AS_PP_IND	2.5	−1.355	0.125	
Technological capabilities indices	AQ_ITC_DS > AQ_ITC_PC	3	−2.310	0.01*	−0.43
	AQ_ITC_AS > AQ_ITC_PC	0	−3.184	0.00*	−0.52
	AQ_ITC_EU > AQ_ITC_PC	9	−0.314	0.422	
	AQ_ITC_AS < AQ_ITC_DS	8	−1.014	0.188	
	AQ_ITC_EU < AQ_ITC_DS	2	−1.095	0.188	
	AQ_ITC_EU < AQ_ITC_AS	8	−1.014	0.188	

Notes:
† Authors' calculations

higher level of investment capabilities was acquired from domestic suppliers (p value = 0.035; $r = -0.26$) than Europe-based suppliers.

Domestic suppliers emerge once again as statistically and significantly higher than Europe-based suppliers in terms of acquired production capabilities (p value = 0.004; $r = -0.35$) and overall acquired ITCs (p value = 0.001; $r = -0.39$). Hypothesis 1a is therefore partially supported.

Based on these findings, we can conclude that for domestic MEPZ firms, Asia-based suppliers lead over Europe-based suppliers as a source of investment capabilities. Asia-based suppliers therefore either have a higher stake, or are better than Europe-based suppliers, in transferring the skills, knowledge and resources required for commissioning or expanding a new facility, securing and disbursing loans and finances, the active monitoring and control of feasibility studies, project preparation and implementation, training and recruitment and engaging in detailed engineering. In other words, Asian suppliers are either more focused than European suppliers on exploiting business opportunities in small developing countries like Mauritius or that their investment capabilities are better suited to the needs of domestic MEPZ firms. Broadman (2007), for example, describes a technological complementarity that exists between South Africa's textile industry and those of China and India, and at a higher level than is the case for other African countries. Similarly, we conjecture that there is a higher technological complementarity between the MEPZ's textile industry and Asia than with Europe. Furthermore, previous studies (for example Ramaswamy and Gereffi, 1998; Kelegama and Foley, 1999) have asserted that newly industrialised East Asian countries have evolved into successful garment input exporters through their ability to lead in buyer-driven commodity chains.

Secondly, domestic MEPZ firms have acquired more investment, production and overall ITCs from domestic suppliers than Europe-based suppliers. Thus, it is deduced that cultural and business ties with domestic suppliers have supported this process, but more importantly that domestic suppliers are capable of playing a significant role as sources of ITCs. This suggests a conscious effort and learning on their part and additionally that local policies and institutions must have potentially aided this process. There are other possible explanations for the superior role of domestic suppliers. First, and as previously explained, domestic firms unlike foreign-owned firms, do not belong to a network that is intrinsically connected to locations that are more technologically advanced. Thus, by being outside the MNE network, domestic firms are compelled to look at national technological capabilities (Lall, 1992, 1993b, 1996) as a source of incentive to invest in ITCs. Second, and following from the previous point, since domestic firms do not have the relative ease of closing down operations and relocating to low-cost countries (which for Asian-owned subsidiaries would be their home country) post-PTA, they have a greater need to rely on national firms and factors to upgrade their ITCs. In view of the anticipated end of the PTA with Europe, it is argued that domestic MEPZ firms and domestic suppliers were both actively motivated to transfer ITCs that would aid their continued survival once the PTA was lifted. Finally, it can also be posited that since the Europe textile industry has downsized and is now more focused on value-adding activities, Europe-based suppliers are at or closer to the technological frontier and consequently they conduct activities that are not applicable to the domestic MEPZ firms, which are still in the transitional stages of technological learning and ITC creation.

Concerning Asian-owned subsidiaries, Table 5 shows that parent companies contribute a significantly higher level of investment capabilities (p value = 0.011; r = −0.36) than Asia-based suppliers. Domestic (p value = 0.044; r = −0.31) and Asia-based suppliers (p value = 0.01; r = −0.37) emerge as statistically and significantly higher sources of acquired production capabilities and overall ITCs (p value = 0.01; r = −0.43; p value = 0.000; r = −0.52) than the parent companies. Our Hypothesis 2a is also partially supported.

The results firstly suggest that parent companies controlled the development of the subsidiaries in terms of skills, knowledge and resources required for expansion and growth. Conversely, it could also imply that Asian-owned subsidiaries were not motivated to acquire investment capabilities through supplier linkages as they were aware that they would eventually exit the local textile industry post-MFA.

In terms of acquired production and overall ITCs, both domestic and Asia-based suppliers play a leadership role while Europe-based suppliers do not. From this finding, we can infer that even if parent companies control the Asian-owned subsidiaries in terms of the transfer of investment capabilities, there is nevertheless independent learning in production and other ITCs. Similarly, it is deduced that cultural and business links with Asia may have favoured learning from Asia-based suppliers over European ones. As Lundvall (1992) explained, with complex and uncertain processes such as innovation, cultural distance is often more of an impediment than geographical and physical distance. Finally, since we posited earlier that domestic suppliers have consciously upgraded their own capabilities, it is axiomatic that Asian-owned subsidiaries would have benefitted from acquired ITCs through this linkage as well.

The second objective of the study is to assess whether supplier linkages facilitated local ITC creation of MEPZ domestic firms and Asian-owned subsidiaries. We correlate all acquired ITC indices for domestic and Asia- and Europe-based suppliers with the created ITC indices of MEPZ domestic firms and Asian-owned subsidiaries. For domestic firms, we used the Pearson correlation test for the acquired ITCs from domestic and Asia-based suppliers since the number of linkages allow for a parametric test. For Europe-based suppliers, we use the non-parametric Kendall tau-b test due to the lower number of linkages.

For Asian-owned subsidiaries, we used only the Kendall tau-b test for the same reason. Statistical significance is based on the one-tailed test due to fact that we use directional hypotheses.

The results for domestic firms, in Table 6, support our Hypothesis 1b. It is seen that acquired investment capabilities (p value = 0.009), capital goods supply capabilities (p value = 0.007) and overall ITCs (p value = 0.045) from domestic suppliers are all positively and significantly correlated to the created levels of ITCs of domestic MEPZ firms. Acquired capital goods supply capabilities (p value = 0.026) from Asia-based suppliers and overall acquired ITCs from the latter (p value = 0.044) and Europe-based suppliers (p value = 0.021) are also positively and significantly correlated to MEPZ domestic firms created levels of ITCs.

Kendall's tau-b results between acquired ITCs from suppliers and created levels of ITCs for Asian-owned MEPZ subsidiaries, in Table 7,

Table 6. Correlation Results of Acquired and Created Technological Capabilities for MEPZ Domestic Firms.

Pearson's correlation		ITC_IND	AQ_DS_IVT_IND	AQ_DS_CG_IND	AQ_DS_PP_IND	AQ_ITC_DS
Domestic suppliers	ITC_IND	Pearson correlation	1	0.430**	0.441**	−0.159	0.315*
		Sig. (1-tailed)		0.009	0.007	0.2	0.045
		N	30	30	30	30	30

		ITC_IND	AQ_AS_IVT_IND	AQ_AS_CG_IND	AQ_AS_PP_IND	AQ_ITC_AS
Asian suppliers	ITC_IND	Pearson correlation	1	0.25	0.352*	0.248	0.311*
		Sig. (1-tailed)		0.087	0.026	0.089	0.044
		N	31	31	31	31	31

Kendall's tau-*b* correlation		ITC_IND	AQ_EU_IVT_IND	AQ_EU_CG_IND	AQ_EU_PP_IND	AQ_ITC_EU
European suppliers	ITC_IND	Correlation coefficient	1	0.202	0.232	0.24	0.319*
		Sig. (1-tailed)		0.1	0.095	0.063	0.021
		N	22	22	22	22	22

Notes:

* Correlation is significant at the 0.05 level (1-tailed)

** Correlation is significant at the 0.01 level (1-tailed)

Table 7. Correlation Results of Acquired and Created Technological Capabilities for MEPZ Asian-Owned Subsidiaries.

Kendall's tau-*b* correlation		ITC_IND	AQ_DS_IVT_IND	AQ_DS_CG_IND	AQ_DS_PP_IND	AQ_ITC_DS
Domestic suppliers	ITC_IND	Correlation coefficient	1	0.236		-0.159	0.087
		Sig. (1-tailed)		0.18		0.273	0.365
		N	20	11		11	11

		ITC_IND	AQ_AS_IVT_IND	AQ_AS_CG_IND	AQ_AS_PP_IND	AQ_ITC_AS
Asian suppliers	ITC_IND	Correlation coefficient	1	0.089		0.096	0.137
		Sig. (1-tailed)		0.313		0.3	0.221
		N	20	19		19	19

		ITC_IND	AQ_EU_IVT_IND	AQ_EU_CG_IND	AQ_EU_PP_IND	AQ_ITC_EU
European suppliers	ITC_IND	Correlation coefficient	1	0.415		0.377	0.377
		Sig. (1-tailed)		0.074		0.084	0.084
		N	20	9		9	9

reveal that there are no statistically significant correlations. It is concluded that Hypothesis 2b is supported.

The results for Hypotheses 1b and 2b clearly answer our second research question, which is: did the MEPZ domestic firms and Asian-owned subsidiaries, which operated under a temporary PTA, equally acquire and absorb ITCs through supplier linkages during their operating lifetime, in order to create new technology locally?

The results reveal that domestic firms, unlike Asian-owned subsidiaries, rely on supplier linkages in order to develop local ITCs. This reinforces the conjecture that domestic MEPZ firms exhibit a higher commitment to local ITC development, through supplier linkages, due to their need to continue to survive and expand post-PTA. Likewise, the results add to the existing literature by showing that export-oriented foreign subsidiaries may fail to engage in local ITC upgrade and development when operating under a temporary PTA. Furthermore, the findings show that domestic suppliers in a developing country like Mauritius can be a source of ITCs to user firms in the same industry.

Regression analysis and discussion

Based on the results above, we can consider the final objective of the study, which is to ascertain the determinants of the absorptive capacity for local ITC creation of domestic MEPZ firms.

Since the sample size of domestic MEPZ firms is 39, we had to limit the number of independent variables to four. This implied dropping one of the four independent variables, namely, *age, training budget, external technical assistance* and *engineers and technicians*. In order to avoid the arbitrary removal of an independent variable, we use the backward stepwise regression method with the independent variables. This method starts with all explanatory variables included in the model and then removes the least significant explanatory variable at each regression step. It therefore only retains, in the final regression model, the most significant explanatory variables. Using the backward method is preferable than using the forward method for example, as the latter is more likely to exclude predicators involved in suppressor effects.

Correlation analysis of the independent and control variables (see Annex 2) shows that the variables *age* and *engineers and technicians* are positively related but the correlation is well below 0.5. Variance inflation factor (VIF) values were computed for all independent variables to check for multicollinearity problems. The VIF values range between 1.1 and 1.4, which are well below the generally accepted cut-off value of 10.0 (Neter *et al.*, 1996). Similarly, all the regressions pass the White test so we reject the hypothesis of heteroscedasticity. Only the final regression models derived through the backward method, for acquired ITCs from domestic, Asia- and Europe-based suppliers are presented in Table 8.

Domestic suppliers

Of the five independent variables, we find that in the first regression model (AQ_DS_IVT_IND) only *training budget* and *external technical assistance* are significantly and negatively related (at 5% levels) to the investment capabilities acquired through domestic suppliers. The second regression model (AQ_DS_CG_IND) reveals that *training budget* and *external technical assistance* are once again significantly and negatively related (at 10% levels) to the capital goods supply capabilities acquired through domestic suppliers. From the final regression model for domestic suppliers (AQ_ITC_DS), we observe that *age* (at 10% level), *training budget* and *external technical assistance* (both at 5% levels) are significantly and negatively related to the overall acquired ITCs through domestic suppliers. The F-statistics (at 1% level) for the models are highly significant and the adjusted R^2 values are acceptable for such a small sample size at 0.229, 0.273 and 0.312, respectively.

Wignaraja (2002) argues that as technologies evolve, a continuous process of training and retraining is needed to supply the technical and managerial skills needed for the implementation of new processes and products. Wignaraja and Ikiara's (1999) study of Kenyan garment and engineering enterprises showed that the training budget has no effect on ITCs. While Wignaraja's (2002) study of garment firms in Mauritius showed that the training budget was positively related to their ITCs.

Table 8. Regression Results for the Determinants of Absorptive Capacity in Domestic MEPZ Firms (N = 39).

		Domestic suppliers			Asia-based suppliers		Europe-based suppliers
		Model 1	Model 2	Model 3	Model 1	Model 2	Model 1
		AQ_DS_IVT_IND	AQ_DS_CG_IND	AQ_ITC_DS	AQ_AS_CG_IND	AQ_ITC_AS	AQ_ITC_EU
(Constant)	Coefficient	1.131	0.717	1.255	0.734	0.794	1.234
	Std error	0.213	0.125	0.247	0.133	0.168	0.184
	t-statistic	5.306	5.743	5.075	5.527	4.718	6.711
Control variable							
Textile		0.366	0.323	0.352	0.007	0.069	−0.989
industry		0.232	0.136	0.168	0.157	0.198	0.217
sector		1.576	2.379**	2.097**	0.045	0.346	−4.562***
Independent variables							
Age				−0.025			
				0.015			
				−1.718*			
Training		−12.307	−6.201	−10.753			
budget		5.793	3.396	4.299			
		−2.124**	−1.826*	−2.501**			

(*Continued*)

Table 8. (*Continued*)

	Domestic suppliers		Asia-based suppliers		Europe-based suppliers	
External	-0.02		-0.011		-0.016	
technical	0.009		0.005		0.007	
assistance	-2.156**		-2.028*		-2.351**	
Engineers		0.004		0.005		0.006
and		0.001		0.001		0.002
technicians		3.435***		3.601***		3.649***
R square	0.291	0.252	0.332	0.271	0.387	0.499
Adjusted R^2	0.229	0.209	0.273	0.230	0.312	0.470
F-statistics	4.661***	5.900***	5.634***	6.521***	5.201***	17.399***

Notes: Significance levels for *t*- and *F*-statistics are ***1%, **5% and *10%.

With regards to external technical assistance, their study also showed that it was positively related to the ITCs of garment firms, while Romijn's (1999) study of engineering firms in Pakistan showed there was no relation between the two variables.

Here the focus is on the determinants for the absorptive capacity of acquired ITCs through supplier linkages and not on the determinants for created ITCs. Thus, as domestic MEPZ firms' expenditure on employee training as a percentage of sales and external technical assistance increases, fewer ITCs are absorbed through domestic supplier linkages. These findings convey that the more resources domestic firms possess, the more they rely on investing in training or hiring external consultants than on absorbing ITCs acquired from domestic suppliers.

The age of the firm is viewed as an important determinant of ITCs as the latter are usually accumulated through experience or learning-by-doing (Arrow, 1962). Deraniyagala and Semboja (1999) for example found that the age of Tanzanian engineering firms is positively related to a production-based technology index. While Romijn (1999) and Wignaraja (2002, 2008a) found that it was not related to the ITCs of firms. From our results, it is ascertained that as domestic firms get older, less ITCs are absorbed through domestic supplier linkages. The results imply, as Penrose (1959) and Romijn (1997), that older domestic firms by virtue of having more operational experience rely on, and develop, internal efficiencies for the absorption of ITCs rather than on domestic supplier linkages.

Asia- and Europe-based suppliers

With regards to Asia- and Europe-based suppliers, our three regression models AQ_AS_CG_IND, AQ_ITC_AS and AQ_ITC_EU reveal that only one of the five explanatory variables — *engineers and technicians* — is positively and significantly related (at 1% levels) to the acquired ITCs of domestic MEPZ firms. The models have highly significant F-statistics (at 1% level) and the adjusted R^2 values are 0.209, 0.230 and 0.470, respectively.

Since the number of engineers in domestic firms conveys both the internal level of skill and is a proxy for firm size, we discuss the results in those terms. The evidence for developing countries that firm size is one of several determinants of firm-level ITCs abounds (for example Lall *et al.*, 1994 on Ghana; Latsch and Robinson (1999) on Zimbabwe; Wignaraja, 2008b). Westphal *et al.* (1990) for example, found that size (as one of four determinants) was significantly and positively related to Thai firms' ITCs. Similar results were found in other developing countries such as Sri Lanka (Wignaraja, 1998) and Kenya (Wignaraja and Ikiara, 1999). Rasiah (2004b) found that for foreign and local firms in the electronics industry in Malaysia, the Philippines and Thailand, larger firms enjoyed the scale and the resources to acquire higher human resources and process technology capabilities. Size did not produce a statistically significant relation with R&D capability owing to the extremely low levels of participation. Romijn (1999) indicated that firm size in relation to the manufacturing complexity of products in Pakistan was, once again, significant and positive. The most pertinent evidence for this study is from Wignaraja's (2002) study of firm-level characteristics, including size, for 40 Mauritian garment firms. In this study, he found that the number of engineers and technicians is also positively related to firms' level of created ITCs through their influence on new quality management methods, equipment maintenance and upgrading, productivity improvement, training and minor adaptations to process technologies. Similar results were found in our study for the acquisition of ITCs through Asia- and Europe-based supplier linkages. Thus, we conclude that in order for domestic MEPZ firms to absorb acquired ITCs through Asia- and Europe-based supplier linkages, they require the presence of skilled in-house engineers and technicians. This also implies that the type of knowledge and skills acquired is probably more advanced and specialised than those acquired through domestic suppliers and therefore requires the intervention of specialists in order to be effectively absorbed.

Contributions and Policy Lessons

Our study contributes in showing the differences in learning from suppliers and how to innovate when domestic firms and foreign subsidiaries operate under a temporary PTA. Firstly, it contributes by revealing that domestic supplier firms in a developing sub-Saharan African country like Mauritius can be an important source of ITCs to both domestic firms and foreign subsidiaries. Secondly, our study reveals that export-oriented foreign subsidiaries may fail to absorb acquired ITCs and engage in local ITC development, despite the presence of appropriate policies and institutions, when operating under a temporary PTA. Thirdly, domestic firms exhibit a higher commitment to the acquisition and absorption of ITCs through supplier linkages and develop local ITC due to their need to continue to survive and expand post-PTA and under world trade liberalisation. Fourthly, the study contributes through its firm-level managerial implications whereby it is revealed that experience in the industry — as measured by the age of firms — investment in training and reliance on foreign consultants and the high number of in-house engineers and technicians in domestic firms lead to a lower reliance on ITC acquisition from suppliers.

Regarding the first contribution, Porter (1990) for example argues that developing domestic suppliers is better than relying solely on foreign ones. Furthermore, he states that the critical underpinnings of competitiveness are present at home: firms will not sustain a competitive advantage in the long run. Additionally, Kelegama and Foley (1999) in their study on impediments to backward domestic supplier linkages in the Sri Lankan garment industry state that with

> *the phase out of the MFA quota system in the year 2005, garment manufacturers in Sri Lanka will have to compete with firms in countries such as Taiwan and Hong Kong most of which have backward linkages to local sources of supply... If there are strong reasons for less backward linkages from a particular industry, does this ultimately mean that the industry will be unable to develop a long-term competitive position in the global economy?*

Based on the results of our study, we posit that the domestic MEPZ suppliers are well poised to continuously develop the capabilities required to support the long-term competitive position of the

MEPZ textile industry. This position is related to the second and third objectives of the study and to the following arguments for policy lessons, because our results for the MEPZ can be applied to other similar textile-based developing countries, especially those operating under PTAs. The examples of Laos and Cambodia are also of pertinence here. Rasiah (2009) argues that even though these two countries have experienced a surge in garment exports, unless they engage in the development of institutional and firm-level ITCs, both countries will find it difficult to retain a significant presence of garment firms once the PTAs are withdrawn. We posit that the capacity of domestic suppliers in the MEPZ to be sources of ITCs and the domestic MEPZ firms' capacity to acquire and absorb ITCs from both domestic and foreign supplier linkages is partly due to the policies and institutional support provided by the Mauritian government.

As Lall (1992, 1993b, 1996) also argued, apart from random firm-level differences, enterprises in any economy react to a common set of incentives when investing in technological effort. They also draw upon a common set of factor markets and institutions, known as the national technological capabilities (NTCs) of the country, for their learning efforts. NTCs become important in technology transfer when there is a market failure at the firm level. The government then intervenes and creates incentives through factor markets and competition.

It was therefore with tremendous foresight that the 1968 post-independence government attached such a high priority to industrial development in its economic strategy. The need for structural transformation of the economy was being felt and moulded as early as the 1970s with the setting up of the MEPZ. The authorities were resolute in their determination to institutionalise a manufacturing sector by encouraging the development of an EPZ thereby diversifying from a mono-crop agricultural sector. The MEPZ firms and subsidiaries benefitted from tax incentives and duty-free access to imported inputs. The policies devised by the government were targeted towards taking advantage of the existing PTA and attracting inward FDI through providing one-stop shop services to foreign investors. Successive

Mauritian governments have for the past decades engaged in actively supporting the textile industry at a national level in order to develop textile firm-level ITCs, providing both domestic and foreign subsidiaries with the same opportunities for technological development and growth. The presence of appropriate institutions has also been argued as being fundamental in supporting the MEPZ (Subramanian and Roy, 2001; Bonaglia and Fukasaku, 2002). Subramanian and Roy (2001) attributed the success of the MEPZ, especially when compared to other African EPZs, to the quality of the support institutions in terms of transparency and their ability to manage rent-seeking behaviour and corruption.

Once again taking into consideration the NTC aspect of firm-level ITC development, Lall (1992) argued that there are various factors that provide incentives for firms to invest in technological effort. One incentive is an efficient labour market with an ample supply of skilled labour. If there is failure in the labour market, the government has to intervene in order to redress the situation. At the national level, various training institutions are in place to ensure a continuous supply of trained and skilled labour to the textile industry. Examples include the Industrial and Vocational Training Board,[7] which provides a Diploma in Clothing Production and the University of Mauritius with specialised production engineering and textile technology related courses from the Faculty of Engineering. These institutions have been strategically in place since the government realised that the MEPZ championed by the textile industry could lead to a strong industrial foundation for the economy. Therefore, it is argued that the availability of managers, engineers and technical staff for textile MEPZ firms and subsidiaries has been ample. Furthermore, the government has taken on the role of training the labour force and even supporting the inflow of foreign shop-floor workers from Asia into the zone.

Likewise, human capital development through on-the-job and external training opportunities allow employees to gain knowledge that is relevant to the tasks they are assigned. This also contributes to

---

[7] Now under the aegis of the Mauritius Institute of Training and Development.

local ITC development. During the field surveys, it was noted that most firms and subsidiaries did not have a formalised training budget or training facility. Several respondents described the firms' engineers as 'QBEs' — qualified by experience — an official title, which conveys that QBEs are specialists by virtue of their numerous years of experience within the industry and through external training and advancement opportunities provided by the firms. Technical training is not formalised and employees are trained on the production floor on an ongoing basis while they carry out their tasks. Thus, this also explains the fact that the government had to take on the role of training the labour force and ensuring an ample supply of skilled employees as described earlier.

Some of the textile-related institutions include the Export Processing Zone Development Authority (EPZDA) — a parastatal institution — which was set up 1992, now renamed Enterprise Mauritius. The EPZDA was geared towards helping MEPZ firms and subsidiaries face international competition, improve skills, manufacture higher value-added products, improve delivery times and enhance creativity in product design. It also addressed the issues critical to the successful transition from a labour-abundant to a skills-intensive economy.

Due to the specificity of the fabric and garment sectors another arm of the EPZDA was set up, namely the Clothing and Textile Centre now called the Textile and Apparel Development Centre, which provides a range of training, consultancy and technical expertise to the industry. Enterprise Mauritius also took over the activities of the Textile Emergency Support Team (TEST), which examined the decline in the textile industry and aimed at its restructuring to enhance international competitiveness. TEST was a high-powered committee set up in 2003 by the government and consisted of representatives from the public and private sectors. TEST also established the Policy Intervention Committee on Textile.

On the marketing front, the body responsible for the promotion of exports was the Mauritius Industrial Development Authority, whose agenda is now managed by Enterprise Mauritius. It focused on the marketing of Mauritian exports, which are primarily textile products, and carried out market surveys and marketing missions in the main Mauritian export markets as well as the regional markets.

All of the abovementioned support organisations and bodies also rely on the services of foreign consultants to improve the MEPZ textile industry. The latest initiative by the government includes the Fashion and Design Institute Bill, which was passed in 2008 by the national assembly. The Institute was created to tap into the high potential of the design sector, to channel existing resources and to re-activate the textile sector.

The quality and good functioning of these institutions in part explain why domestic suppliers have the ability to transfer ITCs and MEPZ domestic firms have developed an absorptive capacity for ITCs acquired through domestic and foreign supplier linkages. Yet, there is no evidence that acquired ITCs through supplier linkages led to local ITC creation in Asian-owned MEPZ firms. The latter had equal access to the support and services of these institutions. This, in turn, raises important questions concerning the absorptive capacity of Asian-owned MEPZ firms. Such a lack of absorptive capacity is deemed as being a reflection of their long-term learning strategies for innovation. Asian-owned subsidiaries did not focus their effort in creating local ITCs based on acquired capabilities from suppliers, nor did they capitalise on the presence of support institutions in Mauritius, because they foresaw their exit from the MEPZ post-MFA and PTA.

Regarding the fourth contribution of our study, we posit that domestic MEPZ firms should not only focus their efforts on absorbing ITCs through supplier linkages, but also concentrate their efforts on investing in training employees, rely on the expertise of foreign consultants and hire more engineers and technicians in order to increase their levels of in-house created ITCs.

Finally, we conclude with the two main limitations of our study. Firstly, we believe that there is a need to investigate whether any kind of reverse learning took place through these supplier linkages. This would elucidate whether the MEPZ domestic firms and foreign subsidiaries have the capacity to contribute to the innovative processes of supplier firms — whether locally based or foreign-based. From the interviews conducted several directors and production managers maintained that there is significant reverse learning from the MEPZ domestic firms and Asian-owned subsidiaries to the foreign suppliers of machinery and equipment. The directors and production managers have asserted that this reverse learning by foreign suppliers is then embodied in those suppliers' products, which are then globally marketed in other textile industries.

Secondly, the study does not analyse the trajectories of firms' ITC accumulation nor the rate at which the capabilities are accumulated. In-depth case studies of technologically advanced MEPZ textile firms, which would explore these rates and trajectories over time, would provide additional insights in innovation practices to other sub-Saharan African and developing country textile firms.

References

Arrow, K. (1962). The economic implications of learning by doing, *The Review of Economic Studies*, **29**(3), 155–173.

Bell, M. and Pavitt, K. (1995). "The development of technological capabilities," in Irfan ul Haque (ed.), *Trade, Technology and International Competitiveness*, in collaboration with Bell, M., Dahlman, S., Lall, S. and Pavitt, K., The World Bank, Washington, DC.

Bell, M. Scott-Kemmis, D. and Satyarakwit, W. (1982). "Limited learning in infant industry: A case study," in Stewart, F. and James, J. (eds), *The Economics of New Technology in Developing Countries*, Frances Pinter, London.

Biggs, T., Shah, M. and Shrivastava, P., (1995). *Technological Capabilities and Learning in African Enterprises*, World Bank Technical Paper No. 288.

Bonaglia, F. and Fukasaku, K. (2002). *Trading Competitively: Trade Capacity Building in Sub-Saharan Africa*, OECD Development Centre Studies, Paris.

Brash, D.T. (1966). *American Investment in Australian Industry*, Harvard University Press, Cambridge, MA.

Broadman, H.G. (2007). *Africa's Silk Road: China and India's New Economic Frontier*, World Bank, Washington, DC.

Busby, J.S. and Fan, I.S. (1993). The extended manufacturing enterprise: Its nature and its needs, *International Journal of Technology Management*, Special Issue on Management — Technology, Diffusion, Implementation, and Management, **8**(3–5), 294–308.

Cammett, M. (2007). Business–government relations and industrial change: The politics of upgrading in Morocco and Tunisia, *World Development*, **35**(11), 1889–1903.

Chen, E.K.Y. (1983). *Multinational Corporations, Technology and Employment*, Macmillan, London.

Chen, L.-C. (2009). Learning through informal local and global linkages: The case of Taiwan's machine tool industry, *Research Policy*, **38**, 527–535.

Clark, K.B. (1998). Project scope and project performance: The effect on parts strategy and supplier involvement in product development, *Management Science*, **35**(10), 1247–1263.

Clark, K.B. and Fujimoto, T. (1991). *Product Development Performance*, Harvard Business School Press, Boston, MA.

Cohen, W. and Levinthal, D. A., (1989). Innovation and learning: The two faces of R&D, *The Economic Journal*,Vol. **99**: 569–596.

Dahlman, C.J. and Westphal, L.E. (1981). The meaning of technological mastery in relation to transfer of technology, *The Annals*, **458**, 12–26.

David, P. (1975). *Technical Choice, Innovation and Economic Growth*, Cambridge University Press, Cambridge, UK.

Deraniyagala, S. and Semboja, H. (1999). "Trade liberalisation, firm performance and technology upgrading in Tanzania," in Lall, S. (ed.), *The Technological Response to Import Liberalisation in Sub Saharan Africa*, Macmillan, London, pp. 57–111.

Dosi, G. (1988). Sources, procedures and microeconomic effects of innovation, *Journal of Economic Literature*, **26**: 1120–71.

Dosi, G. Freeman, C., Nelson, R., Silverberg, G. and Soete, L., (1988). *Technical Change and Economic Theory*, Columbia University Press, New York.

Dunning, J. H., (1995). Reappraising the eclectic paradigm in an age of alliance capitalism. *Journal of International Business Studies*, Vol. **26**, Issue **3**: 461–491

Dutrénit, G. and Vera-Cruz, A.O. (2006). Technological capability accumulation in MNCs' subsidiaries: The case of the Maquilas in Mexico, unpublished paper, COLEF/FLACSO/UAM (Proyecto CONACYT núm. 35947-s).

Ernst, D. and Kim, L. (2002). Global production networks, knowledge diffusion and local capability formation, *Research Policy*, **31**, 1417–1429.

Field, A.P. (2009). *Discovering Statistics Using SPSS*, 3rd edn., Sage Publications, London.

Figueiredo, P.N. (2005). Plugging into globalisation to stay alive and move ahead or standing still to fall behind? evidence of technological capability building from three sets of firms in northern Brazil, *Proceedings of the DRUID Tenth Anniversary Summer Conference on 'Dynamics of Industry and Innovation: Organizations, Networks and Systems'*, Copenhagen, Denmark, June, 2005, 27–29.

Fransman, M. and King, K. (eds) (1984). *Technological Capability in the Third World*, Macmillan, London.

Goldman, S.L. and Nagel, R.N. (1992). Management, technology and agility: The emergence of a new era in manufacturing, *International Journal of Technology Management*, **8**(1–2), 18–38.

Hines, P. (1994). *Creating World Class Suppliers: Unlocking Mutual Competitive Advantage*, Financial Times, Pitman Publishing, London.

Hobday, M. (1995). *Innovation in East Asia: The Challenge to Japan*, Edward Elgar Publishing Ltd, UK.

Hobday, M. (1996). Innovation in Southeast Asia: Lessons for Europe, *Management Decision*, **34**(9), 37–48.

Hobday, M. and Rush, H. (2007). Upgrading the technological capabilities of foreign transnational subsidiaries in developing countries: The case of electronics in Thailand, *Research Policy*, **36**, 1335–1356.

Ivarsson, I. and Alvstam, C.J. (2009). Learning from foreign TNCs: A study of technology upgrading by local suppliers to AB Volvo in Asia and Latin America, *International Journal of Technology Management*, **48**(1), 56–76.

Jonker, M., Romijn, H. and Szirmai, E. (2006). Building technological capabilities to improve performance: A case study of the paper industry in West Java, Indonesia, *Technovation*, **26**(1), 121–134.

Katz, J.M. (1969). *Production Functions, Foreign Investments and Growth: A Study Based on the Argentine Manufacturing Sector 1946–1961*, North Holland, Amsterdam.

Katz, J.M. (1984). Domestic technological innovations and dynamic comparative advantage, *Journal of Development Economics*, **16**(1–2), 13–37.

Kelegama, S. and Foley, F (1999). Impediments to promoting backward linkages from the garment industry in Sri Lanka Institute of Policy Studies, Colombo, Sri Lanka, *World Development*, **27**(8), 1445–1460.

Lall, S. (1980). Vertical inter-firm linkages in LDCs: An empirical study, *Oxford Bulletin of Economics and Statistics*, **42**(3), 203–226.

Lall, S. (1992). Technological capabilities and industrialization, *World Development*, **20**(2), 165–186.

Lall, S. (1993a). *Transnational Corporations and Economic Development*, Routledge, London, New York.

Lall, S. (1993b). Promoting technology development: The role of technology transfer and indigenous effort, *Third World Quarterly*, **14**(1), 95–108.

Lall, S. (1996). *Learning from the Asian Tigers in Technology and Industrial Policy*, Macmillan, London.

Lall, S., Barba-Navaretti, G., Teitel, S. and Wignaraja, G. (1994). *Technology and Enterprise Development: Ghana under Structural Adjustment*, Macmillan, London.

Larsson, S. (1993). New dimensions in organising industrial networks, *International Journal of Technology Management*, Special Issue on Management — Technology, Diffusion, Implementation, and Management, **8**(1–2), 39–58.

Latsch, W. and Robinson, P. (1999). "Technology and the responses of firms to adjustment in Zimbabwe," in Lall, S. (ed.), *The Technological Response to Import Liberalisation in SubSaharan Africa*, Macmillan, London, pp. 148–206.

Liu, X., Wang, C. and Wei, Y. (2009). Do local manufacturing firms benefit from transactional linkages with multinational enterprises in China? *Journal of International Business Studies*, **40**(7), 1113–1130.

Lundvall, B.Å. (1988). "Innovations as an interactive process: From user producer interaction to the national system innovation," in Dosi, G., Freeman, C., Nelson, R., Silverberg, G. and Soete, L. (eds), *Technical Change and Economic Theory*, Printer, London, pp. 349–369.

Lundvall, B.Å. (1992). "User–producer relationships, national systems of innovation and internationalisation," in Lundvall, B.Å. (ed.), *National Systems of Innovation: Towards a Theory of Innovation and Interactive Learning*, Pinter, London, New York, pp. 45–67.

Malerba, F. (1992). Learning by firms and incremental technical change, *The Economic Journal*, **102**, 845–859.

Nelson, R. and Winter, S., (1982). *An Evolutionary Theory of Economic Change*, Cambridge, MA: The Belknap Press of Harvard University Press.

Neter, J., Kutner, M.H., Nachtsheim, C.J. and Wasserman, W. (1996). *Applied Linear Regression Model*, Richard D. Irwin, Inc, Chicago, IL.

Penrose, E.T. (1959). *The Theory of the Growth of the Firm*, Basil Blackwell, Oxford, UK.

Pietrobelli, C. (1997). *Industry, Competitiveness and Technological Capabilities in Chile: A New Tiger From Latin America*, Macmillan, London.

Pisano, G.P. (1996). Learning-before-doing in the development of new process technology, *Research Policy*, **25**(7), 1097–1119.

Porter, M. (1990). The competitive advantage of nations, *Harvard Business Review*, 73–93.

Ramaswamy, K.V. and Gereffi, G. (1998). India's apparel sector in the global economy: Catching up or falling behind, *Economic and Political Weekly*, **17**, 122–129.

Rasiah, R. (ed.) (2004a). *Foreign Firms, Technological Capabilities and Economic Performance: Evidence From Africa, Asia and Latin America*, Edward Elgar Publishing Ltd, Cheltenham, UK.

Rasiah, R. (2004b). Exports and technological capabilities: A study of foreign and local firms in the electronics industry in Malaysia, the Philippines and Thailand, *The European Journal of Development Research*, **16**(3), 587–623.

Rasiah, R. (2004c). "Technological intensity and export incidence in Indonesia," in Rasiah, R. (ed.), *Foreign Firms, Technological Capabilities and Economic Performance: Evidence from Africa, Asia and Latin America*, Edward Elgar Publishing Ltd, Cheltenham, UK, pp. 95–114.

Rasiah, R. (2006). Ownership, technological intensities, and economic performance in South Africa, *International Journal of Technology Management*, **36**(1–3), 166–189.

Rasiah, R. (2009). Garment manufacturing in Cambodia and Laos, *Journal of the Asia Pacific Economy*, **14**(2), 150–161.

Rasiah, R. and Rasagam, G. (2004). "Economic performance, local sourcing and technological intensities in Malaysia," in Rasiah, R. (ed.), *Foreign Firms, Technological Capabilities and Economic Performance: Evidence from Africa, Asia and Latin America*, Edward Elgar Publishing Ltd, Cheltenham, UK, pp. 115–141.

Rasiah, R. and Tamale, H. (2004). "Technology and economic performance in Uganda," in Rasiah, R. (ed.), *Foreign Firms, Technological Capabilities and Economic Performance: Evidence from Africa, Asia and Latin America*, Edward Elgar Publishing Ltd, Cheltenham, UK, pp. 72–94.

Reuber, G.L., Crookell, H., Emerson, M. and Gallais-Hamonno, G. (1973). *Private Foreign Investment in Development*, Clarendon Press, Oxford, UK.

Romijn, H. (1997). Acquisition of technological capability in development: A quantitative case study of Pakistan's capital goods sector, *World Development*, **25**(3), 359–311.

Romijn, H. (1999). *Acquisition of Technological Capability in Small Firms in Developing Countries*, Macmillan Press, London.

Rosenberg, N. (1976). *Perspectives on Technology*, Cambridge University Press, Cambridge, UK.

Rosenberg, N. (1982). *Inside the Black Box*, Cambridge University Press, Cambridge, UK.

Sahal, D. (1981). *Patterns of Technological Innovation*, Reading, Mass: Addison Wesley.

Silverberg, G., Dosi, G. and Orsenigo, L. (1988). Innovation, diversity and diffusion: A self-organisation model, *Economic Journal*, **98**(393), 1032–1054.

Subramanian, A. and Roy, D. (2001). Who can explain the Mauritian miracle: Meade, Romer, Sachs or Rodrik? *IMF Working Paper*, WP/01/116.

Torres, R. (2001). Towards a socially sustainable world economy: an analysis of the social pillars of globalization, Geneva, ILO.

Tyre, M.J. and Orlikowski, W.J. (1996). The episodic process of learning by using, *International Journal of Technology Management*, Special Issue on Unlearning and Learning for Technological Innovation, **11**(7–8), 790–798.

von Hippel, E. (1976). The dominant role of users in the scientific instrument innovation process, *Research Policy*, **5**, 212–239.

von Hippel, E. (1988). *The Sources of Innovation*, Oxford University Press, Oxford, UK.

von Hippel, E. and Tyre, M. (1995). How learning by doing is done: Problem identification in novel process equipment, *Research Policy*, **24**(1), 1–12.

Westphal, L.E., Kritayakirana, K., Petchsuwan, K., Sutabutr, H. and Yuthavong, Y. (1990). "The development of technological capability in manufacturing: A macroscopic approach to policy research," in Evenson, R.E. and Ranis, G. (eds), *Science and Technology: Lessons for Development Policy*, Intermediate Technology Publications, London, pp. 81–134.

Wignaraja, G. (1998). *Trade Liberalisation in Sri Lanka: Exports, Technology and Industrial Policy*, Macmillan, London.

Wignaraja, G. (2002). Firm size, technological capabilities and market-oriented policies in Mauritius, *Oxford Development Studies*, **30**(1), 87–104.

Wignaraja, G. (2008a). Ownership, technology and buyers: Explaining exporting in China and Sri Lanka, *Transnational Corporations*, **17**(2), 1–15.

Wignaraja, G. (2008b). Foreign ownership, technological capabilities and clothing exports in Sri Lanka, *Journal of Asian Economics*, **19**, 29–39.

Wignaraja, G. and Ikiara, G.K. (1999). "Adjustment, technological capabilities and enterprise dynamics in Kenya," in Lall, S. (ed.), *The Technological Response to Import Liberalisation in SubSaharan Africa*, Macmillan, London, pp. 57–111.

WIR (2006). *World Investment Report 2006, FDI from Developing and Transition Economies: Implications for Development*, United Nations Conference on Trade and Development (UNCTAD), United Nations Publications, New York.

Annex 1. Description and Frequency Distribution of Independent and Control Variables for Domestic MEPZ Firms.

Age: Number of years the firms have been in operation in the MEPZ

	≤10	11–20	21–30
Absolute and percentage values	9 (23.1%)	27 (69.2%)	3 (7.7%)

Training budget: Expenditure on employee training as a % of sales

	–	Max	Mean
Percentage values	0.001	0.10	0.0084

External technical assistance: Number of times an external technical consultant or local technology institution was used during a three-year period prior to data collection

	≤10	11–20	21–30	>30
Absolute and percentage values	34 (87.2%)	3 (7.7%)	1 (2.6%)	1(2.6%)

Engineers and technicians: Number of engineers and technicians in the firm

	≤100	101–200	201–300	>300
Absolute and percentage values*	34 (87.18%)	2 (5.13%)	2 (5.13%)	—

Textile industry sector: Dummy control variable, where upstream fabric firms are assigned a value of 1 and downstream garment firms are assigned a value of 0

Fabric firms		Garment firms	
#	%	#	%
15	38.5	24	61.5

Notes: *1 missing value

Annex 2. Correlation Matrix of Control and Independent Variables.

		1	2	3	4	5
1. Age	Pearson correlation	1				
	Sig. (2-tailed)					
	N					
2. Training budget	Pearson correlation	−0.224	1			
	Sig. (2-tailed)	0.171				
	N	39				
3. External technical assistance	Pearson correlation	−0.028	−0.141	1		
	Sig. (2-tailed)	0.864	0.392			
	N	39	39			
4. Engineers and technicians	Pearson correlation	0.399*	−0.017	0.219	1	
	Sig. (2-tailed)	0.013	0.920	0.186		
	N	38	38	38		
5. Textile industry sector	Pearson correlation	0.019	−0.155	−0.216	−0.020	1
	Sig. (2-tailed)	0.911	0.345	0.187	0.906	
	N	39	39	39	38	

Notes: * Correlation is significant at the 0.05 level (2-tailed)

Chapter 7

The Relation Between Internal and External Open Innovation: A Study of Firms Located in the Goomi and Banwol-Sihwa Clusters in South Korea

Joseph Yun Jin-Hyo
Daegu Gyeongbook Institute of Science and
Technology, South Korea

Avvari V. Mohan
Nottingham University Business School
University of Nottingham, Malaysia

Introduction

In the last decade, open innovation (Chesbrough, 2003) has become popular for the practice and study of innovation. This paper presents the results of a survey investigating the relation between 'open innovation factors' (both internal and external to the firm) and other factors termed 'open innovation attitudes', in two clusters in South Korea. Chesbrough's (2003) concept of 'open innovation is explained as the use of purposive inflows and outflows of knowledge to accelerate internal innovation, and expand the markets for external use of innovation, respectively. This paradigm assumes that firms can and should use external ideas as well as internal ideas, and internal and external paths to market, as they look to advance their technology' (Chesbrough, 2003, 133; 2006, pp. 196–203). Thus, there are several factors that affect open innovation from inside the firm itself and outside the firm. In this study we consider certain 'internal open innovation factors' such as 'attitude' and argue that 'open innovation attitude' along with open innovation factors will affect overall innovation performance.

Vanhaverbeke and Cloodt (2006, p. 276) proposed that open innovation research should be investigated at different levels such as individual, firm or organizational, dyad, inter-organizational networks, and national or regional innovation systems, thus indicating the importance of the geographical dimension and geographic specific elements for open innovation. Regional clusters and regional innovation systems are considered important as they aid knowledge flows into firms from different external sources, which is crucial to open innovation (Vanhaverbeke, 2006, p. 216). While the influence of open innovation on firms' performance has been analyzed by studies by authors such as Laursen and Salter (2006), Chen *et al.* (2007), and Yun (2009) we could not find any study about the relation between external open innovation effects and firms' internal open attitude — particularly among firms in clusters where it is expected that there would be external open innovation effects.

Given the above, the aim of this chapter is to investigate the relation between open innovation factors and the internal open innovation attitude and their effect on the innovative performance of firms. To add a geographic dimension the study is conducted in firms located in two different industrial clusters. The clusters chosen for this study are the Banwol-Sihwa and Goomi Clusters in South Korea. The Banwol-Sihwa Cluster is located near to Seoul while the Goomi Cluster is near to Daegu city, the hometown of Samsung Mobile and LG Electronics.

Research Framework, Conceptual Background and Hypotheses

We developed the research framework for this study as in Fig. 1. Open innovation will have an effect on the innovative performance of firms

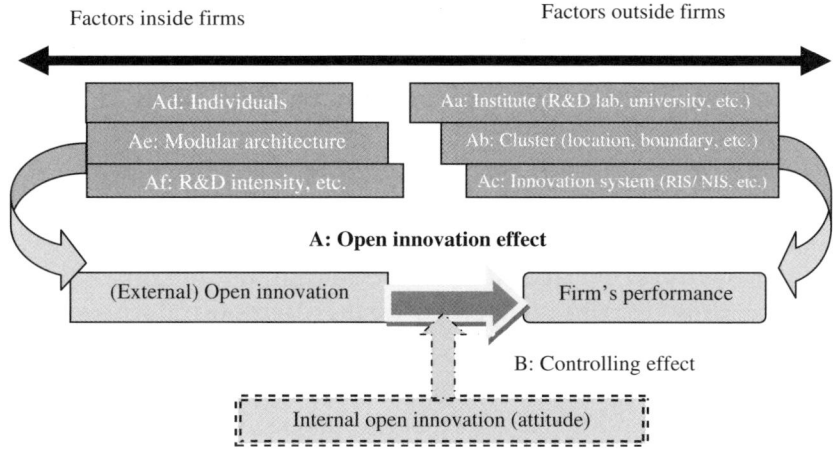

Fig. 1.   Research Framework.

based on factors that are inside and outside the firms. The specific research questions for the study are:

- What is the relation between the internal open innovation attitude of firms and firms' external open innovation?
- Is there any control effect of internal open innovation to the external open innovation effect?

We also wanted to see how these are different in the two clusters as it is assumed that 'external open innovation factors' could be different between the geographic locations — with differences in infrastructure, resources, location benefits, etc.

Open innovation arguments and hypothesis development

Chesbrough (2003) originated the idea of open innovation and identified that it has a huge and positive influence on firms' innovation performance. Through the case study of PARC of Xerox, Chesbrough showed that if a firm uses what is now known as the 'closed innovation' approach, no matter how much it increases its R&D effort, it cannot make complete use of the outcomes of its

R&D (Chesbrough, 2003, pp. 1–19). Adobe, VLSI, GRID, Metaphor, and CTI are firms that Xerox spun off without even acquiring licenses. In addition, Xerox could not develop firms such SynOptics and Microlytis as its essential core even though it knew their potential under the closed innovation paradigm. Chesbrough also analyzed IBM to help understand how a firm transforming from a closed innovation system to an open innovation system could secure growth and develop further (Chesbrough, 2003, pp. 93–112). The case study of IBM helped to further demonstrate how a firm adopting 'open innovation' was able to achieve substantial innovative performance, develop new growth energy, and improve its performance. In addition an analysis of firms such as 3M, Apple, and Intel shows that these firms dynamically acquire new ideas from external sources and develop totally new markets based on their internal open attitude.

3M has evolved from a maker of sandpaper to a manufacturer of hundreds of different products, including adhesives, films, and fiber optics. In almost a century, it has commercialized over fifty thousand products. Its success as an innovator is generally attributed to its corporate culture, which very deliberately fosters creativity by giving employees the freedom to take risks and tinker with new ideas. That culture is a legacy of the '15% rule', which allows technical and scientific employees to use that percentage of their time to pursue ideas unrelated to their official assignments (Luecke, 2003). According to the 3M case, the 'internal open attitude' to new ideas is very important to induce new knowledge and technology from outside. In the case of Intel, instead of academic freedom, intellectual inquiry, and the thrill of scientific discovery, it offers its researchers six months on the manufacturing line, the Noyce Principle of minimum information, and a career path that promises close coordination with manufacturing (Chesbrough, 2003, p. 124). Intel lets researchers develop new ideas through the Noyce Principle, which is also a strategy for the internal open attitude for growth in the company.

Steve Jobs of Apple always tried to scout ideas from outside, and his open attitude to new ideas and products from outside became the culture in Apple. In addition, managing open innovation in a world of intermediate markets for ideas, requires the construction and support of a rich internal innovation network (Chesbrough, 2006, p. 20). Many open business companies such as Qualcomm, Enzyme, Procter & Gamble, and Chicago have their own internal open innovation attitudes, because of their internal innovation networks. An internal innovation network means having an active internal open innovation attitude including a structure and culture that will trigger the internal open innovation attitude. Nonaka (1995, p. 71, pp. 113–116) confirms that the capability for potential knowledge creation is an internal resource that will promote knowledge recognition in an organization, knowledge transition, and making core products. In addition, he lists several factors as the triggers for the capability for potential knowledge creation as an internal resource such as creative vision, autonomy, shock and creative chaos, redundancy, and minimum diversity. Google (2005, pp. 111–112) has a 20% rule, which means that an employee can spend 20% of the work time (1 day per week) on any science and technology job. Many new products such as Google news, Orkut, Froogle, and Google Print are due to the 20% rule. This means that an internal open attitude could promote a diversity of innovation in a firm.

According to West and Gallagher (2006a, p. 84), there are three kinds of innovation models: proprietary (or internal or 'closed'), external and open, as listed in Table 1.

West and Gallagher (2006b, p. 36) described three kinds of R&D according to the degree of openness: proprietary innovation, pooled R&D, and spinout, as shown in Fig. 2. They divided R&D according to the openness of R&D. Proprietary innovation means closed innovation based on internal R&D. Any firm which has a pooled R&D system has open innovation including inward open innovation and outward open innovation. Firms which have spinout R&D have outward open innovation or external open innovation.

In the discussion so far the terms 'closed innovation', 'open innovation', and transition cases from closed to open innovation have been introduced. Chesbrough's model of innovation is divided into two: the closed innovation model and the open innovation model. In this section the concepts and types of open innovation are explained.

Table 1. Models of Innovation and Resulting Managerial Issues.

Innovation model	Management challenges	Resulting management techniques
Proprietary (or internal or 'closed')	Attracting the "best & brightest"	Provide excellent compensation, resources, and freedom
	Transforming research results to development	Provide dedicated development functions to exploit research and link it to market knowledge
External	Exploring a wide range of sources of innovation	Careful environmental search
	Integrate external knowledge with firm resources and capabilities	Developing absorptive capacity and using alliances, networks, etc.
Open	Motivating the generation and use of external knowledge	Provide intrinsic rewards (e.g. recognition) and structure (instrumentality) for contributions
	Incorporating external sources with firm resources and capabilities	As above
	Maximizing the exploitation of diverse intellectual property (IP) resources	Share or give away IP to maximize returns from entire innovation portfolio

Source: West and Gallagher (2006a, p. 84)

According to Chesbrough (2003, p. 43), valuable ideas can come from inside or outside the company and can go to market from inside or outside the company as well — this approach to innovation has been conceptualized as open innovation. He divided 'open innovation' into two categories. The first is 'inward open innovation' through which

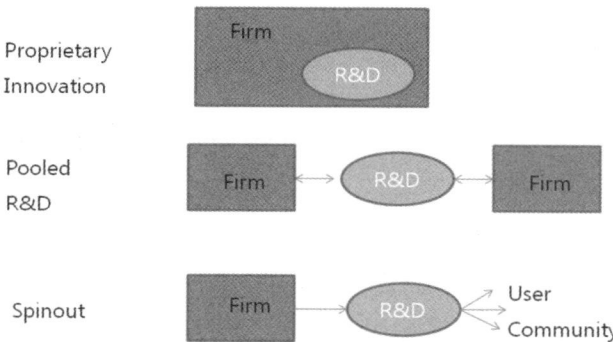

Fig. 2. R&D and Innovation.

Source: West and Gallagher (2006b, p. 319)

firms take new ideas and information from external sources and the second is 'outward open innovation' through which firms transfer information and technology that they do not need in order to maximize the benefits. The first category is technology insourcing, and the second consists of licensing technology to other firms, technology spin-offs to new markets, and transferring product or service innovation to the current market (Chesbrough, 2006b, p. 3).

While open innovation has two sources — internal or external technology — there is an emphasis on the internal attitude or culture of firms for open innovation. There are eight points of differentiation for open innovation. Two of them are the centrality of the business model in converting R&D into commercial value, and the proactive and nuanced role of intellectual property (IP) management, which is directly related with the internal open innovation attitude of a firm (Chesbrough, 2006b, p. 11). The argument is that any firm that has an open attitude or culture to new ideas and new innovation can easily actualize new business models and intellectual property. In addition, there is a new role for internal R&D as a knowledge connector and broker and this 'open innovation thinking' means having an internal open innovation attitude or internal open innovation. Open innovation thinking changes the role of the research function. It expands the role of internal researchers to include not just knowledge generation, but also knowledge brokering (Chesbrough, 2003, p. 56). Thus in the conceptualization of open innovation there is external open innovation and internal open innovation and these two aspects affect each other.

Laursen and Salter (2006) tested and analyzed the relation between open innovation and the performance of firms. They analyzed 2,707 UK manufacturing firms, and empirically tested the relation between open innovation and firms' performance. Even though this study creatively developed variables for open innovation in a firm, there appears to be a weakness in terms of the overlap of the depth and width of open innovation, and the difference from the literal meaning of depth and width based on the Organization for Economic Cooperation and Development (OECD) innovation survey results. Yun (2009) also analyzed firms in the Goomi and Seongseo Clusters to study the relation between open innovation and a firm's performance in different clusters. In this study, the difference of the open innovation effect between neighboring clusters is considered. There does not appear to be any study explicitly considering the different dimensions of open innovation, i.e. internal and external open innovation and their relations. In the next section we explain these aspects further and develop the first hypothesis.

Hypothesis development

First hypothesis: There is a relation between internal and external open innovation

Apple Corporation built its own creative culture under the leadership of Steve Jobs. He organized management retreats as an annual ceremony. Anyone who attends a retreat can take three or four full days to develop their creative ideas. In addition, he gave any team that was involved in new innovative projects such as the Macintosh, iPad, and Pixar (Young and Simon, 2005, p. 58). This policy gives his company an 'open attitude' to new ideas and due to this internal open attitude it has a relation with its external open innovation.

At Apple in the early days, Steve Jobs would go outside the company for creative aspects like product design and advertising. For everything else, Steve blindly followed the "NIH" philosophy — 'not invented here'. The technology had to be created within Apple; if his technical wizards did not know how to do something, they would just hire someone who did. Going outside the company simply was not acceptable. Someone who can't change their ideas is a prisoner of his past. Steve broke out of that prison (Young and Simon, 2005, p. 279). Several of Apple's products such as the Macintosh, iMac, Pixar, and iPad were developed through internal creative and open research but the initial ideas were from outside Apple. Some of the technologies took root through the arrival of key employees at Apple. The Macintosh computer embodied many of the user-interface design concepts created at PARC (Chesbrough, 2003, p. 5).

Google has a 20% rule, which means that any employee can participate in any interesting research or technology job on his or her own volition (Luoyaozong, 2005, p. 111). This rule allowed employees to develop several creative new products such as the Google Deskbar, Google Books, Google News, and Google Alerts. This rule makes Google have an 'internal open attitude' to new products. In addition, Google recruits creative people from all over the world. As a result, it can be argued that the "internal open innovation attitude" has a deep relation with external open innovation. 3M also has its 15% rule, which is similar to Google's. This rule was behind the creation of the Post-it. And it spawned 3M's adhesive tape business, which currently produces more than 700 specialized products for medical, electrical, home, and industrial applications (Luecke, 2003, p. 5).

In addition to the cases discussed so far, managing open innovation in a world of intermediate markets for ideas also requires the construction and support of a rich internal innovation network (Chesbrough, 2006a, p. 20). Indeed, an internal innovation network is essential for the open innovation model and markets such as Intellectual Ventures, InnoCentive, and Ocean Tomo. In conclusion, internal open innovation and external open innovation are related. So, this leads to the first hypothesis (Fig. 3):

Hypothesis 1: There is a relation between internal open innovation and external open innovation.

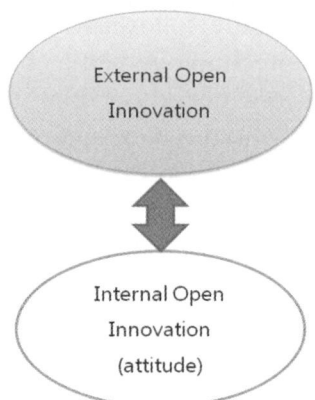

Fig. 3.   Framework for Hypothesis 1.

Second hypothesis: The internal open innovation attitude and its effects

The inventors of a new technology are often not the first to profit from that technology, and one of the reasons for this is the difficulty of transferring new research discoveries into production (Chesbrough, 2003, p. 115). Intel put together an R&D group and a production group in such a way that every new researcher has to work on production from the beginning of their career. In addition, Intel invested in standardizing its equipment between 'lab' (laboratory) and 'fab' (fabrication). These policies allowed the company to develop an internal open attitude. Intel's research philosophy fostered an external orientation to the generation of knowledge (Chesbrough, 2003, p. 130). Indeed, Intel's internal open innovation attitude triggered several mechanisms to access external innovation such as the Intel Technical Journal, the funding of about three hundred external research projects, and lablets.[1]

---

[1] 'Lablets' are small research facilities located adjacent to three leading university research centers — Carnegie Mellon University, the University of California, Berkeley, and the University of Washington — instead of next to Intel fab facilities. As with other parts of its R&D system, Intel manages these new entities in a decidedly untraditional manner (Chesbrough, 2003, p. 123).

Knowledge creation capability rather than organization knowledge is a critical resource in an organization (Nonaka and Konno, 2009, p. 71). Not merely core competences but capability which is used as the know-how at the organization level or probability of future is considered better for open innovation. Nonaka's knowledge creation theory asserts that the interaction between tacit knowledge and coded knowledge creates knowledge in both quantity and quality (Nonaka and Konno, 2009, p. 93). The knowledge creation capability means internal open innovation, and it is one of main resources for knowledge development in the interaction between tacit and coded knowledge. Knowledge firms, which are similar to active external open innovation firms, have several organizational cultures such as an open culture and the not-quantity-but-quality culture, and they stress the importance of communication (Nonaka and Konno, 2009, p. 204). According to Nonaka, an internal open attitude also increases external open innovation (Fig. 4).

Therefore, we propose our second hypothesis:

Hypothesis 2: An internal open innovation attitude will have a modulating effect on the relation between external open innovation and innovative performance.

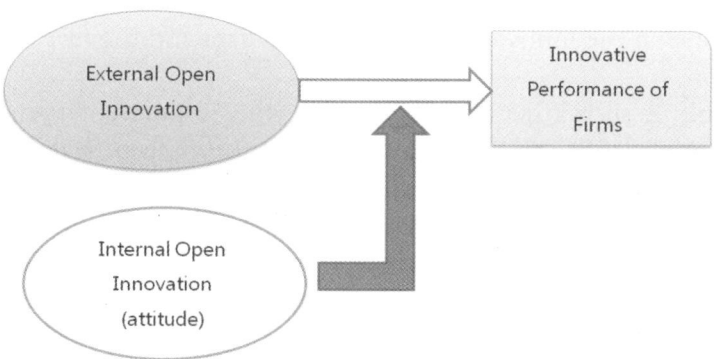

Fig. 4.   Framework for Hypothesis 2.

Here 'modulate' means 'extend', 'increase', and 'expand'. If we analyze the relation between these two facts, we could understand more comprehensively the open innovation process and create open innovation strategies.

Also we would like to explore the effect of the geographic dimension and argue that external open innovation effects may differ in firms located in different regional clusters.

Study Methodology

The data for the analysis was obtained from a survey. Primary data was collected using questionnaires sent out to firms in the Banwol-Sihwa Cluster and Goomi Cluster in South Korea by email. Questionnaires were sent to the CEO or senior general managers of 500 enterprises located in these clusters. We received more than 200 responses. After examining the responses, we ended up with 179 valid questionnaires, which included 99 from Banwol-Sihwa Cluster and 80 from Goomi Cluster.

The survey was conducted in 2008 and the method and types of questions were based on innovation surveys carried out following the OECD *Oslo Manual* and the core Eurostat Community Innovation Survey (CIS) of innovation (Stockdale, 2002; DTI, 2003; OECD, 1997; Laursen & Salter, 2003). There were six questions on external open innovation and five on internal open innovation, and there were questions on the innovation output of the firm and the firm's general situation.

Table 2 shows detailed data about the respondents. There are considerable differences in industry structure, firm scale, year of establishment, and the supply and demand conditions in each cluster. There seems to be a good mix of conglomerates, first-tier vendors, and supplier firms and there are also numerous firms with less than 20 employees in both clusters. There are many chemical and automotive components companies in the Banwol-Sihwa Cluster, while the Goomi Cluster has many video products companies and machinery companies.

Table 2. General Characteristics of the Respondents (*n* = 179).

Classification		Total sum	Banwol-Sihwa Cluster	Goomi Cluster
The number of corporations		179	99 (55.3%)	80 (44.7%)
High-tech approval	High-tech firms	110 (61.5%)	64 (64.6%)	46 (57.5%)
	Non high-tech firms	69 (38.5%)	35 (35.4%)	34 (42.5%)
Supply and demand relations	Conglomerates	44 (24.6%)	24 (24.2%)	20 (25.0%)
	First vendor	77 (43.0%)	37 (37.4%)	40 (50.0%)
	Second vendor	43 (24.0%)	27 (27.3%)	16 (20%)
	Third vendor	15 (8.4%)	11 (11.1%)	4 (5.0%)
Year of establishment	Before 1990	39 (22.3%)	26 (26.3%)	13 (16.3%)
	1990–1999	40 (22.4%)	30 (30.3%)	10 (12.5%)
	2000–2004	72 (40.2%)	28 (28.3%)	44 (55.0%)
	After 2005	28 (15.1%)	15 (15.2%)	13 (16.3%)
Number of employees	Less than 5	19 (10.6%)	6 (6.1%)	13 (16.3%)
	6–10	27 (15.1%)	11 (11.1%)	26 (32.5%)
	11–20	38 (21.2%)	21 (21.2%)	17 (21.3%)
	21–50	49 (27.4%)	35 (35.4%)	14 (17.5%)
	51–100	23 (12.8)	15 (15.2%)	8 (10.0%)
	101–300	17 (9.5%)	9 (9.1%)	8 (10.0%)
	More than 300	6 (3.3%)	2 (2.0%)	4 (5.0%)
Major industry	Textile product	13 (7.26%)	9 (9.1%)	4 (5.0%)
	Compound and chemicals	25 (13.97%)	20 (20.2%)	5 (6.1%)
	Rubber and plastic product	6 (3.35%)	5 (5.1%)	1 (1.3%)
	Steel	11 (6.15%)	9 (9.1%)	3 (4.0%)
	Manufacturing steel and product	20 (11.17%)	12 (12.1%)	8 (10.0%)
	Machinery & equipment	24 (13.41%)	10 (10.1%)	14 (17.5%)

(*Continued*)

Table 2. (*Continued*)

Classification		Total sum	Banwol-Sihwa Cluster	Goomi Cluster
Major industry	Electronics and transformation device	14 (7.82%)	3 (3.0%)	9 (11.3%)
	Motion picture, sound, communication	17 (9.50%)	0 (0.0%)	17 (21.3%)
	Medical, precision, optics, watch	3 (1.68%)	2 (2.0%)	1 (1.3%)
	Automotive and trailer	16 (8.94%)	13 (13.1%)	3 (4.0%)
	Other	30 (16.76%)	16 (16.2%)	14 (17.5%)

Variables for the study

External open innovation independent variables

The transfer of incoming and outgoing knowledge and information happens through the external relations of firms. Therefore, we would like to differentiate internal open innovation from external open innovation. External open innovation has the same meaning as the open innovation concept defined by Chesbrough (2003, p. 43; 2006, p. 15) and Laursen and Salter (2006). This study uses external open innovation channels similar to those used by Laursen and Salter (2006) — which are based on the OECD innovative survey — and slightly modified through translating the questions into Korean. There are 16 open innovation channel variables, which consist of four channels from universities and institutes, six channels from external firms and markets, three channels from public and general information, and three channels concerning firms' personnel and licenses. Each of the 16 channels are measured using a 5-point scale — firms that score many different channels are more 'open' with respect to search breadth than firms that do not (Laursen and Salter, 2006, p. 140). External search depth is defined as the extent to which a firm draws intensively from different search channels or sources of innovative ideas (Laursen and Salter, 2006, p. 140). This concept is constructed by using the average of the degree of openness of the 16 channels. We sum the values of the 16 channels and divide by 16 to measure the depth of external search (Yun, 2009).

We multiply breadth by depth to give a single open innovation independent variable, the level of open innovation (Yun, 2009). Although the introduction of any variable into a well-established area of research is always contentious, the new variable reflects the openness of an innovative search and will enable researchers to better explore the link between an innovative search and innovative performance (Laursen and Salter, 2006, p. 140). Through this we attempt to overcome the limits of Laursen and Salter's (2006) research in which they divided open innovation into depth and width. We multiply these values to give a single variable to measure external open innovation. This overcomes the difficulty of interpretation, which occurs when two open innovation results conflict with each other. Thus we are capable of clearly and consistently measuring the relation between external open innovation and other variables.

Internal open innovation: Moderating variable

Internal open innovation measures the extent of firms' internal open attitude to new innovation, new products, and new processes. Internal open innovation is measured using a 5-point scale ranging from closed innovation to highly open innovation. This variable measures how easily internal teams in firms — Purchasing, Sales, Marketing, R&D, Production, etc. — accept new knowledge and information from each other. We measure this variable according to how many new ideas are taken from other internal departments. We used five channels for internal open innovation following the OECD innovation survey questionnaire. Each of the five channels is measured using the average of the degree of openness of five channels similar to the way width is measured for external open innovation.

Control variables

We control two variables: the intensity of internal R&D effort and firm size. We include 'R&D intensity', measured as firm R&D expenditure divided by firm sales in 2007 as a control variable in order to control the effect on R&D on innovative performance (Laursen and Salter, 2006, p. 141). Firm size (expressed as a logarithm) is measured by the number of employees (LOGEMP) as Laursen and Salter (2006, p. 141). Large firms are better able to acquire the complementary assets that are necessary to guarantee the commercial success of innovative products (Teece, 1986). But small firms might outperform larger firms in terms of creativity, flexibility, and speed, especially when new, disruptive technologies appear (Christensen and Bower, 1996).

To analyze controlling effect, we put the multiple values of firms' external open innovation and internal open innovation as correlative variable. Since each firm has a different way of measuring external and internal open innovation, we will use it after multiplying each standardized value.

Laursen and Salter (2006, p. 142) and Yun (2009) use the length of a firm's existence, STARTUP, the year of establishment, as a control variable. But we do not utilize it as a control variable because the age of a firm is highly correlated with its volume. We do not control for the effect of different industries in this study, in contrast to Laursen and Salter (2006, p. 141), because we want to analyze the cluster effect, which includes the industry effect and among other things (Yun, 2009).

Dependent variable: Firms' performance

We used one proxy variable, which combines three variables aimed at reflecting the various types of innovative performance by firms — which was used by Laursen and Salter (2006) and (Yun, 2009). Because of the difficulty in translating English into Korean, we did not have any other choice but to sum three dependent variables, one of which is for radical innovation and the others are for incremental innovation. It is very difficult to express the difference between the three types of innovation performance in Korean.

This study measures a firm's performance as the number of new products. The performance of firms includes completely new products in the industry or internal to their enterprise and also improvements to existing products. These three variables are the fraction of the firm's turnover for products new to the world market, the fraction of the firm's turnover for products new to the firm, and the fraction of the firm's turnover for products that have been significantly improved (Laursen and Salter, 2006, p. 140).

Analysis and Results

Descriptive analysis

Table 3 shows a strong negative correlation between firm size and R&D intensity. In addition, the correlation between firm size and external open innovation has a *p*-value of 0.10. So, we control firm size and R&D intensity in this study.

Table 4 shows a strong positive relationship between internal open innovation and firm size. Internal open innovation has a positive correlation with R&D intensity. These correlations are similar to the results in Table 3. So, we control for firm size and R&D intensity when we analyze internal open innovation.

Table 4 shows that there is no statistical relationship between internal open innovation and control variables such as firm size and

Table 3. Correlation between External Open Innovation and Control Variables.

		1	2	3
1	EOI (external open innovation) *p*-value	0.135		
2	LOGEMP (firm size) *p*-value	0.101		
3	RDINT (R&D intensity) *p*-value	0.050	−0.406***	
		0.583	0.000	

Notes: * $p < 0.10$, ** $p < 0.05$, *** $p < 0.01$

Table 4. Correlation between Internal Open Innovation and Control Variables.

		1	2
1	IOI (internal open innovation) *p*-value	0.068	
2	LOGEMP (firm size) *p*-value	0.380	
3	RDINT (R&D intensity) *p*-value	0.016	−0.406***
		0.854	0.000

Notes: * $p < 0.10$, ** $p < 0.05$, *** $p < 0.01$

RDINT. Therefore it is possible to use both control variables and the modulating variable in the regression equation.

This study uses multiple regression and analyzes the effect of external open innovation, R&D intensity, and firm size on innovative performance, and the modulating effect of internal open innovation. The statistical method of this research is different from that of Laursen and Salter (2006, p. 141). We did not censor double the dependent variable and directly used new products. But Laursen and Salter (2006, p. 141) censored double the dependent variable as the percentage of innovative sales and therefore by definition it ranges between 0 and 100. A regression model based on censored dependent variables, such as the percentage of new products, is referred to as a censored regression model or a Tobit model (Greene, 2008, p. 871).

According to the results in Table 5, overall external open innovation and firm size have positive and significant effects on a firm's innovative performance. But if we consider the two clusters, the results are different from each other. In the Banwol-Sihwa Cluster, external open innovation, firm size, and R&D intensity do not have any significant effect on a firm's innovative performance. However, in the Goomi Cluster external open innovation and firm size have a positive and significant effect on a firm's innovative performance.

Therefore, if there is a modulating effect of internal open innovation in one of the two clusters, it could indicate that internal open innovation may modulate the effect of external open innovation on a firm's innovative performance depending on location. Because the

Table 5. Multiple-Regression Analysis of the External Open Innovation Effect in Both Clusters.

Dependent variables Independent variables	Total analysis ($n = 121$)			Banwol-Sihwa cluster analysis ($n = 70$)			Goomi cluster analysis ($n = 51$)		
	β (SC)	t	p	β (SC)	t	p	β (SC)	t	p
Constant		-0.749	0.455		1.585	0.118		-1.716	0.093
EOI	0.237***	2.680	0.008	0.301	2.425	0.018	0.275**	2.087	0.042
LOGEMP	0.180**	1.879	0.063	-0.090	-0.682	0.498	0.358***	2.498	0.016
RDINT	-0.020	-0.210	0.834	-0.095	-0.746	0.458	0.032	0.221	0.826
$R2$	0.100			0.084			0.189		
Adjusted $R2$	0.077			0.043			0.137		
F	4.357***			2.030			3.647**		

Notes: The regression analysis coefficient is a standardized coefficient and firm size was measured using the number of employees.

* $p < 0.10$, ** $p < 0.05$, *** $p < 0.01$

effects of external open innovation are different in each cluster, the modulating effect of internal open innovation will also be different in each cluster. So, if there is a modulating effect in any cluster we could say that internal open innovation may modulate the external open innovation effects of a firm's innovative performance.

Measures of correlation

According to the results in Table 6, the first hypothesis can be accepted. Table 6 shows there is a correlation between external open innovation and internal open innovation in total and also in the two clusters. The strong correlation between external and internal open innovation in firms in Banwol-Sihwa Cluster and Goomi Cluster indicates that there is strong interrelation between external open innovation and the internal open attitude of the firms. This results hints that firms with an open culture and systems with respect to new ideas and technology are willing to transfer internal unused ideas or technology for external utilization or commercialization, and accept innovative ideas or crucial information from external channels in order to take advantage of them in developing new products.

Measure of modulating effect

Table 7 shows that for the firms that responded, internal open innovation does not modulate a firm's innovative performance because in

Table 6. Correlation Analysis between External and Internal Open Innovation.

	External open innovation		
	Total firms	Banwol-Sihwa cluster analysis	Goomi cluster analysis
Mean	38.4031	36.2099	40.9411
S.D.	15.67163	14.49345	16.67884
N	151	81	70
Internal open innovation	0.580***	0.556***	0.625***

Coefficient correlation (r), * $p < 0.10$, ** $p < 0.05$, *** $p < 0.01$

Table 7. Analysis of Modulating Effect in Total.

Dependent variables Independent variables	Additional external open innovation (n = 120)			Additional internal open innovation (n = 120)			Additional external and internal interaction (n = 120)		
	β (SC)	t	p	β (SC)	t	p	β (SC)	t	p
Constant		−0.805	0.423		−0.564	0.574		−1.188	0.237
EOI	0.242***	2.727	0.007	0.235**	2.291	0.024	0.195*	1.806	0.074
LOGEMP	0.182***	1.893	0.061	0.181**	1.879	0.063	0.176*	1.829	0.070
RDINT	−0.022	−0.231	0.818	−0.021	−0.219	0.827	−0.023	−0.239	0.812
IOI				0.015	0.148	0.883	0.119	0.886	0.377
EOI × IOIb							0.139	1.183	0.239
Adjusted R2	0.080			0.072			0.075		
ΔR2				−0.008			0.003		
F	4.428***			3.298**			2.928**		

Notes: The regression analysis coefficient is a standardized coefficient and firm size was measured using the number of employees.
Each variable was calculated by multiplying standardized values.
* $p < 0.10$, ** $p < 0.05$, *** $p < 0.01$

Table 8. Analysis of the Modulating Effect in the Banwol-Sihwa Cluster.

Dependent variables Independent variables	Additional external open innovation (n = 69)			Additional internal open innovation (n = 69)			Additional external and internal interaction (n = 69)		
	β (SC)	t	p	β (SC)	t	p	β (SC)	t	p
Constant		1.498	0.139		0.725	0.471		0.183	0.855
EOI	0.306	2.450	0.017	0.303	2.129	0.037	0.270	1.796	0.077
LOGEMP	−0.090	−0.681	0.499	−0.090	−0.675	0.502	−0.082	−0.611	0.543
RDINT	−0.099	−0.772	0.443	−0.098	−0.758	0.451	−0.106	−0.814	0.419
IOI				0.005	0.034	0.973	0.074	0.439	0.662
EOI × IOIb							0.107	0.722	0.473
Adjusted R2	0.045			0.030			0.023		
ΔR2				−0.015			−0.007		
F	2.067			1.527			1.317		

Notes: The regression analysis coefficient is a standardized coefficient and firm size was measured using the number of employees.
Each variable was calculated by multiplying standardized values.
* $p < 0.10$, ** $p < 0.05$, *** $p < 0.01$

Table 9. Analysis of the Modulating Effect in the Goomi Cluster.

Dependent variables Independent variables	Additional external open innovation ($n = 51$)			Additional internal open innovation ($n = 51$)			Additional external and internal interaction ($n = 51$)		
	β (SC)	t	p	β (SC)	t	p	β (SC)	t	p
Constant		−1.716	0.093		−1.030	0.308		−1.219	0.229
EOI	0.275**	2.087	0.042	0.274*	1.762	0.085	0.230	1.366	0.179
LOGEMP	0.358**	2.498	0.016	0.358**	2.463	0.018	0.342**	2.315	0.025
RDINT	0.032	0.221	0.826	0.032	0.218	0.828	0.033	0.224	0.824
IOI				0.002	0.010	0.992	0.125	0.532	0.597
EOI × IOIb							0.143	0.705	0.484
Adjusted $R2$	0.137			0.118			0.109		
$\Delta R2$				−0.019			−0.009		
F	3.647***			2.677**			2.217*		

Notes: The regression analysis coefficient is a standardized coefficient and was measured using the number of employees.
Each variable was calculated by multiplying standardized values.
* $p < 0.10$, ** $p < 0.05$, *** $p < 0.01$

the second and third columns the *F* values are significant, but IOI and EOI × IOI are not significant. In conclusion, internal open innovation appears not to modulate the external open innovation effect for open innovation.

Table 8 shows the results of the regression for external open innovation and internal open innovation — and the results indicate that the relation between external and internal open innovation is not significant among firms in the Banwol-Sihwa Cluster. Incidentally Banwol-Sihwa Cluster is the one nearest to the capital city, Seoul.

Table 9 shows the results of the regression for external open innovation and internal open innovation in the Goomi Cluster are significant. But, as seen in the second and third columns, IOI, and EOI × IOI are not significant. So, we can confirm that for firms in the Goomi Cluster there is no modulating effect of internal open innovation on external open innovation.

According to Tables 7, 8, and 9, Hypothesis 2 is rejected. Therefore, we could not confirm that internal open innovation may modulate external open innovation.

Conclusions and Implications

The statistical analysis leads to several interesting results — including that external open innovation factors and firm size have positive and significant effects on a firm's innovative performance in total. The results from the two clusters were different from each other. In the Banwol-Sihwa Cluster, external open innovation, firm size, and R&D intensity did not have any significant effect on a firm's innovative performance. However, in the Goomi Cluster external open innovation and firm size had a positive and significant effect on a firm's innovative performance. While there was a correlation between external open innovation and the internal open innovation attitude in both clusters, other results showed significant differences for the role of clusters and innovation systems in open innovation. Next we present the results and discuss the implications for the open innovation concept and also for policy and for firms' innovation strategies.

Firms are increasingly drawing in knowledge from external sources in their innovative activities, and modern innovation processes require firms to master highly specific knowledge about different users, technologies, and markets (Laursen and Salter, 2006, p. 146). Regarding open innovation being enhanced by an internal open attitude (as found in the case studies of Google, 3M, and Intel), two new concepts were introduced: external open innovation and the internal open innovation attitude, and we analyzed the relation between them and a firm's innovative performance. In addition, we examined the effects of external open innovation for firms in two clusters: the Banwol-Sihwa Cluster near Seoul and the Goomi Cluster near Daegu, which is the hometown of Samsung Mobile and LG Electronics. Firms in the Goomi Cluster have a positive and significant effect for external open innovation, but firms in the Banwol-Sihwa Cluster do not.

We identified organizations in industries other than "high technology" that are early adopters of the concept. Our results demonstrate that many open innovation concepts are already in use and we discovered that open innovation is not *ipso facto* a recipe for outsourcing R&D. We conclude that open innovation has utility as a paradigm for industrial innovation beyond high-tech to more traditional and mature industries (Chesbrough and Crowther, 2006, p. 229). As Chesbrough and Crowther (2006, p. 229) expressed, open innovation effects exist in diverse technology-based industries. The differences in external open innovation effects in the two clusters is not due to differences in industry type but from differences between the clusters (Chesbrough and Crowther, 2006, p. 229; Yun, 2009). External open innovation is correlated with internal open innovation. In addition, we found that the modulating effect analysis model for firms in the Goomi Cluster is significant even though the modulating effect of internal open innovation to external open innovation is not.

The correlation between external open innovation and an internal open innovation attitude exists in both clusters The modulating effect of internal innovation is significant in one cluster — indicating that for some firms external open innovation has an effect on innovation performance. Accordingly, we confirm that external open innovation has a positive relation with the internal open innovation attitude. Indeed, case studies on the internal open attitude such as those for Google, 3M, and Intel, and several Japanese case studies (Nonaka) can be generalized. The implications are that one should can think about and develop several new strategies and policies to promote external open innovation through the internal open innovation attitude. The modulating effect of the internal open attitude on external open innovation was not confirmed in this study.

Limitations and future research

According to several cases, 3M, Google, and Intel, we could infer that internal open innovation will modulate external open innovation. But in this study, we could not confirm it. The conclusion is that internal open innovation has a positive correlation with external open innovation, and in one cluster, where external open innovation has a significant effect on innovative performance, the modulating effect model is significant. So, further research is required to examine the modulating effect of internal open innovation. We have to examine several firms in diverse clusters and industries to find out the modulating effect.

Second, in this paper, we did not examine internal open innovation policies such as the 15% rule in 3M, the 20% rule in Google, and researchers staying on a manufacturing line for six months. Future research might explore internal open innovation attitudes such as culture, rules, or behavior.

So, future research is required to examine the different dimensions and policies of internal open innovation in individual firms. If we studied diverse forms of internal open innovation, it would be possible to develop a systematic consulting toolkit for firms for open innovation. In addition, we might discover the changing role of internal R&D and invention in firms through a study of individual firms' internal open innovation. Those are core to internal open innovation in firms.

References

Braunerhjelm, P. and Feldman, M. (eds). (2006). *Cluster Genesis: Technology-Based Industrial Development*, Oxford University Press, Oxford, UK.

Breschi, S. and Malebra, F. (eds). (2005). *Clusters, Networks and Innovation*, Oxford University Press, Oxford, UK.

Bresnahan, T., Gambardella, A. and Saxenian, A. (2005). "Old economy inputs for new economy outcomes: Cluster formation in the New Silicon Valley," in Breschi, S. and Malebra, F. (eds), *Clusters, Networks and Innovation*, Oxford University Press, Oxford, UK.

Capello, R. (1999). Spatial transfer of knowledge in high technology milieux: Learning versus collective learning processes, *Regional Studies*, **33**(4), 353–365.

Chen, J., Chen, Y. and Vanhaverbeke, W. (2007). Open innovation strategy and catch-up of Chinese firms, *The Internal Conference for the Chinese Economy*, Seoul National University, Korea.

Chesbrough, H. (2003). *Open Innovation: The New Imperative for Creating and Profiting from Technology*, Harvard University Press, Cambridge, MA.

Chesbrough, H. (2006a). *Open Business Models: How to Thrive in the New Innovation Landscape*, Harvard Business School Press, Boston, MA.

Chesbrough, H. (2006b). "Open Innovation: A new paradigm for understanding industrial innovation," in Chesbrough, H., Vanhaverbeke, W. and West, J. (eds), *Open Innovation: Researching a New Paradigm*, Oxford University Press, Oxford, UK.

Chesbrough, H. (2008). *Open Innovation: The Next Frontier in R&D*, presentation to ALA.

Chesbrough, H. and Crowther, K. (2006). Beyond high tech: Early adopters of open innovation in other industries, *R&D Management*, **36**(3), 229–236.

Chesbrough, H., Vanhaverbeke, W. and West, J. (eds). (2006). *Open Innovation: Researching a New Paradigm*, Oxford University Press, Oxford, UK

Christensen, C. (1997). *The Innovator's Dilemma: When New Technologies Cause Great Firms to Fail*, Harvard Business School Press, Cambridge, MA.

Christensen, C. and Bower, J. (1996). Customer power, strategic investment, and the failure of leading firms, *Strategic Management Journal*, 7(3), 197–218.

Chul-Won, L. (2008). *Let's Enhance the Development of Economy with Open Innovative Paradigm*, Science Technology Police Research Center, Seoul.

Cooke, P. (2005). "Regional knowledge capabilities and open innovation: Regional innovation systems and clusters in asymmetric knowledge economy," in Breschi, S. and Malebra, F. (eds), *Clusters, Networks and Innovation*, Oxford University Press, Oxford, UK.

Cooke, P. (2007). "Theorizing regional knowledge capabilities: Economic geography under 'open innovation'," in Suriñach, J., Moreno, R. and Vayá, E. (eds), *Knowledge Externalities, Innovation Clusters and Regional Development*, Edward Elgar, Northampton.

DTI. (2003). *UK Innovation Survey*, Department of Trade and Industry, London.

Duk-Kyu, B. and Won-hee, L. (2008). *The Status and Effect Analysis of Korean Manufacturing Industry*, Samsung Economic Research Center.

Feldman, M. and Braunerhjelm, P. (2006). "The genesis of industrial cluster," in Braunerhjelm, P. and Feldman, M. (eds), *Cluster Genesis: Technology-Based Industrial Development*, Oxford University Press, Oxford, UK.

Greene, W. (2008). *Econometric Analysis*, Prentice-Hall, Upper Saddle River, NJ.

Hippel, E. (2005). *Democratizing Innovation*, MIT Press, Cambridge, MA.

Jin-Hyo, Y. (2006a) *Korean Technology Policy Theory*, KyoungMoonsa Publishing, Seoul.

Jin-Hyo, Y. (2006b) *New Research and Development*, KyoungMoonsa Publishing, Seoul.

Jin-Hyo, Y., Park, S.-M. and Kun, L. (2006) *Open Innovation: Verification of the possibility of Application in South Korea*, Technology Management Economic Council.

Jin-Hyo, Y. and Sung-duk, H. (2008) *Analysis of Innovative Network and Openness of Local Clusters: Based on the Seongseo and North American Industry Complex*, Science and Technology Policy Research Center, Seoul.

Laursen, K. and Salter, A. (2003). Searching low and high: Why do firms cite universities as a source of innovation? *EMAEE 2003 Conference on the "Knowledge-Based Economies: New Challenges in Methodology, Theory and Policy"*, Augsburg, Germany.

Laursen, K. and Salter, A. (2006). Open for innovation: The role of openness in explaining innovation performance among UK manufacturing firms, *Strategic Management Journal*, **27**, 131–150.

Luecke, R. (2003). *Managing Creativity and Innovation*, Harvard Business Essentials, Boston, MA.

Luoyaozong, Z. (2005). *The Seven Success Lessons from Google*, Xipsaiae Publishing Co, Seoul, translated in 2007.

Miller, W.L. and Morris, L. (1999). *Fourth Generation R&D*, John Wiley & Sons, Inc., New York.

Maskell, P. (2005). "Towards a knowledge-based theory of the geographical cluster," in Breschi, S. and Malebra, F. (eds), *Clusters, Networks and Innovation*, Oxford University Press, Oxford, UK.

Motzek, R. (2007). *Motivation in Open Innovation: An Exploratory Study on User Innovators*, VDM Verlag.

Nonaka, I. and Konno, N. (1995). *Intellectualizing Capability*, Book 21 Publishing Group, Seoul, translated from Korean in 2009.

O'Connor, G. (2006). "Open, radical innovation: Toward an integrated model in large established firms," in Chesbrough, H., Vanhaverbeke, W. and West, J. (eds), *Open Innovation: Researching a New Paradigm*, Oxford University Press, Oxford, UK.

OECD (1997). *Proposed Guidelines for Collecting and Interpreting Technological Innovation Data: The "Oslo Manual"*, Organization for Economic Development and Cooperation, Paris.

Saxenian, A. and Hsu, J. (2005). "The silicon Valley-Hsinshu connection: Technical communities and industrial upgrading," in Breschi, S. and Malebra, F. (eds), *Clusters, Networks and Innovation*, Oxford University Press, Oxford, UK.

Simard, C. and West, J. (2006). "Knowledge networks and the geographic locus of innovation," in Chesbrough, H., Vanhaverbeke, W. and West, J. (eds), *Open Innovation: Researching a New Paradigm*, Oxford University Press, New York.

Stockdale, B. (2002). *UK Innovation Survey*, Department of Trade and Industry, London. Available at http://www.dti.gov.uk/iese/ecotrends.pdf. October 2004.

Suk-Kwan, K. (2008). *Chesbrough's Openness for Innovation*, Seoul Science and Technology Institutes.

Suriñach, J., Moreno, R. and Vayá, E. (eds). (2007). *Knowledge Externalities, Innovation Clusters and Regional Development*, Edward Elgar, Northampton.

Vanhaverbeke, W. (2006). "The interorganizational context of open innovation," in Chesbrough, H., Vanhaverbeke, W., and West, J. (eds), *Open Innovation: Researching a New Paradigm*, Oxford University Press, New York.

Vanhaverbeke, W. and Cloodt, M. (2006). "Open innovation in value networks," in Chesbrough, H., Vanhaverbeke, W. and West, J. (eds), *Open Innovation: Researching a New Paradigm*, Oxford University Press, New York.

West, J. and Gallagher S. (2006a). "Patterns of open innovation in open source software," in Chesbrough, H., Vanhaverbeke, W. and West, J. (eds), *Open Innovation: Researching a New Paradigm*, Oxford University Press, New York.

West, J., Vanhaverbeke, W. and Chesbrough H. (2006). "Open innovation: A research agenda," in Chesbrough, H., Vanhaverbeke, W. and West, J. (eds), *Open Innovation: Researching a New Paradigm*, Oxford University Press, New York.

Wi-Jin, S. (2007). *Searching for Technology Innovation System*, Seoul Technology Policy Institute.

Young, J. and Simon, W. (2005). *iCon: Steve Jobs — The Greatest Second Act in the History of Business*, John Wiley and Sons Inc., New Jersey.

Young-Gil, L., Lee, J.-H. and Young Il, S. (2007). *Paradigm Shift as Open Innovation in the Eye of Patent Analysis*, Korea Technology Innovation Council.

Yun, J.-H.J. (2009). Geographical boundary of open innovation: Sources within and beyond cluster, *Atlanta Conference of Science and Technology*.

Chapter 8

Collaborative Approach Within the Open Innovation Framework: Russian Companies

Daria Podmetina*
Department of Industrial Management,
Lappeenranta University of Technology, Finland

Maria Smirnova
Graduate School of Management,
Saint-Petersburg State, University, Russia

Juha Väätänen
Department of Industrial Management,
Lappeenranta University of Technology, Finland

Marko Torkkeli
Kouvola Research Unit,
Lappeenranta University of Technology, Finland

Introduction

Cooperation plays an important role in the global and turbulent business environment and the need for a collaborative approach has significantly increased in the open innovation era (Enkel *et al.*, 2010). Having cooperation skills is a great advantage for a company's innovativeness, and the capability of utilising external knowledge is a

---

* Corresponding author

287

significant factor in innovation performance (Cohen & Levinthal, 1990).

Cooperation with stakeholders increases the innovation capability of a firm (Lundvall *et al.*, 2002). Companies build links and cooperation in R&D with their stakeholders such as customers, suppliers, competitors and public institutions (Enkel & Gassmann, 2008; Smirnova *et al.*, 2009). The recent trend has been the growing importance of innovation networks (Dittrich & Duysters, 2007; Chesbrough & Prencipe, 2008; Torkkeli *et al.*, 2008). Many studies have shown that external links and cooperation increase a company's innovation capability and have a positive effect on the innovation output (Bayona *et al.*, 2001; Kaufmann & Tödtling, 2001; Klomp & van Leeuwen, 2001; Hagedoorn, 2002; Loof & Heshmati, 2002; Romijn & Albaladejo, 2002; Belderbos *et al.*, 2004; Vivero, 2004; Veugelers & Cassiman, 2005).

Transitional countries such as Russia have typical characteristics of post-communist transitional economies, which significantly affect the companies' stakeholder cooperation strategies. Traditional Soviet industries were vertically integrated and missing horizontal links (Väätänen, 2008). When building external relationships, Russian companies face obstacles such as the instability of relationships in the market, low partner information availability and a high risk of opportunistic behaviour (Johanson, 2007). On the other hand, the Russian market provides a unique opportunity to study the development of innovation strategies in emerging markets. Currently no evidence exists for how Russian companies operate in an environment of market failures and how they identify partners for successful innovation cooperation. The existing literature mainly consists of empirical papers focusing on the effectiveness of innovation processes (Dynkin and Ivanova, 1998), but do not offer any view on how cooperation strategies focus on closing the innovation gap between developed economies and Russia (Cervantes and Malkin, 2001).

This chapter studies cooperation on innovation in Russian companies. Open innovation is analysed based on the Gassmann and Enkel (2004) classification: the outside-in process, the inside-out process and a combination of both processes. We consider that companies possess a portfolio of innovation activities influencing open innovation implementation, which includes in-house R&D, outsourced R&D,

technology acquisition, collaborative external partnerships with suppliers, customers, universities and research organisations and technology commercialisation. We aim to discover the trends and the intensity of cooperation of Russian companies and how this fits into the new open innovation paradigm. Russia is geographically large country consisting of 80 regions. For survey, data collection, we selected best performing regions in terms of innovation indicators.

The chapter is structured as follows: this section has introduced the research topic and set the research objective. The next section reviews the literature of open and closed innovation strategies and cooperation. It is followed by the section that describes the research design, survey data and variables. The section presents the key findings, followed by a discussion of the results, and the final section presents our conclusions.

Literature Review

Towards open innovation

Traditional strategy states that companies have to diversify in order to use opportunities and avoid threats due to market turbulence (Porter, 1979). However, the business environment was still considered relatively stable in the mid to late 1980s. Since the beginning of the 1990s, market and environmental turbulence have increased and companies have been forced to compete and flexibility has become a means for companies' survival (Kotler and Caslione, 2009). What was considered extraordinary and stressful for companies 20 years ago has become an everyday situation for modern companies. Due to the degree of turbulence, increased competition and new technology opportunities, companies have intensified the use of knowledge, both internal and external (Cohen & Levinthal, 1990; Klevorick *et al.*, 1995).

In earlier times, companies were able to control all stages of the innovation process themselves and thus most R&D was produced internally (in-house R&D) (Wheelwright & Clark, 1992). Not only R&D, but new product development (NPD) and technology innovation were conducted within a company's borders. This approach is nowadays referred to as the traditional or closed approach to innovation. It has become obvious that the traditional approach to innovation and R&D does not fit into this changed environment. Thus, many companies have started a transition towards a new, more open policy for innovation. Companies have to develop more open business models if they want to get the best use of their internal R&D, if they want to search for and acquire new technologies and use effectively commercialisation channels, decrease costs and save time (Christensen, 1997). When Chesbrough (2003, 2006) coined the phrase 'open innovation' to describe this new phenomenon, it was at a very appropriate time for describing the latest transformation processes in the field of innovation. Now, the open approach has become essential for many companies' innovation practices. The organised search for new ideas is important for open innovation framework development (Laursen and Salter, 2006). Open innovation can be exploratory (emergent innovation process) and focused (predetermined search) (Holmes and Smart, 2009). Chesbrough (2003) considered that several factors were influential at the beginning of the open innovation era:

(1) improved access to the best available knowledge sources both inside and outside a company because of the increasing availability of an educated labour force;
(2) an increase in the number of possible sources of financing for R&D projects;
(3) companies started to cooperate more and search for ideas and technology outside and incorporate these into their innovation policies.

In this paper, open innovation is analysed based on the Gassmann and Enkel (2004) classification:

(1) the outside-in process — searching for and incorporating the external knowledge of suppliers, customers, competitors, universities and research organisations, etc. — external technology acquisition;
(2) the inside-out process — the transfer of ideas, technology, intellectual property to the market — technology commercialisation;
(3) a combination of outside-in and inside-out processes.

In a more recent work the same authors raise the question of the necessity of finding the optimal ratio between introducing open innovation practices and investing in traditional innovation (Enkel *et al.*, 2010). We consider that companies possess an innovation portfolio that includes in-house R&D, outsourced R&D, technology acquisition, collaborative external partnerships with suppliers, customers, universities and research organisations and technology commercialisation.

Cooperation supports open innovation

Cooperation is the core of the open innovation framework (Chesbrough, 2006) and the number of cooperative partners and the quality of cooperation matter for the success of introducing open innovation principles (Kock and Torkkeli, 2008). Open innovation phenomena evolve a high degree of cooperation with partners such as other companies in the industry, suppliers and clients (Chesbrough, 2003). Customer value increases when companies exploit new ideas and develop new products and technologies both themselves (in-house) (Wheelwright and Clark, 1992) and in cooperation with suppliers or competitors (inter-firm). Cooperation provides an opportunity to access knowledge and technologies in order to increase the innovativeness of the company, decrease costs and risks (Faria and Schmidt, 2007).

There have been multiple studies on the collaborative approach to innovation (Freytag, 2002; Blomqvist and Levy, 2006; Miles *et al.*, 2004; Johnsen and Ford, 2000; Ford and Johnsen, 2001; Hakansson and Eriksson, 1993). Collaborative innovation is an option in addition to in-house R&D and outsourcing (Baglieri and Zamboni, 2005). Its unique advantage is the creation of additional value within the partner relationship (Walter *et al.*, 2001).

The ability to cooperate in R&D or in NPD is valuable for all organisations. Companies that are highly skilled in cooperation (cooperation capability) have access to a large range of technologies and can better manage their R&D resources (Torkkeli *et al.*, 2009). The role of the contribution of external partners and collaboration is difficult to overestimate. Large companies do not fully rely on internal innovation and tend to increase cooperation in R&D activities

(Dodgson, 1993; Freeman and Hagedoorn, 1994) and create their own values for cooperation (Smith and Blanck, 2002).

Decisions about innovation strategies are based on social interaction and the analysis of innovation practices (Neyer *et al.*, 2009). Independently of the level of cooperation, firms need to develop specific organisational competencies to support this type of interaction. Cooperation capability depends on how companies develop and manage partnerships (Dyer and Singh, 1998). The core of cooperation capability is the integration of skills and tacit knowledge with external partners. The motives for cooperation depend on the type of partner (Tether, 2002; Belderbos *et al.*, 2004).

The intensified cooperation in innovation in recent decades indicates a lack of internal resources and capabilities of the companies to satisfy the need for innovation and R&D (Hagedoorn, 2002). The simultaneous implementation of innovation and cooperation strategies in companies has been discussed in many studies. Some companies have decided to cooperate based on their internal R&D expertise, and try to balance internal and external R&D based on this internal knowledge, which is a choice between 'making and buying' (Cassiman and Veugelers, 2002). Companies may externalise if there are internal innovation weaknesses (Keupp and Gassmann, 2009). Other companies cooperate with competitors in product R&D, process R&D or both (Lin and Saggi, 2002).

The literature shows that cooperation is more important for companies with a strong experience of internal research and development, and those companies who cooperate on R&D value this cooperation even more. Based on our observations, companies with experience of internal R&D and R&D cooperation seem to be more eager to expand their innovation business models towards technology acquisition and cooperation in commercialising internal R&D.

Research proposition 1 (P1): Companies with experience of internal R&D cooperate more than companies without internal R&D.

Cooperation with suppliers

Companies can cooperate on innovation with a variety of external parties: suppliers (Hakansson and Eriksson, 1993), competitors

(Clark and Fujimoto, 1991), customers (von Hippel, 1988), research organisations (Gemünden *et al.*, 1996), etc. It is believed that the key sources for innovators are often lead users, suppliers or universities (von Hippel, 1988). Companies use channels (suppliers, users, universities) when they search for innovative opportunities (Laursen and Salter, 2006) and the results of this analysis of UK manufacturing firms shows that the most important channel is the suppliers of equipment, materials, and components, followed closely by clients and customers, which indicates that innovation is determined by relations with suppliers and customers.

In earlier studies (Smirnova *et al.*, 2009) we investigated which groups of external partners were involved in NPD process (suppliers in Russia, suppliers abroad, customers in Russia, customers abroad, intermediaries, shareholders, competitors, consultants, research organisations and partners in joint ventures). Our results indicated that the role of external partners for the firms following the joint NPD approach is higher — they depend more on 'core' stakeholders. At the same time for those firms following their own R&D resources-based NPD strategy, external partners can still be vitally important.

Research proposition 2 (P2): The importance of cooperation is more significant for those companies who have introduced a more diversified innovation strategy such as open innovation.

Some studies have focused on factors that specifically induce companies to cooperate with foreign partners located in other countries for innovative activities (Faria and Schmidt, 2007). The existence of strong relationships between internationalisation and innovation is obvious for many companies, especially when international technology transfer is a form of export *per se* (Filipescu, 2007). Companies' cooperation with foreign suppliers to some degree relates to physical distance, which means that companies export or import to countries that they know well, have experience of and where there is less market uncertainty (Johanson and Vahlne, 1977).

Research proposition 3 (P3): Physical distance matters: Companies value more highly cooperation with domestic partners than with foreign partners.

Research Design

This study is based on an innovation survey of 206 Russian companies collected in 2009. The data collection was conducted within the theoretical framework developed within the international research project 'Innovativeness of Russian Companies', aimed at intensifying the cross-border research cooperation between universities in Finland and Russia. The researchers from both countries who participated in the development of the questionnaire have expertise in marketing, innovation and technology management, international business and transition economies research. The diverse expertise of the participants allowed us to create a unique questionnaire as a multidisciplinary tool for analysing different aspects of activities of Russian companies: innovation activities, international business involvement, marketing, relationship with stakeholders and general business operations. A number of enterprise indicators (size, ownership, employees, education, etc.) were included in order to provide a good understanding of current business operations and the trends of Russian companies.

Sample description and limitations of the study

The questionnaire consists of 110 questions (some questions include two or more sub-questions). The questionnaire was developed based on the recommendations for conducting innovation surveys (Frascati manual, 1993; Oslo manual, 2007) and using the constructs and scales applied in previous research. The survey consisted of ten blocks. Block 1 is the company profile, block 2 asks for general information about the company (age, ownership, privatisation data, number of employees, level of education, business-to-business (B2B) or business-to-customer (B2C) orientation, main clients, main markets, etc.). Block 3 is about the strategy of the firm, its competition and orientation. Block 4 is on innovation activities: the goals and objectives of innovation, barriers and constraints, motivation for innovation and internal R&D. Block 4 consists of specific sub-blocks:

    A — product innovation,
    B — technology innovation,

C — technology and innovation search and acquisition,
D — technology commercialisation,
E — organisational innovation,
F — marketing innovation,
G — innovation output,
H — innovation costs.

Block 5 analyses the cooperation of companies in the innovation process. This block has two sub-blocks: A — the role of cooperation within the company for research and development and B — the role of cooperation with external partners for R&D. Block 6 asks for information on companies' international operations. Block 7 collects data about the market from the company's point of view. Block 8 asks for estimates of the quantitative characteristics of the company. And, finally blocks 9 and 10 gather information about the respondent and collect feedback about the survey, respectively.

The companies surveyed were selected on the basis of representative industrial and regional distribution. The data was collected by the interviewers through visiting companies and interviewing management representatives. Due to the scale of the research, the interviewers needed to visit each company several times. Each questionnaire was filled by hand and later coded to the electronic version in order to increase the reliability of the data and to keep the track of the information. The interviews were conducted in September to December 2009. The limitations of the survey are as follows: (1) the analysis was conducted in only one country and in preselected industries according to the objectives of the study, and the conclusions made using the results may not be valid for other countries without a proper analysis of the data; (2) however, a replication of the methodology applied in this study may provide interesting results for cross-country analysis.

The companies in the sample were mostly medium and large (more than 100 employees); see Table 1. The share of companies conducting internal R&D was high at 78.6%, of which 42.7% conduct R&D systematically and 35.9% irregularly. The R&D intensity

Table 1. Number of Employees in Surveyed Companies

Number of employees	Percentage of companies
less than 20	5.4
20–50	5.9
50–100	5.4
100–250	27.3
250–500	11.7
500–1000	21.0
1000–3000	13.2
more than 3000	10.2

Table 2. R&D Intensity.

R&D intensity	Percentage of companies
0–1.5%	20.7
1.5–3%	38.0
3–5%	14.7
5–10%	9.7
>10%	13.6
No answer	3.3
Total	100.0

(the ratio of R&D expenditure to sales) is between 1.5 and 3.0% for 38% of the companies. This corresponds to an average level of R&D intensity for most high and medium tech industries (Table 2).

Operationalisation

In order to describe the existing patterns of innovation strategies and cooperation of Russian companies a number of variables were applied. The key respondents had to identify cooperation in new product development, internal R&D, acquiring R&D or technology, or commercialising technology and they were asked to estimate the degree of cooperation on a scale from 1 to 5.

Cooperation in new product development

A dichotomous question was used to find out whether external organisations (partners) were involved in the NPD process. The questions on cooperation in NPD asked whether this is with Russian or foreign partners, and if foreign whether they are from the CIS (Commonwealth of Independent States, countries of the former Soviet Union), the EU or other countries, or whether cooperation is with many partners from different countries. The outsourcing of NPD function and involvement of external partners into NPD process is analyzed using dichotomous questions whether new products were developed by external organizations, Russian or foreign (CIS, EU, other countries).

Internal R&D

A dichotomous question was used to measure whether a company conducts internal R&D. The results of the analysis of this dummy question were used in analysing the possible innovation strategies of the firms and to estimate how cooperation depends on the innovation strategy.

R&D acquisition

The companies were asked to select the option that best describes their possible acquisition of R&D: not acquired and acquired — less that 5%, from 5 to 10%, from 10 to 25%, from 25 to 50% and from 50 to 100%. The scale reflects the approximate share of acquired R&D with respect to internal R&D.

Technology acquisition

A dichotomous question on 'technology acquisition' asks if companies acquired technology, and if so whether it is acquired occasionally or often.

Technology commercialisation

A dichotomous question on 'technology commercialisation' asked whether technology was commercialised, and if so whether it was sold occasionally or often.

Role of cooperation with suppliers

The importance of the participation of external stakeholders (suppliers) for the success of R&D and innovation was estimated with a 5-point Likert scale, ranging from not important to absolutely important.

Key Findings

The role of cooperation varies depending on the type of innovation: incremental innovation works through cooperation with existing partners whilst radical innovation requires a company to collaborate more actively with external partners (Nord and Tucker, 1987). External cooperation is very important for the most successful Russian firms and also influences the creation of radically new products (Smirnova *et al.*, 2009). Based on this background, the role of cooperation in NPD was analysed. The number of companies that launched new or significantly modified products (services or concepts for products or services) in 2006–2008 was 89.3%. This number is significantly higher than has been found in other studies on NPD in Russia, namely, 38.8% of companies with NPD (Dynkin and Ivanova, 1998) and 59% in the work of Kadochnikov *et al.* (2004). In 2006–2008, 80.6% of the companies in the sample implemented new or significantly improved technology or production processes. The products were developed mostly by a company itself (65.5%). 36.1% of all companies have developed new products (services) in cooperation with external partners. The empirical results of this study show that Russian companies more intensively cooperate in NPD with local partners than with foreign (Table 3). 10.6% of the

Table 3.   Cooperation in NPD, %.

Cooperation in NPD	36.1	Outsourcing of NPD	10.6
Cooperation with Russian partner	24.8	To Russian organisations	4.4
Cooperation with foreign partner	11.3	To foreign organisations	6.2
• CIS (n = 198)	3.9	• CIS countries (n = 201)	2.4
• EU (n = 195)	5.3	• EU countries (n = 202)	1.9
• Other countries (n = 202)	1.9	• Other countries (n = 202)	1.9

companies outsourced NPD to external organisations, and in this case, to foreign partners more often than to local Russian companies.

In order to extend our analysis of companies' cooperative patterns with the open innovation framework we collected data indicating the role of external partners (both in Russia and abroad) in technology acquisition and technology commercialisation. Companies were asked to estimate the importance of cooperation with competitors, customers, suppliers, sub-contractors (developers and producers), other companies in their own or other industries, universities or research organisations when they are searching for technology to acquire. The data allows us to compare these indicators with those for the importance of technology searches using patent databases, from publications and conferences, technology markets and other sources of new technology. The sample companies were asked to evaluate the importance of technology distribution channels (partners in joint ventures, customers, suppliers, daughter companies, licensing of technology or intellectual property rights (IPR), technology or IPR sales, universities and research organisations, open source and others) when commercialising technology. In R&D cooperation we studied the involvement of external partners in NPD, the modification of products, technology development, technology acquisition, modification of technology, organisational innovation and business processes and in marketing innovation. For the control variable we used company size, ownership and industry.

The traditional categorisation of open innovation as three processes is well known: outside-in process, inside-out process and coupled process (Gassmann and Enkel, 2004; Chesbrough 2007). There is also the classification as inbound and outbound open innovation (Lichtenthaler and Ernst, 2007). There are simplified categorisations for technology acquisition and technology commercialisation. These do not characterise processes as inbound and outbound open innovation as a whole, but provide researchers with the opportunity of analysing parts of a process. In our previous study, we grouped the sample companies depending on the intensity of technology acquisition and commercialisation into nine clusters. The results indicated that experience in technology acquisition is a prerequisite for technology commercialisation. The R&D intensity of companies shows that those which do not sell or acquire technology are the least effective in terms of innovation output and R&D productivity. The synergy effect is observed for companies acquiring and selling technology: companies who sell and buy technology have the highest R&D intensity.

The preliminary descriptive analysis shows that about one third of the sample companies, 31.1%, acquire external technology (23.8% seldom and 5.3% often) and 11.6% commercialise technology (2.9% seldom and 8.7% often).

Next we will analyse the role of cooperation in innovation for companies with different innovation strategies. We define *traditional innovation (closed) strategies* as the strategies used by companies that

(1) do not have internal R&D (21.4%),
(2) have internal R&D (78.6%) and rely purely on their internal R&D (58.6%), do not acquire R&D or technology from outside and do not commercialise their technology through external channels. Companies following the *open innovation* path use external sources of R&D, acquire technology (31.1%) or commercialise technology (11.6%) though external channels.

The majority of companies in the sample conducted internal R&D in the period analysed, 2006–2008 (78.6%). More than 40% of these companies diversified their R&D strategy by acquiring R&D from

Table 4. Internal R&D and R&D Acquisition, %.

	Often	Seldom	Never
Patents (n = 191)	8.9	13.6	77.5
Unpatented inventions (n = 179)	2.8	10.6	86.6
Licences (n = 192)	13.5	18.8	67.7
Know-how (n = 185)	7.0	11.9	81.1
Trademarks (n = 179)	9.5	3.9	86.6

Table 5. Technology Acquisition, %.

	None	1–2	3–10	More than 10
Strategic alliances or other forms of collaboration to develop technology	75.2	7.8	2.9	1.5
Transactions on patent or intellectual property acquisition	69.4	11.7	4.9	1.0
Transactions on highly qualified and professional personnel acquisition	67.5	14.6	3.9	1.9
Technology licence or intellectual property acquisition from third-party organisations	65	14.1	7.3	1.9

outside (Table 4). Most of the companies acquire R&D in the form of licences, trademarks or patents. Companies acquire technology using strategic alliances, licences, qualified personnel acquisition and patents (Table 5).

The role of cooperation, especially with suppliers, depends on the choice Russian companies make regarding the closed and open approach to innovation. The optimal ratio between the open and closed approaches to a company's innovation strategy is an under-studied question (Enkel *et al.*, 2010). However, the role of cooperation is the distinctive factor when comparing strategies. The importance of external stakeholders, where these are suppliers, for the success of R&D and innovation is shown in Table 6. The choice of suppliers as the main important external stakeholders is reflected in many studies (Håkansson and Eriksson, 1993).

Table 6. Importance of the Participation of External Stakeholders (suppliers) for the Success of R&D and Innovation.

Innovation strategy	Share	Suppliers in Russia	Suppliers abroad
No internal R&D	21.4%	3.57	3.0*
Internal R&D	78.6%	4.0	3.9*
Internal R&D and no external R&D acquisition	58.6%	4.13	4.1
Internal R&D and external R&D acquisition	41.4%	3.84	3.78
Technology acquisition	31.1%	4.2*	3.88
No technology acquisition	68.9%	3.76*	3.62
Technology commercialisation	11.6%	4.6**	4.3
No technology commercialisation	88.4%	3.8**	3.6

*sig. at $p < 0.1$ **sig. at $p < 0.05$

Previous research in this field supported the research proposition that cooperation with suppliers is the most essential aspect for innovation. Suppliers and customers have been proved to be the 'core' stakeholders for companies (Smirnova *et al.*, 2009). The importance of the participation of external stakeholders (suppliers) for the success of R&D and innovation was evaluated with the five-point Likert scale, ranging from not important to absolutely important.

Discussion

The role of cooperation for increasing the innovativeness of companies is seen to be even more important for companies from transition economies because the need to compete in local and international markets is of extreme importance. The transition process is the transformation from a centrally planned economy to a market economy through the liberalisation of trade, privatisation and macroeconomic stabilisation (Kornai, 1990; Falke, 2002; Väätänen, 2008). Companies from transitional economies such as Russia experience pressure from both the global turbulence of the market and from the ongoing transformation process within companies. Companies need more resources to compete with foreign rivals and need more knowledge to fill the innovation gap caused by the legacy of the centrally planned economy. Developing the cooperation skills and increasing the innovativeness provides an opportunity for companies to compete successfully both in domestic and international markets.

As discussed earlier, the role of cooperation depends on the type of innovation (Nord and Tucker, 1987; Smirnova *et al.*, 2009). We started our investigation into the role of cooperation with the most common innovation model — the development of new products or product innovation. The NPD process requires investment and the participation of stakeholders such as suppliers, customers and other organisations (von Hippel, 1988) — who then become the key sources of innovation.

The initial findings of this paper show how the process of cooperation is developing in Russia. Considering cooperation in NPD — the most common innovation option — we observe that most companies still try to rely on their own resources. However, one third of the firms have started to cooperate with local partners and about 11% of the companies are cooperating with foreign partners. The companies are more willing to cooperate with partners from Europe following their networks with suppliers and customers. This contradicts the results of our previous study on the internationalisation of Russian companies, which showed that companies tend to expand first in CIS countries due to proximity and physical distance: Russian firms have a common tradition of doing business, a common language, well-understood transportation networks and good communication tools with companies from CIS countries. On the other hand, when a company outsources its NPD function to external organisations, it is more keen to do so with foreign partners from the CIS. Companies explain that this is because of the price/quality ratio, knowledge of the business methods and a common culture.

The role of R&D cooperation has been studied in many scientific papers (Suzumura, 1992; Leiponen, 2001; Tether, 2002; Veugelers and Cassiman, 2005). These papers support the evidence that cooperation on R&D with suppliers, customers or research institutes and universities is important for innovating companies.

Following our observations, the more a company is enrolled in the innovation process, the more sophisticated an innovation model it will implement, and the more significant cooperation is for it (the results are shown in Table 6).

Our analysis proves that the importance of cooperation with external partners, in particular with suppliers, differs for companies with different innovation strategies. Cooperation is important for all companies; however, clear differences are observed for companies based on their innovation strategies. The lowest cooperation importance indicator (cooperation with foreign suppliers) is for those companies with no internal R&D. Companies with internal R&D are characterised as placing more importance on cooperation with local and foreign suppliers than companies with no internal R&D. Companies that have implemented the whole range of the open innovation paradigm including technology commercialisation place the most importance on cooperation with both local suppliers (4.6%) and with foreign suppliers (4.3%).

Concluding the analysis, we found the importance of the stages in the innovation strategies of the Russian companies — companies with more sophisticated innovation approaches place more importance on cooperation with suppliers. This gives empirical support for research propositions P1 and P2.

Companies value more highly cooperation with local suppliers at all stages of innovation — the theory of physical proximity, borrowed from the international business literature, applies in this case. This supports research proposition P3.

Conclusion

This study shows that cooperation with external partners (using the example of suppliers) has an important role for open innovation implementation. Open innovation includes inbound innovation (the search for and acquisition of external knowledge, R&D and technology), outbound innovation (the promotion of internal innovation through external commercialisation channels) and coupled processes (a combination of inbound and outbound innovation).

The results of the study show that companies with more open and sophisticated innovation strategies tend to place more importance on cooperation with suppliers. Open innovation theory considers cooperation as a milestone in the process of implementing open innovation principles in practice. The logic behind this statement is defined by the nature of this externalisation process — actions through a company's borders at all stages of the innovation process always involve a certain level of cooperation with external stakeholders or partners.

In addition, the effects of partner location were evident in the data analysis. Companies value cooperation with domestic suppliers more than with foreign suppliers. This is explained because it is easier to transfer knowledge locally due to proximity, better communications and cultural similarity.

An important aspect of the analysis is that it is based on companies from a transition economy — Russia. Companies from transition economies have a strong need to improve their competitive position though implementing innovation and the best managerial practices. The growing share of innovative companies in Russia during recent years is a very positive indicator of the trend of economic development from a resource and export-dependent economy to a knowledge and innovation-intensive economy.

The results are crucially important to managers because they show how cooperation matters for companies with different innovation strategies. These insights are essential especially now when the internationalisation of Russian companies is increasing on the international markets and their business strategies are interesting for other participants in the European markets.

Based on the findings of this paper, we foresee future research into cooperation with different types of stakeholders and the implementation of the open innovation paradigm.

References

Baglieri, E. and Zamboni, S. (2005). Partnering along the demand chain: Collaboration in new product development process, *21st IMP Conference Proceedings*.

Bayona, C., García-Marco, T. and Huerta, E. (2001). Firms' motivations for cooperative R&D: An empirical analysis of Spanish firms, *Research Policy*, **30**(8), 1289–1307.

Belderbos, R., Carree, M. and Lokshin, B. (2004). Cooperative R&D and firm performance, *Research Policy*, **33**(10), 1477–1492.

Blomqvist, K. and Levy, J. (2006). Collaboration capability — A focal concept in knowledge creation and collaborative innovation in networks, *International Journal of Management Concepts and Philosophy*, **2**(1), 31–48.

Cassiman, B. and Veugelers, R. (2002). R&D cooperation and spillovers: Some empirical evidence from Belgium, *American Economic Review*, **92**(4), 1169–1184.

Cervantes, M. and Malkin, D. (2001). Russia's innovation gap, Organization for Economic Cooperation and Development, *The OECD Observer*, November 2001, 229–239.

Chesbrough, H. (2003). *Open Innovation: The New Imperative for Creating and Profiting from Technology*, Harvard Business Press, Boston, MA.

Chesbrough, H. (2006). *Open Business Models: How to Thrive in the New Innovation Landscape*, Harvard Business School Press, Boston, MA.

Chesbrough, H. (2007). Why companies should have open innovation business models, *MIT Sloan Management Review*, **48**(2), 22–28.

Chesbrough, H.W. and Prencipe, A. (2008). Networks of innovation and modularity: A dynamic perspective, *International Journal of Technology Management*, **42**(4), 414–425.

Christensen, C. (1997). *The Innovator's Dilemma: When New Technologies Cause Great Firms to Fail*, Harvard Business School Press, Boston, MA.

Clark, K. and Fujimoto, T. (1991). *Product Development Performance*, Harvard Business School Press, Boston, MA.

Cohen, W.M. and Levinthal, D.A. (1990). Absorptive capacity — A new perspective on learning and innovation, *Administrative Science Quarterly*, **35**(1), 128–152.

Dittrich, K. and Duysters, G. (2007). Networking as a means to strategy change: The case of open innovation in mobile telephony, *Journal of Product Innovation Management*, **24**(6), 510–521.

Dodgson, M. (1993). *Technological Collaboration in Industry*, Routledge, London.

Dyer, J. and H. Singh (1998). The relational view: Cooperative strategy and sources of interorganizational competitive advantage, *Academy of Management Review*, **23**(4), 660–679.

Dynkin, A., and Ivanova, N. (1998). Technological innovation in Russia, *Research Technology Management*, **41**, Jan/Feb, 44–47.

Enkel, E. and Gassmann, O. (2008). Driving open innovation in the front end. The IBM case, Working paper, University of St. Gallen and Zeppelin University, St. Gallen and Friedrichshafen.

Enkel E., Gassmann, O. and Chesbrough, H. (2010). The future of open innovation, *R&D Management*, **40**(3), 213–221.

Falke, M. (2002). Community interests: An insolvency objective in transition economies? No. 01/02, Frankfurter Institut für Transformationsstudien.

Faria, P. and Schmidt, T. (2007). International cooperation on innovation: empirical evidence for German and Portuguese firms, ZEW Discussion Papers 07-060, ZEW — Zentrum für Europäische Wirtschaftsforschung (Centre for European Economic Research).

Filipescu, D. (2007). *Innovation and Internationalisation. A Focus on the Spanish Exporting Firms*, Research work, doctoral programme: Creation, strategy and management of the firm, Universitat Autonoma de Barcelona, Business Economics Department.

Ford, D. and Johnsen, T. (2001). Managing networks of supplier and customer relationships for technological innovation: Initial case study, *17th IMP Conference Proceedings*.

Freeman, C. and Hagedoorn, J. (1994). Catching up or falling behind: Patterns in international interfirm technology partnering, *World Development*, **22**(5), 771–780.

Freytag, V. (2002). Innovation in cooperation and cooperation innovation, *18th IMP Conference Proceedings*, Dijon, France.

Gassmann, O. and Enkel, E. (2004). Towards a theory of open innovation: three core process archetypes, paper presented at R&D Management Conference.

Gemunden, H. G., Ritter T. and Heydebreck P. (1996). Network configuration and innovation success: An empirical analysis in German high-tech industries, *International Journal of Res Marketing*, **13**(5), 449–462.

Hagedoorn, J. (2002). Inter-firm R&D partnerships: An overview of major trends and patterns since 1960, *Research Policy*, **31**(4), 477–492.

Hakansson, H. and Eriksson, A-K. (1993). Getting innovations out of supplier networks, *Journal of Business to Business Marketing*, **1**(3), 3–34.

Holmes, S. and Smart, P. (2009). Exploring open innovation practice in firm-nonprofit engagements: A corporate social responsibility perspective, *R&D Management*, **39**, 4.

Johnsen, T. and Ford, D. (2000). Managing collaborative innovation in complex networks: Findings from exploratory interviews, *16th IMP conference in Bath.*

Johanson, J. and Vahlne, J.-E. (1977). The internationalization process of the firm — A model of knowledge development and increasing market commitment, *Journal of International Business Studies*, **8**, 23–32.

Johanson, M. (2007). Networks in transition, *Proceedings of the 23th IMP Conference,* Manchester Business School, UK.

Kadochnikov, S., Essine, P. and Slobodyan, S. (2004). What explains the product differentiation of Russian companies: Competitive pressure or technological spillovers? *CERGE-EI Policy Brief*, **3**(June), 1–3.

Kaufmann, A. and Todtling, F. (2001). Science-industry interaction in the process of innovation: The importance of boundary-crossing between systems, *Research Policy*, **30**(5), 791–804.

Keupp, M.M. and Gassmann, O. (2009). Determinants and archetype users of open innovation, *R&D Management*, **39**, 4.

Klevorick, A.K. *et al.* (1995). On the sources and significance of interindustry differences in technological opportunities, *Research Policy*, **24**, 185–205.

Klomp, L. and van Leeuwen, G. (2001). Linking innovation and firm performance: A new approach, *International Journal of the Economics of Business*, **8**(3), 343–364.

Kock, C. and Torkkeli, M. (2008). Open Innovation: A "Swingers' club" or "Going steady"? IE Business School working paper WP08-11, 05.02.2008.

Kornai, J. (1990). The affinity between ownership forms and coordination mechanisms: The common experience of reform in socialist countries, *Journal of Economic Perspectives*, **4**(3), 131–147.

Kotler, F. and Caslione, J. (2009). *Chaotics: The Business of Managing and Marketing in The Age of Turbulence*, Amacom Publishing.

Laursen, K. and Salter, A. (2006). Open for innovation: The role of openness in explaining innovation performance among UK manufacturing firms, *Strategic Management Journal*, 27(2), 131–150.

Leiponen, A. (2001). "Why do firms not collaborate? The role of competencies and technological regimes," in Kleinknecht, A. and Mohnen, P. (eds), *Innovation and Firm Performance: Econometric Exploration of Survey Data*, Palgrave, pp. 253–277.

Lichtenthaler, U. and Ernst, H. (2007). External technology commercialisation in large firms, results of a quantitative benchmarking study, *R&D Management*, 37(5), 383–397.

Lin, P. and Saggi, K. (2002). Under-provision of inputs in joint ventures with market power, *Bulletin of Economic Research*, 54(2), 189–196.

Loof, H. and Heshmati, A. (2002). Knowledge capital and performance heterogeneity: A firm-level innovation study, *International Journal of Production Economics*, 76(1), 61–85.

Lundvall, B.A., Johnson, B., Andersen, E.S. and Dalum, B. (2002). National systems of production, innovation and competence building, *Research Policy*, 31, 213–231.

Miles, R.E., Miles, G. and Snow, C.C. (2004). *Collaborative Entrepreneurship. How Groups of Networked Firms Use Continuous Innovation to Create Economic Wealth?* Stanford University Press, Stanford.

Neyer, A.K., Bullinger, A.C. and Moeslein, K.M. (2009). Integrating inside and outside innovators: A sociotechnical systems perspective, *R&D Management*, 39, 4.

Nord, W.R. and Tucker, S. (1987). *Implementing Routine and Radical Innovations*, Lexington Books, Lexington, MA.

Porter, M.E. (1979). How competitive forces shape strategy, *Harvard Business Review*, March/April.

Romijn, H. and Albaladejo, M. (2002). Determinants of innovation capability in small electronics and software firms in Southeast England, *Research Policy*, 31(7), 1053–1067.

Smirnova, M.M., Podmetina, D., Vaatanen, J. and Kouchtch, S. (2009). Key stakeholders' interaction as a factor of product innovation: The case of Russia, *International Journal of Technology Marketing*, 4(2–3) 230–247.

Smith, P.G. and Blanck, E. (2002). From experience: Leading dispersed teams, *The Journal of Product Innovation Management*, 19(4), 294–304.

Suzumura, K. (1992). Cooperative and noncooperative R&D in an oligopoly with spillovers, *The American Economic Review*, **82**(5), 1307–1320.

Tether, B. (2002). Who co-operates for innovation, and why. An empirical analysis, *Research Policy*, **31**, 947–967.

Torkkeli, M., Podmetina, D. and Väätänen, J. (2009). Knowledge absorption in emerging economy — Role of foreign investments and trade flows in Russia, *International Journal of Business Excellence*, **2**(3/4), 269–234.

Väätänen, J. (2008). *Russian Enterprise Restructuring — The Effect of Privatisation and Market Liberalisation on the Performance of Large Enterprises*, Dissertation, Lappeenranta University of Technology.

Veugelers, R. and Cassiman, B. (2005). R&D cooperation between firms and universities: Some empirical evidence from Belgian manufacturing, *International Journal of Industrial Organization*, **23**(5–6), 355–379.

Vivero, R. (2004). The impact of process innovations on firm's productivity growth: The case of Spain, *Applied Economics*, **34**, 1007–1016.

von Hippel, E. (1988). *The Sources of Innovation*, Oxford University Press, New York.

Walter, A., Ritter, T. and Gemunden, H.G. (2001). Value-creation in buyer-seller relationships: Theoretical considerations and empirical results from a supplier's perspective, *Industrial Marketing Management*, **30**(4), 365–377.

Wheelwright, S. and Clark K. (1992). *Revolutionizing Product Development, Quantum Leaps in Speed, Efficiency, and Quality*, The Free Press, New York.

Chapter 9

Rigidities Considered: Supplier Strategies for Integrated Innovation

Thorsten Teichert
Chair of Marketing and Innovation,
University of Hamburg, Germany

Ricarda B. Bouncken
Chair of Strategic Management and Organization,
University of Bayreuth Prieserstr, Germany

Introduction

Management of innovation is widely perceived as a prominent source of competitive advantage (Balachandra and Friar, 1997; Griffin, 1997) and a crucial strategic issue (Henderson and Clark, 1990; Utterback, 1994) in need of alignment with a firm's overall strategy (Pinto and Prescott, 1988). Among others Cooper and Kleinschmidt (1995) and Cooper (1984) of described five prominent factors of new product performance: process, strategy, organization, culture, and management commitment.

Investigations of success factors focusing on a single organization fail to address issues prevalent outside of the organization. Studies assume that an innovating company acts in an "empty space" without any constraints. This seems less plausible in the context of ongoing innovation activity in supply chains. New product concepts have to be aligned with existing interfaces in both directions of the supply-chain (up- and downstream) to successfully diffuse into the market.

The innovation activities of suppliers are particularly confronted by manufacturers' requirements, such as product and process objectives, frame specifications, and target prices. These requirements can range from more informal and flexible suggestions to tight and formal upstream pre-settings. We refer to these as supply-chain rigidities. Supply-chain innovation rigidities result from a manufacturer's need to manage the integration of several components from different suppliers into a coherent innovation. Rigidities help to coordinate this multi-supplier innovation process; for example, innovations performed by one firm can more easily be integrated into the product concept of a manufacturer (Gilbert *et al.*, 2003). Even though rigidities are important, they have not been considered in previous studies.

As supply-chain rigidities may constitute a major contingency for innovation, the authors of this study believe the lack of rigidity research results in a significant gap in the literature. The more suppliers face innovation rigidities, the more it is questionable whether they can pursue autonomous strategic planning and reap value from their innovation activities. As such, the question of how suppliers can increase success in an environment of rigidities must be answered. These questions include: What are the strategic options? How do soft factors, or dynamic capabilities, particularly in a planning capability and innovation orientation, influence performance and interact with the strategic approach?

This chapter intent is to solve some of the questions in this important puzzle. We will analyze the effects of two strategic approaches for suppliers' success and the relations between strategy and the soft factors of innovation management. Our study will compare effects under conditions of high and low innovation rigidities.

For the strategic approach, we draw upon the distinction between 'deliberate' and 'emergent' strategy formulation (Mintzberg and McHugh, 1985). This integrates the bitter debate of whether strategies are a result of a formal and deliberate planning process or whether they emerge as firms incrementally learn and experiment (Brews and Hunt, 1999). Previous studies have disagreed on whether a formal style of innovation project management is superior to an emergent style (Brown and Eisenhardt, 1995). Given different degrees of supply-chain induced innovation rigidities, it becomes questionable whether innovation can be the object of detailed rationalized and formal planning by a single company, or of a more intuitive *ad hoc* planning, which might better adapt to contingencies. As a result, we analyze the effect of rigidities on the strategic approach and aim to deliver answers to the question of whether suppliers' strategies can either be derived from a formal and deliberate planning process or emerge as suppliers incrementally learn and experiment.

As customer requirements and technology change over time, internal dynamic capabilities may need to adjust according to the changes to achieve product market success. It has been determined that more innovative firms with soft capabilities (Alegre-Vidal *et al.* 2004) are more liberal regarding internal conflict in maintaining creativity (Dyer and Song, 1998) and foster organizational structures that are in the intermediate zone between order and disorder (Brown and Eisenhardt, 1997). As such, an internal innovation orientation will be influential for the success of innovative suppliers. Thus, we not only investigate the strategy–performance link, but also investigate an intermediate effect of internal capabilities, namely suppliers' innovation orientation. We also integrate a second dynamic capability, the planning capability, which acts as a flexible, contingency-orientated, and goal-orientated planning competence.

The results of this study were derived by testing a structural equation model. Our model will explain how two strategic approaches can be transformed into dynamic capabilities and into market performance under different degrees of supply-chain rigidities. A survey of 241 high-tech small and medium-sized enterprises (SMEs) was used for hypothesis testing. Structural equation modeling is used to reveal direct, as well as indirect, effects. While we aim to observe the direct effects of strategy on market success, we also aim to measure both the strategic planning approach to innovation, as well as the dynamic innovation capabilities, as intermediary variables in our analysis. We will apply a moderator analysis to differentiate the causal-effect chain based on environmental settings, i.e. a well- (strong rigidities) and

weakly (few rigidities) defined supply chains. We will also test mediator effects through the planning capability.

In summary, this chapter will attempt to bring light into the black-
box of performance-enhancing innovation strategy and its contingencies in the supply chain. More specifically, we research the relation
between innovation strategy approaches and success under the moderating role of high or low innovation rigidities of the supply chain. To
deduce an even more fine-grained picture, we investigate the intermediary effects of capabilities. Thus, our research will contribute to the
knowledge of innovation strategies, internal capabilities and their performance effects under different contingencies in a supply chain. From
the multi-faceted view and the thorough methodology we can derive
suggestions for effective innovation management in supply chains.

Theory

Innovation rigidities

The assumption that an innovating company acts in an 'empty space'
without any constraints is no longer plausible in the context of ongoing innovation activity by firms in alliances, networks, and particularly in supply chains. The innovative suppliers, which are generally
highly specialized, develop innovative components or modules.
Innovations by several suppliers are combined into a coherent product by a manufacturer. New product concepts and innovation strategies must be aligned with the existing interfaces of the supply chain.
The multi-supplier innovation process requires coordination enabling innovation from several firms to be integrated into the product
concept of a manufacturer (Gilbert *et al.*, 2003). Manufacturers that
need to manage the integration of several components establish innovation rigidities. These can range from more informal and flexible
suggestions, to tight and formal upstream presets on suppliers. We
refer to these as the innovation rigidities of well-defined supply
chains. Rigidities reduce the autonomy of suppliers, but can also
improve suppliers' actions and innovation by providing direction,
and as such, reducing uncertainty. Suppliers may face different

degrees of supply-chain rigidities depending on the power of the supplier, the relation between supply-chain partners, the shape of the supply chain, the dominance of consumer needs, and of the overall industry structure. In particular, under high innovation rigidities, it is unclear if and how suppliers can improve upon their performance by autonomous strategic planning or by their internal innovation capabilities.

Innovation rigidities and strategic approaches

An innovation strategy can be regarded as a timed string of conditional resource allocation decisions to achieve specific goals (Ramanujam and Mensch, 1985). Commonly, an innovation strategy is understood as a description of a firm's targeted innovation position with regard to its competitive environment, in terms of its new product and market development policies (Dyer and Song, 1998). We refer to strategy as a pattern in a stream of decisions that include a commitment to actions and resources, both intended and realized (Mintzberg, 1978). Strategies can either be derived from a formal and deliberate planning process, or emerge as suppliers incrementally learn and experiment (Fredrickson and Mitchell, 1984; Fredrickson and Iaquinto, 1989). According to the Planning School, strategy is a deliberate and 'rational' (Idenburg, 1993, p. 133) process that includes an in-depth analysis of markets and an implementation of the alternatives as a means and an end (Cohen and Cyert, 1973; Guerard *et al.*, 1990). Ansoff (1991) as a proponent of the Planning School states that *a priori* formal planning is necessary for achieving performance. Contrarily, for emergent strategy formulation means and ends are specified simultaneously or intertwined (Fredrickson, 1984; Fredrickson and Iaquinto, 1989). As an emergent strategy does not concentrate on explicit objectives and formal approaches it is necessary to react in a flexible way that muddles through by trial and error (Idenburg, 1993).

Given different high supply-chain rigidities, it becomes questionable whether innovation can be the object of detailed rationalized and formal planning by a single company or of more intuitive *ad hoc* planning, which better applies to contingencies and changes. Furthermore, the fulfillment of *ex-ante* defined innovation goals may not be sufficient to ensure long-term success, because customers, as well as supply-chain requirements, may change over time.

The stronger the supply-chain rigidities a supplier faces, the less opportunity exists for a single supplier's sovereign strategic planning. Changes induced by directives or the requirements of manufacturers might interfere with the supplier's forecasts, goals, and plans. As a result, suppliers might be forced into rapid competency changes. Implementations of deliberate and formal planning might then become obsolete. External changes might require flexibility and *ad hoc* creativity, which are rarely associated with formalized planning. Hence, formal strategic planning cannot provide a secure foundation for formulating a long-term strategy. Furthermore, there are a significant risks of sunk costs associated with the planning process. As such, the positive factors of formal planning are likely to be absorbed by the customers' directives when there are high supply-chain rigidities. Under low supply-chain rigidities, however, suppliers will be able to improve upon their success by deliberate planning, which enables them to set their own agenda for their companies' future.

High rigidities will often exist in the context of powerful downstream partners, particularly large manufacturers. Manufacturers are in the position to dictate the specifications of the innovations provided by their suppliers. If manufacturers are very powerful and have a high internal innovation capability, then SMEs might only exhibit a workbench character. Generally, with growing dependence, and under high rigidities, very frequent changes in manufacturers' demands require higher levels of flexibility from suppliers. The trials and experiences of an emergent strategy approach might improve suppliers' success under high rigidities. An emergent strategy's power lies in intuition, experimentation, creativity, and autonomous testing associated with trial and error. This is not available under high rigidities that may change quickly and exert strict and formal limitations to autonomous creativity and innovation development. Hence, the freedom the emergent strategy approach requires does not exist in an environment of high supply-chain rigidities, which limit the freedom. Thus an emergent strategy approach is only advantageous for achieving long-term competitive advantage in settings of low supply-chain rigidities where suppliers can experiment with ideas, technologies, designs, and diverse interfaces of components. Thus, neither of the strategic approaches will under high rigidities increase their market success. However, internal dynamic capabilities may improve market success, even under high rigidities.

> **Hypothesis 1**: *Supply-chain rigidities moderate the relation of deliberate and emergent strategies and market successes: Both strategic types only increase market success under low supply-chain rigidities.*

Innovation rigidities and dynamic capabilities

A broad spectrum of innovation types have been developed and implemented in supply chains. These innovations range from new components and services for existing products, new designs, new uses, and new technological solutions to completely new products. New products and services developed in supply-chains, as such, can cover incremental, radical, and even breakthrough, innovations. Even though uncertainties increase with growing novelty, supply-chain partners always have to coordinate the innovation task, which is a cross-functional task. As such, the diverse functions of a supplier continuously need to resonate with each other and with the markets for successful achievement and implementation of innovations. Thus, internal dynamic capabilities are necessary to cope with change and achieve product market success. Simpson *et al.* (2006) propose that innovation capabilities impact a firm's number, rate, and type of innovations. Furthermore, Baker *et al.* (2003) postulate that firms can develop routines and structures for innovation. Following this, we identify two dynamic capabilities important for innovation performance in a supply chain. We argue that (1) a smart and flexible planning capability and (2) sustained internal innovation orientation act as important dynamic capabilities in supply-chain innovation. Both can be proactively designed and provide the basis for long-term innovation success.

The **planning capability** refers to the planning expertise, i.e. timeliness, plan content, and fulfillment of objectives, as well as their contribution to the overarching business goals. Planning capabilities are based on assumptions about the organizational environment necessary to contribute to market success. The planning capability, as a dynamic capability, enables a firm to react to changes and contingencies. Planning has an in built flexibility. If suppliers have a dynamic planning capability, they continuously use internal creativity and flexible responses to market and technology changes. Even in environments of high supply-chain rigidities, suppliers can use the presets of their manufacturers to adapt to and transform deliberate planning for product development. The dynamic planning capability increases the identification of components and products that apply to customers' expectations and as such increase market success. Thus, suppliers can increase their performance by deliberate planning under conditions of high and low innovation rigidities. Under low supply-chain rigidities, suppliers use deliberate planning for the development of successful products to increase their market performance. Having developed internal planning capabilities suppliers can also improve upon their success in environments of high supply-chain rigidities if they accommodate the rigidities of their manufacturers into their strategic planning.

Hypothesis 2: *Under high supply-chain rigidities, a supplier's planning capability mediates the relation between deliberate planning and market success: Suppliers achieve success through planning capability when following deliberate planning.*

Innovation orientation can assist a firm's proclivity, openness, and inclination to generate and distribute novel ideas about processes and products within supply chains. Thus, the innovation orientation can increase the success of total innovation programs (Manu, 1992). An innovation orientation contains structures, processes, and positive attitudes toward innovation, critically including people and processes, as well as technology-related issues. This embraces an organization's inclination towards the horizontal and vertical exchange of novel ideas. The integral and highly flexible perspective can be compared with an overarching 'entrepreneurial orientation' (Zhou *et al.*, 2005, p. 54), which has been shown to support innovation success across a broad range of environmental settings, in both less and highly uncertain environments (Tushman and Anderson, 1986; Tushman and O'Reilly, 1996).

An innovation orientation is a dynamic capability that empowers many members of the organization. Ideas from different levels of the organization are used for the development of new products. An innovation orientation provides a high degree of flexibility. The high potential of new ideas and the flexibility allows suppliers under conditions of low and high rigidities to develop and improve upon innovations that apply to the market. Accordingly, an innovation orientation is expected to improve market success under high and low supply-chain rigidities.

Hypothesis 3a: *The innovation orientation increases market success under high and low innovation rigidities.*

In settings of low supply-chain rigidities, suppliers can develop their own routines and structures for innovation. Formal planning can lay out the organizational structure of an innovation orientation. Suppliers can define, as an extension of their formal planning, many organizational devices, e.g. creativity rooms, opportunities for informal vertical and horizontal communication, and teamwork. Additionally, emergent planning, leaving room for experimentation, open communication, trial and error, and feed back slopes can create a framework for an innovation orientation. The fundamental assumptions of the emergent approach correspond highly to the innovation orientation, implying a willingness to move beyond old habits and try new ideas at different levels of the organization. Ignoring the effects of innovation rigidities, both deliberate and emergent strategies can serve as a basis for shaping innovation orientation as vision and planning may provide complementary guidance.

Under high rigidities, suppliers still find it difficult to develop and operate using their own framework for their innovation orientations. Instead, they depend on presets and directives from their manufacturers, which also might change suddenly. Suppliers need to integrate manufacturers' requirements into their planning and the implementation of structures and processes associated with an innovation orientation. This interferes with the potential benefits of an emergent strategy. We argue that suppliers can only develop their innovation orientation by an emergent strategy if they have the freedom to operate, which will exist in an environment of low rigidities. Instead, deliberate planning will also, under high rigidities, provide the processes and structures necessary for an innovation orientation.

Hypothesis 3b: *Supply-chain rigidity moderates the relation between an emergent strategy and an innovation orientation: The emergent strategy only increases an innovation orientation under low rigidities.*

Empirical Study

Sample

Our sample is composed of 241 small- and mid-sized companies within the high-tech sector. We contacted 656 executives personally by phone or by mail, asking them to fill out our questionnaire. To ensure that firms are representative of the industry, all suppliers contacted were carefully selected on the basis of an industry database, which provided information about the size of the firm, as well as the products and services offered. After two rounds of mailings, 242 surveys were returned 241 of which could be analyzed. Consequently, the response rate was 37%.

We compared firms that returned the completed questionnaire with those that did not according to control variables (firm age, firm size, position of the suppliers in the supply chain). We could not find major differences between respondents and non-respondents. The average firm size was 100–150 employees. The firms operated as second-or third-tier suppliers in either the IT or the airline industry, representing software and hardware, respectively. To check the key information quality of our data collection, two researchers made a series of phone calls to verify the position of the key informants in the companies.

Model

Our model is an extension of the standard LISREL models (Joreskog and Aish, 1990). We checked the descriptive statistics of each item (see Table A1 in the Appendix), as well as their normal distribution. Neither skewness nor kurtosis exceeded values of 1, confirming that there were no significant deviations from a normal distribution. To examine the moderating effect of rigidities, we conducted a multigroup estimation. We followed the method of Byrne (2004) in testing moderating effects by multi-group estimations in structural equation modeling. The sign and the statistical significance of the path coefficients and their corresponding *t*-values and chi-square differences served to test the hypothesized relations.

To build the groups, we used a median split of the entire sample to divide the respondents into two subgroups with low or high supply-chain rigidity. The model consists of a two-stage causal effect using supply-chain rigidity as the key moderating effect. Hypothesis 1 postulates that the direct effects of both strategic types on market success are moderated by different levels of supply-chain rigidities. Hence, we expect different effect sizes for these relations for low and high supply-chain rigidity. In Hypothesis 2, we define a moderated mediation: under high supply-chain rigidities, a supplier's planning capability mediates the relation between deliberate planning and market success. Hypothesis 3a demands the analysis of the effect through an innovation orientation on market success in both groups: high and low innovation rigidities. For Hypothesis 3b again we have to check the moderating effect of innovation rigidity on the relation between emergent strategy and innovation orientation.

Measures

Multiple indicators are used to measure the latent constructs. The scales used to measure our constructs were inspired by previous studies. In accordance with previous results, all constructs were measured as reflective indicators. While single constructs might have been formulated as well by formative scales we did not choose this approach both out of content as well as consistency considerations. Most items were measured with 5-point Likert-type scales (1 = strongly disagree, 5 = strongly agree).

Strategic approach

We measured the strategic planning approach with the dimensions (see Table 1) used in previous studies (Leontiades and Tezel, 1980; Robinson and Pearce, 1983; Pearce *et al.*, 1987). Regarding the acquisition of information, the deliberate approach is associated with in-depth research of market changes and risks. In contrast, the emergent approach, in its extreme, does not plan actions in advance. For the processing of information, the means-ends relations and causal effects from market development were analyzed within the deliberate strategy formulation. However an emergent strategy builds upon intuition. In reference to evaluation and decision-making, the deliberate strategy formulation pursues the investigation of different options while at its extreme, the emergent approach uses trial and error.

Innovation orientation

We followed Siguaw *et al.* (2006) and Simpson *et al.* (2006) in distinguishing specific innovation outputs from a broader innovation orientation. More specifically, we took an action-oriented instead of

Table 1. Continuum of Deliberate and Emergent Strategy.

	Deliberate	Emergent
Acquisition of information	Research market opportunities	Actions and market opportunities are not planned in advance
Processing of information	Analysis of the rationale of market growth	Intuition
Decision-making	Development of different options and subsequent decisions	Trial and error

structural view and emphasized the transformation from strategy into specific action (Bouncken *et al.*, 2007). We measured innovation orientation, analogous to market orientation (Kohli and Jaworski, 1990), by the potential it provides for companies' innovation activities. Our construct of innovation orientation was guided by the idea of an organization's inclination towards the horizontal and vertical exchange of novel ideas and focused on the internal innovation process. Innovation is a bottom-up, creative process that requires interdisciplinary exchange and integration within a company for success. Innovation orientation thus aims at overcoming functional barriers and considers how strongly everyone is engaged in innovation behavior. Therefore, we used the following items: a firm's engagement towards (a) the constant search of novel product concepts, (b) the constant refinement and development of products, (c) the fast and cross-functional implementation of innovation, and (d) the horizontal and vertical participation of all personnel in developing novel ideas. These items jointly serve as reflective indicators, as they simultaneously reflect the extent of an innovation orientation.

Planning capability

Planning, as a dynamic capability, was adapted from the study of Bouncken *et al.* (2007). We measured planning capability with four items that describe the degree of planning expertise. All major aspects of planning, as a competence, are covered, i.e. timeliness, plan content, fulfillment of objectives, as well as the contribution to the overarching business goals.

Market success

For market success, we are interested in the market performance of products, instead of technical or short-term measures of success. Subjective measures of performance have been widely used and most studies find high convergent validity with objective measures, such as publicly available accounting data, for selected studies (Worren, *et al.*, 2002). We measured our construct of market success using six indicators.

Two of them measure overall customer satisfaction: whether customers are satisfied with the products and whether their expectations are met (Lam *et al.*, 2004). Three other indicators specifically measure long-term market performance: the loyalty of customers, returing customers, and recommendations of customers leading to additional turnover (Zeithaml *et al.*, 1996). The final item measures the degree of acquired reputation (LeBlanc and Nguyen, 1995). All items simultaneously reflect the market success of a company.

Rigidities

To build the groups, we used a median split to divide the entire sample into two sub-groups with low and high supply-chain rigidity. Prior to the data collection in 2007, we discussed and readjusted our scales on supply-chain rigidities in a workshop with 12 academics and 7 supply-chain managers. Afterwards, items were specified in a pilot study composed of 17 executives from small and medium-sized suppliers in the IT industry. Four items proved to be of importance to differentiate between different settings of supply-chain rigidity: the determination of the behavior of partners in the supply chain, the required fit of a product program, technical compatibility, the volatility of technologies on the market. These items were integrated into an overall score and a median split was applied for each of the two industry groups. This ensured an equal distribution of both industry branches in both subgroups. Out of the 117 observations with high supply-chain rigidity, 72 came from the IT sector and 45 from the airline sector, whereas the 124 observations with low supply-chain rigidity consisted of 68 IT companies and 56 airline suppliers. Thus, possible industry effects could be balanced.

Measurement validity

We estimated the model postulated in Fig. 1 using AMOS 7. In many studies, measurement invariance between models has been ignored. We checked the comparability between the two groups by measuring

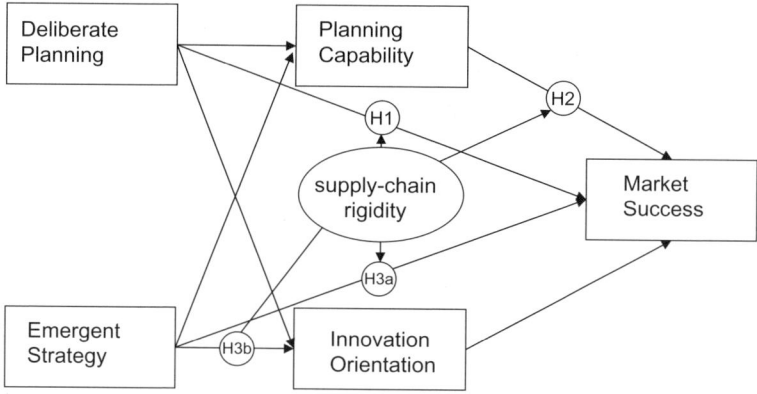

Fig. 1. Causal-Effect Model with Moderator Effects of Supply-Chain Rigidity.

the invariance (Byrne, 2004). After controlling for comparability, we chose a model that constrained measurement weights and intercepts. Compared to the fully unconstrained model, these constraints only lead to a slight decrease in the entire model fit, which was not significant (CMIN 45.459, p-value = 0.160). The overall fit measures indicated a good model fit. The normed chi-square value of 1.32 was much lower than the threshold value of 3.0. Bentler's comparative fit index (CFI), which compares the hypothesized model against an independence model as a baseline model (Arbuckle and Wothke, 1999), is 0.91, which slightly exceeds the required value of 0.90 (Byrne, 2001). The root mean square error of approximation (RMSEA) of 0.036 (90%-interval of 0.027 to 0.045) is significantly lower than the threshold value of 0.08, which indicates a good fit (Browne, 1993).

For the local fit, we find standardized factor loadings above 0.4. All respective *t*-values are above 2.0, indicating that none of the items are to be excluded from the model. Therefore, we do not give the *t*-values in the table in the Appendix. A few indicators did not reach the necessary indicator reliability value of 0.4. Only the indicators of the construct 'deliberate strategy' consistently had an indicator reliability value higher than the threshold value. As a result, all items were used in our model.

Nearly all constructs fulfilled the necessary condition for convergent validity (see Table A2 in the Appendix for details), even though their extracted average variance was moderate. Cronbach's alpha and composite reliability almost always reached the necessary condition of 0.7 (Nunnally and Bernstein, 1994) and 0.6 (Bagozzi and Yi, 1988) respectively. Only the dependent latent variable 'emergent strategy' had a slightly lower Cronbach's alpha value. All of the constructs reached the necessary level of composite reliability. Thus, the measures demonstrated adequate convergent validity and reliability. Overall, we found good convergent validity and reliability, as well as moderate discriminant validity, in the model.

Results

To examine the influence of supply-chain rigidities, we performed a multi-group estimation. We applied a median split to divide the entire sample into low and high rigidity groups. We first allowed (see Table 2)

Table 2.   Model Fits of the Multi-Group Analyses.

	Model	NPAR	Chi²	DF	Delta Chi²	RMSEA	AIC	CFI
1	Unconstrained	142	479.429	362	—	0.037	763.429	0.919
2	Measurement weights and intercepts	105	524.889	399	45.46 df = 37 p < 0.16	0.036	734.889	0.913
3	Structural weights according to hypotheses	102	527.887	402	2.998 df = 3 p < 0.39	0.036	731.887	0.913
4	All structural weights constrained	98	540.46	406	12.573 df = 4 p < 0.01	0.037	736.46	0.907

NPAR: number of parameters
DF: degrees of freedom
AIC: Akaike Information Criterion
CFI: Comparative Fit Index

a free estimation of all measurement and structural coefficients in both groups (For the fully unconstrained model). This model served as the base model for more restrictive models. Enforcing equality in the measurement model (For equal measurement weights and intercepts) resulted in a non-significant difference in chi-squares (45.46, df = 37, p < 0.16). This indicates that the measurement model is invariant across the two groups, ensuring an identity of constructs within both groups. Following this, we restricted the structural coefficients to be equal where we did not expect different causal paths between situations of low and high rigidities. Again, the difference in chi-squares was non-significant (2.998, df = 3, p < 0.39). This indicates that the two groups were not different in the other structural coefficients. Finally, we forced the hypothesized structural differences to be zero (For equality of all structural weights). This fully constrained multi-group analysis did not fit as well as the other models with a significant chi-square difference (12.573, df = 4, p < 0.01) compared to our target model. We conclude that our proposed model fits best to the observed empirical data. This provides a strong signal for the relevance of the proposed moderating effects of rigidities.

Having identified the best-fitting model, we investigated the obtained parameter estimates for the causal effects (see Table 3) and related this empirical evidence to our proposed hypotheses. Hypotheses 1 postulates that both strategy approaches only directly impact market success in the case of low supply-chain rigidities. The results illustrate that both approaches have a significant and positive effect on market success for low rigidities. The emergent strategy (b = 0.211, p = 0.06) and the deliberate strategy (b = 0.196, p = 0.03) affect market success under low rigidities. We find that neither strategy exerts a significant influence on market success in the case of high rigidities (p > 0.8 = 0.7). Thus, our results are in line with Hypothesis 1, confirming that both strategies (deliberate, as well as emergent) only exert a significant direct effect on market success when supply-chain rigidity is low.

In Hypothesis 2, we define a moderated mediation: Under high supply-chain rigidities, a supplier's planning capability should partially

T. Teichert and R.B. Bouncken

Table 3. Structural Parameters and Hypotheses.

Effect related to hypothesis	Path	Low rigidity		High rigidity		Confirmation (✓)/ rejection (x)
		Estimate (S.E.)	t-value	Estimate (S.E.)	t-value	
Causal effects with significant differences under situations of low and high rigidity						
H1	deliberate strategy → market success	0.196 (0.088)	0.026	−0.029 (0.085)	0.729	✓
	emergent strategy → market success	0.211 (0.113)	0.061	0.019 (0.092)	0.834	✓
H2	planning capability → market success	0.093 (0.091)	0.309	0.439 (0.144)	0.002	(✓)
H3b	emergent strategy → innovation orientation	0.401 (0.163)	0.014	0.022 (0.119)	0.855	✓
Causal effects with no significant differences under situations of low and high rigidity						
H3	innovation orientation → market success	0.215 (0.065)	***			✓
No explicit hypothesis, as not the focus	deliberate strategy → planning capability	0.204 (0.048)	***			
	deliberate strategy → innovation orientation	0.338 (0.096)	***			

S.E.: Standard Errors

or fully mediate the relation between deliberate planning and market success. The postulated partial or complete mediation was checked using a comparison of our proposed causal-effects model against a direct-effects only model and against a fully mediated model, each for the group of high rigidities. The first small model only contains the direct paths between planning and market success. The fully mediated effects model contains the indirect effects of both planning models.

Complete mediation exists when (1) the direct effect of the antecedent ('deliberate planning') on market success is significant in the direct-effects only model and (2) is not significant in the extended models. To test for partial versus full mediation, we performed a nested-model comparison. Whereas the difference in chi-square was well above the critical value (Delta Chi² = 21.884, df = 2, p = 0.001) when comparing the direct effects model with the partially mediated model, we did not find a statistically significant improvement between the partially and fully mediated model (Delta Chi² = 1.193, df = 1, p = 0.275). This indicates a partial mediation only. However, planning capability only exerts a significant direct influence on market success if supply-chain rigidity is high (b = 0.42, p = 0.002). The estimate of the direct effect of deliberate planning on market success is insignificant in our full model. Thus, we note a strong tendency towards the confirmation of Hypothesis 2.

Hypothesis 3a stated that the innovation orientation increases market success under high and low innovation rigidities. The results show that innovation orientation always influences market success positively. As such, Hypothesis 3a is confirmed.

Hypothesis 3b stated that innovation rigidity moderates the relationship between emergent strategy and innovation orientation, where the emergent strategy only increases an innovation orientation under low rigidities. The comparison of both groups reveals insights, as an emergent strategy fails to build the capability of innovation orientation in the case of high supply-chain rigidities. However, we find that the emergent strategy has a significant positive effect on innovation orientation under low supply-chain rigidity (b = 0.42, p = 0.014). This supports Hypothesis 3b. We also find that emergence is needed for shaping innovation orientation in the case of low supply-chain rigidities.

Our results are important, as well for the unconstraint as for the constraint causal model (see Table 4): The standardized effects of a deliberate strategy on planning capability as well as on innovation orientation are both significant as well as of similar size in both settings of low and high supply-chain rigidity. Thus, a deliberate innovation strategy seems to strengthen those dynamic capabilities, both under high and low rigidities. This is plausible as the achievement of planned internal capabilities should be independent of supply-chain restrictions. As such, we propose that a reasonable deliberate innovation strategy supports the creation of planning capabilities. The emergent strategy, however, does not rely on such a formal planning process, and thus is unlikely to contribute to an enduring planning capability.

Finally, the total effects of an emergent strategy on market success were found to vanish in settings of high rigidities. A deliberate strategy can still contribute to market success; however, its overall effect is highly reduced (standardized total effects 0.23 compared to 0.65). This stresses the consequences of different degrees of freedom for suppliers in that while the planning impact on market success may be

Table 4. Standardized Direct and Total Effects Under Low/High Rigidity.

	Deliberate strategy	Emergent strategy	Planning capability	Innovation orientation
Standardized direct effects				
Planning capability	0.37/0.38	0	0	0
Innovation orientation	0.42/0.48	0.38/0.03	0	0
Market success	0.44/−0.05	0.36/0.03	0.12/0.41	0.39/0.26
Standardized total effects				
Planning capability	0.37/0.38	0	0	0
Innovation orientation	0.42/0.48	0.38/0.03	0	0
Market success	0.65/0.23	0.51/0.04	0.12/0.41	0.39/0.27

enhanced by less autonomy, strategic action by itself becomes less relevant. Thus, strategic design is of minor relevance for companies facing high restrictions in their innovative activities, due to their embedding in the overall supply chain.

Discussion

The need innovation strategy has long been disputed in the literature (Dosi, 1988). The above mentioned contextual factors of the supply chain demand a strategic design and alignment of companies' innovation activities. We stress that innovation does not happen by chance in an empty space, but instead owes a great deal to a firm's ability to innovate within the entire value chain and to the formulation of strategies. The innovation and performance of suppliers within supply chains and their antecedents along the supply chain, suppliers' strategy, and suppliers' internal innovation orientation have been neglected in the literature so far. This study aimed to explore this complex setting.

This paper discusses the complex areas of innovation strategy, internal capabilities, and performance in supply chains. We clarified how a supplier's innovation strategies and two internal dynamic capabilities, (planning capability and innovation orientation) can cope with manufacturers' rigidities and how these affect performance. We studied a phenomenon neglected in prior studies: how the level of rigidities in supply chains affects suppliers. By introducing the concept of innovation rigidities in the supply chain, we stress that innovation by suppliers is constrained and channeled by manufacturers. Regarding innovation strategy, we build upon the large body of strategy research and transfer the two dominant strategy approaches, the deliberate strategy and the emergent strategy, into the growing research field of supply-chain innovation.

Furthermore, we introduced the important concept of dynamic capabilities in the dynamic setting of innovation in the supply chain. We investigated two important classes of dynamic capabilities: planning capability and innovation orientation. Planning capability is necessary for coping with the changing and challenging contingencies of innovation supply chains, particularly under high rigidities. Our idea of an internal innovation orientation was inspired by the distinction of innovation versus innovativeness and the missing results in this firm level inclination. As such, a long-term proclivity towards innovation was found to exist (Menguc and Auh, 2006). Encouraged by the Resource-Based View (RBV) and its explanation of a sustained competitive advantage, we followed the quest for increased consideration of the internal capability-performance link (Teece *et al.*, 1997).

In essence (Fig. 2), the routes to market success were found to strongly depend on the level of rigidities. Under **low rigidities**, suppliers can follow both strategy approaches to achieve performance. The emergent innovation strategy improves market success through enhanced creativity and experimentation with technologies and designs. As it augments the transfer of ideas and the empowerment of employees, an innovation orientation contributes to market success by following the emergent strategy. The deliberate innovation strategy increases market success as it enables a company to thoroughly plan targets, means, and technologies for innovation. An increased transfer of ideas and empowered employees will help to develop and implement the deliberate innovation strategy and achieve market success.

Under **high innovation rigidities**, suppliers should follow a deliberate strategy. Then they have two options for dynamic capabilities. One option is to establish a high innovation orientation. The creative employees and high information exchange will enable suppliers to build up a high flexibility that can react to the requirements of manufacturers. We argue that the innovation orientation complements both the deliberate planning and rigidities of supply-chain innovation. The other option is to pursue the development of a planning capability. Suppliers can cope with high supply-chain rigidities if they develop the art of flexible and contingency-orientated planning. We found that the planning capability mediates the relation between deliberate planning and market success under high rigidities. Deliberate planning only improves market success under these contingencies

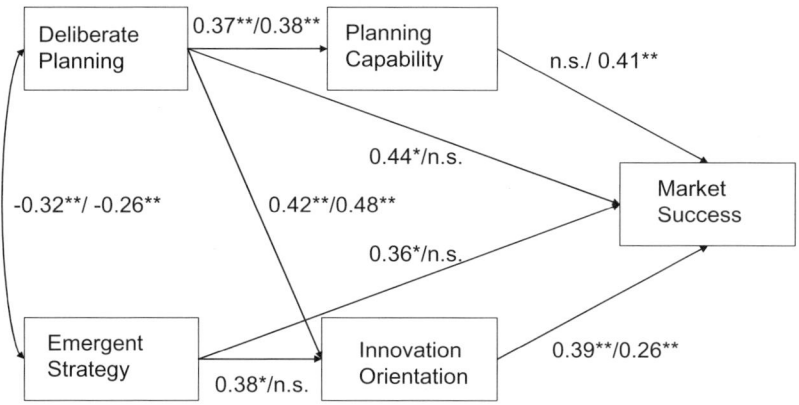

Fig. 2. Standardized Direct Effects in Subgroups of Low/High Supply-Chain Rigidity.

* = significant at p = 5%
** = significant at p = 1%
n.s. = not significant

through the planning capability. Success using a deliberate strategy means that managers must pay more attention to the activities of *ex-ante* rational planning, such as road mapping tools, strategic market assessment, and thus the classic tools of strategic planning.

An important theoretical contribution of this study is the finding that an internal dynamic capability is enhanced by an adequate strategy. Thus, we improve upon the RBV research, which is often accused of lacking concrete suggestions about strategy formulation. Our results for strategies and performance effects bring life into the theoretic discussion about a sustained competitive advantage. More than that, we can derive different adequacies for innovation strategies according to the contingency factor of supply-chain rigidities. We researched long-term market success through internal capabilities and extended the work of scholars who focused on the market orientation-firm performance relationship (Baker and Sinkula, 1999). Extending these studies, we investigated contingency conditions — high and low supply-chain rigidities.

In summary, our research moves beyond prior results on general strategy and planning under high and low uncertainty. High uncertainty partially resembles low supply-chain rigidities, whereas low uncertainty has similarities to a highly defined supply chain. A poorly defined supply chain brings greater autonomy, but increases uncertainty. On the other hand, a highly defined supply chain decreases autonomy and decreases suppliers' uncertainty. To conclude, an emergent general strategy formulation (Mintzberg, 1978) seems suitable under the condition of poorly defined supply chains (high uncertainty).

As always, there are inherent limitations in the study design and thus in the generalizability of the obtained results. First, the database consists of a sample drawn from two specific industry sectors, which are highly dynamic and innovation driven. Supply chains in more static conditions might reveal less emphasis on strategic actions by individual suppliers, which are likely to interfere with long-established routine processes. Further variations in the potential for strategic action should be identified, which may be constrained by overall supplier structures and may vary across different innovation types found in supply chains. Second, and due to the limited access to data sources, we had to rely on subjective success measures and were exposed to a potential common method bias in our data, even though we partially confirmed our obtained measures. Thus, there is need for a cross-validation of the results with additional data, especially for objective measures of long-term company success.

Conceptually, our results contribute to the recently intensified discussion about the importance of dynamic capabilities for linking strategic planning with a company's actions (Teece *et al.*, 2007). We provide a view of innovation orientation and planning capability as dynamic capabilities. Both capabilities show strong intermediary effects for market success. It is reasonable to assume that other capabilities might further explain the process that links overarching strategy with the business environment and which ultimately affects long-term outcomes (Zhou *et al.*, 2005). Thus, future research on the organizational success of supplier companies should follow the multifaceted view proposed by DeSarbo *et al.* (2005) and investigate more thoroughly the interplay between strategic types and internal capabilities, as well as external environmental contingencies on firm performance.

Appendix

Table A1. The Items D1, D2, etc. are Listed in Table A2. Correlation Matrix Including Item Means and Standard Deviations.

Item	Mean	Std. Dev.	D1	D2	D3	D4	E1	E2	E3	P1	P2	P3	P4	I1	I2	I3	I4	M1	M2	M3	M4	M5	M6
D1	3.62	1.02	1.000																				
D2	3.33	1.10	0.593**	1.000																			
D3	3.65	1.01	0.515**	0.525**	1.000																		
D4	3.65	0.96	0.606**	0.542**	0.587**	1.000																	
E1	2.88	1.13	-0.19**	-0.17**	-0.22**	-0.22**	1.000																
E2	2.25	1.10	-0.42**	-0.35**	-0.41**	-0.53**	0.326**	1.000															
E3	2.24	1.07	-0.21**	-0.086	-0.139*	-0.27**	0.361**	0.501**	1.000														
P1	4.05	0.94	0.075	0.189**	0.085	0.149*	-0.019	-0.029	0.106	1.000													
P2	4.22	0.86	0.169**	0.233**	0.103	0.123	0.021	-0.058	0.002	0.579**	1.000												
P3	3.81	0.98	0.090	0.206**	0.208**	0.123	0.002	-0.023	0.033	0.334**	0.386**	1.000											
P4	3.76	1.11	0.109	0.223**	0.142*	0.148*	0.022	-0.102	0.077	0.339**	0.335**	0.382**	1.000										
I1	3.80	0.79	0.208**	0.278**	0.208**	0.216**	-0.148*	-0.17**	-0.055	0.006	0.151*	0.101	0.104	1.000									
I2	3.32	0.97	0.276**	0.249**	0.199**	0.191**	-0.22**	-0.150*	0.000	0.038	0.096	0.132*	0.042	0.425**	1.000								
I3	3.39	0.98	0.238**	0.204**	0.184**	0.152*	-0.19**	-0.140*	0.035	0.020	0.098	0.095	0.016	0.350**	0.677**	1.000							
I4	3.76	0.78	0.179**	0.218**	0.178**	0.174**	-0.084	-0.17**	0.035	0.193**	0.287**	0.152*	0.204**	0.421**	0.355**	0.399**	1.000						
M1	3.94	0.76	0.118	0.075	0.056	0.109	-0.008	-0.028	0.013	0.191**	0.238**	0.315**	0.213**	0.252**	0.153*	0.221**	0.273**	1.000					
M2	3.88	0.90	0.165*	0.151*	0.127*	0.158*	0.020	-0.076	-0.039	0.011	0.144*	0.212**	0.139**	0.237**	0.118	0.145*	0.222**	0.373*	1.000				
M3	4.28	0.74	0.154*	0.141*	0.042	0.076	-0.014	0.011	-0.044	0.091	0.209**	0.213**	0.254**	0.145*	0.128*	0.201**	0.253**	0.359**	0.428**	1.000			
M4	4.00	0.79	0.141*	0.178*	0.084	0.105	0.106	0.058	0.080	0.166*	0.218**	0.272**	0.225**	0.090	0.084	0.140*	0.228**	0.352**	0.345**	0.496**	1.000		
M5	3.61	1.05	0.060	0.091	0.117	0.071	0.103	0.010	0.090	0.078	0.244**	0.268**	0.149*	0.169**	0.109	0.156*	0.223**	0.302**	0.355**	0.472**	0.375**	1.000	
M6	4.40	0.68	0.080	0.053	0.155*	0.092	-0.106	-0.100	-0.051	0.084	0.135*	0.229**	0.147*	0.120	0.111	0.149*	0.280**	0.278**	0.315**	0.440**	0.356**	0.410**	1.000

* = Significant at p = 5%

** = Significant at p = 1%

Table A2. Assessment of Fit of Internal Structure of the Hypothesized Model.

Construct	Item	Standard factor loadings[a]	Indicator reliability	α	AVE
Deliberate	(D1) Research into market opportunities	0.771	0.594	0.83	0.56
	(D2) Analysis of rationale of market growth	0.758	0.574		
	(D3) Development of different options	0.683	0.467		
	(D4) Evaluation of actions taken	0.808	0.652		
Emergent	(E1) Actions and market opportunities are not planned in advance	0.401	0.158	0.69	0.38
	(E2) Intuition	0.873	0.763		
	(E3) Trial and error	0.567	0.319		
Planning capability	(P1) Objectives are always pursued as planned in advance	0.562	0.316	0.76	0.14
	(P2) Planned time frame can always be achieved	0.854	0.73		
	(P3) Planned objectives are always achieved	0.817	0.667		
	(P4) Planning measures always support goal achievements	0.526	0.526		
Innovation orientation	(I1) Constant search for novel product concepts	0.756	0.571	0.71	0.28
	(I2) Constant refinement and development of products	0.777	0.603		

AVE = Average Variance Extracted

(*Continued*)

Table A2. (*Continued*)

Construct	Item	Standard factor loadings[a]	Indicator reliability	α	AVE
	(I3) Fast and cross-functional implementation of innovation	0.588	0.345		
	(I4) Horizontal and vertical participation of all personnel in developing novel ideas	0.587	0.345		
Market success(M1)	Customers' expectations are met	0.457	0.209	0.78	0.13
	(M2) Loyalty of customers	0.479	0.229		
	(M3) Enjoying a good reputation	0.676	0.457		
	(M4) Customers express their satisfaction with the company	0.568	0.323		
	(M5) Recommendations from customers	0.549	0.301		
	(M6) Return customers	0.514	0.265		

Note: [a]All factor loadings are significant ($t > 2.0$ respectively $p < 0.05$), and therefore, s values are not listed.

References

Alegre-Vidal, J.R., Lapiedra-Alcami, R. and Chiva-Gomez, R. (2004). Linking operations strategy and product innovation: An empirical study of Spanish ceramic tile producers, *Research Policy*, **33**(5), 829–839.

Ansoff, H.I. (1991). Critique of Mintzberg, Henry the design school — Reconsidering the basic premises of strategic management, *Strategic Management Journal*, **12**(6), 449–461.

Arbuckle, J. L. and Wothke, W. (1999). *Amos 4.0 User's Guide*. SPSS, Chicago, IL.

Bagozzi, R.P. and Yi, Y. (1988). On the evaluation of structural equation models, *Journal of the Academy of Marketing Science*, **16**(1), 74–94.

Baker, T., Miner, A.S. and Eesley, D.T. (2003). Improvising firms: Bricolage, account giving and improvisational competencies in the founding process, *Research Policy*, **32**(2), 255–276.

Baker, W.E. and Sinkula, J.M. (1999). The synergistic effect of market orientation and learning orientation on organizational performance, *Journal of the Academy of Marketing Science*, **27**(4), 411–427.

Balachandra, R. and Friar, J.H. (1997). Factors for success in R&D projects and new product innovation: A contextual framework, *IEEE Transactions on Engineering Management*, **44**(3), 276–287.

Bouncken, R.B., Koch, M. and Teichert, T. (2007). Innovation strategy explored: Innovation orientation's strategy preconditions and market performance outcomes, *Zeitschrift fü Betriebswirtschaft*, Special Issue **2**, 71–95.

Browne, M. W. and Cudeck, R. (1993). "Alternative ways of assessing model fit", in K. L. Bollen, L (ed), *Testing Structural Equation Models*, Sage Publications, London, pp. 136–162.

Brews, P.J. and Hunt, M.R. (1999). Learning to plan and planning to learn: Resolving the planning school/learning school debate, *Strategic Management Journal*, **20**(10), 889–913.

Brown, S.L. and Eisenhardt, K.M. (1995). Product development: Past research, present findings, and future directions, *Academy of Management Review*, **20**(2), 343–378.

Brown, S.L. and Eisenhardt, K.M. (1997). The art of continuous change: Linking complexity theory and time-paced evolution in relentlessly shifting organizations, *Administrative Science Quarterly*, **42**(1), 1–34.

Browne, M. and Cudeck, R. (1993). "Alternative ways of assessing model fit," in Bollen K.L. (ed.), *Testing Structural Equation Models*, Newburg Park, 136–162.

Byrne, B.M. (2001). *Structural Equation Modeling with AMOS–Basic Concepts, Applications, and Programming*, Lawrence Erlbaum Associates, Mahwah, NJ.

Byrne, B.M. (2004). Testing for multigroup invariance using AMOS Graphics: A road less travelled. *Structural Equation Modeling: A Multidisciplinary Journal*, **11**, 272–300.

Cohen, K.J. and Cyert, R.M. (1973). Strategy — Formulation, implementation, and monitoring, *Journal of Business*, **46**(3), 349–367.

Cooper, R.G. (1984). New product strategies: What distinguishes the top performers? *Journal Product Innovation Management*, **1**(3), 151–164.

Cooper, R.G. and Kleinschmidt, E.J. (1995). Benchmarking the firm's critical success factors in new product development, *Journal of Product Innovation Management*, **12**, 374–391.

DeSarbo, W.S., Di Benedetto, C.A., Song, M. and Sinha, I. (2005). Revisiting the miles and snow strategic framework: Uncovering interrelationships between strategy types, capabilities, environmental uncertainty, and firm performance, *Strategic Management Journal*, **27**(3), 467–488.

Dosi (1988). The nature of the innovative process, The nature of the innovative process, *Technical Change and Economic Theory*, 221–238.

Dyer, B. and Song, X.M. (1998). Innovation strategy and sanctioned conflict: A new edge in innovation? *Journal of Product Innovation Management*, **15**(6), 505–519.

Fredrickson, J.W. (1984). The comprehensiveness of strategic decision-processes — Extension, observations, future-directions, *Academy of Management Journal*, **27**(3), 445–466.

Fredrickson, J.W. and Iaquinto, A.L. (1989). Inertia and creeping rationality in strategic decision-processes, *Academy of Management Journal*, **32**(3), 516–542.

Fredrickson, J. W. & Mitchell, T. R. (1984). Strategic decision-processes — Comprehensiveness and performance in an industry with an unstable environment. *Academy of Management Journal*, **27**(2), 399–423.

Griffin, A. (1997). PDMA research on new product development practices: Updating trends and benchmarking best practices, *Journal of Product Innovation Management*, **14**(6), 429–458.

Gilbert et al. (2003). Strategic commitment to price to stimulate downstream innovation in a supply chain, *European Journal of Operational Research*, **150**(3), 617–639.

Guerard, J.B., Bean, A.S. and Stone, B.K. (1990). Goal-setting for effective corporate-planning, *Management Science*, **36**(3), 359–367.

Henderson, R. and Clark, K. (1990). Architectural innovation: The reconfiguration of existing product technologies and the failure of existing firms, *Administrative Science Quarterly*, **35**(March), 9–30.

Idenburg, P.J. (1993). Four styles of strategy-development, *Long Range Planning*, **26**(6), 132–137.

Joreskog, K.G. and Aish, A.M. (1990). Structural modeling by example — Applications in educational, sociological, and behavioral research, *Contemporary Psychology*, **35**(7), 687–688.

Kamoche, K. and Cinha, M.P.E. (2001). Minimal structures: From jazz improvisation to product innovation, *Organization Studies*, **22**(5), 733–764.

Kohli, A.K. and Jaworski, B. (1990). Market orientation: The construct, research propositions, and managerial implications, *Journal of Marketing*, **54**(April), 1–18.

Lam, S. Y., Shankar, V., Erramilli, M. K., and Murthy, B. (2004). Customer value, satisfaction, loyalty, and switching costs: An illustration from a business-to-business service context. *Journal of the Academy of Marketing Science*, **32**(3), 293–311.

LeBlanc, G. and Nguyen, N. (1995). Cues used by customers evaluating corporate image in service firms. An empirical study in financial institutions, *International Journal of Service Industry Management*, 7(2), 44–56.

Leontiades, M. and Tezel, A. (1980). Planning perceptions and planning results, *Strategic Management Journal*, **1**(1), 65–75.

Manu, F.A. (1992). Innovation orientation, environment and performance: A comparison of US and European markets, *Journal of International Business Studies*, **29**(2), 239–247.

McDermott, C. M. and O'Connor, G. C. (2002). Managing radical innovation: an overview of emergent strategy issues. *Journal of Product Innovation Management*, **19**(6): 424–438.

Menguc, B. and Auh, S. (2006). Creating a firm-level dynamic capability through capitalizing on market orientation and innovativeness, *Journal of the Academy of Marketing Science*, **34**(1), 63–73.

Mintzberg, H. (1978). Patterns in strategy formation, *Management Science*, **24**(9), 934–948.

Mintzberg, H. and McHugh, A. (1985). Strategy formation in an adhocracy, *Administrative Science Quarterly*, **30**(2), 160–197.

Nunnally, J. and Bernstein, I. (1994). *Psychometric Theory*, 3rd edn. New York: McGraw Hill.

Pearce, J.A., Robbins, D.K. and Robinson, R.B. (1987). The impact of grand strategy and planning formality on financial performance, *Strategic Management Journal*, **8**(2), 125–134.

Penrose, E. T. (1995). *The Theory of the Growth of the Firm*, Oxford University Press, Oxford, UK.

Pinto, J.K. and Prescott, J.E. (1988). Variations in critical success factors over the stages in the project life-cycle, *Journal of Management*, **14**(1), 5–18.

Ramanujam, V. and Mensch, G.O. (1985). Improving the strategy-innovation link, *Journal of Product Innovation Management*, **2**(4), 213–223.

Robinson, R.B. and Pearce, J.A. (1983). The impact of formalized strategic-planning on financial performance in small organizations. *Strategic Management Journal*, **4**(3), 197–207.

Siguaw, J.A., Simpson, P.M. and Enz, C.A. (2006). Conceptualizing innovation orientation: A framework for study and integration of innovation research, *Journal of Product Innovation Management*, **23**, 556–574.

Simpson, P.M., Siguaw, J.A. and Enz, C.A. (2006). Innovation orientation outcomes: The good and the bad, *Journal of Business Research*, **59**(10–11), 1133–1141.

Teece, D.J., Pisano, G. and Shuen, A. (1997). Dynamic capabilities and strategic management, *Strategic Management Journal*, **18**(7), 509–533.

Teece *et al.*, (2007). Explicating dynamic capabilities: the nature and micro-foundations of (sustainable) enterprise performance, Strategic Management Journal, **28**(13), 1319–1350

Tushman, M.L. and Anderson, P. (1986). Technological discontinuities and organizational environments, *Administrative Science Quarterly*, **31**(3), 439–465.

Tushman, M.L. and O'Reilly C.A. (1996). Ambidextrous organizations: Managing evolutionary and revolutionary change, *California Management Review*, **38**(4), 8–30.

Utterback, J. (1994). *Mastering the Dynamics of Innovation*, Harvard School Press, Boston, MA.

Worren, N., Moore, K. and Cardona, P. (2002). Modularity, strategic flexibility, and firm performance: A study of the home appliance industry, *Strategic Management Journal*, **23**(12), 1123–1140.

Zeithaml, V.A., Berry, L.L. and Parasuraman, A. (1996). The behavioral consequences of service quality, *Journal of Marketing*, **60**(2), 31–46.

Zhou, K.Z., Kin, C., Tse, Y. and Tse, D.K. (2005). The effects of strategic orientations on technology and market-based breakthrough innovations, *Journal of Marketing*, **69**(April), 42–60.

Chapter 10

Supplier Involvement in Customer New Product Development: New Insights From the Supplier's Perspective

Irina Tiemann*, Nathalie Sick, and Jens Leker
Institute of Business Administration at the Department
of Chemistry and Pharmacy
University of Münster, Germany

Introduction

Research into innovation management has demonstrated that collaborative networks involving external partners may constitute success factors for innovation (Chesbrough, 2006; Nieto and Santamaría, 2007; Tsai and Wang, 2009; von Hippel, 1998). These approaches often focus on customers or users as potential sources of innovation (Baldwin *et al.*, 2006; Bilgram *et al.*, 2008; Foxall, 1989; Harhoff *et al.*, 2003; Souder *et al.*, 1997; von Hippel, 1986). Particularly against the background of a strong shift of value creation to suppliers and an increased search for new raw material substitutes caused by rising raw material costs, suppliers are increasingly considered as initiators of innovation.

Several studies on innovation management have shown that early and extensive supplier involvement in the new product development process

---

*Corresponding author

I. Tiemann, N. Sick, and J. Leker

(NPD) leads to a superior performance for customers, i.e. reduced development times and costs, enhanced product quality and improved productivity (Bonaccorsi and Lipparini, 1994; Clark and Fujimoto, 1991; LaBahn and Krapfel, 2000; Ragatz *et al.*, 2002; Shen and Yu, 2009; Song and Di Benedetto, 2008; Wagner, 2009). In particular, those suppliers providing innovative ideas and new key technologies are of great interest for innovation-driven customers (Bonaccorsi and Lipparini, 1994; Håkansson, 1987; Nishiguchi and Ikeda, 1996; Petroni and Panciroli, 2002; Primo and Amundson, 2002; Schiele, 2006).

Nowadays, many customers recognize the importance of a supplier's contribution to their NPD. The relevance of these contributions has increased as many products are increasingly complex (Johnsen, 2009), especially in research-intensive business-to-business markets, such as the chemical industry. Accordingly, many customers are specifically searching for those suppliers able to provide important impulses and solutions for their NPD and innovation.

However, most of the existing research in this field has focused on the analysis of large and powerful customers. In such settings, suppliers are usually willing to invest in the customer relation and commit to the customer's demanding NPD projects (Johnsen, 2009). The primary challenge for customers is often seen as the selection, evaluation and successful adoption of potential suppliers (De Toni and Nassimbeni, 2001; Hartley *et al.*, 1997; Petersen *et al.*, 2005; Schiele, 2006; Wasti and Liker, 1997). While these research approaches proved to be very valuable in the past, we believe that the rising importance of suppliers as a source of innovation requires new research perspectives. Especially well-performing suppliers with special competencies might easily gain the power to choose their own customers. It therefore appears to be crucial to enlarge the scope of existing research and take into account the supplier's perspective. In this regard, value creation within business relations is an important factor affecting companies' willingness to engage in partnering. Although an increasing amount of research points to the crucial importance of business relations for value creation (Anderson *et al.*, 1994; Biong *et al.*, 1997; Johannessen and Olsen, 2010; Ravald and Grönroos, 1996; Ritala and Hurmelinna-Laukkanen, 2009; Sheth and Sharma, 1997), these research studies concentrate on value creation for customers. As value creation is regarded as crucial for a customer and supplier engaging in a relationship, we take the supplier's perspective and investigate the influences on a supplier's willingness to engage in the NPD of its customers. Thus, our basic research question is: *What factors of a customer relationship influence a supplier's willingness to be involved in customer NPD?*

Addressing the identified shortcomings, this chapter contributes to the existing research by analysing the often neglected supplier perspective. Based on the research of Walter, Ritter and Gemünden, which is one of the few studies to analyse in particular the supplier's perspective (Walter *et al.*, 2001), we explore the suppliers' value creation by different functions of the customer relationship. We further expand the research of Walter *et al.* by analysing whether certain functions of the customer relationship have an effect on the supplier's willingness to be involved in customer NPD. Additionally, we differentiate between innovative and non-innovative suppliers assuming that there are significant inter-group differences in the influence of certain customer relationship functions on the supplier's willingness to be involved in customer NPD.

In our analysis we focus on a single industry to obtain in-depth results and control for possible environmental influences (e.g. industry-specific regulations or R&D intensity). The chemical industry possesses several characteristics that make it an interesting one in which to study supplier integration in customer NPD. First of all, the chemical industry is an important supplier of innovative materials and often triggers innovation in a large variety of downstream industries (e.g. automotive, construction, furniture and also food and beverage and fast moving consumer goods). In particular, chemical companies in European countries usually do not simply focus on price competition due to evolving threats from low-cost countries. They instead concentrate on differentiation through innovation and high quality (Budde *et al.*, 2006). Many downstream manufacturers benefit from the innovation potential of their chemical suppliers and specifically search for those suppliers able to provide important stimuli for their NPD and innovation. Second, the high R&D intensity in this industry means that technological uncertainties may be greater than in other industries. Customers' new products often require new chemical raw materials and unlike the redesign of new mechanical or electronic parts of a product, a technological solution in the chemical industry is often not evident at the outset of a project. Furthermore, the lack of predictability of chemical technology compared to electrical or mechanical engineering means high scale-up challenges from small-scale R&D to large-scale production plants (Cooper and Kleinschmidt, 1993). Therefore, customers are often highly reliant on the supplier's experiences and know-how to help them to reduce uncertainties in their NPD efforts.

An additional peculiarity of the chemical industry that highlights the necessity to explore the chemical supplier perspective is its characteristic of a process industry as opposed to a manufacturing-of-discrete-items industry. This implies that capital equipment investment for a new product may often be quite significant (Cooper and Kleinschmidt, 1993). Thus, new product decisions can affect dependences to a customer due to the high investment costs and possibilities of sunk cost. Finally, the chemical industry is characterized by a number of large and well-known technology-based firms delivering their products to various industries. The challenge of their customers is not mainly to identify potential suppliers but also to achieve their willingness to be involved in their NPD processes. Therefore, analysing a supplier's willingness to integrate into the customer NPD process is of particular importance in the chemical industry.

This chapter is organized as follows. First we introduce the theoretical framework and present the hypotheses to be tested. Then we describe our sample and the variables and constructs. Afterward we present the descriptive statistics and the results of the multivariate analyses. We conclude with a critical discussion of the results obtained, addressing the study's limitations and offering the theoretical and practical implications of our results.

Literature Review and Research Hypotheses

Supplier involvement in customer NPD

Different definitions of supplier involvement in customer NPD have been applied in previous research. In this study we use the definition of van Echtelt *et al.* that differentiates three dimensions of involvement:

resources, tasks and responsibilities. Resources might be innovative ideas, exclusive information and knowledge, specific capabilities or investments that suppliers provide to customers. Tasks are activities within the customer NPD entrusted to the suppliers. Responsibilities might be activities suppliers assume regarding the development of a part, process or service for the benefit of a customer's current or future product development projects (van Echtelt *et al.*, 2008). Supplier involvement represented by these three dimensions could occur at different stages of the customer NPD process.

There are at least five different stages of NPD at which suppliers might be engaged: idea generation; business and technical assessment; product concept development; product engineering and design; and prototype build and pilot test (Handfield *et al.*, 1999). Some studies maintain that earlier involvement at the primary stages of the customer's NPD process is important to the customer's NPD performance (Bonaccorsi and Lipparini, 1994; Clark and Fujimoto, 1991; Esposito and Passaro, 2009; LaBahn and Krapfel, 2000; McIvor and Humphreys, 2004; Ragatz *et al.*, 2002; Wagner and Hoegl, 2006). Suppliers can have specific know-how and add new insights to the idea generation and assessment process of their customers. In the later stages of customer NPD, suppliers can also contribute by participating directly in the customer's NPD team or by taking the responsibility of pilot testing (Muffatto and Panizzolo, 1996; Wasti and Liker, 1997). In particular, for NPD projects that are totally new to the customer or when new technology or new materials are involved, the suppliers' capabilities and competencies are essential at all stages of the customer NPD. In this paper, supplier involvement in customer NPD refers (consistent with Walter, 2003 and van Echtelt *et al.*, 2008) to the supplier resources, tasks and responsibilities provided at all stages of NPD to a focal customer, from the idea stage to the prototype-building and pilot-testing stages.

Direct and indirect functions of the customer relationship

According to a study by Walter, Ritter and Gemünden, seven functions of a customer relation might create value for a supplier. These functions can be differentiated into two categories: direct and indirect (Walter *et al.*, 2001).

In contrast to indirect functions, direct functions have an immediate effect on the supplier firm. These functions are profit, volume and safeguard functions (Lindgreen and Wynstra, 2005). The profit function is a necessary precondition for the survival of a company and thus, an essential function for a supplier (Håkansson, 1987; Purchase *et al.*, 2009). However, the utilization of capacities in order to achieve economies of scale is also very important for a manufacturing company, thus, not only profitability but also the quantity of products sold is crucial for suppliers. Further improvements in cost efficiencies provide the safeguard function. This function is provided by customers who continue buying products from the supplier in difficult periods like depressed markets (Håkansson, 1982). These deals may be less favourable than deals with regular customers but provide some stable business in times of difficulties and reduce the opportunity costs of no business at all (Walter *et al.*, 2001).

Indirect functions of customer relationships have a positive effect on long-term benefits in the future or on exchange in other supplier relations, 'the wider network' (other customers, competitors or other third parties) (Walter *et al.*, 2003). One of the important indirect functions, particularly for innovative suppliers, is the innovation function. Suppliers establish relations with customers who provide benefits for their collaborative innovation efforts e.g. through technology and product expertise. These benefits may positively affect the value of the supplier's offerings to its co-developing customer as well as to other customers (Gemünden *et al.*, 1992; Maidique and Zirger, 1985). The market function of the customer relationship is the process of gaining access to new customers and new markets through referrals and recommendations from current customers. Especially large and well-established customers may provide valuable references to other customers (Walter *et al.*, 2001). A further indirect function is the scout function. Through this function, a supplier obtains important information from outside its organization from a customer. For instance, this information might be relevant market developments, which the supplier might not be able to obtain alone (Håkansson, 1987; Walter *et al.*, 2003). Finally, the access function allows access to third parties (e.g. official authorities, chambers of commerce, banks or trade associations) and reduces the time and costs for procedures such as licensing or business negotiation (Gemünden *et al.*, 1992).

Supplier involvement in customer NPD is often linked to significant efforts and to consumption of limited resources. Due to high investment costs and the risk of sunk costs (Cooper and Kleinschmidt, 1993), suppliers from the chemical industry in particular have to decide which customers to commit to when engaging in customer NPD. Suppliers might be involved in only a few NPD activities for customers, as the problems of property rights and exclusivity increase with the number of customers involved. Suppliers have to carefully assess the benefits associated with each customer. In this regard, the direct functions of the customer relation certainly play an important role. Only customers who provide profitable business will gain the willingness of suppliers to be involved in their NPD. However, the indirect functions might also affect a supplier's willingness to be involved in a customer's NPD. Long-term benefits and network opportunities that are provided by indirect functions are highly important for strategically oriented suppliers. Customers contributing positively to a supplier's product development, providing references to other customers, offering relevant information or assisting in access to important parties ('movers and shakers') will likely gain a supplier's commitment to be involved in their NPD. Therefore, we hypothesise:

Hypothesis 1: The direct and indirect functions of the customer relation have a positive influence on supplier involvement in customer NPD.

Innovation rate and innovativeness

Not all suppliers are equally successful in generating innovation. In our study we differentiate between innovative and non-innovative suppliers. The scientific discussion is still far from reaching a consensus on how to measure the innovativeness of a firm or a product (Bröring *et al.*, 2006). To ensure a generally applicable approach, we use the definition of innovation from the *Oslo Manual*:

A product innovation is the introduction of a good or service that is new or significantly improved with respect to its characteristics or intended uses. This includes significant improvements in technical specifications, components and materials, incorporated software, user friendliness or other functional characteristics. (OECD and Eurostat, 2005, p. 48)

Following the recommendation of the *Oslo Manual* we asked suppliers to estimate the share of total turnover in 2008 with product innovations 'new to the market', 'new to the firm' and 'unchanged or marginally changed', that were introduced in the last three years. According to these estimates and to the German chemical industry report (Torben and Fier, 2009), which indicates the average innovation rate of chemical suppliers with innovations 'new to the market' as 3.9% and the average innovation rate with innovations 'new to the firm' as 14.1%, we classified suppliers into innovative and non-innovative firms. We classified suppliers who indicated their innovation rate was above average as innovative, and suppliers who indicated their innovation rate was below average as non-innovative. According to the widely accepted view that firms have to balance between new products that are high-risk and high-reward (often products with a high-newness level or 'new to the market') and products that are less risky and less profitable (often products with a low-newness level or 'new to the firm') (Cooper *et al.*, 1999), we only consider suppliers that out perform in both categories of innovation ('new to the market' *and* 'new to the firm') as innovative suppliers.

Looking at the innovative and non-innovative suppliers we expect some differences in the influence of direct and indirect functions on supplier involvement in customer NPD. Innovation-driven suppliers are strongly oriented to an efficient innovation generation. The innovation management literature has discussed many success factors for superior innovation performance (Cooper and Kleinschmidt, 1986; Di Benedetto, 1999; Fallah and Lechler, 2008; Lichtenthaler, 2008; Maidique *et al.*, 1984; Mishra *et al.*, 1996; Montoya-Weiss *et al.*, 1994; Rhee *et al.* 2010; Rothwell *et al.*, 1974; Song and Parry, 1996; Verworn, 2009; Zeng *et al.*, 2010). Many of these factors refer to the strong customer/

market orientation (Di Benedetto, 1999; Mishra *et al.*,1996; Montoya-Weiss *et al.*, 1994; Song and Montoya-Weiss, 1998;) and the generation of unique superior products (Cooper and Kleinschmidt, 1996; Mishra *et al.*, 1996; Song and Parry, 1996; Souder and Song, 1997). Hence, a customer's support for NPD, assistance in accessing critical information and mediating open networks are highly relevant in achieving these success factors and thus play an important role for innovative suppliers. Accordingly, innovative suppliers could value the indirect functions of a customer relation higher than the direct functions. Therefore we assume:

Hypothesis 2: The influences of the direct and the indirect functions of customer relations on supplier involvement in customer NPD differ between innovative and non-innovative suppliers.

Research Method

Data collection and sample

In this study we survey suppliers from the chemical industry. In general, the chemical companies can be categorized as companies producing 'commodities' and 'specialities'. According to Budde *et al.*, a speciality business is one that sells products based on performance standards that have higher value added and allow for some product differentiation (Budde *et al.*, 2006). These products are mostly technology driven, and have a relatively small segmented market often categorized according to their application (e.g. microbiocides, catalysts, corrosion inhibitors, coatings, high-performance polymers, plastic additives, flavours, fragrances, etc.) (Abratt and van Altena Lombard, 1993).

Commodities, however, are mature, homogeneous and undifferentiated goods (Kleinaltenkamp, 2000). They are based on mature technology and have only a limited differentiation potential (Leker and Rühmer, 2003). Nevertheless, it should be kept in mind that chemical commodities (e.g. petrochemicals, inorganic chemicals, basic polymers, etc.) are not nearly as commoditized as the 'true' commodities such as copper or crude oil, and therefore still offer more possibilities for differentiation (Budde *et al.*, 2006). In fact, the range from commodities to specialities is a continuous spectrum (Leker and Herzog, 2004). For a sophisticated analysis both types of business should be considered.

For this study, we developed a standardized online questionnaire to address chemical companies in Austria and Switzerland. We pre-tested the comprehensibility of our questionnaire with a small group of experts from the field of innovation management and professionals from the chemical industry. The questionnaires were sent to 236 companies in Austria and 43 companies in Switzerland. The first reminders were sent after one week. After the second week, additional follow-up calls were made, generating an average final response rate of 17.2%. The same level of industrial development and cultural similarities (language, mentality) in both countries allow us to merge both samples. Overall, the final data analysis in this study was based on 48 questionnaires.

Data for the study was obtained from managers of the chemical supplier firms. We gathered the addresses from a commercial address list for chemical companies. For the purpose of this study, we focused on key informants who were engaged in one or more customer relation(s) and have direct contact with customers. Most respondents were sales or marketing managers or CEOs, but also R&D, product and quality management functions were covered as well. For the most part, key informants were from middle management (62.8%). Of the respondents 25.6% were senior management and only 11.6% from lower management positions. In 33.3% of our cases, the companies were commodity manufacturers and 66.7% of the firms were specialties manufacturers. The level of R&D expenditure ranged from 0.5% to 15% with an average of 5.5%. The annual sales volumes and employee numbers are shown in Table 1. The size of their customers ranged from €0.2 M to €10,000 M with an average of €1,195 M. The length of the relationship with the relevant customer ranged from 1 to 35 years with an average of 13.5 years.

Operationalization

After reviewing the existing literature, we developed a set of measures (Table 2). These measures operationalized the supplier

Table 1. Sample Data.

Annual sales volume (€M)	%	Number of employees	%
<25	16.3	<50	14.0
25–49	18.6	50–99	14.0
50–249	34.9	100–499	30.2
250–999	16.3	500–999	18.6
1,000–4,999	0.0	1,000–4,999	7.0
5,000–15,000	4.7	5,000–10,000	4.7
>15,000	9.3	>10,000	11.6
Total	100	Total	100

involvement using five items, covering all stages of possible sup-plier integration (Handfield *et al.*, 1999; Walter, 2003). Following Walter *et al.* we used three items to measure the direct functions of customer relations and four items to measure the indirect func-tions (Walter *et al.*, 2001).* All items were measured on a 7-point Likert scale anchored by 'strongly disagree' (1) and 'strongly agree' (7).

We checked our measures by assessing their reliability and uni-dimensionality. The unidimensionality of the constructs was assessed through exploratory factor analysis. To confirm the relia-bility of the measures, Cronbach's alpha values (Cronbach, 1951) and factor loadings (Iacobucci, 1994) were utilized. Construct validity was assessed via confirmatory factor analysis by assessing the average variance extracted (VE). Applying the Fornell–Larcker criterion (Fornell and Larcker, 1981), we assessed the discriminant validity of the constructs by comparing the VE percentages with the square of the correlation estimates. All VE estimates fulfilled the criterion of being greater than the squared correlation estimates, providing good evidence for discriminant validity (Hair *et al.*, 2006).

---

*Due to the complexity of the original second-order model of Walter *et al.* we used the first-order factors as items in our model.

Table 2.   Overview of Survey Items and Construct Operationalization.

Questionnaire items [Scale 1-7, 'strongly disagree' (1) and 'strongly agree' (7)]	Factor loading	Item reliability
Supplier involvement		
(Five items, Cronbach's α =.906, variance explained = 73.2%, average variance extracted AVE =.666, construct reliability = .908)		
Our company is involved in this customer NPD at the following stages...		
Idea generation	.783	.702
Business and technical assessment	.879	.661
Product concept development	.902	.823
Product engineering and design	.858	.728
Prototype build, test and pilot	.852	.627
Direct functions of customer relationship		
(Three items, Cronbach's α = .707, variance explained = 64.1%, average variance extracted AVE = .466, construct reliability = .716)		
This customer creates value for us by providing the following functions...		
Volume function	.828	.696
Profit function	.756	.271
Safeguard function	.815	.430
Indirect functions of customer relationship		
(Four items, Cronbach's α = .753, variance explained = 57.7%, average variance extracted AVE = .439, construct reliability = .758)		

(*Continued*)

Table 2. (*Continued*)

Questionnaire items [Scale 1-7, 'strongly disagree' (1) and 'strongly agree' (7)]	Factor loading	Item reliability
This customer creates value for us by providing the following functions…		
Innovation function	.733	.452
Market function	.751	.419
Scout function	.786	.438
Access function	.767	.449

Notes: Exploratory factor analysis was performed using SPSS 18.0. Confirmatory analysis was performed by using AMOS 18.0. The goodness-of-fit measures for the overall measurement model are GFI = .754, AGFI = .624 and RMR = 0.089.*

Results

To analyse the differences between the innovative and non-innovative suppliers we initially examined the descriptive statistics. These statistics show that more suppliers from the innovative group indicate their involvement in customer NPD as suppliers than the group of non-innovative suppliers. Of the innovative suppliers 54.3% state that they are involved in customer NPD (averaged over all NPD stages). In contrast, only 37.5% of non-innovative suppliers indicate their involvement in customer NPD. Regarding the different stages of NPD we recognize that, at almost all stages, innovative suppliers state their involvement in customer NPD more often than non-innovative suppliers. In particular, the differences in involvement for the stages of idea generation and business and technical assessment are very pronounced (see Fig. 1).

---

*The goodness-of-fit measures for the overall measurement model do not wholly fulfil the traditional criterion (GFI > .90 and AGFI > .90). However, Anderson and Gerbing state in their research that GFI and AGFI values decrease for a smaller sample size and increasing use of additional indicators (Anderson and Gerbing, 1984). In particular, AGFI is sensitive to sample size; its values decrease by increasing degrees of freedom in relation to sample size (Bagozzi and Baumgartner, 1994). Due to the relative small sample size in our study ($n = 48$), we accept our goodness-of-fit measures, which lie in the rage of other studies with similar sample sizes (Mehrwald, 1999).

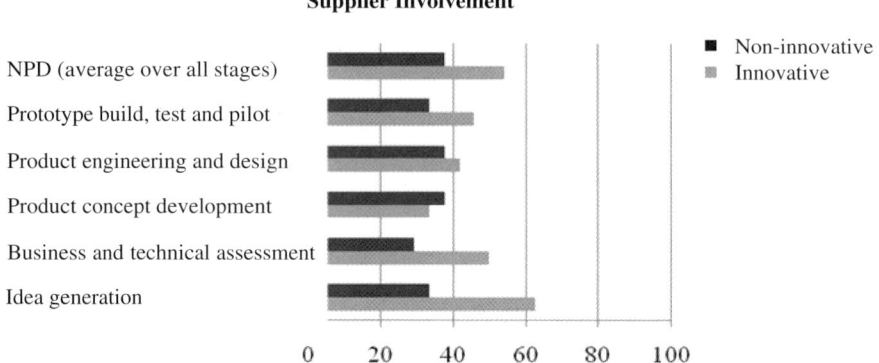

Supplier's percentage specifying their involvement at different NPD stages on a scale, strongly agree' (1) to, strongly disagree' (7) in the range of 5-7.

Fig. 1.   Supplier Involvement in Customer NPD.

Analysing the group differences more closely, we find significant differences between innovative and non-innovative suppliers in their involvement at the idea generation and business and technical assessment stages. Although not statistically significant, the mean values are higher for innovative suppliers for all NPD stages (see Table 3).

Looking at the mean values for direct and indirect functions we also observe higher values for innovative suppliers. However, a significant difference between innovative and non-innovative suppliers exists only for the direct function (see Table 4).

To test our hypotheses and to analyse the relation between the dependent variable 'supplier involvement' and the independent variables (the direct and the indirect functions), we conducted three linear regression analyses. First we tested Hypothesis 1 by including all respondents in the regression analysis. Subsequently, we tested Hypothesis 2 by conducting two isolated regression analyses for both groups (see Fig. 2).

We found a positive relation between the direct functions of customer relationship and supplier involvement in the total sample. However, we could not confirm the influence of indirect functions on supplier involvement. Therefore, Hypothesis 1 cannot be supported.

Table 3. Group Comparison: Supplier Involvement.

	Non-innovative suppliers $n = 24$ Mean (S.D.)	Innovative suppliers $n = 24$ Mean (S.D.)	Mann–Whitney-U-test statistical significance
Supplier involvement at all stages	3.48 (1.83)	4.20 (1.33)	—
Prototype build, test and pilot	3.35 (2.25)	4.17 (1.71)	—
Product engineering and design	3.80 (2.19)	4.00 (1.75)	—
Product concept development	3.75 (1.92)	3.92 (1.50)	—
Business and technical assessment	3.20 (1.88)	4.25 (1.80)	♣
Idea generation	3.30 (1.89)	4.67 (1.55)	*

Notes: S.D. = standard deviation
°significant at $p < .10$; * significant at $p < .05$; ** significant at $p < .01$, *** significant at $p < .001$

Table 4. Group Comparison: Direct and Indirect Functions.

	Non-innovative suppliers $n = 24$ Mean (S.D.)	Innovative suppliers $n = 24$ Mean (S.D.)	Mann–Whitney-U-test statistical significance
Indirect functions	4.70 (1.16)	5.18 (1.18)	—
Direct functions	3.61 (1.49)	4.48 (1.12)	*

Notes: S.D. = standard deviation
*significant at $p < .10$; * significant at $p < .05$; ** significant at $p < .01$, *** significant at $p < .001$

Furthermore, we also found a positive relation between the direct functions and supplier involvement, while we unable to detect any effect of the indirect functions for the non-innovative suppliers'

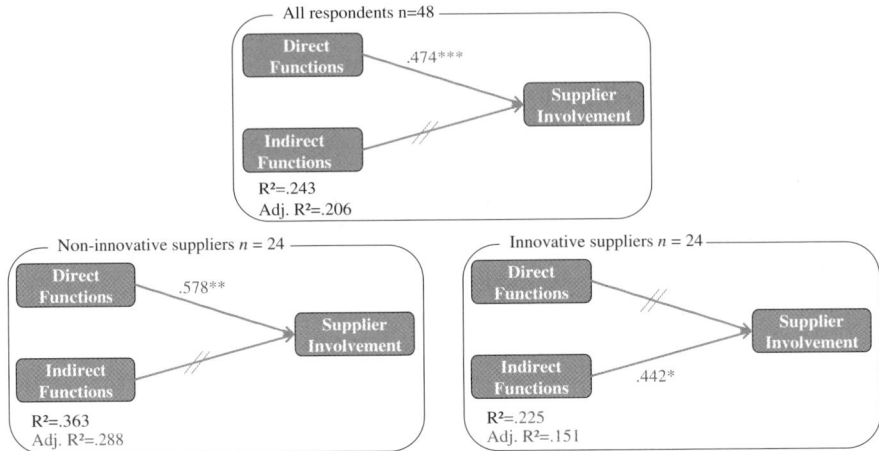

* significant at $p < .05$; ** significant at $p < .01$; *** significant at $p < .001$

Fig. 2.   Regression Analyses.

group. In contrast, we were able to demonstrate the influence of the indirect functions on supplier involvement and that there was no influence of the direct functions for the group of innovative suppliers. Thus, Hypothesis 2 is confirmed.

Discussion: Implications for Theory and Practice

The study presents the results of an empirical survey of suppliers from the chemical industry. Addressing a shortcoming in existing research, we specifically analysed supplier involvement in customer NPD from the often neglected perspective of the suppliers. In particular, we set out to analyse which contributions customers need to offer to increase suppliers' willingness to engage in customer NPD.

We showed in this paper that there are different functions of a customer relationship that can influence the willingness of suppliers to become involved in their customers' NPD processes. Basically, we differentiated between direct and indirect functions of a customer relationship (Walter *et al.*, 2001). In contrast to the direct and mostly apparent functions of a customer relationship that create a direct economic value (e.g. profit and volume) for the suppliers, the indirect functions are often less obvious. But long-term benefits and network opportunities especially, which are provided by indirect functions, are highly important for strategically oriented suppliers. Accordingly, we assumed at first that the direct as well as the indirect functions may influence supplier involvement in customer NPD. However, we could not generally support this hypothesis as we found a significant influence only for direct functions in the total sample. The direct functions seem to be a strong predictor for a supplier's decision to become involved in customer NPD. Only economically secured customer relations appear to be appropriate for the suppliers' willingness to engage in customer NPD. But are the direct functions actually the only triggers for supplier involvement in NPD or are there any differences between innovative and non-innovative suppliers?

To answer this question, we differentiated between innovative and non-innovative suppliers by classifying them into two groups according to their innovation rates. We suggested differences in the influence of the direct and the indirect functions on supplier involvement between the innovative and non-innovative suppliers. The analysis of the descriptive statistics showed several considerable differences between the groups. For instance, the mean values for the direct and indirect functions as well as supplier involvement are consistently higher for innovative suppliers. For the direct functions and supplier involvement, at the idea generation and assessment stages of customer NPD, the group differences are significant. On the one hand, these results show that customers have a tendency to provide a higher level of direct and indirect functions to innovative suppliers. On the other hand, innovative suppliers tend to be more engaged in customer NPD than non-innovative suppliers.

Looking at the regression analyses of the separate groups, we found distinct differences between the correlation of customer relationship functions and supplier involvement. While direct functions have a strong influence on supplier involvement for the non-innovative group, indirect functions are a predictor for supplier involvement for the innovative supplier group. These results support our assumption of a higher relevance for indirect functions for innovative suppliers than for non-innovative suppliers. That does not necessarily mean that innovative suppliers are insensible to the direct return from customer relationships and so neglect customers providing direct functions. In fact, most of the innovative suppliers already enjoy direct value creation in the form of profit, volume and safeguard functions provided by their customers. This conclusion is reflected in the significant mean values difference of the direct functions between innovative and non-innovative suppliers. In fact, innovative suppliers are likely to gain from the profitable situation of being able to continually offer new products and innovation to their customers. Apparently, innovative suppliers require the additional incentives of indirect functions from their customer relationships before becoming involved in their customers' NPD. In this regard, the innovation function plays an essential role. New ideas and technological know-how provided by customers are very important for the successful generation of new products by suppliers. Similarly, gaining access to new markets or customers, to critical information and to third parties is highly relevant for innovative suppliers in order to build a useful network. These results show that mutual support in NPD and open networks are an imperative trigger for the involvement of innovative suppliers.

So far there have only been a few studies focusing on supplier involvement from the supplier's perspective (Johnsen, 2009) and we believe that this study yields relevant theoretical implications for this research stream. With this paper, we contribute to the current research analysing the perspective of a supplier in regard to the willingness to be involved in customer NPD. To the best of our knowledge, this study is one of the first attempts to connect research on value creation through customer relationship functions to research on supplier integration into NPD. In particular, the detailed investigation of customer relationship functions for innovative and non-innovative suppliers offers crucial new insights and starting points for further research – for example to other industries.

Concerning practical implications, the results of this study are of great relevance to the chemical industry as an important supplier of innovative materials and therefore a cooperative partner in NPD with the downstream industry. The results will help suppliers to understand which customer relationship functions can be provided by their customers. This is important to suppliers who want to receive the maximum benefits from their customers. Relationships will be ruined in the long-term by attending to customers' interests without receiving anything in return (Walter *et al.*, 2001).

Customers in turn can use the results to understand which conditions are positively related to the willingness of suppliers to participate in customer NPD. The results show that innovative suppliers need individual handling as value creation, particularly through indirect functions of the customer relationship, is essential. Hence, two practical recommendations for customers of the chemical industry can be deduced. As direct customer relationship functions show less relevance for the engagement of innovative suppliers in NPD than indirect functions, we assume that suppliers will focus on new markets, new products and thus potential future earnings. So, current earnings and other economic factors will not necessarily play a significant role for suppliers to participate in NPD. We would therefore firstly recommend that customers ensure future earnings of NPD for suppliers as incentive for their involvement in the development process with fair and cooperative conditions as a *sine qua non*. With respect to indirect functions and long-term incentives for suppliers, access to strategic networks and relevant strategic information gain importance. So we secondly recommend customers to share available strategic information with their suppliers. Furthermore, customers should provide cooperating suppliers the opportunity to participate in their strategic networks in order to attain and commitment of high-performing innovative suppliers.

As this study represents the first step in our research project on supplier integration in NPD, further investigations will be carried out. Analysing the issues for a larger sample will allow us to consolidate our results and enlarge our research by integrating additional influence factors such as commitment and trust.

References

Abratt, R. and van Altena Lombard, A. (1993). Determinants of product innovation in speciality chemical companies, *Industrial Marketing Management*, **22**(3), 169–175.

Anderson, J.C. and Gerbing, D.W. (1984). The effect of sampling error on convergence, improper solutions, and goodness-of-fit indices for maximum likelihood confirmatory factor analysis, *Psychometrika*, **49**(2), 155–173.

Anderson, J.C., Håkansson, H. and Johanson, J. (1994). Dyadic business relationships within a business network context, *Journal of Marketing*, **58**, 1–15.

Bagozzi, R.P. and Baumgartner, J. (1994). "The evaluation of structural equation models and hypothesis testing," in Bagozzi, R.P. (ed), *Principles of marketing research*, Cambridge University Press, Cambridge, UK pp. 386–422.

Baldwin, C., Hienerth, C. and von Hippel, E. (2006). How user innovations become commercial products: A theoretical investigation and case study, *Research Policy*, **35**(9), 1291–1313.

Bilgram, V., Brem, A. and Voigt, K.-I. (2008). User-centric innovations in the new product development: Systematic identification of lead users harnessing interactive and collaborative online-tools, *International Journal of Innovation management*, **12**(3), 419–458.

Biong, H., Wathne, K. and Parvatiyar, A. (1997). "Why do some companies not want to engage in partnering relationships," in Gemünden, H.G., Ritter, T. and Walter, A. (eds), *Relationships and Networks in International Business Markets*, Elsevier Science, New York, pp. 91–107.

Bonaccorsi, A. and Lipparini, A. (1994). Strategic partnerships in new product development: An Italian case study, *Journal of Product Innovation Management*, **11**(2), 134–145.

Bröring, S., Leker, J. and Rühmer, S. (2006). Radical or not? Assessing innovativeness and its organizational implications for established firms, *International Journal Product Development*, **3**(2), 152–166.

Budde, F., Felch, U.-H. and Frankenmölle, H. (2006). *Value Creation: Strategies for the Chemical Industry*, 2nd edn, Wiley-VCH, Weinheim.

Chesbrough, H. (2006). *Open Innovation: A New Paradigm for Understanding Industrial Innovation*, Oxford University Press, New York.

Clark, K.B. and Fujimoto, T. (1991). *Product Development Performance: Strategy, Organization and Management in the World Auto Industry*, Harvard Business School Press, Boston, MA.

Cooper, R.G. and Kleinschmidt, E.J. (1986). An investigation into the new product process: Steps, deficiencies and impact, *Journal of Product Innovation Management*, **3**(2), 71–85.

Cooper, R.G. and Kleinschmidt, E.J. (1996). Winning businesses in product development: Critical success factors, *Research-Technology Management*, **39**(4), 18–29.

Cooper, R.G., Edgett, S.J. and Kleinschmidt, E.J. (1999). New product portfolio management: Practices and performance, *Journal of Product Innovation Management*, **16**(4), 333–351.

Cronbach, L.J. (1951). Coefficient alpha and the internal structure of tests, *Psychometrika*, **16**(5), 297–334.

De Toni, A. and Nassimbeni, G. (2001). A method for the evaluation of suppliers' co-design effort, *International Journal of Production Economics*, **72**(2), 169–180.

Di Benedetto, C.A. (1999). Identifying the key success factors in new product launch. *Journal of Product Innovation Management*, **16**(6), 530–544.

Esposito, E. and Passaro, R. (2009). The evolution of supply chain relationships: An interpretative framework based on the Italian inter-industry experience, *Journal of Purchasing and Supply Management*, **15**(2), 114–126.

Fallah, M.H. and Lechler, T.G. (2008). Global innovation performance: Strategic challenges for multinational corporations, *Journal of Engineering and Technology Management*, **25**(1–2), 58–74.

Fornell, C. and Larcker, D. (1981). Evaluating structural equation models with unobservable variables and measurement error, *Journal of Marketing Research*, **18**(2), 39–50.

Foxall, G.R. (1989). User initiated product innovations, *Industrial Marketing Management*, **18**(2), 95–104.

Gemünden, H.G., Schaettgen, M. and Walter, A. (1992). "Functional pattern of business relationships", in Valla, J.-P. (ed), *Proceedings of the 8th International Conference on Industrial Marketing and Purchasing*, Lyon.

Hair, J.F., Black, W.C., Babin, B.J., Anderson, R.E. and Tatham, R.L. (2006). *Multivariate Data Analysis*, Pearson Prentice Hall, Upper Saddle River, NY.

Håkansson, H. (1987). *Industrial Technological Development: A Network Approach*, Croom Helm, London.

Håkansson, H. and Turnbull, P. (1982). Inter-company relationships: An analytical framework, working paper 1982/8, Centre for International Business Research, **13**, 49–60.

Harhoff, D., Henkel, J. and von Hippel, E. (2003). Profiting from voluntary information spillovers: How users benefit by freely revealing their innovations, *Research Policy*, **32**(10), 1753–1769.

Hartley J.L., Zirgerand, B.J. and Kamath, B.J. (1997). Managing buyer–supplier interface for on-time performance in product development, *Journal of Operations Management*, **15**, 57–70.

Iacobucci, D. (1994). "Classic factor analysis," in Bagozzi, R.P. (ed), *Principles of Marketing Research*, Blackwell, Cambridge, pp. 279–316.

Johannessen, J.-A. and Olsen, B. (2010). The future of value creation and innovations: Aspects of a theory of value creation and innovation in a global knowledge economy, *International Journal of Information Management*, **30**(6), 502–511.

Johnsen, T.E. (2009). Supplier involvement in new product development and innovation: Taking stock and looking to the future, *Journal of Purchasing and Supply Management*, **15**(3), 187–197.

Kleinaltenkamp, M. (2000). "Business-to-business-marketing", 15th edn. In Gabler (ed.), *Gabler Wirtschafts-Lexikon*, Wiesbaden, pp. 602–607.

LaBahn, D.W. and Krapfel, R. (2000). Early supplier involvement in customer new product development: A contingency model of component supplier intentions, *Journal of Business Research*, **47**(3), 173–190.

Leker, J. and Herzog, P. (2004). "Marketing in der chemischen Industrie", in Backhaus, K. and Voeth, M. (eds), *Handbuch Industriegütermarketing: Strategien-Instrumente-Anwendungen*, Wiesbaden, pp. 1171–1193.

Leker, J. and Rühmer, S. (2003). "Der Einfluss von Wertschöpfungsnetzwerken auf das Innovations management der chemischen Industrie", in Buchholz, W., Bach, N. and Eichler, B. (eds), *Geschäftsmodelle für Wertschöpfungsnetzwerke, Festschrift für Winfried Krüger*.

Lichtenthaler, U. (2008). Externally commercializing technology assets: An examination of different process stages, *Journal of Business Venturing*, **23**(4), 445–464.

Lindgreen, A. and Wynstra, F. (2005). Value in business markets: What do we know? Where are we going? *Industrial Marketing Management*, **34**(7), 732–748.

Maidique, M.A. and Zirger, B.J. (1984). A study of success and failure in product innovation: The case of the US electronics industry, *IEEE Trans. Engineering Management*, (EM–31), 192–203.

McIvor, R. and Humphreys, P. (2004). Early supplier involvement in the design process: Lessons from the electronics industry, *Omega*, **32**(3), 179–199.

Mehrwald, H. (1999). *Das 'Not-invented-here'-Syndrom in Forschung und Entwicklung*, Dt. Univ.-Verl., Wiesbaden.

Mishra, S., Kim, D. and Lee, D.H. (1996). Factors affecting new product success: Cross country comparisons, *Journal of Product Innovation Management*, **13**(6), 530–550.

Montoya-Weiss, M.M. and Calantone, R. (1997). Determinants of new product performance: A review and meta-analysis, *Journal of Product Innovation Management*, **11**(5), 397–417.

Nieto, M.J., Santamaría, L. (2007). The importance of diverse collaborative networks for the novelty of product innovation, *Technovation*, **27**(6–7), 367–377.

OECD and Eurostat (2005). *Oslo Manual, Guidelines for Collecting and Interpreting Innovation data*, 3rd edn, OECD Publishing.

Petersen, K.J., Handfield, R.B. and Ragatz, G.L. (2005). Supplier integration into new product development: Coordination product, process and supply chain design, *Journal of Operations Management*, **23**(3–4), 371–388.

Petroni, A. and Panciroli, B. (2002). Innovation as a determinant of suppliers' roles and performances: An empirical study in the food machinery industry, *European Journal of Purchasing and Supply Management*, **8**(3), 135–149.

Primo, M.A.M. and Amundson, S.D. (2002). An exploratory study of the effects of supplier relationships on new product development outcomes, *Journal of Operations Management*, **20**(1), 33–52.

Purchase, S., Goh, T. and Dooley, K. (2009). Supplier perceived value: Differences between business-to-business and business-to-government relationships, *Journal of Purchasing and Supply Management*, **15**(1), 3–11.

Ragatz, G.L., Handfield, R.B. and Petersen, K.J. (2002). Benefits associated with supplier integration into new product development under conditions of technology uncertainty, *Journal of Business Research*, **55**(5), 389–400.

Ravald, A. and Grönroos, C. (1996). The value concept and relationship marketing, *European Journal of Marketing*, **30**, 19–30.

Rhee, J., Park, T. and Lee, D.H. (2010). Drivers of innovativeness and performance for innovative SMEs in South Korea: Mediation of learning orientation, *Technovation*, **30**(1), 65–75.

Ritala, P. and Hurmelinna-Laukkanen, P. (2009). What's in it for me? Creating and appropriating value in innovation-related coopetition, *Technovation*, **29**(12), 819–828.

Rothwell, R., Freeman, C., Horseley, A., Jervis, V.T.P., Robertson, A.B. and Townsend, J. (1974). SAPPHO updated: Project SAPPHO Phase II, *Research Policy*, **3**, 258–291.

Schiele, H. (2006). How to distinguish innovative suppliers? Identifying innovative suppliers as new task for purchasing, *Industrial Marketing Management*, **35**(8), 925–935.

Shen, C.Y. and Yu, K.T. (2009). Enhancing the efficacy of supplier selection decision-making on the initial stage of new product development: A hybrid fuzzy approach considering the strategic and operational factors simultaneously, *Expert Systems with Applications*, **36**(8), 11271–11281.

Sheth, J.N. and Sharma, A. (1997). Supplier relationships: Emerging issues and challenges, *Industrial Marketing Management*, **26**, 91–100.

Song, M. and Di Benedetto, C.A. (2008). Supplier's involvement and success of radical new product development in new ventures, *Journal of Operations Management*, **26**(1), 1–22.

Song, X.M. and Montoya-Weiss, M.M. (1998). Critical development activities for really new vs. incremental products, *Journal of Product Innovation Management*, **15**(2), 124–135.

Song, X.M. and Parry, M.E. (1996). What separates Japanese new product winners from losers? *Journal of Product Innovation Management*, **13**(5), 422–439.

Souder, W.E. and Song, X.M. (1997). Contingent product design and marketing strategies influencing new product success and failure in US and Japanese electronics firms, *Journal of Product Innovation Management*, **14**(1), 21–34.

Souder, W.E., Buisson, D. and Garrett, T. (1997). Success through customer-driven new product development: A comparison of US and New Zealand small entrepreneurial high technology firms, *Journal of Product Innovation Management*, **14**(5), 459–472.

Torben, S. and Fier, H. (2009). Innovationen Branchenreport: Chemie, Pharma und Mineralölindustrie, **16**(4).

Tsai, K.-H., Wang, J.C. (2009). External technology sourcing and innovation performance in LMT sectors: An analysis based on the Taiwanese Technological Innovation Survey, *Research Policy*, **38**(3), 518–526.

Van Echtelt, F.E.A., Wynstra, F., van Weele, J.A. and Duysters, G. (2008). Managing supplier involvement in new product development: A multiple-case study, *Journal of Innovation Management*, **25**, 180–201.

Verworn, B. (2009). A structural equation model of the impact of the 'fuzzy front end' on the success of new product development, *Research Policy*, **38**(10), 1571–1581.

von Hippel, E. (1986). Lead users: A source of novel product concepts, *Management Science*, **32**(7), 791–805.

von Hippel, E. (1998). *The Sources of Innovation*, Oxford University Press, New York.

Wagner, S.M. (2009). Supplier traits for better customer firm innovation performance, *Industrial Marketing Management*, **39**(7), 1139–1149.

Wagner, S.M. and Hoegl, M. (2006). Involving suppliers in product development: Insights from R&D directors and project managers, *Industrial Marketing Management*, **35**(8), 936–943.

Walter, A. (2003). Relationship-specific factors influencing supplier involvement in customer new product development, *Journal of Business Research*, **56**(9), 721–733.

Walter, A., Ritter, T. and Gemünden, H.G. (2001). Value creation in buyer–seller relationships: Theoretical considerations and empirical results from a supplier's perspective, *Industrial Marketing Management*, **30**(4), 365–377.

Walter, A., Müller, T.A., Helfert, G. and Ritter, T. (2003). Functions of industrial supplier relationships and their impact on relationship quality, *Industrial Marketing Management*, **32**(2), 159–169.

Wasti, S.N. and Liker, J.K. (1997). Risky business or competitive power? Supplier involvement in Japanese product design, *Journal of Product Innovation Management*, **14**, 337–355.

Zeng, S.X., Xie, X.M. and Tam, C.M. (2010). Relationship between cooperation networks and innovation performance of SMEs, *Technovation*, **30**(2010), 181–194.

Part III

Insights From Case Study Research

Chapter 11

Knowledge and Intellectual Property Management in Customer–Supplier Relations

Jaakko Paasi, Tuija Rantala, and Katri Valkokari
VTT Technical Research Centre of Finland

Nari Lee
University of Eastern Finland

Introduction

The development of innovation and new business increasingly involves two or more actors, and often includes a customer and a supplier. Supplier participation in a customer's product development process is not a new phenomenon. The post World War II rise in consumer demand and increased competition led firms to form closer relations with customers (buyers) and suppliers (sellers), especially in the automotive and electronics industries. At the same time, firms developed their business processes. Porter (1985) introduced the concept of a value chain, which consists of a system of strategically important interdependent company functions or activities that create both costs and value. Value chain activities are organised around effective, but routine and repetitive processes and dyadic, hierarchical relationships between the customer and a supplier.

In the early stages of outsourcing supplier involvement was essentially used for the implementation of innovation design in the value chain. Designs were largely developed internally by individual companies, which strictly maintained strategic control of their designs

371

(Chiaromonte, 2006). In the 1990s, a new trend appeared due to changes in the competitive environment (the shortening of technology life cycles, the emergence of new markets, globalisation and dispersed value chains). Firms began searching for new forms of external cooperation and opened up their new innovation and business development processes in both directions in the value chain — upstream towards suppliers and downstream towards customers (see, e.g., Chesbrough, 2003; Bader, 2006; Chiaromonte, 2006; West and Gallagher, 2006; Henkel, 2006; Dittrich and Duysters, 2007; Blomqvist *et al.*, 2008; van de Vrande *et al.*, 2009).

In this new economy, knowledge is the principal asset and its management and protection have become an integral part of a company's competitive strategies (Hanel, 2006). At the same time, as the boundaries between customers and suppliers have become less clear, distributed innovation practices make the management and protection of knowledge difficult (see, e.g., Jacobides and Billinger, 2006; Dittrich and Duysters, 2007; Elmquist *et al.*, 2009). There are no reported best practices on how to share and manage the ownership and rights of the intellectual property (IP) of an innovation output from a joint project. Some literature is available on the management practices of knowledge and IP in research and development collaborations (see, e.g., Bader, 2006; Olander *et al.*, 2009; Luoma *et al.*, 2009), but instead of reporting on best practices and solutions, they report on the diverse types of practices and the challenges resulting from these collaborations.

One possible reason for the shortage of best practices may be that the numerous forms of joint collaborative innovation make it difficult to replicate the knowledge management practices of any one firm. Also, early management practices in customer–supplier relations in the value chain of new business development have typically been divergent. For example, customers may have an 'adversarial' attitude toward their suppliers, or may make more symbiotic arrangements with their key suppliers (Nichiguchi, 1994; Clark, 1989). In the adversarial approach, suppliers are not treated as important collaboration partners, but instead are evaluated primarily on the short-term price of their wares. Additionally, suppliers were expected to take much of the risk associated with variations in supply and demand.

This is very different from symbiotic arrangements where customers, while being strict on issues like quality, cost and on-time delivery, may also share their knowledge with suppliers, help them in solving problems, encourage and support them to modernise their facilities and products, etc. In the new innovation era of the 21st century, these two approaches to the customer–supplier relations are still found in the variety of forms of open or networked innovation.

In this context, this chapter studies *how knowledge and intellectual property are managed in collaborative innovation between customers and suppliers*. We aimed to fill the gap in the research of knowledge management in collaborative innovation by conducting an interview study and analysing the empirical data together with results reported in the literature. We studied the topic by examining the variety of collaboration practices that firms are using today in their customer–supplier relations for innovation and new business development. The relationships are divided into two main categories: *knowledge transaction* relations (where the collaboration focuses on transactions of existing knowledge and IP) and *knowledge co-creation* relations (which refers to the creation of new knowledge and IP).

The chapter is organised according to the following structure. Firstly, the models of inter-organisational innovation and the sharing and protection of knowledge and IP are discussed in the context of the overall theoretical framework. The research methodology and design are then described. The results of the interview study are presented including the central results from the cases and their theoretical implications. Finally, propositions based on the results and their practical implications and limitations are presented and discussed in the concluding section.

Models of Inter-Organisational Innovation

There are several different recognised forms of inter-organisational innovation, varying from partnerships and extended enterprises (Dyer, 2000) to open innovation (Chesbrough, 2003), creation nets (Hagel and Brown, 2006) and co-creation and lead-user innovation (von Hippel, 1988, 2005). Valkokari *et al.* (2012) use the term 'networked innovation' to cover all of these forms of collaboration. Each has special characteristics related to the creation, transfer and protection of knowledge and IP. The paradigm of open innovation is based on the transfer of ideas and IP across company boundaries. For co-creation, creation nets and extended enterprise, the competitive advantage is jointly created and shared by the actors in question. This joint creation and profit sharing, however, may take a variety of forms, depending on factors such as which business models the actors utilise in these relations.

A business model has two main functions: to create value and to capture a portion of that value (Chesbrough and Rosenboom, 2002). For companies in the new knowledge-intensive economy, knowledge and its legally controllable appropriability regime, intellectual property, play an important role in both creating and capturing value (Teece, 1998). In the past, a typical, simplified business model involved developing and manufacturing a product and then selling it with a profit margin. In the new knowledge-intensive economy, while firms are still selling products for profit, their delivery is connected to other products, services or knowledge more than ever before. Accordingly, firms are searching for new innovative business models to be applied to value creation and value capture in their customer–supplier relations (Chesbrough, 2006).

One example of an innovative business model is the interactive utilisation of open-source software (OSS) in a firm's business: this involves donating IP or man-hours to the collaborative development of an open-source project for value creation, and value capturing with the assistance of the open results of the collaborative work or the offering of related products or services (West and Gallagher, 2006). The use of OSS communities is a novel example of inter-organisational innovation and new business development, but it differs from the other forms of customer–supplier innovation and new business development: while OSS communities that act as suppliers include unknown actors, all other customer–supplier relations are formed between known actors.

In one piece of work on novel kinds of inter-organisational innovation relations relevant to the present study, Dittrich and Duysters

(2007) studied the evoltion of R&D collaboration strategies at Nokia Corporation from 1985–2002. They found that Nokia's collaboration strategy changed drastically during this period in terms of the exploration of new knowledge and in the exploitation of innovation output. During the exploration stage, Nokia made use of flexible kinds of legal organisational structures, while in the exploitation stage, Nokia formed legal alliances structured so as to enable long-term collaboration. Nokia became a company engaged in both local and international innovation networks. The supplier network no longer consists of plain subcontracting relations, where the subcontractors offer more or less off-the-shelf knowledge/technology/resources in a classic buyer–supplier relation. There were also examples where the buyer–supplier relation evolved into a close one in which the boundaries between Nokia and its supplier simply faded away. A prerequisite of a closer relation is that the supplier has some special knowledge/technology/resources that are complementary to Nokia's capability. In such a customer–supplier relation, the innovation relation is based on trust and sharing information rather than a formal contract.

While Nokia's is just one example of modern strategies for knowledge exploration and exploitation, the lessons learned could be useful for other firms in Knowledge-intensive industries. However, for sectors other than information technology, there have been few in-depth studies of novel customer–supplier relations that target innovation and new business development.

In the field of inter-organisational structures for knowledge exploration and knowledge exploitation, in general, we can get support from the extant literature. Building on March's (1991) distinction between knowledge generation (exploration) and knowledge application (exploitation), Grant and Baden-Fuller (2004) derived a theory of knowledge management within inter-firm alliances that distinguished between knowledge-acquisition and knowledge-accessing alliances. Knowledge-accessing alliances are for the exploration of new business while knowledge-acquiring alliances are aimed at exploiting an earlier innovation outcome.

Sharing and Protection of Knowledge and Intellectual Property

Managing knowledge and IP within inter-organisational innovation is challenging for both suppliers and customers. According to Polanyi (1966) all knowledge has a tacit component and this tacit component makes the transfer of knowledge (including IP) across organisational boundaries challenging (Teece, 1998; Qvortrup, 2006). A transaction involving IP rights alone is usually not adequate for creating new products or services: the transfer of tacit knowledge is also required. Therefore, inter-organisational collaborative arrangements are often seen as an alternative for the IP transaction in order to innovate. Such collaborative arrangements, however, always contain additional risks (Pisano and Teece, 1989; Enkel *et al.*, 2005).

Negotiations for collaboration require open communication and evidence of technological knowledge. At the same time, there is a major risk of losing strategic knowledge: a customer may use the knowledge for its own purposes or trade it with a supplier's competitor or *vice versa* (Enkel *et al.*, 2005; Blomqvist *et al.*, 2008). The negotiations may also end in disputes regarding the ownership of ideas arising form the innovation process when the supplier's and the customer's knowledge are combined (Hagedoorn, 2003). A customer may feel that it owns all the ideas generated in the process and this may cause conflict if the supplier already had the knowledge that the customer believed it had jointly developed but the supplier had not proactively clarified the legal status (contamination of another's knowledge). The opposite can also occur especially if the supplier is a large company and the customer is a small to medium-sized (SME), enterprise because SMEs have less bargaining power in negotiations than large firms (Blomqvist *et al.*, 2008; Olander *et al.*, 2009). In order to avoid such problems, a variety of knowledge-protection methods is used in collaborative relations: in addition to the formal protection methods of IP, firms are actively using contractual and informal methods of knowledge protection (Kitching and Blackburn, 1999; PRO INNO Europe, 2007; Leiponen, 2008; Olander *et al.*, 2009; Luoma *et al.*, 2010). For example, nondisclosure agreements

(NDAs) are commonly used in most inter-organisational innovation relations.

Contracting is an essential part of establishing and managing any innovation relation and the contracting capability is one of the central assets of an innovative firm (Lee, 2008). But the ability to create and maintain trust in these relations is even more critical because trust covers expectations about what others will do in situations that cannot be explicitly specified in the contract (Blomqvist *et al.*, 2008), even when flexible, open-ended terms are employed (Nystén-Haarala *et al.*, 2009). Contracts and trust are not mutually exclusive and they equally create a supportive framework for both the successful exploration of new knowledge in an inter-organisational innovation relation and in the exploitation of the innovation outcome.

While the management of knowledge sharing and input into the process of innovation is challenging in customer–supplier relationships, knowledge and IP as inputs may be anticipated or even known to the collaborating partners in advance. On the other hand, the management of the IP related to the outcome of a joint innovation is perhaps more challenging. This is because the results of the collaboration and the path (i.e. how the results were obtained) are seldom known beforehand. Furthermore, IP rights are modelled on the idea that one inventive idea or creation correlates to a legal right to a single product. Consequently, there is a substantial gap between innovation practice and the model that IP law uses in areas where multiple entities are involved in the creation and use of IP and where coordination is required (Lee, 2009). Accordingly, although the number of joint patents has increased during the past few decades, joint ownership of patents is generally seen by lawyers and firms alike as a second-best option that, if possible, should be avoided (Hagedoorn, 2003).

If the parties prefer to avoid joint ownership, alternative arrangements for the ownership and rights to use the innovation outcome should be sought in a customer–supplier relation. In a traditional relation model, a customer owns the results because it invested in the R&D either through direct compensation to the supplier or in the price of purchased products or services. On the other hand, the extant literature suggests a correlation between the appropriation of IP and innovativeness (see, e.g., Levin *et al.*, 1987). The party that obtains the rights to a newly created knowledge asset tends to improve it, build on it and use it in a variety of applications (Leiponen, 2008). Accordingly, control-right allocation may therefore have dynamic effects on the supply relation. Leiponen (2008) has shown that in long-term customer–supplier relations, controlling rights over jointly created knowledge assets should optimally be allocated to the partner that is best positioned to later make non-contractible investments, such as innovation and quality improvements, in the asset. While strictly controlling the IP may often be strategically important for a customer, the customer should gauge the benefits of a more optimal allocation of control rights in terms of this strategic goal through boosted incentives for long-term suppliers. In practice, this may not always be so straightforward. Bader (2006) has suggested that the more experience a partner has with IP issues in R&D collaborations, the more capable the partner is in establishing its interests in IP. In addition, the better the strategic fit between the partners, the more likely it is that a balanced IP model that satisfies both parties can be found. Furthermore, the more open the information exchange philosophy of the partner, the more likely it is that balanced collaboration contracts with respect to IP can be closed (Bader, 2006).

Research Methodology and Design

Although the extant literature mentioned above reports several empirical results and specific theories about the management of knowledge and IP in open or networked innovation (e.g. Bader, 2006; West and Gallagher, 2006; Dittrich and Duysters, 2007; Blomqvist *et al.*, 2008; Leiponen, 2008; Olander *et al.*, 2009), the literature is either too general or too specific. The field is also still evolving and the extant literature may not correspond to state-of-the-art practices. Therefore, the objective of the study is to bridge the gap between the existing underdeveloped theories and the practical managerial need for how knowledge and IP should be managed in innovation collaboration between customers and suppliers.

Because we are studying phenomena of open and collaborative innovation practices that are still relatively novel and evolving, we focus on qualitative data and use a multiple case study method to assist in building our theory (Eisenhardt, 1989; Yin, 2003; Eisenhardt and Graebner, 2007). The present study has an interpretative orientation and aims to understand the phenomena from the inside rather than the outside. The main research question of the paper is the following: *How are knowledge and IP managed in collaborative innovation between customers and suppliers?* This is further implemented through sub-questions that address the collaboration and innovation practices of the firms:

- *What kinds of collaboration practices are the firms currently using in their customer–supplier relations?*
- *How do the firms share and protect their knowledge in these relations in the phases of exploitation and exploration?*
- *How do they treat the outcome of the collaboration (IP, tacit knowledge)?*

Answers to the research questions are based on a large interview study about IP management practices in inter-organisational relations conducted from February to October 2009; 36 firms in Finland and in the Netherlands were studied by using semi-structured theme interviews. The interviews went beyond knowledge and IP management in customer–supplier relations to cover a broad range of themes on IP management practices but in this paper we focus exclusively on the customer–supplier relations.

The empirical material of the study was collected by a group of 5 researchers (including the authors of this paper) who interviewed a total of 48 managers from 20 Dutch and 16 Finnish companies in face-to-face meetings. The firms represented different fields of industry and different firm sizes, bringing diversity to the empirical material and maximising the variety in the data (see Table 1). The criteria for the selection of a firm into the study was that the firm was generally known to be innovative and was among the leading companies in its branch of industry. The roles of both customers and suppliers

Table 1. List of the Firms in the Interview Study.

Organisation	Industry/products/services	Personnel (2008)
ABN AMRO	Finance, banking	50,000
Arcusys	IT services	12
Blancco	Software, ICT	37
Consolis	Construction industry	9,000
Corus Group	Steel industry	42,000
Damen Shipyards	Shipbuilding	2,100
DSM	Chemical industry	23,000
Dun Agro	Agriculture	3
Forcit Defence	Chemical industry	5 (Forcit 220)
Fugro	Technical consultancy, geospatial industry	13,000
Image Wear	Clothing industry	500
Imtech WPS	Parking technology systems	150
Koppert	Biological systems — pollination systems and integrated pest management	250
KPN	Telecommunications and ICT services	43,500
Krohne Altometer	Technology products and measurement solutions	315
Laitosjalkine	Textile and footwear industry	80
Medisize	Manufacturing industry	1,000
Metso Automation	Industrial automation industry	1,500
Nammo	Defence industry	1,800
Nokia Research Center	Telecommunications	500
Norit X-Flow	Water purification systems	1,600
Outotec	Metals and mining industry	2,000
Philips Lighting	Lighting industry	40,000
Rabobank	Finance, banking	60,000

(*Continued*)

Table 1. (*Continued*)

Organisation	Industry/products/services	Personnel (2008)
River Diagnostics	Measuring and testing equipment, healthcare and medical industry	26
Sandvik Mining and Construction	Mining and construction	17,000
Stevens Id Partners	Engineering and designing	10
Strukton Rail	Railway construction and maintenance services	3,500
Tamlink	Technology transfer	70
ThyssenKrupp Accessibility	Accessibility industry	1,100
Tremco Illbruck	Building material industry	1,000
UPM	Forest industry	24,000
Vaisala	Measuring and testing equipment	1,100
Vebego	Cleaning, facility and personnel services	30,000
Wihuri Oy Wipak	Plastics industry	3,600
Xsens Technologies	3D motion measurement systems	40

were well represented in the group of interviewed firms. Some of the firms could be customers in one value network and suppliers in another. During the interviews we also found that there were a few active customer–supplier relations among the interviewed companies. That, however, did not bring any additional aspects into the study.

The duration of a typical interview was 1–1.5 hours, and two interviewers were generally involved. Moreover, one author of this chapter participated in every interview, which made it easier to create a standard approach for the interviews in both countries.

Semi-structured theme interviews were chosen as the main source of empirical material, because the study was partly explorative in nature and the meanings of concepts needed to be discussed with the interviewees. The interviewees were specifically senior corporate, R&D, business unit or IP managers. An interview usually began by enquiring into the company's business and its role and position in the business environment of the firm. The deeper inter-organisational relations of the firm were then discussed, the main focus being on innovation and new business creation and products. Step by step, more specific questions relating to knowledge and IP management practices within the firm and in their inter-organisational relations were investigated. The interview material was supplemented by product and company presentations and agreement templates from some of the companies. In some cases, the interviewees were also asked additional questions later in order to elucidate the company's practices and motives.

Almost all interviews were recorded (we always asked and received permission for recording) and transcribed. The interviewers also made their own notes during the interviews. The analysis of the interview data was based on a computer-assisted analysis of the transcribed data combined with the notes taken during the interviews. Search codes for the computer-assisted analysis were taken largely from the extant literature.

The interview material was analysed by the authors of this paper, at first from the viewpoints of 'the kind of inter-organisational practices companies currently have in their innovation and new business development' and 'how they are managing knowledge and IP in these relations in general'. The results of a preliminary analysis were presented and discussed in two large workshops with the representatives of the interviewed firms: one in the Netherlands and one in Finland. The focus of the analysis and theory-building then moved on to customer–supplier relations and the authors then began addressing the research questions of the paper. The theory-building process involved iteratively incorporating the case data of the interviews, emerging theory and the extant literature.

Interview Results

Collaboration practices

The interviews showed that almost all the firms carry out innovation activities with their customers and suppliers. The detailed forms and practices of the collaboration, however, varied considerably. The managers mentioned that the management of knowledge and IP is often challenging in these relations.

One challenge identified in the interviews was related to the way in which companies understand the term 'intellectual property' and use it in association with the firm's practices. In the words of one interviewee: 'At our firm we understand IP as intellectual property rights plus the know-how that can be covered by an NDA and other agreements'. While this is just one (but nevertheless representative) example, most managers said that tacit knowledge (or know-how) plays an extremely important role in their innovation and expressed their desire to isolate and control the tacit knowledge relating to collaborative innovation. The managers interviewed typically attempt to achieve this through different contracts (NDAs, employee agreements, collaboration agreements, etc.) in conjunction with company policies. Some firms even use the term 'intellectual property' in contracts with a broader meaning — not just as IP rights that are granted and protected by IP laws.

The early literature on open innovation addresses the role of IP as an instrument for the in-and-outflows of knowledge in accelerating internal innovation and in expanding the markets for external use of innovation (see, e.g., Chesbrough, 2003, 2006; Lichtenthaler, 2008). Our case studies, however, highlighted early collaboration between customers and their suppliers in the exploration of new knowledge. Nearly all of the respondent firms reported active collaborations with their customers or suppliers in their R&D or new product development activities. There was no difference between manufacturing firms and service firms in that regard. Our results are in line with those of van de Vrande *et al.* (2009). A sole transaction of explicit IP in a customer–supplier relation is rare in the case of innovation and new business development among the interviewed firms. When an IP transaction occurs, it is usually supported by the transfer of tacit knowledge. A collaborative co-creation of new knowledge may include background IP as a starting point, and it may end up in the transaction of an IP related to the innovation outcome, but the combination of the customer's tacit knowledge with the supplier's tacit knowledge was at the core of most of the collaboration practices between a customer and a supplier.

The following interviewee's response to the question about the firm's collaboration practices is characteristic of the change that has occurred:

> *Yes, of course we work with suppliers. When we introduce something new on a market, it's always done with at least one or two other parties. Until three or four years ago it was quite a linear process: we had an idea, we organised the partners and started up the development project. Now it's a little bit different, because you start at a very early stage in the innovation process already together with your partner, develop the ideas together and then go into a joint project.*

The response shows that collaboration with the supplier is inevitable, but the pattern of exchange has changed.

In addition to the various types of collaboration, traditional subcontracting is still a commonly used model in customer–supplier relations. Many customers, however, considered subcontracting differently from other forms of collaboration. The words of one customer explain why: 'I pay them for what they do for me, so it's not a cooperation. In cooperation, the costs are shared (one way or another)'. Subcontracting without sharing costs is not regarded as a collaboration but rather a unilateral transaction.

We observed a variety of practices both for the transfer of knowledge and for the co-creation of knowledge, including inside-out and outside-in licensing and selling of IP, joint venturing, explorative joint-projects, exploitative joint-projects, use of open-source communities as learning or solution platforms, etc. Each of the practices has its own special characteristics and poses challenges related to knowledge and IP management. According to our results, the situation is further complicated by the fact that the business models that the actors utilise in these relationships have an influence on knowledge and IP management.

Sharing and protection of knowledge in the exploration and exploitation of knowledge

Most of the interviewed managers mentioned a contract as the most important method of protecting knowledge in their innovation efforts with their customers and suppliers. Those firms typically explored new knowledge together with their customers and suppliers by signing a brief NDA or a more extensive collaboration agreement at the beginning of the joint project. When providing the motivation for such agreements, one interviewee said:

> *It starts with people, let's say gentlemen's agreements. But to make sure that it goes from a personal relationship to a company relationship, we need confidentiality agreements.*

Another interviewee explains:

> *In the past, collaboration was sometimes based on gentlemen's agreements, but after one big case, which had a negative influence on our stock exchange value, we started to pay closer attention to contracting.*

Even a single negative influence affects the motivation to collaborate informally.

Typically, the reasons for not entering into a contract in the early exploration phase include cases where the joint innovation occurs unintentionally and cases that rely on gentlemen's agreements. In the latter case, the collaboration is based on trust rather than on a contract.

Trust was generally seen as highly important in innovation: "Trust is necessary for co-creation to allow open sharing of knowledge." In many companies, however, contracts and trust were not considered exclusive: they were seen as complementary. Managers also said: "There must be the right balance between them." This 'right balance' between trust and contracts was generally described as challenging:

> *That depends on culture. Let's say, when you are collaborating with a foreign company from a 'low-trust' country, you should have early and thick formal contracts, but when collaborating with a company from a 'high-trust' country, you need only thin contracts.*

More than one interviewee expressed that 'paying too much attention to contracts at the very beginning of joint work kills innovation.' These managers considered contracts important but stated that if too much focus is placed at the start of the collaboration on 'bureaucratic issues' and on dividing the potential benefits of the innovation outcome instead of focusing on practices supporting the actual collaboration, it is likely to have a negative impact on the results of the collaboration or even bring the collaboration to a halt. 'You have to bake the pie before you divide it up'.

Informal protection methods such as secrecy and publishing were commonly mentioned among the most preferred ways to protect knowledge. While publishing is related to the innovation outcome and the exploitation phase (by publishing your results you can obtain a freedom of action and prevent others from owning the rights to the results), secrecy as a protection method is also applicable in the exploration phase of new knowledge. Companies would generally like to control the kind of knowledge and the degree of it that they will share with their customers and suppliers.

Knowledge sharing is pronounced during the knowledge-exploration phase. Most of the interviewed firms explored new business by co-creating new knowledge together with their customers and suppliers. A good example of co-creating:

> *Ideas typically surface at the interface. I mean, when you interact, you both bring in. So it's like, hey, I have this idea, now describe your specific situation to me. That will lead to attempting the idea, evolving it, building on it, and then you get the great idea. But it's a dialogue, and it's always at the interface, the great ideas.*

This example describes a relations between a customer and a supplier where knowledge can be openly shared without the fear that it will later harm the business in one way or another. However, at times the fear is justified.

The firms were selective in terms of choosing collaboration partners. There has to be a good reason and motivation for collaboration. The statement: 'We have the know-why and they have the know-how', describes a typical situation between a customer and a supplier. In a situation like this one, there is a good fit for the exploration phase of knowledge. However, this does not necessarily mean that the firms are fit to collaborate in the exploitation phase. In a successful innovation relation, a good fit is needed for both phases.

Some firms are actively using OSS communities as suppliers. The challenge in using open-source communities is that it is not possible to know all the actors involved in the community, which makes the management of knowledge challenging in these co-creative relations. One interviewee noted that:

You must be very careful when operating inside an open-source community so that you do not inadvertently share any critical information that your competitor should not know, because they may also be there.

Formal protection methods especially patents and trademarks play an important role in the protection of innovation outcomes. Half of the interviewees mentioned patents as an important way to protect their knowledge. Those whose firms do not actively use patenting as a protection method gave business-related arguments such as: 'if you patent it, the information goes public', 'if you cannot control infringements of your patents, why patent the technology?', and 'patenting is too expensive a way of protecting our knowledge'.

When discussing customer–supplier relations in the interviews, the managers did not explicitly mention whether their companies distinguish between strategies for knowledge sharing and protection in the exploration phase of new knowledge and those used during the exploitation phase of the innovation outcome. Implicitly, however, it is obvious that many firms pay more attention to the management of knowledge and IP in the exploitation than in the exploration phase of new business.

Managing the innovation outcome

The interviews showed that firms are actively collaborating and searching for new methods in the exploration of new business, but the same cannot be said for the exploitation of the collaborative innovation outcomes. Although there were good examples of new practices and models to exploit the results, in most of the cases from the interview study the exploitation of results relied more on traditional business models, and novel innovation practices were limited to the exploration of knowledge.

The following is a good example of a case where the exploitation of collaborative innovation results was done using a traditional model:

> *We have strategic cooperation with a supplier, which delivers a vital part of our product. We didn't pay them for the development. We have the IP but they have the first right for delivery and they amortise their development costs in the goods they supply. The downside is that we could make more profit if we could save a euro on materials, but that would require a new construction and a new development project with them (which is not of direct interest to the supplier in the model used for collaboration).*

This is a very common example of a successful co-creation between a customer and a supplier where the rights to the joint innovation outcome were transferred to the customer. Through this IP transaction, the customer got full control of the rights of its product. However, in this same transaction, the customer lost control that would allow further improvement of the joint innovation. Obviously, this is an example of the non-optimised allocation of rights discussed in the section 'Sharing and protection of knowledge and intellectual property' and in the study by Leiponen (2008).

There were also cases where the allocation of rights promoted innovativeness on the part of both the customer and the supplier. As an example:

> *We collaborate with a big material supplier. When they are developing new features for their materials, they sometimes provide us with samples for testing. Although we don't get IP rights to the materials, because we are a small company in comparison to them, the collaboration is very beneficial for us. It promotes our own product development and we gain a competitive advantage by more quickly releasing new products based on these materials on the market.*

The following is an example of those few cases where the collaborative innovation was followed by a novel way of exploiting the innovation outcome:

> *We lacked a good proprietary technology. Instead of developing it ourselves, we decided to team up with another company. Five years earlier, we would have tried to develop it ourselves, but at that point we said no. If we tried, it would either take muck longer or the end product would be inferior than if we had teamed up with somebody. So what we did was that we signed a deal with them, defined a joint development program, and obtained an exclusive licence. Both companies benefit from because we had opted for a licensing model all the sales and the licensing revenues are shared between us. To me that is a modern example of how you do innovation, because you really derive a lot of strength from your partner, but you also bring very good things to the table.*

As the interviewee notes this is a good modern-day example of successful collaboration between a big company and a small technology supplier that has special knowledge in both the exploration and exploitation of new business. In terms of the exploitation of the innovation outcomes, the interesting point is how the exploitation was made operational through a licensing model in which both parties gained revenues from the sales. This definitely represents a novel way to exploit the innovation outcome.

The case above is also an excellent example of a good "fit" between the companies in both the exploration and exploitation phases. This is not always the case. The following two cases describe the situation.

> *A lot of innovation comes from customers. Sometimes we have a promising technology and we work with a lead customer to generate the first application using it. But we typically arrange it in such a way that we also get the results back we use, which for other applications. It's a win-win situation, because the client can make use of our technology, but we also are able to use the results of that collaboration in different fields. So it's innovation with the customer for their product, but also to enhance other possibilities.*
>
> *It is often difficult to operate with a manufacturer. We want to have a new apparatus for our process. We know what we want to have, and they know how to make it. But they do not want to make it just for us but for everyone also our competitors. But the joint innovation is between us and the manufacturer.*

In the first case, the firms (a customer and a supplier) and their intentions fit well both in the exploration of new business and in the exploitation of the results. In the second case, there is not an adequate fit for the exploitation of the innovation outcome. In the latter case, it is the voice of a customer whose supplier is a large firm. There were also several cases in which the opposite occurred: A big firm in the role of the customer wants to own all the rights to the joint innovation so that it can seek out alternative suppliers for the innovation.

Our results on the fit of firms are in line with the findings of Bader (2006), who studied IP management practices in R&D collaborations at four large service innovation companies (IBM, SAP, Swisscom and Swiss Re). The results are also in accordance with those of Chesbrough and Schwartz (2007), who noted that business objective and business model alignment increases the chances of success in co-development partnerships.

In the cases presented in this section, the IP for the joint innovation was allocated to one of the partners. In fact, all the companies interviewed said that they have few, if any, joint patents that resulted from collaboration in innovation. The companies tend to avoid joint patenting as much as possible.

> *We don't favour joint patenting, and that is not only because of the increased bureaucracy it entails. It's what the management of joint patents through the life cycle of the patent involves. Twenty years is a long time and a lot can happen. There can be changes in the interests and ownerships of the firms. And that can make things very complicated.*

Theoretical Implications

The term 'intellectual property'

Knowledge plays an extremely important role in inter-organisational innovation in all its various forms. It is part of the firm's resources and represents capability in terms of the exchange of a special resource that makes a difference to a firm's performance. Legal protection of the tacit part of knowledge, however, is unclear. Only explicit, codified knowledge can have clear legal protection (Teece, 1998). Firms would like to isolate and control the tacit knowledge from inter-organisational innovation. Attempts to do so include contracts, company policies, and the use of the term 'intellectual property' in contracts in a broad sense.

The very term 'intellectual property' as a legal expression is not uncontested (Gordon, 2003) and may include various patterns of human interaction as shown in the World Intellectual Property Organization definition (WIPO, 1979). Under national laws, IP law may include, among others: patents, copyright, trademarks, trade secrecy, rights to the topography of integrated circuits, industrial design rights, plant breeder's rights, publicity rights, and database rights. Regardless of whether certain knowledge is protected as an IP right, firms contractually and behaviourally control and isolate the knowledge and other intangible resources related to innovation and may view any controllable knowledge as the IP of the firm.

The practice, which differs from firm to firm, may cause misunderstandings and consequent problems in inter-organisational innovation.

Thus it is crucial to align the practice of the firms and to do so all parties need to have one coherent understanding of the term. Accordingly, the term 'intellectual property' may include not only IP rights that are granted and protected by law but also knowledge and other intangible resources whose use may be controlled by contracts, policies, organisation and process routines and norms, both physically and technically.

Collaboration practices for innovation in customer–supplier relations

In order to understand and manage the complexity of knowledge and IP management in novel customer–supplier relations, we derived a typology of the main types of collaborative practices in these relations. We found that these practices generally involved either the co-creation of new knowledge (knowledge exploration) or transactions involving existing knowledge (exploitation of innovation outcomes). That finding allowed us to apply the theory of Grant and Baden- Fuller (2004) on knowledge management within inter-firm alliances and to extend it to customer–supplier relations with unequal partners. Accordingly, we divided the novel customer–supplier relations in innovation and new business development into two main categories according to whether the focus was on the exploration or exploitation of knowledge: *knowledge co-creation relations for knowledge exploration* (analogous to knowledge-accessing alliances) and *knowledge transaction relations for knowledge exploitation* (analogous to knowledge-acquiring alliances).

In the knowledge co-creation relationships, the focus is on the creation of new knowledge and IP. In a customer–supplier relation, this happens with a known partner (or partners, when the relation involves networking). In both cases the relation is closed in the sense that the actors can agree on issues relating to the knowledge and IP management during and after the collaboration. The motivation behind the explorative collaboration could be in interactive learning with no direct commercial targets (R&D, benchmarking of best practices, etc.). There could also be direct commercial goals in the explorative collaboration, which should be achieved by sharing and combining some special tacit knowledge of the actors, possibly with background IP, and thus the co-creation of innovations. The use of open-source communities either as learning platforms or as solution platforms is increasing also in the business-to-business economy in customer–supplier relations. For example, local service suppliers of a customer in a global net- work may learn from one another by sharing their experiences and thus improve their competitive advantage as a local service supplier in a customer's global network. A customer may interactively use an OSS community or innovation mediator communities (e.g., Allio, 2004) as solution suppliers, just to mention a few examples. A typology of knowledge co-creation relations is shown in Fig. 1.

In the knowledge transaction relations, the focus is on the existing knowledge and IP and the new business is built on that. In a customer–supplier relation where the focus is on the development of the customer's business, the customer acquires knowledge in some form from the supplier. However, because the customer's acquisition of the ownership of the knowledge is different from obtaining the rights to use this knowledge, one should consider both the outside-in and the

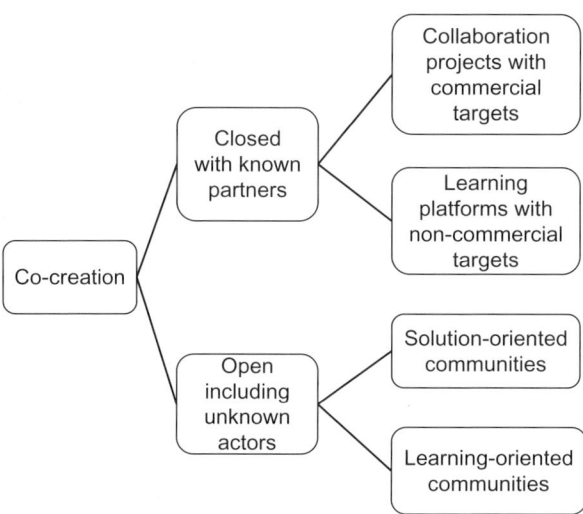

Fig. 1. Typology of Knowledge Co-creation Relations.

inside-out viewpoints of knowledge transaction. Cross-licensing (a special combination of outside-in and inside-out transactions of IP) is the third form of knowledge transaction, but it was found to be so rare in customer–supplier relations that we decided not to focus on it. Outside-in transactions may take place either in closed relations with known actors or in open relations involving unknown actors. An example of the latter is the licensing of OSS, where an open-source community (acting as a supplier) holds full ownership of the code but specifies usage rights to the customer. Closed forms of outside-in transaction include buying, licensing and contracting the knowledge from a supplier to a customer. In buying, the customer may obtain exclusive rights to the knowledge or, alternatively, the transaction may result in joint ownership of the knowledge between the customer and the supplier. In buying, the IP transaction could be accompanied by the transfer of the tacit knowledge necessary for the utilisation of the explicit IP through expert services (both rights and know-how) or through venturing or merging (both rights and business). In licensing, a customer may get either exclusive or non-exclusive rights to use a supplier's IP. Contracting of knowledge refers to classical subcontracting work by a supplier using existing knowledge. A typology of knowledge transaction relations is shown in Fig. 2.

In the inside-out viewpoint, a supplier offers its knowledge and IP to a customer. The mechanisms are the same as in the outside-in but the viewpoint is different.

Exploration of knowledge in customer–supplier relations

The empirical data highlighted two important aspects for achieving a solid frame-work that supports innovation in customer–supplier relations: trust and agreements. The interviewees expressed how challenging both aspects were in the context of innovation and new business creation. Trust and agreements are also inter-connected and both are necessary in accordance with the results of Blomqvist *et al.* (2008).

To find the right balance between trust and agreements at an early stage of the knowledge exploration phase (in practice, at the beginning of an innovation design and development project), it seems that

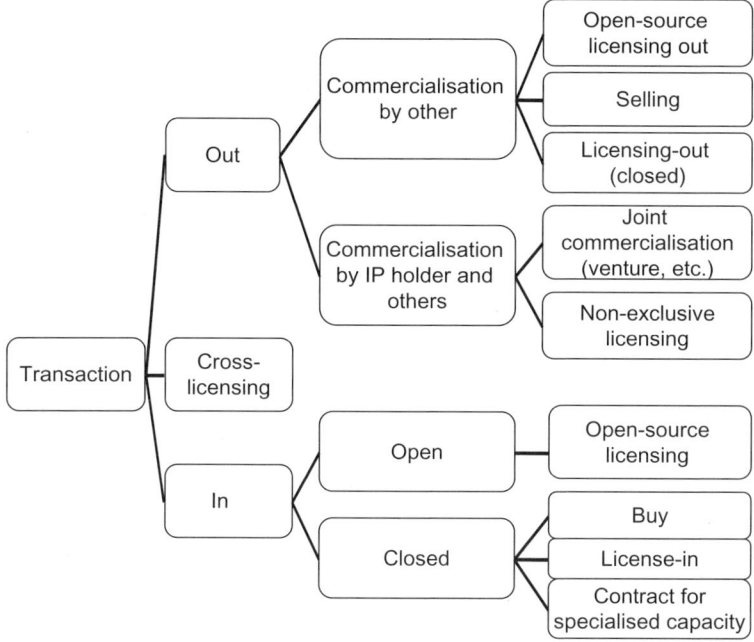

Fig. 2. Typology of Knowledge Transaction Relations.

one should conclude a brief but adequate formal agreement where the parties agree on the intentions of the collaboration, on the main points of the development project and on the main points for the exploitation of the potential innovation outcome without going into too much detail.

Drafting a brief but adequate contract requires that both parties have a good level of contracting capability. The previous experience of the parties has a strong effect on its success. The firms should also understand what is strategically important to close and to avoid protecting any knowledge that is already known within the industry.

Exploitation of innovation outcomes in customer–supplier relations

The typology of knowledge co-creation and knowledge transaction relations aids firms in the management of knowledge and IP in their customer–supplier relations by distinguishing between collaboration models for the exploration of new business and those which target the exploitation of innovation outcomes. The knowledge transaction relations offer a variety of models for exploiting existing IP.

If the existing business models of the customer and the supplier do not seem to fit with respect to the exploitation of the innovation outcome, it is possible to produce a new business model for the exploitation where both parties can win and thus are motivated to work towards a successful joint effort. A business model may be created for the sharing of IP, the sharing of profits, the transfer of IP (for example, through venturing), etc. The typology of knowledge transaction relations offers typical contractual elements for the business models to develop.

Conclusions and Practical Implications

In this chapter, we have studied knowledge and IP management practices in innovation collaboration between customers and their suppliers. Interviews with managers from 36 firms in Finland and in the Netherlands showed that almost all of the firms carry out innovation activities with their customers and suppliers. However, different forms and practices in these innovation relations are increasingly emerging. Furthermore, IP law and the IP rights defined by the laws seem to stimulate innovation by single companies and not joint innovation. As a result, the firms found the management of knowledge and IP in these relations very challenging. To support knowledge and IP management in customer–supplier relations, we distinguished between the exploration of new business and the exploitation of the innovation outcomes.

Based on the extant literature and our empirical results, we suggest three propositions as the contribution of the study: (1) a typology of inter-organisational innovation practices between customers and suppliers, (2) contracts that strike a balance between trust and agreements at the beginning of the exploration phase, and (3) business models for the typology of knowledge transaction relations in order to make the exploitation of collaborative innovation outcomes operational.

Proposition 1a: *The joint exploration of new business takes place in a variety of different knowledge co-creation relations, which can be described by a typology.*

Proposition 1b: *The exploitation of an innovation outcome takes place in customer–supplier relations through transactions of existing IP, which can be described by a typology.*

Our first theoretical contribution is the typologies of inter-organisational innovation practices in customer–supplier relations. A distinction can be made between the typologies of customer–supplier relations the exploration of new business or for the exploitation of an existing innovation outcome. We distinguish between the co-creation of knowledge and knowledge co-creation relations for the exploration of new business from transactions of IP for the exploitation of innovation outcomes. In both of these typologies, IP is understood broadly to include not only IP rights that are granted and protected by law but also knowledge and other intangible resources whose use may be controlled by contracts and policies. Both knowledge co-creation and knowledge transaction relations between customers and their suppliers contain a rich variety of different forms and practices, forming a typology of inter-organisational innovation practices in customer–supplier relations.

Proposition 2: *A concise formal agreement concluded at an early stage of the exploration phase helps companies share knowledge.*

The second contribution of our study is related to finding the right balance between trust and formal contracts, which is crucial in the successful management of knowledge in inter-organisational innovation. This contribution is operationally related to the management of knowledge and IP at the beginning of the collaboration but its influence covers the entire life cycle of the innovation. A prerequisite to the successful joint exploration of new business in a customer–supplier relation is that both parties are open and share their knowledge. In such a relation, the boundary between the firms is no longer clear. The right balance between trust and agreements is needed so that the sharing of knowledge may successfully take place, formally and informally. Therefore, we argue that one needs a concise formal agreement by an early stage of the exploration phase. The brief agreement may include the customer's and the supplier's agreement to the overall intent to collaborate, the main points of the development project, the definition of the IP and points for the sharing and exploitation of the outcome — all without too much detail. The initial agreement must not only take into account the exploration phase but also anticipate the exploitation of the potential innovation outcome and thus incorporate flexibilities for contingencies.

Proposition 3: *Business models that encourage both the customer and the supplier to innovate and direct their best efforts to the work positively influence to the exploitation of collaborative innovation.*

The third contribution is related to the innovation outcome and gaining competitive advantage for both the customer and the supplier. It highlights the importance of the business model in the exploitation of the innovation outcome, which results from a collaboration between a customer and a supplier. If the existing business models of the customer and the supplier are not aligned with respect to the exploitation of the innovation outcome, they should try to find a new business model for the exploitation in which both parties can win and are encouraged to innovate. Our typology of knowledge transaction relations describes the paths and underlying contractual elements on which a business model could be based.

Limitations of the study

In this study we aimed to obtain a broad perspective of the subject and therefore we chose innovative firms from several branches of industry. While this approach allows for a good general overview to be developed, it also raises validity limitations (Gibbert *et al.*, 2008). First, basic terms related to the research framework of the study (such as IP and open innovation) were understood quite differently in different branches of industry and in different firms. This simple difference brought additional challenges to linking the interview data (practice) with the extant literature (theory) although the semi-structured form of the interviews allowed us to quickly become familiar with the particular lingo of a firm during an interview. On the other hand, the finding that firms may understand basic terms differently is one of the outcomes of the study. Second, although the total number of case companies was not small, there were aspects in the study for novel forms of collaboration for which the empirical data was limited to a few cases. Also the number of firms per industrial sector was too small to perform any sectoral analysis of the results although it is well known that there are sectoral differences in the innovation patterns of firms (Tidd *et al.*, 1997).

The three propositions were the result of a qualitative analysis of the interview data. The first proposition is such that all of the interviewees could identify their businesses in the typology. The second and the third propositions are based on a smaller number of cases. However, this does not mean that the other firms would consider the propositions erroneous or unsuitable to their business practices: it is simply because collaborative innovation practices are not yet fully developed in many firms. Most of the firms that were interviewed apply the novel forms of open or networked innovation in the exploration of new business but still use traditional ways to exploit the results of innovation. This limits the possibilities as they may disregard some of the potentials that a customer– supplier partnership could offer in new business development. The validity of Propositions 2 and 3 could be better tested after the firms have had more experience in open or networked innovation accompanied by the development of practices in both knowledge exploration and the exploitation of the innovation outcomes.

Practical implications

The practical implications of our results for the management of knowledge and IP in customer–supplier relations are three fold. Firstly, the sharing of knowledge through open or networked innovation needs to be coordinated with the need to control the knowledge flow. While an open innovation practice demands sharing knowledge sharing needs to be connected to the necessary controls to generate mutual profit from the outcome and to provide the motivation collaboration for regarding the inputs. The fact that many customers have historically adopted an almost adversarial attitude towards their suppliers while others have seen them as symbiotic partners adds further complexity in this new era of a knowledge-intensive economy and open or networked innovation.

Secondly, the typology of knowledge co-creation and knowledge transaction relations may help a manager to structure the variety of novel forms of open and networked innovation. With the help of this structure a manager should understand that knowledge and IP should be managed differently in the exploration and exploitation phases of collaboration and then how management should be performed in both phases.

Thirdly, our results suggest that managers should carefully consider how to optimally allocate the rights of the innovation outcome after the collaboration project is complete. Managers should also think about new innovative business models for the exploitation of the innovation so that both parties will be motivated to give their best effort during and after the development project.

References

Allio, R.J. (2004). CEO interview: The InnoCentive model of open innovation, *Strategy and Leadership*, **32**, 4–9.

Bader, M.A. (2006). *Intellectual Property Management in R&D Collaborations: The Case of the Service Industry Sector*, Physica-Verlag, Heidelberg.

Blomqvist, K., Hurmelinna-Laukkanen, P., Nummela, N. and Saarenketo, S. (2008). The role of trust and contracts in the internationalization of technology-intensive born globals, *Journal of Engineering and Technology Management*, **25**, 123–135.

Chesbrough, H. (2003). *Open Innovation: The New Imperative for Creating and Profiting From Technology*, Harvard Business School Press, Cambridge, MA.

Chesbrough, H. (2006). *Open Business Models: How to Thrive in the New Innovation Landscape*, Harvard Business School Press, Cambridge, MA.

Chesbrough, H. and Rosenboom, R. (2002). The role of the business model in capturing value from innovation: Evidence from Xerox Corporation's technology spin-off companies, *Industrial and Corporate Change*, **11**, 529–555.

Chesbrough, H. and Schwartz, K. (2007). Innovating business models with co-development partnerships, *Research-Technology Management*, **50**, 55–59.

Chiaromonte, F. (2006). Open innovation through alliances and partnership: Theory and practice, *International Journal of Technology Management*, **33**, 111–114.

Clark, K. (1989). Project scope and project performance: The effect of parts strategy and supplier involvement on product development, *Management Science*, **35**, 1247–1263.

Dittrich, K. and Duysters, G. (2007). Networking as a means to strategy change: The case of open innovation in mobile telephone, *Journal of Product Innovation Management*, **24**, 510–521.

Dyer, J.H. (2000). *Collaborative Advantage: Winning Through Extended Enterprise Supplier Networks*, Oxford University Press, Oxford, UK.

Eisenhardt, K. (1989). Building theories from case study research, *Academy of Management Review*, **14**, 532–550.

Eisenhardt, K. and Graebner, M. (2007). Theory building from cases: Opportunities and challenges, *Academy of Management Journal*, **50**, 25–32.

Elmquist, M., Fredberg, T. and Ollila, S. (2009). Exploring the field of open innovation, *European Journal of Innovation Management*, **12**, 326–345.

Enkel, E., Kausch, C. and Gassmann, O. (2005). Managing the risk of customer integration, *European Management Journal*, **23**, 203–213.

Gibbert, M., Ruigrok, W. and Wicki, B. (2008). What passes as a rigorous case study? *Strategic Management Journal*, **29**, 1465–1474.

Gordon, W. (2003). "Intellectual property," in Cane, P. and Tushnet, M. (eds), *Oxford Handbook of Legal Studies*, Oxford University Press, Oxford, UK. pp. 617–646.

Grant, R. and Baden-Fuller, C. (2004). Knowledge accessing theory of strategic alliances, *Journal of Management Studies*, **41**, 61–84.

Hagedoorn, J. (2003). Sharing intellectual property rights — An exploratory study of joint patenting amongst companies, *Industrial and Corporate Challenge*, **12**, 1035–1050.

Hagel III, J. and Brown, J.S. (2006). Creation nets: Harnessing the potential of open innovation, Working Paper. Available at http://www. johnseelybrown.com/.

Hanel, P. (2006). Intellectual property rights business management practices: A survey of the literature, *Technovation*, **26**, 895–931.

Henkel, J. (2006). Selective revealing in open innovation processes: The case of embedded Linux, *Research Policy*, **35**, 953–969.

Jacobides, M. and Billinger, S. (2006). Designing the boundaries of the firm: From "make, buy, or ally" to the dynamic benefits of vertical architecture, *Organizational Science*, **17**, 249–261.

Kitching, J. and Blackburn, R. (1999). Intellectual property management in the small and medium enterprise (SME), *Journal of Small Business and Enterprise Development*, **5**, 327–335.

Lee, N. (2008). "From tangibles to intangibles–Contracting capabilities for intangible innovation," in Nystén-Haarala, S. (ed.), *Corporate Contracting Capabilities*, University of Joensuu Publication, **21**, pp. 33–50.

Lee, N. (2009). Exclusion and coordination in collaborative innovation and patent law, *International Journal of Intellectual Property Management*, **3**, 79–93.

Leiponen, A. (2008). Control of intellectual assets in client relationships: Implications for innovation, *Strategic Management Journal*, **29**, 1371–1394.

Levin, R., Klevorick, A., Nelson, R. and Winter, S. (1987). Appropriating the returns from industrial research and development, *Brookings Papers on Economic Activity*, **3**, 783–820.

Lichtenthaler, U. (2008). Open innovation in practice: An analysis of strategic approaches to technology transactions, *IEEE Transactions on Engineering Management*, **55**, 148–157.

Luoma, T., Paasi, J. and Valkokari, K. (2009). Intellectual property in inter-organisational relationships, *Proceeding of 2009 ISPIM Symposium*, New York.

March, J.G. (1991). Exploration and exploitation in organizational learning, *Organization Science*, **2**, 427–440.

Nichiguchi, T. (1994). *Strategic Industrial Sourcing: The Japanese Advantage*, Oxford University Press, Oxford, UK.

Nystén-Haarala, S., Lee, N. and Lehto, J. (2009). Hard and soft contracting, *Proceedings of 2009 International Project Management Association Congress*, Helsinki.

Olander, H., Hurmelinna-Laukkanen, P. and Mähönen, J. (2009). What's small size got to do with it? Protection of intellectual assets in SMEs, *International Journal of Innovation Management*, **13**, 349–370.

Pisano, G. and Teece, D. (1989). Collaborative arrangements and global technology strategy: Some evidence from the telecommunications equipment industry, *Research on Technological Innovation, Management and Policy*, **4**, 227–256.

Polanyi, M. (1966). *The tacit dimension*. Peter Smith, Gloucester, MA.

Porter, M. (1985). *Competitive Advantage: Creating and Sustaining Superior Performance*, Free Press, New York.

PRO INNO Europe (2007). *A memorandum on removing barriers for a better use of IPR by SMEs. A report for the directorate-general for enterprise and industry by an IPR Expert group*, PRO INNO Europe.

Qvortrup, L. (2006). Knowledge society and educational institutions–Towards a sociological theory of knowledge, *Agora*, **8**.

Teece, D.J. (1998). Capturing value from knowledge assets: The new economy, markets for know-how, and intangible assets, *California Management Review*, **40**, 55–79.

Tidd, J., Bessant, J. and Pavitt, K. (1997). *Managing Innovation. Integrating Technological, Market and Organizational Change*, Wiley, Chichester.

Valkokari, K., Paasi, J. and Rantala, T. (2012). Managing knowledge within networked innovation, *Knowledge Management Research and Practice*, **10**, 27–40.

van de Vrande, V., de Jong, J., Vanhaverbeke, V. and Rochemont, M. (2009). Open innovation in SMEs: Trends, motives and management challenges, *Technovation*, **29**, 423–437.

von Hippel, E. (1988). *On the Sources of Innovation*, Oxford University Press, Oxford, UK.

von Hippel, E. (2005). *Democratizing Innovation*, MIT Press Cambridge, MA.

West, J. and Gallagher, S. (2006). Challenges of open innovation: The paradox of firm investment in open-source software, *R&D Management*, **36**, 319–331.

WIPO (1979). Convention Establishing the World Intellectual Property Organization.

Yin, R.K. (2003). *Case Study Research: Design and Methods*, Sage Publications, Thousand Oaks, CA.

Chapter 12

Procurement Procedures for Supplier Integration and Open Innovation in Process Development Projects

Per Erik Eriksson and David Rönnberg Sjödin
Centre for Management of Innovation and Technology
in Process Industry,
Luleå University of Technology, Sweden

Introduction

The era of open innovation is characterized by increased benefits from collaborative relations (Chesbrough, 2003b, 2003a; Enkel *et al.*, 2009). Empirical research into open innovation has mostly focused on firms in high-tech industries. However, recent investigations have found that open innovation practices are utilized also in mature industries (Chesbrough and Crowther, 2006). In fact, the occurrence of open innovation is independent of industry characteristics and the phenomenon is found in many different types of industrial settings (Lichtenthaler, 2008). Hence, the bias towards high-tech industries seems unjustified and additional studies within mature industries are vital. In this study, we therefore investigate open innovation practices within firms in process industries (e.g. metal and minerals, pulp and paper, chemicals and food).

Process firms are typically active in mature industries, with tight cost control and an emphasis on process innovation (Hutcheson *et al.*, 1995). The development and installation of new process technology frequently necessitate major input from equipment suppliers, and due to the complex and customized nature of process technology (Lager and Frishammar, 2010), strongly integrated and collaborative buyer-supplier relations are typically required (Lager and Hörte, 2005; Chronéer and Laurell-Stenlund, 2006). In essence these kinds of collaborative relations relate to the coupled process of both inbound and outbound innovation. This implies co-creation with complementary partners through alliances, cooperation or joint ventures during which reciprocity in terms of give and take are crucial for success (Enkel *et al.*, 2009).

However, from a managerial perspective, firms are still struggling to find suitable practices to facilitate supplier integration and open innovation (Chesbrough and Crowther, 2006). In addition, the existing literature about how such supplier integration and open innovation practices should be organized and managed is scarce. Previous studies either (1) focus on an overall strategic level, describing the choice of suitable governance modes (van de Vrande *et al.*, 2006; Cassiman and Chiara Di Guardo, 2009) (e.g. joint venture, licensing agreement, equity alliance, non-equity alliance, etc.), thus lacking illuminating detail of how to manage supplier integration, or (2) are on a too detailed level, describing one or a few specific procurement-related procedures such as partner selection (Stump and Heide, 1996; Hoetker, 2005), contract formalization (Woolthuis *et al.*, 2005; Carson *et al.*, 2006), incentive systems (Stump and Heide, 1996) and collaborative design (Ro *et al.*, 2008), thereby lacking a comprehensive perspective on how various interconnected procedures together facilitate supplier integration. This article aims to address this managerial problem and gaps in the open innovation literature by adopting a life-cycle perspective on procurement for supplier integration and open innovation practices in the process industries. *The purpose of this study is to explore how process firms can organize and manage supplier integration and open innovation practices when developing and installing new process equipment.*

In the next section we first review previous research within the fields of open innovation, collaborative development and complex procurement, in order to establish a conceptual background for our research topic. Then the method and research approach are described, leading to a section that provides empirical findings. Subsequently, a life-cycle-based procurement model is developed, based on our empirical findings. This is followed by conclusions, implications and suggestions for future research.

Literature Review and Conceptual Background

In a case study of the development and construction of process plant facilities for pharmaceutical production, Eriksson (2008) developed a framework based on the industrial buying behaviour literature and transaction cost economics in order to obtain a comprehensive view of the entire buying process. The framework focuses specifically on how procurement decisions concerning design responsibility, partner and subcontractor selection, contract formalization, payment, performance evaluation and the use of collaborative tools facilitate competitive or collaborative project governance. This distinction between competitive and collaborative project governance corresponds to closed versus open innovation practices (Chesbrough, 2003a). In this study we therefore adapt Eriksson's (2008) framework in order to investigate how a broad range of procurement procedures can facilitate supplier integration and open innovation.

However, the original framework lacks a distinction of how procurement procedures may differ at different stages in the life cycle of process equipment. As different stages contain distinct problems and opportunities, the collaborating firms may behave differently in terms of routines and practices performed, and utilize different types of mechanisms and procedures (e.g. in terms of contracts, collaborative tools and incentive structures) at different stages (Langner and Seidel, 2009). Hence, we argue that there are strong interdependences among stages, and as a buyer there are several major decisions to be made and actions to be taken during the entire buying process, from the initial concept design to the operation of the final product. Since these decisions will affect the governance of the development project in terms of supplier integration and open innovation, the conceptual framework needs to be based on an explicit life-cycle perspective.

Who performs the work at different stages?

Drawing on a life-cycle model of process equipment presented in Lager and Frishammar (2010) we divide the development process into five distinct stages (see Fig. 1). These stages, consisting of the concept

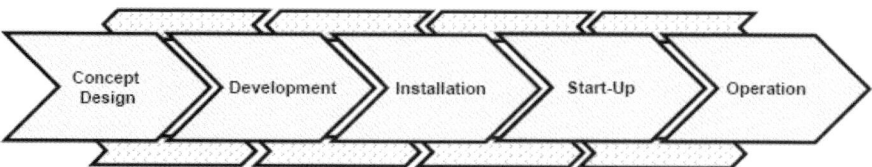

Fig. 1. The Life Cycle of Process Equipment.

design, development, installation, start-up and operation, are sequential but also interconnected and somewhat overlapping. The work in the stages can be performed by the process firm (closed innovation by the buyer), by the supplier (closed innovation by the supplier) or jointly by both the process firm and key suppliers in collaboration (open innovation). The decision on who performs the work should be based on the specific characteristics of the development project's different stages. As such, we highlight the fact that being totally open in development activities is not always the most suitable option (Enkel *et al.*, 2009; Lazzarotti and Manzini, 2009). Instead, different degrees of 'openness' may be suitable at different stages.

Concept design

The development of new or improved process equipment may be prompted by the equipment supplier's recognition of a need for such equipment on the market — or, alternatively, individual process firms may in their strategic production and development plans have identified a need for specific process equipment that is not currently available on the market (Lager and Frishammar, 2010). When a process firm identifies a need, the concept design can be performed in-house or jointly with an equipment supplier, indicating open innovation. Prior research on development projects suggests that key suppliers should be identified early so that they contribute in the collaborative design work (Petersen *et al.*, 2005), especially when the technology is new to the actors (Parker *et al.*, 2008). During this early development work it is important to articulate the needs of the process firms and translate these into a product concept (Cooper, 1988a; Khurana and

Rosenthal, 1997). A product concept is the objective of the development process and is a statement of both the technology and the customer benefits (Montoya-Weiss and O'Driscoll, 2000). Since this stage strongly affects equipment performance and costs in the following development stage, it is crucial that the collaborative partners have carefully discussed and agreed upon equipment specifications and preliminary operating and investment costs for such equipment (Cooper, 1988b).

Development

When the client has a deep knowledge of and interest in the required technology, development is often performed by the client together with consultants before suppliers are identified, in order to develop a detailed design as a solid basis for competitive bidding (Song *et al.*, 2009). However, this approach results in a divorce between development and construction/installation, since construction planning cannot affect the design (Pietroforte, 1997; Dubois and Gadde, 2002). This separation results in long project durations (Pietroforte, 1997) and decreased innovation (Rutten *et al.*, 2009), due to the lack of joint problem-solving (Korczynski, 1996). Another option, available when the client is more interested in the final function rather than the details of the technology, is to identify a supplier very early based on the concept design, after which the supplier is responsible for further development. This facilitates solutions with high constructability because it will be a supplier-focused design (Tam, 2000). The drawback is diminished client influence in the design work. Between these extremes, where development relies heavily either on the client or the supplier, there are alternatives in which the client and the suppliers together with consultants cooperate in developing the design. This approach is called joint development (Eriksson and Nilsson, 2008) or concurrent engineering, since it makes parallel and integrated design and assembly possible (Gil *et al.*, 2008; Errasti *et al.*, 2009). Such early involvement of suppliers and the integration of development and construction/installation facilitates cooperation (Palaneeswaran *et al.*, 2003) and innovation (Dulaimi *et al.*, 2003; Ling, 2003; Caldwell *et al.*, 2009) due to joint problem-solving in the early stages. In the process industry it is important that concurrent engineering does not only involve internal collaboration among different functions and departments but also collaboration with external actors such as equipment suppliers and installation subcontractors (Gunasekaran, 1998). To facilitate useful supplier input, relations should preferably be based on long-term collaboration and trust, rather than on short-term competitive bidding practices (Ro *et al.*, 2008). The early involvement of suppliers in concurrent engineering is often argued to be suitable for development projects characterized by high complexity, uncertainty, time pressure and customization (Grandori, 1997; Brown *et al.*, 2001; Eriksson and Pesämaa, 2007). Concurrent engineering increases the suppliers' understanding of customers' needs and improves teamwork and joint problem-solving and for these reasons it has been shown to improve both costs and time performance (Errasti *et al.*, 2009; Song *et al.*, 2009). The earlier the suppliers are involved in this phase, the more they can contribute to the product being developed.

Installation

The assembly and installation of the developed product/process are typically performed by the supplier or subcontractors. It may, however, be important for the client to engage in collaboration in this stage too, since buyer–supplier integration during installation accelerates effective use of the process equipment (Athaide and Klink, 2009). When concurrent engineering is adopted, construction planning and assembly of the product can be initiated before all development work is finished (Gil *et al.*, 2008). For products with challenging characteristics in terms of complexity, customization, time pressure and uncertainty, there are normally many suppliers who have to interact when assembling the equipment or a whole plant, which results in reciprocal interdependence among the different actors (Grandori, 1997). The output of Supplier A is often the input to Supplier B, at the same time as Supplier A requires design information from Supplier B so as to initiate assembly work. In these cases it is important to establish collaborative relations among the suppliers, often referred to as a broad partnering team, in which all key actors are integrated (Eriksson and Nilsson, 2008).

Start-up

When the equipment has been installed, the start-up activities are initiated. Due to the complexity and strategic importance of the production process, the start-up stage is a key part of these development projects (Lager and Frishammar, 2010). In particular, the complete transfer of the technology and know-how related to the equipment, from the supplier to the engineers and operators of the process firm, is essential for effective utilization (Lee *et al.*, 2010) However, previous studies have shown that making use of new equipment in process plants is a weak area for process firms (Agarwal *et al.*, 1984). Due to this fact, it is important during the contract negotiations that both parties agree on how the start-up stage is to be managed. Consequently, a suitable organization and integration of all available resources at the start-up stage is essential (Frazier *et al.*, 1996; Bagsarian, 2001).

Operation

In the operation stage, cooperation may also be important. Burger and Cann (1995) suggest that collaborative post-purchase strategies enacted by the supplier affect the level of trust and the extent to which the product is used and integrated into the buyer's organization. Hence, post-purchase activities are a valuable form of partnership (Burger and Cann, 1995). During this stage, buyers can provide suppliers with rich information on the idiosyncratic characteristics of their operating environment (Athaide *et al.*, 2003). Moreover, users are increasingly being regarded not just as passive adopters of equipment innovation — they may develop their own fine-grained adjustments of the equipment during operation, which suppliers can imitate (Von Hippel, 2005). Users regularly modify their current machines, equipment and software to better satisfy process needs, if these needs are not met by the market (Von Hippel, 2005). This is common in process firms, since process equipment often requires fine tuning for many months or even years before it is working optimally (Lager, 2010). Therefore, interaction between buyer and supplier in this post-installation work may enhance the innovation's production performance (Athaide and Klink, 2009). Recent research into the process industry has also found that suppliers often wish to market after-sales services in order to expand their business (Jalkala *et al.*, 2009).

Procurement procedures

Prior research has found that the buyer's decisions regarding partner selection, contract formalization, payment, subcontractor selection, collaborative tools and performance evaluation heavily affect project governance (Eriksson, 2008). Next, we therefore discuss how these procurement decisions affect supplier integration and open innovation in development projects.

Partner selection

Regardless of whether the work is to be performed jointly or by a supplier, the buyer first has to select a suitable supplier. Traditionally, clients focus on the lowest bid price in competitive tendering (Kadefors, 2005), in order to select the supplier who will perform the work at the lowest cost. The drawback is that such competitive tendering increases the risk of conflicts (Kadefors, 2005) and hampers long-term development in lasting relations (Ahola *et al.*, 2008). The alternative is to acknowledge that the basis of any collaboration is having the right partner for collaboration (Emden *et al.*, 2006). Partner selection involves efforts that are undertaken by the buyer *ex ante* to verify the supplier's skills (e.g. technical expertise and manufacturing capacity) and motivation (e.g. business philosophy and reputation) to perform as needed (Ouchi, 1979; Stump and Heide, 1996; Wathne and Heide, 2004). The issue is finding a partner with the appropriate technical knowledge and ability, strategic intent and long-term collaborative orientation (Emden *et al.*, 2006). A careful selection of competent suppliers can therefore facilitate innovation (Manley, 2008; Bosch-Sijtsema and Postma, 2009; Caldwell *et al.*, 2009) and collaboration, through trust, commitment and shared values (Ouchi, 1979; Stump and Heide, 1996). Relevant evaluation criteria when selecting partners in collaborative development projects include earlier references, technical competence, collaborative ability and a willingness to change (Clegg *et al.*, 2002; Rahman and Kumaraswamy, 2004; Kadefors *et al.*, 2007; Bosch-Sijtsema and Postma, 2009).

Contract formalization

Competitive market relations rely heavily on legal rules and formal documents (Blois, 2002) since little change is anticipated and since complete contracts are more legally binding in court (Macneil, 1978; Woolthuis *et al.*, 2005). Contracts then function as safeguards, specifying all future contingencies and penalties for non-performance (Woolthuis *et al.*, 2005). However, research has shown that formalization decreases trust and increases opportunism, for which reason relational norms should be used as safeguards instead (Heide and John, 1992; Ghoshal and Moran, 1996). By developing shared norms the parties establish an implicit sense of acceptable and deviant behaviour (Aulakh and Gencturk, 2000), increasing trust and making it possible to decrease formalization (Das and Teng, 1998; Parkhe, 1998), i.e. trust replaces contracts. However, recent research has shown that formalized contracts may be beneficial also in transactions characterized by high complexity, customization and uncertainty, if they are coupled with trust and relational norms, i.e. contracts complement trust (Woolthuis *et al.*, 2005). Such an approach, in which formal contracts are coupled with relational norms, may be especially suitable in situations where knowledge leakage is apparent.

In addition, to succeed in collaborative development, sharing of information, research plans and vision are vital (Kreiner and Schultz, 1993). However, the knowledge exchanged may be passed to competitors (Enkel *et al.*, 2005), and this knowledge leakage may lead both parties to become protective, especially concerning their core capabilities (Chesbrough and Schwartz, 2007). To enable open innovation practices, firms need to protect their knowledge from unintended use (Slowinski *et al.*, 2006), through legal as well as non-legal methods. Legal methods include linking formal agreements to the activities of the collaboration, while non-legal methods include ensuring that employees in both firms discuss what information must be shared, may be shared and may not be shared with the partner (Slowinski *et al.*, 2006).

Payment

According to Eisenhardt (1985) and Gencturk and Aulakh (1995), output-based compensation (e.g. fixed prices) leads to an emphasis on price and competition. In order to decrease opportunism (Wathne and Heide, 2000) and increase cooperation in relational contracting, profit sharing (incentives) together with joint objectives should be used (Olsen *et al.*, 2005; Spekman and Carraway, 2006). Incentive-based payment with gain share/pain share arrangements provides a supplier with extrinsic motivation to perform well, since it increases the likelihood that the benefits (e.g. cost savings due to increased constructability) of improved collaboration and successful joint problem-solving are shared equitably among the partners (Crespin-Mazet and Ghauri, 2007; Kadefors and Badenfelt, 2009). The gain share/pain share mechanism also serves as a vital symbol in signalling the importance of collaboration and integration (Badenfelt, 2008; Kadefors and Badenfelt, 2009). In complex development projects where many interdependent partners are integrated, incentives based on group performance are vital (Eriksson and Nilsson, 2008). By establishing gain share/pain share arrangements and bonus opportunities in which benefits from successful performance are shared, the partners are motivated to work jointly towards a joint objective instead of sub-optimizing their own individual efforts (Korczynski, 1996; Olsen *et al.*, 2005). Thus, such incentives also facilitate innovation (Dulaimi *et al.*, 2003; Caldwell *et al.*, 2009).

Subcontractor selection

A domestic contract means that subcontractor selection is made by the contractor (supplier), while the client selects the subcontractors in nominated contracts (Shoesmith, 1996). In market relationships, contractors have total freedom to select their subcontractors, leaving the client with no control of who performs specialist work (Shoesmith, 1996). Domestic contracts therefore indicate a *laissez-faire* approach, while nominated contracts entail control and authority. Despite a subcontractor's large effect on project performance, a contractor's procurement of subcontractors in domestic contracts is traditionally unsophisticated and unaffected by collaboration in client–contractor relations (Saad *et al.*, 2002; Alderman and Ivory, 2007). The selection can also be made jointly by both the client and contractor in collaboration, indicating a concern for both parties' interests (Eriksson and Nilsson, 2008). Such joint selection facilitates subcontractors' involvement in the value-adding activities of development projects (Saad *et al.*, 2002; Eriksson and Nilsson, 2008), which enhances innovation (Eriksson *et al.*, 2007; Manley, 2008).

Collaborative tools

In collaborative development projects the buyer and supplier interact to create the product. Joint activities (Heide and John, 1990) or collaborative tools may therefore be appropriate in order to facilitate flexibility, integration and collaboration (Joshi and Stump, 1999; Cheung *et al.*, 2003; Bayliss *et al.*, 2004). Earlier investigations proposed that joint action, which entails activities that are performed jointly by the partners rather than unilaterally, is a central element of buyer–supplier integration (Jaspers and van den Ende, 2006; Barnes *et al.*, 2007; Duffy, 2008). A distinct feature of collaborative relations is therefore the focus on joint activities and collaborative tools such as the establishment of joint objectives, joint office building, team-building activities, partnering facilitating, joint IT tools and joint risk management (Bayliss *et al.*, 2004; Olsen *et al.*, 2005; Eriksson, 2008).

Performance evaluation

The evaluation and control of work in progress and the final product can either be executed by the client, by the supplier or jointly. When the client inspects the finished product or monitors a supplier's ongoing performance, a high focus on competition is facilitated (Hennart, 1993; Korczynski, 1996). Such tight monitoring of supplier behaviour and performance increases the risk of opportunism and hampers cooperation (Korczynski, 1996; Ruuska *et al.*, 2009). In collaborative development projects, self-inspection by the supplier, which is related to trust (Das and Teng, 2001), is more suitable (Hagen and Choe, 1998; Eriksson and Nilsson, 2008). The joint evaluation of performance can be performed in a workshop at the end of the project, during which the benefits and drawbacks of both the work methods and the final product/process can be discussed (Eriksson and Nilsson, 2008).

Empirical Method

Our research strategy involved two exploratory case studies, in order to capture a more complete and contextual assessment of the complex and iterative activities that constitute the process of achieving supplier integration in collaborative development projects in process industries (Hutcheson *et al.*, 1995). The choice of the case-study method is further justified given the aim of getting a more detailed understanding of how collaborations are organized and managed (Yin, 2003) from a process perspective (Pratt, 2009).

To investigate collaborative practices within the process industries, two process firms in the metals and minerals industry were selected by means of judgement sampling (Denzin and Lincoln, 1994), henceforth referred to as X Corp and Y Corp. The case setting is particularly interesting as the development of process equipment for the metals and minerals industry provides several challenges. The operations include heavy materials that wear and tear equipment, idiosyncratic process needs and a critical requirement for reliable equipment. Both firms have their corporate headquarters and main R&D departments in northern Europe, but sell their products in a global market. Empirical data was collected mainly through in-depth interviews as they provide insightful information and can be focused directly on research topics (Yin, 2003). The main unit of analysis was the collaborative relations among equipment suppliers and process firms, focusing on general tendencies and patterns of collaborative relations, rather than on distinct projects. However, relevant and interesting examples from specific projects are provided in order to illustrate key problems and opportunities.

This paper is underpinned by 28 interviews, ranging in length from one to two hours, with an average of about 90 minutes. The respondents were selected after a dialogue with the participating firms, based on their involvement in and knowledge of collaborative development projects. Deliberate effort was spent on getting respondents from both strategic and operational levels in the firms. The respondents varied in age, years of employment, academic training and position, and were therefore able to contribute with diverse perspectives. The different positions of the respondents included: vice-presidents, various department managers (e.g. technical support, R&D and facilities), project managers, production managers, marketing managers, engineers and technical specialists. The interviews were semi-structured and guided by a list of questions designed on the basis of the literature review in order to capture a life-cycle perspective on the collaborative development process. Departures from specific questions were permitted; the format of the interviews was accordingly adapted and changed slightly to pursue interesting and particularly relevant new facets as they emerged. Both authors conducted interviews in order to obtain investigator triangulation (Denzin, 1978).

In addition, approximately 20 hours of document studies were performed, focusing on partnering charters, incentive arrangements and tendering and contractual documents. To create an overlap between data collection and data analysis, frequent discussions among the authors were held as well as continuous taking of field notes. Each interview was summarized and transferred into a spreadsheet for further analysis. The spreadsheet was structured as a conceptually ordered display (Miles and Huberman, 1994). To facilitate the analysis, several research questions were conceptually clustered together in rows according to the general theme that they were exploring (Miles and Huberman, 1994). Each theme was explored and summarized and later discussed by the researchers to arrive at a joint result. To further increase reliability (transparency and future replication), a case-study protocol was constructed together with a case-study database, containing case-study notes, documents and the narratives collected during the study, all with the aim of facilitating retrieval for future studies (Yin, 2003).

The qualitative process data formed an empirical data pattern, which described why and how the procurement procedures were performed in the process firms. The empirical patterns were then compared to the theoretical predictions in order to investigate differences and similarities between the process data and theory, i.e. a pattern-matching analysis was performed (Yin, 2003). Although case studies are not devoid of generalizations (Gibbert *et al.*, 2008), generalizability is problematic with a research design like the current one. Nevertheless, the main objective is to employ analytical generalization — from empirical observation to theory.

Empirical Results

Who performs the work in different stages?

The respondents agreed that a collaborative approach to the buying process (often referred to as partnering) was of utmost importance in addressing the challenges faced when developing process technology. However, the degree of collaboration varies among the stages. The two design stages were considered critical for making sure that a good product concept for equipment is developed. Consequently, the respondents were typically in favour of joint development activities in these stages. In particular, if the equipment is highly complex and customized (e.g. an entire production plant), it is important to establish collaboration with key suppliers during these early stages. However, many respondents suggested that concept design is often performed internally to a high degree, while development after the purchase decision is performed mainly by the equipment supplier. Intense interaction and joint problem-solving in the early stages are primarily motivated by the fact that it is much easier and cheaper to make changes to equipment during early development than in later stages where development costs increase significantly.

However, a plant manager at Y Corp described a tendency for myopia concerning early investment decisions:

> *Unfortunately, sufficient work is not always put into the early stages. When we make investment decisions it is usually because of a need for increased capacity, and when we need it we need it fast, it is almost like investing in panic.*

When the concept design is finalized, the process firm makes the decision to proceed or not with the project. If a positive decision is taken, the project is formally started as soon as possible and more resources are allocated. Suppliers are then selected and contracted so that they can be involved in concurrent engineering (i.e. overlapping design and assembly/installation), in order to save time and utilize their competence. Parallel design and construction are vital due to the high time pressure of most projects, and the integration also serves as a key factor for enhancing cooperation. Equipment manufacturers might, however, be reluctant to collaborate intensively during product development as core knowledge may be shared by the process firm with the supplier's competitors.

The vice-president at Y Corp highlighted this issue:

> *A reason why we might not collaborate as much as we should at this stage may be that the equipment supplier wants to protect its knowledge. They are not interested in letting us in and letting us understand what is unique in their development process, as they perceive the risk of us using this knowledge to develop our own equipment.*

The installation stage is the most complex in terms of interdependence and interaction among a large variety of suppliers and subcontractors. If a project involves an entire production plant, the number of people and firms involved in it peaks during this stage, making it very difficult to coordinate the large number of heterogeneous activities. Collaboration is here somewhat less intense in the different buyer–supplier dyads, but is instead intensified among the suppliers in the project network.

In the start-up phase, a substantial amount of joint effort is required, as problems during start-up might affect the performance of the whole plant and impose high costs due to production disturbances. Consequently, personnel from the equipment manufacturer are usually very much involved in the start-up process at the plant to get the equipment to work properly, transfer operational knowledge and make sure that an efficient start-up is achieved.

In the operation stage the degree of collaboration decreases and the work is mainly performed by the process firm. This may in some cases be related to a fear on the part of the process firm that the equipment manufacturers might learn too much about the production process, which is regarded as the process firm's core capability.

A department manager at X Corp further elaborated on this issue:

> *We do things in our maintenance and we do things in our process to adapt the equipment to suit our process. The critical matter is really how we run our process, and that is something that we do not want anyone to know about.*

Procurement procedures

Both process firms utilized a broad range of procurement procedures in different ways during the different stages, in order to facilitate supplier integration and open innovation practices.

Partner selection

As mentioned above, partner selection is often performed before the development stage or even during concept design, in order to involve suppliers early in the development. If suppliers are involved in the concept design, they are selected based on their competences and earlier achievements, since it is not possible to estimate an expected price of the equipment at this early stage. After the concept design is finished, the process firm and the supplier negotiate a price for the final product. If they fail to agree a price or if the process firm is disappointed with the supplier's concept design, a new partner is selected.

When selecting a partner to collaborate for the development, installation and start-up stages, a general search of competent suppliers is typically performed by the process firm's R&D department. This can usually be done through the network of employees at the firm using personal contacts. A bid invitation is generally sent out to suppliers that are believed to have the necessary technical competences. The selected suppliers then send their proposals for how they would solve the problem and the proposals are evaluated. Both process firms base their selection procedures on multiple criteria and earlier experiences of the partners.

Furthermore, price may not always be an important criterion as suggested by a process development specialist at Y Corp:

> *If we have two or three suppliers with different products where the price ranges 20–30% the lowest prices may not be the best deal, the more expensive equipment may for example be more reliable.*

The explicitly low focus on lowest price facilitates harmonious relations in which all actors are allowed to make money. In most cases, the suppliers chosen are well known within the process industry and new entrants are indeed rare. Furthermore, the long-term survival of the equipment suppliers is important to process firms, since they operate in a very specific context with high entry costs for firms without the necessary knowledge of the operating environment in the process industry. If an equipment supplier does not reap sufficient benefit from collaboration, they will be unwilling to take part in future collaborations.

Contract formalization

In the concept design stage, the process firms typically want to uphold some degree of competition and keep their options open, for which reason they are reluctant to contract only one supplier for a certain piece of equipment unless necessary. At the same time, it is impossible to agree upon a purchase price for the equipment at this early stage due to the high uncertainties. An option employed by

X Corp is to contract one or two key suppliers as consultants during this stage. Subsequently, the partners enter the main contract, covering the development, assembly and start-up stages. Respondents at both firms suggested that it is important to have clearly written contracts, but it is even more important to avoid getting caught in the contract. It is the contract objective that is important not the contract itself. A vital aspect of handling diverging objectives is a letter of understanding, which states both parties' objectives for the collaboration and how the results will be used. In a recent development project at X Corp such collaborative contractual clauses (also called a partnering charter) were appended to the standard contract. Although they were not considered crucial for the collaborative climate, the process of establishing them constituted a useful team-building exercise. Moreover, respondents at both firms suggested that such a document should also include how intellectual property rights, patents and drawings should be handled. It is also important to state how responsibility is handled when something goes wrong.

The most critical risk in collaborative development projects is the potential of transmitting core knowledge to competitors. As an example, X Corp described a situation during the 1990s where blueprints of one of their plants were widely spread throughout the industry. Consequently, the process firms usually have a policy of using nondisclosure agreements, in order to hinder the leakage of important information. In cases where the risk of spreading critical information is low this policy may be relaxed.

However, it can be hard to unlearn knowledge that has been acquired in a collaboration as suggested by a process development specialist at Y Corp:

> *If you end up in a similar project with another supplier it is hard to not think of experiences from earlier projects.*

Moreover, both firms avoid taking out patents because this would reveal how their processes are structured. Contracts preventing equipment manufacturers from selling the equipment to competitors are formed in most cases. However, an exception is made when the equipment is not particularly important and this is also a way of improving the market potential for the equipment supplier. However, in many cases the equipment developed is not of any use to competitors since they have very different processes. Accordingly, the respondents identified a sometimes irrational fear of sharing information in the buyer–supplier dyad. Noting that a better knowledge of what can be shared and what cannot, could lead to more open collaborations. In order to spread development costs over several buyers, equipment could be made available to companies in non-competing industries.

Payment

If suppliers are involved in the concept design, payment is mostly in the form of cost reimbursement, that is, they get paid for the hours they work as consultants. During the rest of the project, payment is often based on incentives connected to a target price or sometimes there is a traditional fixed price payment. Rewards and incentives, such as time bonuses, are viewed as important to ensure good collaboration that focuses on the outcome rather than on self-interest. X Corp has sometimes used gain share/pain share arrangements coupled with bonus opportunities in development projects. The size of these bonuses deserves some reflection. If bonuses are to affect attitudes and behaviour, many respondents argued that they have to be relatively large. Hence, bonus opportunities were amplified from approximately 1–2% to 5% of the project value in the most recent development projects. Perhaps the most important point to make regarding payment is that gain share/pain share arrangements and bonus opportunities should be tied to group performance rather than performance within individual contracts. Traditionally, incentives have been connected to a supplier's individual performance, which hampered collaboration between contracts. In the most recent project at X Corp the gain share/pain share arrangements and bonus opportunities were tied to the group performance, so that the individual partners did not have any incentive to sub-optimize their own performance. This was perceived to be very beneficial. Some caution is, however, called for regarding incentives. Respondents at X Corp pinpoint that incentives require trust and cooperative relations among the partners in order to function well otherwise the suspicion of potential opportunism may grow under the surface. Moreover, respondents at Y Corp indicated that there had been discussions about implementing long-term bonuses to ensure that equipment suppliers were committed to maintaining and adapting the equipment even after the formal project had ended. However, the Y Corp respondents did not like this option as it would entail paying more for the same piece of equipment.

Subcontractor selection

Subcontractors are mostly not involved in the concept design and if they are, the equipment manufacturer selects and involves them without much interaction with the process firm. In subsequent stages of the project, the process firms are often involved in choosing the equipment manufacturer's component suppliers. This has mostly to do with the operations and service departments' familiarity and experience with a particular component, which promotes more efficient operations and maintenance. The process firms also put high importance on being involved in the selection of reliable subcontractors for the installation of the equipment as this is of critical importance. This has led to some subcontractors being banned from working with the process firms after particularly bad experiences. Due to the lack of resources, the process firms normally collaborate with some of the partners only in the selection of subcontractors. Although the actors consider this collaboration beneficial, it requires time and resources and does not eliminate the risk of selecting unsuitable subcontractors. In recent development projects at X Corp a few poorly performing subcontractors were actually jointly selected. A positive effect of joint selection is, however, that the actors share the risks and cannot blame each other for a poor selection; they have to take joint action to decrease the negative effects of unsuitable choices. It is more important to involve key subcontractors in the partnering team. This is often done to some extent but the respondents agreed that it should be done to a larger extent.

Collaborative tools

A problem with collaboration in the concept design stage is that the buyer organization has not yet been formally established, since the formal buying decision is taken when the concept has been developed and an approximate price can be estimated. Hence, the process firms lack the human resources to collaborate intensively with many suppliers at the same time. Nevertheless, it is important to initiate the collaboration process and facilitate communication at this early stage by establishing joint objectives to enhance a win-win situation, holding workshops to facilitate joint problem-solving and conducting team-building activities.

When the formal buying decision has been taken, further investments in collaborative tools are made during concurrent engineering activities. During development it is important to focus on describing and effectively communicating the requirements to the equipment manufacturer, who should take responsibility to ensure that the equipment delivers as intended, by trying harder to understand the process firm's needs. X Corp has utilized a broad range of collaborative tools in their development projects: start workshops, joint IT-tools, joint objectives, partnering questionnaires, follow-up workshops, team-building, facilitating and conflict resolution. All respondents at X Corp were positive about these activities and found them effective for improving relations and collaboration among all actors. Since all projects were large in monetary terms, the costs of performing these activities were not considered unreasonably high. Of the collaborative tools, joint objectives are especially important. In general the most pressing differences in goals and objectives are costs, as both partners have tight cost constraints because of the economic reality of the firms, and the collaboration may suffer as a result. Consequently, respondents suggested that it is important to consider the equipment suppliers' goals to make sure that they will still be willing and able to collaborate in the future.

Additionally, internal collaboration requires some attention. When organizing a collaborative development project, it is important to involve the whole organization to create commitment and to utilize all relevant knowledge within the firm. Consequently, collaborative projects are usually organized with people from many different areas of the organization such as R&D, operations and purchasing. Project teams from both firms create a management team that is involved in extensive discussions, creating specifications of requirements and agreements.

Performance evaluation

In both firms, performance evaluation is mostly conducted in traditional ways, that is, the buyer controls both work in progress and the final product to a high degree. Self-inspection by suppliers is not perceived to work very well. This motivated X Corp to devote more focus to this issue in their most recent development project. Key suppliers were asked to improve their self-inspection, which was frequently discussed during monthly meetings. Partnering was then considered as a suitable base for improved self-inspection, but although some improvement was achieved, there is still a long way to go in order to reach satisfactory results. Partnering also serves as an appropriate base for joint performance evaluation in the form of a workshop when a project is complete. X Corp hold this type of workshop after every project, in order to discuss good and poor achievements, problems and benefits experienced by the project actors. These experiences may then be transferred to the next project, facilitating continuous improvement.

Discussion and Model Development

In the introduction we argued that earlier literature lacks a life-cycle perspective on how to organize and manage supplier integration and open innovation. Our literature review provided a greater understanding of the importance of a life-cycle perspective on the development of new process equipment and how a broad range of interconnected procurement procedures affects supplier integration. Our empirical results, summarized in Table 1, further showed how these procurement

Table 1. Summary of Empirical Findings.

	Concept design	Development	Installation	Start-up	Operation
Who performs the work?	Mainly the process firm, sometimes with input from supplier. If suppliers are involved, collaboration may be rather intense but the process firm also wants to uphold some degree of competition.	Mainly the supplier, with input from process firm. Suppliers may be reluctant to collaborate intensively due to fear of knowledge leakage.	Mainly the supplier, with input from process firm. Intense collaboration among suppliers is coordinated by process firm in large complex projects.	Intense collaboration between process firm and supplier enhances knowledge transfer and learning.	Process firm operates the equipment and is reluctant to collaborate with supplier due to fear of knowledge leakage.
Partner selection	Competences, references, reputation and earlier experiences are evaluated.	Suppliers are mostly procured for the development, installation and start-up stages together. If supplier was involved in concept design a mutual agreeable price is negotiated. If concept design was performed internally trustworthy and competent suppliers are invited to bid and selected based on multiple criteria (e.g. competences, references, reputation, earlier experiences and price).			Not applicable.

(Continued)

Table 1. (*Continued*)

	Concept design	Development	Installation	Start-up	Operation
Contract formalization	When one or more suppliers are involved, consultant contracts are utilized due to their reversible nature.	Main contract covers development, assembly/installation, and start-up of the equipment. Although clearly written formal contracts are important it is vital to not get caught in the contract, but rather establish relationships based on collaboration and mutual commitment. Jointly developed collaborative contractual clauses may be appended to the formal contract. Non-disclosure agreements are used rather than patents in order to avoid knowledge leakage.			Not applicable.
Payment	Cost reimbursement due to difficulties of estimating a final price in this early stage.	Sometimes a traditional fixed price for a product delivered but sometimes incentive-based payment connected to a negotiated target price. Bonus opportunities connected to delivery times and health and safety targets are sometimes offered. Incentives/bonuses should be connected to group performances rather than individual contracts in order to avoid sub-optimizations.			Not applicable.
Subcontractor selection	Subcontractors are mostly not involved in concept design but when they are, the supplier manage the selection.	Subcontractors of high monetary and strategic importance are often selected jointly in order to obtain better prices and more capable partners. This decreases but do not eliminate the risk of unsuitable selections. If poor performing subcontractors have been chosen jointly the supplier and process firm can work jointly to improve the situation instead of blaming each other.			Not applicable.

(*Continued*)

Table 1. (*Continued*)

	Concept design	Development	Installation	Start-up	Operation
Collaborative tools	Due to lack of resources before the formal buying decision, collaborative tools are often not utilized to a very high extent.	After the formal buying decision has been taken, more investments in collaborative tools are made. Initial workshops, joint IT-tools, follow-up workshops, team-building and facilitator are sometimes used to increase the integration among buyer and suppliers.			Not applicable.
Performance evaluation	Evaluation of the quality of the concept design work and documents are often not performed adequately due to lack of time and resources.	Control of both work in progress and the final product is mostly conducted in traditional ways by the process firm. The suppliers' self-inspection processes are not perceived to work very well. This is an identified improvement area.			Not applicable.

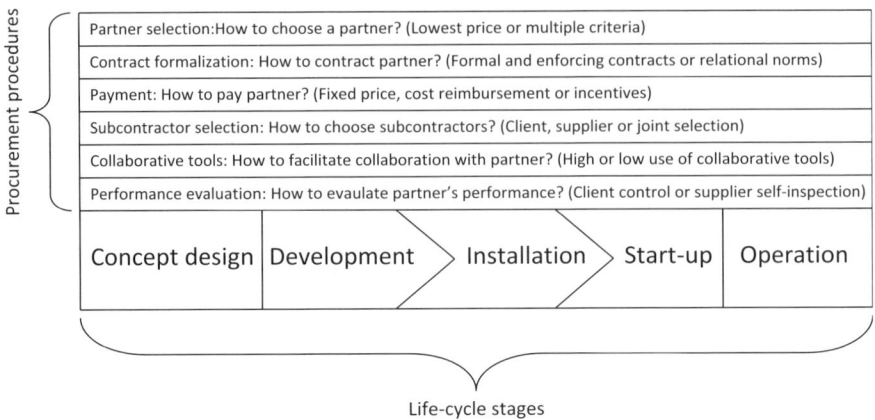

Fig. 2. The Supplier Integration Model.

procedures varied during the different life-cycle stages. Hence, it seems useful to merge the life-cycle perspective provided by Lager and Frishammar (2010) and the comprehensive procurement framework developed by Eriksson (2008) in order to obtain a conceptual model that can increase our understanding of how to organize and manage supplier integration and open innovation.

In Fig. 2, we show the model developed from the literature review and our empirical findings. At the bottom of the figure the five life-cycle stages provide a process perspective of the development of process equipment. Our empirical findings show that process firms adopt three different procurement approaches during the five stages: the first is during concept design, the second during development, installation and start-up and the third is during operation. The boundaries separating these procurement approaches, resulting in limited interconnections between stages, are illustrated in Fig. 2 by the straight lines following the concept design and start-up stages. At the top of the figure the six procurement decisions serve as the means to facilitate closed or open innovation, depending on which alternatives are chosen. Hence, the buying firm should choose from these procurement procedures in order to facilitate different degrees of supplier integration and open innovation during different stages.

Our empirical results clearly illustrate the model's applicability by describing how the two process firms chose three different procurement-based approaches to open innovation during the five life-cycle stages:

(1) During concept design, supplier integration practices are performed to some extent, but the process firms hesitate in relying heavily on a single partner since this actor cannot be selected based on competitive tendering at this early stage. If partners are involved, they are selected based on competence and earlier experience, since it is not possible to estimate a price at this stage. Suppliers are contracted as consultants paid through cost reimbursement. Collaborative tools are utilized only to a limited extent, since the client's budget is very tight before the formal buying decision, which will end this stage.

(2) After a positive buying decision the project begins and key suppliers are contracted for the development, installation and start-up stages. Our results indicate that strong supplier integration was chiefly based on careful partner selection coupled with incentives and collaborative tools (e.g. a joint project office, joint project objectives, joint IT tools, partner facilitating and team-building activities). In order to coordinate collaboration among suppliers, a broad partnering team can be established in which all key actors interact and share the rewards arising from their collaborative efforts in the network, rather than sub-optimizing their performance through dyadic contracts (Eriksson, 2008; Caldwell *et al.*, 2009). However, prior research has shown that clients generally focus on dyadic relations although interdependencies among different types of suppliers make a network perspective more suitable (Ford, 2004; Roseira *et al.*, 2010). Although collaborative tools are considered very useful, partner selection is, however, the most important procedure. If a buyer selects the wrong partner, it appears to be very difficult to transform an adversarial relationship into a cooperative one with incentives and collaborative tools. Performance evaluation in terms of self-regulation is problematic but joint evaluation

workshops after completed projects are deemed to be very useful.

(3) During operation of the equipment, supplier integration is weak, resulting in limited interconnections between the operation stage and the preceding stages. The reason for this is that process firms fear knowledge leakage of core competences. The low level of collaboration is thereby logical and in line with the reasoning presented by Chesbrough and Schwartz (2007), who argued that core capabilities should be developed in-house and shared only sparingly. In contrast, suppliers are keen on increased integration in order to obtain operational data about the equipment, facilitating further development.

Theoretically, a number of different procurement approaches are possible during the life cycle, that is, either one all-encompassing procurement strategy during the entire life cycle or different strategies, each covering one or several stages. However, choosing different procurement strategies for each stage will lead to a divorce between the activities in the development process. We argue that a comprehensive procurement approach is required in order to achieve an overlap and synergies across activities in different stages. As such, a collaborative open innovation approach not only depends on the collaborative procurement practices being aligned across stages, but more importantly it depends on the chosen procurement approach overlapping several stages, that is concurrent engineering (Brown *et al.*, 2001; Eriksson and Pesämaa, 2007). Previous research has highlighted that concurrent engineering, which is mostly adopted in new product development in manufacturing industries, is even more important in process innovation projects in the process industry (Gunasekaran, 1998). Such an overlapping approach is important for the two process firms as the development of process equipment is characterized by high complexity, uncertainty, time pressure and customization. Moreover, our empirical results illustrate how difficult and important it is to choose appropriate procurement procedures tailored to the demands and challenges posed in each stage. Our model can serve as a guide for dealing with this predicament.

Conclusions, Limitations and Further Research

By adopting a life-cycle perspective on procurement, we provide a model on how to organize and manage supplier integration and open innovation practices when developing and installing new process equipment. Theoretically, the paper fills two gaps in the open innovation literature. First, a life-cycle-based procurement perspective is required in order to address the interconnections both among different procurement procedures, but also among different life-cycle stages of the process equipment. We contribute to the theory by merging a life-cycle perspective and a comprehensive framework including a broad range of procurement procedures, into a supplier integration model. Second, we contribute to the theory by developing this model based upon empirical results from process development projects in mature industries, an area neglected in previous research. We provide relevant and novel insights into how a broad range of cooperative procurement procedures works and interacts when managing supplier integration and open innovation during different stages of a development project in process industries.

In addition this study contributes to management practice by helping process firms and equipment suppliers to assess and manage their open innovation practices through a collaborative procurement perspective. First, the merging of the life-cycle perspective and procurement procedures highlights the need for interaction and coordination among the internal functions of R&D, operations and procurement in process firms at an early stage. In particular, the life-cycle perspective is important as a large percentage of the process equipment life-cycle cost is determined during the design stage. Second, the model developed underlines how choices among the different procurement procedures can lead to different degrees of supplier integration and collaboration. Accordingly, it is important from an early stage to discern and decide on the future needs for collaboration in a project and adapt the procurement procedures accordingly. On a more detailed level, the findings show that the rare use of broad partnering teams, who share incentives based on the group's performance, are not difficult to set up and can result in significant improvements in collaboration across contractual relations in a network of suppliers, instead of the traditional focus on performance in dyadic relations. To this end, the life-cycle-based procurement model can serve as an illustrative framework, guiding practitioners in organizing and managing supplier integration and open innovation practices.

One limitation of this study is that the findings and the developed model are based on the perspective of two process firms. However, we argue that the model could be applied by equipment suppliers in order to increase their awareness of how different procurement procedures affect collaboration during different stages. Still, future studies should be encouraged to include the supplier's perspective in order to increase our understanding of how collaborative procurement procedures affect supplier integration. It would also be interesting to search for and investigate cases in which collaboration between a process firm and suppliers occur at the operational stage, in order to identify the problems and opportunities faced by the actors in strategically important activities. Another relevant approach would be to quantitatively investigate these types of collaborative development projects in order to make more general conclusions and also to compare different types of process industries (e.g. pulp/paper, food and metals/minerals).

References

Agarwal, J.C., Brown, S.R. and Katrak, S.E. (1984). Taking the string out of project startup problems, *Engineering and Mining Journal*, **9**, 62–76.

Ahola, T., Laitinen, E., Kujala, J. and Wikström, K. (2008). Purchasing strategies and value creation in industrial turnkey projects, *International Journal of Project Management*, **26**(1), 87–94.

Alderman, N. and Ivory, C. (2007). Partnering in major contracts: Paradox and metaphor, *International Journal of Project Management*, **25**(4), 386–393.

Athaide, G. and Klink, R. (2009). Managing seller–buyer relationships during new product development, *Journal of Product Innovation Management*, **26**(5), 566–577.

Athaide, G.A., Stump, R.L. and Joshi, A.W. (2003). Understanding new product co-development relationships in technology-based industrial markets, *Journal of Marketing Theory and Practice,* **11**(3), 46–59.

Aulakh, P. and Gencturk, E. (2000). International principal-agent relationships: control, governance and performance, *Industrial Marketing Management,* **29**(6), 521–538.

Aylen, J. (2010). Open versus closed innovation: Development of the wide strip mill for steel in the United States during the 1920s, *R&D Management,* **40**(1), 67–80.

Badenfelt, U. (2008). The selection of sharing ratios in target cost contracts, *Engineering Construction and Architectural Management,* **15**(1), 54–65.

Bagsarian, T. (2001). Avoiding startup stumbles, *Iron Age New Steel,* **17**(2), 16–19.

Barnes, B., Naudé, P., and Michell, P. (2007). Perceptual gaps and similarities in buyer-seller relationships. *Industrial Marketing Management,* **36**(5), 662–675.

Bayliss, R., Cheung, S., Suen, H., and Wong, S.-P. (2004). Effective partnering tools in construction: A case study on MTRC TKE Contract in Hong Kong, *International Journal of Project Management,* **22**(3), 253–263.

Blois, K. (2002). Business to business exchanges: A rich descriptive apparatus derived from Macneil's and Menger's analysis, *Journal of Management Studies,* **39**(4), 523–551.

Bosch-Sijtsema, P. and Postma, T. (2009). Cooperative innovation projects: Capabilities and governance mechanisms, *Journal of Product Innovation Management,* **26**(1), 58–70.

Brown, D., Ashleigh, M., Riley, M. and Shaw, R. (2001). New project procurement process, *Journal of Management in Engineering,* **17**(4), 192–201.

Burger, P. and Cann, C. (1995). Post-purchase strategy: A key to successful industrial marketing and customer satisfaction, *Industrial Marketing Management,* **24**(2), 91–98.

Caldwell, N., Roehrich, J. and Davies, A. (2009). Procuring complex performance in construction: London Heathrow Terminal 5 and a private finance initiative hospital, *Journal of Purchasing and Supply Management,* **15**(3), 178–186.

Carson, S., Madhok, A. and Wu, T. (2006). Uncertainty, opportunism, and governance: The effects of volatility and ambiguity on formal and relational contracting, *Academy of Management Journal*, **49**(5), 1058–1077.

Cassiman, B. and Chiara Di Guardo, M. (2009). Organising R&D projects to profit from innovation: Insights from co-opetition, *Long Range Planning*, **42**(2), 216–233.

Chesbrough, H. (2003a). *Open Innovation: The New Imperative for Creating and Profiting from Technology*, Harvard Business School Press, Boston, MA.

Chesbrough, H. (2003b). The era of open innovation, *MIT Sloan Management Review*, **44**(3), 35–41.

Chesbrough, H. and Crowther, A. (2006). Beyond high tech: Early adopters of open innovation in other industries, *R&D Management*, **36**(3), 229–236.

Chesbrough, H. and Schwartz, K. (2007). Innovating business models with co-development partnerships, *Research Technology Management*, **50**(1), 55–59.

Cheung, S. O., Suen, H., and Cheung, K. (2003). An automated partnering monitoring system — Partnering temperature index, *Automation in Construction*, **12**(3), 331–345.

Chronéer, D. and Laurell-Stenlund, K. (2006). Determinants of an effective product development process: Towards a conceptual framework for process industry, *International Journal of Innovation Management*, **10**(3), 237–269.

Clegg, S., Pitsis, T., Rura-Polley, T. and Marosszeky, M. (2002). Governmentality matters: Designing an alliance culture of inter-organizational collaboration for managing projects, *Organization Studies*, **23**(3), 317–337.

Cooper, R.G. (1988a). Predevelopment activities determine new product success, *Industrial Marketing Management*, **17**(3), 237–247.

Cooper, R.G. (1988b). *Winning at New Products*, Kogan Page, London.

Crespin-Mazet, F. and Ghauri, P. (2007). Co-development as a marketing strategy in the construction industry, *Industrial Marketing Management*, **36**(2), 158–172.

Das, T. and Teng, B.-S. (1998). Between trust and control: Developing confidence in partner cooperation in alliances, *Academy of Management Review*, **23**(3), 491–512.

Das, T. and Teng, B.-S. (2001). Trust, control, and risk in strategic alliances: An integrated framework. *Organization Studies,* **22**(2), 251–283.

Denzin, N.K. (1978). *Sociological Methods: A Source Book,* McGraw-Hill, New York.

Denzin, N.K. and Lincoln, Y.S. (1994). *Handbook of Qualitative Research,* Sage Publications, London.

Dubois, A. and Gadde, L.-E. (2002). The construction industry as a loosely coupled system: Implications for productivity and innovation, *Construction Management and Economics,* **20**(7), 621–632.

Duffy, R. (2008). Towards a better understanding of partnership attributes: an exploratory analysis of relationship type classification, *Industrial Marketing Management,* **37**(2), 228–244.

Dulaimi, M.F., Ling, F.Y. and Bajracharya, A. (2003). Organizational motivation and inter-organizational interaction in construction innovation in Singapore, *Construction Management and Economics,* **21**(3), 307–318.

Eisenhardt, K. (1985). Control: Organizational and economic approaches, *Management Science,* **31**(2), 134–149.

Emden, Z., Calantone, R.J. and Droge, C. (2006). Collaborating for new product development: Selecting the partner with maximum potential to create value, *Journal of Product Innovation Management,* **23**(4), 330–341.

Enkel, E., Kausch, C. and Gassmann, O. (2005). Managing the risk of customer integration, *European Management Journal,* **23**(2), 203–213.

Enkel, E., Gassmann, O. and Chesbrough, H. (2009). Open R&D and open innovation: Exploring the phenomenon, *R&D Management,* **39**(4), 311–316.

Eriksson, P.E. (2008). Achieving suitable coopetition in buyer–supplier relationships: The case of Astra-Zeneca, *Journal of Business to Business Marketing,* **15**(4), 425–454.

Eriksson, P.E. and Nilsson, T. (2008). Partnering the construction of a Swedish pharmaceutical plant: Case study, *Journal of Management in Engineering,* **24**(4), 227–233.

Eriksson, P.E. and Pesämaa, O. (2007). Modelling procurement effects on cooperation, *Construction Management and Economics,* **25**(8), 893–901.

Eriksson, P.E., Dickinson, M. and Khalfan, M. (2007). The influence of partnering and procurement on subcontractor involvement and innovation, *Facilities*, **25**(5/6), 203–214.

Errasti, A., Beach, R., Oduoza, C. and Apaolaza, U. (2009). Close coupling value chain functions to improve subcontractor manufacturing performance, *International Journal of Project Management*, **27**(3), 261–269.

Ford, D. (2004). Guest Editorial: The IMP group and international Marketing, *International Marketing Review*, **21**(2), 139–141.

Frazier, W.C., Scott, S. and Beach, T. (1996). Project team starts up Rainy River's Recycled Pulp Plant at Kenora, Ont, *Pulp and Paper*, **70**(11), 69–73.

Gencturk, E. and Aulakh, P. (1995). The use of process and output controls in foreign markets, *Journal of International Business Studies*, **26**(4), 755–786.

Ghoshal, S. and Moran, P. (1996). Bad for practice: A critique of the transaction cost theory, *Academy of Management Review*, **21**(1), 13–47.

Gibbert, M., Ruigrok, W. and Wicki, B. (2008). What passes as a rigorous case study? *Strategic Management Journal*, **29**(13), 1465–1474.

Gil, N., Beckman, S. and Tommelein, I. (2008). Upstream problem solving under uncertainty and ambiguity: Evidence from airport expansion project, *IEEE Transactions on Engineering Management*, **55**(3), 508–522.

Grandori, A. (1997). An organizational assessment of interfirm coordination modes, *Organization Studies*, **18**(6), 897–925.

Gunasekaran, A. (1998). Concurrent engineering: A competitive strategy for process industries, *The Journal of the Operational Research Society*, **49**(7), 758–765.

Hagen, J. and Choe, S. (1998). Trust in Japanese interfirm relations: Institutional sanctions matter, *Academy of Management Review*, **23**(3), 473–490.

Heide, J.B. and John, G. (1990). Alliances in industrial purchasing: The determinants of joint action in buyer–supplier relationships, *Journal of Marketing Research*, **27**(1), 24–36.

Heide, J.B. and John, G. (1992). Do norms matter in marketing relationships? *Journal of Marketing*, **56**(1), 32–44.

Hennart, J.-F. (1993). Explaining the swollen middle: Why most transactions are a mix of market and hierarchy, *Organization Science,* 4(4), 529–547.

Hoetker, G. (2005). How much you know versus how well I know you: Selecting a supplier for a technically innovative component, *Strategic Management Journal,* 26(1), 75–96.

Hutcheson, P., Pearson, A. and Ball, D. (1995). Innovation in process plant: A case study of ethylene, *Journal of Product Innovation Management,* 12(5), 415–430.

Jalkala, A., Cova, B., Salle, R. and Salminen, R. (2009). Changing project business orientations: Toward a new logic of project marketing, *European Management Journal,* in press.

Jaspers, F. and van den Ende, J. (2006). The organizational form of vertical relationships: dimensions of integration, *Industrial Marketing Management,* 35(7), 819–828.

Joshi, A. and Stump, R. (1999). The contingent effect of specific asset investments on joint action in manufacturer–supplier relationships: an empirical test of the moderating role of reciprocal asset investments, uncertainty, and trust, *Journal of the Academy of Marketing Science,* 27(3), 291–305.

Kadefors, A. (2005). Fairness in interorganizational project relations: Norms and strategies, *Construction Management and Economics,* 23(8), 871–878.

Kadefors, A. and Badenfelt, U. (2009). The roles and risks of incentives in construction projects. *International Journal of Project Organisation and Management,* 1(3), 268–284.

Kadefors, A., Björlingson, E. and Karlsson, A. (2007). Procuring service innovations: Contractor selection for partnering projects, *International Journal of Project Management,* 25, 375–385.

Khurana, A. and Rosenthal, S.R. (1997). Integrating the fuzzy front end of new product development, *Sloan Management Review,* 38(2), 103–120.

Korczynski, M. (1996). The low-trust route to economic development: Inter-firm relations in the UK engineering construction industry in the 1980s and 1990s, *Journal of Management Studies,* 33(6), 787–808.

Kreiner, K. and Schultz, M. (1993). Informal collaborations in R&D: The formation of networks across organizations, *Organization Studies,* 14(2), 189–209.

Lager, T. (2010). *Managing Process Innovation: A Strategic Perspective on Process Innovation and Technology Management in the Process Industries,* Imperial College Press, London.

Lager, T. and Frishammar, J. (2010). Equipment supplier/user collaboration in the process industries: In search of enhanced operating performance, *Journal of Manufacturing Technology Management,* forthcoming.

Lager, T. and Hörte, S.-Å. (2005). Success factors for the development of process technology in process industry, Part 2: A ranking of success factors on an operational level and a dynamic model for company implementation, *International Journal Process Management and Benchmarking,* 1(1), 104–126.

Langner, B. and Seidel, V. (2009). Collaborative concept development using supplier competitions: Insights from the automotive industry, *Journal of Engineering and Technology Management,* 26(1–2), 1–14.

Lazzarotti, V. and Manzini, R. (2009). Different modes of open innovation: A theoretical framework and an empirical study, *International Journal of Innovation Management,* 13(4), 615–636.

Lee, A.H.I., Wang, W.-M. and Lin, T.-Y. (2010). An evaluation framework for technology transfer of new equipment in high technology industry, *Technological Forecasting and Social Change,* 77(1), 135–150.

Lichtenthaler, U. (2008). Open innovation in practice: An analysis of strategic approaches to technology transactions, *IEEE Transactions on Engineering Management,* 55(1), 48–157.

Ling, F.Y. (2003). Managing the implementation of construction innovations, *Construction Management and Economics,* 21(6), 635–649.

Macneil, I. (1978). Contracts: Adjustments of long-term economic relations under classical, neoclassical and relational contract law, *Northwestern University Law Review,* 72(6), 854–905.

Manley, K. (2008). Implementation of innovation by manufacturers subcontracting to construction projects, *Engineering Construction and Architectural Management,* 15(3), 230–245.

Miles, M. and Huberman, M. (1994). *Qualitative Data Analysis,* Sage Publications, London.

Montoya-Weiss, M.M. and O'Driscoll, T.M. (2000). From experience: Applying performance support technology in the fuzzy front end, *The Journal of Product Innovation Management,* 17(2), 143–161.

Olsen, B., Haugland, S., Karlsen, E. and Husoy, G. (2005). Governance of complex procurements in the oil and gas industry, *Journal of Purchasing and Supply Management*, **11**(1), 1–13.

Ouchi, W. (1979). A conceptual framework for the design of organizational control mechanisms, *Management Science*, **25**(9), 833–848.

Palaneeswaran, E., Kumaraswamy, M., Rahman, M. and Ng, T. (2003). Curing congenital construction industry disorders through relationally integrated supply chains, *Building and Environment*, **38**(4), 571–582.

Parker, D., Zsidisin, G. and Ragatz, G. (2008). Timing and extent of supplier integration in new product development: A contingency approach, *Journal of Supply Chain Management*, **44**(1), 71–83.

Parkhe, A. (1998). Building trust in international alliances, *Journal of World Business*, **33**(4), 417–438.

Petersen, K., Handfield, R. and Ragatz, G. (2005). Supplier integration into new product development: Coordination product, process and supply chain design, *Journal of Operations Management*, **23**(3–4), 371–388.

Pietroforte, R. (1997). Communication and governance in the building process, *Construction Management and Economics*, **15**(1), 71–82.

Pratt, M. (2009). For the lack of a boilerplate: Tips on writing up (and reviewing) qualitative research, *Academy of Management Journal*, **52**(5), 856–862.

Rahman, M. and Kumaraswamy, M. (2004). Potential for implementing relational contracting and joint risk management, *Journal of Management in Engineering*, **20**(4), 178–189.

Ro, Y., Liker, J. and Fixson, S. (2008). Evolving models of supplier involvement in design: The deterioration of the Japanese model in US auto, *IEEE Transactions on Engineering Management*, **55**(2), 359–377.

Roseira, C., Brito, C. and Henneberg, S. (2010). Managing interdependencies in supplier networks. *Industrial Marketing Management*, **39**(6), 925–935.

Rutten, M., Dorée, A. and Halman, J. (2009). Innovation and interorganizational cooperation: A synthesis of literature, *Construction Innovation*, **9**(3), 285–297.

Ruuska, I., Artto, K., Aaltonen, K. and Lehtonen, P. (2009). Dimensions of distance in a project network: Exploring Olkiluoto 3 Nuclear Power Plant Project, *International Journal of Project Management*, **27**(2), 142–153.

Saad, M., Jones, M. and James, P. (2002). A review of the progress towards the adoption of supply chain management (SCM) relationships in construction, *European Journal of Purchasing and Supply Management,* **8**(3), 173–183.

Shoesmith, D. (1996). A study of the management and procurement of building services work, *Construction Management and Economics,* **14**(2), 93–101.

Slowinski, G., Hummel, E. and Kumpf, R.J. (2006). Protecting know-how and trade secrets in collaborative R&D relationships, *Research Technology Management,* **49**(4), 30–38.

Song, L., Mohamed, Y. and AbouRizk, S. (2009). Early contractor involvement in design and its impact on construction schedule performance, *Journal of Management in Engineering,* **25**(1), 12–20.

Spekman, R. and Carraway, R. (2006). Making the transition to collaborative buyer–seller relationships: An emerging framework, *Industrial Marketing Management,* **35**(1), 10–19.

Stump, R. and Heide, J.B. (1996). Controlling supplier opportunism in industrial relationships, *Journal of Marketing Research,* **33**(4), 431–441.

Tam, C.M. (2000). Design and build on a complicated redevelopment project in Hong Kong: The Happy Valley Racecourse redevelopment, *International Journal of Project Management,* **18**(2), 125–129.

van de Vrande, V., Lemmens, C. and Vanhaverbeke, W. (2006). Choosing governance modes for external technology sourcing, *R&D Management,* **36**(3), 347–362.

von Hippel, E. (2005). *Democratizing Innovation,* MIT Press, Cambridge, MA.

Wathne, K. and Heide, J.B. (2000). Opportunism in interfirm relationships: Forms, outcomes, and solutions, *Journal of Marketing,* **64**(4), 36–51.

Wathne, K. and Heide, J.B. (2004). Relationship governance in a supply chain network, *Journal of Marketing,* **68**(1), 73–89.

Woolthuis, R., Hillebrand, B. and Nooteboom, B. (2005). Trust, contract and relationship development, *Organization Studies,* **26**(6), 813–840.

Yin, R. (2003). *Case Study Research, Design and Methods,* Sage Publications, London.

Chapter 13

Organising Innovation Processes With Suppliers*

Tina B. Aune
Trondheim Business School, HiST, Norway and
Department of Industrial Economics and Technology Management,
Norwegian University of Science and Technology, Norway

Espen Gressetvold [†]
Trondheim Business School, HiST, Norway

Introduction

Globalisation and increased speed in business intensify competition and most companies need to innovate continuously to ensure long-term competitiveness. To achieve this, suppliers play an important role in many companies' innovation processes. This phenomenon has won growing recognition both among companies and among academics (e.g. Clark and Fujimoto, 1991; Kamath and Liker, 1994; Dyer, 1996; Hoegl and Wagner, 2005).

Suppliers are important in innovation processes because of the extensive knowledge and capabilities they possess in relation to a company's products and technologies (Gadde and Håkansson, 2001;

---

*The chapter is a revised version of the article 'Supplier Involvement in Innovation Processes: A Taxonomy', by Tina B. Aune and Espen Gressetvold, presented in a Special Issue on Open Innovation and the Integration of Suppliers, in the *International Journal of Innovation Management*, 2011, 15(1), 121–143.
[†]Corresponding author

Sobrero and Roberts, 2001). Supplier involvement offers advantages for the product or process innovation itself, such as reductions in the time-to-market, reductions in development costs and quality improvements (Clark and Fujimoto, 1991; Ragatz *et al.*, 1997). It also offers advantages for the company, such as knowledge development, joint learning (Teece, 1992; Nonaka and Takeuchi, 1995; Kash and Auger, 2005), a higher level of specialisation and a focus on the company's own core competences (Hamel and Prahalad, 1994). Recognition of the importance of suppliers in innovation processes fits well with the concept of 'open innovation', advocated notably by Chesbrough (Chesbrough, 2003; Chesbrough and Garman, 2009) and adopted by others (e.g. Teece, 2007; Lafley and Charan, 2008; Bergman *et al.*, 2009).

The purpose of the chapter is to classify and analyse different ways of organising innovation processes with suppliers. Empirically, this purpose is motivated by a study of innovation processes conducted by the paper mill Norske Skog Skogn (NSS) with its supplier ABB, and third parties. Over a period of more than 30 years, ABB has been involved in a number of technological innovations aimed at improving NSS's paper machines, leading to the development of a comprehensive customer–supplier relation. Although the innovation processes have been conducted using the same customer–supplier relation, the variation in the ways that they are organised is striking.

From the perspective of the literature, the purpose is motivated by work that calls for variety in ways of organising innovation processes with suppliers (e.g. Clark and Fujimoto, 1991; van Echtelt *et al.*, 2008; Wynstra *et al.*, 2003). Inter-organisational theory provides different models or taxonomies for the management of supplier relations both from a dyadic perspective (Kamath and Liker, 1994; Araujo *et al.*, 1999; Gadde and Snehota, 2000; Wynstra and ten Pierick, 2000) and from a network perspective (Harland *et al.*, 2001). These models focus on different supplier interfaces; however, less emphasis has been placed on the organisation of a single innovation process.

Inspired by both the empirical data and the literature, the chapter proposes a taxonomy that addresses the variations in supplier involvement in innovation processes by exploring the degree of customer–supplier cooperation and the scope of company involvement on the supply side. This taxonomy introduces a novel way of classifying and analysing the organisation of such complex processes, and, even more importantly, of questioning their organisation.

The chapter is structured as follows. First, a literature review and the taxonomy are presented. This is followed by the method, empirical data and analysis. A concluding section discusses the results of the study and derives some implications for theory and for managers.

Literature Review and Taxonomy

The taxonomy presented in this section considers the customer–supplier relationship and introduces four ways to organise innovation processes with suppliers (see Fig. 1). The taxonomy has two dimensions: the *degree of cooperation between the customer and the supplier* throughout the innovation process, and the *scope of company involvement on the supply side* in this process.

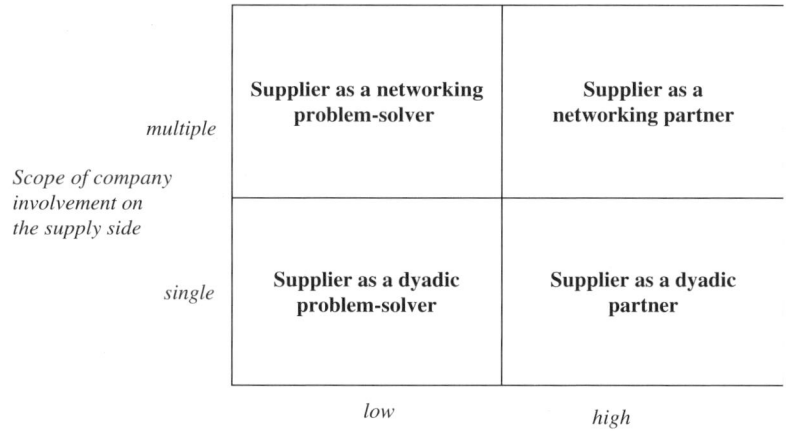

Fig. 1. A Taxonomy for Organising Innovation Processes with Suppliers.

In the following, these two dimensions are discussed in more depth, starting with the *degree of cooperation*. In the organisation of innovation processes with suppliers, this dimension is regarded as highly relevant among practitioners and researchers (e.g. Bidault *et al.*, 1998). Some studies that focus on the degree of cooperation with suppliers make use of concepts such as arm's length versus partner (Dwyer *et al.*, 1987), a low degree versus a high degree of concurrent involvement (Alderman *et al.*, 2001) or use of a short-term approach versus the development of a long-term relationship (Gadde and Snehota, 2000). Whenever the customer, as part of an innovation process, engages a supplier that develops a solution with little or no dialogue, or there exist clear-cut specifications that make contact between the two superfluous, the degree of cooperation is regarded as low. Accordingly, the supplier is referred to as a *problem-solver* in relation to this innovation process. If, however, the customer and the supplier cooperate extensively on central parts of or throughout the whole innovation process, the degree of cooperation is regarded as high. Accordingly, the supplier is referred to as a *partner* in relation to this innovation process.

Naturally, there are borderline cases, i.e. innovation processes where it is difficult to determine whether the degree of cooperation should be regarded as low or high. After all, the continuous scale between the low and high degrees of cooperation is divided into two for classification purposes. One operational way to classify the degree of cooperation between two parties that conduct an innovation process is to divide that process into a number of stages from problem definition to deployment, and measure the intensity of cooperation in each stage along a continuum ranging from no interactive relationship to joint performance of activities (Biemans, 1991). However, the question of whether the overall degree of cooperation between two companies is low or high is still a matter of judgement. More important than identifying an exact dividing line between the two is the recognition of the effects that follow when one seeks to increase the degree of cooperation with a supplier, e.g. by encouraging joint learning, or decreasing it, e.g. by introducing a clear division of work.

The other dimension, the *scope of the company's involvement on the supply side* in the innovation process, is also a much discussed subject in innovation studies (e.g. DeBresson and Amesse, 1991; Johnsen, 2009). Much attention has been focused on the use of a dyadic versus a multilateral or network approach to suppliers in innovation processes (e.g. Håkansson and Eriksson, 1993; Richardson, 1993; Takeishi, 2001; Wynstra *et al.*, 2001; Faems *et al.*, 2005; O'Sullivan, 2006). When the customer involves a single supplier as part of an innovation process, i.e. the scope of the innovation process is regarded as restricted to these two parties, the supplier relation is referred to as *dyadic*. If, however, the customer involves multiple companies on the supply side, the supplier that is part of the customer–supplier relationship is referred to as *networking*.

Again, there are borderline cases, such as innovation processes where it is difficult to determine whether an indirect counterpart should be regarded as part of this process. Such difficulties may be due to companies' different perceptions regarding the surrounding business network (Holmen and Pedersen, 2003). For example, a company may lack insight into whether the counterpart involves third parties, or it can be difficult to determine which companies ought to be regarded as participating in the innovation process and which ones ought to be disregarded. Again, more important than searching for the exact dividing line between the two is the recognition of the effects that follow from increasing or reducing the number of companies involved in an innovation process.

The taxonomy introduces four approaches for organising innovation processes with suppliers. In the following, these are discussed in more detail.

Supplier as a dyadic problem-solver

This approach refers to an innovation process regarded to involve a *single* supplier and where the degree of cooperation between the customer and the supplier in this process is regarded as *low*.

This approach has received considerable attention within the field of management. This way of organising an innovation process builds on the principles of dealing with a direct supplier on an individual basis and of achieving a clear-cut division of work (Ellram and

Hendrick, 1995). This approach resembles a discrete transaction, limited to the exchange of a product for financial resources (Dwyer *et al.*, 1987). Such an exchange is characterised by a short time perspective, limited or no exchange of knowledge and price as a main concern. A benefit primarily associated with this approach is related to efficiency over a short-term perspective, i.e. a solution that may require fewer resources (Sobrero and Roberts, 2001).

The involvement of a supplier as a dyadic problem-solver in the innovation process entails certain requirements for the product at hand. The first alternative is that it should be easy to partition and distribute the work between the two parties. This is also referred to as task partitioning, a technique of partitioning a piece of work into a number of tasks and subtasks (von Hippel, 1990; Holmen and Kristensen, 1998). A second alternative is that the innovation process is in the main handed over to the supplier, leaving no complex interfaces between the two (Clark, 1989).

The customer may initiate the innovation process by communicating its needs to the supplier, e.g. in the form of functional requirements or more precise product specifications (Araujo *et al.*, 1999). However, the supplier may also initiate the process by developing a solution prior to making contact with the customer. By doing so, the supplier takes on a highly independent role in the development process (Lakemond *et al.*, 2006).

Supplier as a dyadic partner

This approach also refers to an innovation process regarded as involving a *single* supplier; however, this time the degree of cooperation between the customer and the supplier in this process is regarded as *high*.

This approach is also quite common, as it builds on the widely used principle of dealing with suppliers directly and on an individual basis in the organisation of innovation processes (Bidault *et al.*, 1998). As part of this approach, the customer and the supplier cooperate extensively throughout the innovation process, which may lead to considerable learning for the two parties (Araujo *et al.*, 1999). At the same time, such cooperation is a resource-demanding process, which emphasises the need for careful consideration of the costs and benefits associated with it.

Increased product complexity strengthens the need to cooperate with suppliers (Kamath and Liker, 1994; Alderman *et al.*, 2001). Furthermore, if both the customer and the supplier possess knowledge that is needed in the innovation process, and this knowledge is of a tacit and 'sticky' nature, this may call for a high degree of cooperation (von Hippel, 1994; Sobrero and Roberts, 2001).

The cooperation between the customer and the supplier may take place through an integrated, systematic way of working together, or be based on a more *ad hoc* approach, where contact is made as problems occur (Lakemond *et al.*, 2006). Furthermore, there exist several methods and techniques to efficiently obtain a high degree of cooperation between the two throughout an innovation process, such as the use of guest engineers to enable the communication of complex, dynamic information directly with suppliers (Slack and Twigg, 1999) and ESI (Early Supplier Involvement), which includes co-design activities and joint concept development (Bidault *et al.*, 1998).

Supplier as a networking problem-solver

This approach refers to an innovation process in which the supplier is regarded as one of *multiple* companies participating in the process, and where the degree of cooperation between the customer and the supplier in this process is regarded as *low*.

Although not as widely studied as a dyadic approach, a network approach to organising innovation processes with suppliers is definitely gaining increased attention (e.g. Håkansson and Eriksson, 1993; Dyer, 1996; Dyer and Nobeoka, 2000; O'Sullivan, 2006). This strategy may be cost efficient in the sense that the customer may reap some benefits from the supplier's business network, while at the same time avoiding the costs of entering into a high degree of cooperation (Hallén *et al.*, 1991). The concept is also referred to as network delegation as opposed to network intervention (Johnsen and Ford, 2005).

This approach involves a network of companies in the innovation process, while at the same time there is a low degree of cooperation between the customer and the supplier. A study by Staudenmayer *et al.* (2005) suggests that modular products and industries require interaction with a web of partners, corresponding with the idea of open innovation (Chesbrough, 2003) and extensive research into industrial networks (e.g. Håkansson, 1987; Axelsson and Easton, 1992; Baraldi, 2009). Typically, products that are compound or entail several different technologies tend to involve a network of companies in their development, because of the need to supplement the in-house knowledge and capabilities of the company that develops them (Araujo *et al.*, 1999; Alderman *et al.*, 2001). At the same time, the low degree of cooperation with the supplier indicates that at least parts of this innovation process should be easy to partition and hand over to a supplier.

One way of organising such innovation processes is for the supplier to involve sub-suppliers that handle parts of the innovation. This way of organising an innovation process is in line with conventional methods within supply chains and supply networks, such as when a first-tier supplier teams up with second- or third-tier suppliers (Dyer, 1996). Furthermore, it follows the logic of specialisation and economies of scale (Teece, 1992). A different way of organising such an innovation process may require that the customer and the supplier, despite their low degree of cooperation, jointly cooperate with one or several third parties as part of this process.

Supplier as a networking partner

This approach also refers to an innovation process in which the supplier is regarded as one of *multiple* companies participating in the process; however, this time the degree of cooperation between the customer and the supplier in this process is regarded as *high*.

By cooperating closely with a supplier and at the same time involving a network of companies in the innovation process, the customer creates the possibility for the joint shaping and utilisation of knowledge, capabilities and ideas from a number of companies (Faems *et al.*, 2005). These ideas on how to shape innovation and solve technical challenges may even come from the network, rather than from individual companies (e.g., Powell *et al.*, 1996; Dooley and O'Sullivan, 2007; Huston Sakkab, 2006). However, organising an innovation process through the use of a network of companies has to be weighed against the costs, as the processes of networking may be resource demanding (Hallén *et al.*, 1991).

Like the foregoing approach, this one is typically well suited for innovation processes that include compound and complex products that require several technologies and a high degree of cooperation among several parties. Sometimes, such innovation processes are referred to as systemic as opposed to autonomous ones (Teece, 1992).

For the organisation of such complex innovation processes, a customer may encourage the companies on the supply side to cooperate with each other and openly share knowledge in the process of improving and innovating. Toyota has been identified as making use of such methods, creating a type of network that can be referred to as 'highly interconnected' and with 'multiple pathways' (Dyer and Nobeoka, 2000). By interacting directly with these companies during the innovation process, the customer can be said to make use of the technique of network intervention (Johnsen and Ford, 2005). On its own initiative, the customer may also involve one or several third parties in the innovation process, in this way turning the supplier into a networking company. Although the supplier has no direct relations with these third parties, they all become part of the network of companies that are involved in the innovation process. Such business networks consist of relationships that are connected, and that interact and mutually influence each other (Anderson *et al.*, 1994). It is not uncommon for a customer to organise an innovation process by acting as a channel for information itself, rather than facilitating the development of direct relationships between the suppliers or other companies in the innovation process (Wynstra *et al.*, 2001, 2003).

Methods

The empirical data underlying the chapter consist of a single case study centred on the involvement of ABB in four embedded innovation processes at NSS. Their customer–supplier relationship is the focal one of the study, where the unit of analysis is at the level of an individual innovation process.

Although the innovation processes are organised as projects, they are referred to as innovation processes. In line with the purpose of the chapter, this is done in order to direct primary attention towards the organisation of innovation on an inter-organisational level, rather than the challenges related to project management.

The research was carried out in the period 2006–2008, involving interviews with purchasers, engineers, project managers and maintenance managers. In total, 15 interviews were conducted: nine with NSS and six with ABB, all face to face, following a semi-structured interview guide.

Several guided tours of NSS's plant were arranged, which included inspection of some of the technical innovations in focus. The company provided technical and administrative documents on some of the innovation processes, in addition to other material, such as annual reports and detailed descriptions of the papermaking process.

Several visits were made to ABB's unit based in Trondheim, which is also NSS's main contact point. Whilst participating in innovation processes with NSS as the customer, this unit has involved several other ABB units, mainly located elsewhere in Norway or in other Nordic countries. Although ABB is a conglomerate with many locations in more than 100 countries, in this study it is regarded as one actor/company. This simplification seems reasonable, since ABB's Trondheim unit is NSS's main contact point, and has managed the innovation processes being considered. Furthermore, the purpose of this study is to elaborate on the organisation of innovation processes with suppliers, i.e., the focus is on the cooperation between NSS, ABB and third parties, and not on ABB's internal organisation across different units.

After 11 of the 15 interviews had been conducted, and subsequent to the collection of the secondary material, an initial version of the case description was developed. Following this, a workshop at NSS was arranged, involving three researchers and seven employees from NSS's maintenance and engineering departments. The taxonomy was recognised as relevant by participants from NSS, who commented that it appeared to be a useful tool for discussing the organisation of their company's innovation processes. It was also agreed that more interviews should be conducted to investigate topics that had emerged as important for this study, but had not yet been properly covered. These more targeted interviews proved to be essential for this case study, as they contributed knowledge that fitted well with some aspects of the taxonomy that had not been investigated in depth at that stage.

Case studies are:

> *empirical inquiries that investigate a contemporary phenomenon within its real life context, when the boundaries between the phenomenon and context are not clearly evident and in which multiple sources of evidence are used* (Yin, 1994, p.13).

This statement covers several important aspects characterising the empirical data in this study, as the innovation processes are contemporary, difficult to separate from other ongoing processes in NSS and ABB and were mapped through interviews, documents, presentations, discussions and observations.

The research process can be described as interactive, where the theoretical foundation and the research question are shaped, reformulated and refined throughout the collection of the empirical data. This process can therefore be said to draw on the principles of 'systematic combining' (Dubois and Gadde, 2002). Accordingly, the search for empirical data became more targeted as the taxonomy emerged.

Introduction to NSS and ABB

In this section NSS, ABB and their relationship are introduced, followed by a presentation of the papermaking process at NSS. In the following section, innovation processes involving the parties are presented and analysed.

NSS, ABB and their relationship

NSS was founded in 1962 and is one of 19 paper mills owned by the Norske Skog Group. The Norske Skog Group is headquartered in

Oslo, Norway, whereas NSS is located in Skogn, Norway, which is 600 km north of Oslo. NSS has played an important role in the creation of the Norske Skog Group, as the headquarters were located in Skogn from the time of establishment for more than three decades. Today, the Norske Skog Group controls paper mills on four continents, and its operating revenue in 2007 was approximately 3.6 billion euros, making it the world's second largest producer of newsprint. NSS is the second largest of these 19 paper mills, producing more than 600,000 tonnes of newsprint per year and employing some 515 people.

NSS produces newsprint using three machines: PM1, PM2 and PM3, built in 1966, 1967 and 1982 respectively. PM1 and PM2 are referred to as sister machines and share many technological similarities. However, each of them has been upgraded on an individual basis in order to meet specific requirements from customers, thus making them different in certain technical dimensions. As PM3 was built more than a decade after the other two, it differs substantially with respect to the technology used. It also produces about half of NSS's total output. More than 90% of the newsprint is exported to customers worldwide, predominantly to the UK and continental Europe from NSS's own port facilities. NSS's production is currently based on pulp from wood and recovered paper.

ABB is a global engineering company that operates in 100 countries and employs around 110,000 people; it had revenues of 18.6 billion euros in 2007. Its full name, Asea Brown Boveri, stems from the merger between Asea and Brown Boveri in 1988.

Both Asea and Brown Boveri were suppliers of NSS prior to their merger, and ever since the establishment of the paper mill in 1962. The formation of ABB strengthened its relationship with NSS, and a large number of innovation processes have been conducted in cooperation between the two companies. Through these innovation processes as well as other joint activities, ABB and NSS have developed a comprehensive and well-functioning business relationship with close personal contacts and a high degree of trust.

The papermaking process at NSS

The general papermaking process, used by NSS's three paper machines, PM1, PM2 and PM3, is shown in Fig. 2. Pulp enters the *headbox*, a chamber at the start of the paper machine that disperses the pulp and loads it onto a moving wire mesh where water is removed. The newly created paper, which contains 90% water, is then passed on to the *press section*, which removes most of the water. Next, the paper enters a *dryer section* where it is dried by steam-heated rollers. Then, the paper moves through a series of rollers in the *calender section* for further smoothing. Finally, the paper is wound onto a roll in the *reel-winding section* before it is placed in paper storage for final cutting and shipping.

Even though the basic structure of the three paper machines at NSS has remained unchanged since their establishment, the machines have all been substantially rebuilt and modernised over the years. This has led to considerable increases in productivity as well as improvements in paper quality. As part of this process, every year a team of managers and engineers suggests several improvements for the three paper machines, many of which involve ABB. NSS has always had extensive knowledge on the technical aspects of its paper machines in-house, but as part of NSS's strategy this knowledge is increasingly held by suppliers. For NSS, therefore, an important issue when making suggestions for improvements is deciding which tasks should be handled in-house and which should be handled by suppliers.

ABB installed most of the process control systems for the three paper machines. A process control system (see Fig. 2) monitors and controls many process variables such as pressure, flow, temperature and tank levels during pulp production, stock preparation, coating and applying additives. This system can be divided into three subsystems: DCS (the distributed control system), QCS (the quality control system) and Drives. DCS controls the flow of pulp and the variable speed drives and motor control centres. QCS provides measurement of all sheet parameters in order to maintain paper quality. The Drives subsystem refers to smaller motors involved in the papermaking process.

Presentation and Analysis of Four Innovation Processes

This section presents and analyses four innovation processes that involve NSS, ABB and third parties. These four processes cover each of the four cells in the taxonomy presented in Fig. 1.

Improvement of basis weight measurement modules

One of the four innovation processes included in this study is NSS's initiative to improve paper quality by reducing variances in thickness. NSS's customers require uniform paper, i.e. a constant weight per unit area. This requirement is handled by a basis weight measurement module, which uses sensors at the end of the papermaking process to adjust the flow of pulp in the headbox of the paper machine (see Fig. 2). This module is part of QCS, which was installed by ABB.

Although this module had been in operation for several years, NSS experienced occasional problems due to static electricity in this module on PM1. NSS believed that these problems were caused by

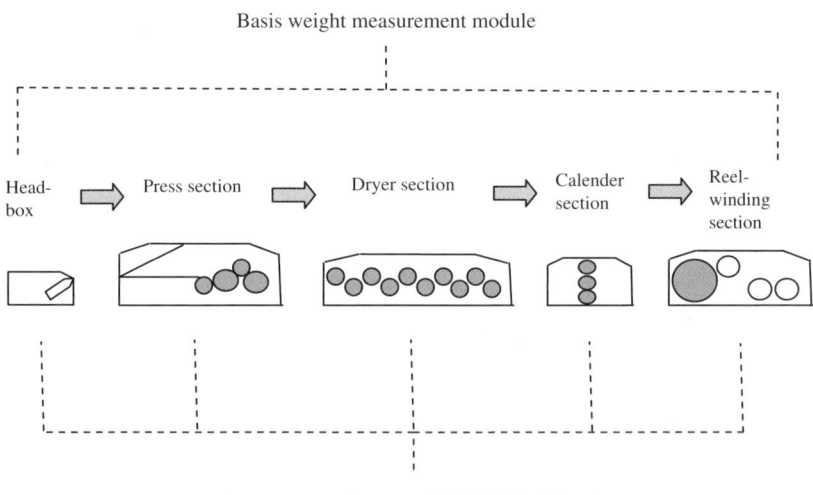

Fig. 2. The Papermaking Process.

temperature fluctuations and initially attempted to solve them internally but failed. NSS then consulted ABB. ABB had supplied similar solutions to several customers but it was not aware of the problems that NSS had experienced. ABB conducted investigations of similar equipment at a number of its other customers and found a solution that it believed would solve NSS's problems. The solution included a component that was part of ABB's stock but had not yet been applied to this type of equipment. Other than providing ABB with some information on its problems, NSS was not actively involved in this innovation process. ABB on its own adjusted the component for NSS's paper machine, installed it and tested it. Following a verification of this solution for PM1 it was also installed on PM2.

Analysis

This innovation process involves one supplier. This approach seems rational as ABB had supplied the original basis weight measurement module and by itself it was able to provide a well-functioning solution to NSS's problem. Furthermore, the level of cooperation between the parties can be regarded as low, as NSS restricted its participation to communication of the problem. Obviously, NSS must have had great trust in ABB when handing over a critical assignment in this way. Also, there were several factors that enabled ABB to solve NSS's problem with little contact between the companies, such as knowledge of the previous technological solution, knowledge of NSS's process control system in general and a comprehensive relationship between the two. Accordingly, in this innovation process ABB is a *dyadic problem-solver* for NSS.

Upgrading of process control system

After several years of operation, NSS wanted to upgrade the process control system on PM2. NSS expected this upgrade to result in improved paper quality as well as increased speed of the paper machine. Parts of the existing process control system had been installed by ABB, which had also been involved in other, minor improvements of the process control system on this paper machine. ABB was engaged in this innovation process, which would include upgrading of QCS, DCS and Drives. As this upgrade was limited to the process control system itself, NSS did not involve any companies other than ABB.

Throughout the early phases of the process, NSS and ABB agreed to implement an industrial IT system named 800xA, a solution that had already been developed by ABB and which allowed single-point data access for the entire paper machine. The 800xA system was considered cutting-edge by ABB and PM2 was the first paper machine in Norway where this technology was installed. Several technical challenges had to be dealt with, which necessitated considerable cooperation between the two companies. As employees at the two companies knew each other well from earlier innovation processes, the information sharing and joint development of technical specifications proceeded smoothly.

Prior to the installation of the upgraded equipment, the two parties jointly conducted a factory acceptance test at NSS's facilities. Throughout this test, the parties solved some minor, unexpected difficulties and made some adjustments. Following this, PM2 was shut down for 14 days while NSS and ABB worked together around the clock for the necessary reconstruction and installation.

Analysis

This innovation process also involves one supplier, which seems to follow as a consequence of its scope. However, for this innovation process, the level of cooperation between NSS and ABB can be regarded as high. First, they cooperated in determining the parts of the process control system that needed to be upgraded. Later, they cooperated extensively during the installation of 800xA as well as the factory acceptance test. In many ways, the nature of this innovation process can be said to have encouraged such a high degree of cooperation. Two complex technologies, the new process control system and the existing paper machine, needed to be combined; at the same time two companies, each with superior knowledge of one of these technologies, needed to synchronise their activities and resources. Accordingly, for this innovation process ABB is a *dyadic partner* with NSS.

Installation of new headbox

NSS initiated a process that included the installation of a new head-box (see Fig. 2) and corresponding process control system on PM1. This was motivated by problems in both paper quality and production stops. The problems with paper quality were due to variations in the basis weight profile. NSS's customers require paper with little variation. In addition, these variations interfered with the stability of the production process and could potentially lead to production stops. Since PM1 was built in 1966, NSS had increased the speed of this paper machine, making it even more sensitive to such variations.

The headbox receives signals from QCS in order to adjust the distribution of the pulp that enters the papermaking process. The headbox had been supplied by Metso, a world-leading maker of paper machines with headquarters in Finland. This company had also supplied all three paper machines at NSS, and NSS regards its relationship with this company as even more comprehensive than the one it has with ABB. ABB had supplied the existing process control system for feeding the pulp into the headbox along with the connected QCS system.

NSS decided to involve ABB and Metso in this innovation process. Although NSS acted as the project manager, it was of the opinion that the solutions to the technological challenges were likely to be found through cooperation between ABB and Metso. Therefore, from the initiation of this innovation process NSS encouraged a high degree of cooperation between these two companies. NSS knew that ABB and Metso would be able to cooperate efficiently as they had installed the existing technologies at NSS that would now be replaced, and had worked together in relation to several other innovations.

Metso replaced the headbox and carried out other mechanical changes while ABB re-programmed the process control system. This required extensive cooperation between the two suppliers including joint testing. These parts of the process required a great deal of open-ness, which was challenging because ABB and Metso are competitors in some areas. Most of the technical challenges were solved between ABB and Metso, and NSS did not cooperate closely with either of them throughout this innovation process.

Analysis

This innovation process involved NSS, ABB and Metso, which, given the technical challenges, seems natural. Right from the initiation of the process, NSS communicated its needs to ABB and Metso, leaving the two of them to cooperate throughout the development of the techni-cal solution. NSS can be said to have used network delegation as a technique to organise the process in a way that required a low degree of cooperation with ABB. Obviously the technical aspects concerning this innovation did not require the two to cooperate closely through-out the development. In addition, efficient delegation by NSS was likely to be facilitated by the high degree of trust it has in ABB through their well-developed relationship. In addition, ABB and Metso held considerable insight into the existing technologies at NSS, reducing their need to cooperate with this company. Accordingly, in this innovation process ABB is a *networking problem-solver* for NSS.

Upgrading of PM1

After several years of operation, NSS decided to upgrade PM1 (this was some years before the installation of the new headbox at PM1 as presented earlier). This upgrade was motivated by a desire to improve paper quality and to increase productivity, and included the replace-ment of both the process control system and some mechanical parts. NSS was of the opinion that the existing process control system lacked a well-defined path for further upgrades and it therefore wanted to replace the system altogether. This system had been installed by two companies, one of which was Brown Boveri, i.e. it had been installed at NSS prior to the merger between Asea and Brown Boveri to form ABB in 1988.

To minimise the number of suppliers, NSS asked ABB to coordinate delivery of the three parts of the new process control system that would be installed: QCS, DCS and Drives. However, even though Brown Boveri had installed the parts of the existing process control system at NSS, ABB had limited knowledge of the system because of strategic decisions taken several years before. Following the merger between Asea and Brown Boveri, the newly created company, ABB, chose to build further on Asea's system rather than on Brown Boveri's within this field. As a consequence, when NSS wanted to replace its process control system, ABB had limited knowledge of the existing system that had been installed by Brown Boveri. Therefore, ABB and NSS decided that they had to cooperate extensively on the specifications in the early stages of this innovation process. In addition, the two parties cooperated on the mapping of the process control system, which included many drives, signals and valves.

Also at this time, NSS asked Metso to upgrade the mechanical components. In the early phases of this innovation process, ABB and Metso cooperated in order to solve specific challenges related to the interface between the process control system and these mechanical parts. NSS saw the necessity of this cooperation, and encouraged it.

NSS regarded this innovation process as technically challenging, requiring a high degree of cooperation among the three companies (NSS, ABB and Metso). Such cooperation took place during the installation of SymZS, a zone-controlled roll in the press section of the paper machine (see Fig. 2). SymZS, delivered by Metso, removes water from the paper through a dewatering process that applies an even distribution of loads. ABB developed and installed a communication link between SymZS and the systems, DCS and QCS. NSS, ABB and Metso all cooperated in order to adapt SymZS for the press section of the paper machine, which included developing mechanical solutions to adjacent parts of the paper machine.

During the implementation phase, all three companies — NSS, ABB and Metso — were involved in the factory acceptance test to ensure that the new system performed satisfactorily. Following the implementation, the speed of PM1 was increased by 200 metres/minute, representing a substantial productivity increase.

Analysis

This innovation process also involves NSS and the two suppliers, ABB and Metso. ABB cooperated with both NSS and Metso throughout the development and implementation of the process control system that was installed on PM1. SymZS is one of several challenging elements that required ABB to work with NSS and Metso. Again, NSS took a leading role through encouraging ABB and Metso to cooperate on these technical challenges. With regard to NSS and ABB, their degree of cooperation for this innovation process can be regarded as high. One important reason for this was the innovation process itself, as ABB had limited knowledge of the existing process control system at NSS, and therefore needed to cooperate to learn more about how the new solution should be developed. Again, their well-established relationship seemed to provide a good foundation for this way of organising the innovation process, as the two parties were able to cooperate in an efficient way on several technical challenges. Accordingly, in this innovation process ABB is a *networking partner* with NSS.

Conclusions

The analysis shows the differences in both the scope of company involvement on the supply side and the degree of cooperation between two parties in the focal customer–supplier relation, covering all four cells in the taxonomy. Furthermore, the analysis indicates that the taxonomy is well suited to the classification of innovation processes that involve suppliers. The taxonomy covers only a fraction of the different ways that innovation processes can be organised with suppliers. However, by focusing on two dimensions that appear to be important from both a theoretical and an empirical point of view, it provides some guidelines on how to analyse and organise such complex processes.

Discussion

From the four innovation processes presented in the empirical data, it is evident that the observed variety may stem from a number of root causes, apart from chance. Three of them are presented here.

First, the nature of the innovation process itself is, of course, important with respect to its organisation. In terms of the empirical data, the innovation process where NSS involved ABB as a dyadic problem-solver seemed to be of a kind where the tasks were relatively easy to partition between the two parties without comprehensive cooperation or coordination. In contrast, the process where NSS involved ABB as a partner seemed to require considerable technological collaboration and joint solving of problems. In another innovation process, the technological challenges induced NSS to involve ABB as a networking supplier by involving Metso as well.

Second, the companies themselves played a pivotal role in the organisation of the innovation processes, as their capabilities and willingness may hinder or advance cooperation and the involvement of other parties. In the innovation processes that involved Metso, the technological challenges were given as one reason for this organisation. However, NSS itself also played a very active role, ensuring that ABB took on a networking role through encouraging it to cooperate with Metso in order to solve certain challenges.

Third, business relations are important when organising an innovation process, as they represent valuable assets that the companies have invested in and developed over time, and which can be utilised in a variety of ways. The customer–supplier relationship between NSS and ABB can be characterised as comprehensive, long-lasting and with a high degree of trust. It played an important role in facilitating the efficient use of ABB as a problem-solver in one of the innovation processes. In another process, it facilitated the involvement of ABB as a networking supplier where a majority of the technical challenges were solved through cooperation with Metso. In several ways, their well-developed customer–supplier relationship seems to enable and facilitate the efficient organisation of innovation processes together.

With regard to a different aspect, the presented taxonomy is not only relevant for how innovation processes are organised with suppliers. The scope may be broadened, and one way to do so is to focus on how to organise inter-organisational innovation processes in general. Another way is to go beyond innovation processes and focus on other kinds of projects or change processes that take place on an inter-organisational level. Examples might include inter-organisational IT projects or construction projects. As such, the taxonomy deals with the inter-organisational side of business strategy; it is centred on questions such as with whom to cooperate and to what degree.

Theoretical implications

The chapter considers the inter-organisational side of innovation processes and builds on the principles underlying a network approach to innovation (e.g. Anderson *et al.*, 1994; Powell *et al.*, 1996). A specific focus is on the contributions of the supply side in innovation (e.g. Dyer, 1996). Some of the principles of 'open innovation' are concerned with a broad-based external search for technology, knowledge and companies that may be of importance to a company and its innovation process (Chesbrough, 2003). Because the chapter addresses the organisation of specific relationships on the supply side for innovation processes, it can be seen as exploring one field of 'open innovation' in greater depth.

The chapter highlights the need for a variety of approaches to organising innovation processes with suppliers. This represents a step away from 'one best way', instead relying on mid-range theories for organising, or analysing such innovation processes, and should accordingly be captured by theory. The need for variety in organising innovation has also been recognised by others. Chesbrough and Teece (1996) introduced a two-by-two matrix that suggests that a company either brings in external parties or organises the process internally, depending on the type of innovation (autonomous versus systemic) and the need for capabilities (existing externally versus needing to be created) as the two dimensions. The taxonomy presented in the chapter focuses more strongly on business relations and introduces two dimensions that are central in the literature on business research in general and also in relation to suppliers and innovation processes. However, a contribution to the theory is made by combining the two, thus identifying and comparing four distinctly different approaches to organising innovation processes with suppliers.

Another implication concerns the variety of opportunities that is provided by a well-established relationship when organising innovation processes. Several studies indicate that there is a need for variety when organising innovation processes (Kamath and Liker, 1994; Araujo *et al.*, 1999; Wynstra and ten Pierick, 2000). However, and drawing on the empirical data of this study, a contribution is made to theory by indicating that this variety can and should take place even within one customer–supplier relation.

Furthermore, implications are identified for the development and use of business relations when organising innovation processes. Traditionally, a low degree of cooperation between a customer and a supplier is associated with the absence of a business relationship, i.e. pure transactions, whereas a high degree of cooperation is associated with the presence of a business relation. This study, however, focuses on the degree of cooperation for a specific innovation process, which can be regarded as an 'episode' occurring within the framework of the business relation, making the picture more complicated. Thus, if there is a low degree of cooperation between the two during an innovation process, i.e. the supplier acts as a problem-solver, this will be the exploitation of any well-established relationship (Sobrero and Roberts, 2001). If, however, there is no established relationship between the two at the time of the initiation of the innovation process, the low degree of cooperation will not contribute significantly to the development of one. In a similar vein, if there is a high degree of cooperation, this will lead to both the exploitation of and further development of a well-established relationship. If there is no established relationship when the innovation process is initiated, a high degree of cooperation will contribute to the development of such a relationship. The development of a relationship is both resource intensive and time consuming, and the innovation process may not benefit fully from it. Thus, a question for companies is whether or not to invest heavily in the development of a relationship if the purpose is to conduct one innovation process only. This addresses the underlying dilemma of aiming at either short-term or long-term benefits when involving suppliers in innovation processes (Wynstra *et al.*, 2001; Dunn and Young, 2004).

Managerial implications

For companies, the organisation of innovation processes with suppliers raises a number of questions. How can a company strengthen its employees' understanding of how the innovation process should be organised? Should the supplier act as a partner? How should the innovation process be organised in order to further the company's business network? The taxonomy may form a starting point when addressing these kinds of questions in planning and implementation, as well as when considering innovation processes. In the following, some ways to make use of the taxonomy are introduced.

A company may use the taxonomy when creating a shared understanding among its employees of how to organise an innovation process, such as the number of companies it seeks to involve and the degree of cooperation it seeks with each of them. This may in turn lead to employee behaviour that is more consistent throughout the innovation process. Employees with different backgrounds often see things in different ways. This may create several concurrent approaches for the degree of cooperation with the same counterpart. As an example, it may be helpful for an engineer and a purchaser to attempt to reach a common understanding with respect to the desired degree of cooperation for each of the suppliers that are involved in an innovation process. Similarly, the taxonomy may form a starting point for discussions among several companies in a search for a shared understanding, or agreement, on how to organise an innovation process.

Secondly, a company may use the taxonomy when searching for an appropriate way to organise an innovation process, for example by questioning the degree of cooperation it seeks with a counterpart as part of this process. In this way, if a company realises that a high degree of cooperation with a supplier may benefit an innovation process, it may seek to achieve this at an early stage by communicating clearly, sharing knowledge and creating an atmosphere of trust. In a similar vein, a company may consider whether to involve third parties in the innovation process, and if so, with which companies these third parties should hold direct and indirect relationships. As an example, an innovation process may benefit from a company establishing relationships and cooperating with its supplier's suppliers. Similarly, a company can often influence the degree of cooperation between its suppliers in relation to an innovation process.

Thirdly, a company may use the taxonomy to connect the two processes of developing innovations and developing its network of business relationships. This can be achieved by the company by defining the priorities for the business relationships it wants to develop. Then, using the taxonomy, the company can seek to organise its innovation processes in a way that supports the long-term, strategic process of developing its network of business relationships. This type of strategy may be relevant for a company that develops new products with suppliers, some of whom could potentially be involved in activities such as manufacturing components or after-sales services. A company may also use an innovation process actively to encourage the establishment of direct relations between several of its suppliers, for example as part of a strategy of building a supply network that functions more effectively over time.

References

Alderman, N., Thwaites, A. and Maffin, D. (2001). Project-level influences on the management and organisation of product development in engineering, *International Journal of Innovation Management*, **5**(4), 517–542.

Anderson, J.C., Håkansson, H. and Johanson, J. (1994). Dyadic business relationships within a business network context, *Journal of Marketing*, **58**(4), 1–15.

Araujo, L., Dubois, A. and Gadde, L.-E. (1999). Managing interfaces with suppliers, *Industrial Marketing Management*, **28**(5), 497–506.

Axelsson, B. and Easton, G. (1992). *Industrial Networks: A New View of Reality*, Routledge, London.

Baraldi, E. (2009). User-related complexity dimensions of complex products and systems (CoPS): A case of implementing an ERP system, *International Journal of Innovation Management*, **13**(1), 19–45.

Bergman, J., Jantunen, A. and Saksa, J.-M. (2009). Enabling open innovation processes through interactive methods: Scenarios and group decision support systems, *International Journal of Innovation Management*, **13**(1), 139–156.

Bidault, F., Despres, C. and Butler, C. (1998). The drivers of cooperation between buyers and suppliers for product innovation, *Research Policy*, **26**(7), 719–732.

Biemans, W.G. (1991). User and third-party involvement in developing medical equipment innovations, *Technovation*, **13**(3), 163–182.

Chesbrough, H.W. (2003). *Open Innovation: The New Imperative for Creating and Profiting from Technology*, Harvard Business School Press, Boston, MA.

Chesbrough, H.W. and Garman, A.R. (2009). How open innovation can help you cope in lean times, *Harvard Business Review*, **87**(12), 68–76.

Chesbrough, H.W. and Teece, D.J. (1996). When is virtual virtuous? Organizing for innovation, *Harvard Business Review*, **74**(1), 65–73.

Clark, K.B. (1989). Project scope and project performance: The effect of parts strategy and supplier involvement on product development, *Management Science*, **35**(10), 1247–1263.

Clark, K.B. and Fujimoto, T. (1991). *Product Development Performance*, Harvard Business School Press, Boston, MA.

DeBresson, C. and Amesse, F. (1991). Networks of innovators: A review and introduction to the issue, *Research Policy*, **20**(5), 363–379.

Dooley, L. and O'Sullivan, D. (2007). Managing within distributed innovation networks, *International Journal of Innovation Management*, (3), 397–416.

Dubois, A. and Gadde, L.-E. (2002). Systematic combining: An abductive approach to case research, *Journal of Business Research*, **55**(7), 553–560.

Dunn, S.C. and Young, R.R. (2004). Supplier assistance within supplier development initiatives, *The Journal of Supply Chain Management*, **40**(3), 19–29.

Dwyer, F.R., Schurr, P.H. and Oh, S. (1987). Developing buyer–seller relationships, *Journal of Marketing*, **51**(2), 11–27.

Dyer, J.H. (1996). Specialized supplier networks as a source of competitive advantage: Evidence from the auto industry, *Strategic Management Journal*, **17**(4), 271–291.

Dyer, J.H. and Nobeoka, K. (2000). Creating and managing a high-performance knowledge-sharing network: The Toyota case, *Strategic Management Journal*, **21**(3), 345–367.

Ellram, L.M. and Hendrick, T.E. (1995). Partnering characteristics: A dyadic perspective, *Journal of Business Logistics*, **16**(1), 41–64.

Faems, D., Van Looy, B. and Debackere, K. (2005). Interorganizational collaboration and innovation: Toward a portfolio approach, *Journal of Product Innovation Management*, **22**(3), 238–250.

Gadde, L.E. and Håkansson, H. (2001). *Supply Network Strategies*, John Wiley & Sons, Chichester.

Gadde, L.E. and Snehota, I. (2000). Making the most of supplier relationships, *Industrial Marketing Management*, **29**(4), 305–316.

Håkansson, H. (ed.) (1987). *Industrial Technological Development: A Network Approach*, Croom Helm, London.

Håkansson, H. and Eriksson, A.K. (1993). Getting innovations out of supplier networks, *Journal of Business-to-Business Marketing*, **1**(3), 3–34.

Hallén, L., Johanson, J. and Seyed-Mohamed, N. (1991). Interfirm adaptation in business relationships, *Journal of Marketing*, **55**(2), 29–37.

Hamel, G. and Prahalad, C.K. (1994). *Competing for the Future*, Harvard Business School Press, Boston, MA.

Harland, C.M., Lamming, R.C., Jurong, Z. and Johnsen, T.E. (2001). A taxonomy of supply networks, *Journal of Supply Chain Management*, **37**(4), 21–27.

Hoegl, M. and Wagner, S.M. (2005). Buyer–supplier collaboration in product development projects, *Journal of Management*, **31**, 530–548.

Holmen, E. and Kristensen, P.S. (1998). Supplier roles in product development: Interaction versus task partitioning, *European Journal of Purchasing and Supply Management*, **4**(2/3), 185–193.

Holmen, E. and Pedersen, A.C. (2003). Strategizing through analyzing and influencing the network horizon, *Industrial Marketing Management*, **32**(5), 409–418.

Huston, L. and Sakkab, N. (2006). Connect and develop, *Harvard Business Review*, **84**(3), 58–66.

Johnsen, T.E. (2009). Supplier involvement in new product development and innovation: Taking stock and looking to the future, *Journal of Purchasing and Supply Management*, **15**(3), 87–197.

Johnsen, T.E. and Ford, D. (2005). At the receiving end of supply network intervention: The view from an automotive first tier supplier, *Journal of Purchasing and Supply Management*, **11**(4), 183–192.

Kamath, R.R. and Liker, J.K. (1994). A second look at Japanese product development, *Harvard Business Review*, **72**(6), 154–170.

Kash, D.E. and Auger, R.N. (2005). From a few craftsmen to an international network of alliances: Bosch diesel fuel injection systems, *International Journal of Innovation Management*, **9**(1), 19–45.

Lafley, A.G. and Charan, R. (2008). *The Game Changer: How You Can Drive Revenue and Profit Growth With Innovation*, Crown Business, New York.

Lakemond, N., Berggren, C. and van Weele, A. (2006). Coordinating supplier involvement in product development projects: A differentiated coordination typology, *R&D Management*, **36**(1), 55–66.

Nonaka, I. and Takeuchi, H. (1995). *The Knowledge-Creating Company*, Oxford University Press, New York.

O'Sullivan, A. (2006). Why tense, unstable, and diverse relations are inherent in co-designing with suppliers: An aerospace case study, *Industrial and Corporate Change*, **15**(2), 221–250.

Powell, W.W., Koput, K.W. and Smith-Doerr, L. (1996). Interorganizational collaboration and the locus of innovation: Networks of learning in biotechnology, *Administrative Science Quarterly*, **41**(1), 116–145.

Ragatz, G.L., Handfield, R.B. and Scannell, T.V. (1997). Success factors for integrating suppliers into new product development, *Journal of Product Innovation Management*, **14**(3), 190–202.

Richardson, J. (1993). Parallel sourcing and supplier performance in the Japanese automobile industry, *Strategic Management Journal*, **14**(5), 339–350.

Slack, N. and Twigg, D. (1999). The organisation of external resources through guest engineers, *International Journal of Innovation Management*, **3**(1), 27–62.

Sobrero, M. and Roberts, E.B. (2001). The trade-off between efficiency and learning in interorganizational relationships for product development, *Management Science*, **47**(4), 493–511.

Staudenmayer, N., Tripsas, M. and Tucci, C.L. (2005). Interfirm modularity and its implications for NPD, *Journal of Product Innovation Management*, **22**(4), 303–321.

Takeishi, A. (2001). Bridging inter- and intra-firm boundaries: Management of supplier involvement in automobile product development, *Strategic Management Journal*, **22**(5), 403–433.

Teece, D.J. (1992). Competition, cooperation, and innovation: Organizational arrangements for regimes of rapid technological progress, *Journal of Economic Behavior and Organization*, **18**(1), 1–25.

Teece, D.J. (2007). Explicating dynamic capabilities: The nature and microfoundations of (sustainable) enterprise performance, *Strategic Management Journal*, **28**(13), 1319–1350.

van Echtelt, F.E.A., Wynstra, F., van Weele, A.J. and Duysters, G. (2008). Managing supplier involvement in new product development: A multiple-case study, *Journal of Product Innovation Management*, **25**(2), 180–201.

von Hippel, E. (1990). Task partitioning: An innovation process variable, *Research Policy*, **19**(5), 407–418.

von Hippel, E. (1994). 'Sticky information' and the locus of problem solving: Implications for innovation, *Management Science*, **40**(4), 429–439.

Wynstra, F. and ten Pierick, E. (2000). Managing supplier involvement in new product development: A portfolio approach, *European Journal of Purchasing and Supply Management*, **6**(1), 49–57.

Wynstra, F., van Weele, A. and Weggemann, M. (2001). Managing supplier involvement in product development: Three critical issues, *European Management Journal*, **19**(2), 157–167.

Wynstra, F., Weggemann, M. and van Weele, A. (2003). Exploring purchasing integration in product development, *Industrial Marketing Management*, **32**(1), 69–83.

Yin, R.K. (1994). *Case Study Research: Design and Methods*, 2nd edn, Sage Publications, London.

Chapter 14

Managing the Fuzzy Front End: Intra-Firm Versus Inter-Firm Networks

Jacob Høj Jørgensen*, Erik Stavnsager Rasmussen,
and René Chester Goduscheit Bergenholtz
Department of Marketing & Management
University of Southern Denmark, Denmark

Carsten Bergenholtz
Department of Business Administration
Aarthus University, Denmark

Introduction

The innovation process is typically divided into a series of succeeding stages and the fuzzy front end (FFE) is the first stage. A wide stream of research applies an intra-firm paradigm and focuses on how a manufacturer can control and influence the environment (Cooper, 2005; Cooper and Kleinschmidt, 1987). In contrast to this approach, the paradigm of open innovation and inter-firm collaboration has become increasingly influential over the last decade (Chesbrough, 2003). In this paradigm, the locus of innovation is considered to be located in the interstices between firms (Powell *et al.*, 1996). Companies can engage in such inter-firm collaborations for many different activities, e.g. innovation, logistics, marketing and sales (Bergenholtz and Waldstrøm, 2011; Moller and Halinen, 1999; Hagedoorn, 2002; Nooteboom, 2004). The focus of this paper is on inter-firm collaboration where

---

*Corresponding author

innovation is the main part of the collaborative effort. Innovation in this respect refers to the research and development (R&D) activity devoted to increasing scientific or technical knowledge and the application of that knowledge to the creation of new and improved products and processes (Hagedoorn, 2002).

Contractual innovation partnerships have been widely researched (Ahuja, 2000; Child *et al.*, 2005; Faems *et al.*, 2005; Hagedoorn, 2002; Nooteboom, 2004; Sampson, 2007; Sorenson and Stuart, 2008; Gilsing *et al.*, 2007). The research has provided useful insights into the dynamics and tendencies in formal R&D partnering relations. This chapter, however, focuses on collaboration between independent companies *prior* to such formal agreements as joint ventures or other contractual agreements. Thus, the focus is on how a focal firm can orchestrate a loosely coupled network (Dhanaraj and Parkhe, 2006). While Dhanaraj and Parkhe (2006) focus on the entire innovation process, the present article focuses on the first phase of the innovation process, which is often referred to as the fuzzy front end due to its intangible and ambiguous nature (Brun *et al.*, 2009). The FFE phase consists of idea generation, product definition and project evaluation (Murphy and Kumar, 1997). It is where the innovation process begins by allowing new ideas for incremental or radical products or service concepts to emerge (Richard and Donald, 2008; Verworn *et al.*, 2008). Such early involvement of suppliers and customers has been shown to reduce development times (Guptar and Wilemon, 1990; Sanchez and Perez, 2003).

Management of FFE in an inter-firm setting has barely been examined (Ojasalo, 2008), and hence the research objective of the paper is to investigate how management methods applied in an intra-firm FFE setting can be transferred to an inter-firm FFE setting. To answer this question, a longitudinal in-depth case study of a focal firm and its innovation partners is performed, in order to examine the characteristics and structure of the FFE phase in an inter-firm perspective.

In an intra-firm setting the early FFE phase is often carried out with a low degree of formalisation, in order to facilitate creative input. However, as illustrated in the present case study of an inter-organisational setting, the unstructured process and low degree of formalisation in the early FFE can entail an unstable network, since innovation partners might discard the project. We suggest that as the FFE

Table 1.   Three Forms of Collaboration (Powell, 1990).

	Hierarchy (intra-firm collaboration)	Network (inter-firm collaboration)	Market
Normative basis	Employment relationship	Complementary strengths	Contract, property rights
Means of communication	Routines	Relational	Prices
Tone or climate	Formal/bureaucratic	Open-ended, mutual benefits	Precision or suspicion
Actor preferences or choices	Dependent	Interdependent	Independent
Methods of conflict resolution	Fiat/supervision	Reciprocity and reputation	Haggling

process becomes an inter-firm collaboration, the management of the FFE also changes and calls for new management practice in this phase.

The article identifies two types of structure relating to the degree of formalisation which should be considered: the structure of the *content* and the structure of the *process*. The outcome of the case-study analysis is a number of preliminary considerations concerning the balance of these two types of structure.

In the following section, the methodological approach is made explicit. Secondly, the literature on the inter-firm collaboration dichotomy is presented. Thirdly, the traditional intra-firm FFE phase is characterised. After a presentation of the methodology and research setting, the case is analysed in relation to the management methods applied in the FFE, followed by a presentation of findings and managerial implications.

Inter-firm Collaboration

Powell (1990) presents a taxonomy of three overall forms of collaboration: hierarchies, networks and markets.

Table 1 shows the essential differences between the three kinds of collaboration. The distinction between a hierarchy and a network is equivalent to the difference between intra-firm and inter-firm relations. It should be noted that this may also be the case on an inter-unit level within an organisation. Even though some sort of hierarchy might exist between two companies in a network (in terms of size, intellectual properties, economic and staff resources, etc.), the normative basis, communication, tone, etc. will differ from the intra-firm and inter-unit collaboration. We argue that these differences have significant theoretical and managerial implications for the FFE, and so the intra- and inter-firm settings can therefore be assumed to set different standards and demands for a collaborative process.

An inter-firm network is not founded on the same degree of routines and formal tone as a hierarchy, and the direct means of power, such as fiat and supervision, will not be feasible in a network (Powell, 1990). The reciprocity, interdependence and complementary relationship between the companies involved in a network make the sources of influence and power much more subtle, and for this reason, Orton and Weick (1990) refer to such an interdependent collaboration as 'a loosely coupled system'.

In spite of these challenges, Chandy and Tellis (1998) were able to show that by gathering information from external organisations, a company could obtain a better understanding of current and potential customer needs. Furthermore Powell *et al.* (1996, p. 118) state that:

> *Sources of innovation [...] are commonly found in the interstices between firms, universities, research laboratories, suppliers, and customers.*

The characteristics of the three forms of collaboration illustrate the challenges confronting a focal company that initiates an inter-firm network. The focal company does not have the benefit of being able to impose a given behaviour on the other participants, as would be the case in a hierarchy. Furthermore, it does not have a contract to rely on in case of inexpedient behaviour of the other participants, as is often the case in a market relationship (Child *et al.*, 2005). Without a written contract or an employment relationship, there is a permanent risk that the other participants will exit from the network (Dhanaraj and Parkhe, 2006; Gulati, 2007).

However, the hybrid between markets and hierarchies also provides opportunities for the focal company. If the focal company manages to convince the other participants in the network about the potential in the network collaboration, the network can prove to be an adaptable and flexible form of organisation that is light on its feet (Gulati and Kletter, 2005; Powell, 1990; Provan and Kenis, 2008). A sense of mutual benefits, complementary strengths and reciprocity will be a substantial driver for collaboration in the network. In order to succeed in creating this sense of communality and a common goal, the focal company has to be able to push the right buttons.

The fuzzy front end

The fuzzy front end is the first phase of the innovation process, and initiates the process by producing ideas for incremental or radical products or service concepts. The term 'fuzzy' refers to the intangible and ambiguous nature of this particular stage of the innovation process (Brun *et al.*, 2009; Brun, 2008). There are uncertainties and unknown issues concerning the needs of the customers, uncertainty about what competitors are doing, and uncertainty about which product and process technologies should be used. Uncertainty concerning strategy alignment, required resources, capabilities and company limits may prevent an opportunity from proceeding to the more structured new product development (NPD) phase (Kim and Wilemon, 2002b; Kijkuit and van den Ende, 2007).

The FFE is of interest because it significantly effects the outcome of the innovation project (Frishammar *et al.*, 2011; Kim and Wilemon, 2002a; Qingyu and William, 2001; Verworn *et al.*, 2008). As ideas are generated in the front end, this is both the most troublesome and weakest part of the innovation process, and at the same time it is the phase with the biggest potential (Reid and de Brentani, 2004). The outcome of the FFE is a well-defined concept with clear development requirements, and a business plan that is aligned with the corporate strategy (Kim and Wilemon, 2002b).

According to Moenaert *et al.* (1995), a company proposes a product concept and determines whether or not it should invest resources to develop the idea through the FFE. Based on the process developed by Cooper (1988), Murphy and Kumar (1997) define the

predevelopment stages as consisting of idea generation, product definition and project evaluation.

In this article, the FFE is defined as:

*the period between when an opportunity is first considered and when an
idea is judged ready for development. (Kim and Wilemon, 2002b, p. 269)*

The FFE phase thereby includes the development of the concept
but not the concrete product.

The management of the FFE in intra-firm settings is essential, and
unsuccessful management of this phase has been shown to have a
significant effect on the outcome, in particular due to the (un)certainty
and (un)equivocality involved (Frishammar *et al.*, 2011; Murphy and
Kumar, 1997; Verworn *et al.*, 2008). If a project enters the development phase without sufficient preparation, there is a high risk of uncertainty and ambiguity, which will lead to project delays and budget
escalations (Thomke and Fujimoto, 2000). Furthermore, Clark and
Fujimoto (1991) point out that engineering changes occurring late in
the development are both costly and time consuming.

In the conventional intra-firm perspective on the early innovation
process, a loose idea or opportunity is still an internal process within
the company. Hence, an idea in development is still easy to change or
to reject. Traditionally, management at this stage is characterised by a
low degree of formalisation, and the management methods applied
are unstructured and experimental (Kim and Wilemon, 2002b), as it
is not decisive to formalise in a hierarchy where authority is clearly
defined. There are management methods that support the creative
process and the desire to explore new ideas and opportunities
(Martins and Terblanche, 2003).

Here, creativity is defined as the generation of new and valuable
ideas for products, services, processes and procedures by individuals
or groups (Martins and Terblanche, 2003) within the specific organisational context of an inter-firm setting.

Ideas that are put forward may later become formalised projects
in an NPD process, or they may simply disappear without notice.

Some survive in other projects and some are discarded. Meetings are held without agendas and on an accidental basis or due to a coincidence of events. The FFE phase is in general carried out by an individual or a small project team (Kim and Wilemon, 2002b). There is little or no budget allocated to the activities. It is in many respects a very informal phase of the innovation process and Montoya-Weiss and O'Driscoll (2000) describe the process as being often ill defined.

While some of the challenges of an FFE setting are similar across intra- and inter-firm settings, some features are clearly different (see Table 1). The actors in an inter-firm setting are interdependent and different actors have different interests. The decision-making process is hence very different, which is the main reason why Dhanaraj and Parkhe (2006) talk about 'orchestrating' innovation networks rather than governing or managing them. This could potentially have a substantial effect on the collaborative process of generating ideas in the FFE.

Additionally, as a focal firm invites external network partners to participate in this often unformalised stage of an innovation process, they should consider that their partners will expect some kind of tangible outcome. This is related to the issue of resources. A company within this logic of economic exchange usually does not pay to collaborate with another company. Still, networks involve a significant amount of cost spent in developing the formal and informal relations with the network partners (Harrigan, 1985). The invited partners might need to travel in order to participate, and they most certainly will need to spend time participating. It is one thing is to meet informally in the premises of your own firm, but it is quite different to spend considerable resources preparing, travelling and participating in meetings with the sole purpose of providing potential innovation partners with valuable input.

Finally, inter-firm networks can be assumed to involve more heterogeneous knowledge than intra-firm networks, since different firms have different core competencies and the involved networks of social relations are less dense (Colombo *et al.*, 2011. Such a network structure implies more heterogeneous partners and knowledge (Kilduff and Tsai, 2003), which again entail managerial challenges.

This chapter focuses on the balance of structure in the practical organisation of a development process. On the one hand, it is important to ensure a continuous flow of concrete output from the fuzzy phase of an innovation process, and, on the other, it important to focus on the structure of the content, allowing network partners to provide creative input to concept development.

Methodology

The paper is based on a single case study of a Danish inter-firm network within the energy sector. Since the actual processes and dynamics of the relations and ongoing processes were of primary interest, a case-study design following Yin (2009) and Flyvbjerg (2006) seemed the most appropriate choice of research design. Additionally, Dyer and Wilkins (1991) pointed out the value of performing a single case study in order to get an in-depth understanding of the relevant processes, rather than applying Eisenhardt's (1989) pattern-searching case(s) study approach.

In 2005, the focal company K was about to initiate a network and the issue of how to handle the FFE phase was important both from a theoretical point of view but also from K's point of view. This provided the opportunity for a longitudinal study, where the research could develop along with the evolution of the particular network (Ring and Van de Ven, 1994).

Furthermore, Oliver and Ebers (1998) and Steen *et al.* (2011) emphasise the need for comprehensive descriptions and qualitative studies in inter-organisational settings, since inter-organisational collaborations are particularly complex to investigate. Therefore, a qualitative approach has been chosen. The data on which the present paper is based are partly observations of meetings, in-depth interviews with the companies involved in the process and relevant archival data. During the process, all data, including interviews, observations, letters, email, secondary data, etc., were registered in a 'case book' to ensure that no information was lost in the process.

Over a period of one year, the focal company organised four network meetings with the purpose of concept development. The researchers participated in all four network meetings. The duration of each network meeting was between four and eight hours. One of the network meetings was documented on an audio recorder and transcribed. Due to the fact that the initiating organisation did not feel comfortable about having the other three network meetings audio recorded, these three meetings were documented through field notes.

Following the four network meetings, the researchers carried out 14 interviews with representatives from 9 of the 11 participating companies. Two companies did not wish to participate in personal interviews. The interviews were set up as explorative interviews covering a variety of aspects of the network process with a specific focus on the management (or lack of) of the FFE in the inter-firm collaboration. The questions in these interviews explored theoretical constructs and they were not aimed at verifying or falsifying specific relations between parameters. The duration of the interviews was between 50 minutes and 1 hour and 55 minutes. All interviews were recorded and transcribed and the interpretations of them have been discussed by at least three researchers. Thus, the different data sources have been triangulated (Jick, 1979) and the interpretations have also been triangulated since different researchers with different theoretical standpoints were present at the network meetings (Rasmussen *et al.*, 2009). The aim of these triangulating actions is to ensure that all relevant alternative interpretations have been included. Via analytical generalisations (Yin, 2009), the current theory on the management of inter-firm collaborations in the FFE is hence developed on the basis of this case.

Overall, the case-study method has been used to describe the relevant parameters for inter-firm collaboration in FFE projects, and, furthermore, it has been explained why these parameters are relevant. In addition to the qualitative data collection, the network partners involved were surveyed. Even though the network consists of organisational actors, collaborations take place between individuals, and it is therefore vital to untangle these different levels of analysis (Zaheer *et al.*, 2010). Therefore, a questionnaire was sent to 32 people (of whom 31 responded) with the purpose of clarifying the network structure of the inter-firm and inter-personal relations between the relevant partners.

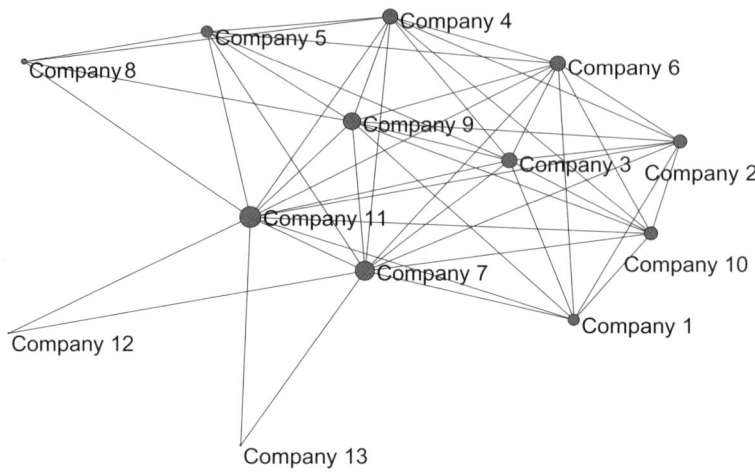

Fig. 1. Network Structure at the August 2006 Meeting.

Case Background

The case started with K holding introductory meetings with potential network partners at their company premises. The purpose of these meetings was clear to both parties involved: K would present their idea for a digital platform for business-to-customer services within the energy area, and wanted to find out whether the potential partner was interested in participating in the development of this project. At the end of each meeting, K invited interested partners to participate in a future meeting to which all interested parties were invited. Two months after the final introductory meeting, all interested network partners participated in a meeting held at K's meeting facilities. The purpose of this meeting was communicated as a chance to meet the other participants and to provide new ideas to the concept development of the platform.

Figure 1 gives a visual illustration of the network structure of the overall inter-firm network.

Size of nodes based on degree measure in Netdraw, which is a software tool supplied with UCINET (Borgatti *et al.*, 2002).

The density is fairly low, which also underlines the fact that this setting cannot be compared to an intra-firm setting, where the density is usually assumed to be higher. As the figure illustrates, the network structure consists of a mix of minor cliques and more peripheral actors without any single actor being the clear centre of the network. Some of the main players in the figure are the main actors in the Danish energy sector.

Case analysis

All the comments below are based on the transcribed interviews about the process and thus represent the respondents' afterthoughts about the process and the meetings. All quotes have been translated from Danish.

At the first meeting, which was chaired by one of K's directors, K presented their perspective for the digital platform. Their presentation included specific functionalities that should be incorporated in the platform as well as a detailed flow chart illustrating how information flows in the system should be structured. From the focal company's view, this was retrospectively seen as a major reason why the meetings did not make significant progress. As the director of the focal company said:

> *And I think that when we started [the project], we were probably too far down into the funnel – meaning that we were ready – mentally more ready to make decisions than they [the other participants] were because they were still way back there. You can say it is our fault, because we probably drove too fast...* (Company 1, director of the focal company)

During the six-hour-long meeting at K, there was much discussion and brainstorming concerning a wide variety of issues. The main topics were price, market potential and the functionality of the product. The discussions became very narrow and focused on problem-solving rather than concept development.

The representative from a major manufacturer of heating and water controls expressed a degree of disappointment, as he felt that the project had great potential:

> *They [the focal company] began by talking about the solution and functionalities too early, instead of dealing with the long-term*

perspective. We never discussed the framework for this project.
(Company 4, a major manufacturer of heating and water controls)

As the interviewees elaborated on the issue of the framework –
what we denote the 'structure' – they emphasised the lack of not only
an open discussion of project visions, but also the focal company's
openness towards product architecture, product functionality and an
overall business model. In this respect, the participating network partners perceived the framework as being too narrow and restrictive.

At the end of the first meeting, the general assumption was that
nothing new had appeared in regard to the concept development of
the platform (see Table 2). The focal company's initial presentation
had not been further developed or modified in any way. A close customer of the focal company and a utility provider, who had a major
interest in the project, gave their impressions of the meeting in the
following way:

> *We did not feel that anything new was put forward in regard to Project
> X. Nothing at all. And this is what you expect.* (Company 3, a close
> customer and utility provider)

In response, K suggested a second meeting to be held one month
later where new participants with different backgrounds would be
invited in addition to the present participants. The purpose of this
second meeting would be to focus on creative thinking and idea generation concerning the platform.

The first meeting ended with K handing out questionnaires to the
participants with the purpose of finding out which participants would
still like to be involved in the development of the platform. The participating network partners expressed their wish to receive minutes
from the meeting and K agreed that minutes would be put on their
website. Furthermore, it was agreed that K would hold individual
meetings with the participants.

The second meeting was postponed for four months and the minutes were not put on the website. Even though all of the participants
had answered positively in the questionnaire, some of them did not
show up at the second meeting. A considerable group of participants

did not think that there was a concrete outcome and therefore they chose not to participate in the second meeting. In this respect, the *'framework'* can be seen to be related to the issue of, e.g. agendas, a clear purpose for meetings, follow-up meetings, and meeting minutes. In this sense, there was not an adequate framework or structure for the practical organisation of the development process.

> *I was in a workshop meeting... And since then I have actually not heard anything from them... I think I felt a little like the others – no new ideas were put forward.* (Company 2, a high-end audio and television manufacturer)

The interviews with the company participants showed that all participating companies expected an outcome from the meetings. This could be either: (1) new ideas in regard to the concept development, or (2) a follow-up meeting to explain in which direction the project was moving and detailing the next steps and any progress in the project.

Table 2 provides an overview of the participants' perception of the outcome from the first two network meetings.

Both from the perspective of the focal organisation and the meeting participants, no new ideas were provided throughout the process. It could be argued that the reason why some of the participants chose not to attend the second meeting was because the project had no relevance for them. However, the interviews revealed that this was not the case. All participating companies found the project interesting and with great potential and relevance.

Respondents 2, 3, 8 and 9 did not perceive any tangible outcome in the form of either new ideas or project progress and ended their participation in the project.

At the first meeting, the management of the focal company had prepared a written agenda. The internal criteria for success for the meeting was that they would perceive new valuable input to the concept development for Project X and that the vast majority of the invited companies would express a positive interest in continued participation.

Table 2. Overview of Participants' Perception of the Outcome From the First Two Network Meetings.

	Participant outcome		Result
	Follow up (with indication of progress)	New ideas	Participant in second meeting
Company 1 – Major IT solution provider (project leader of the funding organisation)	N/A	None	N/A
Company 2 – High-end audio and television manufacturer	No	None	No
Company 3 – Utility provider	No	None	No[1]
Company 4 – Major manufacturer of heating and water controls	Yes	None	Yes
Company 5 – Engineering company	None	New perspectives	Yes
Company 6 – Utility provider	Yes	None	Yes[2]
Company 7 – Web portal developer	Yes	None	No
Company 8 – Major telecommunications company (II)	None	None	No[3]
Company 9 – Electrical equipment manufacturer	None	None	No

Notes

[1]The initial representative from Company 3 sent a substitute, as he felt that the project was going nowhere. Later he re-joined the project after the project vision was modified according to their specific needs.

[2]The representative from Company 6 intended to participate in the second meeting but was unable to make it. He was in close contact with the focal company and participated in later meetings.

[3]The initial representative from Company 8 dropped out of the project after the first meeting as he felt that there was no vision for the project. To attend the following meeting, he sent a lower ranking colleague as a gesture to the other participating companies. This was also done in order to nurse some customer relations – it was not to be perceived as a wish to stay involved in the project.

The internal success criteria were partly fulfilled. The meeting did not provide any new inputs but the participants all expressed interest in continued participation. Still, the case analysis shows that this expression of interest was based on the precondition that the meeting would provide a tangible outcome. As this was not the case for four out of the eight participants, they chose to drop out of the project.

Meanwhile, the management of K agreed that it would be preferable to apply an unstructured management method with a low degree of formalisation. This was done in order to make all partners in the project equal. The director of the focal company made this decision explicit at the first meeting:

> *It was correct to say: 'This is not [K] – it is us [a network of compa-nies]. We are doing this together. I will not stand on the podium and conduct. We want this to be a network. We might be coordinators of some part of it, but you must be aware that we do not run it.'*
> (Company 1, director of focal company)

As illustrated in Fig. 2, K entered the project with a very specific vision of the concept and the final product functionalities. This led to

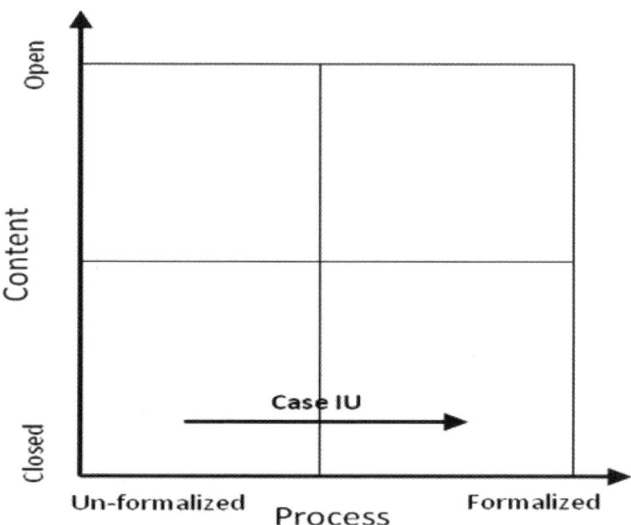

Fig. 2. The FFE for Project X.

a closed presentation of the project and the concept, which prevented any creative input from the invited innovation partners.

As the project progressed, the working process became more structured and formalised. At this time, however, the majority of the invited network partners had already decided to leave the project.

Discussion

From our analysis of the case, we argue that an ill-defined work process and unstructured management methods with a low degree of formalisation do not seem to be suitable for handling the FFE in an inter-firm setting based on a non-contractual collaboration.

We found, in addition to the existing literature on FFE management, that in an inter-firm setting two analytical levels of structure should be considered:

1. The structure of the content: open versus closed
2. The structure of the work process: formalised versus unformalised

The structure of the content is related to the creative processes concerning the concept that is to be developed during the FFE. If the concept is presented as a closed concept with specified technologies, functionalities and information flows, the participants will be discussing the project within the structure of that concept. If the concept is presented as an open concept with multiple alternatives for technology, functionality and information flows, it is more likely that the participants will offer some creative input (Basadur *et al.*, 2000). In our case, K presented the digital platform as a closed concept, which led to a lack of creative input from the participating innovation partners.

As Dhanaraj and Parkhe (2006) point out and the case findings illustrate, the involved actors are interdependent and hence decisions should not just be made by a single authority. In an open innovation context you want actual collaboration (Miles *et al.*, 2010), which implies that idea development should not be closed but open for significant new input. Furthermore, given the low density for such an inter-firm network it is quite heterogeneous, which means that firms will provide significantly different input (Kilduff and Tsai, 2003; Gilsing *et al.*, 2007). A closed concept structure would filter out such input.

The structure of the process refers to the work process for concept development. Is there a clear purpose for the meeting with an agenda, a chair and success criteria? Is the outcome of each meeting made explicit with minutes and follow-up meetings? This case has shown that for the first meeting in the network, the purpose of the meeting was clear but its outcome was very unclear. Even though the participants explicitly asked for a tangible outcome in the form of minutes, these were never provided. Instead, the outcome was presented as a future meeting, which was then postponed for four months. Since there are costs associated with meetings (Harrigan, 1985) some form of incentive to attend is important. Furthermore, due to the interdependent nature of the involved firms, it is important to treat collaborating firms as equals (Powell, 1990; Dhanaraj and Parkhe, 2006).

Figure 3 illustrates the differences between undertaking an FFE phase in an inter-firm setting and an intra-firm setting with the aim of reaching the goals of the FFE phase: a well-defined concept, clear development requirements and a business plan aligned with corporate strategy.

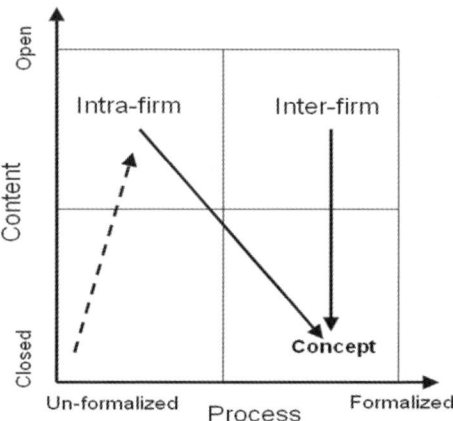

Fig. 3. The FFE Phase Comparing the Inter-Firm and Intra-Firm Settings.

In the intra-firm setting, the process can be initially unstructured and gradually become more structured as the involvement of personnel becomes clearer and the concept takes form (Kim and Wilemon, 2002a, 2002b). Or, as the dotted line illustrates, it can also start as a somewhat closed concept developed by a small group or an individual, which is challenged by colleagues, and, as a result, becomes open. In the inter-firm setting, it appears central that the process starts with an open concept, whereas collaboration is based on a structured and formalised process.

Managerial implications

According to our in-depth case study and analytical approach, it seems reasonable to claim that there ought to be a fair structure for the process in order to ensure a successful outcome for the participants of the FFE in an inter-firm innovation setting.

An informal meeting in an intra-firm perspective is quite different from an 'informal' meeting in an inter-firm perspective. On the one hand, participants who do not perceive a tangible outcome are likely to quit the project. On the other hand, if there is too much structure in the concept that is to be developed, it seems to suppress the creative input from the innovation partners.

The challenge in regard to structure when undertaking an FFE in an inter-firm setting is thus to balance the two levels of structure ensuring the following:

1. The concept is presented as open so that creative input from participants is encouraged.
2. A clear and structured work process is provided in order to ensure explicit and continuous information about the output and progress of the process.

This balance is illustrated in Fig. 4. We suggest that the sum of the levels of the two structures in an inter-firm FFE phase should be approximately constant. At the beginning of the project, the process must be very conform, which may help to persuade the participants

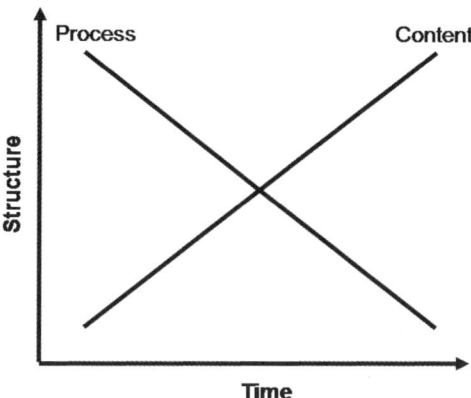

Fig. 4. Two Levels of Structure.

that the project is moving forwards – that it is still beneficial to stay involved. At this early stage of the FFE, the structure is the main driver in the project. As the concept become more concrete during the FFE phase, the specific content of the project gradually substitutes the process as the main driver that keeps the innovation partners involved in the project.

As a direct fiat cannot be used in such inter-firm settings, the challenge for the focal company is to structure the concept development work process and the creative thinking process in a way that provides tangible output and allows the recombination of knowledge and thereby new ideas (Brown and Duguid, 2000). If this balance is not reached, there is a risk that if the partners do not see continuous development and progress in the process they will lose their commitment to the project.

Overall we suggest that organisations that wish to carry out inter-firm development projects should become more aware of the challenges of balancing the structures of the content and the process. Based on our case study we suggest that organisations develop specific managerial guidelines for project managers for inter-firm development projects. However, the guidelines will vary from one organisation to another, from one project to another and from one industry to another, depending on the intensity of the collaboration, the common history and relations of the innovation partners and the scope of the development project. In this regard educational programmes for project managers should recognise the challenge of structural balance and should allow participants to discuss and develop more context-specific practices.

In our case study, we saw that as a consequence of neglecting the importance of appropriate FFE management in an inter-firm setting, the focal company had great difficulties in re-engaging the innovation partners who abandoned the project – which also applies to any new projects. In other words the focal organisation has only one shot, which stresses the importance of appropriate management.

As discussed earlier, the need for a successful balance of the structures of the content and the process may also apply in an intra-firm setting at an inter-unit level within an organisation, depending on the hierarchy between the units and the distance between them.

Prior to a project's start, management can use the following questions as an indicator of the importance of the structural balance for an innovation project:

- Information level: Will the participants receive information on the project status and progress?
- Non-project-related network activities: Do the innovation partners regularly meet, apart from activities related to the development project?
- Network history: Do you have strong relations with the innovation partners based on a history of successful collaboration?
- Divergent thinking: Will the innovation partners challenge the basic scope of the project?

If the answer to the majority of the above questions is 'no', the success of the FFE to an increasing degree is dependent on a suitable balance of the structure of the process and the structure of the content.

Conclusion

This chapter has discussed the differences of undertaking an FFE phase of an innovation process in an intra-firm versus an inter-firm innovation setting. In regard to the form of collaboration, the latter is characterised as a *network* where no direct power can be employed as opposed to an intra-firm setting, which is traditionally characterised as a *hierarchy*. Through an in-depth case study analysis we focused on two main differences:

(1) The structure of the content: whether the concept is formulated as an open or a closed concept.
(2) The structure of the work process: whether there is a clear purpose to meetings and whether the outcome of each meeting is made explicit.

The focal company K had very high ambitions for the project, and was prepared to use great resources to make it succeed. Similarly, many of the network partners had quite high expectations, and were willing to invest manpower and money. Why then did it not succeed? In our opinion, the answer can be found in the two results above: process and content. The focal company did not manage to balance the structure of the *content* and the structure of the *process* properly. In future studies multi-case studies could test the proposed distinction between the structures of the content and the process. Such studies could also involve different industries and different network structures, in order to examine whether and how these contingencies matter.

References

Ahuja, G. (2000). Collaboration networks, structural holes, and innovation: A longitudinal study, *Administrative Science Quarterly*, **45**(3), 425–455.

Basadur, M., Pringle, P., Speranzini, G. and Bacot, M. (2000) Collaborative problem solving through creativity in problem definition: Expanding the pie, *Creativity and Innovation Management*, **9**(1), 54–76.

Bergenholtz, C. and Waldstrøm, C. (2011). Inter-organizational network studies: A literature review, *Industry and Innovation*, **18**(6), 539–562.

Borgatti, S.P., Everett, M.G. and Freeman, L.C. (2002). *Ucinet for Windows: Software for Social Network Analysis*, Analytic Technologies, Harvard, MA.

Brown, J.S. and Duguid, P. (2000). *The Social Life of Information*, Harvard Business School Press, Boston, MA.

Brun, E. (2008) Ambiguity reduction in new product development, *International Journal of Innovation Management*, **12**(4), 573–597.

Brun, E., Steinar, S.A. and Gjelsvik, M. (2009). Classification of ambiguity in new product development projects, *European Journal of Innovation Management*, **12**(1), 62.

Chandy, K.R. and Tellis, J.G. (1998). Organizing for radical product innovation: The overlooked role of willingness to cannibalize, *Journal of Marketing Research*, **35**(4), 474.

Chesbrough, H. (2003). *Open Innovation: The New Imperative for Creating and Profiting from Technology*, Harvard University Press, Cambridge.

Child, J., Faulkner, D. and Tallman, S.B. (2005). *Cooperative Strategy*, Oxford University Press, Oxford, UK.

Clark, B.K. and Fujimoto, T. (1991). *Product Development Performance: Strategy, Organization, and Management in the World Auto Industry*, Harvard Business School Press, Boston, MA.

Colombo, M.G., Laursen, K., Magnusson, M. and Rossi-Lamastra, C. (2011). Organizing inter- and intra-firm networks: What is the impact on innovation performance, *Industry and Innovation*, **18**(6), 531–538.

Cooper, R. (2005). *Product Leadership — Pathways to Profitable Innovation*, Basic Books, New York.

Cooper, R.G. (1988). Predevelopment activities determine new product success, *Industrial Marketing Management*, **17**(3), 237.

Cooper, R.G. and Kleinschmidt, E.J. (1987). Success factors in product innovation, *Industrial Marketing Management*, **16**(3), 215.

Dhanaraj, C. and Parkhe, A. (2006). Orchestrating innovation networks, *Academy of Management Review*, **31**(3), 659–669.

Dyer, G.W. and Wilkins, A.L. (1991). Better stories, not better constructs, to generate better theory: A rejoinder to Eisenhardt, *Academy of Management Review*, **16**(3), 613–619.

Eisenhardt, K. (1989). Building theories from case study research, *Academy of Management Review*, **14**(4), 532–550.

Faems, D., Van Looy, B. and Debackere, K. (2005). Interorganizational collaboration and innovation: Toward a portfolio approach, *Journal of Product Innovation Management*, **22**(3), 238–250.

Flyvbjerg, B. (2006). Five misunderstandings about case-study research, *Qualitative Inquiry*, **12**(2), 219–245.

Frishammar, J., Floren, H. and Wincent, J. (2011). Beyond managing uncertainty: Insights from studying equivocality in the fuzzy front end of product and process innovation projects, *IEEE Transactions on Engineering Management*, **58**(3), 551–563.

Gilsing, V.A., Lemmens, C.E.A.V. and Duysters, G. (2007). Strategic alliance networks and innovation: A deterministic and voluntaristic view combined, *Technology Analysis and Strategic Management*, **19**(2), 227.

Gulati, R. (2007). *Managing Network Resources*, Oxford University Press, Oxford, UK.

Gulati, R. and Kletter D. (2005). Shrinking core, expanding periphery: The relational architecture of high-performing organizations, *California Management Review*, **47**(3), 77–104.

Guptar, A.K. and Wilemon, D.L. (1990) Accelerating the development of technology-based new products, *California Management Review*, **32**, 24–45.

Hagedoorn, J. (2002) Inter-firm R&D partnerships: An overview of major trends and patterns since 1960, *Research Policy*, **31**(4), 477–492.

Harrigan, K.R. (1985). *Strategies for Joint Ventures*, Lexington Books, Lexington, MA.

Jick, T.D. (1979). Mixing qualitative and quantitative methods: Triangulation in action, *Administrative Science Quarterly*, **24**(4), 602.

Jukka, O. (2008). Management of innovation networks: A case study of different approaches, *European Journal of Innovation Management*, **11**(1), 51.

Kijkuit, B. and van den Ende, J. (2007). The organizational life of an idea: Integrating social network, creativity and decision-making perspectives, *Journal of Management Studies*, **44**, 863–882.

Kim, J. and Wilemon, D. (2002a). Strategic issues in managing innovation's fuzzy front-end, *European Journal of Innovation Management*, **5**(1), 27.

Kim, J. and Wilemon, D. (2002b). Focusing the fuzzy front end in new product development, *R&D Management*, **32**(4), 269–279.

Kilduff, M. and Tsai, W. (2003). *Social Networks and Organizations*, Sage Publications, London.

Martins, E.C. and Terblanche, F. (2003). Building organizational culture that stimulates creativity and innovation, *European Journal of Innovation Management*, **6**(1), 64.

Miles, R.E., Snow, C.C., Fjeldstad, O.D., Miles, G. and Lettl, C. (2010). Designing organizations to meet 21st century opportunities and challenges, *Organizational Dynamics*, **39**(2), 93–103.

Moenaert, R.K., De Meyer, A., Souder, W.E. and Deschoolmeester, D. (1995). R&D/marketing communication during the fuzzy front-end, *IEEE Transactions on Engineering Management*, **42**(3), 243.

Moller, K.K. and Halinen, A. (1999). Business relationships and networks: Managerial challenge of network era, *Industrial Marketing Management*, **28**(5), 413–427.

Montoya-Weiss, M.M. and O'Driscoll, T.M. (2000). From experience: Applying performance support technology in the fuzzy front end, *The Journal of Product Innovation Management*, **17**(2), 143.

Murphy, S.A. and Kumar, V. (1997). The front end of new product development: A Canadian survey, *R&D Management*, **27**(1), 5–15.

Nooteboom, B. (2004). *Inter-firm Collaboration, Networks and Strategy; an Integrated Approach*, Routledge, London.

Oliver, L.A. and Ebers, M. (1998). Networking network studies: An analysis of conceptual configurations in the study of inter-organizational relationships, *Organization Studies*, **19**(4), 549.

Orton, J.D. and Weick, K.E. (1990). Loosely coupled systems: A reconceptualization, *Academy of Management Review*, **15**(2), 203–224.

Powell, W.W. (1990). "Neither market nor hierarchy: Network forms of organization", in Staw, B.M. and Cummings, L.L. (eds), *Research in Organizational Behavior*, JAI Press, Greenwich, pp. 295–336.

Powell, W.W., Koput, K.W. and Smith-Doerr, L. (1996). Interorganizational collaboration and the locus of innovation: Networks of learning in biotechnology, *Administrative Science Quarterly*, **41**(1), 116–145.

Provan, K.G. and Kenis, P. (2008). Modes of network governance: Structure, management, and effectiveness, *Journal of Public Administration Research and Theory*, **18**(2), 229–252.

Qingyu, Z. and William, J.D. (2001). The fuzzy front end and success of new product development: A causal model, *European Journal of Innovation Management*, **4**(2), 95.

Rasmussen, E.S., Jorgensen, J.H., Goduscheit, R.C. and Bergenholtz, C. (2009). Innovation, product development, and new business models in networks: How to come from case studies to a valid and operational theory, *Revue Sciences de Gestion*, **70**, 103–120.

Reid, S.E. and de Brentani, U. (2004). The fuzzy front end of new product development for discontinuous innovations: A theoretical model, *Journal of Product Innovation Management*, **21**(3), 170–184.

Richard, K.R. and Donald, D.T. (2008). Critical success factors for the fuzzy front end of innovation in the medical device industry, *Engineering Management Journal*, **20**, 3, 36.

Ring, P.S. and Van de Ven, A.H. (1994). Developmental processes of cooperative interorganizational relationships, *Academy of Management Journal*, **19**(1), 90.

Sanchez, A.M. and Perez, M.P. (2003). Cooperation and the ability to minimize the time and cost of new product development within the Spanish automotive supplier industry, *The Journal of Product Innovation Management*, **20**(1), 57–69.

Sampson, R.C. (2007). R&D alliances and firm performance: The impact of technological diversity and alliance organization on innovation, *Academy of Management Journal*, **50**(2), 364–386.

Sorenson, O. and Stuart, T.E. (2008). Bringing the context back in: Settings and the search for syndicate partners in venture capital investment networks, *Administrative Science Quarterly*, **53**, 266–294.

Steen, J., Macaulay S. and Kastelle, T. (2011). Small worlds: The best network structure for innovation. *Prometheus*, **29**(1), 39–50.

Thomke, S. and Fujimoto, T. (2000). The effect of 'front-loading' problem-solving on product development performance, *Journal of Product Innovation Management*, **17**(2), 128–142.

Verworn, B., Herstatt, C. and Agahira, A. (2008). The fuzzy front end of Japanese new product development projects: Impact on success and differences between incremental and radical projects, *R&D Management*, **38**(1), 1.

Vlaar, P.W.L., Van Den Bosch, F.A.J. and Volberda, H.W. (2007). Towards a dialectic perspective on formalization in interorganizational relationships: How alliance managers capitalize on the duality inherent in contracts, rules and procedures, *Organization Studies*, **28**(4), 437.

Yin, R.K. (2009). *Case Study Research: Design and Methods*, Sage Publishing, Beverly Hills.

Zaheer, A., Gözübüyük, R. and Milanov, H. (2010). It's the connections: The network perspective in interorganizational research, *Academy of Management Perspective*, **24**(1), 62–77.

Chapter 15

How New Product Development Service Suppliers Exchange Knowledge in Open Innovation Processes

*Gabriele Colombo, Claudio Dell'Era, and Federico Frattini**
Department of Management,
Economics and Industrial Engineering,
Politecnico di Milano, Italy

Introduction

Open innovation has been one of the most debated topics in technology and innovation management research in the last decade (Chesbrough, 2003; Gassmann, 2006). It has been proposed as a new paradigm for industrial innovation management, according to which firms use 'purposive inflows and outflows of knowledge to accelerate innovation, and to expand the markets for external use of innovation, respectively' (Chesbrough *et al.*, 2006, p. 1). The effect of open innovation on management practice has been significant as well. Not only firms in high-tech, high-velocity industries (Chesbrough, 2003) but also companies competing in more mature, asset-intensive markets (Chesbrough and Crowther, 2006), have increasingly applied the open innovation principles. The literature has unquestionably shown that effectively acquiring and integrating external knowledge is a

* Corresponding author

critical challenge for innovative firms (Chesbrough, 2003; Chesbrough *et al.*, 2006). However, surprisingly very limited attention has been devoted to understand how the exchange process can be managed by the 'supplier' of the external knowledge, despite its fundamental role in the process. The chapter attempts to address this gap by focusing on a particular category of external knowledge suppliers, i.e. new product development service providers. NPD service providers secure their clients through a wide array of knowledge-intensive services; they are able to support all the steps of an NPD process, such as technology and market scouting, concept generation, design, engineering, testing, rapid and virtual prototyping and 3D-modelling services.

However, it is in the first phases of the NPD process that the relation between the NPD service provider and its clients is particularly challenging, because of the tacitness of the knowledge to be exchanged and the considerable level of market and technical uncertainty characterizing scouting and concept generation activities (Borja de Mozota, 2003). Tacitness in the early phases of an NPD process stems from the need of an NPD service provider to delve deeply into the client's rich body of experience concerning the industry's evolutionary trends, the customers' requirements, the products' meanings and languages, the socio-cultural dynamics, as well as its vision and mission, the organizational culture and values (Philips, 2004). These pieces of knowledge are very hard to codify in written specifications and require extensive face-to-face interactions, where trust plays a critical role (Bstieler, 2006), in order to be properly conveyed and assimilated. Furthermore, the first activities in the NPD process are very complex, uncertain and involve a significant deal of creativity, which makes it particularly complex to predict progress at the beginning of a provider–client relation and to anticipate those exceptions that might affect its development.

Starting from these premises, the aim of the chapter is to investigate how an NPD service provider organizes and manages the relationships with its clients in the early stages of the development process, so as to facilitate the transfer and integration of knowledge into the clients' innovation process. The focus is on two main dimensions of the knowledge exchange relationship: (1) the process followed to exchange knowledge and integrate it in the client's innovation process; (2) the organization of this process. These issues are investigated using a rich empirical basis gathered in the scope of a multiple case study analysis. The case study focuses on three projects undertaken by a leading NPD service provider (denoted as *Service Supplier* in the remainder of the chapter for confidentiality reasons) with three of its most important clients. Besides contributing to the recent debate on open innovation, the findings of the chapter have important practical implications. They provide managers of NPD service providers with a number of suggestions about which approaches could be used to administer their relations with clients, so as to ease the exchange and integration of knowledge and, ultimately, increase the customer's satisfaction. The structure of the chapter is as follows. The next section briefly reviews the literature that is relevant for the purpose of this chapter. Afterwards, the methodology used in the empirical analysis will be presented. The fourth section illustrates and discusses the main results of the analysis and, finally, conclusions are drawn and some avenues for future research are outlined.

Overview of the Literature

The purpose of this section is to provide an overview of three streams of research that are relevant for the purpose of the chapter, i.e. open innovation, NPD service providers and inter-organizational knowledge exchange.

Open innovation

Open innovation has been unquestionably one of the most debated topics in management research over the last decade (Chesbrough, 2003; Christensen *et al.*, 2005; Gassmann, 2006; Vanhaverbeke, 2006). It can be described as an emerging innovation management paradigm, which suggests that firms should strategically commit themselves to make the most out of their knowledge abundant external environment, with the aim of improving innovation performance and, ultimately, creating economic value. Open innovation is therefore all about exchanging knowledge and technology with a wide population of external organizations, such as universities, clients, competitors, firms from other industries, individuals, NPD service providers and suppliers.

In recent years, some important contributions have deepened and further clarified the open innovation concept. Dahlander and Gann (2010) identify four distinct open innovation processes: sourcing, acquiring, revealing and selling. Sourcing and acquiring are inbound processes for integrating a firm's internal knowledge base with external knowledge, while revealing and selling are outbound processes for gaining the most from innovation outcomes. In the same vein, van de Vrande *et al.* (2009) operationalized the open innovation concept according to two main dimensions, i.e. technology exploration (an inbound process) and technology exploitation (an outbound process), identifying within these dimensions eight specific open innovation practices.

Another important stream of research within the open innovation literature explores the contexts where open innovation practices have been applied. The 'early adopters' of open innovation were mainly large, multinational corporations, working in high-technology, high-velocity industries, e.g. Intel (Chesbrough, 2003), Air Products and Chemicals (Tao and Magnotta, 2006), Nokia (Dittrich and Duysters, 2007), DSM (Kirschbaum, 2005), Procter & Gamble (Houston and Sakkab, 2006) and IBM (Dittrich *et al.*, 2007). However, more recent empirical analyses have shown that firms from mature, asset-intensive industries (Chiaroni *et al.*, 2010; Chesbrough and Crowther, 2006; Buganza *et al.*, 2011), small to medium-sized enterprises (van de Vrande *et al.*, 2009) as well as service companies (Chesbrough, 2011a, 2011b) have started to use the emerging innovation management paradigm.

Finally, recent research has mainly adopted the viewpoint of the firm willing to take advantage of open innovation and has investigated the major issues that should be addressed in order to streamline the implementation and adoption of the new paradigm. Some scholars have studied the organizational implications of open innovation and, in particular, the changes to a firm's organization that are needed to evolve from a 'closed' to an 'open' approach (Chiaroni *et al.*, 2010; Gassmann, 2006). Others have investigated the use of information and communications technology and knowledge management systems that can support the implementation of open innovation processes (Dodgson *et al.*, 2006; Huston and Sakkab, 2006). A further stream of research has documented how innovative firms can use innovation networks to anticipate and manage radical technological changes (Dittrich and Duysters, 2007; Dittrich *et al.*, 2007). More recently, scholars have examined how firms can take advantage of open innovation by licensing technologies that have not been used internally (Bianchi *et al.*, 2010; Lichtenthaler, 2009), showing how this is particularly relevant during periods of economic downturn (Chesbrough, 2009; Di Minin *et al.*, 2010).

Even though theoretical and empirical research on open innovation has shown that exchanging knowledge with external organizations requires carefully designed managerial and organizational practices, in terms of both processes and organization, very limited research has been carried out so far to understand how the exchange process can be organized and managed by the 'supplier' of the external knowledge. It is reasonable to assume that the effectiveness with which a firm interacts with an external organization for knowledge exchange purposes does not merely depend on the managerial approaches adopted on the side of the knowledge recipient. It is also the proficiency with which the knowledge supplier organizes and manages the exchange process that matters in this respect. The chapter helps to close this gap in the open innovation literature by focusing on a particular type of 'knowledge supplier', with which open innovation firms have been increasingly partnering for acquiring useful knowledge, i.e. new product development service providers.

NPD service providers

NPD service providers have been traditionally depicted as 'knowledge brokers' (Sutton, 2002; Hargadon, 2003), i.e. 'firms that span multiple markets and technology domains and innovate by brokering knowledge from where it is known to where it is not' (Hargadon, 1998, p. 210). NPD service providers play a critical role in knowledge transfer and exchange processes (Hargadon and Sutton, 1997; Hargadon, 1998) because of their particular characteristics (Muller and Zenker, 2001): (1) their knowledge intensity; (2) their consulting function, which promotes the effective and efficient absorption of transferred knowledge into the recipient organization; (3) their inter-active or client-related nature: the strong linkages they create with clients stimulate the integration of transferred knowledge into the recipient organization's innovation process.

Traditionally, the literature on NPD services has investigated four main issues: (1) the role of NPD service providers as partners in tech-nological collaboration (Chatterji,1996; Chatterji and Manuel, 1993); (2) the knowledge-brokering role played by NPD service providers, which can also foster the birth and growth of technology-intensive industries (Hargadon and Sutton, 1997; Hargadon, 1998); (3) the effect of NPD service providers on national or local economies (Mansfield and Lee, 1996; Windrum and Tomlinson, 1999); (4) the effect of NPD service providers on companies' innovative performance (Katsoulacos and Tsounis, 2000; Kessler *et al.*, 2000; MacPherson, 1997a, 1997b, 1997c). This brief synthesis of the literature indicates that NPD service providers have been studied mainly from an industrial economic perspective so far, and that management research has dealt with NPD services only from the point of view of a firm that has estab-lished a relation with a service provider. Research into the organization and management of NPD service providers is very limited indeed (some exceptions are the works by Chiesa *et al.*, 2004, 2007, 2008).

Nevertheless, in recent years, a new stream of literature investigat-ing the organization and management of NPD service providers has emerged (Jeppesen and Lakhani, 2010; Boudreau *et al.*, 2011; Terwiesch and Xu, 2008). In particular, this literature focuses on web-based intermediaries, i.e. a new class of NPD service providers that leverage web potentiality to connect firms with innovation problems to potential solvers all over the world. Such providers organize their ser-vices by making many individuals, called solvers, compete to identify solutions to a firm's innovation problems (Jeppesen and Lakhani, 2010; Boudreau *et al.*, 2011; Terwiesch and Xu, 2008). The peculiarity of these particular kinds of NPD service providers lies in their ability to easily explore different knowledge domains (Boudreau *et al.*, 2011) by leveraging a crowd of potential solvers. Indeed, attracting many individuals with different backgrounds and competences increases the likelihood of obtaining unexpected solutions or ideas from unknown knowledge domains (Terwiesch and Xu, 2008; Boudreau *et al.*, 2011).

However, despite the relevance of such contributions in deepening our comprehension of the organization and management of NPD service providers, web-based intermediaries deliver highly codified solutions referred to well defined innovation problems, that are hence easily transferrable to clients. Limited attention has instead been devoted so far to understand the organization and management practices adopted by NPD service suppliers to exchange knowledge with their clients during the upstream phases of the NPD process, where knowledge to be exchange is highly tacit and the uncertainty surrounding the outcomes of the knowledge exchange process is particularly soaring.

Starting from this analysis, it emerges that studying how a supplier of NPD services organizes and manages the relations with its clients during the upstream phases of the NPD process, so as to facilitate knowledge transfer and integration, is a topic that deserves future investigation. The chapter adds therefore to the body of research that has been briefly reviewed, by focusing on the process and organizational variables NPD service providers should rely on, in order to support an effective knowledge exchange process.

Inter-organizational knowledge exchange

There are two major variables that might affect the ease with which knowledge and technology can be exchanged between organizations: the characteristics of the knowledge itself and the ability to anticipate the content and outcomes of the knowledge exchange process.

The first factor refers to the distinction between tacit and codified (or explicit) knowledge (Polanyi, 1962). Tacit knowledge 'indwells in a comprehensive cognizance of the human mind and body' (Polanyi, 1962, p. 4), is highly personal or firm specific and hence hard to formalize into blueprints or written instructions (Nonaka and Takeuchi, 1995; Marwick, 2001). It is the specific expertise that a firm acquires with time and therefore it is very hard to communicate and transfer between organizations without continuous personal, face-to-face communication (Marcotte and Niosi, 2000). Explicit knowledge, in contrast, is codified (Nonaka and Takeuchi, 1995; Marcotte and Niosi, 2000), i.e. it is knowledge in a symbolic form (e.g. blueprints, written instructions and formal languages). When knowledge is codified it is standardized, easily available to firms and the communication and human factors are less problematic (Marwick, 2001).

The second factor refers to the uncertainty surrounding the content and outcomes of the knowledge exchange process. When the outcomes of a collaboration are uncertain, cannot be foreseen in advance, involve a significant deal of creativity and are highly variable, it is particularly complex to predict those exceptions that might affect development activities. As suggested by information-processing contingency theory (Tushman and Nadler, 1978; Egelhoff, 1982), under these conditions the information needed to coordinate R&D and innovation activities is hard to codify and exchange without misunderstandings and high costs. This increases the challenges a supplier faces when managing relations with clients.

These theoretical lenses represent the basis for a thorough analysis of the different process and organization solutions adopted by an NPD service provider to ease knowledge exchange and integration with clients during the early phases of a collaborative development process.

Research Design and Methodology

As previously mentioned, the chapter focuses on new product development (NPD) service providers and it investigates how they organize collaborative relations with clients during the upstream phases of an NPD process, i.e. technology and market scouting and concept generation. Even though NPD service providers collaborate with their clients during different phases of an NPD process, the earlier stages have specific challenges: knowledge exchanged between an NPD service provider and a client is typically tacit (Chiesa *et al.*, 2008) and the uncertainties in both project scope and product life cycle are particularly high (Verganti, 1997, 1999). This makes them particularly relevant for our analysis for both theoretical and practical reasons. In particular the analysis focuses on two main levers, which an NPD service provider can use to address these challenges: the collaboration process and its organization.

Due to the complex system of variables that characterize the problem, we use a case study methodology that allows us to develop a holistic and contextualized analysis. We believe that this method is suited to the exploratory nature of this research as it allows us not only to explore the phenomenon in all its complexity, but also to identify those variables that we deem critical (Eisenhardt and Graebner, 2007). Therefore, our case studies have an exploratory intent, are retrospective and multiple in nature (Yin, 1984). The case studies focus on three projects undertaken by a leading NPD service provider (named *Service Supplier*) with some of its most important clients.

Service Supplier is a design and innovation consultancy based in the US with offices in Italy and Japan. The company's core disciplines include brand experience, design strategy, organizational innovation and product innovation. The company was founded in 1983 and it employs today approximately 180 people with an annual turnover of about €2 million. It has worked with clients in several industries: medical, consumer, computer, automotive, hospitality and financial services. The company has won 14 IDSA/BusinessWeek International Design Excellence Awards since 2003 and developed more than 330 design and utility patents. For the purpose of our research, we analysed first the typical approaches that *Service Supplier* uses to manage and organize relations with its clients during the service delivery process. This analysis, whose major findings are presented in the first paragraph of the next section, is based on three in-depth direct interviews carried out with designers and managers from *Service Supplier*. Then we have adopted a second unit of analysis (i.e. a single collaborative innovation project) to investigate how *Service Supplier* adapts the standard approaches found in the previous step to the characteristics of each of its project (the results of this analysis are presented in the second paragraph of the next section). For this purpose, we identified three projects aimed at the development of incremental innovation in the consumer market, which *Service Supplier* has recently carried out in collaboration with three clients. These projects are heterogeneous from several perspectives: industry type, business model and size (both in employees and annual turnover), as well as the expected output of the projects. A description of the three clients can be found in Table 1.

Table 1. Case Studies Overview.

Name	Description	Industry	Business model	Size	Expected output of the project with *Service Supplier*
Client A	In June 1973, *Client A* made its debut among sports footwear manufacturers. Tennis shoes were the first product made, followed by models for basketball, volleyball, athletics and football and finally sports clothing. Its involvement in both the design and fine tuning of the products together with their image led the company to become a leader in tennis and football. During this period, *Client A* expanded into the export market. International growth continued rapidly and ten years later the brand was being distributed in more than 60 countries around the world. Today, the performance segment has been strengthened, in line with a new corporate mission. Special focus is given to footwear and technical clothing for football and tennis, also supporting the brand's worldwide leadership with products that are on the cutting edge in terms of innovation and design. In parallel, based on production, technical and stylistic know-how, an idea has been developed for men's and women's leisure clothing and footwear with a sport-inspired image with regards to fabrics, colours and styles.	Footwear	B2C	500 employees €311 M turnover	COMPONENT *Client A* wanted to develop a shock-absorption system for its tennis shoes.

(*Continued*)

Table 1. (*Continued*)

Name	Description	Industry	Business model	Size	Expected output of the project with *Service Supplier*
Client B	*Client B Group* is a world leader in the production of automatic snack and beverage vending machines and is a major international player in both the HoReCa (hotel, restaurant and café) and the office coffee service sectors. *Client B Group* was formed in 2000, following the merger of two long-established vending companies. The newly formed group flourished and in 2007, *Client B Group* responded to market demands for an even wider range of products through several acquisitions. These companies brought specific capabilities to *Client B Group* such as competences in espresso coffee technology for portioned dispensing machines and competences in the design and production of payment systems. These new capabilities enhanced *Client B Group*'s product line and therefore *Client B Group* is ideally placed to consolidate its presence in the burgeoning cashless technology marketplace.	Vending machine	B2B	1,800 employees €400 M turnover	SCENARIO *Client B* decided to collaborate with *Service Supplier* in order to develop concepts for the vending machine of the future.

(*Continued*)

Table 1. (*Continued*)

Name	Description	Industry	Business model	Size	Expected output of the project with *Service Supplier*
Client C	*Client C* is one of the world's leading international appliance companies. Each year, some 40 million consumers in more than 150 countries choose *Client C* products, such as cookers and cooktops, ovens, fridges and freezers, dishwashers, washing machines, tumble dryers, room air conditioners and vacuum cleaners. With a presence in more than 100 countries *Client C* is a truly international company. *Client C* products include refrigerators, dishwashers, washing machines, vacuum cleaners and cookers sold under well-respected brands. The founding father of *Client C* established the principles by which the company still thrives. His dream for improving the quality of life has had a fundamental effect on homes around the world. Today *Client C*, 90 years later, is a global leader in household appliances and appliances for professional use. 'Thinking of you' expresses the *Client C* offering: to maintain continuous focus on the consumer, whether it's a question of product development, design, production, marketing, logistics or service.	Household appliances	B2C	55,000 employees €11,000 M turnover	PRODUCT *Client C* started the collaboration with *Service Supplier* in order to produce a synthesis of the results it had achieved after a year of internal concept generation activities. *Client C* asked *Service Supplier* to develop an operating model, i.e. a prototype that looks and works like the new household appliance.

The decision to focus on incremental innovation projects in the consumer domain affects the generalizability of the findings. The development of radical innovations might require different organizational endeavours for a collaborative project, e.g. the establishment of a full-time joint team, co-located in the same place. This might have a significant effect on the ease with which tacit knowledge can be exchanged as well as changing the uncertainty regarding the development process. The reader should be aware of these generalizability concerns.

Two in-depth interviews were carried out to gather empirical evidence for each innovation project, together with a brief questionnaire, which was useful for collecting background data such as the client's turnover, number of employees, business model, expected output and timing of the collaboration with *Service Supplier*. Both interviews used a protocol that is able to track the decision-making process in the collaboration with *Service Supplier*. The first interview was with senior managers and designers from *Service Supplier*, while the second was with NPD project managers and team members from each client, who were identified in collaboration with *Service Supplier* during the first interview.

All interviews were carried out by at least two of the authors. Before starting the data analysis, we retrieved additional information from secondary sources for data triangulation. The content analysis was developed by each author, coding the principal phases of the innovation process (Eisenhardt, 1989). In order to increase the robustness of the interpretations, some of the different interpretations by the three authors were corroborated by re-contacting the interviewees by phone and a synthetic report for each case study was shared with the interviewees to obtain final approval.

Results and Discussion

A detailed description of the three case studies is given in the appendix. The analysis of this rich empirical evidence suggests that *Service*

Supplier employs standard approaches to administer knowledge exchange and integration throughout its dealings with its clients. However, these methods are put into practice according to specific criteria that take into account the heterogeneity of the clients and their collaborative NPD projects. The common approaches applied by *Service Supplier* regardless of the nature of its clients are presented in the next section, and the reasons why it differentiates in how these methods are put into practice are in the following section.

Standard approaches for knowledge exchange and integration

Service Supplier adopts specific solutions for the innovation process and the collaborative organization to ease knowledge exchange and integration with its clients.

Innovation process

Service Supplier collaborates with its clients according to a standard sequence of activities right from the outset of the relationship (see Fig. 1). Specifically, the collaboration starts with a kick-off meeting in which the client presents a rough brief of the project to *Service Supplier*. The kick-off meeting ends with a preliminary schedule of

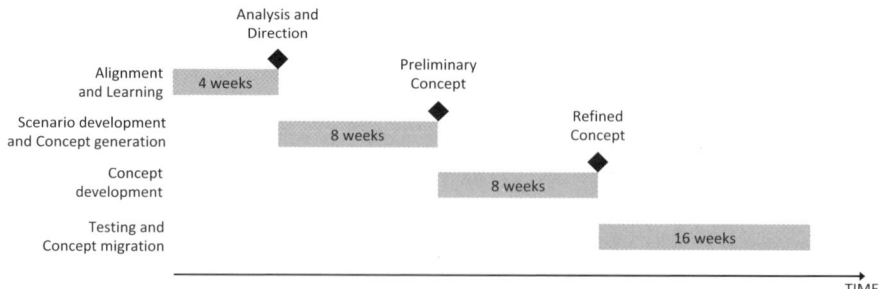

Fig. 1.   Innovation Process Adopted by *Service Supplier*.

activities and meetings for the next one or two weeks, according to the length of the project. After the kick-off meeting, there is a very critical activity called *alignment and learning*. The aim of this phase is twofold. First, *Service Supplier* gathers and interprets, through several face-to-face meetings with the client's managers, the client's needs and then it identifies the client's organizational culture (*alignment*). This task is of paramount importance in refining the original brief of the project and arriving at an agreement for the collaboration, both for the NPD service provider and the client. This activity lasts on average one week. After the scope of the project and the client's needs and culture are fully understood, *Service Supplier* often proposes changes in the first draft of the project schedule, the progression of the team meetings and the critical milestones of the project.

Second, the characteristics of the market where the client sells its products are thoroughly investigated by *Service Supplier*, with the aim of identifying useful insights for the development of the new product (*learning*). This task is supported by a set of user-needs analysis tools such as interviews with key users and ethnography, as used with *Client A*. An analysis of competing products is part of the process. These preliminary activities end with the identification of the development directions for the concept, both in terms of client needs and market opportunities (*analysis and direction* milestone). After the alignment and learning phase, which lasts on average four weeks, *Service Supplier* starts the *scenario development and concept generation* phase. This stage can be either focused on a scenario analysis, as for *Client B*, or aimed at developing a new concept for products or components, as for *Client A*. Designers and engineers develop a number of product concepts to illustrate the types of product that are both technically feasible and would best meet the requirements of the target specification. This activity usually requires eight weeks and ends with the presentation of the preliminary concepts to the client (*preliminary concept* milestone). Next, the *concept development* phase starts, which has an average duration of eight weeks. During this phase, *Service Supplier* defines the product's specifications and creates the CAD/CAM drawings and models needed to produce a small batch of prototypes (*refined concept* milestone). Starting from these, *Service Supplier* creates the prototypes and tests them. If the prototypes pass the tests, the *testing and concept migration* phase ends with a 'green light' for production process development and engineering activities (which last on average sixteen weeks). This can be seen for *Client A* and *Client C*, whereas the collaboration with *Client B* was stopped before the concept development phase started.

While the innovation process depicted in Fig. 1 resembles to some extent a traditional NPD process as described in the well-established pertinent literature (Ulrich and Eppinger, 1995), there are some important aspects that are worth emphasizing.

In particular, our analysis indicates that *Service Supplier* carefully manages and devotes significant time and resources to the first phases of the collaborative NPD process, i.e. alignment and learning. The presence and relevance of the alignment and learning activities are a major difference compared to traditional NPD processes (Ulrich and Eppinger, 1995). Although the realignment of the team and organization is a critical activity in NPD projects undertaken within a single firm (Shilling and Hill, 1998), for a collaboration with an NPD service provider the need to establish a highly formalized alignment activity is higher, because it involves people working for different firms (the NPD service provider and the client), who do not know each other and do not share the same culture and values. This makes the management of the alignment and learning activities more complex. In particular, developing a deep knowledge of the client's culture, needs and expectations for the collaboration is particularly challenging because this type of knowledge is highly tacit and confidential. Strong interactions and several face-to-face meetings are fundamental in order to acquire such knowledge and this suggests the need for a more formalized process.

The importance of the alignment and learning phase is due to two additional reasons. First, it is fundamental in creating trust between *Service Supplier* and its clients. As noted in the management literature (Zaheer *et al.*, 1998; Adler, 2001), trust is the main coordination mechanism that should be used to administer collaborations that are uncertain in nature, cannot be pre-programmed and require creative collaboration. Markets and hierarchies are not effective coordination mechanisms for the management of these types of project (Adler, 2001).

> *The first phase of the collaboration is fundamental in establishing a good and trusting relationship with the client. How you are dressed, how you talk with the other team members, what you know about their products and experience... all these aspects impact on how you are accepted by the client's team. [...] The most critical issue during the alignment and learning phase is to develop trust and a personal relationship with people who do not believe in the project. It is obviously much more difficult in shorter projects.* (Project and design manager, *Service Supplier*, on project collaboration with *Client B*)

Some interesting aspects emerge regarding trust formation when comparing the three projects. *Client C* had already collaborated with *Service Supplier* in the past, and in particular with the senior designer who participated in the development project. In this context of prior reciprocal knowledge, one single face-to-face meeting was sufficient to ensure a proper alignment and the creation of a trusting relationship. However, *Service Supplier* had never collaborated with *Client A* or *Client B* before, and the projects required at least three personal meetings between the project teams in order to create an adequate level of trust. In the same vein, the way that *Service Supplier* forms a project team is a fundamental lever in enabling the creation of trust with a client organization, as will be further explained in the next section.

Second, if the alignment and learning phase is poorly executed, it can undermine the project's chances of success.

> *In order to make the project continue smoothly I really have to understand the client's needs. I can develop the best product in the world from a technical point of view. It won't be enough if the client wants something different.* (Product manager, *Service Supplier*, on project collaboration with *Client C*)

The client's objectives and expectations are analysed, interpreted and interiorized during this phase of the process by the NPD service provider, together with any peculiarities of the industry. This often leads *Service Supplier* to reiterate the first draft of the design brief in a document where its own interpretation of the problem is given. This brief[1] is a critical tool through which *Service Supplier* and its clients share reciprocal knowledge and align themselves before project activities start.

The cases for *Client A* and *Client B* testify the challenges inherent the alignment and learning phase. Focusing too much on the technical attributes of the products (*Client A*) and misunderstanding the real needs of the client (*Client B*), prevented *Service Supplier* from fully satisfying the two clients. Misunderstandings during the alignment and learning phase can be prevented by adopting consolidated project management tools. Several authors have stressed the importance of the so-called 'scope management process' (Pinto and Slevin, 1988; Clark, 1999). By undertaking a formal scope management process, i.e. scope planning, scope definition, scope verification and scope change control, *Service Supplier* could improve the outcomes of alignment and learning, making the knowledge about the client's need more explicit and manageable during the whole project life cycle.

Finally, our analysis identifies an intriguing trade-off during the alignment and learning phase. On the one hand, it is true that a good alignment and leaning phase with the client improves the chances of creating a trusting relationship and of satisfying the client. However, delving too deeply into the client's culture and system of values might prevent *Service Supplier* from identifying particularly innovative solutions to the client's needs (Tushman and O'Reilly, 2004; Weiss, 2004). Therefore, *Service Supplier* must balance these contrasting needs through collecting insights and suggestions about the project from other designers and engineers not directly involved in its execution. The cases of *Client A* and *Client B* are paradigmatic in this

---

[1]According to Borja de Mozota (2003), the design brief starts concept generation and consists of three main elements: the design project objective, information about the client company and information about the project.

respect. *Service Supplier* provided a room in its offices to display the prototypes and its client's products in order to encourage designers and engineers to try them out, give their impressions and opinions and hence stimulate the organization's ability to think out-of-the-box.

Collaborative organization

In the previous paragraph we pointed out the importance of trust as a coordination and transfer mechanism for tacit knowledge exchange during the alignment and learning phase. The ability of *Service Supplier* to build a trusting relationship with its clients during this critical stage mainly depends on the composition of the team for the NPD project.

A *Service Supplier* team has a standard configuration, which comprises a 'core team' eventually supported by an extended team. Each member has specific competencies and is in charge of carrying out a given set of activities. The core team has three people. The *key account* is in charge of managing the relationship with the client and typically has significant experience in new business development and marketing. This employee holds milestone meetings with the clients and acts as the formal interface between *Service Supplier* and the client's top management (and especially the *project leader* of the client's team). Within *Service Supplier*, a key account can be simultaneously responsible for a maximum of four projects, depending on their strategic importance. The second key role in the core team is the *project and design manager*, who is responsible for managing and developing the project. Typically this role is assigned to a senior designer with significant experience in strategic and product design. Besides actively participating in the project, this employee is in charge of scheduling and controlling its progress. Surprisingly, this administrative role is not given to a person with an engineering background. This is largely due to the history of *Service Supplier*, which was born as a pure design company and, as a result, its culture has always encouraged designers to develop strong project management capabilities, which is very uncommon in other design firms. The third member of the core team is usually a *concept developer* with product design experience, who supports the team especially during the scenario development and concept generation phases. Technical knowledge is typically ensured, when necessary, by temporarily extending the team to comprise a *product manager* and a *product developer*.[2] An additional concept developer may be part of the extended team performing the more time-consuming or knowledge-specific activities, such as reading white papers and specialized literature or developing prototypes and defining the specifics and the materials of the product[3] (see Fig. 2).

Although the structure of the *Service Supplier* team is rather traditional, some aspects deserve special attention. First, it appears that a critical point to which *Service Supplier* pays particular attention is to build the team on the basis of the motivation of the prospective members. Obviously, the human resources included in one team are chosen on the basis of their skills, i.e. technical competencies, previous experience in the industry and relational capabilities. However, a prerequisite in this selection process is a strong motivation to take part in the project:

> *For our designers, money and working hours are not important. A designer wants to work on something that he really enjoys.* (Product developer, *Service Supplier*, on project collaboration with *Client C*)

Our analysis indicates that the motivation of the team members is particularly critical because it helps build trust with the client organization, where extensive personal contacts and face-to-face meetings

---

[2] The project developed in collaboration with *Client C* is an exception in this respect: the complexity of the technical problems concerning the project objectives and the absence of a traditional key account in the core team forced *Service Supplier* to include a product manager in the core team.

[3] The concept developer in the core team has the same competences and is responsible for the same activities as the one in the extended team. The only difference between the two is their importance in the project. The concept developer in the core team has a key role in developing the project and in managing the interface with the product developer in the client team. In contrast, the concept developer in the extended team serves as an additional resource who mainly works in the back office to speed up project activities.

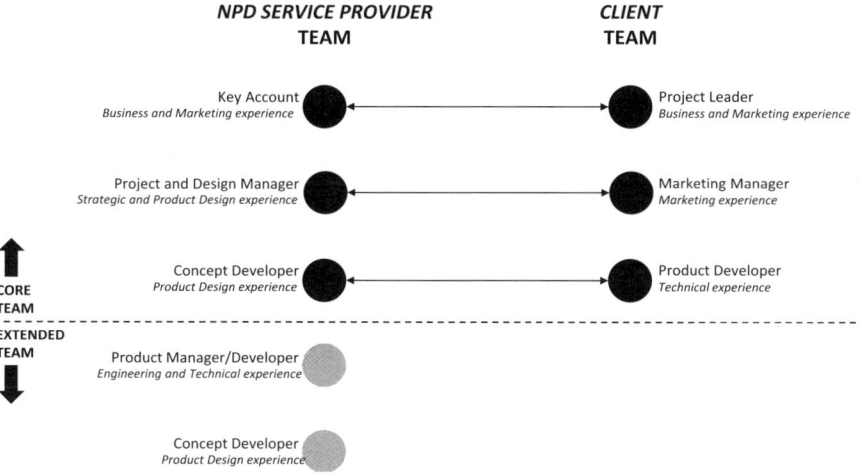

Fig. 2.   Collaborative organization adopted by *Service Supplier*.

require a special commitment in order to be successful. As noticed above, trust is the fundamental coordination mechanism in managing projects characterized by a high level of uncertainty. For the same reason, cultural affinity, languages spoken and personality traits are all critical aspects that *Service Supplier* takes into careful consideration in the creation of the team. For instance, for *Client A*, *Service Supplier* decided that one of the main criteria for the key account role was that the prospective key account spoke the same language as the client and was very close to the client culturally and in personality. What should be noticed is that trust is built through a personal relationship between a member of the *Service Supplier* team and somebody on the client's team. The client's team usually has a simple structure (see Fig. 2). A *project leader* is in charge of coordinating a group of people from both the technical and marketing departments. The analysis suggests that horizontal communication flows exist between the two teams and that they occur mainly at the same 'hierarchical' level (e.g. the product manager and product developer of the *Service Supplier* team are in a close relationship with the client's employees who have a technical background). Horizontal communications and interactions are fundamental in order to transfer tacit knowledge. This kind of knowledge is embedded in the people within the organization, i.e. it is sticky (von Hippel, 1994). Therefore, in order to figure out a complete picture of the client's needs and expectations, *Service Supplier* should gather information at different organizational levels. Hence, it is interesting to emphasize that, during the alignment and learning phase, *Service Supplier* pays particular attention to identifying and understanding the personal characteristics and cultural background of each member of the client's team. This often causes *Service Supplier* to slightly change the composition of its team to favour the establishment of a trusting relationship between the respective members.

Another aspect that deserves attention is that the *Service Supplier* team often plays a critical role in 'championing' the innovation process within the client's team (Schon, 1963; Chakrabarti, 1974; Howell and Higgins, 1990). In other words, they are often asked to support the project leader in convincing and motivating the whole team about the correctness of the decisions taken during the development process, as is clear for *Client A* and *Client C*. This is useful in reducing the perceived uncertainty over the project by the client's team, by strengthening the motivation of its members:

> *We have developed a scoring tool. It was nothing more than an Excel sheet created to rate different product concepts. The project leader asked us for a tool to convince and motivate his team regarding the quality of the concept chosen.* (Project and design manager, *Service Supplier*, on project collaboration with *Client A*)

In other words, by leveraging the trust built with the client during the early stages of the collaborative process, the *Service Supplier* team uses its reputation and well-respected competencies to motivate the client's team to pursue ambitious goals and overcome the unavoidable barriers that surface during a development project.

Tailoring the approaches of knowledge exchange and integration to the peculiarities of each project

The analysis of the empirical evidence further suggests that *Service Supplier* adapts the standard approaches and strategies for knowledge exchange and integration described above to the peculiarities of each collaborative project. Several variables can be identified as influencing the way *Service Supplier* applies these standard approaches in practice. Table 2 synthesizes the effects of the major contingent variables on the standard practices adopted by *Service Supplier*. A thorough discussion on the topic follows.

Client collaboration attitude

The amount of time and resources that *Service Supplier* devotes to the alignment and learning phase of a collaborative process is heavily influenced by the previous experience of the client in collaborating with NPD service suppliers; this is referred to as the *client collaboration attitude*. This is clear for *Client C*, which suggests that firms that have already collaborated with external consultants in their innovation activities are more inclined and able to transfer critical information and tacit knowledge about their competencies, needs and competitive advantage. This substantially reduces the barriers the NPD service provider has to overcome to acquire and integrate this critical knowledge from the outset of the process.

> *The kick-off meeting was held in a room with all the concept sketches hanging on the walls. What they had previously told us about their work was visible on the wall. We exchanged our cell phone numbers, defined how to share information and arranged the next meetings. After another meeting we clearly understood the scope of the project. We were ready to start.* (Project and design manager, *Service Supplier*, on project collaboration with *Client C*)

Furthermore, when *Service Supplier* starts working with a client it has already collaborated with, it often employs a simplified structure for the core team, where there is no key account and the project and design manager is given more responsibility for managing the relationship with the client, as with *Client C*:

> *I had more responsibilities than I usually have. I was in charge of both the practical issues of the project, such as planning and controlling,*

Table 2.   Effect of Contingent Variables on the Management Practices Adopted by the *Service Supplier*.

Classification of case		Client collaboration attitude			Timing of client collaboration			Provider collaboration role		
		Client A	Client B	Client C	Client A	Client B	Client C	Client A	Client B	Client C
Innovation process		*Client A* was not familiar with collaborating with external NPD providers and this was the first time that *Service Supplier* had worked with them. Furthermore, *Service Supplier* had no previous experience in the footwear industry	*Client B* was not familiar with collaborating with external NPD providers and this was the first time that *Service Supplier* had collaborated with the company	*Client C* had already collaborated with *Service Supplier* and it was accustomed to working with consultants in the innovation process, e.g. it had other internal groups collaborating with external NPD service providers	*Service Supplier* was involved in the NPD project from the beginning with the aim of designing a new shock-absorption system	*Service Supplier* was involved in the NPD process from the beginning with the aim of elaborating scenarios about what the vending machine of the future would be	*Service Supplier* was involved in the NPD process in the concept development phase with the aim of formalizing and synthesizing six concepts already developed by Client C	*Service Supplier* represented a 'source' of innovation since it had to provide radically new concepts for one of *Client A*'s products	*Service Supplier* represented a 'source' of Innovation since it had to provide radically new scenarios for vending machines of the future	*Service Supplier* represented a 'facilitator' of Innovation since it had to synthesize and formalize concepts already developed by *Client C* internally
Alignment and learning		(Alignment) *Service Supplier* needed to perform four face-to-face meetings in order to complete the alignment phase	(Alignment) *Service Supplier* gained knowledge about the client in three face-to-face meetings.	(Alignment) *Service Supplier* fully understood the scope of the project after one meeting held in a room with sketches of the preliminary concepts on the walls	(Alignment) The collaboration started with a thorough analysis of the needs and the capabilities of the client. It took two weeks and was focused on better defining the project brief taking into account the client's capabilities	(Alignment) *Service Supplier* needed to understand the client's needs. The accomplishment of this task required several interactions between *Service Supplier*'s and the client's teams	(Alignment) The two teams defined how to exchange information, documents and PowerPoint presentations. After the first meeting, *Service Supplier* understood the scope of the project. This phase took one day	(Learning) *Service Supplier* carried out web and literature searches on similar products. Furthermore, it surveyed the key users of the product, both professionals and amateurs. Finally *Service Supplier* developed a tool to test different shock-absorption systems. This activity took three weeks	(Learning) *Service Supplier* dedicated three weeks to develop a map of the entire supply chain for the product. During this preliminary task *Service Supplier* identified the distributors as a new and important stakeholder	(Learning) There was not a detailed learning phase, since *Service Supplier* had to synthesize concepts already developed. The interviews were used to test the client's reactions to new features
Collaborative organization	*NPD service provider team*	The composition of the team followed the traditional structure: a key account supported by people with both design and engineering backgrounds	Two senior designers were involved in the project. One of them was mainly in charge of managing the relationship with the client, i.e. he had the role of key account, while the other had the role of project and design manager	In contrast to the other projects, there was no key account. Thus *Service Supplier* increased the responsibilities of the senior designer	The team set up by *Service Supplier* had a mix of design, technical and strategic competences with the product manager and product developer who became more important as the project entered its final phase	The core and extended teams created by *Service Supplier* comprised only people with design and strategic competences	The core team created by *Service Supplier* comprised a project and design manager, a concept developer and a product manager. The extended team included a product developer			
	Client team	The team comprised a project leader, a marketing manager and a product developer			The team comprised a project leader, a marketing manager and a product developer	The team comprised a project leader from the marketing department and two other marketing managers	The team comprised a project leader from the R&D department, a marketing manager and two product developers			

and the relational issues, such as taking care of relations with the client. (Project and design manager, *Service Supplier,* on project collaboration with *Client C*)

Because reciprocal trust had been built during previous relationships, the key account role was not as critical for the success of the project, thus explaining the unusual configuration of the team.

The timing of client collaboration

Although the focus of our analysis is on the early stages of the NPD process, substantial differences can be observed, e.g. between *Client A*, where *Service Supplier* was involved in the very preliminary, unstructured concept generation activities, and *Client C*, where the client had already performed concept generation internally and collaborated with *Service Supplier* for the testing and concept migration activities. Our analysis indicates that the earlier the stage at which *Service Supplier* is involved in the client's NPD process, the more critical the alignment and learning phase is for the NPD service supplier, because it is much more difficult to codify the objectives of the collaboration and to understand the needs and requirements of the client, i.e. the knowledge to be exchanged is highly tacit and the uncertainty over the outcomes of the project is higher. Therefore, *Service Supplier* has to devote more time and resources in order to be properly aligned with the client. *Service Supplier* spent two weeks aligning with *Client A* and only one week on the projects with the other two clients. Nevertheless, as reported in Table 2 and discussed above, the effort *Service Supplier* is required to put into alignment and learning depends not only on the timing of the client collaboration, but also on the client collaboration attitude. However, despite the similar effect of these two variables, they explain the empirical evidence in different ways. The timing of client collaboration affects the amount of tacit knowledge that needs to be exchanged in order to be fully aligned. The sooner the collaboration starts, the more tacit knowledge has to be shared between the counterparts. In contrast, the client collaborative attitude influences the ease with which tacit knowledge can be transferred. Taking as constant the amount of tacit knowledge to be exchanged, the higher the client's attitude to collaborate with NPD service providers and with *Service Supplier*, the shorter the time required to exchange and integrate this body of knowledge, and consequently the shorter the time required to align the NPD service provider with its client.

A second aspect to emphasize is that the earlier the stage of involvement of the NPD service supplier, the lower the degree of formalization and the rigidity of the collaborative process. Although milestones and schedules are set out and shared by *Service Supplier* and its client at the beginning of a project, they are much more flexible and are often adjusted as long as development activities continue (as for *Client B*). Furthermore, when the NPD service provider is involved later in the NPD process, the temporal milestones are tighter, which requires closer monitoring and control of the development process. This is clear for *Client C*:

> *We had a very short lead time to finish the project. At the very beginning of the project we even planned the date and the hour of the final meeting. We had to fix the agendas of all the people involved with very short notice. We had no contingency for mistakes.* (Project and design manager, *Service Supplier*, on project collaboration with *Client C*)

This evidence can be explained by considering that the last phases of an NPD process are characterized by a lower level of uncertainty, which makes the implementation and use of formalized project management techniques easier.

Finally, the later the stage in which *Service Supplier* is involved in a collaborative NPD process, the stronger the role played by the product developer within the client's team, since technical competencies are more relevant as an NPD project moves downstream. It is possible to observe that in the projects that ended during the later stages of the NPD process, the technical members of the client team increased their decision-making power and their presence. The heterogeneous importance of people with a technical background in the client team has an effect on the organizational power of the product manager or developer inside *Service Supplier's* team. In particular, the higher the importance of the technical department in the client team, the higher the relevance of the product manager or developer within the *Service Supplier* team. Again, this is related to trust and to the ease with which knowledge and information can be exchanged between the counterparts:

> *In the project the engineer had a very important role. The customer's technical department usually looks at us (designers) suspiciously. The engineer should be trusted by them.* (Project and design manager, *Service Supplier*, on project collaboration with *Client C*)

In this respect, while the extended teams in both projects with *Client A* and *Client C* foresaw the presence of a product manager and a product developer, for *Client B* these roles were not involved, neither in the core nor in the extended team.

Provider collaboration role

The analysis of the case studies indicates that the NPD service provider can play two distinct roles throughout the collaboration with the client. It can be a 'source' of innovation (Fischer, 2001; Hipp, 2000), as for *Client A*, where *Service Supplier* was required to provide new concepts for a critical component of a new product. Alternatively, it can play a 'facilitator' role (Fischer, 2001; Hipp, 2000), as with *Client C*, where *Service Supplier* helped the client make a decision about which concepts should be given higher priority.

It seems that if the NPD service provider acts as a 'source' of innovation it needs to devote much more time and resources to the alignment and learning phase of the collaborative process because it is required to develop a substantial competence regarding the market, the users and the competitiors, so as to propose new components and product designs. This is clear if we compare the time required by the NPD service provider to fully understand *Client A*'s market (three weeks), where *Service Supplier* played the role of 'provider,' and for *Client C* (one week), where *Service Supplier* played instead the role of 'facilitator', i.e. it worked on concepts already developed by the client firm. The existence of already developed concepts means the knowledge to be exchanged is more explicit and reduces the overall uncertainty for a project since some relevant decisions have already been taken.

Conclusions

The research presented in this chapter starts from the premise that as a result of the increasing diffusion of open innovation practices, a soaring number of innovative companies find themselves entrenched in a strongly interconnected network of heterogeneous actors with different types of inter-organizational relations established for knowledge exchange. Among these external actors, NPD service providers have expanded their role as brokers and providers of critical specialized knowledge and technology.

This chapter adopts the viewpoint of an NPD service provider and investigates the approaches that it can employ to favour knowledge exchange with its clients throughout the service delivery process. The research shows that the NPD service provider should use the configuration of the innovation process and the organization of the collaborative relationship to address two critical barriers to the success of the relationship with its clients, i.e. the tacit nature of the knowledge to be exchanged and the difficulties in predicting the content of collaboration activities.

Managerial implications

Although the research is exploratory in intent, we believe that the chapter has relevant practical implications. In particular, it can be of help to managers of NPD service providers with several practical insights, gathered from the experience of one of the world's leading players in the industry, about how a collaborative relationship with client firms can be organized and managed so as to increase the capability of transferring tacit and complex knowledge and hence improve competitiveness. The major strategies identified in the chapter that an NPD service provider can use are summarized in Fig. 3.

The chapter further illustrates that putting these approaches into practice requires that the NPD service provider takes into account the distinctive characteristics of each client (e.g. in terms of previous experience in working with providers of knowledge-intensive business services) and the peculiarities of the specific collaborative project (e.g. in terms of the phase of the NPD process where the contribution of the service supplier is required and the major role it is asked to perform, whether as a 'source' of new concepts and ideas for innovative products or simply as a 'facilitator', which helps the client prioritize and select concepts and ideas already developed). Figure 4 shows the collaboration practices the NPD service provider should adopt according to the collaboration context:

- The commitment of resources and the attention paid to alignment and learning should be high if the client does not have previous experience in working with providers of knowledge-intensive business services (KIBS). This is particularly important if the NPD service provider starts to collaborate from the beginning of the innovation process and it is seen by the client as a source of knowledge.
- The key account and the project and design manager have important roles in an NPD service provider team especially when the service provider is involved early in the innovation process for a client that is not used to collaborating with KIBS providers. When the provider acts a facilitator, the concept developer and the product manager or developer are the key actors in the team.
- Finally, the project leader and the marketing manager in the client team are the most important interfaces between the client and the service provider, especially for new collaborations aimed at designing new scenarios and concepts.

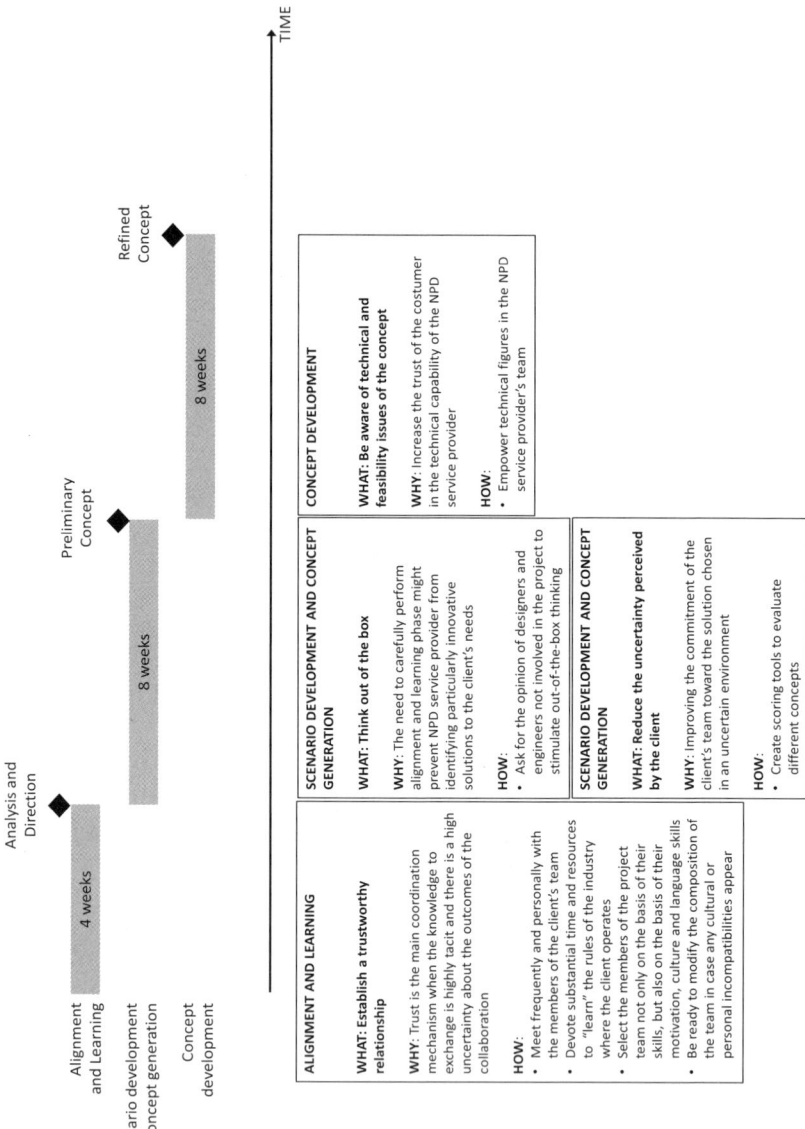

Fig. 3. Strategies for Effective Knowledge Exchange and Integration.

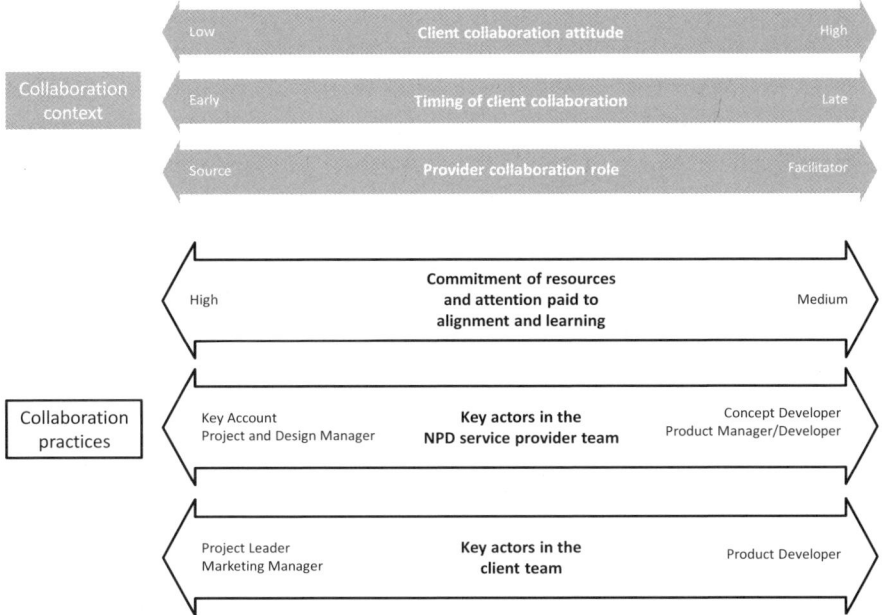

Fig. 4. Managerial Guidelines for Collaboration Practices.

We also believe that the chapter can benefit managers working in those companies that are following the principles of the open innovation paradigm and which have been increasingly relying on suppliers of specialized knowledge and technology, among which new product development service providers are growing in importance. These managers can see how the service suppliers organize the service delivery process, which could help to improve and facilitate the establishment of a trusting relationship. First and foremost, our analysis suggests that managers working in the client firm should promote continuous communication and information exchange with the members of the supplier's team. This can be achieved perhaps through introducing appropriate incentives and rewards for the people taking part in a co-development project or by promoting the co-location of joint development activities. This may be important for overcoming the unavoidable psychological bias toward exchanging knowledge with external parties, which is likely to hinder effective alignment and learning by the service provider. Our analysis shows that this aspect is especially important for the success of the whole project. Second, it would be useful for managers working in the client firm to clarify at the beginning of a co-development project the role that they would like the service provider to play, whether primarily as a source of knowledge or as a facilitator. Our analysis shows that this can affect how the service provider organizes the project team. Therefore, it is of particular importance to define this aspect at the outset of the collaborative relationship.

Finally, the chapter provides some practical insights that could be useful to policymakers interested in bolstering firms' innovation and competitiveness. Besides providing firms with funds that target the use of the services offered by an NPD provider, our analysis suggests that an effective initiative would be to promote joint work between a firm's engineers and designers and a service provider's employees, so as to create trust and mutual knowledge. Furthermore, sponsored training initiatives, where a firm's engineers and product managers are shown the advantages, challenges, ways of working and operational routines that characterize NPD service providers, are likely to improve attitudes to collaboration, therefore reducing the time and resources needed to align each party before development activities can start.

Research implications

Regarding the implications for research, the chapter is one of the first attempts in the recent open innovation debate, to investigate inter-organizational relations for knowledge exchange from the viewpoint of the provider of the knowledge. Furthermore, it contributes to the development of a deeper theoretical understanding of how NPD service provider firms organize themselves, a topic that has not yet received adequate attention in spite of the importance that these services have assumed in most of the industrialized economies in recent years. Consistent with research on collaborative NPD, the chapter points to the importance of trust in determining the success of this kind of inter-organizational relationship. Furthermore, it encourages researchers to investigate the managerial and organizational determinants underlining trust formation, which have been only explored in this research. Moreover, an interesting opportunity for future research would be the investigation of attitudinal and personality traits of the people involved in a collaborative NPD process with the aim of assessing their effect on trust formation, the client's satisfaction and, ultimately, on the successful completion of the project. This would contribute to the recent research (Rothaermel and Hess, 2007) that explored the micro-foundations of a firm's capabilities in innovation management. Another interesting issue to explore relates to the generalizability of this study. We focused our analysis on incremental innovation projects for consumer markets. However, it would be interesting to discover if the process and organizational solutions identified by our research are useful also for the development of radical new products, which usually challenge the client's competencies and established organizational routines.

Appendix: Description of the Case Studies
Client A

Client A was a leader in the shoe industry but in the early 2000s its market position worsened due to increased competition. In order to face this challenge, *Client A* decided to reinforce its technical credibility through the commercialization of an innovative shock-absorption system for its tennis shoes. The new system was aimed at satisfying the needs of both professional and non-professional players, and the firm had to communicate clearly the added value and the innovative elements of the design. The development of the new system for the tennis shoes was only the first step within a broader innovation strategy pursued by *Client A*. Indeed *Client A* started the collaboration project with the intention of migrating the technology and design of the new system to footwear for other sports such as football including five-a-side football.

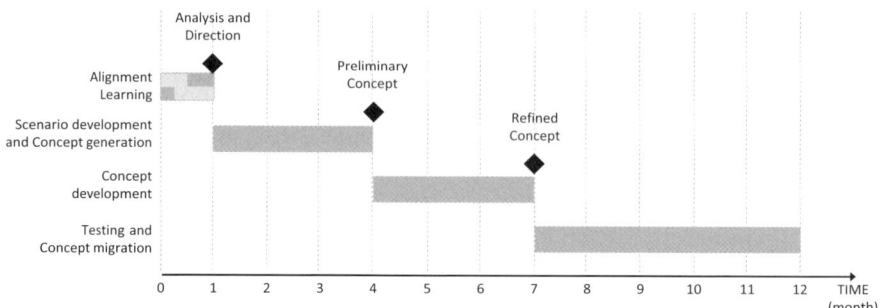

Fig. 5. Innovation Process Adopted by *Service Supplier* During the Collaboration with *Client A*.

Innovation process

The collaboration process started with a project kick-off meeting (September 2004) and its overall duration was 12 months (see Fig. 5). At this first meeting, *Client A* presented the project to *Service Supplier* and, afterwards, two meetings were scheduled for the following week. The first activities performed by the NPD service provider were to better understand the scope of the collaboration, i.e. to align *Service Supplier*'s team with the objectives of the client by taking into account its existing capability. Due to the tacit nature of the knowledge that the NPD supplier had to acquire at this stage, there was the need for continuous face-to-face contact between the *Service Supplier* team and the client. Furthermore, this was the first time that *Service Supplier* had collaborated with *Client A* and, more importantly, it was the first time it had worked in the footwear industry. Furthermore, *Client A* was not used to collaborating with NPD service providers during its NPD activities. Therefore a significant effort was required to align the *Service Supplier*'s team and *Client A*'s team. The collaboration included a deep analysis of the needs and the capabilities of the client. Understanding *Client A*'s development and production processes, reviewing its products and technology and performing a benchmarking of the relevant competitors' products were essential for the success of the project. This information was gathered in collaboration with *Client A*'s team in four face-to-face meetings. First, *Service*

Supplier performed an analysis of *Client A*'s products with the aim of understanding the technical functionality and advantages of the shoe and it identified *Client A*'s competences. Second, *Service Supplier* asked *Client A* to evaluate the different products of its competitors, in order to understand *Client A*'s evaluation criteria. Only after this stage was a detailed schedule of the project activities and milestones agreed (the alignment activity lasted two weeks).

During these early activities *Service Supplier* collected data and information about the shoe market in order to learn about the client's competitive environment. During this phase *Service Supplier* also conducted searches of the web and relevant literature for similar products to better understand the market context. Furthermore, *Client A* helped *Service Supplier* with the identification of the main key users, both professionals and amateurs. Surveys and focus groups were employed in this phase. Moreover, customers were monitored whilst using their tennis shoes. During this activity *Service Supplier*'s project team collaborated with the University of Cremona to develop a tool that could be used to test the mechanical response of the shoes to different movements of the feet (the learning activity lasted three weeks). At the end of the alignment and learning phase *Service Supplier* presented the preliminary findings to *Client A* in order to discuss the areas of opportunity identified and to select the more promising directions to explore and develop in the next phases of the program (the analysis and direction milestone).

Starting from the results presented for the analysis and direction milestone, *Service Supplier* developed different concepts for the absorption system. At the end, five detailed concepts were proposed to *Client A* through the use of 2D sketches. In order to enhance the creativity of its project team, *Service Supplier* allowed designers who were not involved in the project to contribute by identifying interesting concept ideas. An entire room of *Service Supplier*'s offices in Milan was used to display *Client A*'s and competitors' shoes. The designers could look at them, try them out, take them home, leave a comment or suggest an idea to improve them. The five initial concepts were reduced to three and presented for the preliminary concept milestone (the scenario development and concept generation phase lasted three months).

In order to help *Client A* in the selection of the most promising concepts, *Service Supplier* developed an *ad hoc* dashboard, which used a traditional scoring evaluation method. This was used to corroborate a critical decision taken by the *Client A* team during the concept selection phase. It was *Client A*'s project leader who asked *Service Supplier* to develop and use this tool, which was very much appreciated by the whole team. Starting from the selected concept, 3D CAD drawings were created and a small shoe batch was produced for the refined concept milestone (the concept development phase lasted three months).

The prototypes were used to test and refine the concepts with the aim of defining the best production process. *Service Supplier* defined the specifics of the products and developed the bills of material, taking into account the skills and the competences already owned by *Client A* (the testing and concept migration phase lasted five months).

Collaborative organization

The *Service Supplier* core team comprised three people (see Fig. 6): the key account, who was accountable for managing the relationship with the project leader and had significant experience in new business development and marketing; the project and design manager, selected from the *Service Supplier*'s senior designers with responsibility for developing a product consistent with the strategic objectives defined by *Client A*; a junior designer in charge of performing the analysis of the user's needs and the concept realization (concept developer). Despite his limited technical experience, the concept developer was selected because of his strong motivation to take part in this project. For the same reason, the key account was chosen on the basis of his cultural and language skills since he came from the same country as the project leader. The extended team benefited from the presence of two additional designers, who were heavily employed on the most time-consuming activities, such as desk and field researches in the learning phase and concept development (concept developers). Furthermore, the extended team comprised a senior and a junior engineer. They were mainly involved in the final phases of the project, but in the early phases they checked the choices of the core team in

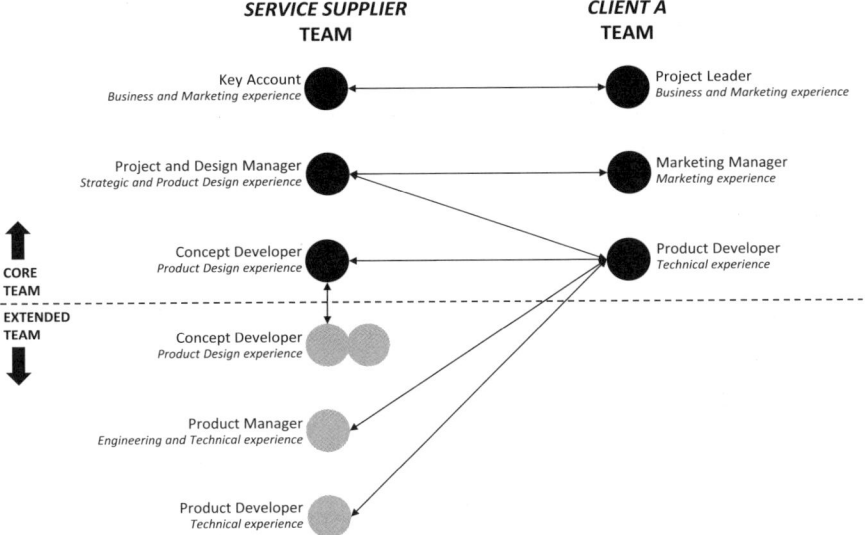

Fig. 6. Collaborative Organization Adopted in the Collaboration Between *Service Supplier* and *Client A.*

order to guarantee the technical feasibility of the developed concepts (product manager and product developer).

Client A's team comprised the project leader, who was mainly involved in strategic and commercial decisions, the marketing manager, who collaborated with the project and design manager in the identification of project priorities and was responsible for the concept initially defined in collaboration with the project leader, and the product developer, who represented the real interface with *Service Supplier* in terms of product implementation.

Project and collaboration results

The shock-absorption system developed by the project was never launched on the market, though some ideas from the project were employed in other products. The main reason for this poor outcome was an excessive focus on the product's technical aspects. Indeed the senior designer of the project was too focused on creating the best shoe from a technical perspective, without taking into account what the client really wanted.

Client B

Client B is a world leader in the vending machine industry and it is ahead of its competitors in terms of technical and innovation capabilities. However, in 2005 it decided to collaborate with *Service Supplier* in order to create scenarios about what the vending machine of the future would be, in order to maintain its leading market position. The lead time for the entire project was around four months.

Innovation process

After the presentation of a short project brief by *Client B* during the kick-off (March 2006), *Service Supplier* looked very carefully at the characteristics of its client (see Fig. 7). Had it already developed radically innovative products? What are *Client B*'s needs? How can *Service Supplier* answer such needs? Finding an answer to these questions was necessary to *Service Supplier* for understanding the project scope, i.e. to align *Service Supplier*'s team with the needs of the client. Since the focus was on the development of new scenarios for future vending machines, in this preliminary phase *Service Supplier* did not focus much on the capabilities of *Client B*. *Service Supplier* needed to meet and talk with different key people within

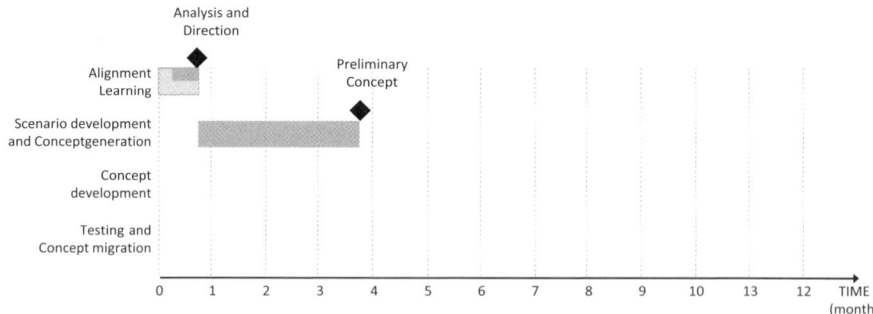

Fig. 7.   Innovation Process Adopted by *Service Supplier* During the Collaboration with *Client B*.

Client B in order to determine the project's scope and clearly identify the project's objectives. These tasks lasted around one week and required three face-to-face meetings, due to the difficulty in codifying the scope of the collaboration (the alignment activity lasted one week).

Furthermore, *Service Supplier* needed to better understand the vending machine market and to learn about the client's competitive environment in order to identify the variables that would affect the vending machine of tomorrow. To achieve this objective, *Service Supplier* spent two weeks developing a map of the entire supply chain for the product (the learning activity lasted three weeks). Whilst it was performing this preliminary task, *Service Supplier* identified a major weakness in *Client B*: it had always developed products by looking at the needs of the final users of the vending machines, without taking into account the needs and requirements of other important stakeholders such as distributors. Through intense research, based on an analysis of white papers and scenario analysis, *Service Supplier* developed several interesting insights for the vending machine of the future. These insights were presented and validated by the client during a formal meeting (the analysis and direction milestone).

Starting from the issues identified for the analysis and direction milestone, *Service Supplier* developed three new scenarios for future vending machines. In the scenario development and concept generation phase designers who were not directly involved in the project participated in two brainstorming sessions in order to increase creative capabilities. They were invited to use and comment on some of the existing vending machines developed by *Client B*, located within *Service Supplier*'s offices. For the preliminary concept milestone meeting three new scenarios were proposed to *Client B* (the scenario development and concept generation phase lasted three months).

Collaborative organization

Service Supplier executed the project employing a core team comprising two senior designers with significant experience in strategic and product design: *Service Supplier* usually has only one senior designer in each project. One of them was in charge of managing the relationship with the client (key account) while the other was assigned the role of project and design manager. Both were full time on the project. Furthermore, a junior designer was allocated to the project with the aim of helping the team in searching for information about future trends in the vending machine industry (concept developer). The team was also supported by an extended team, with another two junior designers (concept developers). These additional resources were involved in specific tasks mainly with the aim of supporting the core team in the labour-intensive research phase (see Fig. 8).

Client B's team comprised a project leader with significant experience in new business development and marketing and two marketing managers. Two employees from the R&D Department (product developers) took part in some meetings with *Service Supplier* mainly with the aim of ensuring the technical feasibility of the proposed scenarios.

Project and collaboration results

Client B was very satisfied with the output of the collaboration. It judged the concepts proposed as interesting future developments of their traditional vending machines. However, *Client B* was unable to transform these preliminary concepts into products due to problems

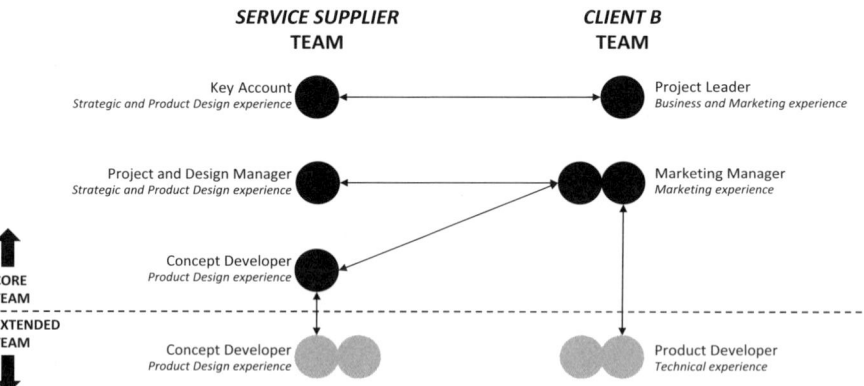

Fig. 8. Collaborative Organization Adopted in the Collaboration Between *Service Supplier* and *Client B*.

with technical modifications of the existing product line. *Service Supplier* had not considered this aspect during the development of the project since the scope was bounded by the identification of future scenarios. This is due to a partial misalignment between the output of the collaboration and the needs of *Client B* and shows the importance of a careful alignment between the NPD service supplier and its client from the outset of the project.

Client C

Client C was aware of the importance of innovation in its turbulent competitive environment. As a result of a continuous idea generation process, it had internally developed a set of six new features for a household appliance through brainstorming. Every two weeks employees from R&D in Germany, the marketing manager from the France Division, the chief engineer from the Sweden Division and a group of designers from the Italy Division met together to develop these new features. *Client C* asked *Service Supplier* to formalize and synthesize their work by creating an operating model for the household appliance, i.e. a model that looks like and works like the new product. The lead time for the project was very short, about two months. *Client C* had already collaborated with *Service Supplier* and it was accustomed to performing similar collaborative tasks.

Innovation process

The project started with a kick-off meeting (in June 2005) that was held in a room with the sketches of the new features, developed during the brainstorming, hanging on the four walls (see Fig. 9). Because of the short time available to carry out the project (two months), meetings for the following week were immediately scheduled and the two teams defined how to exchange information, documents and PowerPoint presentations. After the first meeting, *Service Supplier* was clear about the scope of the project: to realize an operating model of the household appliance incorporating the most promising features

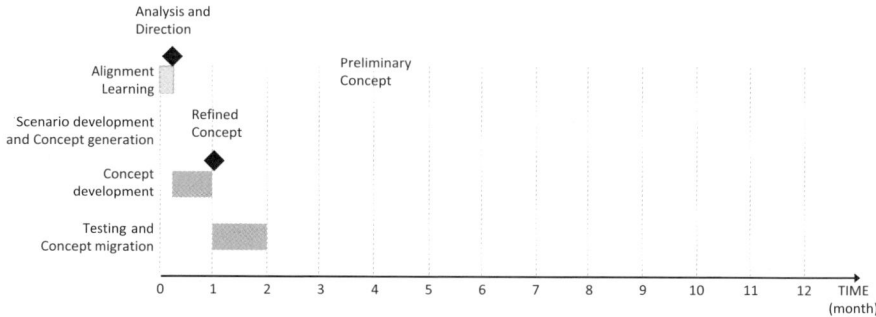

Fig. 9. Innovation Process Adopted by *Service Supplier* During the Collaboration with *Client C*.

already developed, i.e. a model that looks like and works like the new product. At the end of the first week *Service Supplier* created an exact schedule of the entire project. The main milestones and the internal meetings were established early (the alignment and learning activities were developed in parallel and lasted one week).

After the analysis and direction milestone, the concept development phase started. Since *Client C* had already developed six preliminary concepts, the concept generation phase was not performed collaboratively. *Service Supplier* tested the suitability of the new features for *Client C*'s customers by carrying out 30 in-depth interviews. Each interview lasted about one hour. Half of them were conducted in France while the other fifteen were in the UK. Interviews started with a short investigation of the current advantages and disadvantages of the new features developed by *Client C*. Furthermore, in order to stimulate the discussion and to replicate an 'in-store situation', the interviewees could open and look at three products with different features. The 'in-store simulation' concluded with the customers' ranking the features developed by *Client C* and the preferred combinations of them.

Using this information, *Service Supplier* refined and improved the six concepts developed by *Client C*. *Service Supplier* developed scoring tools to evaluate the different options. *Client C* assessed the preliminary concepts with this tool and expressed their confidence in the decisions that had been taken. From the six initial concepts, three

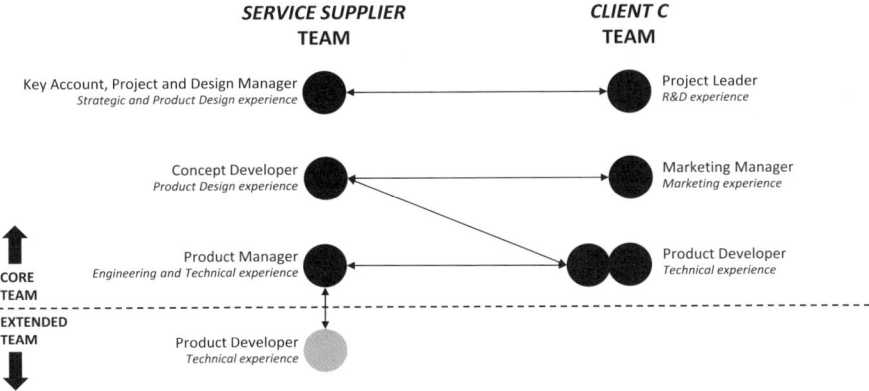

Fig. 10. Collaborative Organization Adopted in the Collaboration Between *Service Supplier* and *Client C.*

reached the next phase and passed the refined concept milestone (the concept development phase lasted around one month).

After the refined concept milestone, *Service Supplier* focused on the product architecture definition and the identification of appropriate materials. *Service Supplier* checked the integration of the components of the whole product through CAD drawings. Physical prototypes were tested in a real-life context with key customers using ethnographic methodologies. The members of both the *Service Supplier* team and the client's team took part in this test. The project ended with a definition of the product requirements (the testing and concept migration phase lasted around one month).

Collaborative organization

The *Service Supplier* core team was led by a senior designer, who directly interacted with the *Client C* project leader from the R&D department. In this project, the senior designer covered both the role of key account, taking care of commercial and relational aspects, and the project and design manager, planning the project and co-elaborating its strategic objectives. *Service Supplier* normally had different people for the roles of key account and project and design manager. However, the employees who specialized in business development were at that time already involved in other projects. Moreover, *Client C* was accustomed to collaborating with external NPD service providers and it had already collaborated with *Service Supplier* (specifically with the same senior designer). This made it much easier to establish trusting relationships with the client's team from the outset of the collaborative relation. A junior designer (concept developer) interacted directly with the marketing manager, while the product manager, who had significant experience in engineering and technical development, was the interface with the product developer came from the technical office. In this project the role of the product manager was particularly important. Indeed, designers are usually considered with suspicion by the engineering department of the client firm. Therefore, it was critical that the product manager from *Service Supplier* gained the trust of the client's engineering department. He had to demonstrate that he was able to answer their questions and to show that he had understood how the project was to be developed. Since the collaboration was aiming to develop an operating model, the engineering department had an important role in the project. *Service Supplier*'s team was supported by a product developer with significant technical experience.

Client C's team comprised a project leader from the R&D department, a marketing manager who interacted with the concept developer and two employees from the operations department (product developers).

Project and collaboration results

The collaboration was very successful. The project was completed on time and the selected features have been produced and installed in several models of the household appliance. Furthermore, the client was very satisfied with the outcome of the collaboration. *Client C* wrote one of the best reference letters ever received by *Service Supplier*. In particular, the ability of *Service Supplier* to meet the strict deadline and its ability to build a very multidisciplinary team in a short period were greatly appreciated by the client.

References

Adler, P.S. (2001). Market, hierarchy, and trust: The knowledge economy and the future of capitalism, *Organization Science*, **12**(2), 215–234.

Bianchi, M., Cavaliere, A., Chiaroni, D., Frattini, F. and Chiesa, V. (2010). Organisational modes for open innovation in the bio-pharmaceutical industry: An exploratory analysis, *Technovation*, **31**(1), 22–33.

Borja de Mozota, B. (2003). *Design Management: Using Design to Build Brand Value and Corporate Innovation*, Allworth Press, New York.

Boudreau, K., Lacetera, N. and Lakhani, K. (2011) Incentives and problem uncertainty in innovation contests: An empirical analysis, *Management Science*, **57**(5), 843–863.

Bstieler, L. (2006). Trust formation in collaborative new product development, *Journal of Product Innovation Management*, **23**, 56–72.

Buganza, T., Chiaroni, D., Colombo, G. and Frattini, F. (2011). Organisational implications of open innovation: An analysis of inter-industry patterns, *International Journal of Innovation Management*, **15**(2), 423–455.

Chakrabarti, A. (1974). The role of champion in product innovation, *California Management Review*, **17**, 58–62.

Chatterji, D. (1996). Accessing external sources of technology, *Research-Technology Management*, **39**(2), 48–56.

Chatterji, D. and Manuel, T.A. (1993). Benefiting from external sources of technology, *Research-Technology Management*, **36**(6), 21–26.

Chesbrough, H. (2003). *Open Innovation: The New Imperative for Creating and Profiting from Technology*, Harvard Business School Press, Boston, MA.

Chesbrough, H. (2009). Use open innovation to cope in a downturn, *Harvard Business Review*, June, 1–9.

Chesbrough, H. (2011a). Bringing open innovation to services, *MIT Sloan Management Review*, **52**(2), 85–80.

Chesbrough, H. and Crowther, A.K. (2006). Beyond high-tech: Early adopters of open innovation in other industries, *R&D Management*, **36**(3), 229–236.

Chesbrough, H., Vanhaverbeke, W. and West, J. (2006). *Open Innovation: Researching a New Paradigm*, Oxford University Press, Oxford, UK.

Chesbrough, H. (2011b). The case for open services innovation: The commodity trap, *California Management Review*, **53**(3), 5–20.

Chiaroni, D., Chiesa, V., De Massis, A. and Frattini, F. (2008). The knowledge bridging role of technical and scientific services in knowledge-intensive industries, *International Journal of Technology Management*, **41**(3/4), 249–272.

Chiaroni, D., Chiesa, V. and Frattini, F. (2010). Unraveling the process from closed to open innovation: Evidence from mature, asset-intensive industries, *R&D Management*, forthcoming.

Chiesa, V., Manzini, R. and Pizzurno, E. (2004). The externalisation of R&D activities and the growing market of product development services, *R&D Management*, **34**(1), 53–63.

Chiesa, V., De Massis, A., Frattini, F. and Manzini, R. (2007). How to sell technology services to innovators: Evidence from nanotech Italian companies, *European Journal of Innovation Management*, **10**(4), 510–531.

Chiesa, V., Frattini, F. and Manzini, R. (2008). Managing and organising technical and scientific service firms: A taxonomy and an empirical study, *International Journal of Services Technology and Management*, **10**(2/3/4), 211–234.

Christensen, J.F., Olesen, M.H. and Kjaer, J.S. (2005). The industrial dynamics of open innovation: Evidence from the transformation of consumer electronics, *Research Policy*, **34**(10), 1533–1549.

Clark, A. (1999). A practical use of key success factors to improve the effectiveness of project management, *International Journal of Project Management*, **17**(3), 139–145.

Cooper, R.G. (1990). Stage-gate-systems: A new tool for managing new products, *Business Horizons*, **33**(3), 44–56.

Di Minin, A., Frattini, F. and Piccaluga, A. (2010). Fiat: Open innovation in a downturn (1993–2003). How the Italian carmaker successfully transformed its R&D strategy to maintain its technological capabilities, *California Management Review*, forthcoming.

Dittrich, K. and Duysters, G. (2007). Networking as a means to strategy change: The case of open innovation in mobile telephony, *Journal of Product Innovation Management*, **24**(5), 510–521.

Dittrich, K., Duysters, G. and de Man, A.-P. (2007). Strategic repositioning by means of alliance networks: The case of IBM, *Research Policy*, **36**, 1469–1511.

Dodgson, M., Gann, D. and Salter, A. (2006). The role of technology in the shift towards open innovation: The case of Procter & Gamble, *R&D Management*, **36**(3), 333–346.

Egelhoff, W.G. (1982). Strategy and structure in multinational corporations: An information-processing approach, *Administrative Science Quarterly*, **27**, 435–458.

Eisenhardt, K.M. (1989). Building theories from case study research, *Academy of Management Review*, **14**, 532–550.

Eisenhardt, K. and Brown, S. (1999). Patching: Restitching business portfolio in dynamic markets, *Harvard Business Review*, **77**(3), 72–82.

Eisenhardt, K.M. and Graebner, M.E. (2007). Theory building from cases: Opportunities and challenges, *Academy of Management Journal,* **50**(1), 25–32.

Eisenhardt K. and Sull, D. (2001). Strategy as simple rules, *Harvard Business Review,* **79**(1), 106–116.

Fischer, M.M. (2001). Innovation, knowledge creation and systems of innovations, *Annals of Regional Science*, **35**(2), 199–216.

Gassmann, O. (2006). Opening up the innovation process: Towards an agenda, *R&D Management*, **36**(3), 223–226.

Hargadon, A.B. (1998). Firms as knowledge brokers: Lessons in pursuing continuous innovation, *California Management Review*, **40**(3), 209–227.

Hargadon, A. (2003). *How Breakthroughs Happen. The Surprising Truth About How Companies Innovate*, Harvard Business School Press, Boston, MA.

Hargadon, A.B. and Sutton, R.I. (1997). Technology brokering and innovation in a product development firm, *Administrative Science Quarterly*, **42**(4), 716–749.

Hipp, C. (2000). 'Information flows and knowledge creation in knowledge-intensive business services: Scheme for a conceptualization', in Metcalfe, J.S. and Miles, I. (eds), *Innovation Systems in the Service Economy*, Kluwer Academic Publishers, Boston, MA.

Howell, J. and Higgins, C. (1990). Champions of technological innovation, *Administrative Science Quarterly*, **35**(2), 317–341.

Huston, L. and Sakkab, N. (2006). Connect and develop: Inside Procter & Gamble's new model for innovation, *Harvard Business Review*, **84**(3), 58–66.

Iansiti, M. and MacCormack, A. (1997). Developing products on Internet time, *Harvard Business Review*, **75**(5), 108–117.

Jeppesen, L.B. and Lakhani, K.R. (2010). Marginality and problem solving effectiveness in broadcast research, *Organization Science*, **21**(5), 1–18.

Katsoulacos, Y. and Tsounis, N. (2000). "Knowledge-intensive business services and productivity growth: The Greek evidence," in Boden, M. and Miles, I. (eds), *Services and the Knowledge-Based Economy*, Continuum, London.

Kessler, E.H., Bierly, P.E. and Gopalakrishnan, S. (2000). Internal vs. external learning in new product development: Effects on speed, costs and competitive advantage, *R&D Management*, **30**(3), 213–223.

Kirschbaum, R. (2005). Open innovation in practice, *Research-Technology Management*, **48**(4), 24–28.

Lichtenthaler, U. (2009). Outbound open innovation and its effect on firm performance: Examining environmental influences, *R&D Management*, **39**(4), 317–330.

MacPherson, A. (1997a). The contribution of external services inputs to the product development efforts of small manufacturing firms, *R&D Management*, **27**, 127–144.

MacPherson, A. (1997b). The role of external technical support in the innovation performance of scientific instruments firms: Empirical evidence from New York State, *Technovation*, **17**, 141–151.

MacPherson, A. (1997c). A comparison of within-firm and external sources of product innovation, *Growth and Change*, **28**, 289–308.

Mansfield, E. and Lee, J.-Y. (1996). The modern university: Contributor to industrial innovation and recipient of industrial support, *Research Policy*, **25**, 1047–1058.

Marcotte, C. and Niosi, J. (2000). Technology transfer to China: The issues of knowledge and learning, *Journal of Technology Transfer*, **25**(1), 43–57.

Marwick, A.D. (2001). Knowledge management technology, *IBM Systems Journal*, **40**(4), 814–830.

Muller, E. and Zenker, A. (2001). Business services as actors of knowledge transformation: The role of KIBS in regional and national innovation systems, *Research Policy*, **30**, 1501–1516.

Nonaka, I. and Takeuchi, H. (1995). *The Knowledge Creating Company*, Oxford University Press, Oxford, UK.

Philips, P.L. (2004). *Creating the Perfect Brief: How to Manage Design for Strategic Advantage*, Allworth Press, New York.

Pinto, J.K. and Slevin, D.P. (1988). Critical success factors across the project life cycle, *Project Management Journal*, **19**, 67–75.

Polanyi, M. (1962). The logic of tacit inference, *Philosophy*, **41**, 1–18.

Rothaermel, F.T. and Hess, A. (2007). Building dynamic capabilities: Innovation driven by individual, firm, and network-level effects, *Organization Science*, **18**(6), 898–921.

Schon, D. (1963). Champions for radical new innovations, *Harvard Business Review*, **41**, 77–86.

Shilling, M.A. and Hill, C.W.L. (1998). Managing the new product development process: Strategic imperatives, *Academy of Management Executives*, **12**(3), 67–81.

Sutton, R. (2002). Weird ideas that spark innovation, *Sloan Management Review*, **43**(2), 83–87.

Tao, J. and Magnotta, V. (2006). How air products and chemicals identifies and accelerates, *Research Technology Management*, **49**(5), 12–18.

Terwiesch, C. and Xu, Y. (2008). Innovation contests, open innovation, and multiagent problem solving, *Management Science*, **54**(9), 1529–1543.

Tushman, M.L. and Nadler, D.A. (1978). Information-processing as an integrating concept in organizational design, *Academy of Management Review*, **3**(3), 613–624.

Tushman, M.L. and O'Reilly, C.A. (2004). The ambidextrous organization, *Harvard Business Review*, **82**(4), 74–81.

Ulrich, K. and Eppinger, S.D. (1995). *Product Design and Development*, McGraw-Hill, New York.

van de Vrande, V., de Jong, J.P.J., Vanhaverbeke, W. and de Rochemont, M. (2009). Open innovation in SMEs: Trends, motives and management challenges, *Technovation*, **29**, 423–437.

Vanhaverbeke, W. (2006). "The interorganisational context of open innovation," in Chesbrough, H., Vanhaverbeke, W. and West, J. (eds), *Open Innovation: Researching a New Paradigm*, Oxford University Press, Oxford, UK.

Verganti, R. (1997). Leveraging on systemic learning to manage the early phases of product innovation projects, *R&D Management*, **27**(4), 377–392.

Verganti, R. (1999). Planned flexibility: Linking anticipation and reaction in product development projects, *Journal of Product Innovation Management*, **16**, 363–376.

von Hippel, E. (1994). 'Sticky information' and the locus of problem solving: Implications for innovation, *Management Science*, **40**(4), 429–439.

Weiss, E. (2004). Functional market concept for planning technological innovations, *International Journal of Technology Management*, **27**, 320–330.

Windrum, P. and Tomlinson, M. (1999). Knowledge-intensive services and international competitiveness: A four country comparison, *Technology Analysis and Strategic Management*, **11**(3), 391–405.

Yin, R.K. (1984). *Case Study Research, Design and Methods*, Sage Publications, London.

Zaheer, A., McEvily, B. and Perrone, V. (1998). Does trust matter? Exploring the effect of interorganizational and interpersonal trust on performance, *Organization Science*, **9**(2), 141–159.

Chapter 16

Managing Offshore Development: A Cultural Perspective

Petra Edoff, Christer Norström, and Ylva Wretås
School of Innovation, Design and Engineering
Mälardalen University, Sweden

Introduction

As global competition is increasing, organizations are looking for new ways to decrease costs and gain innovation. For organizations involved in global product development of complex systems these are the main challenges for staying competitive. A recent trend emphasizes that the capabilities and resources for managing product development increasingly reside outside a company's boundaries. Many argue that the earlier and more extensive involvement of suppliers in product development will enhance productivity, speed, and product quality (Clark, 1989) but this also poses challenges. As companies increasingly compete in a global arena choosing the right partner is essential. Goldbrunner *et al.* (2006) claim that organizations benefit when they configure their supplier network for cost and manage them for value. Offshore outsourcing is one of the solutions that companies use to reduce costs through a supplier's economies of scale and lower wages (Bengtsson *et al.*, 2009). Other reasons to outsource are for strategic motives, to gain access to local market (Goldbrunner *et al.*, 2006; Mao *et al.*, 2008), or to gain access to new technology, competence, and innovation (Bengtsson *et al.*, 2009). Brown and Wilson (2005) give the definition: "Offshore outsourcing, or offshoring, refers to the procurement of goods or services by a business or organization from an outside foreign supplier, typically to gain the benefits of labour arbitrage" (Brown and Wilson, 2005, p vii). Initially many companies started offshore development using their vendors for testing and maintenance. As the relation matures, advanced product development tasks are outsourced to the offshore development center and clients also start to demand innovative results. In this chapter, product development includes everything from fulfilling a requirement specification from the client to more independent development as well as the creation of new independent services and products. However, as tasks become more complex the cultural differences and working methods are evident. In order to facilitate innovation from collaboration with suppliers, more integration is needed. These are the issues that need to be considered to facilitate collaboration in an efficient way.

Current research has identified several factors for successful outsourcing; Supplier competence in technology and quality control (Boutellier *et al.*, 2008; Primo and Amundson, 2002), interface management and communication (Boutellier *et al.*, 2008; Primo and Amundson, 2002; Van Looy *et al.*, 2005), Amount of direct interaction with supplier (Primo and Amundson, 2002), legislation and contracts (Mao *et al.*, 2008), the nature of supplier involvement (Primo and Amundson, 2002; Clark, 1989), trust (Sherwood and Covin, 2008; Mao *et al.*, 2008; Doney *et al.*, 1998), and the maturity of collaboration (Sherwood and Covin, 2008). A recent special issue on the outsourcing of innovation and R&D described research gaps relating to the performance implications of outsourcing and how to best manage outsourced projects once they are decided (Stanko and Calantone, 2011). Much research has been carried out on intercultural aspects in business (Trompenaars and Hampden-Turner, 1997; Hofstede and Hofstede, 2005; Adler and Gunderson, 2008); however, current research has only to a limited extent addressed the cultural aspects of efficient outsourcing in product development (Avison and Banks, 2008). Long-distance cultural collaborations put a greater demand on all these factors, not only in managing but also in understanding the underlying patterns that guide the behavior determine the efficiency of projects. In the past ten years, a large number of outsourcing contracts have increasingly been awarded to firms in developing countries because educated workers in these countries (India and China in particular) are willing to work for much lower wages (Brown and Wilson, 2005). While the clients of outsourcing are concentrated in North America, Western Europe, and Japan, India has been the leading destination (Mao *et al.*, 2008). Western clients seem to fall too easily for the argument that in a globalized world, distance, borders, and place no longer matter. This is in contrast to the study on global software outsourcing (GSO) by Heeks *et al.* (2001): "Players in this global game still retain cultural values rooted in a particular locale. The overseas development center is a powerful tool for synching and, thus, for raising project success rates and moving up the GSO value chain, but it has its limits. Western processes, systems, capabilities, and so forth can all be imposed. However, some cultural 'stains' underpinning these dimensions are hard for this global tide to wash away. Clients must learn to live with this" (Heeks *et al.*, 2001, p. 59).

This chapter will use an exploratory case study of a Swedish high-tech company (SHTC) and its Indian service provider (ISP) to give further insight into how cultural differences can influence the success of offshoring collaboration as well as providing a framework for managers when developing an offshore relation. The client–supplier relation is studied to map the current situation as well as identify possible efficiency improvements. To achieve efficiency in this set-up demands effective communication to understand the requirements, to adapt to changes in the requirements, to understand the technology that is the basis for implementing the requirements, and to deliver the results on time, on budget, and with the requested quality. The case-study analysis revealed that at the time of the study, the single most important factor on the progress of the relation was due to cultural issues, such as limited awareness and strategies for handling cross-cultural variations. Consequently, in this paper we will focus on the intercultural aspects of the relation between a client and a supplier with respect to product development efficiency. We will include organizational culture, national culture, as well as contextual factors to demonstrate the cross-cultural variations between two companies, one in Sweden and one in India

SHTC   ISP

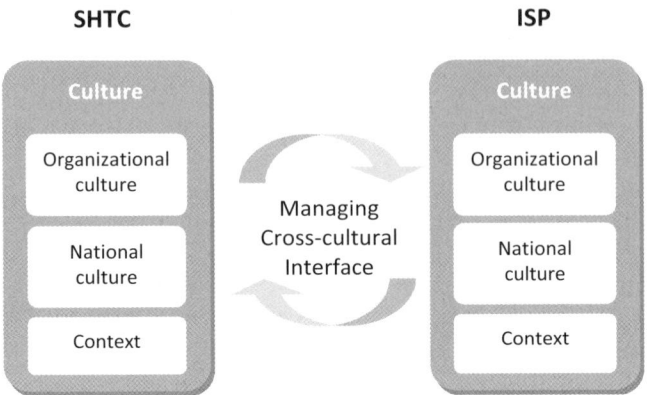

Fig. 1.   Focus of Study.

(Fig. 1). We have chosen to study this factor in-depth and to present theoretical as well as managerial insights into managing offshore outsourcing between Sweden and India.

The outline of this paper is a reflection of the research contribution. As this study used an exploratory approach, the appearance of cultural effects on collaboration is the conclusion and so an overview of the case study will precede the theoretical framework. The chapter will start with an overview of the case study, the research approach, data collection and analysis. The theoretical framework includes a general introduction to culture followed by a literature overview of organizational culture, national culture, and contextual factors in relation to outsourcing. The case-study perspectives on culture will be divided into three levels in our analysis: understanding, relating to, and managing the intercultural process. Finally, the theoretical framework is combined with the case study in a model that could guide companies in handling cross-cultural variations.

An outsourcing relation between SHTC in Sweden and ISP in India

SHTC is a Swedish Fortune 500 company, which develops software-intensive systems and operates business to business. Even though its products are

Table 1. Case Overview: Characteristics of the Projects and Companies.

Dimensions	Case-study characteristics
Nature of products	Complex software-intensive product, long competence transfer
Nature of projects offshored	Maintenance and support Product development (partial and complete products)
Openness	ISP has limited access to database under a "need-to-know basis," due to SHTC company regulations and policies
Knowledge management system	SHTC CMMI level 3, ISP CMMI level 5
Attrition	SHTC low attrition in general, managerial shifts occurred ISP 14.6% in general, 4.8% in ODC
Collaboration mode	Client–supplier

complex and require significant effort and budget for development, SHTC operates with a strict budget focusing on achieving the lowest possible cost when developing and implementing state-of-the-art technology. One of the strategies for delivering at low cost but keeping labor flexibility has been to outsource a large part of its development to low-cost countries. SHTC has several development sites globally, where projects are outsourced to ISP. We focus on one of the sites located in Sweden.

ISP is a consultancy company with consultants in 50 countries. The company provides IT services, business solutions and outsourcing to global businesses. ISP has been working on several projects for SHTC since the business relation started in 2000. The supplier performs both maintenance and product development in an offshore development center (ODC) in Hyderabad, India. There are about 500 people employed at the ISP ODC working directly for SHTC. The projects range from direct customer support, product maintenance to product development in cooperation with SHTC engineers.

A summary of the projects and companies is given in Table 1.

SHTC managers have varying experience in outsourcing and managing teams abroad. Significant attrition at managerial level has resulted in limited knowledge and coordination internally towards its supplier. ISP has an advanced knowledge management system, which enables them to transfer employees between projects without losing efficiency. However, SHTC has several times requested ISP to decrease its rate of attrition, as it fears that the time and money spent educating ISP staff on SHTC systems will have a marginal effect. ISP is also struggling to be proactive and achieve results due to its limited access to information regarding SHTC products and overall strategies. As the collaboration has continued both parties have communicated a wish to move towards a partnership but this is yet to be defined.

Research Approach

Our research aimed to develop a holistic and in-depth understanding of the evolution of an offshore development in terms of the client–supplier relation and to describe the views of the stakeholders in context, in an "interpretive case study." Our intention was to identify, isolate, and then explore the factors that either helped progress or hindered the development of the relation. The case study is based on interviews with 40 respondents (9 from SHTC and 31 from ISP) over a period of three months as well as an analysis of business review documentation and meetings (e.g. management day including all managers involved in the projects of both companins and regular meetings with key respondents), which were combined to triangulate the data.

We selected the case since it involves a wide range of outsourced projects, giving us insight in how elapsed time, strategic content, interaction between the sites, and organizational compatibility influenced the efficiency of the relation. We had research access to both the Indian and Swedish participants on all levels of the organizations in both India and Sweden. Two field trips to India were made; there were six days of interviews, participation in management days (two days), and informal discussions, which took place in corridors and the dining hall. In order to limit the effects of ethnocentrism due to our cultural origin and ideological convictions, we developed the interview guide and interpreted the results together with colleagues from Sweden and India (including a representative from Welingkar Institute of Management Development and Research in Mumbai). One of the results of the collaboration with Welingkar was the decision to interview team members

Table 2.   Overview of Data Collection.

Data collection	SHTC	ISP	Time
Interview	4 development managers	1 client general manager	3 months' data collection in spring 2008
	2 partnership managers	1 client offshore development center manager	
	1 manager from support	6 program managers	
	1 product manager	7 project managers	
	1 team member	15 team members	
		1 HR manager	
Observation	Meetings, management days 8 managers	Management days 22 project or program managers	2008–2009 2 days, fall 2008
Business review documentation	Steering committee reports and management guidelines	Business review report HR strategy and personnel training program	Written 2007–2009

and their team managers separately to make sure that no hierarchal influence affected the answers. The interviews were semi-structured and formulated to cover different aspects of the relation and working process; cultural perspectives were not asked about specifically until the end of the interview to avoid bias from the respondents.

An overview of the data collection process is given in Table 2.

The interviews were recorded and transcribed, while the informal discussions gave further insight into the organizational culture and work setting, and the management day gave us an opportunity to present the data and analysis for feedback and validation. It also led to the management at different levels discussing strategic issues with us, and the presentation of the findings and the discussions that followed helped

Table 3. Organizational Characteristics of Data Sample.

Organizational characteristics	SHTC	ISP
Organizational level	Managers (3 levels)	Managers and engineers (5 levels)
Organization size	Big multinational	Big multinational
Industry	Software-intensive systems – product oriented	Software-intensive systems – consultancy
Headquarters location	Sweden	India
Departmental affiliation	1 unit, 3 departments	1 unit
Demographical variables	On average older, higher technical experience	On average younger, lower technical experience
	Minority female employees	Minority female employees

broadening the communication between the companies. After transcription, detailed notes were made on the issues emphasized by the respondents and thereafter examined in relation to theory. Our interpretations were discussed among the authors as well as the case participants, which helped to clarify and refine our interpretation. Thus, even though the interview questions were inspired by the literature, the analysis of the data was made within the case and the theoretical frame was developed continuously throughout the process.

Ronen and Shenkar (1985) discuss the need to use diverse measurements in the same study for clustering the results, apart from measuring cultural differences. It is valuable to mention these different factors and consider how they influence the overall results of the study, as shown in Table 3.

Respondents from all hierarchal levels were interviewed at ISP. At SHTC, the respondents were managers at different levels since they are the only employees involved in the collaboration from the SHTC side and thus were representative for the relation as such. One reason for picking this case was that even though both organizations have departments in both countries, the relation is investigated from the headquarters point of view. We were thus able to evaluate the national and organizational cultures of ISP and SHTC, and their influence on the relation. The goal of the empirical study was twofold: first, to gain a snapshot of current issues emphasized by the respondents, and second to elaborate on the challenges they saw ahead. Even though the respondents were asked about the influence of cultural issues both directly and indirectly, the extent to which these would influence the results of the study was not revealed until the analysis of the data. The element of surprise is important when analyzing a case study (Siggelkow, 2007) as well in cultural analysis (Schein, 1992). Cultural analysis involves "raising issues of context and meaning, and bringing to the surface underlying values" (Smircich, 1983, p. 355). In general, cultural differences are seen as more common than the commonalities we all share, a bias which can be described as heterocentrism. At the same time, it is common to focus on problems, misunderstandings, and cultural clashes, rather than the things shared in common (Stier, 2009). The "problems" are highlighted here to justify the attention given to the cultural perspective (from a managerial perspective), while the true message is that understanding and strategies can contribute to a more efficient collaboration both in terms of perception and results. It is our belief that cross-cultural collaborations have as much potential for success as intra-cultural ones!

Theoretical Framework

The central aspect of this chapter is the case study rather than testing existing theory, thus we use an inductive approach. We have combined theory in an eclectic way to provide an understanding of bridging different disciplines. Culture is a concept used in a variety of disciplines; the contexts and the complexity of the different concepts are overwhelming. Even though culture has been thoroughly researched in the social disciplines, this chapter fills a gap with a focus on offshoring product development, as well as the description and comparison between Sweden and India. Avison and Banks (2008, p. 250) noted: "Relatively little work has been done on the deeper effects of cross-cultural communication within the delivery of offshore projects or services." We will provide some practical examples of how culture plays a part in overall performance in the relation between SHTC and ISP.

The insights that emerge from linking two concepts are a function of the basic conceptions of, in this case, culture and outsourcing that the researchers bring to the situation. The following sections give an overview of how the concept of culture can be seen from national and organizational perspectives, as well as the framing contextual factors (such as regional issues and the religious perspective). This framework will be used to describe the different perspectives on culture, while the case study illustrates its role in offshore outsourcing between Sweden and India. We will then analyze what the combination of organizational culture, national culture, structure, and contextual factors bring to the offshore outsourcing relation.

Culture

"Culture is to society what memory is to the person. It specifies designs for living that have proven effective in the past, ways of dealing with social situations, and ways to think about the self and social behavior that have been reinforced in the past" (Triandis, 1989, p. 511). "Culture includes language, technology, economic, political, and educational systems, religious and aesthetic patterns, social structures, and so on" (Triandis, 1989). Schein (1992) defines culture as a "pattern of shared basic assumptions that the group learned as it solved its problems of external adaptation and internal integration, that has worked well enough to be considered to be valid and, therefore, to be taught to new members as the correct way to perceive, think, and feel in relation to these problems" (p. 12). Culture can be described on different levels, from concrete manifestations to deeper values and assumptions, which are taken for granted. The visible organizational structures and processes can be called the *artifacts* of culture. It includes all the visible phenomena of culture such as language, technology, clothing, and rituals. Even if something is visible it does not mean it is easy to interpret its meaning as symbols can be ambiguous and interpreted subjectively. *Espoused values* include strategies, goals, and philosophies. They are conscious manifestations of culture, which match the underlying values to a variable extent. The *basic underlying assumptions* illustrate the unconscious beliefs that are taken for granted including perceptions, thoughts, and feelings (Schein, 1992). Management practices differ on an individual level, on an organizational level within a culture and there are national differences. We will start by explaining the concept of organizational culture.

Organizational culture: Concepts of culture and organizational analysis

Smircich (1983) gives an overview of the intersection between culture and organizational analysis found in different research themes, such as comparative management and corporate culture. Culture can be seen as a root metaphor "to frame the study of organization as a social phenomenon" (Smircich, 1983, p. 353), focusing on language, symbols, myths, stories, and rituals. Culture has been used in research as a background factor, an organizational variable, as well as a metaphor for conceptualizing organization. The overall similarity is that "the idea of culture focuses attention on the expressive, non-rational qualities of the experience of organization. It legitimates attention to the subjective, interpretive aspects of organizational life" (Smircich, 1983, p. 355). Smircich discuss the different themes in organization and management research relating to culture:

* Comparative management — seek patterns of belief and attitudes and managerial patterns across countries
* Corporate culture — seek to outline how these dimensions are interrelated and their influence on critical organizational processes and outcomes
* Cognitive organization theory — consider organizations as systems of thought, charting the rules by which organization members coordinate their actions
* Symbolic organization theory — interpret patterns of symbolic actions that create a sense of organization, such as language

- Organization theory influenced by anthropology or psychodynamics – try to understand how organizations form and practice manifest unconscious processes

Organizational culture is conceptually closely related to other concepts such as organizational climate and occupational culture. According to Denison, "[c]ulture refers to the deep structure of organizations, which is rooted in the values, beliefs, and assumptions held by organizational members" (Denison, 1996, p. 624). He continues, "[c]limate, in contrast, portrays organizational environments as being rooted in the organization's value system" (p. 624). Both perspectives, however, examine the internal social psychological environment of organizations in relation to individual perception and the effect on organizational adaptation (Denison, 1996). Thus, both climate and culture are relevant for this study.

In this study, we will use the concept of organizational culture to describe the set of values and routines that guides behavior within an organization, at the same time distinguishing the organization from others. However, big multinational companies can display different cultures when located in different countries. Apart from contextual factors, the underlying culture characterized by the nation in which the organization operates is relevant.

National culture and outsourcing

Globalization entails both diversification and standardization, but while you can find the same products all over the world, management practices still differ across cultures (Newman and Nollen, 1996). There have been several attempts to conceptualize and measure cultural differences among nations and relate them to management practices, the most well-known survey results include Hofstede and Hofstede (2005) and Trompenaars and Hampden-Turner (1997). Trompenaars and Hampden-Turner (1997, p. 3) state that "as markets globalize, the need for standardization in organizational design, systems and procedures increases. Yet managers are also under pressure to adapt their organization to the local characteristics of the market, the legislation, the fiscal regime, the socio-political system and the cultural system. This balance between consistency and adaptation is essential for corporate success."

National culture has also been researched in terms of its effect on strategic decision-making (Schneider and De Meyer, 1991), joint venture dissolution (Park and Ungson, 1997), choice of entry mode (Kogut and Singh, 1988), and new product development (Nakata and Sivakumar, 1996). Nakata and Sivakumar explain that each firm chooses a culture, whether consciously or not, when for instance establishing a new R&D site. They conclude that the national factor can influence the outcome along with the more traditional factors of technical capabilities, financial resources, logistics, and market access.

Trompenaars and Hampden-Turner (1997) define culture as the way people solve problems, particularly in relation to other people, time, and the external environment. They claim that all humans have to face basic problems of survival but the solutions that each human finds differ. Ronen and Shenkar (1985) underline that nationality alone cannot fully capture cultural values but national boundaries delineate the legal, political, and social environments within which organizations and workers operate. This study tries to avoid stereotypes, which are sometimes apparent in the literature on national culture (Nicholson and Sahay, 2001), but a literature survey provides guidelines on general aspects that are important to consider. The results from global surveys on culture by Trompenaars and Hampden-Turner (1997) and Hofstede and Hofstede (2005) are shown in Table 4, emphasizing those dimensions, or dilemmas, of culture where Sweden and India differ the most.

Culture is part of a socialization process that starts in childhood and the variance between individualistic and collectivistic cultures can be seen in parenting. Collective cultures preach obedience, reliability, and proper behavior, while the primary concerns of parents in individualistic cultures are self-reliance, independence, and creativity. "The smaller the family size, the more the child is allowed to do his or her own thing" (Triandis, 1989, p. 510). Most Indians tend to rely on an external locus of control, subjugate themselves to nature, which means that the future is perceived as uncertain and out of reach of

Table 4. Literature Review of National Differences Between Sweden and India.

Sweden	India
Individualistic (Trompenaars and Hampden-Turner, 2007; Hofstede and Hofstede, 2005)	Collectivistic (Trompenaars and Hampden-Turner, 2007; Hofstede, 2005; Panda and Gupta, 2004)
Autonomous and action oriented (Isaksson, 2008)	Dependence and conformity (Gopalan and Rivera, 1997)
	High power distance (Hofstede and Hofstede, 2005; Hofstede, 2007; Panda and Gupta, 2004)
Low power distance (Hofstede and Hofstede, 2005)	Primacy of personal relationships, diffuse culture (Gopalan and Rivera, 1997; Panda and Gupta, 2004)
Primacy of work goals, specific culture (Isaksson, 2008; Trompenaars and Hampden-Turner, 1997)	Ascribed status (Trompenaars and Hampden-Turner, 1997)
Achieved status (Trompenaars and Hampden-Turner, 1997)	Particularistic, situational behavior (Trompenaars and Hampden-Turner, 1997; Panda and Gupta, 2004)
Universalist (Trompenaars and Hampden-Turner, 1997)	

their control. This is combined with a past time orientation, which causes tremendous pressure to conform to traditional practices and beliefs, accounting for e.g. religious and astrological beliefs. Behaviors displaying dependence, conformity, and approval-seeking are rewarded over creativity, independence, and showing initiative. At the same time, Indian employees attach greater importance to the superior–subordinate relationship than productivity and work goals (Gopalan and Rivera, 1997). Panda and Gupta (2004) claim that while high ideals are preached, they are not practiced; instead family and material interests are prioritized. Indians are motivated to achievement not for the sake of achievement but for the enhancement of family status (p. 39).

A study by Hofstede (2007) comparing the perceived goals ascribed to successful business leaders in four countries shows that the Indian respondents prioritize: family interests, continuity of the business, personal wealth, and power. The least important factors were staying within the law, creating something new, and responsibility towards employees. This is in contrast to the three strengths of Swedish management found by Isaksson (2008): "Big picture" preference and a high-level of delegation; change and action oriented; and inclusive and non-confrontational. The modern Swedish management style is meritocratic, autonomous, and anti-hierarchal, biased to team working, reluctant to glorify star performers, non-confrontational and conflict-avoidant, as well as action oriented. Somewhat paradoxically, even though Sweden has a rather individualistic culture the Swedish tradition of organizing work stresses the role of the individual as well as the group. Employees enjoy following directives, as long as they are loosely set and goal oriented. Swedes always expect to be part of a team but at the same time prefer to work autonomously. Isaksson (2008) illustrates this paradox with the communal coffee breaks, which are common in Sweden, contrasting the small talk around the coffee machine, which is more common in other cultures. Another aspect of Swedish culture is that the social ties within a work team focus on a common commitment to a specific cause or goal rather than personal relationships. As companies have suppliers all over the world, learning and development of knowledge can become problematic because of cultural differences (Bosch-Sijtsema and Postma, 2009). However, companies can benefit from culturally diverse partners, for example in understanding different markets and different customer behaviors.

While culture has been widely researched, its influence on offshore outsourcing is not widely acknowledged (Nicholson and Sahay, 2001). One attempt to explore this issue is a case study on the globalization of software outsourcing by Nicholson and Sahay (2001), discussing collaboration between Britain and India. India still remains the unquestioned leader for offshore development for European and North American companies. Indian companies are nowadays veterans in the software outsourcing business and are able to use their experience as well as references from multinational companies (Ali Babar *et al.*, 2007). Ali Babar *et al.* (2007) discovered that Indian as opposed to Vietnamese practitioners did not mention the understanding of a client's culture in gaining trust, but they were mostly referring to American clients. American clients have been common in India for a long time and there is a great deal of influence from American MBAs in education in India, which can explain why this combination of cultures is seen as normal.

Nakata and Sivakumar (1996) studied the relation between national culture and new product development (NPD) and found that a high degree of individualism promotes NPD at the initiation stage as it can benefit from drive and personal vision. On the other hand, a high degree of collectivism promotes NPD during the implementation stage as it benefits from cooperation and a unified purpose. The same pattern was shown in terms of power distance, where a low degree of power distance favors the initial stages of NPD by encouraging contributions of diverse ideas regardless of hierarchal position.

Context and traditions in relation to culture

The big Swedish R&D companies are increasing their share of research and development work in low-salary countries (Ahlbom, 2007). Meanwhile the low-salary countries of Asia are rapidly approaching the frontiers of knowledge and innovation in the hope that new areas of commercial activities can be explored and exploited in the global market (Singh, 2006). India has a well-developed national innovation system but spending is less than one percent of GDP. The supply and quality of researchers in India is high compared to other Asian countries, promoting the establishment of foreign affiliate R&D centers (Singh, 2006). India has experienced rapid economic growth, which now makes it the fourth largest economy and its GDP is increasing 8% annually (Goldbrunner *et al.*, 2006). Sweden, on the other hand, has been labeled as one of the world's most creative and competitive nations. Florida (2005) ranked Sweden as first in a Global Creativity Index based on research in 45 countries. Sweden was ranked fourth on the Global Competitiveness Index 2007–2008 (Porter *et al.*, 2007). Between 2007 and 2010, Sweden has consistently been ranked fourth on this index, while in the same period India was, on average, in 49th place, out of 133 countries (World Economic Forum, 2009). Although Sweden has gains much praise in research regarding innovation, because of its small size it is always affected by the larger countries and therefore relies on collaboration to maintain its global position.

One can never exclude the context when trying to explain cultural differences and other problems that can arise in global business. Sweden and India are different in more than size and economy, e.g. there are differences in labor regulations, demographics, education systems, as well as the history and current status of the specific industry. These contextual factors can be seen as the most general artifacts of culture but there are also regional differences that can have big influence. Panda and Gupta (2004) revealed in their study that while there were some common cultural preferences in India, one could also find location-specific cultural preferences, associating them with the degree of infrastructure development in these locations. They argue that "cultural change is context sensitive and depends on the historical and cultural legacy inherited by a location" (p. 27). This relates to some of the criticism directed at the search for average national scores such as the research by Hofstede and Trompenaars. Singh (1990) argues that general descriptions and average national cultural scores are less valid in culturally plural countries such as India and China, which are diverse and have distinct sub-cultures. He prefers to identify a distinct segment and determine its sub-cultural identity, such as industrial organization. However, one should note that Hofstede (Hofstede and Hofstede, 2005; Hofstede, 2007) investigated the relative positions of countries rather than giving a general description of the characteristics of management in each society. Singh (1990) investigated cultural aspects in organizations in India, differentiating between the public and private sectors, as well as international companies, and found all of them to have a distinctive niche in the cultural sphere. The scores for international companies were in line with those for the UK, the US, and Canada, which is not surprising since it matches the companies' origins and thus their cultures. Many managers internalize both Indian and Western values, combining a childhood in an Indian cultural context with training in Western management practices (Fusilier and Durlabhji, 2001). The lack of uniformity in values makes doing business in India highly complex for the outsider.

Radhkrishnan (2009) discusses the concept of social exclusion in India and how globalization is reinforcing some of the old systems. The types of exclusion in globalizing India include: displacement, fragmented labor, and educational deprivation. The latter has implications from an offshoring perspective, since not all of the talented people in Indian have the opportunity to enter higher education and they will have difficulties in benefitting from the global knowledge-based economy. Sweden, on the other hand, is a secularized country with free education for all and a social security system to aid the less fortunate. The statistics show a clear picture for the differences in education level: 22% of the people in Sweden are graduates (SCB, 2009) compared to about 8% in India (Radhkrishnan, 2009). These examples of culture boil down to the question of how to handle cross-cultural collaboration and whether understanding and an attempt to move closer to a partner, through a "negotiated culture perspective," is of any use in global business. Should we focus on choosing complementing cultures to collaborate with, or are there methods that can be used to adjust culture to suit the present needs of a collaboration?

Perspectives on Culture Related to the SHTC-ISP Relation

The companies have different perceptions of the relevance of whether they should adapt to cultural variations or not. ISP is trying to learn how to please their client, through both behavior and working methods. The case-study results show that the managers from SHTC can be divided into two groups: (1) managers addressing the cultural differences and trying to work around them, and (2) managers who find cultural differences difficult and use the same working methods as usual. The first group has developed new reporting systems and increased interaction and feedback to improve the efficiency within the relation. The managers who have not addressed the cultural differences claim that inefficiency is due to the younger, less-experienced engineers at ISP compared to those at SHTC. The different perspectives from SHTC managers also reflect their view on the future of the relationship, which is now described as in "preparing mode for partnership." One SHTC manager is still "pleased, but not satisfied," and it is clear that the more qualitative perception and understanding of a potential partner can sometimes influence strategic decisions as much as key performance indicators. This paper emphasizes the need for awareness of cultural variations for the purpose of taking the steps needed to reconcile cultural dilemmas. Adding the cultural aspect as an essential factor for efficiency in outsourcing, we wish to highlight how cultural differences can cause misunderstandings and frustration in a supplier–client relation, which often originate from a combination of organizational, national, as well as contextual (e.g. regional and religious) backgrounds. An understanding of the origin of cultural differences can guide companies in handling these differences systematically.

We propose a framework for dealing with cultural factors from a management perspective. The cultural factors have been divided into two sets in our analysis. The first set of factors is manageable by the companies involved in the business relation and the other factors can only be related to. We have also provided managerial measures for these cross-cultural variations, which can be used to achieve higher performance in a business relation.

Managing Cross-Cultural Interfaces

Figure 2 shows the process for managing a cross-cultural interface in an offshoring collaboration, which will be the basis for our discussion.

Cultural factors to understand and relate to

There are some factors fundamentally rooted in each society, which can be described as cultural values. Knowing these factors is the first step toward understanding a culture and accepting them is a necessary part of a business relation. The underlying assumptions of the culture in an organization according to Schein (1992) and the nationally rooted cultural values emphasized by Hofstede and Hofstede (2005) and Trompenaars and Hampden-Turner (2007) fit into this category. The

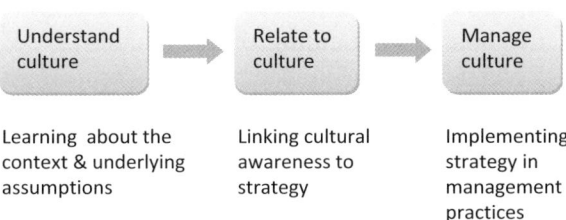

Fig. 2. The Intercultural Process.

underlying values are something that cannot be expected to change within an offshore outsourcing relation but they are important to relate to. Individuality versus team orientation is an important aspect that is influenced by culture (Trompenaars and Hampden-Turner, 1997; Hofstede and Hofstede, 2005).This cultural dilemma is reflected in whether people regard themselves as individuals or as part of a group. Individualistic societies tend to have looser ties between individuals and personal responsibility is higher (Hofstede and Hofstede, 2005). Sweden is an individualistic culture (Trompenaars and Hampden-Turner, 1997; Hofstede and Hofstede, 2005), which influences the degree to which a person is proactive or creative as an employee. Individualistic-oriented people tend to take responsibility for themselves and their own development. A society that instead favors the collective, develops team-oriented individuals who feel a larger responsibility for the context and look at developments in a more holistic sense. Losing face (Trompenaars and Hampden-Turner, 1997; Bullis, 1998; Lau, 2004) is another well-known aspect of Asian culture that represents the behavior of conforming to social pressure and contacts. The tendency to focus on ascribed rather than achieved status and the higher degree of power distance within an organization, are other ways in which India and Sweden differ. When working in a global context it is important to be aware of the differences in the way that verbal and non-verbal communication are used (Trompenaars and Hampden-Turner, 1997). Touching other people, the space appropriate between people as well as assumptions about privacy are all features of non-verbal communication. To wiggle the head in India means that you agree, but in Sweden it is interpreted as a "no." There have been some efforts to educate employees in cultural differences at the start of new projects, but since this practice is not yet widespread in the organizations, it means that employees do not yet have a shared perspective and understanding of the situation.

Cultural factors to understand, to relate to and that are manageable

When entering an offshore relation it is obvious that there will be differences at both national and organizational levels. While the national

Table 5. Artifacts and Espoused Values Demonstrated at SHTC and ISP.

	SHTC	ISP
Organizational culture	Centralized structure	Centralized structure
	Individual process of working (communicating in personal meetings)	Centralized process of working (instant messaging and email)
	Fragmented use of knowledge management system	Centralized knowledge management system
	Openness for criticism and discussions, opportunities to skip hierarchal levels with suggestions	Fear of causing loss of face Centralized decision-making Reward systems on performance
	Individual freedom to test ideas	Centralized and structured idea and implementation process
	Individual performance gives status	Ascribed status

differences are difficult to alter, some differences in the organizational culture can be changed in terms of the interface set-up. These cultural factors describe the organizational way of working, as well as the personal tendencies of reacting to the working environment. These aspects must be understood from a cultural context but it is also essential to adapt certain processes to achieve an efficient product development interface. Organizational structures and processes are examples of the visible and manageable aspects of organizational culture (artifacts and espoused values according to Schein, 1992). For the two companies, these are shown in Table 5.

A decentralized organizational structure with personal responsibility for completing tasks is common in Sweden (Isaksson, 2008). Swedish engineers may have their own processes for completing tasks. A team orientation can be seen in ISP's large number of centralized processes. It is important to understand the organizational interface in order to achieve an efficient business relation. While the young IT

engineers at ISP enjoy email and instant messaging, the Swedish culture
and work atmosphere promotes less interaction. ISP's process-oriented
way of working put greater demands on knowledge sharing and processes compared to SHTC. ISP has developed a sophisticated system
for new employees and it has a knowledge system to move employees
between projects without losing efficiency.

Ali Babar *et al.* (2007) noted that Indian companies are veterans in
the software outsourcing business, but what aspects are they veterans
on? Our respondents from ISP explained that their previous experiences with clients from the US and Belgium did not apply when solving
the problems that arose with the Swedish client. One program manager
noted that the American clients wanted quantitative performance measures to justify the choice of outsourcing supplier, but they trusted them
with new product development. This contrasts with the SHTC tendency to gradually increase the complexity of outsourced projects over
a number of years, with an emphasis on maintenance projects.

*An individuals' ability to be, for example, flexible, proactive, or
creative* can be constrained by processes, ethical considerations, and
loss of face. ISP employees are bound to several systems of processes
that make them inflexible in terms of thought, but the systems are
adaptable to a client's project. The number of processes and regulations can be reduced but an individual's inclination for flexibility is
harder to change. SHTC would like their supplier to act more proactively, showing that they are sufficiently mature to take on new and
more advanced projects. Indian engineers may work proactively but
they are required to settle decisions at a team level, as well as according to their own company process, in addition to matching their
client's process. The respect for seniority (and power distance and
ascribed status) can be seen in hierarchal differences but foremost in
the way individuals relate to the formal structure and titles. ISP
employees have great respect for their managers and the client, which
influences their behavior when their managers or client are present.
The case study shows that the risk of losing face influences the actions
of ISP employees in several ways such as when openly discussing
ideas, giving feedback to their manager, or taking action without first
addressing the hierarchal levels. Employees need to play by the rules

to progress in an organization and career tracks vary with culture. This is also one of the reasons why people from India are often afraid to admit their failings (Bullis, 1998), which is frustrating for the client – deadlines may be missed due to optimistic time planning.

Organizational prerequisites for creativity and innovation

At SHTC there is often a creative climate since employees have both deep knowledge and individual freedom to test ideas. The Swedish respondents described a culture defined by problem-solving; it takes little effort to solve a problem by gathering a small group and implementing the results. The individualistic culture in Sweden, in combination with low power distance (Trompenaars and Hampden-Turner, 1997; Hofstede and Hofstede, 2005), enables them to be proactive in solving problems, and at the same time there are no hierarchal barriers that affect the communication and collaboration among employees, as shown by Nakata and Sivakumar (1996). Although ISP uses centralized tools and processes for capturing ideas, the type of creativity differs from that typical in Sweden. Lau (2004) explains that in Asia creativity is seen as positive if it serves the greater good in society. If we consider creativity as a combination of novelty and usefulness it may be that Asians put emphasis on the usefulness aspect to a higher extent. At the same time, they are much more concerned with social influence and their contribution to society than being innovative. Another way of putting it, is that Western societies are more likely to produce individuals who are task-involved, or intrinsically oriented, while Eastern societies develop ego-involved, or extrinsically oriented, people. Lau (2004, p. 281) explains: "One must be careful not to engage in activities that will diminish his/her face. This situation sets up a dynamic struggle between creative thought, pursing one's own ideas, versus conforming to society thereby enhancing socially determined self-esteem." Lau (2004) also says that the most efficient way to express creativity is to take advantage of innate tendencies and talents, not to force oneself to behave in a manner that is inconsistent with one's natural inclinations. This suggests that an understanding of the cultural foundation of creative behavior will explain an employee's contribution on the innovation scale, and can also help managers develop a working process and a reward system that encourage employees in developing a specific type of creativity and innovation. Although our case study partially confirms these statements, one should note that "stereotyping" innate tendencies of creativity may not be helpful in increasing the efficiency in a longer perspective. By not giving suppliers either the prerequisites or opportunities to demonstrate innovative results, they will probably not be able to demonstrate them either.

Our research support the results of Nakata and Sivakumar (1996), since Sweden and SHTC with a higher degree of individualism are seen as superior in executing NPD at the initiation stage, as it can benefit from drive and personal vision. On the other hand, ISP (with a higher degree of collectivism) has made a great effort in its process and knowledge management during the implementation and maintenance of products with stable performance indicators.

Motivation

SHTC has struggled to find ways to motivate employees at the offshore development center. Bullis (1998) claims that foreign managers do not understand an Indian's deep psychological need for validation and the primacy of the family in workers' values. The family-oriented aspects relating to motivation correspond to the results of Panda and Gupta (2004) and Hofstede (2007). At ISP employees are used to receiving feedback in terms of written grades and awards, which influences their chance of advancement within the company. SHTC managers do not follow these procedures, thus hurting the feelings of their employees and lowering motivation. Ascribed status (Trompenaars and Hampden-Turner, 1997) is important for somebody's status in the community and well-being for their family (Panda and Gupta, 2004). We will not make assumptions regarding the influence of contextual differences due to religious traditions, but research on social exclusion (Radhkrishnan, 2009), karma (Gopalan and Rivera, 1997), and related topics could provide more insight into religious or regional values in relation to motivation. Motivational factors also explain some of the cultural differences in regards to *attrition*. The Swedish client was troubled concerning the relatively high attrition rate at ISP, which became one of the biggest challenges for ISP managers. However, there are differences in the national context — in Sweden the industry is fairly mature and SHTC is experienced and is one of the market leaders in their field globally. In India on the other hand, the whole IT industry is not yet mature. The employees are fairly young and new to the business and they do not know what to expect for the future, which affects their behavior and motivation. Their desire to increase their competences and to progress in their careers does not correspond to the client's need to keep knowledge within the offshore development center. The companies have decreased the attrition rate by implementing a job rotation to Sweden, a reward system, and career advancement within ISP.

Conclusion and Further Research

In summary, is it about choosing the right project or using methods to develop collaboration and increase efficiency? One interpretation of our results is that both companies need to acknowledge and understand that SHTC has the resources for innovation while ISP has the building blocks for professional implementation and maintenance. In this sense SHTC is deficient: track records show that on several occasions ISP has fixed bugs according to an error report but the same error reappears later due to the lack of organizational memory at SHTC. Ten years into the relation between SHTC and ISP, it is clear that it is not a lack of quality or technical competence which causes the most problems and frustration within the relation, but rather deficiencies in communication, openness, and mutual understanding. One would imagine that the main sources of inefficiency would have been solved during the years, but it is clear that cultural factors demand more time, as well as an internal commitment, to make them work for a project rather than against. Structures, routines, and distance management are in place, but a lack of understanding for each other's perspective hampers the communication and efficiency of the collaboration.

National culture, organizational culture, and traditions are intertwined, and all of them influence the efficiency of offshore outsourcing
relations. Religious and regional traditions may not be the first things
considered when entering into an outsourcing relation, but in some
cases they can help to increase understanding and trust, as well as help
in the planning and execution of product development projects. In the
same way that contextual factors can explain the attrition patterns of
ISP in this case study, they can create insight into the religious holidays
in India and the two-month summer leave, which is non-negotiable in
both Swedish law and culture. The motivation cycle for young engineers at ISP is that they want to start a career, go abroad, get married,
and then stay in India to start a family, etc. The underlying pattern of
attrition is useful information for career planning not only for ISP managers but for SHTC as well. The relation between SHTC and ISP
started as a collaboration between the Swedish office and the Indian
center, but as the number of outsourced projects grew, SHTC Italy
started using ISP for projects too. ISP has expressed a degree of frustration regarding the differences in communication with the Italian office
because specifications, routines, and communication modes did not
match ISP's previous experience with handling projects for SHTC
Sweden. This is a clear indication for how, at least sometimes, the
national culture highly influences collaboration by altering the organizational culture from one office to another in a radical way.

We have provided an overview of the cross-cultural issues to consider when managing offshoring between Sweden and India. Managers
can benefit from applying our framework, within the context of their
collaboration, as the basis for developing a strategy for offshore collaboration. This framework can be used in combination with more
traditional measures, such as the supplier's competence (technology
and quality) and costs. Cultural understanding creates knowledge of
each other's strengths and weaknesses, thereby creating the ability to
form and organize a collaboration to give the largest potential efficiency. The managerial implications can be summarized as:

- Understand, relate and manage the cultural variations that apply
  for the specific offshore development center

- Understand the differences between the cultures through the theoretical framework (e.g. Hofstede and Hofstede, 2005) and undertake any necessary precautions
- Take advantage of the combination of specific that the specific cultural match between the organizations allows
- Understand the receptive organization as well as employee motivation (e.g. family, status, international contacts, and career path)
- Open up communication between the client and supplier through intercultural socializing, partly as a joint effort, e.g. workshops

In this paper we have studied the outsourcing of product development from a European company to an Indian supplier in an offshore development center. The success factors for outsourcing are described in detail in the literature. We have studied the effect of a lack of intercultural understanding on effective communication and product development efficiency, which has not to any extent been presented in the literature. Our analysis shows that cultural factors influence the success of outsourcing in terms of quality of communication between partners, but also has an effect on the organizational structures, work processes and as a basis for decision-making when developing a supplier–client relation. The cultural factors were divided into two sets in our analysis. One set of factors is manageable by the companies involved in the business relation and the other set the companies can only relate to. In this chapter we have addressed the fields of innovation management, supplier management, and NPD, bridging the fields of cross-cultural management and intercultural communication. We have provided an overview of the existing literature on national as well as organizational cultures, which can be used as a framework in further studies on outsourcing relationships, as well as other types of inter-organizational collaboration in NPD (e.g. open innovation). As globalization continues to affect all areas of business, the influence of culture will become more evident within innovation management. Our results indicate that research needs to deal with all facets of culture within innovation management and NPD to fully understand the implications for companies in these times of the globalization and democratization of the development of highly complex products and services. In addition, it is questionable whether the discourse of innovation can be described as a general rather than a Western construction, which will be much more evident when the integration of suppliers in product development expands in terms of the intercultural interface. The incremental (*kaizen*) and radical (*kaikaku*) changes in production systems (Imai, 1986) stand out as two of the few examples in the innovation literature that build on the Eastern conception and practice of innovation.

This research has to be further developed in order to understand the main issue: how cultural differences affect development efficiency in different industrial sectors as well as for different types of outsourcing. Also further research is needed on how to benefit from cultural differences when a client decides to outsource. In future research we will investigate the cross-cultural interface during product management transfers. Further studies comparing different cultures and validating our framework is needed.

References

Adler, N.J. and Gundersen, A. (2008). *International Dimensions of Organisational Behavior*, Thomson, Case Western Reserve University.

Ahlbom, H. (2007). Nu ökar svensk FoU men mest utomlands, *Ny teknik*: April 4.

Ali Babar, M., Verner, J.M. *et al.* (2007). Establishing and maintaining trust in software outsourcing relationships: An empirical investigation, *Journal of Systems and Software* **80**(9), 1438–1449.

Avison, D. and Banks, P. (2008). Cross-cultural (mis)communication in IS offshoring: Understanding through conversation analysis, *Journal of Information Technology*, **23**(4), 249.

Bengtsson, L., Von Haartman, R. and Dabhilkar, M. (2009). Low-cost versus innovation: Contrasting outsourcing and integration strategies in manufacturing, *Creativity and Innovation Management*, **18**(1), 35.

Boutellier, R., Gassmann, O. and von Zedtwitz, M. (2008). *Managing Global Innovation Uncovering the Secrets of Future Competitiveness*, 3rd edn, Springer, New York.

Brown, D. and Wilson, S. (2005). *Black Book of Outsourcing: How to Manage the Changes, Challenges, and Opportunities*, John Wiley & Sons, Hoboken, NJ.

Bullis, D. (1998). *Doing Business in Today's India*, Greenwood Publishing Group, Incorporated, Westport, CT, p. 135.

Clark, K.B. (1989). Project scope and project performance: The effects of parts strategy and supplier involvement on product development, *Management Science*, **35**(10), 1247–1263.

Denison, D.R. (1996). What is the difference between organizational culture and organizational climate? A native's point of view on a decade of paradigm wars, *The Academy of Management Review*, **21**(3), 619–654.

Doney, P.M., Cannon, J.P. *et al.* (1998). Understanding the influence of national culture on the development of trust, *The Academy of Management Review*, **23**(3), 601–620.

Florida, R. (2005). *The flight of the Creative Class: The New Global Competition for Talent*, Harper Collins Publishers Inc., USA.

Fusilier, M. and Durlabhji, S. (2001). Cultural values of Indian Managers: An exploration through unstructured interviews, *International Journal of Value-Based Management*, **14**(3), 223.

Goldbrunner, T., Doz, Y., Wilson, K. and Veldhoen, S. (2006). The well-designed global R&D network, *Booz Allen Hamilton Resilience Report*.

Gopalan, S. and Rivera, J. (1997). Gaining a perspective on Indian value orientations: Implications for expatriate managers, *International Journal of Organizational Analysis*, **5**(2), 156.

Heeks, R., Krishna, S. *et al.* (2001). Synching or sinking: Global software outsourcing relationships, *IEEE Software*, **18**(2), 54–60.

Hofstede, G. (2007). Asian management in the 21st century, *Asia Pacific Journal of Management*, **24**(4), 411–420.

Hofstede, G. and Hofstede, G.J. (2005). *Cultures and Organizations. Intercultural Cooperation and Its Importance for Survival. Software of the Mind*, 2nd edn, Profile Books, London.

Imai, M. (1986). *Kaizen (ky'zen), the Key to Japan's Competitive Success*, 1st edn, Random House Business Division, New York, NY.

Isaksson, P. (2008). Leading companies in a global age: Managing the Swedish way, *VR 2008:14 VINNOVA (Swedish Governmental Agency for Innovation Systems)*, Stockholm.

Kogut, B. and Singh, H. (1988). The effect of national culture on the choice of entry mode, *Journal of International Business Studies*, **19**(3), 411–432.

Lau, S. (ed.) (2004). *Creativity: When East Meets West*, World Scientific Publishing Company, Incorporated, River Edge, NJ, p. 420. Available at http://site.ebrary.com/lib/malardalen/Doc?id=10106583&ppg=441

Mao, J.-L., Lee, J.-N. and Deng, C.-P. (2008). Vendor's perspectives on trust and control in offshore development systems outsourcing, *Information and Management*, **45**, 482–492.

Marques, M.J., Alves, J. and Saur, I. (2005). *University–Industry Networks for Innovation*, Department of Management and industrial Engineering, University of Aveiro. Available at www.regional-studies-assoc.ac.uk/events/aalborg05/marques.pdf

Nakata, C.S. and Sivakumar, K. (1996). National culture and new product development: An integrative review, *Journal of Marketing*, **60**(1), 61.

Newman, K.L. and Nollen, S.D. (1996). Culture and congruence: The fit between management practices and national culture, *Journal of International Business Studies*, **27**(4), 753–779.

Nicholson, B. and Sahay, S. (2001). Some political and cultural issues in the globalisation of software development: Case experience from Britain and India, *Information and Organization*, **11**(1), 25–43.

Panda, A. and Gupta, R.K. (2004). Mapping cultural diversity within India: A metaanalysis of some recent studies, *Global Business Review*, **5**(1), 27–49.

Park, S.H. and Ungson, G.R. (1997). The effect of national culture, organizational complementarity, and economic motivation on joint venture dissolution, *The Academy of Management Journal*, **40**(2), 279–307.

Porter, M.E., Schwab, K. and Sala-I-Martin, X. (2007). *The Global Competitiveness Report 2007–2008*, World Economic Forum, Palgrave Macmillan.

Primo, M.A.M. and Amundson, S.D. (2002). An exploratory study of the effects of supplier relationships on new product development outcomes, *Journal of Operations Management*, **20**(1), 33–52.

Radhkrishnan, P. (2009). Globalization and exclusion: The Indian context, *Global Asia*, **1**(4), 64–73.

Ronen, S. and Shenkar, O. (1985). Clustering countries on attitudinal dimensions: A review and synthesis, *The Academy of Management Review*, **10**(3), 435.

SCB (2009). *Educational attainment of the population*, Statistics Sweden.

Schein, E.H. (1992). *Organizational Culture and Leadership*, 2nd edn, John Wiley & Sons.

Schneider, S.C. and Meyer, A.D. (1991). Interpreting and responding to strategic issues: The impact of national culture, *Strategic Management Journal*, **12**(4), 307–320.

Sherwood, A.L. and Covin J.G. (2008). Knowledge acquisition in university–industry alliances: An empirical investigation from a learning theory perspective, *Journal of Product Innovation Management*, **25**(2), 162–179.

Siggelkow, N. (2007). Persuasion with case studies, *Academy of Management Journal*, **50**(1), 20.

Singh, J.P. (1990). Managerial culture and work-related values in India, *Organization Studies*, **11**(1), 075.

Singh, L. (2006). *Innovations and Economic Growth in a Fast Changing Global Economy: Comparative Experience of Asian Countries*, MPRA paper No. 80.

Smircich, L. (1983). Concepts of culture and organizational analysis, *Administrative Science Quarterly*, **28**(3), 339–358.

Stanko, M.A. and Calantone, R.J. (2011). Controversy in innovation outsourcing research: Review, synthesis and future directions, *R&D Management*, **41**(1), 8–20.

Stier, J. (2009). The blindspots and biases of intercultural communication studies: A discussion on episteme and doxa in a field, *Annual conference for the Nordic Network for Intercultural Communication: Borås*.

Triandis, H.C. (1989). The self and social behavior in differing cultural contexts, *Psychological Review*, **96**(3), 506–520.

Trompenaars, F. and Hampden-Turner, C. (1997). *Riding the Waves of Culture: Understanding Cultural Diversity in Business*, 2nd edn, Nicholas Brealy Publishing, London.

Van Looy, B., Martens, T. and Debackere, K. (2005). Organizing for continuous innovation: on the sustainability of ambidextrous organizations, *Creativity and Innovation Management*, **14**(3), 208.

World Economic Forum (2009). *The Global Competitiveness Report 2009–2010*. Available at https://members.weforum.org/pdf/GCR09/GCR20092010 fullreport.pdf

Chapter 17

Wearing Different Hats: How Absorptive Capacity Differs in Open Innovation

Lance Newey
University of Queensland Business School
University of Queensland, Australia

Introduction

In pursuing their performance objectives, the open innovation paradigm encourages firms to consider resources outside of their boundaries (Almirall and Casadesus-Masanell, 2010; Chesbrough, 2003; Chesbrough *et al.*, 2006; Dodgson *et al.*, 2006). Such openness can be inbound or outbound (Gassmann and Enkel, 2004), leading some firms to potentially develop an imbalance of skills from favouring one over the other (Chesbrough, 2003). Yet, interorganizational new product development (INPD) is an area where, to stay competitive, firms can be compelled to be skilful at both. This is because within the process the same firm may at first act as a customer to an upstream supplier (outside-in) and then become the supplier to a downstream customer (inside-out).

Being skilful at these shifting roles requires different types of absorptive capacity (Cohen and Levinthal, 1990; Lane *et al.*, 2006; Zahra and George, 2002). Absorptive capacity is defined as 'the ability of a firm to recognize the value of new external information, assimilate it, and apply it to commercial ends' (Cohen and devinthal, 1990,

p. 128). Firms' prior related knowledge is seen as a critical contingency governing whether and how firms detect and transform knowledge in their environments into commercial value. How firms recognize and evaluate the value of new external information can also differ depending on their needs and purposes at any one time. In the first instance, the firm integrates suppliers through customer absorptive capacity while in the second case it requires supplier absorptive capacity to engage customers. Supplier absorptive capacity is defined as the absorptive capacity required while acting as a supplier and likewise for customer absorptive capacity. The focus of and way that absorptive capacity is leveraged is different in both cases. While many have acknowledged the important role of absorptive capacity in open innovation (Lichtenthaler, 2009; Lichtenthaler and Lichtenthaler, 2009; Rothaermel and Alexandre, 2009), empirical research that links absorptive capacity to the different types of open innovation is lacking.

In this chapter, we connect the themes of open innovation, supplier integration and absorptive capacity in the context of interorganizational new product development. Specifically, we ask: how does absorptive capacity differ across different types of open innovation such as inbound versus outbound? We contribute by arguing that in INPD firms can assume multiple identities and the way that absorptive capacity needs to be leveraged is different across these identities. Using longitudinal process research (Langley, 1999; Pettigrew, 1997) to investigate how several firms undertook the research, development and commercialization of a groundbreaking new anti-influenza drug, we show that the ability of firms to develop absorptive capacity both as a supplier and customer serves as an important contingency governing whether firms profit from INPD. Firms thus need to cultivate, at least, a dual identity involving supplier and customer absorptive capacity.

We contribute to the open innovation literature by shedding new light on the nuanced role of absorptive capacity when firms occupy positions in INPD that entail them acting as both a supplier and customer at different points. This also adds to the supplier integration literature (e.g. Das *et al.*, 2006; Petersen *et al.*, 2003) by showing that firms can have multiple identities where, on the one hand, they may act as the customer of a supplier only to then become a supplier themselves. In INPD, both identities are reinforcing and we show how absorptive capacity needs to be built in order for this reciprocity to be beneficial. Our shifting, multiple identity viewpoint extends the supplier integration literature, which can often depict an organization as purely a supplier, ignoring its possible shifting identity in circumstances such as INPD.

Finally, we also add to the absorptive capacity literature by shifting the unit of analysis to understanding cycles of absorptive capacity between suppliers and customers. This way we overcome current perspectives that focus on absorptive capacity as a purely supply-side phenomenon where firms use it to achieve some output valued by a customer. Customers too need absorptive capacity and our contribution is to expose and elaborate absorptive capacity as a demand-side learning ability that enables customers to also 'recognize the value of new information' and co-create value propositions (Cohen and Levinthal, 1990).

We set about making our contributions by first reviewing the relevant literature, highlighting the limitations of existing open innovation, supplier integration and absorptive capacity perspectives. We then combine insights from these literature streams as a way to glean a fresh, yet informative, explanation of the role of absorptive capacity in INPD. We then expound our theory-building, process-research design. Data analysis follows along with the induction of theoretical propositions addressing our research question. We conclude with implications for theory and practice.

Open Innovation, Supplier Integration and Absorptive Capacity

Based on Chesbrough (2003), Gassmann and Enkel (2004) see open innovation as either inbound (bringing knowledge in) or outbound (distributing knowledge out). Capturing the broad sweep of ways to be open, Dahlander and Gann (2010) have taken Gassmann and Enkel's distinction a step further by noting that both inbound and outbound forms can be pecuniary or non-pecuniary in nature. The result is a two-by-two matrix where there are two forms of inbound innovation — acquiring (pecuniary) and sourcing (non-pecuniary) and two types of outbound innovation — selling (pecuniary) and revealing (non-pecuniary).

INPD is an interesting area of open innovation where all four types of openness can be undertaken. What may start as a non-pecuniary relation between collaborating scientists from different institutions can soon become pecuniary with the clarifying of commercial options. For those that pursue openness via INPD, the increasing de-verticalization of the value chain has meant firms specialize in different stages of the innovation process. For example, according to some (Markides and Geroski, 2004) small entrepreneurial firms are best equipped to specialize in creating new markets leaving large firms with the core competencies to scale up these markets. Access to new innovation and the greater gains from scaled-up markets provide incentives for these upstream and downstream firms to collaborate (Mora-Valentin *et al.*, 2004). The intensity of knowledge exchange between collaborators in new product development can differ with modular component interfaces requiring less intense interactions than more complex configurations that require firms to learn from each other (Grant and Baden-Fuller, 2004). It is these latter instances that most interest us here.

INPD is an area where there has been considerable process innovation placing pressure on firms to learn new skills in user- (Buur and Matthews, 2008; von Hippel, 2005) and supplier-driven innovation (Das *et al.*, 2006). This process innovation involves new ways for firms to access, convert and exploit knowledge in the context of a specific network of participants.

Supplier and customer integration

A number of studies report the benefits of supplier (Petersen *et al.*, 2003; Rosenzweig *et al.*, 2003) and customer (Buur and Matthews, 2008; von Hippel, 2005) integration in new product development. These relations, though, may be curvilinear, where costs start to outweigh benefits at some tipping point (Das *et al.*, 2006). An assumption underpinning many of these studies is that suppliers and customers are different entities and that integration is with an external party. In INPD, however, the one firm may act as both supplier and customer and the challenge of integration is internal as well as external. As an open innovator, integration must occur with outside partners but this integration must be coordinated internally so that how the firm acts as a customer to one outside partner needs to inform how it acts as a supplier to another. Although some have recognized the need at times to synchronize external and internal collaboration (Barki and Pinsonneault, 2005; Hillebrand and Biemans, 2004; Sanders and Premus, 2005), empirical work is needed to more closely specify how this occurs. Our conceptual route for doing so is by recognizing firms' shifting identities between supplier and customer in INPD. This shifting identity arises from the systemic nature of INPD (Newey and Shulman, 2004).

INPD system formation and performance: The role of absorptive capacity

The INPD literature recognizes that, in circumstances of complementarity and intense knowledge exchange, arrangements can take on the properties of a system (Brusoni *et al.*, 2001; Gerwin, 2004; Rothaermel and Deeds, 2004). INPD systems form when 'open' firms share a common goal, requiring coordinated effort (Gerwin, 2004). The ultimate value from the INPD process comes through the value created by a final product that is offered to an end user.

For the requisite number of firms to join the system, each downstream partner needs to perceive value in the work offered by those upstream and be confident that they can transform those inputs into a more developed value proposition. System performance depends on how well these outside-in and inside-out open innovation processes can be sustained across the various collaborators. Absorptive capacity is, therefore, a critical knowledge-based capability driving these system dynamics (Cohen and Levinthal, 1990; Lane *et al.*, 2006; Todorova and Durisin, 2007; Zahra and George, 2002). Path-dependent prior related knowledge underpins the absorptive capacity of an actor to perceive the value offered by another, to perceive how it can further extend the developing knowledge and then develop its own value proposition in the hope of gaining a desired return on the learning and knowledge-creation investments (Cohen and Levinthal, 1990; Newey and Zahra, 2009; Zahra and George, 2002).

Two main existing insights inform the role of absorptive capacity in affecting inbound and outbound processes in INPD. First, absorptive capacity is a learning capability comprising four processes: knowledge acquisition, assimilation, transformation and exploitation (Zahra and George, 2002). INPD can then be seen to entail a series of these absorptive capacity transactions between upstream and downstream firms. Each downstream firm must acquire, assimilate, transform and exploit knowledge from those upstream as well as the wider knowledge network.

Second, the efficiency with which these processes are undertaken between firms is affected by their relative absorptive capacity (Lane and Lubatkin, 1998). This notion recognizes that firms do not have an equal capacity to learn from other firms. The ability of two firms to learn from each other is jointly determined by their relative characteristics that help form a learning context. The aim of this relative absorptive capacity can be to offer the downstream partner the sort of clear inputs it needs to continue acquiring, assimilating, transforming and exploiting knowledge along its pathway when developing a value proposition for another firm downstream or an end user.

Despite these insights several issues remain vague. First, while intuitively we can see that the processes of knowledge acquisition, assimilation, transformation and exploitation can aid INPD, we lack empirical research detailing how these processes in fact unfold over time both within and across firms working on product development (Lane *et al.*, 2006; Newey and Zahra, 2009). Second, Lane and Lubatkin (1998) shifted Cohen and Levinthal's firm-level unit of analysis to focus on the 'student–teacher pairing' consisting of a learning dyad between two collaborating firms (Cohen and Levinthal, 1990). However, in INPD, we feel that the appropriate characterization of the relation between upstream and downstream firms is more that of supplier–customer than teacher–student. This imagery is important because it influences how we understand absorptive capacity processes between collaborating firms. It also can help us to better understand how firms integrate and coordinate in systemic ways.

So, it would be good to study a case example that involves multiple upstream and downstream partnerships distributed across the different stages of product development and that are all united by the common purpose of sharing in the value created by the final product. We report such a study next.

Research Setting and Design

Our research design has a theory-building purpose achieved via a longitudinal case study of the development of a groundbreaking anti-influenza drug from idea through to market launch. We build on the theory for open innovation and absorptive capacity using a process-research method. Process research focuses on the study of processes as a sequence of individual and collective events, actions and activities unfolding over time in context (Langley, 1999; Pettigrew, 1997). The particular case we chose was instructive as it highlights the challenges associated with interfirm knowledge integration, thus throwing into clearer relief the processes of absorptive capacity between firms.

To protect the anonymity of informants, we refer to the drug as Flustop. We have also disguised the names of the key actors including scientists and firms. Consistent with the focus of our research question, the INPD effort surrounding this drug involved a series of intermediate products exchanged between upstream firms and institutions and downstream partners, finally culminating in a final product released to an end-user market.

Data collection and analysis

The 'chain of evidence' (Yin, 2003) for building a theory required us to focus on the constructs of open innovation, supplier–customer relationships and absorptive capacity. Figure 1 charts the relevant chronology and the series of supplier–customer relations. We now elaborate on our operationalization of each of the focal constructs.

Open innovation: Our research question seeks to address how absorptive capacity differs across different types of open innovation. We wish to be able to draw inferences about the relation between open innovation and absorptive capacity, thus requiring us to code

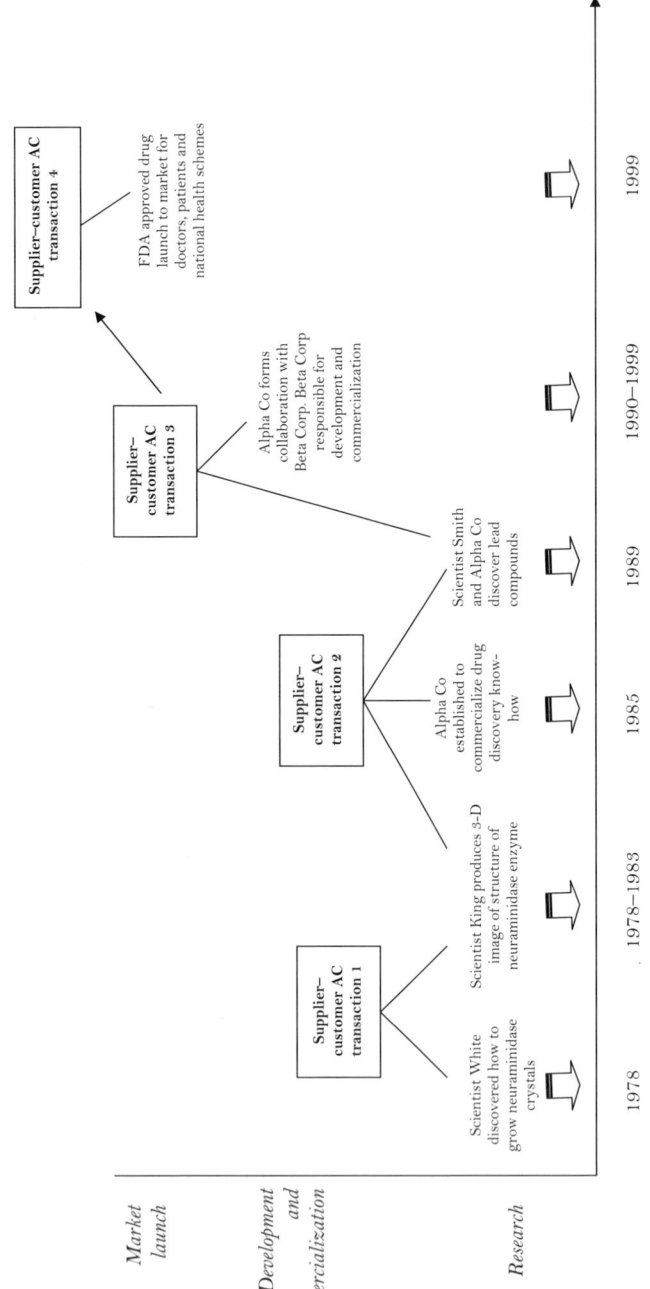

Fig. 1. The Flustop INPD Process.

open innovation as it manifests in our data. We use Dahlander and Gann's (2010) framework of inbound–outbound and pecuniary–non-pecuniary axes of open innovation — as a way to code the nature of open relations.

Supplier–customer relations: Our case example is a situation of loosely coupled supplier–customer relations. Upstream firms have been coded as 'suppliers' because they offer something valued by a downstream partner, who behaves as a purchasing customer. These relations came together here for the first time as a result of an opportunistic development of a radical innovation that required the searching out and combining of previously disconnected skill sets at different stages of the product development. Even though these were not established supplier–customer relations, their close interactions took on the form of supply and demand that mirror typical supplier–customer relations. This allowed for the drawing of inferences regarding supplier–customer activities. Table 1 documents all these actors, their contribution to the product development effort as well as the number of interviews that were conducted with each. In total, over an 18-month period, we conducted 40 interviews with key informants.

Absorptive capacity: While numerous competing conceptualizations of absorptive capacity exist (e.g. Lane *et al.*, 2006; Todorova and Durisin, 2007), we operationalized Zahra and George's (2002) dimensions. Our qualitative operationalization mirrors that adopted elsewhere (Newey and Zahra, 2009). We coded statements as pertaining to prior related knowledge when informants mentioned how their existing knowledge or expertise was relevant to some new information that was acquired. Typical interview questions included: 'How were you able to interpret the meaning of this incoming data?' or 'Did you need to know much about chemistry in order for you to understand what Scientist Y did?' Knowledge acquisition was defined and coded as the gathering of information from internal and external sources. Example questions included: 'What new information did you acquire that became the basis of your work?' or 'How did you acquire information about the market?'

Knowledge assimilation is the processing of acquired knowledge for interpretation and understanding. We coded statements as

Table 1. Key Informants.

Informant	Institution	Stage in product development	Number of interviews	Role
Scientist White	University	Early research	6	Discovered how to grow neuraminidase crystals. Triggered off the whole drug discovery and development process
Scientist King	University	Early research	2	Discovered the 3-dimensional molecular structure of neuraminidase crystals
Scientist Smith	University	Research	5	Discovered lead compounds to inhibit function of neuraminidase
CEO	Alpha Co	Research	2	First CEO of Alpha Co responsible for overseeing drug discovery work
Board Member	Alpha Co	Research	5	Served as board member in Alpha Co for the duration of the drug's research, development and commercialization
Patent attorney	Alpha Co	Research	2	Responsible for Alpha Co intellectual property strategy
CFO	Alpha Co	Research	1	Hired to help grow Alpha Co from drug discovery proceeds
CEO Australian subsidiary of Beta Corp	Beta Corp	Development	4	Licensed-in compounds from Alpha Co into Beta Corp
Director of commercial strategy — anti-infectives	Beta Corp	Development and commercialization	7	Commercial assessment of and strategy for anti-influenza drug
Head of development	Beta Corp	Development and commercialization	2	Medical, regulatory and product strategy
Flu project research leader	Beta Corp	Research and development	2	Biological validation
Clinical project leader	Beta Corp	Development and commercialization	2	Late-phase clinical studies, product registration, launch and marketing

assimilation when actors described how knowledge was dispersed to other actors within the firm or alliance as well as how sense was made of it. Firm-level inquiries of assimilation asked: 'How was that new information distributed to relevant parts of the organization for interpretation and evaluation?' and 'What sense did you make of the data?'

Knowledge transformation was regarded as the process of combining acquired and assimilated knowledge with existing knowledge. We coded interview text as transformation when actors spoke of how they used acquired knowledge to produce new proprietary knowledge in relation to the drug. We asked interviewees: 'What new understandings emerged in your work?' 'How did these new understandings emerge?' and 'What unique value did you add in your knowledge creation?'

Exploitation focused on those activities relating to what the actor did to try to gain some sort of desired benefit from their 'product'. We observed exploitation to be an incremental and progressive process. That is, in the first instance, we interpreted exploitation as occurring in the form of what an actor did with transformed knowledge. This may not have entailed some sort of commercial transaction but merely the passing of the transformed knowledge back to an upstream partner for further development on their part. So, exploitation was defined broadly to mean what an actor did to further progress their transformed knowledge. Ultimately though, this incremental process of exploitation culminated when either intermediate products were sold to downstream partners or when the last firm in the chain took Flustop to market. We captured exploitation by asking: 'What did you do with your transformed knowledge?' and 'What desired value did you seek from your product?' Our question recognized that 'product' could be intermediate or final.

Looking at a singular collaboration in the INPD process, we constructed an initial theoretical framework of how we viewed the role of absorptive capacity in INPD. The eventual result was the set of propositions developed in this chapter. In the spirit of replication logic (Eisenhardt, 1989), we then tested to see whether the model accurately captured the data pattern across all collaborations in the system. We then probed the data further to induce some key propositions about INPD and absorptive capacity. Apart from absorptive capacity, we considered other knowledge-based capabilities such as knowledge transfer and integration to determine if they were better interpretations of the data. While these constructs were relevant, in the end we felt that none of these alternatives captured the range of knowledge-based activity in the data better than absorptive capacity.

The Flustop Story and Analysis

As per Fig. 1, we focus on four absorptive capacity transactions in the development of Flustop. These were the points of supplier–customer relations within the process. Our method for presenting the data and showing our theoretical interpretation of that data is to first narrate what occurred in each transaction then interpret the data through the absorptive capacity lens with the aim of developing new theory.

Absorptive capacity transaction 1: Scientists White and King

Through a series of experiments in the 1960s and 1970s, scientists discovered that the neuraminidase enzyme played a key role in enabling the replication of the influenza virus within host organisms. Then in 1978, while working on a neuraminidase project, Scientist White, an organic chemist working at the Australian National University, made a groundbreaking discovery. Scientist White recalls:

> *I'd made up some sialidase [neuraminidase] protein this day and I noticed a sheen coming off the solution. I took it to the microscope and that was that. I know organic chemistry, I know what crystals look like and I knew I'd stumbled on the sialidase [neuraminidase] crystal.*

In absorptive capacity terms, Scientist White had recognized the value of his discovery: he had figured out how to grow crystals of neuraminidase.

'I didn't know what to do with them,' and so he sought the opinion of a number of colleagues. Eventually, Scientist White was introduced to Scientist King, who at the time was working at the Division of Protein Chemistry at Australia's Commonwealth Scientific and Industrial Research Organization (CSIRO). Scientist King had expertise in protein crystallography. This 'involves working out the 3-dimensional structures of protein molecules using crystals of the protein and x-rays as the probe'.

Scientist King perceived the value of Scientist White's discovery. Nobody had developed the explicit knowledge about how to grow crystals of the neuraminidase enzyme. The discovery was valuable because crystals would allow the closer determination of the structure of the enzyme. Scientist King originally believed that this was a way to develop influenza vaccines. Both Scientist King and Scientist White recognized that there were different strains of influenza virus and so more and better crystals were needed to test for the neuraminidase structure in different strains. So, an iterative process ensued where both Scientist White and Scientist King would grow more crystals and Scientist King would then study the structure and determine 'the position of all the 15 thousand or so atoms in the neuraminidase molecule'. King reflected that 'when you use this technique you start out by getting a rough picture of the molecule and then you use a process called refinement where you optimize the quality of the picture that you have to the raw data that you've collected. That's a long and fairly tedious process.'

Eventually, this collaborative exercise of growing crystals from different strains of virus and getting a refined picture of the enzyme structure yielded a significant breakthrough. Scientist King said:

> We produced a picture of what's effectively a sort of cavity on a protein molecule... We thought that if it were possible to design a molecule that was complementary in shape to that little cavity we could stop the enzyme from doing an important job that it has to do for the virus.

In 1985, this knowledge then became the trigger for the setting up of Alpha Company in the hope that Scientist King had discovered a way to make an anti-influenza drug (Fig. 1).

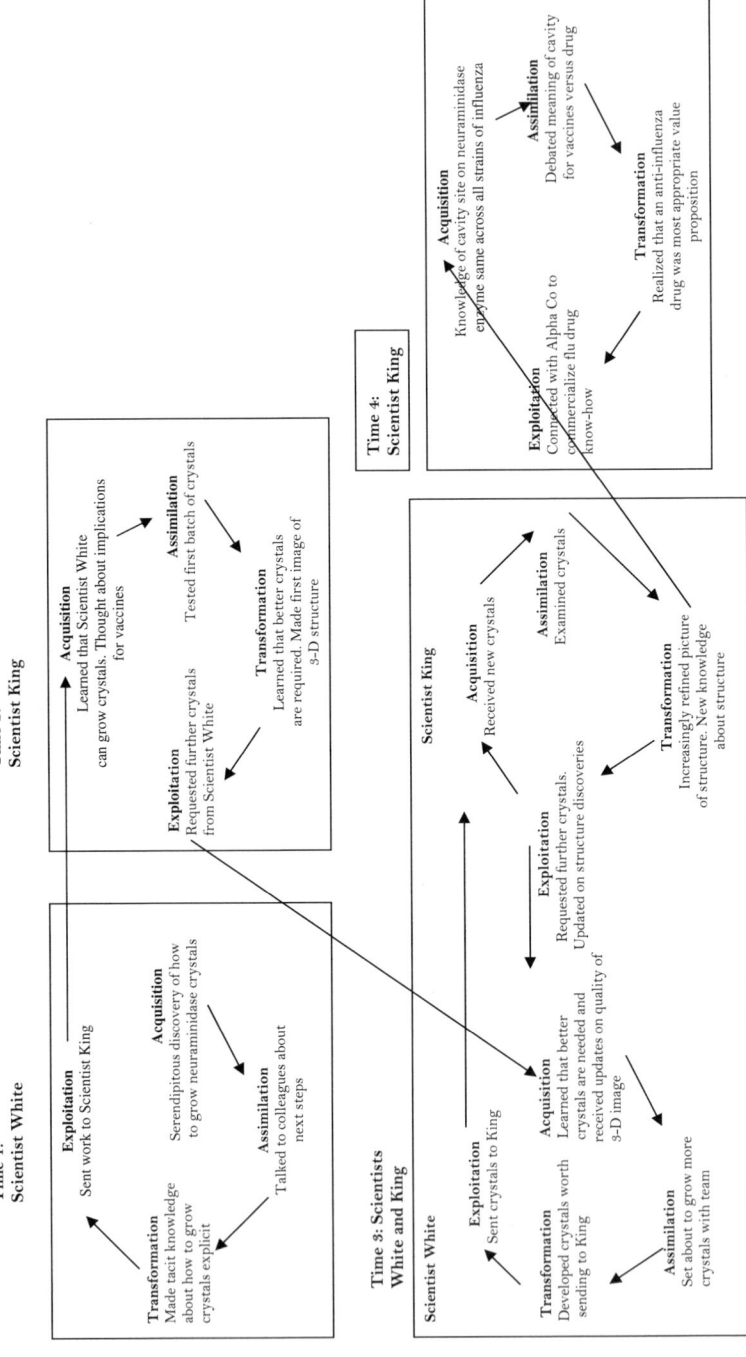

Fig. 2. Data Pattern for Absorptive Capacity Transaction 1.

Analysis

Figure 2 codes this narrative in terms of absorptive capacity. We see that absorptive capacity was essential in enabling both actors to produce something of value that would, in turn, enable them to realize various ambitions (Times 1–4). Further, we see an 'open' innovation arrangement where the actors considered themselves part of a wider knowledge network and where their collaboration involved iterative outside-in and inside-out innovation processes (Gassmann and Enkel, 2004). In Dahlander and Gann's (2010) terms the open relationship was initially one of sourcing and revealing before progressing to a more pecuniary relation once the commercial pathway became clearer. The absorptive capacity lens helps us to dissect these processes of sourcing and revealing and progression to a pecuniary relation.

At the individual level, absorptive capacity is an ability that helps people to create new knowledge and exploit it towards some desired end (Time 1). Scientist White's remarks that 'making pots of money was not a motivation' but rather 'all we wanted to do was discover new things' that would bring scientific prestige. However, in order for him to realize the full potential of his discovery he had to convince someone else who had the complementary skill set to take the work further. Scientist King was effectively a customer of Scientist White. Scientist King had to perceive the value proposition for himself and to extricate himself from a project in Germany before coming back to Australia to work full-time on the neuraminidase project (Time 2). In turn, in order for Scientist King to realize the full potential of his work he had to develop a value proposition that would be meaningful to another downstream customer, whether for vaccine or drug development. This entailed collaboration with Scientist White, pooling their respective expertise (Time 3).

A process of co-specialization ensued where Scientist King would give feedback relating to the picture quality emanating from the quality of the crystals supplied by Scientist White. This feedback would then guide Scientist White's work (acquisition and assimilation) and in particular how he went about transforming his initial discovery. He needed to continue to improve his explicit knowledge of how to grow better crystals until crystals were produced that enabled Scientist King to create the knowledge he needed to constitute a value proposition for a downstream partner. This downstream partner was Alpha Co and would constitute a pecuniary shift in the nature of the project.

We propose:

Proposition 1: The upstream supplier's absorptive capacity to develop a value proposition affects the downstream customer's absorptive capacity to develop a value proposition.

This holds because clearly without the work of Scientist White (supplier) then Scientist King (customer) had nothing to contribute. In addition, how well Scientist White was able to develop a value proposition affects whether Scientist King was able to 'recognize the value' of that new knowledge.

Proposition 2: The downstream customer's ability to develop a value proposition is affected by:
(2a) the deployment of absorptive capacity processes in contributing its own specialized expertise; and
(2b) the co-specialized absorptive capacity processes with the upstream supplier.

This proposition recognizes the difference in the contributions of the various parties to the intellectual property (IP) ultimately produced by the downstream customer. The latter's ability to develop a value proposition is aided by work done in collaboration with the upstream supplier and this work involves iterative cycles of absorptive capacity processes (cycles of feedback between White and King about crystal and picture quality). But, in addition, this collaborative work merely aids the downstream customer as it deploys its absorptive capacity in contributing its own specialized contribution (King's individual work in trying to determine the neuraminidase structure).

Absorptive capacity transaction 2: Scientist King, Scientist Smith and Alpha Co

In 1985, the work of Scientists White and King had attracted the interest of a group of entrepreneurs who had started a small company, which we will call Alpha Co. What had attracted these entrepreneurs, indeed excited them, was the proposition that Scientists White and King had discovered a way to make an anti-influenza drug for all strains of influenza. This know-how was perceived to become the basis for the growth of Alpha Co via a public floatation. At the same time, Scientists White and King would be given equity in Alpha Co.

Investment money did indeed flow in and Alpha Co executives and the board contracted out the drug discovery work to Scientist Smith at the Victorian College of Pharmacy in Australia. Scientist Smith was given the objective of discovering a lead compound that could in fact block the action of the neuraminidase enzyme and be able to demonstrate the proof of principle of enzyme inhibition via the drug. This work resulted in a suite of patented compounds that did in fact block the action of the enzyme. Scientist Smith stated:

About two years on in that process as we were going down that pathway, [Scientist King] and his colleagues, had then refined the structure and that sharpened the whole thing up. We reapplied then the computational chemistry software and indeed it was very predictive. We had some benchmarks in there that told us it was predicting exactly where things should go... now we can go back in and apply software in to modify that compound or indeed other compounds to make active drugs.

This was an iterative process between Scientist King, Scientist Smith and their respective teams. The latter would develop compounds and the former would examine how tightly the compound bound to the neuraminidase cavity site. In turn, this information would help in further drug design. Eventually, a lead compound was developed that showed clear efficacy *in vivo*. This became an attractive value proposition for Beta Corp, a large pharmaceutical company, which had expertise in dry powder inhalers. The compound that Smith had designed required an inhaled administration and so a pharmaceutical company was sought that specialized in that sort of drug delivery mechanism.

Analysis

Figure 3 captures the data in terms of the cycles of absorptive capacity that operated across Alpha Co, Scientist Smith, Scientist King through to the eventual connection with pharmaceutical giant Beta Corp. Consistent with Proposition 1, the behaviour of each actor can be understood in terms of leveraging absorptive capacity to be able to offer a value proposition to a downstream customer. King's ability to bring in knowledge from White and work away at transforming it ultimately meant that Alpha Co had something to which they could contribute and receive value from a downstream customer (Times 1–4). This was originally a non-pecuniary open innovation relationship of sourcing and revealing between King and Smith (Dahlander and Gann, 2010). Once a compound was developed then a pecuniary relationship developed between Alpha Co and Beta Corp.

Without King's ability to develop a value proposition via ongoing processes of knowledge acquisition, assimilation, transformation and exploitation, then Alpha Co would have had nothing to, in turn, acquire, assimilate, transform and exploit. In addition, as we have seen in transaction 1, King used his absorptive capacity in a way that would enhance the likelihood that an entrepreneurial start-up like Alpha Co would perceive value in the form of a potential company growth vehicle.

While King's work had enough value for Alpha Co entrepreneurs to recognize the value, it was not yet sufficiently mature for Smith to use in his process of developing a value proposition. Smith then used absorptive capacity to acquire knowledge about the disease process and used this knowledge to develop an early compound, which showed some neuraminidase inhibition. Acknowledging the limitations of his early work, however, led King to continue to use absorptive capacity processes to improve his value proposition to Smith (Time 3). King acquired and assimilated information from Smith about what was wrong with the early images and then used inventive means to transform the early results into a more refined image that Smith could actually use to improve his work (Time 3). A better lead compound was then available as a value proposition to a large pharmaceutical company.

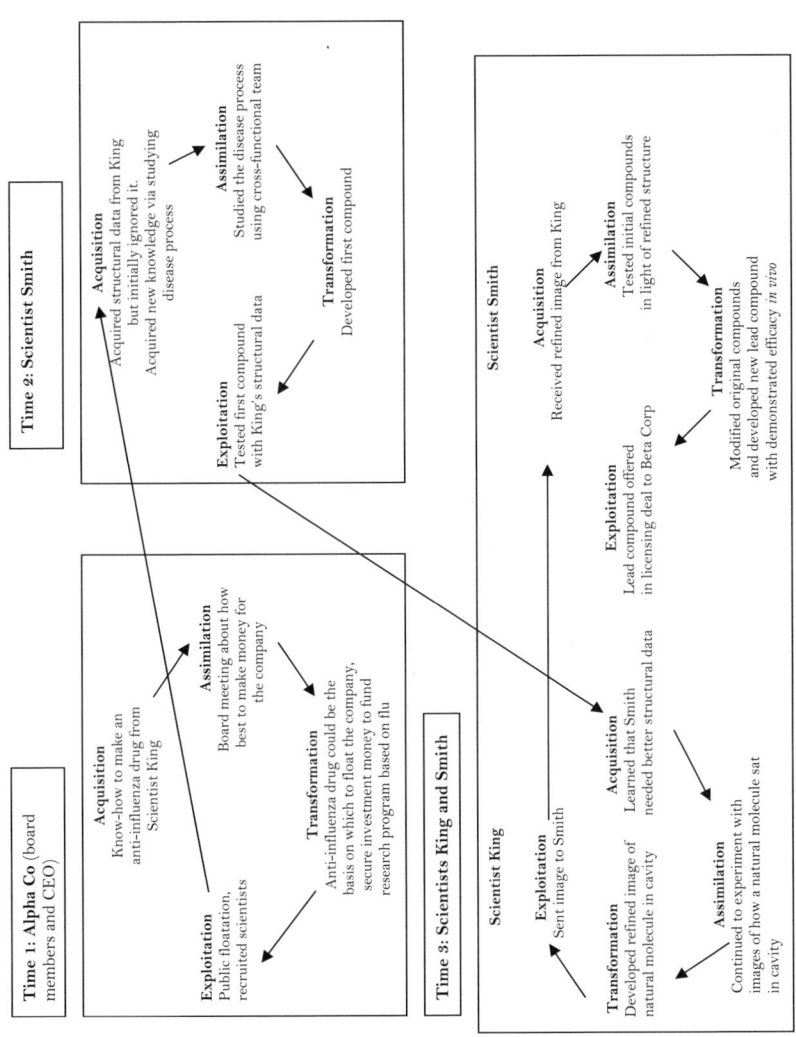

Fig. 3. Absorptive Capacity Transaction 2.

Times 2 and 3 in Figure 3 also offer support for Proposition 2. Time 2 shows that Smith used his own absorptive capacity, unaided by King's discoveries, to develop the first compound. Time 3 shows that the co-adaptive absorptive capacity processes of King and Smith allowed Smith to develop a better compound by illuminating what the design of the drug compound needed to be to more tightly bind to the neuraminidase cavity. So, it was the combination of both independent and interdependent absorptive capacity processes that resulted in the ability of the downstream partner to develop a value proposition.

What we can see is that the supplier–customer absorptive capacity transactions affect the way that the processes of acquisition, assimilation, transformation and exploitation are undertaken. Knowing who your customer is and learning what value means to them is a key informational challenge. In turn, this influences the sorts of questions that are asked by the upstream partner (knowledge acquisition: for example, what is lacking in the current structural image?), how the information is made sense of by various actors (assimilation: if Smith wants a more refined image then this is what I need to do), how various alternative solutions are evaluated (transformation: will this be more appealing to Smith than the other image?) and finally exploited (do we have a value proposition that maximizes Smith's perception of value to him and that enhances his ability to offer a value proposition to his customer?).

The downstream customer also uses absorptive capacity processes to enhance the relationship with their supplier but with the greater goal in mind that recognizes that their role will switch from customer to being a supplier to someone else downstream. Each actor in the process plays the role of supplier and customer at some point, with each role necessitating a different way of acquiring, assimilating, transforming and exploiting knowledge.

King was first a customer of White and then became a supplier to Alpha Co. Alpha Co was first a customer of King and then became a supplier to Beta Corp. Depending on the role adopted at any one time, the absorptive capacity processes of the focal actor are different.

In the first instance, King used absorptive capacity as a customer taking crystals from White, processing them and seeing what the structural image revealed. Slowly but surely, the structural data became clearer and clearer (acquisition, assimilation, transformation) and inspired a shift in value proposition away from vaccines to drugs (transformation and exploitation). At that point then and armed with such a value proposition, the customer of King became clear — a small drug discovery firm. King's absorptive capacity processes then took on a different texture — that of a supplier not a customer. Knowledge was now being acquired about what the customer needed.

Similarly, Alpha Co was, at first, the customer of King. Alpha Co's customer absorptive capacity involved working with King, acquiring and assimilating structural data from him and then being able to offer feedback as to how the data needed to be improved in order for Alpha Co to reach the standard of value proposition needed. The standard of value proposition needed by Alpha Co was dictated by the pharmaceutical in-licensing standards of the time. So, when a lead compound was discovered, Alpha Co switched to supplier absorptive capacity and it then started working with the customer (Beta Corp) to acquire, assimilate, transform and exploit information about its needs.

The main aim of customer absorptive capacity then concerns working with the supplier to determine what value proposition the customer can create and determine who the best customer of that value proposition will be. Key skills include combining absorptive capacity processes with a supplier, being able to assess the offerings of the supplier, being able to articulate needs and efficiently co-adapt knowledge outputs towards a desired value proposition. Supplier absorptive capacity has the aim of attracting a customer and working with the customer towards the latter's desired value proposition. Key skills involve working with a particular customer, being able to understand its needs, understand who its customer is and what it will desire, understand the business model of the customer and how what you can offer as a supplier aids its business objectives.

Each firm in the INPD process therefore must be able to wear both these hats as the role switches from customer to supplier. We can now assert a third proposition:

Proposition 3: Successful INPD depends on the ability of each firm that takes a lead role at a product development stage(s) to leverage both customer and supplier absorptive capacity as the situation demands.

We also advance:

Proposition 4: In INPD, customer absorptive capacity processes of a focal firm are positively related to its supplier absorptive capacity.

This proposition holds because when it is a customer, a firm guides the efforts of the supplier towards a value proposition that the firm will need when its role switches to that of supplier. So, Alpha Co (through Scientist Smith) motivated King to work towards structural imagery that could confirm how tightly the lead compound was binding to the neuraminidase cavity. When it became a supplier to Beta Corp, Alpha Co would need this data in order to alleviate Beta Corp's concerns over the safety and efficacy risks of the drug. So, forward-looking firms will undertake customer absorptive capacity processes in a way that is mindful of what their needs will be when they adopt the role of supplier.

Absorptive capacity transactions 3 and 4: Alpha Co, Beta Corp and final customer markets

The initial point of contact with Beta Corp came via the latter's Australian operation. The CEO of Alpha Co approached the CEO of Beta Corp Australia with the story that they had active compounds for flu and that the drug design necessitated an inhaled delivery device. Indeed, the CEO of Beta Corp Australia said that he was 'pretty compelled by the argument that they'd evolved the understanding of the role of neuraminidase in the replication cycle of flu and that they'd solved the crystal structure and as a consequence of that the story that rational drug design would follow'. Upon licensing the compounds, the Australia CEO needed a technical sponsor in Beta Corp's UK-based

R&D. He found such a sponsor, the head of drug discovery for anti-infectives, a man with whom he had an established personal friendship.

The immediate scientific objective then was to further the biological validation of the Alpha Co compounds. The medicinal chemists found positive activity in the early *in vitro* screens of the compound against all flu strains. They then found very exciting results during animal modelling. These results were enough to trigger further investment. Chemical development became involved in order to produce larger quantities of the drug and optimize the route of scaled-up manufacture. In addition, Alpha Co continued to work with another scientific team charged with developing compound substitutes that would serve to develop the intellectual property portfolio against competitive intervention.

While excitement was building within Beta Corp's scientific sections, the reaction to Flustop was quite the opposite within commercial circles. A commercial team was assigned to the Flustop project at the time when the biological validation triggered development scale-up of the compound. The director of commercial strategy for anti-infectives pointed out that a number of problems interfered with commercial development. First, the early commercial analyses did not support investing in Flustop relative to other projects in the portfolio such as herpes. The commercial team was then left to champion a cause that it did not believe was in the best interests of the company.

The director also discussed how other parts of the organization failed to 'recognize the value' in the Flustop project. Beta Corp comprises various operating companies, which gave the company a presence in each of the major geographic markets of the world. From the outset, these operating companies were not interested in Flustop. The director related that he spent all his time 'negotiating with operating companies to get them to come to the party. The problem was that if they didn't like what was being suggested, they just ignored it. When it came to [Flustop], the problem was that the commercialization challenges were so significant and so different from what any of the operating companies had to deal with before, that for a lot of them it was all too difficult for them to really contemplate.'

This internal indifference to the project was compounded by the project's newness, which plagued information acquisition. The director reported that problems arose with the Flustop development because the company was 'looking to break new ground'.

> *The financial, time and learning costs of developing relationships and expertise with new physicians every time you enter a new therapy area are huge. There was lots of learning going on but we were not particularly skilled at asking questions of regulators, nor potential customers at the outset.*

The results from the human clinical trials dealt a near fatal blow to the drug's prospects in the marketplace. The drug displayed only a marginal therapeutic benefit consisting of symptomatic relief 2.6 days in advance of a control group. The drug was subsequently launched but was met with a very weak response from the various markets. The key markets for Flustop consisted of doctors who would prescribe the drug, end users who would take the drug and national health schemes who would subsidize the drug. In the early days after launch, all three markets failed to recognize the value in the Flustop value proposition.

Analysis

Times 1 and 2 in Fig. 4 capture the absorptive capacity patterns we observed in the analysis of the data around transactions 3 and 4. The data support Propositions 2 through 4. In terms of Proposition 2, Beta Corp was able to put a value proposition to a variety of markets (doctors, flu sufferers and health schemes) and this value proposition did result from a combination of their own independent efforts as well as some more minor input from Alpha Co. The Beta Corp data reveals co-evolutionary processes of knowledge acquisition, assimilation, transformation and exploitation across different organizational functions and levels of management (Fig. 4).

Consistent with Proposition 3, Beta Corp also leveraged customer absorptive capacity in its dealings with Alpha Co, relaying what it needed in a value proposition in order for a deal to be done. This involved cycles of acquiring and assimilating knowledge

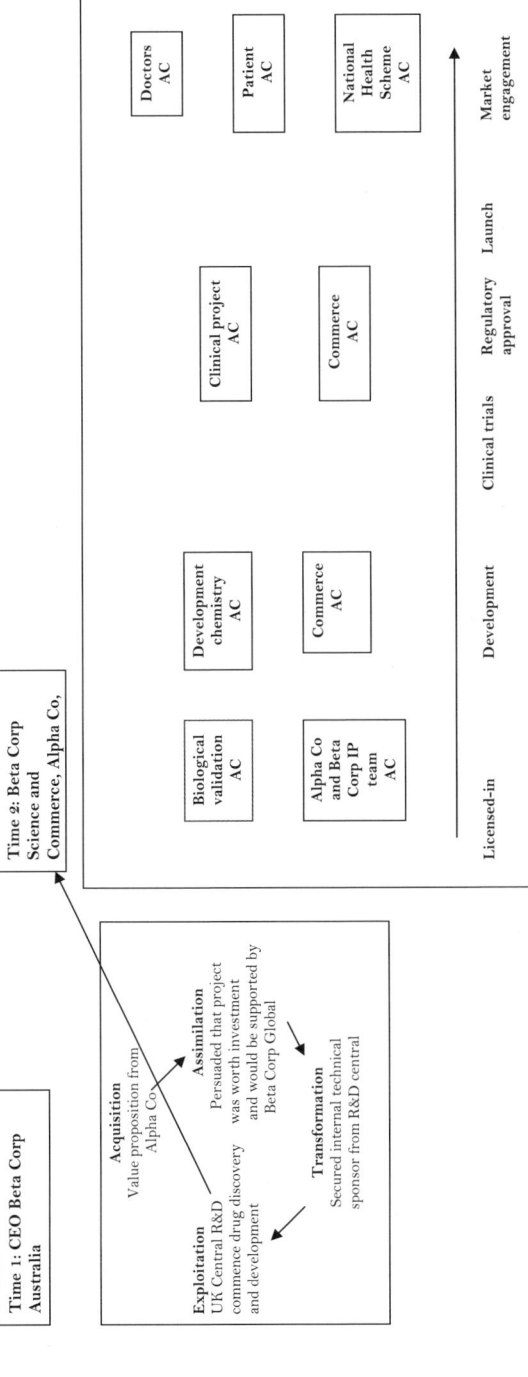

Fig. 4. Absorptive Capacity Transactions 3 and 4 — Alpha Co, Beta Corp and End Users.

about lead compounds, testing them for how well they bound to the cavity site and then transforming and exploiting this information by guiding future drug design attempts. In turn, Beta Corp then had to use supplier absorptive capacity in working towards being able to offer a value proposition to the marketplace. Figure 4 highlights that this process involved cross-functional cycles of absorptive capacity as different functions (e.g. medicinal chemistry, development chemistry and commerce) acquired, assimilated, transformed and exploited knowledge across the stages of product development.

Further, as with Proposition 4, processes involved in Beta Corp's customer absorptive capacity enabled it to fund and guide the work of Alpha Co in maturing the drug candidates to a point where they were able to assess if there was *in vivo* activity. This allowed for smoother transmission and championing of the project by the Australian CEO of Beta Corp to internal technical sponsors. The latter were then able to 'recognize the value' of the project and engage their own absorptive capacity processes in further biological validation. The latter was a necessary step to then, in turn, allow other internal sections to 'recognize the value' and trigger further cycles of absorptive capacity.

However, the data reveal that both the commercial team and the operating companies did not 'recognize the value' in the Flustop project. From the central commercial team's perspective all analyses indicated that the project money was better going to the existing franchise area of herpes. The operating companies saw that Flustop would require a 'paradigm shift' in the business model and the way they undertook sales and supply chain management. Beta Corp was used to chronic diseases that were predictable in terms of sales and distribution. Influenza was difficult to predict and required significant re-education of the public. The director of commercial strategy revealed the effects of this negative evaluation by saying that a 'junior marketing executive' was appointed to champion the cause in the major operating companies. This signalled the lack of priority to be given to subsequent cycles of knowledge acquisition, assimilation, transformation and exploitation.

We see another interesting dynamic emerge in the Beta Corp data that critically affected both supplier and customer types of absorptive capacity and the success of inbound and outbound innovation. When using customer absorptive capacity, the commercial team within Beta Corp failed to 'recognize the value' in the Flustop project. In turn, this profoundly affected the intensity of the effort applied to supplier absorptive capacity in developing a drug for commercial sale. In using customer absorptive capacity, end users, such as doctors, national health schemes and patients, failed to 'recognize the value' in the Flustop value proposition, ultimately resulting in lower than expected sales.

We learned that achieving the desired level of intensity of effort within and between the customer and supplier absorptive capacity efforts of an organization is affected by whether the project team members perceive value in the project for themselves. We call these mental models — value schema — referring to how actors define value for themselves and their beliefs about how best to realize that value (Porac and Thomas, 2002; Walsh, 1995). The critical link is between an actor's value schema and the project value proposition. Actors ask whether working on a project will be worth all the effort for themselves, based on how they define value. Without a favourable appraisal, neither customer nor supplier absorptive capacities are likely to receive the effort and integration required in linking inbound and outbound open innovation initiatives.

Therefore we propose:

Proposition 5: The efficiency of supplier and customer absorptive capacities is a function of the fit between the project value proposition and the actor's value schema. The better the fit the more integrated and intense the supplier absorptive capacity effort and the more likely it will positively influence customer absorptive capacity and vice versa.

Implications, Future Research and Limitations

Our research quest was to develop a better understanding of the relationship between open innovation, supplier integration and absorptive capacity. Our literature review pointed out that while researchers recognize that firms can be open in different ways, we lack an understanding of how these differences affect absorptive capacity. Further, we noted that the context of INPD is an area where different types of openness are at play, thus providing a context for studying possible heterogeneity in the role of absorptive capacity. In addition, we pinpointed the different roles that firms play — customer and supplier — as potential sources of absorptive capacity heterogeneity across different open innovation methods. Our case analysis illuminates several key theoretical implications for each of these literatures.

We contribute to the open innovation literature by shedding new light on the nuanced role of absorptive capacity when firms occupy positions in INPD that entail them acting as both a supplier and customer at different points. In our data, actors needed to wear two hats. They needed to use absorptive capacity processes as a supplier and then a customer. King was a customer of White but then became a supplier to Alpha Co. Alpha Co was a customer of King but then became a supplier to Beta Corp. The actors are saying to themselves: how can we be a good customer in a way that will, in turn, also lead us to be a good supplier?

We learn that although firms can be open in different ways such as outside-in and inside-out (Gassmann and Enkel, 2004) these different ways have corresponding role identities in the innovation process. As a consequence, the role of absorptive capacity can differ according to the particular identity assumed. More specifically, outside-in open innovation requires customer absorptive capacity while inside-out involves supplier absorptive capacity. Our identity-based perspective thus extends the insight that firms are open in different ways. In addition, each absorptive capacity type requires different knowledge and skills, thus potentially offering a lens through which to answer why some firms profit more than others from open innovation.

If customer absorptive capacity corresponds to inbound innovation and supplier absorptive capacity to outbound then it calls into question Dahlander and Gann's (2010) framework for differentiating different types of openness. In their scheme, pecuniary inbound innovation equates merely to 'acquiring' and outbound to 'selling'. However, our research shows that both inbound and outbound forms of open innovation involve the full gamut of absorptive capacity processes — acquisition, assimilation, transformation and exploitation. So, these knowledge-based processes *per se* were not the key point of difference in the way that firms were open but rather the identity they assumed when deploying those processes. We therefore extend the discussion about the different ways that firms can be open by pointing to role identity as a basis for comparison. When firms are open as customers they use absorptive capacity differently than when they are open as suppliers. Table 2 further highlights these distinctions. Table 2 reflects our data by showing that different questions, goals, orientations and mindsets are involved in customer versus supplier absorptive capacity.

There is a potential link here with organizational identity research. Organizational identity encapsulates the collective cognitive

Table 2. Supplier–Customer Absorptive Capacity Processes.

Absorptive capacity process	Supplier	Downstream customer
Acquisition	What value proposition can we create? Who will be our customer? What does value mean to that customer? Who do we need to get information from, what information and how?	How do we get access to value propositions?
Assimilation	Who internally will need this information when we get it? What does the acquired information mean for our project's progress?	How does the supplier's value proposition enable or hinder us from developing a value proposition for our customer?
Transformation	Have we got what we need in a value proposition?	How can we collaborate with the supplier for a win-win value proposition?
Exploitation	How best do we need to communicate the value proposition to attract an actual customer transaction?	Do we have something that is ready for our customer?

categorization of organization members in defining 'who are we?' (Pratt and Foreman, 2000; Scott and Lane, 2000). On a more micro-level, firms can have multiple identities, including 'we are a customer of x', 'we are a supplier to y' or 'we only deal with chronic diseases with predictable demand patterns and that use established distribution channels'. Future research could use identity theory to help further unpack firm-level absorptive capacity. How does identity-based absorptive capacity development differ from or complement product- or technology-based development? What are the strengths and weaknesses of identity-based absorptive capacity development? Future absorptive capacity research could also build on our notion of value schema. How are value schema and identity linked? When value schema and identity are linked/not linked around a project, what are the effects on project outcomes? How can value schema enhance or constrain absorptive capacity?

In terms of the absorptive capacity literature, Propositions 1 and 2 assert that a transaction between a supplier and a customer (business-to-business or business-to-customer) becomes an important unit of absorptive capacity analysis beyond just the firm and interfirm (Lane and Lubatkin, 1998) levels that have dominated attention. The relation between a supplier and a downstream customer profoundly shapes the way that absorptive capacity processes are undertaken. Understanding our data and the collaborations between actors (e.g. Scientist King and Scientist Smith) required us to understand how they used absorptive capacity in the transactions between supplier and customer. Just looking at one side of this transaction only, for example time 1 in Fig. 2, overlooks the rich nuances of absorptive capacity leverage that unfold over time as a result of the collaboration. We come to understand how and why an actor leverages absorptive capacity through its interaction with a supplier or a customer. Future research may test how competing systems of firms undertake cycles of supplier and customer absorptive capacity and how this affects their relative time-to-market, costs and market performance.

Also, the current supply-side bias of existing absorptive capacity conceptualizations needs to be complemented by a demand-side recognition that customers also need absorptive capacity. In fact, it is the absorptive capacity of the customer that helps them to perceive the value in what the upstream actor is offering and whether they should engage in a transaction. This carries an important implication for how we define absorptive capacity. Definitions that hold to Cohen and Levinthal's condition of 'apply to commercial ends' reach a boundary condition with end users. End-user customers also need absorptive capacity (e.g. flu sufferers and doctors) but exploitation for them does not involve some commercial end. At the least, our work suggests modifying Cohen and Levinthal's (1990) 'apply to commercial ends' stipulation to 'apply to desired ends'.

The supplier integration literature sometimes carries the assumption that who is the supplier and who is the customer are stable ascriptions. This ignores how one firm may need to act as both. Our research highlights that the same firm's interactive cycles between customer and supplier absorptive capacities drives its success in INPD. As a customer, the firm must recognize the value of the upstream or horizontal partner's work. But then it may actively engage that supplier in transforming the developing product in a way that allows it the best opportunity for exploitation. In turn, this transformation and exploitation process is informed by supplier absorptive capacity as the firm now identifies potential customers and learns how they define value for themselves. This information becomes the basis for how the product is shaped to particular customers. The particular skill here involves getting the firm's customer and supplier absorptive capacities to synchronize. We thus add to that literature seeking to understand how firms can synchronize their internal and external integration in new product development (Barki and Pinsonneault, 2005; Hillebrand and Biemans, 2004; Sanders and Premus, 2005). This also points towards the merits of future research exploring an identity-based view of capability development in organizations dedicated to open innovation.

Our model is limited to a specific instance of radical innovation involving groundbreaking knowledge across multiple vertical alliances. Other industries, cases, large samples and collaborative configurations in new product development would pose important further tests of the boundary conditions and validity of the model. In addition, our notion of an INPD system presupposes that all constituent firms are united by a common focus on seeking a share of the returns from a final product. In some circumstances, firms may be content to prioritize upfront payments through licensing of intermediate products and desire no stake in the final product. This would remove an incentive for these firms to coordinate as a system. The propositions therefore are more narrowly focused on those firms for whom a share in final product value is a key goal.

Finally, the chapter has important implications for practice. First, our findings show that absorptive capacity is critical to open innovation, both inbound and outbound. The ability to recognize the value, secure the relationship and co-create mutual value propositions can act as a competitive advantage. This is because it can mean the difference between those that act entrepreneurially on perceived opportunities and those that fail to 'see the light'. The absorptive capacity lens offers a way to ensure that open innovation investments actually lead to returns. This is because the concept identifies key underlying processes that require attention and development as well as the key skills needed for each of those underlying processes.

Particularly with radical innovations, relations involving intense knowledge exchanges are underpinned by the ability of partners to co-generate and co-adapt new knowledge to each other's needs. Firms also need to wear at least two different absorptive capacity hats — one as a supplier and one as a customer. Different questions, mindsets, relationships and goals underpin each, pointing towards the need for differential skill development. Both customer and supplier types of absorptive capacity feed each other, pointing towards the importance of internal integration processes that synchronize each of the four absorptive capacity processes across the two types (supplier and customer). Finally, the Beta Corp experience attests that project members need to 'recognize the value' for themselves in a project if they are to apply the desired levels of effort to acquiring, assimilating, transforming and exploiting. One useful link to make here is to ensure alignment between project goals and project members' performance incentive schemes.

Conclusions

Open innovation can involve firms collaborating in new product development. The nature of this collaborative process can mean that firms may have to act as both a supplier and customer at some point. Understanding how to integrate suppliers depends on the customer absorptive capacity of the downstream firm and this requires the firm understanding how it will, in turn, need to act as a supplier to another downstream firm. Firms thus have multiple identities and these identities must inform each other at the project level. Wearing two hats as both supplier and customer sheds new light on the different ways that absorptive capacity needs to be developed and leveraged if firms are to succeed through open innovation. These insights help inform how firms may build the skills necessary to make their open innovation investments more likely to succeed.

References

Almirall, E. and Casadesus-Masanell, R. (2010). Open versus closed innovation: A model of discovery and divergence, *Academy of Management Review*, **35**(1), 27–47.

Barki, H. and Pinsonneault, A. (2005). A model of organizational integration, implementation effort, and performance, *Organization Science*, **2**(16), 165–179.

Brusoni S., Prencipe, A. and Pavitt, K. (2001). Knowledge specialization, organizational coupling and the boundaries of the firm: Why do firms know more than they make? *Administrative Science Quarterly*, **46**, 597–621.

Buur, J. and Matthews, B. (2008). Participatory innovation, *International Journal of Innovation Management*, **12**(3), 255–273.

Chesbrough, H. (2003). *Open Innovation: The New Imperative for Creating and Profiting From Technology*, Harvard Business School Press, Boston, MA.

Chesbrough, H., Vanhaverbeke, W. and West, J. (2006). *Open Innovation: Researching a New Paradigm*, Oxford University Press, Oxford, UK.

Cohen, W.M. and Levinthal, D.A. (1990). Absorptive capacity: A new perspective on learning and innovation, *Administrative Science Quarterly*, **35**, 128–152.

Dahlander, L. and Gann, D.M. (2010). How open is innovation? *Research Policy*, in press.

Das, A., Narasimhan, R. and Talluri, S. (2006). Supplier integration: Finding an optimal configuration, *Journal of Operations Management*, **24**, 563–582.

Dodgson, M., Gann, D. and Salter, A. (2006). The role of technology in the shift towards open innovation: The case of Proctor & Gamble, *R&D Management*, **36**(3), 333–346.

Eisenhardt, K.M. (1989). Building theories from case study research, *Academy of Management Review*, **14**(4), 532–550.

Gassmann, O. and Enkel, E. (2004). Towards a theory of open innovation: Three core process archetypes, *R&D Management Conference*, Lisbon, Portugal, July 5–6, pp. 1–18.

Gerwin, D. (2004). Coordinating new product development in strategic alliances, *Academy of Management Review*, **29**(2), 241–257.

Grant, R.M. and Baden-Fuller, C. (2004). A knowledge accessing theory of strategic alliances, *Journal of Management Studies*, **41**(1), 61–84.

Hillebrand, B. and Biemans, W.G. (2004). Links between internal and external cooperation in product development: An exploratory study, *Journal of Product Innovation Management*, **2**(21), 110–122.

Lane, P.J. and Lubatkin, M. (1998). Relative absorptive capacity and inter-organizational learning, *Strategic Management Journal*, **19**(5), 461–477.

Lane P.J., Koka, B.R. and Pathak, S. (2006). The reification of absorptive capacity: A critical review and rejuvenation of the construct, *Academy of Management Review*, **31**(4), 833–863.

Langley, A. (1999). Strategies for theorizing from process data, *Academy of Management Review*, **24**(4), 691–710.

Laursen, K. and Salter, A. (2006). Open for innovation: The role of openness in explaining innovation performance among UK manufacturing firms, *Strategic Management Journal*, **27**, 131–150.

Lichtenthaler, U. (2009). Absorptive capacity, environmental turbulence and the complementarity of organizational learning processes, *Academy of Management Journal*, **52**(4), 822–846.

Lichtenthaler, U. and Lichtenthaler, E. (2009). A capability-based framework for open innovation: Complementing absorptive capacity, *Journal of Management Studies*, **46**(8), 1315–1338.

Markides, C.C. and Geroski, P.A. (2004). *Fast Second: How Smart Companies Bypass Radical Innovation to Enter and Dominate New Markets*, Jossey-Bass, San Francisco, CA.

Mora-Valentin, E.M., Montoro-Sanchez, A. and Guerras-Martin, L.A. (2004). Determining factors in the success of R&D cooperative agreements between firms and research organizations, *Research Policy*, **33**, 17–40.

Newey, L.R. and Shulman, A.D. (2004). Systemic absorptive capacity: Creating early-to-market returns through R&D alliances, *R&D Management*, **34**(5), 491–500.

Newey, L.R. and Zahra, S.A. (2009). The evolving firm: How dynamic and operating capabilities interact to enable entrepreneurship, *British Journal of Management*, **20**, S81–S100.

Petersen, K.J., Handfield, R.B. and Ragatz, G.L. (2003). A model of supplier integration into new product development, *Journal of Product Innovation Management*, **20**, 284–299.

Pettigrew, A.M. (1997). What is a processual analysis? *Scandinavian Journal of Management*, **13**(4), 337–348.

Porac, J.F. and Thomas, H. (2002). "Managing cognition and strategy: Issues, trends and future directions," in Pettigrew, A., Thomas, H. and Whittington, R. (eds), *Handbook of Strategy and Management*, Sage Publications, Thousand Oaks, CA, pp. 139–164.

Pratt, M. and Foreman, P.O. (2000). Classifying managerial responses to multiple organizational identities, *Academy of Management Review*, **25**(1), 18–42.

Rosenzweig, E.D., Roth, A.V. and Dean Jr, J.W. (2003). The influence of an integration strategy on competitive capabilities and business performance: An exploratory study of consumer products manufacturers, *Journal of Operations Management*, **21**(4), 437.

Rothaermel, F.T. and Alexandre, M.T. (2009). Ambidexterity in technology sourcing: The moderating role of absorptive capacity, *Organization Science*, **20**(4), 759–780.

Rothaermel, F.T. and Deeds, D.L. (2004). Exploration and exploitation alliances in biotechnology: A system of new product development, *Strategic Management Journal*, **25**, 201–221.

Sanders, N.R. and Premus, R. (2005). Modeling the relationship between firm IT capability, collaboration, and performance, *Journal of Business Logistics*, **1**(26), 1–23.

Scott, S.G. and Lane, V.R. (2000). A stakeholder approach to organizational identity, *Academy of Management Review*, **25**(1), 43–62.

Todorova, G. and Durisin, B. (2007). Absorptive capacity: Valuing a reconceptualization, *Academy of Management Review*, **32**(3), 774–786.

von Hippel, E. (2005). *Democratizing Innovation*, MIT Press, Cambridge, MA.

Walsh, J.P. (1995). Managerial and organizational cognition: Notes from a trip down memory lane, *Organization Science*, **6**(3), 280–321.

Yin, R.K. (2003). *Case Study Research: Design and Methods*, Sage Publications, Thousand Oaks, CA.

Zahra, S.A. and George, G. (2002). Absorptive capacity: A review, reconceptualization and extension, *Academy of Management Review*, **27**(2), 185–203.

Chapter 18

Generativity in Open Innovation Ecosystems: The iPhone and Android*

Björn Remneland-Wikhamn
School of Business, Economics and Law
University of Gothenburg, Sweden

Jan Ljungberg, Magnus Bergquist, and Jonas Kuschel
Department of Applied IT
University of Gothenburg, Sweden

Introduction

Advances in science and technology have created promising new opportunities for industries and economies to create value, which also have made them more complex as innovations can contain specialized knowledge from various disciplines. Under these conditions, firms are said to benefit from acting more open (Chesbrough, 2003) within cross-organizational innovation systems (Cooke, 2001), clusters (Porter, 1998), or ecosystems (Moore, 1995) rather than as sole competitors. New relations emerge as companies strive to meet the challenges of increased user demands, higher R&D costs, and shorter product life cycles, which put the organization's capacity to adapt and innovate into focus (Teece, 2007). Such complexities cause liaisons that form more or less

---

*This chapter is a reworked and extended version of a previously published paper, Remneland-Wikhamn *et al.* (2011). Open innovation, generativity and the supplier as peer: The case of Iphone and Android, *International Journal of Innovation Management*, 15(1), 205–230.

viable ecosystems for R&D and innovation (Rohrbeck *et al.*, 2009). These relations emerge in order to jointly manage certain innovation challenges, explicitly linking the dynamics of value creation and value capture to an interdependent structure (Adner and Kapoor, 2010). An innovation ecosystem perspective is thus sensitive to the presence and roles of different actors besides the focal firm, such as suppliers, complementors, and customers.

The diffusion of various forms of digital technology experienced in modern economies has acted as a disrupting force (Christensen, 2000), providing novel opportunities for distribution and transformation of knowledge across geographical, physical, and organizational boundaries. Mobile computing and communication technology have started to merge with Internet-generated services (Kenney and Pon, 2011), a transition which has been accelerated by strong actors such as Google and Apple. The integration is paradoxically enhanced by a separation in layers (e.g. hardware, operating systems, and applications) among producers (Zittrain, 2008), which creates possibilities for new actors to partake in value creation. Participating in the development of new applications does not require extensive knowledge in hardware, and *vice versa*. This is one important part of what Zittrain (2006, 2008) calls *generative capacity* or *generativity*, i.e. a technology's capacity to enable the generation of new valuable uses that are easy to distribute and in turn could be sources of further innovation.

The purpose of this chapter is to analyze how generativity relates to open innovation ecosystems. More specifically we address the question of how generative capacity attracts external actors to contribute with extensive value. The chapter sets out to explore the proposed shift in power relations among actors in such value ecologies, and investigate the role of suppliers and complementors within distributed and innovation processes. To discuss these areas, we will draw on a comparative case study of two mobile phone platforms — the *iPhone* and *Android*. The mobile phone industry, as well as the two cases, was selected to highlight new forms of external involvement. The two cases have similarities but also differences in how they approach generativity.

In the chapter we suggest that the external actors in innovation ecosystems will receive a more participatory and creative function.

Contributors such as suppliers, customers, and other stakeholders in an affiliated network do not only produce parts of the product, they are involved in innovating, developing, marketing, and branding the products and services in relation to the shared platform, which at the same time constitutes the evolution of the platform. We therefore argue that these generative forces are important to understand and utilize when moving toward an open and distributed innovation model. Hence, in innovation ecosystems there is a need for firms to reflect upon how they can implement generativity in terms of organizational structure, intellectual property, and technological infrastructure, and not least to consider the managerial implications in transforming the organization from a closed firm to a focal actor able to harness the generative capacities developed in open innovation ecosystems.

The chapter presents a general discussion pointing to the increased distribution of innovation activities in society due to digitalization and IT advances. This is followed by an introduction to Zittrain's (2006, 2008) views about the concept of generativity, which will be used as a theoretical lens in the analysis of open innovation initiatives. The mobile phone industry is then briefly outlined and the two cases (iPhone and Android) are presented, followed by an analysis based on Zittrain's (2008) dimensions of generativity. The chapter ends with a concluding discussion about the managerial challenges within open innovation ecosystems.

Peer Producers in Open Innovation Ecosystems

Although it has long been accepted that organizations act in open systems (Thompson, 1967) strongly affected by the external environment (e.g. Lawrence and Lorsch, 1967) and its stakeholder demands (Freeman, 1984), open innovation (Chesbrough, 2003, 2006, 2011) has in recent years gained much attention in academic as well as industry settings. The notion is sometimes criticized as being "old wine in new bottles" (Trott and Hartmann, 2009; Mowery, 2009) or too vague and imprecise (Dahlander and Gann, 2010; di Benedetto, 2010) but the overall growing interest in the collaborative organization of innovation is difficult to disregard. Chesbrough defines open innovation as an organization's purposive inflow and outflow of knowledge across its boundaries in order to accelerate innovation and expand market opportunities (Chesbrough, 2003; Chesbrough *et al.*, 2006) or strengthen the business model (Chesbrough, 2006). Recently he also linked the notion to the emerging service economy (Chesbrough, 2011).

The "openness" in Chesbrough's terms refers to an exchange or bargain of ideas and intellectual property with external associates such as customers, suppliers, partners, or competitors. Open innovation is contrasted with "closed" innovation, where firms keep tight control over their R&D processes in terms of both who can contribute to the value production and who are allowed to claim value from the generated results. In open innovation processes horizontal as well as vertical borders between various co-producing actors tend to fade.

On the consumer side, the blurring of boundaries has been captured by Toffler's (1980) notion of *prosumer*, which suggests that users take an active part in developing the content of the innovation as co-producers. For instance, in some online services (e.g. online communities, virtual worlds, matchmaking services, and other Web 2.0 services) the users' activities make up most of the platform's total value. The opposite side of the value chain, the supplier perspective, has not been addressed as much in the open innovation literature, except for the two special issues of the *International Journal of Innovation Management* in 2010 and 2011. However, the research on supply-chain management suggests that suppliers have a unique position when innovating to increase end-user value due to their expert knowledge in at least parts of the joint value proposal (Bessant *et al.*, 2003).

In open innovation ecosystems, interdependencies between the various participators are strong, and coordination can be marked by both collaboration and competition. Firms for instance often take initiatives to encourage ecosystem partners to favor their specific technology platforms (Adner and Kapoor, 2010) but have less control over service development and partners' affiliations with competitors. Innovation in open ecosystems generates more insecurities than in traditional closed innovation and firms need to orchestrate these challenges actively (Teece, 2007).

The disruptive movement toward a digitalized economy has indeed enhanced cross-border value production but also shifted power relations and control mechanisms among actors across the whole value chain. One example of this is when users or customers develop or modify innovations in what von Hippel (2005) refers to as "user innovations." The benefit of innovation initiatives being distributed and democratized is that users can develop solutions nearer to what they want instead of relying only on imperfect agents to translate their needs. Von Hippel highlights "lead users" as the main external source for innovative and value-adding contributions and others (e.g. Franke and Shah, 2003; Lettl *et al.*, 2006; Pillar and Walcher, 2006) have shown empirical evidence from various industries of users' innovative initiatives.

An illustrative example of a voluntaristic production mode (i.e. where users or other developers on their own initiative contribute to innovation and development) is open-source software. The typical open-source project is a loosely coupled community, where work is totally delegated, relying on a high amount of voluntaristic contributions but coordinated by one or a few developers. One of the most well-known examples is the operating system Linux. The development of Linux is entirely distributed; anyone can download the code, contribute to it, send it back, and if it is considered good enough it will be included in the core product. The contributors come from all over the world and most of them have never met face to face. The identities of the interacting persons in an open-source community do not matter in principle (Demil and Lecocq, 2006) but the reputation and status of a participating person may matter (Bergquist and Ljungberg, 2001).

Open source can in its purified form be described as a production mode where the outcomes as well as the required knowledge resources are considered as common resources, and where the aim of the process is to contribute to public good. The way to accomplish this is through peer production, i.e. self-selected and decentralized individual action (Benkler, 2006). What has happened over the last decade is that open source to a large extent has been intertwined with the commercial software market, leading to a plethora of new business models and new sorts of software suppliers. While individual developers contributing to communities do so by a complex set of social motivations, guided by the norms and values established in open-source communities, firms engaged in open source tend to be driven by economical and technical motivations (e.g. Bergquist and Ljungberg, 2001; Bonaccorsi and Rossi, 2003).

The type of organizing and production process that is represented by open-source projects has been likened to a bazaar (e.g. Demil and Lecocq, 2006; Ljungberg, 2000; Raymond, 1999), i.e. a marketplace where people enter and leave, sell, buy, and exchange goods. The characteristics of the bazaar are that actors are not coordinated by price mechanisms (as in markets), formal hierarchies (as in firms), or strong ties/long relations (as in networks); there is no selection of members or contracting parties; and there is no definitive delimitation of roles between users and producers and no enforced work roles (Demil and Lecocq, 2006). This community-based production mode also resembles what could be described as a "civic community logic" (Boltanski and Chiapello, 2005; Rolandsson *et al.*, 2011), emphasizing informal and personal relations, transparent peer production, and software as common goods.

One attempt to explain the development toward a new production mode beyond the open-source example is Benkler's notion of "commons-based peer production" (Benkler, 2006). The predominant understanding of the organizing of economic production is that individuals engage in productive activities either as employees in firms following the directions of managers, or as individuals in markets following price signals (Coase, 1937; Williamson, 1975). Benkler (2006) describes commons-based peer production as a third mode of production, where large aggregations of individuals independently search for opportunities to be creative. This new mode of production may not conquer the old modes, but rather it tends to co-exist and rely on firms and markets, resulting in blurred boundaries between value creation and value capture, in what could be described as a value ecosystem. Collaborating firms can capture, elaborate on, and capitalize value created outside the company, but may also be obliged to contribute to value creation where the appropriation of invested resources is out of control (e.g. Chesbrough and Appleyard, 2007; Dahlander and Magnusson, 2005; Fitzgerald, 2006; O'Mahony, 2003; Ven and

Verelst, 2008). This joint development of value creation is still an emerging phenomenon where the borders between commons based and proprietary, open and closed, firms and communities, peer production and market are not always clear cut. The point here is that this development toward peer production (commons based or not) opens up a new role for the supplier as a peer, i.e. a developer or contributor that decides to contribute by its own initiative. Thus, the supplier contributes to a commons-based or commercial project in which the appropriation of the supplier's invested resources emanate from the potential customer base and will be boosted by community-related benefits in the form of economic or social value.

To summarize, advances in IT have promoted new intermediary opportunities to match supply and demand, build relations and cross-pollinate creative ideas. Patent auctions, intermediary markets (e.g. Dodgson *et al.*, 2006), crowd sourcing (e.g. Brabham, 2008), online communities (e.g. Sproull *et al.*, 2007), and various other forms of Web 2.0 platforms (O'Reilly, 2007) are examples of such activities. By promoting a critical mass of engaged participants followed by escalating network effects (Shapiro and Varian, 1998) and diffusion mechanisms (Rogers, 1995), mass collaboration has shown its potential in not only open-source projects but in other innovation activities as well. Innovation ecologies are here manifested by the interdependencies and relations across participating stakeholders. One common denominator for these phenomena is that they all have a system design that enhances the generative capacity, as they invite users and developers to generate new innovative features and applications that are easy to distribute and in turn could be sources for further innovation by other users and developers. Viewed in this light, an IT infrastructure with high generative capacity could be seen as the technical foundation of commons-based peer production in innovation ecologies.

The concept of generativity

Generativity as a notion has been used in various settings linked to innovation and design (e.g. Avital and Te'eni, 2009; Hopkins *et al.*,

2011; Lane and Maxfield, 1996; Swan and Scarbrough, 2005). In this chapter we will focus on Zittrain's (2006, 2008) use of the term, as he discusses specifically a (digital) technology's capacity to enable voluntaristic and spontaneous innovation driven by large, heterogeneous, and uncoordinated crowds of people. The modular construction of the PC and the open architecture of the Internet are both important examples where this form of generative capacity is flourishing. Zittrain describes five principal factors for generativity: leverage, adaptability, ease of mastery, accessibility, and transferability. *Leverage* means the degree to which a technology provides help in performing certain tasks. A computer has for instance higher leverage in aiding advanced calculating than a pen and a paper. *Adaptability* means how flexible and modifiable the technology is in performing different tasks. A paper has high adaptability in the sense that it can be written on but also be used to wrap things. *Ease of mastery* is related to how simple the technology is to use for broad user groups and how much previous knowledge is required in order to capture its full potential. An airplane is for instance more difficult to master than a bicycle. *Accessibility* involves how easy it is to get access to the technology, e.g. its availability for ordinary users. A very expensive or rare technology has lower accessibility than a cheap and common one. The level of *transferability* indicates how easily changes and updates in the technology are distributed to its users. Open-source software has for instance higher transferability than proprietary software, in that contributions are open for a wide community to modify and share. These five conditions, according to Zittrain, contribute to the generativity of a technology and enhance the possibilities for suppliers, producers, and users to become involved in adding new distributed value and further innovation.

Zittrain gives several examples on the relation between generativity and control. One would intuitively assume that the two notions are in opposition to each other, since control is often portrayed as hindering creativity by streamlining thoughts and actions to a certain predetermined direction. Control is thus linked to power in the sense that one actor's will is enforced upon other actors. Actors can utilize technology to put themselves in the position of gatekeepers (Allen, 1971) or inscribe program-of-actions (Callon, 1991) to coordinate the networks and users. Digital Rights Management (DRM) is nowadays often integrated in innovations to control the behavior of users, stopping them from tinkering without authorization. However, control can also be viewed as a prerequisite of external involvement, in terms of for instance protecting and promoting various levels of openness, providing guidance to potential contributors, and rewarding value-creation above free-riding. The tools for generativity, such as the technology infrastructure, intellectual property rights, and organization mechanisms, are therefore in the spotlight. Generativity changes the control focus rather than dissolving it, and affects the whole ecosystem of manufacturers, suppliers, vendors, and users (Zittrain, 2006). This transition raises the question of how generativity specifically relates to the involvement of external actors in value production. This is the aim of this chapter, by drawing on a comparative case study from the mobile phone industry.

The Mobile Phone Industry in Change

The mobile phone industry is under rapid development. It has in recent decades moved from merely dealing with connecting voices to providing integrated services and add-ons, which have transformed the (mobile) telephone into a device capable of restructuring users' lives (e.g. Ling, 2004). Mobile communication and its fusion with the Internet has generated synchronization opportunities for email, calendar and notes, location-based services linked to online maps and GPS positioning, audio-visual services such as capturing and sharing digital photos, videos, and music, and other forms of leisure services such as games and online community applications (e.g. Lindgren *et al.*, 2002). This development has been enhanced by the availability of free tool kits for distributed application development (Bergvall-Kåreborn *et al.*, 2011).

A few studies have considered the mobile phone industry from an open innovation perspective. For instance, Dittrich and Duysters (2007) investigated how Nokia strategically dealt with the changing technological environment in terms of exploration and exploitation in the years 1985–2002, and Lee *et al.* (2008) argued that mobile phone firms increasingly engage in exploitation-oriented alliances, standards, networks, and co-patenting.

Mobile technology is often described as consisting of several interrelated layers (e.g. Fransman, 2002; Zittrain, 2008) from infrastructural hardware to software applications. As such it includes developers of the technology platform, the operating system, the user interface, and applications, but also the network and service providers and mobile portal providers (e.g. Maitland *et al.*, 2002; Sabat, 2002). The various actors and roles constitute a wide association of relations and dependencies, which have increased in complexity as each layer has progressed. As mentioned earlier in the chapter, Zittrain (2008) among others has argued that the separation of these layers enhances the possibilities for new actors to enter the ecological system with fresh ideas.

One could argue that we are moving from a value-chain perspective toward what has been described as value ecosystems (Chesbrough and Appleyard, 2007). The concept of the value chain, popularized by Porter (1985), has been widely used to analyze how different actors are involved in creating value within the IT and mobile phone industry (e.g. Barnes, 2002; Maitland, *et al.*, 2002; Olla and Patel, 2002; Sabat, 2002). The idea behind the value chain is that products or offerings pass through a sequential chain of activities, each adding value to the process. Rülke *et al.* (2003) use a value-chain analysis to map the ecology of mobile commerce (m-commerce), involving the set of competencies, investments, and activities required to create and deliver value via the mobile phone. They argue that the m-commerce value chain has passed through three generations: the first was built around analog cellular voice services in the mid-1980s, the second generation was based on digital voice and data, and the third generation is based on the wireless Internet. As the industry matures, more elements have been added to the process, making it increasingly difficult for one single enterprise to provide competitive solutions to end users.

Peppard and Rylander (2006) propose that a value network would be a more appropriate metaphor than a value chain, since the old linear model does not accurately describe value creation in a digitalized economy. This is similar to the ideas of Freeman and Liedtka (1997) who introduced a stakeholder view as well as those of Kothandaraman and Wilson (2001) who suggested a value-nets view. Peppard and Rylander used Network Value Analysis (NVA) to analyze the evolution of the mobile services ecosystem, including defining and mapping the network's objectives, participants, value dimensions, and value linkages, concluding that mobile phone operators should emphasis a strategy of cooperation and partnering in service and content offerings. Also the proponents of a value-chain perspective discuss the problematic use of the chain metaphor representing value creation in the mobile phone industry. Maitland *et al.* (2002) agree in their analysis of the European mobile phone market that horizontal linkages or value nets and networks are important for understanding value creation. Olla and Patel (2002) choose the oxymoron "value chain network" to describe the telecom industry in the UK.

In sum, one could argue that the mobile phone industry has matured (Fransman, 2002; Maitland, *et al.*, 2002), shifting the value-adding focus from improving and adding technology and design features to providing interactive mobile services. Many of these services explore totally new territories, which makes it difficult to estimate their possibilities for success *ex ante* (Mathew *et al.*, 2004). When users to a large extent contribute to the generation and adoption of content, the growth and application of such mobile services are much in the hands of large-scale end-user experimentation than to planned stage-gate implementations (Mylonopoulos and Sideris, 2006). Hence, there is a significant movement from "technology push" to "market pull," influencing the more traditional mobile phone developers to add software features to their devices, but also attracting new actors to enter the market. This transition highlights the need to reflect on the evolving strategies for generativity, in terms of inducing openness in order to build a critical mass of content, engagement, and attention, but also using control to protect intellectual property rights and business models.

Case Description: The iPhone and Android

As a study into the shift in hegemony of the mobile phone industry in relation to generativity and external value creation, two mobile phone platforms will be introduced and analyzed: the iPhone and Android. The empirical material was collected through various public sources, such as news articles, official blogs, recorded public interviews, and press releases.

iPhone

The iPhone, launched by Apple on June 29, 2007, has been hugely successful in terms of sales of devices as well as software applications. Until the end of 2010, 90 million devices had been distributed. When Apple's CEO gave an introductory speech for the iPhone launch at the MacForum 2007, he started by saying:

> *This is a day that I have been looking forward to for two and a half years. Every once and a while a revolutionary product comes along that changes everything.*
>
> *... Apple has been very fortunate, it's been able to introduce a few of these in the world. In 1984, we introduced the Macintosh. It didn't just change Apple — it changed the whole computer industry. In 2001, we introduced the first iPod, and it didn't just change the way we listen to music, it changed the entire music industry. Well, today we introduce three revolutionary products in this class. The first one is a widescreen iPod with touch controls. The second is a revolutionary mobile phone. And the third is a breakthrough Internet communications device. So three things...*
>
> *... These are not three separate devices. This is one device, and we are calling it iPhone. Today, Apple is going to reinvent the phone. (Steve Jobs, MacForum 2007)*

The development of the iPhone was initiated in a joint project with Cingular, a wireless phone company now belonging to AT&T. However, Apple developed most of the iPhone's hardware and software in-house, which led to the filing of more than 200 patents including for instance the multi-touch screen, scrolling, and zooming.

> *We have invented a new technology called multi-touch which is phe-*
> *nomenal. It works like magic. You do not need a stylus, it is far more*
> *accurate than any touch display that has ever been shipped. It ignores*
> *unintended touches, it is supersmart, you can do multi-finger ges-*
> *tures on it — and boy have we patented it! (Steve Jobs, MacForum*
> *2007)*

Some of the hardware was also acquired as intellectual property from small state-of-the art high-tech firms. One such example is FingerWorks, founded by a doctoral student and a professor from the University of Delaware with a focus on multi-touch surface keyboards. Since its launch, the iPhone has been the subject of numerous law suits. In 2009, Nokia sued Apple for infringement of ten patents on various wireless technologies, which was followed by a countersuit against Nokia for infringement of 13 of Apples patents, such as display graphics, teleconferencing, and power conservation. The "war" between the different mobile phone platforms (e.g. iPhone, Android, and Windows Mobile) has since then escalated, leading to several more lawsuits and a high degree of competition over existing intellectual property rights.

The operating system, iPhone OS, is based on a proprietary variant of the, in parts open-sourced, operating system Mac OS X Leopard. Also the Graphical User Interface (GUI) was developed in-house, and is considered a core value feature for the iPhone as it is designed for optimal user experience. For instance, the keyboard is integrated into the GUI based on the multi-touch functionality.

> *We gonna start with a revolutionary user interface. It is a result of*
> *years of research and development and of course it is an interplay of*
> *hardware and software. ... [The other smartphones] all have these*
> *control buttons that are fixed in plastic and are the same for every*

application. Every application wants a slightly different user interface, a slightly optimized set of buttons just for it. And what if you think of a great idea six months from now, you can't run around and add a button to these things, they are already shipped. (Steve Jobs, MacForum 2007)

The platform is designed to only run applications approved by Apple and identified with a cryptographic signature. On July 10th, 2008, Apple opened an online distribution channel named the *App Store*, where users of the iPhone and iPod Touch can browse and download applications directly to their devices, either free of charge or on average for a small cost. When it was launched the store contained 500 third-party applications, including 125 freeware programs. One year later it had over 55,000 available applications and there had been more than 1 million downloads in total. By October 2011, about 425,000 approved third-party applications had been added to the App Store. In early 2010, Apple also launched a tablet-like media device known as the iPad based on the same touch-based operating system as the iPhone.

Android

The Open Handset alliance (OHA) was established on November 5, 2007. OHA is a consortium of around 50 companies from the mobile phone industry including leading operators, handset manufacturers, semiconductor firms, software developers, and commercialization vendors, with a shared goal of developing open standards for mobile devices. At the same time, Android was announced — a new, open-sourced, mobile phone operating system.

This alliance shares a common goal of fostering innovation on mobile devices and giving consumers a far better user experience than much of what is available on today's mobile platforms. By providing developers a new level of openness that enables them to work more collaboratively, Android will accelerate the pace at which new and compelling mobile services are made available to consumers. (Press release, November 5, 2007)

Android was originally a small Palo Alto startup, acquired by Google in 2005 and later transferred to the Open Handset alliance. Since the first release of the mobile phone operating system, several new updates have been launched. The Android initiative can be described as being open on three axes: toward the mobile phone industry (i.e. manufacturers, operators, vendors, etc.), toward users, and toward application suppliers. To support the mobile phone industry, the whole stack of codes for Android was released under an open-source license and runs on the Linux kernel. The members of the Open Handset alliance agree upon shared technical standards for Android in order to enforce compatibility between hardware and software. At the same time, Android encourages the contributing actors to customize and differentiate the look-and-feel of the features they develop within these compatibility boundaries. Openness in relation to the users means that Android gives them increased freedom to control their experiences in terms of the applications installed and used. Most programs can be deleted or replaced and the system is designed so that user data can easily be ported to new applications. Regarding the openness toward application suppliers, Jason Chen, an Android developer from Google, stated:

> *When we say Android is open for developers, it is a couple of important things. The first and foremost is that you as developers don't need to get permission to ship an application. There is no application certification for Android, and there is also no hidden or privileged APIs so there is no additional level of access or things that you have to do to get your device or application out on the market and to be able to take full advantage of the Android platform. ...The other way that Android is open to user developers is at a technical level. And the way we like to sum this up is really there are three key things ... and that is that you can integrate, extend, and replace existing components in the Android stack. (Jason Chen, Android developer, Google, 2008)*

The Android team has developed tools for guiding application suppliers in emulating and debugging code in the Android framework. Android has also started "challenges" in order to mobilize programmers to start generating applications for the system. The first challenge opened on January 3, 2008, and generated almost 1,800 new applications. On October 22, 2008, *Android Market* was made available to Android users as a distribution channel for browsing and downloading applications, similar to the iPhone App Store. The application for the store was developed and managed by Google and is nowadays preinstalled on all Android handhelds. As of July 2011, over 250,000 official third-party applications had been added. As with most of the Android features, Google's Android Market is not an exclusive downloading tool. Any competitor can build their own "store" and suppliers can find other distribution channels to cater for end-users. For instance, in 2011 Amazon launched the Amazon Appstore to distribute apps on Android devices (and Apple sued Amazon for violating Apple's trademark by using the term "appstore").

iPhone and Android: A Generativity Lens

For both the iPhone and Android, involving external actors in innovation is an important driver for value creation across the innovation ecosystem. The comparative case study highlights two somewhat different approaches to distributed involvement, which will be discussed using Zittrain's definition of generativity (Zittrain, 2008), as introduced earlier, in terms of leverage, adaptability, ease of mastery, accessibility, and transferability. The analysis is summarized in Table 1.

Leverage

The generative capacity in terms of leverage means the extent to which the mobile phone system acts as a lever for users and suppliers of applications to accomplish their goals. Both the iPhone and Android are aimed at the premium market segment, suggesting that they need to offer their users and application developers a solution with high potential leverage. With the iPhone, Apple has from the

Table 1. Summary of the Comparison between the iPhone and Android.

Aspect of generativity	iPhone	Android
Leverage	Apple's standardized and uncomplicated approach together with a huge mass of potential users provides strong levers for application suppliers to create new applications for the platform.	Android's open ecosystem of collaborating actors pushes the development of hardware and software forward, enhancing the platform's leverage potential.
Adaptability	As the gatekeeper for which applications are allowed into the App Store, Apple might censor disruptive innovation. There is hence a rather low adaptability for suppliers in relation to Apple's rules, but a rather high adaptability within these rules. Users have, due to the huge number of diverse applications, many possibilities for adapting a phone's content to their specific needs.	All manufacturers need to adjust the operating system to their technology. Suppliers face uncertainty in terms of "forking" and the emergence of new business areas. Suppliers have many opportunities to adapt their applications to a wide range of services both in relation to the technology and other applications' functionalities. Users have freedom to add, replace, and remove applications according to their own needs.
Ease of mastery	For suppliers, the Apple and iPhone communities provide programming tools and support. The App Store is an easy to use and effective distribution channel. For users, the iPhone is a highly user friendly device, integrating hardware, operating system, GUI, and applications. The focus is on reliability, an intuitive design, standardized program layouts, etc.	For suppliers, ease of mastery is complicated by the vast number of variations of handheld devices, distribution channels, etc. Ease of mastery is, however, enhanced because all APIs are available and the operating system is open source. Handheld device manufacturers develop their own GUIs, which makes ease of mastery specific for each phone and brand.

(Continued)

Table 1. (*Continued*)

Aspect of generativity	iPhone	Android
Accessibility	The programming language Objective C reduces accessibility for some developers. Suppliers also risk not gaining access to potential users due to Apple's role as a gatekeeper in the App Store. The ease of adding and downloading applications to the phone through the App Store enhances access for suppliers as well as users.	Android supports a well-known programming language (Java) making the platform accessible for many potential programmers. Suppliers are free to add innovative applications without asking anyone for permission. Users have many channels to gain access and to add new applications. Users can also "root" their phones to increase accessibility and adaptation even further. The freedom can enhance the feeling of accessibility for some users and reduce it for others.
Transferability	The iPhone's transferability is restricted by Apple to a one-way interaction between the user and the company. Direct sharing between users and devices is not allowed. Updates must be reaccredited by App Store, which slows down transferability. However, it is very easy for users to update an iPhone directly or via iTunes. "Jailbreaking" an iPhone has emerged among users as a way to increase transferability.	Suppliers have many channels to access users, which can blur possibilities for distribution and marketing or increase suppliers' efforts in different ways. Google-owned Android Market has, however, become the main entrance for applications on Android phones. Users can share applications through the Internet and install them directly on an Android phone or via a computer. Applications can be shared through peer-to-peer communities.

start focused on providing advanced built-in technologies and an operating system integrated with an intuitively designed phone, one which is also a general entertainment and utility device. For Android, several different handheld manufacturers work separately or jointly in advancing technological features adapted for the operating system. New models with different designs and performance are frequently released, pushing the development further. The technological infrastructure for both iPhone and Android handhelds is constructed so that it is easy for external suppliers to add new applications and take full advantage of the built-in features and sensors, such as the touch screen, GPS positioning, camera recorders, Wi-Fi, calibration tools, etc. The devices are built using separate layers easily reachable for external suppliers through common Application Programming Interfaces (APIs).

With standardized instructions and templates for application suppliers, the iPhone system has a unified look-and-feel, making externally developed applications familiar to users. Together with straightforward payment functions and distribution channels, the iPhone is attractive to external programmers, who have generated a huge number of applications. This critical mass of applications makes the mobile device highly customizable for each user's specific needs, and the critical mass of users has created a lucrative market for application suppliers.

Android has fewer standards compared to the iPhone, creating a freer but also somewhat more chaotic environment for application developers. Android has put more emphasis on the generative aspects in that they allow for interaction and information exchange between the programs and databases locally installed on a mobile device. This allows application developers to build on other developers' work and ideas, which has increased the possibilities for a more complex user experience. Programmers can take advantage of features already installed, such as online maps, barcode scanners, and contact lists when designing new functions.

The ability to download applications after a device has been shipped clearly extends its leverage as a utility and entertainment device; each mobile phone can be tailored to a user's unique needs and wants. By providing innovative applications for the iPhone or Android, companies can also leverage their offerings by integrating services with mobile technology and the ubiquitous presence. For instance, Facebook and Twitter have gained in value because users have access to their services wherever they are and can use a mobile phone's built-in camera to publish online.

Adaptability

Adaptability as a facet of generative capacity is the extent to which a mobile system can perform a variety of different tasks and how open it is for innovative and adaptive development. Android and the iPhone provide opportunities for the end user to install applications with a wide range of purposes, including games and entertainment, utilities, social networking, music, productivity, navigation, etc. With hundreds of thousands of applications and millions of active users, it is even possible to talk about "long tail" opportunities (Anderson, 2006) where niche programs of "non-hit items" can find a market. Apple has maintained a gatekeeping role over the iPhone and restricts the applications that are allowed to enter their App Store. The compulsory terms, which both guide and restrict a developer's creative work, are written down in the iPhone SDK (software development kit) Agreement. These include for instance prohibitions of pornographic and offensive content, abuse of Digital Rights Management, and the installation of executable code that can call other frameworks and APIs not approved by Apple. The principles provide clear directions to suppliers, with a low adaptability of the rules but a high adaptability within the rules. At the same time, it also imposes a risk of censorship to users and application suppliers if Apple decides that an application does not meet the required standard or poses a threat to Apple's idea of how the phone should function. A much debated case was when Google tried to launch an application called "Google Voice Apps" for the iPhone during the fall of 2009. What this program does is to provide extended services, such as voice mail with automatic transcription and call notification. The service can also replace the device's phone number with a

"Google number," which offers low-cost international calls, free SMS, etc. The application, although highly appreciated by many users, was rejected by Apple due to the fact that it was said to emulate features that come with the actual phone and its predefined network provider.

With Android, negotiations of standards occur between all the Open Handset alliance members, with Google as a main influential actor. The alliance partners participate in a distributed innovation ecosystem where everyone can contribute to the development of the Android value ecology, pushing both hardware and software technology forward. Each handset manufacturer has to tailor new releases of the open-source operating system to their specific devices, and being involved early in the development process saves time and eases implementation. Google has taken a leading role in developing the operating system and for the release of Android 2.0 (also called Eclair) they worked closely with Motorola and Verizon in developing the phone Droid before the source code was revealed openly to the rest of the alliance partners. A couple of months later, Google launched (together with HTC) the Google branded handheld device Nexus One, which possibly complicated the alliance's balance of competition and collaboration a bit further. In August 2011, Google and Motorola Mobility announced that an agreement had been reached where Google acquired Motorola Mobility, but strongly pointed out that Android will still remain open.

There is the risk of forking (Lerner and Tirole, 2001) in open-source projects through the emergence of subgroups and multiple standards and software versions within the community. As Android provides a quite high degree of freedom and adaptability for any developer or developer group, the system can be applied also in business areas other than mobile phones, such as mini-PCs, computer tablets, televisions, and even automotive platforms. The whole project, due to its adaptability openness, faces huge coordination and compatibility challenges. From the user's perspective, however, the adaptability must be considered high in terms of the possibilities to tailor the mobile phone exactly to one's needs. For common features, such as a browser, media player, and a phone book, preinstalled applications exist, but they can be to a large extent removed or replaced. New programs can be downloaded from various sources.

Ease of mastery

Ease of mastery measures the degree of skill and knowledge needed to be able to understand and work with the functionalities of the mobile system. For users, ease of mastery is linked to user friendly and familiar design and commands, sensibility in the touch screen, clear instructions, easy account setup, few failures, breakdowns and interruptions, and a smooth and fast communication between hardware and software. For Android phones and in particular the iPhone, much effort has been expended in making it easy for users to master the devices, simplifying their experience through agile GUIs and state-of-the-art technology. The iPhone benefits in this sense because Apple has full control over the development processes for the hardware, the operating system and the GUI, supporting only one type of handheld device (although in several releases). Android, on the other hand, is integrated in a variety of different handheld devices, most of them with their own GUI implementation and some even with slight customizations of the Android stack. Hence, the user friendliness and design is to a large extent contingent on the work of each manufacturer.

The ease of mastery for users also involves the process of downloading applications and upgrading the system with new releases. Apple has control over the only distribution channel, App Store, which provides a smooth and easy way for users to install new content. Also Android phones have, with the preinstalled Android Market, a way of searching and downloading applications similar to the App Store. The fact that the Android system does not block application developers from using other forms of program distribution allows alternative sources to emerge. This gives increased freedom to the actors in the ecosystem, but it might also lead to confusion for less advanced users when they have to navigate among many different distribution channels.

For external application providers, ease of mastery implies support for programming, testing, distributing, marketing, and charging for their applications. For both Android and the iPhone, toolkits and standard forms have been developed to guide and simplify programming tasks. Large communities support and give feedback in the process. Distribution channels such as the App Store and Android Market provide a cheap and effective means to connect supply with demand. Ease of mastery is further maintained by the iPhone because Apple has maintained overall control of the mobile platform and providers have one single contact when designing their services. Android suppliers have to take into consideration a number of different manufacturers and devices. On the other hand, their work is simplified by the fact that the operating system and APIs are freely revealed as open source.

Accessibility

Accessibility as an aspect of generativity is the ease of access to the technology along with the tools and information to master it. A typical example of a technology with high accessibility is an ordinary PC, which comes in a wide range of prices, and can be opened and reconfigured without too much difficulty. For a user with the necessary skills it is relatively easy to start writing code for it. Transferring this concept to mobile phones, accessibility can be divided into hardware and software accessibility. On the hardware level, the platforms compared are not easily accessible for users and developers. Whereas a PC can be modified with new drives, more memory, or extended with hardware connected via USB or FireWire, mobile phones have a limited set of possibilities to add or reconfigure hardware. Accessibility in terms of adding and developing software is different. Both systems are highly accessible for program suppliers with helpful tools and instructions, which makes it easy to both program and launch new applications at low cost.

For the iPhone, the programming language is Apple's Objective C, which limits the accessibility for new application suppliers who first need to learn that particular language. Apple supports suppliers with a free iPhone SDK, tools, frameworks, development best-practices, design methods, sample code, technical documentation, and guides for creating iPhone applications. Android offer similar resources for its suppliers but applies a more open and accessible system, with an SDK for Android and Android Development Tools (ADT) as a plug-in for the open-source development platform Eclipse, and the programming language is the well-known Java. Most of the system code is revealed as open source.

The iPhone is built around the idea that its content and experience should be accessible for end users. To secure this, Apple has limited certain aspects for application suppliers, such as the programming language, distribution channels, specific rules on design and content, etc. Due to Apple's rather strict policies and sometimes long lead times, suppliers risk not gaining access to potential users when applying for acceptance of an application into the App Store, which is the sole source of downloads for users. Once accepted by Apple, however, applications are accessible to millions of iPhone users directly from their own handheld devices. The App Store provides a good overview of available applications to users and suppliers but the large number of applications in a single place can also generate an overload of information.

Android allows more freedom for the development of applications, but the lower restrictions could also be seen as increasing the risk of diluting quality and user friendliness. Android phones have Google's Android Market as a preinstalled distribution channel, which works in a similar way to the App Store but has to date less content. Developers and users are also free to start their own channels for distributing applications. An even more elaborate way of tinkering with an Android phone is to "root" it. Rooting is a process where the user can become the superuser (root) of the phone and replace the operating system provided by the manufacturer in flash memory by a different version. New opportunities then emerge for the phone such as running a wider range of applications and performing hardware-related activities such as overclocking the processor. The freedom and "openness" of an Android platform provides high accessibility to users and suppliers with interest and knowledge in the technology, but the complexity of many parallel opportunities and channels can also reduce the feeling of accessibility for less skilled users.

Transferability

Transferability measures how easily changes in the technology can be transferred to other users. A fully transferable technology means that adaptations made by skilled users can easily be conveyed to less-skilled users. For the iPhone and Android transferability is the extent to which the system is capable of transferring applications, improvements, and updates to other developers and users. Generativity in terms of transferability differs depending on the layer considered. For hardware development, the iPhone has rather low transferability since Apple does most of the work in-house. Android handheld manufacturers also mainly develop hardware internally, but have to raise standardization decisions with the Open Handset Alliance, which thereby opens up the matter for discussion and debate. The transferability for the operating system is considered high for Android, as it is based on Linux and open-source software. However, Google has, in the development of new versions of the operating system, worked closely with certain handheld device manufacturers (such as Motorola for the Eclair release), giving them a head start. The iPhone's operating system is closed and it is not possible to transfer applications between users. For the iPhone as well as Android, new updates of the operating system are quite easily transferable to existing device owners.

Android has several ways of transferring applications, updates, and additions to applications. Although Android Market is the main channel for file transfer, peer-to-peer transfers are also possible between phones and applications can be downloaded to a computer and then copied and installed on a phone. Links with direct access to applications are published on the Internet, which can be used to download and install them on a phone. These features support transferability between both users and suppliers. The users of the iPhone must download all applications from the App Store, either via the built-in function in an iPhone or by using iTunes and transferring the application to the iPhone through USB. Direct sharing of applications between users is not allowed by Apple. To change an iPhone so that the App Store is no longer the sole distribution channel for applications and to be able to run unofficial code, some users have applied a method called "jailbreaking." Several alternatives are available, mostly providing free software, but paid applications also exist. Programs that have been rejected by the App Store can in this way find a market and, although not sanctioned by Apple, this strengthens the platform's transferability and thus at least one dimension of its generative capacity. Jailbreaking might not be considered illegal *per se* but it voids Apple's warranty on the device. It is, as mentioned before, also possible to open up Android phones through "rooting." From the perspective of generativity, however, jailbreaking is an act of transferability (since it allows the transfer of applications and updates between users) while rooting is a way to increase accessibility (since it allows users to manipulate the device on a deeper level). However, Android's open transferability and rooting and jailbreaking iPhones increase the risk of receiving a virus. For instance, in May 2011, a trojan virus called DroidDream was released on the Android Market in the form of free, pirated versions of existing priced apps. This allowed hackers to steal information from users. Governance structures, such as the iPhone's rather restricted App Store policies, protect users from potential malware and other risks caused by "unprotected" programs.

Different Forms of Generative Ecosystems

Both the iPhone and Android are highly generative ecosystems. The main difference is the way that generativity in terms of the infrastructure is configured. Apple has with the advent of the iPhone and App Store reshaped the mobile phone market, bringing commercial and brand success in their effort to challenge developers, suppliers, and vendors of mobile phones and mobile applications with a new technological platform. Apple clearly imposes a high level of control but also provides support to developers and it is easy to supply software and services to end users. Open Handset Alliance-based Android has chosen a similar but also to some extent different path with more open relations between hardware manufacturers, vendors, software developers, and users, which calls for higher demands on compatibility between different stakeholders but is also open for new initiatives.

The choice of metaphor for the two distribution channels — "store" and "market" — are symbolic of the iPhone and Android in general. In a store, such as Bloomingdale's or Walmart, sections and brands are placed within the ordered premises of the store. Designers and suppliers have the freedom to develop whatever products they want, but the store owner acts as the gatekeeper to what will be distributed through the store. This makes it possible to maintain quality and a consistent product range, which helps to build a strong unified store brand while at the same time allowing approved suppliers to nurture their own brands in a controlled manner. iPhone application developers have one effective channel for reaching potential customers, a quality check that their software meets the standard, and a ready-to-use e-commerce solution. On the downside, there is less flexibility and the risk of a slow cycle for approving new applications. Android Market, on the other hand, can metaphorically be described as the digital equivalent to a souk in Marrakech or a bazaar in Dhaka. The market is characterized by less hierarchical structure and control over who is selling what, compared to a store. Each stand has thus more individual freedom, but receives also less support from the overall system in terms of logistical accessibility and user recognition. Android application developers do indeed have guidance in the form of an SDK, tools, frameworks, methods, and best practices and Google has taken a lead as provider of Android Market, but in comparison to the iPhone, Android developers must rely more on their own capacity to brand their products and to reach users.

The two approaches described transform suppliers into peer producers. For the iPhone, the generative aspect of inviting external developers to participate in innovation is selective and concentrated at the later stages of the value chain (i.e. application development). For Android, generativity is a pervasive element throughout the whole platform (hardware, operating system, applications, etc.). In the management literature, suppliers are often portrayed as mere contractual deliverers of tasks agreed before hand, within an overall project or value chain and bound by the customer's carefully specified terms. The prevailing view of the relation between a firm and suppliers is that the firm is in control of the process and fully owns the outcomes. New phenomena such as iPhone's App Store and the Android Market provide arenas for peer production, where external developers creatively provide value to the communities of iPhone and Android users, respectively. As such, peer production promotes a new type of supplier and a new type of supplier relation. The generative aspects of the innovation process have strengthened suppliers' as well as other stakeholders' opportunities to boost value for themselves and for the whole value ecosystem.

Conclusion and Managerial Implications

This chapter has shown that generativity is an important component of open and distributed innovation. In the two examples of collaborative innovation processes analyzed it is generativity — not openness — that builds the aggregated value. The case studies show the various degrees and forms of generativity and the activities performed by the various actors include elements of both openness and control as a means of supporting and facilitating the generative efforts. To some extent control hinders generativity because external suppliers of application software need to ask permission before their applications are accepted as content. However, control also facilitates generativity because toolkits, standards, and guidelines have been developed for suppliers. Similarly openness can be both generative and a hindrance. It allows new ideas and possibilities but in some cases a lack of management hinders exploration and exploitation of the generative capacities of a platform because the actors themselves must create the paths for innovation.

Furthermore we have described a form of value creation where the boundaries between the production and consumption of value are highly overlapping. In opposition to the idea of a sequential chain of stepwise, path-dependent contributions, we have described the emergence of complex relations where generativity is the main driver for progress. In this setting, the innovative work of producers, suppliers, and users melds together into an open innovation ecosystem. This has similarities to the open-source movement and commons-based peer production in the sense that the innovative efforts are distributed over large, unspecified crowds and that each contribution can easily diffuse to the rest of the ecosystem. There are differences because the source code of each application has not necessarily been revealed to others for further development. On the other hand, since the network of users and application developers meet on online forums and rating sites, and apply other means of feedback communication, potential contributors to the value ecology can estimate which services and features are appreciated and which are not.

When the innovation process extends outside the hierarchical structure of an organization, the firm's control mechanisms need to be changed in order to facilitate value creation. Dynamic capabilities (Teece, 2007), business models (Chesbrough, 2006), complementary asset strategies (Teece, 1986), and other forms of indirect steering are then highlighted as a way to capture value from the shared processes. In this chapter we shown the need to consider how (digital) technology supports generative processes in an innovation ecosystem. When firms move toward digitalization, managers need to carefully assess how relations can be enhanced and governed, for instance through the configuration of the technological infrastructure, the use of intellectual property, and the necessary organizational structure.

The aim of this comparative case study was not to make judgments on which alternative is more generative than the other, but rather to show that a generative design can take many different forms. We also theoretically elaborate the notion of generativity, which we argue is a central feature when designing for open innovation. We strongly believe that further research on generativity — both quantitative and qualitative — would enrich the understanding of how open and distributed innovation processes work in practice.

References

Adner, R. and Kapoor, R. (2010). Value creation in innovation ecosystems: How the structure of technological interdependence affects firm performance in technology generations, *Strategic Management Journal*, **31**(3), 306–333.

Allen, T.J. (1971). Communications, technology transfer, and the role of technical gatekeeper, *R&D Management*, **1**(1), 14–21.

Anderson, C. (2006). *The Long Tail: Why the Future of Business is Selling Less of More*, Hyperion, New York.

Avital, M. and Te'eni, D. (2009). From generative fit to generative capacity: Exploring an emerging dimension of information systems design and task performance, *Information Systems Journal*, **19**(4), 345–367.

Barnes, S. (2002). The mobile commerce value chain: Analysis and future developments, *International Journal of Information Management*, **22**(2), 91–108.

Benkler, Y. (2006). *The Wealth of Networks: How Social Production Transforms Markets and Freedom*, Yale University Press, New Haven.

Bergquist, M. and Ljungberg, J. (2001). The power of gifts: Organizing social relationships in open source communities, *Information Systems Journal*, **11**(4), 305–320.

Bergvall-Kåreborn, B., Björn, M. and Chincholle, D. (2011). Motivational profiles of toolkit users: iPhone and Android developers, *International Journal of Technology Marketing*, **6**(1), 36–56.

Bessant, J., Kaplinsky, R. and Lamming, R. (2003). Putting supply chain learning into practice, *International Journal of Operations and Production Management*, **23**(2), 167–184.

Boltanski, L. and Chiapello, E. (2005). *The New Spirit of Capitalism*, Verso, New York.

Bonaccorsi, A. and Rossi, C. (2003). Why open source software can succeed, *Research Policy*, **32**(7), 1243–1258.

Brabham, D. (2008). Crowdsourcing as a model for problem solving: An introduction and cases, *Convergence*, **14**(1), 75–90.

Callon, M. (1991). "Techno-economic networks and irreversibility," in Law, J. (ed), *A Sociology of Monsters: Essays on Power, Technology and Domination*, Routledge, London, pp. 132–161.

Chesbrough, H. (2003). *Open Innovation: The New Imperative for Creating and Profiting from Technology*, Harvard Business School Press, Boston, MA.

Chesbrough, H. (2006). *Open Business Models: How to Thrive in the New Innovation Landscape*, Harvard Business School Press, Boston, MA.

Chesbrough, H. (2011). *Open Services Innovation: Rethinking Your Business to Grow and Compete in a New Era*, Jossey-Bass, San Francisco, CA.

Chesbrough, H. and Appleyard, M. (2007). Open innovation and strategy, *California Management Review*, **50**(1), 57–76.

Chesbrough, H., Vanhaverbeke, W. and West, J. (2006). *Open Innovation: Researching a New Paradigm*, Oxford University Press, USA.

Christensen, C.M. (2000). *The Innovator's Dilemma: When New Technologies Cause Great Firms to Fail*, Harper Business, New York.

Coase, R.H. (1937). The nature of the firm, *Economica*, **4**(16), 386–405.

Cooke, P. (2001). *Knowledge Economies: Clusters, Learning and Co-operative Advantage*, Routledge, New York.

Dahlander, L. and Gann, D. (2010). How open is innovation? *Research Policy*, **39**(6), 699–709.

Dahlander, L. and Magnusson, M. (2005). Relationships between open source software companies and communities: Observations from Nordic firms, *Research Policy*, **34**(4), 481–493.

Demil, B. and Lecocq, X. (2006). Neither market nor hierarchy nor network: The emergence of bazaar governance, *Organization Studies*, **27**(10), 1447–1466.

di Benedetto, A. (2010). Comment on "Is open innovation a field of study or a communication barrier to theory development?" *Technovation*, **30**(11–12), 557–557.

Dittrich, K. and Duysters, G. (2007). Networking as means to strategy change: The case of open innovation in mobile telephony, *Journal of Product Innovation Management*, **24**(6), 510–521.

Dodgson, M., Gann, D. and Salter, A. (2006). The role of technology in the shift toward open innovation: The case of Procter and Gamble, *R&D Management*, **36**(3), 333–346.

Fitzgerald, B. (2006). The transformation of open source software, *Management Information Systems Quarterly*, **30**(3), 587–598.

Franke, N. and Shah, S. (2003). How communities support innovative activities: An exploration of assistance and sharing among end-users, *Research Policy*, **32**(1), 157–178.

Fransman, M. (2002). Mapping the evolving telecoms industry: The uses and shortcomings of the layer model, *Telecommunications Policy*, **26**(9–10), 473–483.

Freeman, E. and Liedtka, J. (1997). Stakeholder capitalism and the value chain, *European Management Journal*, **15**(3), 286–296.

Freeman, E.R. (1984). *Strategic Management: A Stakeholder Approach*, Pitman, Boston.

Hopkins, M.M., Tidd, J., Nightingale, P. and Miller, R. (2011). Generative and degenerative interactions: Positive and negative dynamics of open, user centric innovation in technology and engineering consultancies, *R&D Management*, **41**(1), 44–60.

Kenney, M. and Pon, B. (2011). Structuring the smartphone industry: Is the mobile Internet OS platform the key, *Journal of Industry, Competition and Trade*, **11**(3), 239–261.

Kothandaraman, P. and Wilson, D. (2001). The future of competition value-creating networks, *Industrial Marketing Management*, **30**(4), 379–389.

Lane, D. and Maxfield, R. (1996). Strategy under complexity: Fostering generative relationships, *Long Range Planning*, **29**(2), 215–231.

Lawrence, P.R. and Lorsch, J.W. (1967). Differentiation and integration in complex organizations, *Administrative Science Quarterly*, **12**(1), 1–47.

Lee, Y.G., Lee, J.H., Song, Y.I. and Kim, H.J. (2008). Technological convergence and open innovation in the mobile telecommunication industry, *Asian Journal of Technology Innovation*, **16**(1), 45–62.

Lettl, C., Herstatt, C. and Gemuenden, H.G. (2006). Users' contributions to radical innovation: Evidence from four cases in the field of medical equipment technology, *R&D Management*, **36**(3), 251–272.

Lindgren, M., Jedbratt, J. and Svensson, E. (2002). *Beyond Mobile: People, Communications and Marketing in a Mobilized World*, Palgrave Macmillan, Basingstoke.

Ling, R. (2004). *The Mobile Connection: The Cell Phone's Impact on Society*, Morgan Kaufmann Publishers, San Francisco, CA.

Ljungberg, J. (2000). Open source movements as a model for organising, *European Journal of Information Systems*, **9**(4), 208–216.

Maitland, C., Bauer, J. and Westerveld, R. (2002). The European market for mobile data: Evolving value chains and industry structures, *Telecommunications Policy*, **26**(9–10), 485–504.

Mathew, J., Sarker, S. and Varshney, U. (2004). M-commerce services: Promises and challenges, *Communications of the Association of Information Systems*, **14**(26), 1–19.

Moore, J.F. (1995). *The Death of Competition: Leadership and Strategy in the Age of Business Ecosystems*, Harper Business, New York.

Mowery, D.C. (2009). Plus ca change: Industrial R&D in the "third industrial revolution," *Industrial and Corporate Change*, **18**(1), 1–50.

Mylonopoulos, N. and Sideris, I. (2006). Growth of value added mobile services under different scenarios of industry evolution, *Electronic Markets*, **16**(1), 28–40.

Olla, P. and Patel, N. (2002). A value chain model for mobile data service providers, *Telecommunications Policy*, **26**(9–10), 551–571.

O'Mahony, S. (2003). Guarding the commons: How community managed software projects protect their work, *Research Policy*, **32**(7), 1179–1198.

O'Reilly, T. (2007). What is Web 2.0? Design patterns and business models for the next generation of software, *Communications and Strategies*, **65**(1), 17–37.

Peppard, J. and Rylander, A. (2006). From value chain to value network: Insights for mobile operators, *European Management Journal*, **24**(2–3), 128–141.

Pillar, F. and Walcher, D. (2006). Toolkits for idea competitions: A novel method to integrate users in new product development, *R&D Management*, **36**(3), 307–318.

Porter, M.E. (1985). *Competitive Advantage: Creating and Sustaining Superior Performance*, Free Press, New York.

Porter, M.E. (1998). Clusters and the new economics of competition, *Harvard Business Review*, **76**(6), 77–90.

Raymond, E.S. (1999). *The Cathedral and the Bazaar: Musings on Linux and Open Source by an Accidental Revolutionary*, O'Reilly and Associates, Sebastopol, CA.

Rogers, E.M. (1995). *Diffusion of Innovations*, 4th edn, The Free Press, New York.

Rohrbeck, R., Hölzle, K. and Gemünden, H.G. (2009). Opening up for competitive advantage: How Deutsche Telekom creates an open innovation ecosystem, *R&D Management*, **39**(4), 420–430.

Rolandsson, B., Bergquist, M. and Ljungberg, J. (2011). Open source in the firm: Opening up professional practices of software development, *Research Policy*, **40**(4), 576–587.

Rülke, A., Lyer, A. and Ghiasson, G. (2003). "The ecology of mobile commerce: Charting a course for success using value chain analysis", in

Mennecke, B. and Strader, T. (eds), *Mobile Commerce: Technology, Theory, and Applications*, Idea Group Publishing, Hershey, PA, pp. 122–144.

Sabat, H. (2002). The Evolving Mobile Wireless Value Chain and Market Structure, *Telecommunications Policy*, **26**(9–10), 505–535.

Shapiro, C. and Varian, H.R. (1998). *Information Rules: A Strategic Guide to the Network Economy*, Harvard Business School Press, Boston, MA.

Sproull, L., Dutton, W. and Kiesler, S. (2007). Introduction to the special issue: Online communities, *Organization Studies*, **28**(3), 277–281.

Swan, J. and Scarbrough, H. (2005). The politics of networked innovation, *Human relations*, **58**(7), 913–943.

Teece, D. (1986). Profiting from technological innovation: Implications for integration, collaboration, licensing and public policy, *Research Policy*, **15**(6), 285–305.

Teece, D. (2007). Explicating dynamic capabilities: The nature and micro-foundations of (sustainable) enterprise performance, *Strategic Management Journal*, **28**(13), 1319–1350.

Thompson, J. (1967). *Organizations in Action*, McGraw-Hill, New York.

Toffler, A. (1980). *The Third Wave*, Morrow, New York.

Trott, P. and Hartmann, D. (2009). Why "open innovation" is old wine in new bottles, *International Journal of Innovation Management*, **13**(4), 715–736.

Ven, K. and Verelst, J. (2008). The impact of ideology on the organizational adoption of open source software, *Journal of Database Management*, **19**(2), 58–72.

von Hippel, E. (2005). *Democratizing Innovation*, MIT Press, Cambridge, MA.

Williamson, O.E. (1975). *Markets and Hierarchies: Analysis and Antitrust Implications*, Free Press, New York.

Zittrain, J. (2006). The generative Internet, *Harvard Law Review*, **119**, 1975.

Zittrain, J. (2008). *The Future of the Internet and How to Stop it*, Yale University Press, New Haven, CT.

Chapter 19

Crossing Horizons: Leveraging a Cross-Industry Innovation Search in the Front-End of the Innovation Process

Sabine Brunswicker*
Fraunhofer Institute for Industrial Engineering, Germany
Ulrich Hutschek
Zeppelin Universtity, Germany

Introduction

The current discourse both in research and practice in innovation management suggests that we are currently facing a new era of innovation (Chesbrough, 2003; Gassmann, 2006; Piller, 2003; von Hippel, 1988). The new paradigm — open innovation — claims that enterprises have to *purposively* open their innovation activities in order to connect internal and external ideas and to profit from innovation (Chesbrough, 2003, 2006; RTM, 2007; Vanhaverbeke, 2006). Prominent case studies demonstrate that firms have discovered the value to be gained from tapping into external sources of innovation (Nambisan and Sawhney, 2007a; RTM, 2007); recent quantitative empirical research indicates that the paradigm shift is having a real impact on firms' innovation performance (Laursen and Salter, 2006; Drechsler and Natter, 2008). Firms can draw on a range of external

---

* Corresponding author

sources to search for new ideas such as customers, consumers (Brockhoff, 1998; von Hippel, 1988), universities and suppliers (Laursen and Salter, 2006; Walter *et al.*, 2007). Increasingly those suppliers matter most who supply knowledge and ideas in the quest for innovation rather than tangible components (Johnsen *et al.*, 2006). 'Idea suppliers' can also be found in different industries (Gassmann and Zeschky, 2008). Examples such as the BMW I-Drive show that searching for technological solutions in different industries can open the solution space and can help to alleviate the problem of 'industry blindness' (Gassmann and Zeschky, 2008; Dürmüller, 2007).

In innovation-related research domains, it is widely acknowledged that novel ideas often emerge from the combination of unconnected pieces of knowledge (Gassmann and Zeschky, 2008; Amabile and Khaire, 2008; de Bono, 1968). The systematic search for isomorphic relations between apparently unrelated knowledge domains, markets or technological functions has been addressed in the research on innovation and technology management prior to the discussion on open innovation (Pfeiffer, 1971; Jantsch, 1967; Weiss, 2004). In creativity research, analogies and lateral thinking are considered important means to overcome the problem of the bounded rationality of social actors and support the structured identification of novel ideas (Simon, 1959). However, these different theoretical views and methodological approaches have hardly been linked to open innovation and external innovation searching. Indeed, the current discussion hardly addresses the question of *how* firms can systematically search for innovation inputs for fuzzy search fields (such as a fuzzy customer need) at the front end by interacting with firms and organisations from different industries.

The paper is structured as follows: First we present the state of the art in cross-industry innovation methods and introduce related theoretical concepts and methodologies. We critically discuss the dimensions of an innovation search across industries and link it with existing concepts. Next we propose a framework that guides managerial practices when developing and implementing a cross-industry innovation with fuzzy search fields in the front end of the innovation process. The framework was developed in a participatory action research project. Finally, we discuss the results of a pilot, managerial implications and potential future research directions.

State of the Art and Conceptual Discussions — External Innovation Search, Cross-Industry Knowledge and Innovation Planning

Open innovation and external search for new ideas in the fuzzy front end

Traditionally established firms relied on their own Research and Development (R&D) departments and favoured a 'closed' innovation model where all innovation is under the firm's control (Chesbrough, 2003, 2006; RTM, 2007; Vanhaverbeke, 2006). This 'closed innovation model' is in contrast with the open innovation paradigm that describes a new cognitive framework for a firm's strategy to profit from innovation (Chesbrough, 2003; Fredberg *et al.*, 2008). It supports firms seeking to adapt both their innovation models and processes in order to purposively use inflows and outflows of knowledge to accelerate internal innovation on the one hand and to expand markets for the external use of its innovation on the other (Chesbrough, 2003). From a firm's perspective inflows and outflows can occur throughout various phases of innovation value chain (Hansen and Birkinshaw, 2007; Koen *et al.*, 2002; Brunswicker and Kianto, 2009). In the front end of a firm's innovation value chain, search and problem-solving activities relate to fuzzy problems (see, e.g., Koen *et al.*, 2002) while an external search is even more difficult.

Gassmann and Enkel (2004) differentiate between three archetypes of open innovation processes: (1) outside-in processes, (2) inside-out processes, and (3) coupled processes. Outside-in processes aim to enrich the firm's own 'knowledge base' through the integration of suppliers, customers and other external knowledge sources. In inside-out processes, firms commercialise internally developed ideas and technologies and do not turn them into products to offer to their own customers. Coupled processes build on strong ties with innovation network partners (e.g. strategic alliances) and are characterised by formally established collaboration activities and co-development partnerships (Gassmann and Enkel, 2004; Gassmann, 2006).

Theoretically open innovation is linked to the knowledge-based view of the firm and to organisational learning (Grant, 1996; March, 1991). Following these theoretical perspectives, knowledge is perceived as an overwhelmingly important and productive resource and the primary source of Ricardian rents (Grant and Baden-Fuller, 2004). Organisational learning enables a firm to explore new opportunities, to innovate and to achieve a sustainable competitive advantage (March, 1991).

A firm's external innovation search strategy plays a crucial role in outside-in processes (Laursen and Salter, 2004, 2006). Recent quantitative empirical research confirms that the 'breadth' of an external search — meaning the diversity of external sources for the innovation input — has a positive impact on a firm's innovation performance (Laursen and Salter, 2006). Indeed, firms can search among a range of different external actors (Nalebuff and Brandenburger, 1996; Brunswicker and Kianto, 2009). For example, they can establish linkages with customers (Nalebuff and Brandenburger, 1996; Walter *et al.*, 2007), end consumers (Brockhoff, 1998; von Hippel, 1988) and direct suppliers (Walter *et al.*, 2007; Schiele, 2010). It is crucial to maintain linkages with research institutes and universities in order to remain up to date with emerging technologies (Laursen and Salter, 2006; Cohen and Levinthal, 1990). Well-tested technologies and novel ideas can also be found among actors from different knowledge domains and from outside the firm's industry (Gassmann and Enkel, 2004; Gassmann, 2006).

Analogical problem-solving and the search for technological solutions in new product development

Searching different knowledge domains is rooted in conceptual discussions on 'analogical problem-solving' (Jacobs *et al.*, 2005; Gentner, 1983; Gick and Holyoak, 1980) and 'lateral thinking' (De Bono, 1968). In creativity research and cognitive psychology, analogies are perceived as 'devices' for conveying that two situations or domains share a relational structure despite arbitrary degrees of difference in the objects that make up the domains (Gentner, 1983; Hesse, 1966).

Analogical problem-solving is described as a process of structural mapping from a source context of prior experience to a current target context (Gick and Holyoak, 1980). The term 'analogy' refers to the successful identification of similarities among a source and a target domain (Jacobs *et al.*, 2005). Theoretical discussions about analogies differentiate between *formal* analogies (a one-to-one correspondence between different interpretations of the same formal theory) and material analogies (pre-theoretic analogies between observables) (Hesse, 1966). Similarities between the source domain and the target domain are either superficial or structural (Jacobs *et al.*, 2005).

Analogies are the backbone of structured methodologies and tools for problem-solving (Dahl and Moreau, 2002; Gassmann and Zeschky, 2008). For example, TRIZ or Synectics build upon analogical thinking to identify solutions for a well-specified (mostly technological) problem (Schild *et al.*, 2004).

New product development can also be perceived as a problem-solving activity (Pfeiffer, 1980). It has been recognised that analogical problem-solving and the search for technological solutions in different industries can enhance product development processes (Gassmann and Zeschky, 2008; Schild *et al.*, 2004). Tapping into different knowledge domains challenges current thinking patterns and helps to overcome the constraints of bounded rationality (Gassmann and Sutter, 2008; Gassmann and Zeschky, 2007a, 2008; Dürmüller, 2007; Simon, 1959). Technologies that are already tested and utilised in other industries can significantly affect a firm's innovation performance if adapted to the firm's context. In addition, tested technological solutions from other industry domains can increase the efficiency and lower the risk of innovation activities (Gassmann and Zeschky, 2007a).

To better link analogical problem-solving and new product development processes, Gassmann and Zeschky (2008) propose a systematic process model to exploit analogical thinking and to search for technological solutions employed in different industry domains. Based on a case study they conclude that analogical thinking does not happen merely by accident but can be supported by a structured process. Their cross-industry innovation (CII) process includes three major phases and is embedded in a firm's concept development phase (Fig.1). First, a concrete problem is abstracted from a specific technological problem area. Second, analogical solutions are investigated. Third, various

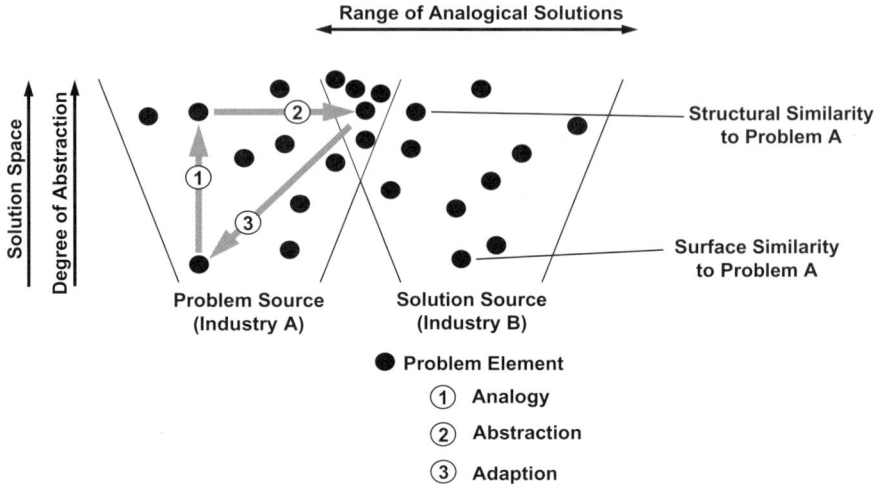

Fig. 1. Cross-Industry Innovation Process; see Gassmann and Zeschky (2008).

solutions are assessed from a technological and a market perspective (Gassmann and Zeschky, 2007b, 2008). To successfully integrate the cross-industry innovation activities in the innovation and new product development processes, they add two 'integration' phases — one prior and one after the cross-industry innovation process (Gassmann and Zeschky, 2008) — to successfully align the CII process with other activities in the innovation process. This CII process is a rare example of a management framework employed to systematically exploit technological knowledge from different domains. However, it concentrates on finding technological solutions for well-defined technological problems. It does not integrate the market perspective. In addition it does not include any interactive involvement of organisations from different industries. Thus, it needs to be enriched with relevant concepts in innovation management and innovation planning that integrate the market perspective of innovation.

Innovation planning and external innovation searching

Innovation can be conceptualised as the interaction of technology and market spheres (Weiss, 2004; Pfeiffer, 1971). Thus, an external search at the front end of the innovation process does not relate to a technological problem only. It relates to a 'fuzzy' search field defined by developments and interactions between the market and the technology domain (Jantsch, 1967; Weiss, 2004; Koen *et al.*, 2002; Pfeiffer, 1971). at turn, innovation planning processes at the front end cannot be separated from strategic planning of business areas. Innovation planning integrates market *and* technology planning (Abell, 1980; Mintzberg *et al*, 1995).

In prior research on innovation management, the principle of isomorphism and functional analysis have been applied to guide an external search for know-how and information at the front end (Pfeiffer, 1971; Jantsch, 1967). Following these principles, all existing and potential technological innovation can be perceived as the result of the constructive combination of technological functions and characteristics that perform certain market functions. The functional market concept has been developed to support firms in planning technological innovation in hyper-competitive environments (Pfeiffer, 1971; Weiss, 2004). It leverages the idea of isomorphic relations and functional analysis in the early phases of the innovation process. Based on functional considerations of technologies, the functional market concept creates relations between problems and solutions independent of market and cognitive boundaries. It helps firms look beyond their industry boundaries and systematically exploits 'function thinking'. This thinking starts with a customer's problem and separates the technology or a particular product from its context. It results in an abstract description of a 'functional market' (Pfeiffer, 1971; Weiss, 2004) and guides the search for alternative technology performing this function outside a firm's technological knowledge base.

Innovation strategies and innovation planning aim to enhance, extend and complement firms' competencies and technological knowledge bases. The competency-based and the knowledge-based views of the firm suggest that a firm's competencies and knowledge assets create a competitive advantage (Prahalad and Hamel, 1990; Grant, 1996). Thus, firms need to decide wisely whether to build new competency purely internally or to interactively learn from others

(Grant, 1996; Lee and Veloso, 2008). Chesbrough and Schwartz (2007) suggest that there are three different types of technological capabilities that are relevant to develop an innovation. However, the decision to search externally has different implications, namely (Chesbrough and Schwartz, 2007; Prahalad and Hamel, 1990): (1) *Core technological capabilities* are the key sources of a firm's distinctive advantages and added value. They should be managed rather closely. (2) *Critical technological capabilities* are those that are vital to the success of a firm's product but are not core capabilities of the firm. Here, an external search or co-development partnerships might be an option. If firms open their innovation processes for critical capabilities they can improve their value propositions without heavily investing in R&D. (3) *Contextual capabilities* are those required to complement the offering but provide rather little differentiation. A cross-industry innovation search is most relevant for critical capabilities that are vital to the firm's success and added value.

Search method and knowledge partitioning

Firms face various options regarding how they search and what they search for externally. Nambisan and Sawhney (2007a, 2007b) differentiate innovation inputs along a continuum with two contrasting ends: *raw ideas versus market-ready products.* Deciding what to search for is partly shaped by four variables: the *expected reach* (or *variety*), the *costs*, the *risk involved* and the *speed* with which an idea can be brought to market (Nambisan and Sawhney, 2007a). Indeed, not only the transaction costs but also the transaction value guide decisions about how to implement analogical problem-solving (Vanhaverbeke and Cloodt, 2006).

Firms can search in many different ways (Pisano and Verganti, 2008). New and emerging intermediary markets can create a range of additional search channels and methods that reduce search and transaction costs (Nambisan and Sawhney, 2007a, 2007b; Pisano and Verganti, 2008). *Broadcast search* is a search and problem-solving approach that is leveraged via online communities such as InnoCentive.

It implies that firms provide 'problem information' to a large group of 'unknown' outsiders in order to open the solution space; it has been proven successful for scientific problems and it provides access to a large variety of new ideas (Pisano and Verganti, 2008; Lakhani *et al.*, 2006): the premise of broadcast search is the central insight that knowledge is unequally and widely distributed in society (Lakhani *et al.*, 2006; von Hippel, 1988). In contrast, firms such as Alessi rely on small expert networks to search for new solutions to design problems (Pisano and Verganti, 2008). Expert networks or bilateral relations leverage the expertise of selected organisations or actors to tackle more complex problems that require expert knowledge (Pisano and Verganti, 2008).

Modularity influences decisions concerning which search method should be adopted. A complex system — e.g. a product architecture or an organisational design — is said to exhibit *modularity* in design if its parts can be designed independently but will work together to support the whole (Baldwin and Clark, 2006; Lee and Veloso, 2008; Sanchez and Mahoney, 1996). *Modularity* is high in nearly decomposable systems (Sanchez and Mahoney, 1996). For a fuzzy 'search field', such as a customer need and its underlying market functions, knowledge may not be easily partitioned upfront (Lee and Veloso, 2008; von Hippel, 1990). In addition knowledge from different industries may be rather *sticky* and more difficult to access and absorb (von Hippel, 1988).

Cognitive distance and absorptive capacity

Cognitive distance is another important concept that illuminates the external innovation search process and a firm's ability to absorb external knowledge. It concerns differences in how individual people see, interpret and evaluate the world (Nooteboom *et al.*, 2005; Cohen and Levinthal, 1990; Li *et al.*, 2008). For an external innovation search, cognitive distance relates to at least three areas: product market, technology and science (March, 1991; Li *et al.*, 2008). Greater degrees of cognitive distance tend to yield opportunities for highly novel solutions. At a certain point, however, cognitive distance can become so great that the mutual understanding required to exploit analogical opportunities begins to erode. According to Nooteboom (1999) the seeker and the solver(s) must be sufficiently close in cognition and language to enable meaningful communication By default, a cross-industry innovation search implies that the knowledge distance in product markets is high. However, a functional analysis of product-market systems may reveal structural similarities between them and thus ease the identification of potentially relevant innovation inputs from different industry domains (Weiss, 2004; Pfeiffer, 1971). Technological distance influences a firm's ability to absorb external knowledge. Thus, it is another important variable to be considered when developing a cross-industry innovation search strategy.

Research Strategy and Methodology

This research follows an action and participatory research strategy (Mintzberg *et al.*, 1995; Checkland and Holwell, 2007) called that leverages a combined approach participatory action research (PAR, see Whyte *et al.*, 1991). Existing research on cross-industry innovation indicates that there is a lack of processes to guide managerial actions and interventions to develop and implement a cross-industry innovation search strategy. Participatory research allows the researcher to develop and test a new 'intervention'. It creates direct insights and reflections in practice.

Following action research principles, this research went through the following major phases: *planning, acting* and *reflection of actions.* In the planning phase, we identified the problem and the need for an external idea search. Then, we developed a managerial framework for cross industry innovation to guide managerial actions and interventions. In the action phase this framework was tested by the research team in close collaboration with innovation managers from the automotive sector and a cross-industry 'partner', namely, a medical firm. After completing the acting phase, we reflected the actions. The results supported the adaption and refinement of the managerial model.

A Management Framework for Cross-Industry Innovation Searching

The question of how firms can search for external knowledge at the front end of the innovation process in different industries has hardly been addressed in current discussions on open innovation. Existing frameworks for cross-industry innovation focus on technological problems. This paper links relevant theories and concepts such as analogical problem-solving in cognitive psychology, the principle of isomorphism and functional analysis in innovation planning with the outside-in dimension of open innovation. The following section discusses relevant factors for a systematic cross-industry innovation search. It also outlines a systematic process that offers managerial guidance in the search for *novel solution principles* and *application ideas* for a fuzzy search field at the front end.

A framework for developing a cross-industry innovation search strategy

When developing a cross-industry search strategy there are four dimensions that guide managerial actions and interventions:

(1) Search field (*Where to open?*): An external innovation search starts by deciding 'where to open' the search for external innovation inputs. A firm's overall strategy and innovation targets act as a 'strategic corridor' (Porter, 1985). The search field is characterised by two dimensions: market and technology. Both the market and the technology dimensions of innovation are addressed when defining the search field (Pfeiffer, 1971). The search field describes market trends and potential value propositions that yield value to existing or future customers (Teece, 1986; Chesbrough, 2006) and links it with a firm's technological competency to perform these market functions (Prahalad and Hamel, 1990; Pfeiffer, 1971, 1980; Weiss, 2004). Both dimensions can be assessed along a continuum with two contrasting ends.

The market functions yield a customer value ranging from high to low. Similarly, a firm's technological competency to perform this market function can be described as ranging from core to critical and to contextual. The 'search field' in focus may have a high customer value and relate to a firm's contextual technological competencies (but not to a core technological competency).

(2) Search domain (*Where to search?*): The search domain (or solver domain) answers the question 'where to search' and describes potential solvers from a different industry that show an isomorphic relation with the seeking firm (Pfeiffer, 1971; Weiss, 2004; Jantsch, 1967). System and functional analysis are important in identifying abstract functional relations between market functions from different industries and knowledge domains. Structural similarities in terms of abstract market functions increase the attractiveness of the industry and search domain. In addition the technological distance or proximity influences the attractiveness of the solver domain (Nooteboom, 2002). Nowadays service providers and new types of intermediaries support the identification of potential search domains.

(3) Search objective (*What to search?*): The decision on what to search is a crucial one. Firms need to understand the trade-offs of different innovation inputs. For example, firms might search for a large number of raw ideas. In contrast, others might be interested in more detailed and elaborated solution principles, rough product concepts or even marketable products (Baldwin and Clark, 2006; Nambisan and Sawhney, 2007a). This decision depends on the accepted risk, the accepted costs, the required speed and the expected number of ideas. Raw ideas are relatively easy to get and do not cause noteworthy costs; however, the time for commercialisation is rather long. Marketable products carry lower risk and faster commercialisation potential. However, they are not easily accessible and they are more expensive. In addition the 'novelty' level and the modularity of the knowledge in the search field constitute the search objective.

(4) Search method (*How to search?*): The contemporary world is creating new search channels and methods. Simply, search

methods can be classified along a continuum ranging from a group of unknown outsiders, called a *broadcast search*, to an expert search of small network (or even a bilateral relations) with close interactions. A *broadcast search* leverages the large accumulation of knowledge amongst the wider community of scientists, researchers and users (Lakhani *et al.*, 2006; von Hippel, 1988). It may alleviate the problems of a local search and it significantly increases the variety and number of proposed solutions. It works best if firms can easily evaluate the proposed solutions at low costs. In contrast, expert networks or bilateral relations leverage the expertise of specifically selected actors to tackle more complex problems that require expert knowledge (Pisano and Verganti, 2008). Indeed, for search fields that can hardly be modularised and require expert knowledge, bilateral relations and expert networks may yield fewer but more promising innovation inputs. Direct interaction provides the knowledge-sharing context required to create an appropriate understanding of the search field, market functions and alternative solution principles (Weiss, 2004).

These four dimensions should not be treated independently because they interact and influence one another. For example, the appropriate search method links the search objective with the required innovation input.

A two-stage process model for implementing a cross-industry innovation search project

The CII framework and existing methodologies in new product development such as TRIZ focus on technological problems. The existing literature on innovation planning and open innovation suggests that the potential of an external and 'interactive' search in different industries can be leveraged at the front end for newly identified market trends. However, managers lack practical advice on how to implement such a cross-industry innovation search. A systematic process supports them in the interactive search for novel solution principles

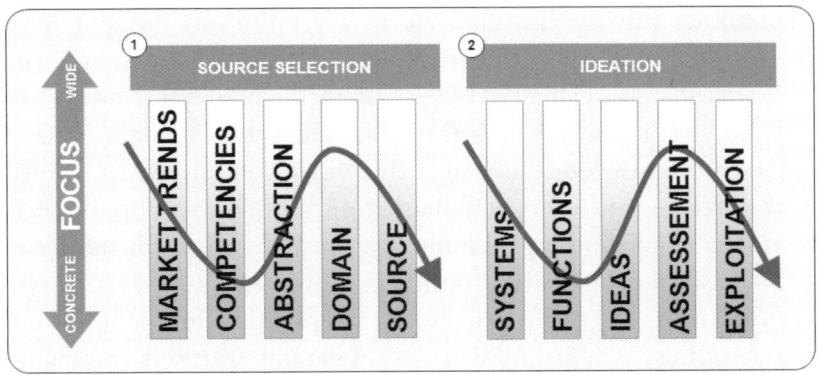

Fig. 2. Two-Stage Cross-Industry Innovation Search Process.

('product substances' rather than raw ideas) that perform new market functions related to a fuzzy 'customer need'.

Extending the conceptual discussions and the framework developed by Gassmann and Zeschky (2008) we propose a two-stage process (Fig. 2) for a cross-industry innovation search within fuzzy search fields at the front end. It integrates existing theoretical perspectives and concepts such as functional market analysis, system analysis and the principle of isomorphism (Weiss, 2004; Pfeiffer, 1971; Jantsch, 1967) and leverages an external search as a means to open the solution space for a market-induced search field. Thus, it tackles the question of 'how' to implement open innovation and search externally for a fuzzy customer problem. As market functions for fuzzy customer needs of complex products such as cars require expert knowledge, it leverages an interactive and expert search method. An interactive approach creates the required knowledge-sharing context (Bergman, 2009). It has two major stages: (1) source selection and (2) ideation; throughout each stage analogical processes and functional analysis change the level of abstraction of the search and problem-solving activities to reveal isomorphic relations.

Both stages are well aligned with the internal innovation processes to ensure the successful integration of open innovation activities and internal innovation processes.

Source selection

The first stage encompasses the selection of the search field and the target selection. It has five major steps:

- Market-trend analysis: Market trends and future market requirements are the starting point when developing a cross-industry innovation search strategy. In the first step, potential value propositions and related market functions should be analysed and assessed. Those market functions that may yield high customer value in the future and show high attractiveness are investigated more closely in the following steps. During this phase a close interaction between the R&D, Marketing and Business Development Functions is required.
- Competency analysis: In the second step, the technological competencies of the firm to perform the market functions should be investigated in more detail. Competencies are classified as core, critical or contextual. Both the market dimension and the technological competency constitute a potential search field. The search field to be chosen should show both high customer value and leverage the firm's critical competencies. The search field defines 'where' to open up to external influences.
- Abstraction: During the abstraction phase, the market need should be separated from its industry and market context. The 'search field' is an abstract 'functional market problem'. As proposed by the functional market concept, abstraction supports the creation of relations between problems and solutions independent market and industry contexts.
- Domain selection: After abstraction, select the search domain. Here, both the proximity of the 'functional markets' and the technological distance should be taken into consideration. The search domain should reveal structural similarities of market functions. In addition the technological distance should be within acceptable boundaries. Other variables influence the decision regarding which industry as well, such as: R&D intensity, the dominant innovation type (product versus process) and the maturity.

- Source selection: In the final step, select the potential candidates for participation in the interactive ideation phase. Cultural and language issues might be considered as well. Once the organisations are identified, they receive a formal invitation to participate.

Ideation phase

The second stage is about generating ideas for novel solution principles in an interactive manner. Just like the first stage, the ideation stage leverages analogical problem-solving. It systematically exploits system and functional analysis as proposed by prior research (Weiss, 2004; Pfeiffer, 1971, 1980; Jantsch, 1967). The ideation stage is the core activity of a cross-industry innovation project. It is executed in an interactive setting, that is, in moderated workshops. Representatives from both the idea seeker and the solution provider take part in this stage.

In the preparation for the ideation stage, some critical aspects need to be considered: briefing of the participants providing information about the objective and scope of the project, legal aspects such as confidentiality agreements and an agreement on usage rights after the idea generation phase. In addition both parties should discuss potential exploitation options after completion of the ideation stage, ranging from a collaborative development project to technology licensing. Only if there is mutual understanding and agreement on the potential outcome, can the second stage be successfully executed.

There are five major steps:

- System analysis: The system analysis step investigates relations between customer needs, market functions, products and solution principles from 'seeker' and 'solution provider' perspective. System analysis reduces the problem without substantial deviation (Pfeiffer, 1971; Weiss, 2004; Jantsch, 1967). A system analysis framework guides the participants of the workshop in better understanding the functional market problem and isomorphic relations between customer needs and market functions both in the seeker and the solver domains. It is the starting point for identifying solution principles and technologies in different industry domains. Experienced moderation and guiding questions support the system analysis.

- Functional analysis: After the system analysis, the relation between selected solution principles and technological functions is further decomposed. This provides the starting point for the generation of new combinations that perform abstract market functions.
- Idea generation: In the idea generation step, workshop participants construct new combinations of technologies and characteristics to identify novel solution principles. These solution principles should perform the market functions specified in the 'search field'. However, project 'spill overs' might occur as well.
- Assessment: In the assessment step, the individual ideas and the overall outcome of the idea generation are assessed by the 'seeker'. The objective is to assess whether and how individual technologies and new solution principles can be further utilised. As a result of this step, the seeker has a pool of assessed ideas and options for further developing these ideas.
- Exploitation preparation: In the final step, measures are defined to successfully leverage the results of the ideation stage. Ideas are selected, discarded or 'put on hold'. Decisions about the scope and content of follow-up activities are made, e.g. co-development projects or technology licensing.

Results of Piloting and Discussion

A participatory action research approach was selected to develop a framework with high practical value. Thus, a research collaboration with a German car manufacturer was initially set up. The aim of the collaboration was to create direct insights and value for the car manufacturer when developing and testing the new framework. Both the framework and the process were developed in direct interaction with the innovation management group and experts from R&D and Marketing. One researcher was located at the site of the firm when developing and prototyping the process. Relevant contextual information and tacit knowledge were collected such as the firm's strategic processes and core technological competencies.

The pilot with the car manufacturer was aimed at deriving the 'proof of concept'. In the first stage, an interdisciplinary team specified the search field. After functional abstraction of the market, the research team searched the appropriate domain for organisations to participate in the *interactive* ideation stage. The search led to the medical engineering industry where a promising project partner was found.

During the *ideation stage* workshops were moderated by experienced researchers. To create the required knowledge context and to ease the system and function analysis, concrete 'use cases' of the different industries were included in the workshop sessions. For example, the relations between technologies, solution principles, products and 'market functions' were elaborated in use cases in operating rooms. During the ideation stage, technologies and solution principles were identified in the domain of medical devices, which will provide the basis for new application ideas and market functions for the manufacturer.

The pilot created value for both sides: the 'seeker' and the 'solver'. On the one hand, the seeker was able to search effectively and efficiently for already tested technologies and solution principles that offer new application areas and perform new market functions for a fuzzy search field at the front end. The pool of new ideas was not 'raw' but characterised by a high potential for successful exploitation. As the technology and solution principles were already proven in the chosen industry, the risks and costs for further developing the generated ideas are lower, compared to 'in-house' development of a totally new technology. In addition there is a low competitive risk as participants act in different industries. On the other hand, the 'solver' from the medical industry gained access to a new potential for commercialising their know-how, e.g. via licensing.

The action was reflected and evaluated by the workshop participants via both structured feedback forms and direct interviews with the participants. The average satisfaction with the outcome of the workshop (with eight participants) was 3.1 on a scale from 1 (not satisfied) to 4 (highly satisfied).

The review produced the following additional results:

Interactive expert search and mutual learning: The transfer of 'proven' knowledge from different industry domains for a fuzzy search field at the front end requires learning on the part of both the 'seeker' and the 'solver'. Thus, it cannot be treated purely as a transaction. A bilateral and direct interaction with experts was confirmed to be an appropriate search method. The functional abstraction and system analysis for identifying isomorphic relation was eased in interactive sessions. The interactive ideation stage also resulted in more elaborated solution principles and application ideas and not just raw ideas. Expert knowledge was required for both the identification of abstract relations and the assessment of new application ideas. Thus, bilateral interaction with a small number of experts was confirmed to be appropriate. It is important to pay attention to the set-up of the workshops and the profile of the workshop participants as both the context of the 'seeker' and the "solver" have to be fully understood.

Alignment with internal planning and ideation processes: The alignment of external and internal innovation processes was also identified as a key success factor both in planning of the cross-industry initiative and in further exploitation of new ideas. It ensures that the initiative is aligned with the overall innovation strategy and that newly generated ideas are further developed and exploited. A successful exploitation of the results requires appropriate processes and internal competencies. In addition a firm's culture drives the adoption of externally generated ideas. The phrase 'not invented here' is common in manufacturing industries and thus openness to outside influences is a facilitator of absorption and exploitation of new ideas.

Balance of structure and creative freedom during ideation: The results confirmed that functional thinking supports both stages: source selection and ideation. However, there is the risk that too much structure and process reliance hinders creativity and the identification of solution principles that do not directly relate to the abstract market function that is the focus of the ideation stage. So-called project 'spill overs' (i.e. reasonable idea outcomes that are not related to the search field and the related market functions) may also occur and should not be neglected. Thus, the moderation of the workshop needs to balance structure (to guide the idea generation) with sufficient degrees of freedom (to create new application ideas).

This research takes important steps towards a structured and integrated framework for developing a cross-industry innovation search strategy at the fuzzy front end. It takes a functional perspective for a fuzzy search field in the front end rather than a product or technology perspective. This alleviates the constraints of existing products and markets. It is unique as it links existing research on analogical problem-solving in new product development and functional analysis in innovation planning with open innovation. The interactive expert search ensures that the appropriate learning takes place, which is required to identify more elaborate application ideas rather than a large number of new ideas. It also facilitates the assessment of proposed ideas.

Overall the framework does not treat openness as a binary variable. An open innovation strategy needs to be developed case-by-case and we need to consider boundary conditions and contingencies such as a firm's technological competency, the complexity of the problem and the fit with a firm's business model. The first application of this process has been very encouraging. Currently, a long-term review is being executed and its results will provide further insights.

Limitations and Further Research Directions

The research created some concrete insights and reflections when developing and applying a managerial framework for a cross-industry search. It proposes an integrated managerial framework including a systematic processes model and discusses insights drawn from piloting. However, there are some limitations that need to be kept in mind.

First, discussions and lessons learned were drawn from participatory action research in the manufacturing industry. In turn, the development and implementation might have been influenced by contingencies such as the characteristics of the industry domain and the modularity of the firm's knowledge in the innovation search field. Whether this is a constraint needs to be further investigated. Further insight can be drawn from additional case studies in other industries that complements our results and further improves the existing framework. In addition further research should pay attention to the constraints of open innovation and an external search. Indeed, whether to open up to external influences or not is a strategic decision that implies constraints on appropriation and intellectual property protection, to name but a few. It also requires new internal processes to create value from openness. If the proposed framework is further applied with these research questions in mind, additional crucial insights can be drawn.

Second, the pilot posed additional ideas on how we could further extend the framework in future research. For example, additional methods such as a broadcast search should be tested. Such research may yield additional insights into the relation between complexity and appropriate search methods for cross-industry innovation.

References

Abell, D.F. (1980). "Defining the business," *The Starting Point of Strategic Planning*, Prentice Hall, London.

Amabile, T.M. and Khaire, M. (2008). Creativity and the role of the leader, *Harvard Business Review*, **86**(10), 100–109.

Baldwin, C. and Clark, K. (2006). The architecture of participation. Does code architecture mitigate free riding in the open source development model? *Management Science*, **52**(7), 1116–1127.

Bergman, J. (2009). Enabling open innovation process through interactive methods, scenarios and group decision support systems, *International Journal of Innovation Management*, **13**(1), 139–156.

Brockhoff, K. (1998). *Der Kunde im Innovationsprozess*, Vandenhoeck & Ruprecht, Göttingen.

Brunswicker, S. and Kianto, A. (2009). Taking a closer look into open innovation in SME: The interplay of openness, performance and innovation management practices, *Proceedings of R&D Management Conference*, Wien.

Checkland, P. and Holwell, S. (2007). "Action research — Its nature and validity, information systems action research," in Kock, N. (ed.), *An Applied View of Emerging Concepts and Methods*, Springer, Boston, MA.

Chesbrough, H.W. (2003). The era of open innovation, *MIT Sloan Management Review*, **44**(3), 35–41.

Chesbrough, H.W. (2006). *Open Business Models. How to Thrive in the New Innovation Landscape*, Harvard Business School Press, Boston, MA.

Chesbrough, H.W. and Schwartz, K. (2007). Innovating business models with co-development partnerships, *Research Technology Management*, **50**, 55–59.

Cohen, W.M. and Levinthal, D.A. (1990). Absorptive capacity: A new perspective on learning and innovation, *Administrative Science Quarterly*, **35**(1), 128–152.

Dahl, D.W. and Moreau, P. (2002). The influence and role of analogical thinking during new product ideation, *Journal of Marketing Research*, **39**(1), 47–60.

de Bono, E. (1968). *New Think: The Use of Lateral Thinking in the Generation of New Ideas*, Basic Books, New York.

Drechsler, W. and Natter M. (2008). Open innovation — Management trend with impact? An empirical investigation of antecedents, drivers and performance outcomes, Working Paper, Goethe University Frankfurt, Frankfurt.

Dürmüller, C. (2007). Cross-industry innovation: Der lohnende Blick über den eigenen Gartenzaun, *Innovation Management*, **03–06**(1), 100–102.

Fredberg, T., Elmquist, M. and Ollila, S. (2008). *Managing Open Innovation. Present Findings and Future Directions*, VINNIVA and Chalmers University of Technology.

Gassmann, O. (2006). Opening up the innovation process: Towards an agenda, *R&D Management*, **36**(3), 223–228.

Gassmann, O. and Enkel, E. (2004). Towards a theory of open innovation: Three core process archetypes, *Proceedings of the R&D Management Conference (RADMA)*, Lisbon, Portugal, July 6–9, 2004.

Gassmann, O. and Sutter, P. (2008). *Praxiswissen Innovations Management — Von der Idee zum Markterfolg*, Hanser, München.

Gassmann, O. and Zeschky, M. (2007a). Dem Zufall auf die Sprünge helfen, *Technische Rundschau*, **3**, 8–9

Gassmann, O. and Zeschky, M. (2007b). Radikale innovation ist nicht planbar wie ein produktionsprozess, *Innovation Management*, September–November (3), 8–10.

Gassmann, O. and Zeschky M. (2008). Opening up the solution space: The role of analogical thinking for breakthrough product innovation, *Creativity and Innovation Management*, **17**(2), 97–106.

Gentner, D. (1983). Structure-mapping: A theoretical framework for analogy, *Cognitive Science*, **7**, 155–170.

Gick, M.L. and Holyoak, K.J. (1980). Analogical problem solving, *Cognitive Psychology*, **12**, 306–355.

Grant, R.M. (1996). Toward a knowledge-based theory of the firm, *Strategic Management Journal*, **17**, 109–122.

Grant, R.M. and Baden-Fuller, C. (2004). A knowledge accessing theory of strategic alliances, *Journal of Management Studies*, **41**(1), 61–84.

Hansen, M.T. and Birkinshaw, J. (2007). The innovation value chain, *Harvard Business Review*, **85**(6), 121–130.

Hesse, M. (1966). *Models and Analogies in Science*, University of Notre Dame Press, Notre Dame, In.

Jacobs, C., Statler, M. and Ross, J. (2005). Reforming strategy: Analogical reasoning as strategic practice, *Scandinavian Journal of Management*, **24**, 133–144.

Jantsch, E. (1967). *Technological Forecasting in Perspective*, Organization for Economic Cooperation and Development (OECD), Paris.

Johnsen, T., Phillips, W., Caldwell, N. and Lewis, M. (2006). Centrality of customer and supplier interaction in innovation, *Journal of Business Research*, **59**, 671–678.

Koen, P.A., Ajamian, G.M., Boyce, S., Clamen, A., Fisher, E., Fountoulakis, S., Johnson, A., Puri, P. and Seibert R. (2002). "Fuzzy front end: Effective methods, tools and techniques," in Belliveau, P. (ed.), *The PDMA Toolbook for New Product Development*, Wiley, New Yark.

Lakhani, K.R., Jeppesen, L.B., Lohse, P., and Panetta, J. (2006). The value of openness in scientific problem solving, Working Paper, Harvard Business School.

Laursen, K. and Salter, A. (2004). Searching high and low: What types of firms use universities as a source of innovation? *Research Policy*, **33**, 1201–1215.

Laursen, K. and Salter, A. (2006). Open for innovation: The role of open-ness in explaining innovation performance among U.K. manufacturing firms, *Strategic Management Journal*, **27**(2), 131–150.

Lee, J. and Veloso, F.M. (2008). Interfirm innovation under uncertainty: Empirical evidence for strategic knowledge partitioning, *Journal of Product Innovation Management*, **25**, 418–435.

Li, Y., Vanhaverbeke, W. and Schoenmakers, W. (2008). Exploration and exploitation in innovation: Reframing the interpretation, *Creativity and Innovation Management*, **17**(2), 107–126.

March, J.G. (1991). Exploration and exploitation in organizational learning, *Organization Science*, **2**(1), 71–87.

Mintzberg, H., Quinn, J.B. and Ghoshal, S. (1995). *The Strategy Process*, European Edition, Prentice Hall, London.

Nalebuff, B. and Brandenburger A. (1996). *Coopetition — Kooperativ Konkurrieren*, Campus, Frankfurt.

Nambisan, S. and Sawhney, M. (2007a). A buyer's guide to the innovation bazaar, *Harvard Business Review*, **86**(6), 109–118.

Nambisan, S. and Sawhney, M. (2007b). Marktreife Erfindungen, *Harvard Business Manager*, **29**(6), 19–20.

Nooteboom, B. (1999). *Inter-firm Alliances: Analysis and Design*, Routledge, London.

Nooteboom, B. (2002). A cognitive theory of the firm, White paper, Rotterdam.

Nooteboom, B. vanhaverbeke, W., Duysters, G, Gilsing, V., and van den Oord, A. (2005). Optimal cognitive distance and absorptive capacity, *Research Policy*, **36**(7), 1016–1034.

Pfeiffer, W. (1971). Allgemeine Theorie der technischen Entwicklung, Vandenhoeck & Ruprecht, Göttingen.

Pfeiffer, W. (1980). "Innovationsmanagement als know-how management," in Hahn, D. (ed.), *Führungsprobleme industrieller Unternehmen*, Berlin Walter de Gruyter, New York.

Piller, F. (2003). Von open source zu open innovation, *Harvard Business Manager*, **25**(12), 114.

Pisano, G.P. and Verganti R. (2008). Which kind of collaboration is right for you? The new leaders in innovation will be those who figure out the best way to leverage a network of outsiders, *Harvard Business Review*, **86**(12), 78–86.

Porter, M.E. (1985). *Competitive Advantage: Creating and Sustaining Superior Performance*, Free Press, New York.

Prahalad, C.K., and Hamel, G. (1990). The core competence of the corporation, *Harvard Business Review*, May–June, 79–91.

RTM (2007). Implementing open innovation. RTM interviews Larry Huston and Nabil Sakkab about Procter & Gamble's experience with its 'connect and develop' innovation model, *Research Technology Management*, **50**(2), 21–25.

Sanchez, R. and Mahoney, J.T. (1996). Modularity, flexibility, and knowledge management in product and organization design, *Strategic Management Journal*, **17**, 63–76.

Schiele, H. (2010). Early supplier integration: The dual role of purchasing in new product development, *R&D Management*, **40**(2), 138–153.

Schild, K., Herstatt, C. and Lüthje C. (2004). How to use analogies for breakthrough innovations, White paper, Hamburg.

Simon, H. (1959). Theories of decision-making in economics and behaviour science, *The American Economic Review*, **49**(3), 253–283.

Teece, D.J. (1986). Profiting from technological innovation. Implications for integration, collaboration, licensing and public policy, *Research Policy*, **15**, 285–305.

Vanhaverbeke, W. (2006). The inter-organizational context of open innovation, Chesbrough, H.W. *et al.* (eds.), in *Open Innovation: Researching a New Paradigm*, Oxford University Press, Oxford.

Vanhaverbeke, W. and Cloodt M. (2006). "Open innovation in value networks," in Chesbrough H.W. *et al.* (eds.). *Open Innovation: Researching a New Paradigm*, Oxford University Press, Oxford, UK.

von Hippel, E. (1988). *The Sources of Innovation*, Oxford University Press, New York.

von Hippel, E. (1990). Task partitioning: An innovation process variable, *Research Policy*, **19**(5) 407–418.

Walter, A. Ritter, T. and Riesenhuber, F. (2007). Innovation development in supplier-customer relationships: Does it give suppliers a bigger piece of the pie? *Zeitschrift für Betriebswirtschaft*, Special Issue (4), 1–19.

Weiss, E. (2004). Functional market concept for planning technological innovations, *International Journal of Technology Management*, **27**(2/3), 320–330.

Whyte, W.F., Greenwood D.J. and Lazes P. (1991). "Participatory action research," in Whyte, W.F. (ed.), *Through Practice to Science in Social Research, Participatory Action Research*, Sage, Newbury Park, London, New Delhi.

Summary and Future Directions

Joe Tidd
University of Sussex, UK
Alexander Brem
University of Erlangen-Nuremberg, Germany

The concept of open innovation is currently popular in the management and policy literature on technology and innovation. However, despite the large volume of empirical work many of the proposed prescriptions are fairly general, rather than specific to particular contexts and contingencies. As Huizingh (2011, p. 9) argued in his recent review of open innovation: 'case studies may contrast high- and low-performing open innovation adopters to increase our understanding of why and how the effectiveness of certain practices is context dependent... We still lack knowledge about how to do it and when to do it'. More specifically, Groen and Linton (2010) ask for a clearer distinction or relation between open innovation and supply-chain innovation and management. These have been the central aims of this book.

However, proponents of open innovation tend to offer universal, and often universally positive, prescriptions but recent research casts doubts on this view (Trott and Hartmann, 2009). More specifically, research on product and service innovation suggests that the specific mechanisms and outcomes of open-innovation models are very sensitive to context and contingency (Tidd and Bessant, 2013; Bessant and

Tidd, 2011; Tidd and Hull, 2006). We would therefore expect the nature of interactions with distributed external actors to be highly context dependent (Blindenbach-Driessen and van den Ende, 2006). This is not surprising since the open or closed nature of innovation does not entail a simple shift from being closed to open as often suggested in the literature (Mowery, 2009), but following Pavitt's (1984) taxonomy of the sources of innovation we know that patterns of innovation differ fundamentally — by sector, firm and strategy. Therefore there is a need to examine the mechanisms that help to generate successful open innovation in specific contexts (Enkel *et al.*, 2009; Huizingh, 2011). Fredberg *et al.* (2008) identify aspects of open innovation requiring further research, including the locus of the innovation process, the extent of collaboration and the organizational structures, capabilities and processes required. Gassmann *et al.* (2010) propose that alliance structures for creating value in open innovation are not well understood, particularly in the service sector.

In this book we aim to contribute to a shift in the debate from potentially misleading general prescriptions, and provide some empirical insights into the precise mechanisms and potential limitations of open innovation in one particular context: the supplier–customer interaction. We identify specific mechanisms that generate or restrict innovation with a particular focus on the intensity and quality of partner and supplier relations and interactions.

Open vs. Closed Innovation

The original idea of open innovation was that firms should (also) exploit external sources and resources to innovate, a notion that is difficult to contest (Tidd and Bessant, 2013). However, wider dissemination of this thesis (Chesbrough, 2003) shows that it is difficult to research and implement (Chesbrough *et al.*, 2006), to the point it has now become 'all things to all people', lacking explanatory or predictive power (Tidd and Bessant, 2013). Empirical evidence for the utility of open innovation is limited and practical prescriptions overly general (Trott and Hartmann, 2009). Individual case studies are frequently not generalizable, while studies based on various community innovation surveys (Laursen and Salter, 2006; Poot *et al.*, 2009) provide only simple counts of external sources and partnerships. Thus, they may suffer from survivor bias and also reveal little about the mechanisms of and limitations to open innovation.

The phenomenon of open innovation is not new (Mowery, 2009) and innovation that exploits external networks through a process of recursive learning and testing is a classic organizational response to the complexity or uncertainty of technology and markets (Freeman, 1991). Thus, the well-established innovation networks literature potentially can contribute much to the debate on open innovation. Innovation networks are more than an aggregation of bilateral collaborative relations or dyads (Belussi and Arcangeli, 1998). Variations in the degree and type of such interactions typically produce dynamic, inherently unpredictable sets of relations, that make network-based innovation fundamentally different from the trial-and-error process found within individual firms (Bidault and Fischer, 1994).

The open-innovation model emphasizes why a firm acquires valuable resources from external firms and shares internal resources for new product and service development. But the question of how a firm sources external knowledge and shares internal knowledge in an interfirm collaboration is less clear. Vanhaverbeke *et al.* (2007) argue that a firm should develop routines and structures for knowledge transfer in order to access and assimilate valuable resources and facilitate the open-innovation process. This means that a firm has to develop routines for knowledge to flow between firms in order to contribute to new product or service development. Managing different types and degrees of inter-firm relationship with external companies in order to create value will involve different degrees of openness for innovation purposes (van de Vrande *et al.*, 2006; Dittrich and Duysters, 2007). Open innovation demands greater attention to the management of knowledge flows, and has to be accompanied by control to coordinate sources and activities that are not owned by the company (Remneland-Wikhamn *et al.*, 2011) while maintaining the motivation of partners to contribute (Klioutch and Leker, 2011).

Some studies argue that there is not a simple dichotomy between the open and closed approaches (Mowery, 2009; Trott and Hartmann,

2009). The studies suggest that further research should pay more attention to exploring the different degrees and types of openness and the extent to which a firm can benefit from external and internal resources and knowledge in the innovation process. This view provides an opportunity to investigate the use of various collaboration strategies available to a company and the types and contexts of sources of innovation (Lazzarotti and Manzini, 2009). Recently, some studies have begun to identify different types of openness; for example, Lichtenthaler (2008) defines two dimensions, the extent of external technology acquisition and the extent of external technology exploitation, to investigate a company's behaviour in an innovation process. Furthermore, Birkinshaw (2007) proposes that a hybrid open model, located between the traditional closed model and a fully open model, may exist. The characteristics that can be used to analyse a firm's processes include: whether knowledge is concentrated or dispersed, the different degrees of control and the different degrees of trust and reciprocity. Von Zedtwitz and Gassmann (2002) argued that firms need some degree of control, such as a formal or informal relation with partners, inorder to implement open innovation. Moreover, van de Vrande *et al.* (2006) examined the choice of governance modes for external technology sourcing with external partners for different degrees of uncertainty. They proposed that, under a high level of technological and market uncertainty, less hierarchical governance modes should be adopted.

The connection between the different types and intensity of inter-firm relations and development outcomes has also been discussed in previous studies (e.g. Littler *et al.*, 1998; Takeishi, 2001; Von Corswant and Tunälv, 2002; Bstieler, 2006; Fliess and Becker, 2006; Cousins and Lawson, 2007). A few studies have gone further and found that the connection between different inter-firm relations and the development outcome may depend on different degrees of project complexity (Meyer and Utterback, 1995; Griffin, 1997) and project novelty (Eisenhardt and Tabrizi, 1995; Ragatz *et al.*, 2002). Accordingly, the connection between inter-firm relations and development outcomes is likely to vary in certain circumstances, such as project complexity and newness.

Future Directions

The simplistic distinction between open and closed development processes, assessed in terms of internal versus external sources, may be less relevant than the *quality of the external relationships*, assessed in terms of the intensity of interactions and the richness of knowledge sharing, moderated by the *type of project or technology*. Lane and Maxfield (1996) suggest successful innovative collaborations result from situations where two organizations with different perspectives and capabilities share a commitment to a common direction, interact in a recurring manner and value, and monitor and nurture their relation. Such generative relations can 'induce changes in the way participants see their world and act in it and... give rise to new entities, like agents, artifacts, even institutions' (Lane and Maxfield, 1996, p. 216). Importantly, Lane and Maxfield emphasize that the precise nature of the benefits derived from generative relationships cannot be anticipated. Swan and Scarborough (2005) refer to generative interactions rather than relationships, to describe situations involving successful innovation in which knowledge integration is facilitated by network coordination.

There is recent but growing evidence that it is this *generative potential* of such relationships that is a critical condition for the success of open innovation (Hopkins *et al.*, 2011; Remneland-Wilkhamn *et al.*, 2011), rather than the use of open innovation or external sources *per se*. Indeed, this collection of conceptual and empirical work confirms that traditional internal knowledge routines and capabilities, such as cross-disciplinary working and complementary assets, in combination with external knowledge networks and partnerships, can promote such generative interactions. This is very different to simply outsourcing development or importing external knowledge. An obvious implication of this is that open forms of innovation are not a substitute for building internal capabilities but rather act as valuable complementary capabilities (Tidd, 2012). A better understanding of the mechanisms that contribute to generative interactions and outcomes will result in more precise prescriptions for open innovation (Huizingh, 2011).

References

Atuahene-Gima, K. and Ko, A. (2001). An empirical investigation of the effect of market orientation alignment on product innovation, *Organization Science*, **12**(1), 54–74.

Ausster, E. (1992). The relationship of industry evolution to patterns of technological linkages, joint ventures, and direct investment between the US and Japan, *Management Science*, **17**, 1–25.

Bahemia, H. and Squire, B. (2010). A contingent perspective of open innovation in new product development projects, *International Journal of Innovation Management*, **14**(4), 603–627.

Belussi, F. and F. Arcangeli (1998). A typology of networks: Flexible and evolutionary firms, *Research Policy*, **27**: 415–28.

Bessant, J. and Tidd, J. (2011). *Innovation and Entrepreneurship*, Wiley, Chichester.

Bidault, F. and Fischer, W.A. (1994). Technology transactions: Networks over markets, *R&D Management*, **24**(4), 373–86.

Birkinshaw, J. (2007). Open Innovation and in-sourcing of external technologies, *Keynote speech in EURAM conference*, Paris, France, May 16–19.

Blindenbach-Driessen, F. and van den Ende, J. (2006). Innovation in project-based firms: The context-dependency of success factors, *Research Policy*, **35**: 545–61.

Bstieler, L. (2006). Trust formation in collaborative new product development, *Journal of Product Innovation Management*, **23**, 56–72.

Chesbrough, H. W. (2003). *Open Innovation: The New Imperative for Creating and Profiting From Technology*, Harvard Business School Press, Boston, MA.

Chesbrough, H., Vanhaverbeke, W. and West, J. (2006). *Open Innovation: Researching a New Paradigm*. Oxford University Press, Oxford, UK.

Clark, K.B. and Fujimoto, T. (1991). *Product Development Performance*, Harvard University Press, Boston, MA.

Clark, K.B. and Wheelwright, S.C. (1993). *Managing New Product and Process Development: Text and Cases*, Harvard Business School Press, Cambridge, MA.

Cooper, R.G. and Edgett, S. (1999). Critical success factors for new financial services, *Marketing Management*, **5**(3), 26–37.

Cousins, P.D. and Lawson, B. (2007). The effect of socialization mechanisms and performance measurement on supplier integration in new product development, *British Journal of Management*, **18**, 311–326.

Daft, R.L., Lengel, R.H. and Trevino, L.K. (1987). Message equivocality, media selection, and manager performance: Implications for information systems, *MIS Quarterly*, **11**, 355–366.

DenHertog, P. and Bilderbeek, R. (1999). Conceptualising service innovation and service innovation patterns, *Research Programme on Innovation in Services(SIID) for the Ministry of Economic Affairs*, Dialogic, Utrecht.

Dittrich, K. and Duysters, G. (2007). Networking as a means to strategy Change: The case of open innovation in mobile telephony, *The Journal of Product Innovation Management*, **24**, 510–521.

Dyer, J.H. and Hatch, N.W. (2006). Relation-specific capabilities and barriers toknowledge transfer: Creating advantage through network relationships, *Strategic Management Journal*, **27**, 701–719.

Dyer, J.H. and Nobeoka, K. (2000). Creating and managing a high-performance knowledge-sharing network: The Toyota case, *Strategic Management Journal*, **21**, 345–367.

Enkel, E., Gassmann, O. and Chesbrough, H. (2009). Open innovation: Exploring the phenomenon, *R&D Management*, **39**(4): 311–316.

Eisenhardt, K.M. and Tabrizi, B.N. (1995). Accelerating adaptive processes: Product innovation in the global computer industry, *Administrative Science Quarterly*, **40**, 84–110.

Emmanuelides, P.A. (1993). Towards an integrative framework of performance in product development projects, *Journal of Engineering and Technology Management*, **10**, 363–392.

Fasnacht, D. (2009). *Open Innovation in the Financial Services: Growing through Openness, Flexibility and Customer Integration*, Springer-Verlag, Berlin.

Fliess, S. and Becker, U. (2006). Supplier integration — Controlling of co-development processes, *Industrial Marketing Management*, **35**, 28–44.

Forfás (2006). *Services Innovation in Ireland: Options for Innovation Policy*, *Forfásreport*, Dublin, Ireland. Available at http://www. forfas. ie/ media/forfas060928_services_innovation_full_report. pdf.

Fredberg, T., Elmquist, M. and Ollila, S. (2008). Managing open innovation-present findings and future directions. VINNOVA Report. VINNOVA — VerketförInnovationssystem/Swedish Governmental Agency for Innovation

Systems, Stockholm, Sweden. Available at http://www. openinnovation. eu/download/vr-08–02. pdf.

Freeman, C. (1991). Networks of Innovators: A synthesis of research issues, *Research Policy*, **20**(5), 499–514.

Gallouj, F. and Weinstein, O. (1997). Innovation in services, *Research Policy*, **26**, 537–556.

Gassmann, O., Enkel, E. and Chesbrough, H. (2010). The future of open innovation, *R&D Management*, **40**, 213–221.

Gorovaia, N. and Windsperger, J. (2010). The use of knowledge transfer-mechanisms, *Knowledge and Process Management*, **17**, 12–21.

Griffin, A. (1997). Modeling and measuring product development cycle time across industries, *Journal of Engineering and Technology Management*, **14**, 1–24.

Groen, A.J. and Linton, J.D. (2010). Is open innovation a field of study or a communication barrier to theory development?, *Technovation*, **30**, 554.

Hagedoorn, J. and Narula, R. (1996). Choosing organizational modes of strategic technology partnering: International sectoral differences, *Journal of International Business Studies*, **27**, 265–284.

Hales, M. and Tidd, J. (2009). The practice of routines and representations in designand development, *Industrial and Corporate Change*, **18**, 551–574.

Hauptman, O. and Hirji, K.K. (1999). Managing integration and co-ordination in cross-functional teams, *R&D Management*, **29**(2), 179–191.

Hopkins, M. M., Tidd, J., Nightingale, P. and Miller, R. (2011). Generative and degenerative interactions: Positive and negative dynamics of open, user-centric innovation in technology and engineering consultancies, *R&D Management*, **41**(1), 44–60.

Huizingh, E.K.R.E. (2011). Open innovation: State of the art and future perspectives, *Technovation*, **13**(1), 2–9.

Kald, M., Nilsson, F. and Rapp, B. (2001). On strategy and management control: The importance of classifying the strategy of the business, *British Journal of Management*, **11**(3), 197–212.

Klioutch, I. and Leker, J. (2011). Supplier involvement in customer new product development: New insights from the supplier's perspective, *International Journal of Innovation Management*, **15**(1), 231–248.

Lane, D. and Maxfield, R. (1996). Strategy under complexity: Fostering generative relationships, *Long Range Planning*, **29**(2), 215–231.

Laursen, K. and Salter, A. (2006). Open for innovation: The role of openness in explaining innovation performance among UK manufacturing firms, *Strategic Management Journal*, **27**(2), 131–150.

Lazzarotti, V. and Manzini, R. (2009). Different modes of open innovation: A theoretical framework and an empirical study, *International Journal of Innovation Management*, **13**, 615–636.

Lichtenthaler, U. (2008). Open innovation in practice: An analysis of strategic approaches to technology transactions, *IEEE Transactions of Engineering Management*, **55**, 148–157.

Littler, D., Leerick, F. and Wilson, D. (1998). Collaboration in new technology based markets. *International Journal of Technology Management*, **15**, 139–159.

Mante, A. and Sydow, J. (2007). Inter-organizational routines: Coordinating R&D practices in international alliances, *International Conference on Organizational Routines: Empirical Research and Conceptual Foundations*, Strasbourg, France, May 25–26.

Meyer, M. H. and Utterback, J.M. (1995). Product development cycle time and commercial success, *IEEE Transactions on Engineering Management*, **42**, 297–304.

Moenaert, R. K., De Meyer, A., Souder, W.E. and Deschoolmeester, D. (1995). R&D/marketing communication during the fuzzy front-end, *IEEE Transactions on Engineering Management*, **42**, 243–258.

Mowery, D.C. (2009). Plus ca change: Industrial R&D in the third industrial revolution, *Industrial and Corporate Change*, **18**(1), 1–50.

Nylen, U. (2007). Interagency collaboration in human service: Impact of formalization and intensity on effectiveness, *Public Administration*, **85**, 143–166.

Pavitt, K. (1984). Sectoral patterns of technical change: Towards a taxonomy and a theory, *Research Policy*, **13**, 343–373.

Petersen, K. , Handfield, R. and Ragatz, G. L. (2003). A model of supplier integration into new product development, *Journal of Product Innovation Management*, **20**, 284–299.

Petersen, K., Handfield, R. and Ragatz, G.L. (2005). Supplier integration into new product development: Coordinating product, process and supply chain design, *Journal of Operation Management*, **23**, 371–388.

Poot, T., Faems, D. and Vanhaverbeke, W. (2009). Toward a dynamic perspective on open innovation: A longitudinal assessment of the adoption of internal and external innovation strategies in the Netherlands, *International Journal of Innovation Management* **13**(2), 177–200.

Pratt, M. (2009). From the editors: For the lack of a boilerplate — Tips on writing up (and reviewing) qualitative research, *Academy of Management Journal*, **52**(5), 856–862.

Ragatz, G.L. , Handfield, R.B. and Petersen, K.J. (2002). Benefits associated with supplier integration into new product development under conditions of technology uncertainty, *Journal of Business Research*, **55**, 389–400.

Remneland-Wilkhamn, B., Ljungberg, M., Bergquist, M. and Kuschel, J. (2011). Open innovation, generativity and the supplier as peer, *International Journal of Innovation Management*, **15**(1), 205–230.

Schweitzer, F.M., Gassmann, O. and Gaubinger, K. (2011). Open innovation and its ability to embrace turbulent environments, *International Journal of Innovation Management*, **15**(6).

Sheer, V.C. and Chen, L. (2004). Improving media richness theory: A study of interaction goals, message valence, and task complexity in manager-subordinate communication, *Management Communication Quarterly*, **11**, 76–93.

Souder, W.E., Sherman, J.D. and Davies-Cooper, R. (1998). Environmental uncertainty, organizational integration, and new product development effectiveness: A test of contingency theory, *Journal of Product Innovation Management*, **15**, 520–533.

Swan J. and Scarborough H. (2005). The politics of networked innovation, *Human Relations*, **58**(7), 913–943.

Takeishi, A. (2001). Bridging inter-and intra-firm boundaries: Management of supplier involvement in automobile product development, *Strategic Management Journal*, **22**, 403–433.

Tether, B.S. and Metcalfe, J.S. (2004). "Services and systems of innovation," in Malerba, F. (ed), *Sectoral Systems of Innovation: Concepts, Issues and Analyses of Six Major Sectors in Europe*, Cambridge University Press, Cambridge, UK.

Thomas, A.S. and Ramaswamy, K. (1996). Matching managers to strategy: Further tests of the miles and snow typology, *British Journal of Management*.

Tidd, J. (1993). Technological innovation, organisational linkages and strategic degrees of freedom, *Technology Analysis and Strategic Management*, **5**(3), 273–285.

Tidd, J. (2012). *From Knowledge Management to Strategic Competence.* Imperial College Press, London.

Tidd, J. and Bessant, J. (2013). *Managing Innovation: Integrating Technological, Market and Organizational Change*, Wiley, Chichester.

Tidd, J. and Bodley, K. (2002). The effect of project novelty on the new product development process, *R&D Management*, **32**(2), 127–138.

Tidd, J. and Hull, F. (2006). Managing service innovation: The need for selectivity rather than 'best-practice', *New Technology, Work and Employment*, **21**(2), 139–161.

Trott, P. and Hartmann, D. (2009). Why open innovation is old wine in new bottles, *International Journal of Innovation Management*, **13**(4), 715–736.

Van de Vrande, V., Lemmens, C. and Vanhaverbeke, W. (2006). Choosing governance modes for external technology sourcing, *R&D Management*, **36**, 347–363.

Vanhaverbeke, W., Cloodt, M. and Van de Vrande, V. (2007). Connecting absorptive capacity and open innovation, *Centre for Advanced Study (CAS) Workshop on Innovation in Firms*, Asker, Norway, October 30–November 1.

Verworn, B. (2009). A structural equation model of the impact of the 'fuzzy front end' on the success of new product development, *Research Policy*, **38**, 1571–1581.

Von Corswant, F. and Tunälv, C. (2002). Coordinating customers and proactive suppliers- A case study of supplier collaboration in product development, *Journal of Engineering and Technology Management*, **19**, 249–261.

Von Zedtwitz, M. and Gassmann, O. (2002). Market versus technology driven in R&D internationalisation: Four different patterns of managing research and development, *Research Policy*, **31**, 569–588.

Womack, J.P. and Jones, D.T. (1996). *Lean Thinking*, Simon and Schuster.

Index